P9-DDN-439

REVIEWER PRAISE OF BOOKS BY DOUGLAS GRAY

The Canadian Snowbird Guide

"…an invaluable guide to worry-free part-time living in the U.S. …by one of Canada's bestselling authors of business and personal finance books…"

—*The Globe and Mail*

"…Gray has written a reference book, thoughtful and complete, and prepared with the authoritative research skills and knowledge of a fastidious solicitor… as practical as a sunhat on a Tampa afternoon, and that alone warrants it a place on every southbound RV's bookshelf."

—*Quill & Quire*

The Canadian Guide to Will and Estate Planning
(with John Budd)

"…An informative, practical guide…the authors…cover all the bases."

—*The National Post*

"…A bargain for its price, it should be part of every family's library."

—*The Globe and Mail*

Making Money in Real Estate

"Gray delivers the goods. It is all-Canadian, and not a retread book full of tips that are worthless north of the U.S. border. It's chock-full of practical streetsmart strategies and advice, pitfalls to avoid, samples, what-to-look-out for, checklists and information."

—*Business in Vancouver*

"…provides consumer insights into securing the best deal and avoiding the pitfalls…Gray's legal background has given him valuable insights."

—*The Edmonton Journal*

"Outstanding…peppered with practical no-nonsense tips…invaluable information throughout."

—*Calgary Herald*

THE
CANADIAN SNOWBIRD GUIDE

FOURTH EDITION,
REVISED & UPDATED

EVERYTHING YOU NEED TO KNOW ABOUT
LIVING PART-TIME IN THE USA & MEXICO

BEST-SELLING BOOKS BY DOUGLAS GRAY

PERSONAL FINANCE/RETIREMENT PLANNING TITLES

- *The Canadian Snowbird Guide: Everything You Need to Know about Living Part-time in the US.A. and Mexico*
- *The Canadian Guide to Will and Estate Planning* (with John Budd)
- *Risk-Free Retirement: The Complete Canadian Planning Guide* (with Tom Delaney, Graham Cunningham, Les Solomon and Dr. Des Dwyer)

REAL ESTATE TITLES

- *Making Money in Real Estate: The Canadian Guide to Profitable Investment in Residential Property*
- *101 Streetsmart Condo-Buying Tips for Canadians*
- *Real Estate Investing for Canadians for Dummies* (with Peter Mitham)
- *The Complete Guide to Buying and Owning Recreational Property in Canada*
- *Mortgages Made Easy: The All-Canadian Guide to Home Financing*
- *Home Buying Made Easy: The Canadian Guide to Purchasing a Newly-Built or Pre-Owned Home*
- *Condo Buying Made Easy: The Canadian Guide to Apartment and Townhouse Condos, Co-ops and Timeshares*
- *Mortgage Payment Tables Made Easy*

SMALL BUSINESS TITLES

- *Start and Run a Profitable Consulting Business*
- *Start and Run a Profitable Business Using Your Computer*
- *Have You Got What It Takes? The Entrepreneur's Complete Self-Assessment Guide*
- *Marketing Your Product* (with Donald Cyr)
- *The Complete Canadian Small Business Guide* (with Diana Gray)
- *Home Inc.: The Canadian Home-Based Business Guide* (with Diana Gray)

- *Raising Money: The Canadian Guide to Successful Business Financing* (with Brian Nattrass)
- *The Complete Canadian Franchise Guide* (with Norm Friend)
- *So You Want to Buy a Franchise?* (with Norm Friend)
- *Be Your Own Boss: The Ultimate Guide to Buying a Small Business or Franchise in Canada* (with Norm Friend)
- *The Canadian Small Business Legal Advisor*

SOFTWARE PROGRAMS

- *Making Money in Real Estate* (jointly developed by Douglas Gray and Phoenix Accrual Corporation)

THE CANADIAN SNOWBIRD GUIDE

FOURTH EDITION, REVISED & UPDATED

EVERYTHING YOU NEED TO KNOW ABOUT
LIVING PART-TIME IN THE USA & MEXICO

DOUGLAS GRAY

John Wiley & Sons Canada, Ltd.

Library and Archives Canada Cataloguing in Publication Data

Gray, Douglas A.
    The Canadian snowbird guide : everything you need to know about living part-time
in the U.S.A. and Mexico / Douglas Gray. — 4th ed.

Includes bibliographical references and index.
ISBN 978-0-470-15375-8

    1. Canadians—Retirement—United States.   2. Canadians—Retirement—Mexico.
3. Retirees—Canada—Finance, Personal.   4. Canadians—United States—Finance, Personal. 5. Canadians—Mexico—Finance, Personal. I. Title.

HG179.G732 2007   332.0240086'96   C2007-905876-0

Production Credits
Cover design: Jason Vandenberg
Interior text design: Tegan Wallace
Front Cover Photos: Top Left: Stockbyte; Top Right: Photodisc; Middle Left: Photodisc;
    Middle Right: Photodisc; Bottom Left: Stockbyte; Bottom Right: Slobo Mitic
Back Cover Photos: Top Right: Stockbyte; Middle Left: Photodisc; Bottom Right: Slobo Mitic
Printer: Quebecor—Fairfield/Martinsburg

John Wiley & Sons Canada, Ltd.
6045 Freemont Blvd.
Mississauga, Ontario
L5R 4J3

Printed in Canada

1 2 3 4 5 QW 11 10 09 08 07

Table of Contents

Acknowledgements

I am indebted to many individuals, too numerous to mention, who have given generously of their time and expertise in the preparation of this book. I am also grateful for the helpful assistance given to me by various federal, provincial, and state governments, medical insurance companies, financial planning and seniors' associations, and tax experts and authorities. In particular, I appreciated the excellent information provided by the Foreign Affairs and International Trade Canada through their superb publications and websites. Selected parts of this information have been adapted and used in this new edition.

I would also like to express my appreciation to Richard Brunton, CPA, of Boca Raton, Florida, for all his generous feedback on cross-border tax issues. Richard is also the publisher of *Brunton's U.S. Tax Letter for Canadians*, and kindly consented to the use of some of the material in his recent newsletters. I would like to thank John Budd, CFA, chartered accountant and tax and estate planning expert in Toronto, Ontario, for his kind assistance. John is my co-author of the book *The Canadian Guide to Will and Estate Planning*.

I appreciated the time and expertise of two U.S immigration lawyers, Larry Behar of Fort Lauderdale, Florida, and Eileen Martin of Buffalo, N.Y., in vetting the chapter on immigration and customs issues. Larry is the author of the book *How to Immigrate to the USA*.

Thanks to David Cooper of Century 21 Carousel Realty in Phoenix, Arizona, for his candid and constructive suggestions. Also, thanks to Bernard Rowe, CHFC, CLU, CFP and Archie Blaikie, RFP, CFP, CHFC, CLU, both professional financial planners in Vancouver, B.C., for their manuscript critiques.

Many thanks to Julie Taylor, who reviewed the chapter on Mexico and gave many excellent suggestions. If you are considering being a Snowbird in Mexico, you should read her excellent book: *Mexico: The Trick Is Living Here*, 2nd edition. Julie is an expat American who is living in Mexico. Her website to download the book is www.home-sweet-mexico.com.

I would like to thank Leo and Arlene Hevey, of Belleville, Ontario, for their enthusiastic example of how rewarding the Snowbird lifestyle can be. They have been most helpful with feedback and suggestions on the issues and concerns of being a part-time resident in the United States. As their guest on numerous visits to the United States over the years, I have shared first-hand their activities, pleasures, friendships, and rejuvenating experiences as Canadian Snowbirds.

I would also like to thank the staff of John Wiley & Sons for their support, professionalism, and insightful feedback throughout.

Last but not least, I would like to express my appreciation to Don Loney, Executive Editor, of John Wiley & Sons, for his patience and encouragement in the development of this book. I have had the pleasure of knowing Don for over 16 years. I have indeed been fortunate to work with such a consummate professional in the publishing business.

CHAPTER 1

The Snowbird Lifestyle

INTRODUCTION

The thought of spending Canada's cold winter in a warm and sunny place—for many people, a U.S. Sunbelt state or Mexico—appeals to millions of Canadian retirees. This trend is increasing every year, as Canada's population ages. Because Canadians are living longer and staying healthier, retirement could last 30 years, and many Canadians choose to spend part or all of those winter months in a warmer climate—hence the term "Snowbirds." Another term used while you are staying in the U.S. or Mexico is "winter visitor."

With proper planning, the Snowbird lifestyle can provide the most active, stimulating, and enjoyable experience of your retirement years. It could enhance your quality of life immeasurably. About two-thirds of Snowbirds leave Canada for the United States or Mexico in late October or early November and return sometime before the end of April. The other third prefer to wait until January and stay in the South for up to three months. Snowbirds can therefore have the best of both countries during various seasons, enjoying a wide range of outdoor activities.

Living in the South during the winter can also be very affordable. In fact, you may find that you come out ahead financially. This is because of the savings from the lower cost of living in the U.S. or Mexico. You can rent a mobile home/ RV pad for a small amount, starting from about CDN$300 per month. You can buy a used mobile home (fixed in place) in a park, for about CDN$7,000, and find it meets all your needs. There are some good bargains, especially at the end of the season in April. When you amortize that cost over 10 years, it becomes very affordable. You also have use of all the facilities and amenities at a mobile home/RV park, which is generally included in your pad lease fee.

Naturally, expenses can be higher in some parks, but you would normally select the type of park or condominium community that meets your budget as well as other needs. In addition, you are saving money on heating costs at home in Canada during the winter. Even taking into account the cost of your out-of-country emergency medical insurance, you could be breaking even or paying just a bit more than if you stayed at home in Canada all winter. It is this type of attractive economic reality that is also a contributing factor to the decision of many to winter in the South.

The Snowbird lifestyle also provides considerable net financial benefits to the Canadian taxpayer. Because Snowbirds can be active outdoors all year round, their physical and mental health is enhanced accordingly. In many areas of Canada the weather curtails outdoor or social activities.

In addition, many Canadians establish close friendships with U.S. Snowbirds from northern U.S. states. This is because of the feeling of community and friendship in mobile home/RV parks and other retirement developments. Many Americans visit their Canadian Snowbird friends between May and September, stimulating the economy in Canada through tourism.

Many Snowbirds also have friends, relatives, and family from Canada who visit them for short periods down South. If that might occur in your case, read Chapter 6 on insurance. Advise them why it is so critical for them to have out-of-country emergency medical insurance.

Having said all that, the Snowbird lifestyle is not for everyone. It is just another retirement option. As will be discussed shortly, it is wise to try it for a month or so by renting. In other words, evolve into the lifestyle in a step-by-step fashion to see if you like it and it meets your various needs.

This chapter covers a variety of preliminary issues to consider. For example, it considers the things involved in being a Snowbird in the U.S. or Mexico. Also covered will be the rental option, where to stay, how to get there, what to do once you get there, tips on saving money, safety and security issues, pets and other issues.

If you are considering the option of retiring outside Canada on a full-time basis, refer to Chapter 11.

SNOWBIRDING IN THE UNITED STATES

As you might expect, the U.S. is the most popular Snowbird location. A common language and culture, familiarity, proximity, and accessibility make it the destination of choice for the vast majority of Canadian Snowbirds.

This and the next eight chapters relate mainly to the U.S. experience. Most of the Appendix reference material and sources of information are also relevant to being a seasonal resident in the U.S.

Many Canadians don't realize the wide range of issues that they need to consider when being a part-time resident in the U.S. For your protection and peace of mind, you need to be familiar with these issues and the options available to you regarding tax, estate planning, legal, housing, insurance, immigration and customs issues, retirement and financial planning, and more.

SNOWBIRDING IN MEXICO

In response to a lot of interest on the topic, this fourth edition of the book includes Mexico as a potential Snowbird option. Mexico is rich with culture and diversity, and over a million Canadian tourists visit there every year. Several places in Mexico are popular retirement communities for Canadian and American part-time or full-time residents.

However, there are numerous differences on some key issues when living in Mexico from what you are accustomed to in Canada or in the U.S.; these differences are covered in Chapter 10.

SNOWBIRDING OUTSIDE THE U.S. OR MEXICO

U.S. purchases are easier and less complicated than buying vacation property in popular retirement places like Mexico, the Caribbean countries, Portugal, and elsewhere. That is because there is a well-established protocol for dealing with Canada-U.S tax issues. The greater the distance from Canada, and the less developed the area, the more challenges you would face:

- National and local laws
- Regulations about foreign ownership
- Financing
- Exchange rates
- Crime
- Political stability
- Local attitudes towards foreigners
- Quality of medical services
- Medical insurance
- Tax issues
- Renting your vacation home from afar or having a local agent
- Your rights and obligations in the country as a foreigner.

If you are considering buying abroad, here are some general cautions you need to consider.

Do Your Due Diligence Research Thoroughly

This is a critical step. Fortunately, in the age of the Internet, you can do a great deal of your primary research from the comfort of your own home. Once you have worked up a checklist of questions that you want answered, you can then go to the local consulate of the country that you are interested in going to. You can also speak with the Canadian government department dealing with information and assistance for Canadians abroad. Seeking legal and tax advice on the implications of your situation—from both Canadian advisors and advisors in the country of interest to you—is very important.

The federal government has an excellent, information-rich website to assist Canadians in getting a reality check on other countries, and the steps that need to be taken. Go to www.voyage.gc.ca, which is operated by Foreign Affairs and International Trade Canada. This site provides country profiles, information on current issues, travel reports, travel warnings, publications, maps, a traveller's checklist, information on dual citizenship, advice on packing medical supplies, and much more.

You can contact the Canadian consulate closest to where you are considering buying a vacation property and ask for candid feedback on the range of issues that you need to deal with—for example, learning to speak the language reasonably well to communicate effectively. Alternatively, maybe you are thinking of buying in an international resort where the English language is commonly spoken.

You also need to check on any immunizations that are required for the area.

Once you decide you want to explore the pros and cons more seriously, you should visit the area first-hand. (Maybe you already have done so many times, which is why you have considered buying a vacation property there.) Once you have done your advance research, create a realistic list of pros and cons of buying a vacation home outside of Canada or the United States. You may want to rent a home or apartment in the area of your interest as a long-term stay for up to six months before you make up your mind. That option is popular and affordable in many countries, to attract Canadian Snowbirds who like to spend the winter months in a warm climate.

After your research, you need to do a risk/reward assessment, and then think about it a second time. You want to keep your life simple and keep your financial security intact.

Political Uncertainties

If you buy a property in a country where the political situation is tenuous, or there is a history of instability or a polarized society, that presents a whole host of additional problems. It is really not worth the hassle. If this scenario is even remotely relevant to your situation, proceed with great caution.

Foreign Laws

In addition to the foreign laws regarding property ownership, you also want to become thoroughly acquainted with the laws and regulations of the country, and what your rights are as a nonresident and non-citizen. If you are renting a property, there are many other issues you need to deal with.

Financing

Getting financing for nonresidents is not an option in most foreign countries. You will have to arrange your own financing in Canada, through a home-equity loan on your own home or adding an additional mortgage on to it, in order to pay for the vacation property outside Canada or the United States.

Owning Rental Properties Abroad

Owning a property in your own name in another country may not be possible. The first thing you need to find out is whether non-citizens or nonresidents are permitted to own property. Some countries do not allow you to own property unless you are a citizen, or you can't own property on the ocean, although inland purchases may be allowed. Sometimes a way around any restriction is to buy a property through a local resident whom you know, or through an agent, such as a law firm, on your behalf. All these options involve increased risk for obvious reasons. The less direct control you have, the more risk. Special permits could be required, as well as fees, taxes, etc.

Get a legal opinion from several lawyers in the area who are familiar with real estate law and foreign ownership. The Canadian consulate in the area could be a source of referral to legal advice, and provide other cautions.

Renting for Income

If you own a vacation home in Canada that is located a long distance from your primary residence, it can be a logistical challenge, especially if you are arranging rentals from afar. If you own a vacation home in a foreign country, the challenges can be compounded considerably. You will need to rely on others, e.g., property agents or lawyers, to look after your interests. The more people assisting you, the less net revenue you receive. It can also be more difficult to rent in a foreign country, unless you own a luxurious villa in an international resort area in high demand.

You would also need to check on the local and national tax laws where the property is located, and the cost of filing tax returns. The Canada Revenue Agency will require you to annually disclose, in your tax return, your worldwide income from all sources.

Expert Legal and Tax Advice

If you are thinking of renting a vacation home in Canada or the United States, you need to have expert tax advice. If you are thinking of renting a vacation home or buying or selling one abroad, you really need to make sure you have talented and objective legal and tax advice.

As you can see, there are a number of complications, implications, and cautions when buying vacation real estate outside Canada. For further information, refer to my books, *The Complete Guide to Buying and Owning Recreational Property in Canada* and *101 Streetsmart Condo Buying Tips for Canadians*.

KEY FACTORS TO CONSIDER

Planning is very important. With research and preparation, you will maximize your enjoyment of your U.S. stay and minimize unexpected and unwanted surprises.

Here is an overview of some of the important preliminary issues you need to consider.

Renting to Try It Out

For your first Snowbird experience, you may wish to familiarize yourself with the area for a month or so to see if you like it. After doing your research, you should be able to shortlist where you would like to go. Rental accommodation options include renting a motor home or RV, mobile home (on a permanent foundation), manufactured home (prefabricated in many cases), apartment, condominium, or house.

Where to Stay

There are many possible places to stay. The most popular U.S. Sunbelt states are Florida, Arizona, Texas, and California. You might want to be based in one area and just take side trips for a day or several days to sightsee. Or you might want to use a recreational vehicle (RV) and travel through various states. There are many factors to consider in choosing where to stay, depending on your interests and needs. For example, do you prefer varied terrain, spectacular scenery, or hot weather? Do you prefer a dry or humid climate? Maybe you prefer the ocean, the mountains, or the desert. Do you like the proximity of city life or a rural ambience? Friends could also be a factor drawing you to one place or another. Contact the local Chamber of Commerce for more information, as well as doing a Google search on the Internet. Check with your local library for videos, DVDs and books of the state and specific city you are considering. Also speak with other people you know who are Snowbirds from that location.

How to Get There

You have lots of options for how to get to your Sunbelt home. You could fly down, drive your car, or have someone else drive it for you. There are companies who will do that for a fee. Or perhaps you have an RV.

Contact your local automobile club to obtain travel guides and detailed trip-planning schedules. Look at travel books for the specific areas or states you are travelling through. These can be found in libraries or your local bookstore.

If you are driving, remember that there are many discounts for seniors for accommodation, restaurants, and so on. Ask. If you are a member of a seniors' association, find out if it offers travel-related discounts. There are also seniors' discounts available if you are flying, so make enquiries.

If you are planning to fly, long hours of physical inactivity or crossing time zones can contribute to jet lag or fatigue, and it can take several days for your natural body cycle to adjust. Heeding the following advice while you are on the plane will aid the process:

- Walk around whenever it is convenient.
- Change the position of your body at least every hour, even when you are dozing.
- Wear a sweater or jacket to deal with fluctuating temperatures.
- Wear loose-fitting clothing with an expandable waistband to make movement more comfortable.

- Leave your shoes on. Since your feet tend to swell during flight, you may have trouble getting your shoes back on if you take them off.

- Drink plenty of nonalcoholic fluids, which prevent dehydration. The air conditioning in the cabin tends to have a dehydrating effect.

- Avoid a heavy intake of alcohol, since a drink has a greater impact during flight because of the effects of air pressurization.

- Avoid carbonated beverages and heavy meals, since they tend to cause discomfort.

- If you are going through time changes, lessen the impact by changing your sleeping schedule two or three days before you leave.

What to Do When You Get There

One of the many reasons the Snowbird lifestyle is so attractive is the wide range of available activities. You are bound to meet many kindred spirits and form new friendships. Some of the activities that may interest you include these:

- Participating in regularly scheduled social activities at the mobile home park, RV park, or other retirement community. Refer to Appendix A for an activity schedule of a sample mobile home/RV park.

- Participating in social activities through local social clubs that have regular events and members who are part-time or full-time Canadians in the U.S.

- Participating in recreational activities such as golfing, swimming, tennis, shuffleboard, cards, bingo, dancing, and keep-fit exercises.

- Travelling to explore new sights and scenery as part of a tour group, in your own car or RV, or in a convoy with others. Possibly taking a cruise.

- Taking continuing education courses through local university, college, or school board adult education programs for retirees. Courses are offered on almost every subject you can imagine and can be taken for credit or just to expand your knowledge. Also consider the many excellent programs available through Elderhostel. You may wish to pursue a hobby. There are many different types of hobbies or crafts that are inexpensive and creative or challenging.

- Subscribing to local newspapers to find out what is happening in your community.

Tips on Saving Money

There are many ways of saving money as a senior. Get into the habit of asking if there is a seniors' discount, and comparison-shop. Here are some other ways to save money:

- **National seniors' associations**

  Various Canadian and U.S. associations for Snowbirds or seniors have membership benefits such as discounts on travel packages, cruises, accommodation, meals, tourist attractions, and currency exchange.

- **Long-distance discount rates**

  You can save a lot of money with various programs set up by the major long-distance companies in the U.S. and Canada. Comparison-shop to see who has the best rate package for your needs in each country. Before you commit yourself to a particular company, make sure you have the program's details clearly spelled out in writing.

- **State tourism catalogues**

  Most states have incentive packages or special seasonal promotions to coax travelers to spend tourist dollars there. These could include discounts, dollar-at-par offers, and coupon books for use for attractions, entertainment, accommodations, meals, RV rentals, and so on. Contact the specific state tourism departments and ask for the tourist information package.

- **Transportation discounts**

  Almost every company offering bus, train, or plane transportation has seniors' discounts.

- **Outlet malls**

  There are many of these malls throughout the United States, especially in the Sunbelt states. They offer discount prices on a wide range of name-brand products. Find out why particular items are discounted— whether they are seconds, inventory overruns or surplus, off-season items, or low-demand items.

- **Seniors' guides**

  Contact Health Canada (see the Appendix) for a directory of moneysaving discounts and free services for seniors in Canada for government-related amenities, such as museums, parks, and trains.

Many provinces also have similar discount policies for seniors for such provincially owned attractions.

- **Local Chamber of Commerce**

  One of the main purposes of a local Chamber of Commerce is to stimulate economic activity in the community. One way of doing this is to offer a special tourist discount package for the services and products of chamber members. Contact the Chamber of Commerce in areas where you are visiting.

- **Local newspapers**

  Many local newspapers in key Sunbelt areas have special Snowbird discount subscription packages for seasonal residents. In addition, frequently there are visitor discount-package coupons for local products or services given to seasonal subscribers by the newspaper's advertisers.

- **Banks, trust companies, credit unions, and savings and loans institutions**

  Almost all of these institutions have discounts on services to seniors. In addition, many major Canadian financial institutions, as well as several U.S. ones in Sunbelt states, have developed additional discounts or other unique programs especially for the needs of Canadian Snowbirds. These could include U.S.-dollar credit cards, Canadian-dollar accounts, lack of holding periods on Canadian cheques deposited in a U.S. bank account, currency exchange-rate commission discounts, and mortgages for U.S. real estate.

- **Advance supply of medication**

  If you are on medication, have your doctor prescribe enough medication to cover your needs before you leave Canada, so that you don't have to buy medication in the United States. Generally, you can get a three-month supply at a time in most provinces. You would then need to reorder the medication for a further three months and arrange to have it sent to you.

- **Annual discount books**

  Several companies sell books listing a wide variety of discounts on restaurants, attractions, and events. The books are published annually and are generally valid from November I through October 31 or December I through November 30. If you are residing for up to six months in an area close to a major city, you may want to check into these types of books. The books generally cost about US$30. If you go out a lot, or frequently entertain visiting relatives or friends, you may find that you can save a lot of money with these books. One major company, Entertainment Publications, has a toll-free number for information: 1-800-374-4464.

Safety and Security

One of the main concerns of any Snowbird is safety and security. To ensure that you do not have a bad experience, you need to find out about how to upgrade your home security before you leave, and learn about travelling precautions, city travel, and special areas of risk. Here is where you can obtain information to assist you:

- **Travel Information Service of the Department of Foreign Affairs and International Trade (Canada)**

  This service continually monitors and assesses potential risks to Canadians in all countries outside Canada. For example, a travel information report is available on Florida, including specific precautions to avoid being a victim of crime. Contact the Travel Information Service before your departure date. They can be reached 24 hours a day, seven days a week at 1-800-267-6788. The website is: www.dfait-maeci.gc.ca.

- **Local police department**

  You could contact the police in the place you are planning to stay to obtain crime statistics in the area and precautions to follow.

- **State tourism offices**

  These offices can provide you with travel safety tips and cautions in specific areas (e.g., Florida).

- **Travel agencies**

  Various travel agencies have free booklets and pamphlets giving general safety tips and tips specific to certain areas

- *Seniors' Guidebook to Safety and Security*

  This book is published by the RCMP Crime Prevention Branch. Contact your closest RCMP office.

- **Travel guides**

  Your auto club (CAA or AAA affiliate offices) produces travel guides that include travel safety tips and cautions.

If you have access to the Internet, you can also obtain the information immediately.

Precautions When Travelling in the U.S.

The same rules apply in the United States as at home, only more so. You are usually at greater risk than locals; as everywhere, tourists and non-locals could be targeted. Accordingly, you should follow these rules:

- Know where you are and where you are going at all times. Carefully plan road trips in advance.
- Do not pick up hitchhikers.
- Keep valuables out of sight, and never leave them in a parked vehicle.
- Leave a copy of your itinerary and proof of citizenship (for example, Canadian birth certificate or certificate of Canadian citizenship as well as a copy of your passport) with a family member or friend who can be contacted in an emergency.
- Phone home regularly if you do not have a fixed schedule.
- Keep a separate record of your travellers' cheques, credit cards, and medical insurance, and ensure that the information is also available to someone back home.
- Do not carry your passport, tickets, identification documents, cash, credit cards, and insurance papers together. Keep them separate so that in the event of theft or loss you do not lose everything.
- Use the safety deposit box at your hotel. Never leave valuables in your room.

Obtaining Medical Advice Before You Depart

Health Canada strongly recommends an individual risk assessment by your own family doctor or a travel medicine provider prior to travelling. Based on your health risks, vaccinations and any special precautions to take during your trip can be determined. This is particularly important if you are travelling outside the U.S. Health Canada's website with travel health information is: www.hc-sc.gc.ca. Also check out the Canadian government website: www.voyage.gc.ca.

a) Vaccinations

Before travelling to any foreign destination, for example Mexico, find out well in advance of your trip if you need any special vaccinations or preventive medications for such illnesses as yellow fever, typhoid, meningitis, Japanese encephalitis, hepatitis, or malaria. An International Certificate of Vaccination for yellow fever may be a legal requirement to enter certain countries. Your doctor, the local office of the Canadian Society for International Health (www.csih.org), or Health Canada (www.hc-sc.gc.ca) or Foreign Affairs and International Trade Canada (www. www.dfait-maeci.gc.ca) can provide you with this information.

Start your vaccination shots *at least* three months before you leave. In some cases, you may need several inoculations with waiting periods between each injection.

Make sure that your routine immunizations are up to date. If you were not exposed to certain diseases as a child, or were not immunized, you could be at an increased risk of contracting diseases such as tetanus, diphtheria, polio, measles, mumps, or rubella (German measles). All adults should ensure they are protected from tetanus and diphtheria by receiving a booster shot every 10 years.

b) Medication

If you take medication, be sure to pack an extra supply in case you are away for longer than expected. Carrying a duplicate of your original prescription is highly recommended—especially when travelling to a country that is particularly sensitive about drugs. Also, carry an extra (written) prescription that lists both the generic and the trade names of the drug, in case your medication is lost or stolen. This is also a good idea if you wear glasses or contact lenses—having the written prescription makes it easier to replace them.

- *Important:* Do not try to save luggage space by combining medications into a single container. Keep all medications in the original, labelled container to avoid problems.

Find out whether your medication is sold in the country you are visiting. Also check to see that it is legal. Some over-the-counter medications in Canada are illegal in other countries or require a prescription. Obtaining a note from your doctor that states the medical reasons for your prescription and the recommended dosage is also encouraged.

If you need syringes for a medical condition such as diabetes, it is very important that you take along an appropriate supply. As well, you should carry a medical certificate that shows they are for medical use.

If you have a pre-existing medical condition that could present a problem while you are travelling, it is wise to wear a MedicAlert bracelet. Through the MedicAlert Foundation, your vital medical facts become part of a database that can be accessed 24 hours a day from anywhere in the world. Call 1-800-825-3785 for membership information.

c) On Your Return

If you should become sick or feel unwell on entering Canada, see your doctor. Inform the doctor, without being asked, that you have been travelling or living outside Canada, and explain where. Likewise, if you were ill while travelling, see your doctor on your return and explain your travel history and any treatment you received.

If you have been in a malarial area and develop fever during the first year after return (especially in the first two months), see your doctor immediately. Ask for a referral to a doctor specializing in tropical medicine. Remember that:

- Anti-malarial pills do not guarantee protection against malaria
- Malaria must be ruled out by one or more thick and thin blood film examinations.

d) Supplemental Health Insurance

Do not rely on your provincial health plan to cover the total cost if you get sick or are injured while you are abroad. At best, your health plan will cover only a small portion of the bill. It is your responsibility to obtain and understand the terms of your supplementary insurance policies. Some credit cards offer their holders health and travel insurance; do not assume the card alone provides adequate coverage. Refer to the chapter on insurance. There are a number of things you need to ask about your policy:

- Does it have an in-house worldwide emergency hotline you can call if you are in trouble? Check to see if it is open 24 hours a day, seven days a week; whether the operators are multilingual; and if nurses or physicians are on staff.
- Does it pay foreign hospital and related medical costs and, if so, does it pay "up front" or expect you to pay and be reimbursed later?

- Does it provide for your medical evacuation to Canada?
- Does it pay for any required medical escort (doctor/nurse) to accompany you back to Canada?
- Does it exclude pre-existing medical conditions? (If such conditions exist for you, notify your insurance company and get an agreement in writing that you are covered for these conditions. Otherwise, you could find your claim "null and void" under a pre-existing condition clause.)
- Does it allow for cash advances if a hospital accepts only such payment?
- Does it pay for the preparation and return to Canada of your remains, should you die while travelling?

Carry details of your insurance with you. Also, tell your travel agent, a friend or relative at home, and your travelling companion how to contact your insurer. Get a detailed invoice from the doctor or hospital before you leave the country. There is nothing more frustrating than trying to get the proper paperwork when you are thousands of kilometres away. Remember, always submit original receipts for any medical services or prescriptions you received while travelling abroad, but retain a copy for your files. Most insurance companies will not accept copies or faxes.

Services Provided to Snowbirds by the Canadian Government

The Canadian government offers a wide range of emergency and other forms of assistance to Canadians in the U.S., Mexico, and in most countries throughout the world. Services are provided through the Foreign Affairs and International Trade Canada. Their website is: www.dfait-maeci.gc.ca. In the U.S. the main Canadian embassy is in Washington, DC, but there are Canadian consulates in Miami, Los Angeles, Atlanta, Boston, Dallas, Buffalo, Chicago, Detroit, New York, Minneapolis, and Seattle.

There is also an honourary consul in San Juan, Puerto Rico. The Australian consulate general in Honolulu, Hawaii, will assist Canadians in an emergency.

The consulate offices provide a range of services:

- Advice and support in the event of an accident, illness, or other emergency
- Communication with relatives and friends
- Assistance during natural disasters

- Support and assistance in the event of a death
- Identification of sources of information on local laws, regulations, and facilities
- Assistance in the event of an arrest—ensuring equitable treatment informing relatives and friends, and helping make arrangements for a lawyer
- Help with arrangements for friends and relatives to transfer funds in emergencies
- Interventions with local authorities, if required
- Notarial services such as certification of documents
- Emergency passport replacement services.

Emergency services are available 24 hours, 7 days a week. After normal business hours, calls to Canadian consular offices in the U.S. (or any Canadian consular office throughout the world) are automatically forwarded to Ottawa. Alternatively, you may call Ottawa collect directly at (613) 996-8885. The daytime Ottawa number for enquiries about Canadian consular operations and emergency services for Canadians outside Canada is toll-free at 1-800-267-6788. However, this number is only accessible from within Canada.

If you want travel information on geographic areas of potential risk to Canadians, contact the previous number. The office is open 24 hours, 7 days a week. If you want the travel information faxed to you immediately, on a 24-hour, 7-day basis, phone 1-800-575-2500. This number is only accessible from within Canada. You will have to phone collect to the (613) 996-8885 number from the U.S. or other parts of the world if you want travel information, or alternatively, phone any Canadian consular office during or after business hours. For a list of the current consular office locations and phone numbers in the U.S., Mexico, or Costa Rica, refer to the website for the Department of Foreign Affairs and International Trade Canada at: www.dfait-maeci.gc.ca. Also, ask any Canadian consular office for a free copy of a booklet called *Crossing the 49th* and a list of their other excellent publications. They are available by phoning any of the above numbers.

If you want information on what you can or cannot bring back to Canada, Customs and Excise Canada has a 24-hour, 7-day telephone service to answer your questions. The toll-free number inside Canada is 1-800-461-9999.

Pets

Many people like to take their pets with them for an extended Snowbird stay. Check to see if the mobile home park or RV park you are considering has restrictions on pets. Additionally, there are requirements before you can leave the country with your pet, and enter the U.S. or Mexico.

You need to ensure that your pet has current rabies shots and a health certificate before you leave Canada. Your vet can give you advice regarding potential health risks in the geographic area in which you will be staying. Certain states have diseases that your pet could contract. Take a sufficient supply of any medication or special foods that your pet may require, in case they are not readily available there.

Mail

You will want to be able to have people communicate with you while you are away. You have several options:

a) Canada Post

Arrange with Canada Post to do a temporary redirection. This service is available at monthly rates. The cost is nominal. Remember to account for your travel time between addresses. For example, if you're taking six days to drive home from your Snowbird address, is your mail heading south while you're heading north?

If you are going out of town for a shorter period of time, you can use a "hold mail" service instead. Sold by the week (with a two-week minimum), this service assures that your mail is held for you for a specified period of time, during which nobody can access it. When the hold mail period ends, the mail is delivered to your address.

b) Friends Sending Mail Down for You

Some people prefer to arrange for a friend, relative, or next-door neighbour to bundle their mail, remove all the junk mail, and send it on every two to four weeks.

c) Renting a Mail Box in the U.S.

Depending on where you are staying, you might already have a mail box. If not, you can easily rent a mail box at any U.S. postal service outlet, or a private mail box rental company.

d) Canadian Consulate Services

One of the services available to you if you are out of the country is to arrange for mail to be sent to the Canadian consulate office closest to where you are staying. This is not customary in the U.S. but it is in Mexico. You need to make arrangements to pick up the mail. It will not be sent to you.

Voting in Canadian Elections

In the event a federal or provincial election is called in Canada while you are down south, you are still entitled to vote by means of an absentee ballot. Elections Canada provides for enumeration and voting by mail. Reach them through Canadian embassies and consulates, or contact them at:

> Elections Canada
> 1595 Telesat Court
> Ottawa, Ontario
> K1A 0M6
> 1-800-463-6868 (within Canada only)
> www.elections.ca

If you want information about a provincial election so you can do a mail-in absentee ballot, contact your provincial elections office, or the riding office of your elected provincial representative.

Tips Before Leaving Canada

√ Thoroughly plan your Snowbird vacation before you leave by taking the time to do your research. The more preparation time, the more the enjoyment. The appendices in this book provide helpful information.

√ If you are planning to stay in an area you have not stayed in before, find out how safe it is before you go. Obtain information from the local police, the local automobile club, and the state tourist bureau.

√ Compare various discount plans with seniors' associations and decide which ones will save you the most money. Also check into seniors' and other discounts you can use in the United States.

√ If you are considering staying at a retirement community or in an RV park or mobile home park, contact the management and get names as references of others who reside there. Contact several of them and ask questions to ensure that the place is compatible with your needs.

√ Arrange with Canada Post to have your mail forwarded to your address in the United States.

√ If you are trying the Snowbird lifestyle for the first time, consider renting for the first year rather than buying.

√ Subscribe to local newspapers in the Snowbird area of interest to you, to keep aware of issues and information of interest. When you are living in the United States, many popular Snowbird destinations have regular radio news reports specifically for Canadians.

Home Exchanging as a Snowbird Option

INTRODUCTION

Snowbirds traditionally think of buying or renting in a warm southern state, or Hawaii or Mexico, or some country like Portugal or Australia. A creative option, however, is to exchange your home if you live in a high-demand area, or own a recreational second home in a resort or attractive tourist area.

You might occasionally envy those who have a timeshare in a resort area, because they can trade their timeshare allotment (of a week or a month in their home location) for a timeshare in some exotic or tropical area of the world.

If you own vacation property in Canada, you could rent your winter or all-season property periodically or seasonally, assuming that local bylaws or condo bylaws permit that, and use the money to cover all or part of your travel costs anywhere you want. For example, if you own a chalet or condo in a ski resort area, you could rent it out while you spend up to six months in the U.S. Sunbelt, Mexico, or some other desirable locale.

If you own your own vacation property, you also have many advantages over the timeshare option when it comes to using your property for other appealing purposes—quite apart from the capital gains appreciation or the pride of ownership and control over your property. For example, you could exchange your winter, summer, or all-season property with others in warm climates of the world, such as Australia, or typical snowbird states such as California, Arizona, Texas, or Florida.

The main attraction of home exchanging is that you could exchange with another owner anywhere in the world. You might like to try this option to see if you prefer a certain country or geographic location before you decide to spend a lot of time there as a Snowbird in the future.

WHAT IS A HOME OR VACATION EXCHANGE?

You probably know people who have done home exchanges, or perhaps you are familiar with the terminology but not the details of the process.

Home exchanging has become a very established and popular trend over the past 20 years. It means exchanging your vacation home and/or primary residence with other people's homes for a short time, such as a long weekend if they are in travelling distance, or a week to a month, or long-term for up to six months or a year. Home exchanges are available everywhere in the world, and can be simultaneous or non-simultaneous. Exchanges frequently include the use of a car.

Home exchanging allows you to travel almost anywhere in the world inexpensively, with your accommodation being free. Your only costs are the airfare; tourist activities; fuel for the car, if it is included; and meals. As you would be eating and driving anyway at home, the net outlay can be very minimal, especially if you are using airline points or get cheap flight deals. So you can easily vacation away from your vacation home, and experience new adventures, sights, scenes, people, and culture.

Money rarely changes hands between exchangers. It is almost an unwritten philosophical rule that one exchanger not pay another. Although one type of housing accommodation might be more luxurious than another, this is usually offset by the location or attractiveness of the area; for example, a Whistler chalet for an apartment in the centre of Paris.

Here are some points to consider about the home exchange option:

PROFILE OF A TYPICAL EXCHANGER

Well, there is no typical exchanger profile. They range from 30 years to 80-plus; from retirees with a desire to travel to parents with young children not old enough for school; from teachers with the summer off as well as Christmas and Easter breaks, to parents with school-age children who want to travel in the summer; from a single person or couple taking a sabbatical from work, with or without kids, to adults who want to experience a year or two in different parts of the world by having a continuous series of sequential exchanges, or a long-term exchange in various countries. Some people wish to travel around the world for many years, and knock off each item on the checklists from the various books on the theme of "places to see before you die" before they pass on to the ultimate extended vacation in the hereafter.

The common denominator is a love of travel, and the joy that comes from new experiences, and exploring diverse and different parts of the world.

A VACATION HOME PROVIDES FLEXIBLITY

You are presumably only using your vacation home part of the year. If it is located in a year-round access location, and particularly a developed recreational or resort area, then it would be in high demand and more desirable for exchange guests any time of the year. This will make your exchanging easier.

It is generally easier to get a vacation home ready for visitors than it is a primary residence, especially if you periodically rent your vacation home, and have drawer or closet space already cleaned out to be used by your guests. If you rent, you are accustomed to people you don't know using your property. You probably don't have as many personal possessions and clothing in your vacation home as in your primary home.

You also have flexibility in arranging an exchange with your vacation home, as the timing does not have to match your usage. This will be explained in more detail in the next point.

SIMULTANEOUS AND NON-SIMULTANEOUS EXCHANGES

The most common format is a simultaneous exchange where two parties exchange with one another at the same time. The times do not have to be of equal duration. It is whatever is arranged. For example, you might be spending four weeks in Europe, and want to spend a week in several different areas. You might exchange two weeks of your primary home and/or vacation property for two weeks in a Tuscan villa in Italy, then trade another two weeks of your vacation home for one week in Paris or Rome, and just have the freedom to roam the remaining week or travel between the above exchanges.

Another format is the non-simultaneous exchange (you don't exchange at the same time). You can bank—or the other exchangers bank—the use at a future time to be agreed or determined at some later date. For example, you might be planning to visit relatives next summer for two months, leaving your vacation home available for that period. You could arrange for exchangers in other parts of the world to use your vacation home during your absence. You would then use those banked exchanges in the future when it is more convenient for your travel scheduling. In practical terms, it does not create an issue in most cases whether you are using someone's primary residence or vacation home or both. With enough lead time, flexibility in scheduling when they are going to be away on vacation is easy to arrange.

You could also make arrangements for friends or relatives to make their homes available as part of a package of potentially available offerings. This is helpful for exchangers who want to travel in your province or other parts of Canada, for example. In exchange, you could ask them to do likewise. You will find the availability of two or more properties as an enticing menu offering is becoming more common on exchange websites.

HOME EXCHANGE WEBSITES AND CATALOGUES

When you are considering how to expose your vacation property or primary home for exchange purposes, and see what offerings exist that might interest you, there are several options available.

As most people throughout the world are computer literate and use the Internet as their primary source of research information, the most popular option is using a home-exchange website. There are many companies in Canada, the U.S., and internationally that provide this type of matchmaking service. Refer to Appendix B: Helpful Websites for some of the most popular exchange sites.

These exchange websites are automated and generally—but not always—restrict access, to allow only fellow exchange members. There is often an annual fee to become a member, which is nominal and ranges from about $75 to $200 or more, depending on the features that you select. Possibly you want to profile both your primary residence and vacation home, with separate profiles. There is usually a discounted fee for a second listing. The way it works is that you are automatically notified through your email when someone is interested in doing an exchange with you. You take the communication from there, and either decline or start exploratory discussions. Many of the exchange websites use a member exchange email address that is then sent to your personal email address, to avoid or minimize your being spammed, where the general public might have access to the exchange site. You can then choose to use your own email address or not. In some sites, only members can see the email address that you have given.

Many home exchange sites also have additional features available for you to offer if you wish, such as vacation rentals, long-term exchanges, homesitting, and simultaneous or non-simultaneous options.

To find companies that do online home exchanges, search under "home exchanges," "home swaps," or "house exchanges." If you rent out your vacation home, and are listed on various owner-direct rental sites, many of those sites also have a feature that you can display on your listing to show your home's availability for exchanges. To optimize your marketing and odds of finding an attractive match, consider listing your home on two, three, or more exchange sites. Although all exchange sites have listings throughout the world, some may be more heavily weighted in listings from certain parts of the world than others.

Some of the larger online home exchange companies also have seasonal catalogues with their listings, since those print catalogues pre-dated, of course, the online format. In most cases, you have a choice of including your listing in the catalogue or online or both, with prices adjusted accordingly. (Most people now have their listing online only; however, for a modest extra cost, having your listing in the catalogue could enhance your marketing.)

WHAT INFORMATION IS IN THE HOME EXCHANGE LISTING?

When you check out the various online sites, you will see they have similar user-friendly formats, with template fields and prompts for you to complete, so that there is consistency and ease of navigation and comprehension for the viewer. All the main exchange sites have a place for photos of your home; sometimes 12 or more photos can be uploaded. Using high-quality digital photos is important to enhance the look and feel of your home, and make it more inviting to the prospect. You can put brief descriptions under the photos in many cases.

The sites have a description of your property, which you provide, plus a checklist of home features and amenities, features of the geographic area and location, and distance from the closest major city or airport or train station. Your listing will also state the various locations that you wish to travel to, at what times of the year, and the duration of exchange. In some cases, people state they are open to offers, available at any time of the year, by scheduling arrangement. You can also state whether you are interested in simultaneous or non-simultaneous exchanges, and whether you have your primary home as well as vacation home available, and whether you have a car available. You could also list other recreational craft you have available for use, such as boats, canoes, kayaks, bikes, etc.

Your listing also sets out the owner's conditions, such as no pets, no smoking, no children, how many exchanges you have done in the past, your occupation, languages spoken, contact information, etc.

It does not take long to input your site information, and you can easily modify it any time you want, in real time. If you have a website, you can link to that site from your listing.

PASSIVE OR ACTIVE MARKETING

Once your listing is in, you can either wait until the world metaphorically knocks your door down with compelling exchange offers or take the initiative yourself. If you have a vacation home in a well-known and desirable location, you will get exchange offers. However, it is important to set up your own online initiative to ensure you find potential exchanges in the location of interest to you. Once you are a member of an exchange site, you can search by the country, city, or geographic area you want to visit, and see who has listings there. If any listing seems attractive to you, it will say where they want to go and when. If there is a geographic match of interest, that is a good start. If not, you can contact them anyway and sell them on why they should exchange with you.

If you get offers that are not timely for your interest, reply courteously that the time is not right for you, but keep them on your computer in an organized fashion in case you want to contact them in the future. If you get offers that don't interest you, simply send a courteous but straightforward reply.

It is a good technique to prepare an interesting overview letter for those you want to exchange with or who contact you for an exchange. Some exchange websites have more space than others for descriptive narrative. Your overview letter can give more information that might help persuade interested parties, such as what you and your family do, your interests, what you are looking for in an exchange, and the attractive features and amenities of your home and general area that make it an interesting place to visit.

EXCHANGING WITHOUT A CAR

Many home exchanges include the use of a car. If you are comfortable with doing so, you can include your car as part of a simultaneous exchange, or lend one of your cars (if you have more than one) for a non-simultaneous exchange. Insurance implications are discussed on the next page.

There are circumstances, however, when including a car is not necessary or desirable. The exchange family may have their own car, or decide to rent one because they want to travel throughout the province or into another province. If an exchange is your primary residence in a major city, or your vacation home is in a major resort area, a car may not be needed if public transportation is adequate, or if the beach or centre of town is within walking distance. If you are exchanging with someone located in downtown Paris, Rome, London, or New York, you may find that a car is not desired anyway, since parking can be difficult or expensive, and public transportation is more convenient.

If you are not including a car in your exchange arrangement, make sure you emphasize this in your listing or subsequent letter to a prospective exchanger.

INSURANCE COVERAGE

You want to make sure that your primary home, vacation home, and automobile insurance covers any accident, theft, or fire, if you are exchanging with someone else. If you have a vacation home with rental coverage, you should be fine. If you are usually the sole user of your vacation home, and do not carry rental insurance, or are exchanging with your primary residence, you should check with your insurance company and policy. It is likely that your policy will cover use of your home by guests for shorter periods, but for extended periods there could be notification and approval protocols in advance required by your insurance company.

If you are also exchanging the use of your car, check with your insurance broker to ensure that you will be covered if someone else is using it with your authorization.

Confirm your conversations with your insurance broker in writing to make sure there is no misunderstanding and request confirmation of the desired coverage—you don't want to rely on the broker's verbal assurances alone. Each insurance company is different and each policy is different, so don't assume anything.

You also want to check how you will be covered while using an exchange car in another country. Will your car and homeowner personal liability insurance coverage apply, or will you be covered by the policy of the exchange owner? Make sure these issues are clarified in advance in writing. Be prepared for discrepancies between insurance laws, policies, and practices in different countries. You don't want to run the risk of not being insured if you have an accident in another country. The results could be financially devastating.

In addition, you should have an agreement in writing with the person you are exchanging with, dealing with issues such as who pays the deductible portion on any insurance claim relating to the use of each other's home and car. You don't want to have any misunderstandings.

Refer to Chapter 6, Insurance Needs and Options.

GETTING EXPANDED PERSONAL LIABILITY PROTECTION

It is prudent to extend the third-party liability protection on the use of your personal car to at least $5 million, and preferably up to $15 million if you can. The premiums are reasonable, and it is worth it for peace of mind. You can imagine the risk if you had a car accident using the exchange guest's car or even your own car with a home exchange in the United States, and someone were seriously injured. An additional line of protection is to extend your personal liability protection under your homeowner policy to the maximum allowable by paying an extra premium, up to $10 million if you can. Again, these premiums tend to be modest, relative to the protection that covers you for anyone suing you personally. Make sure you understand the fine print of the coverage and any exclusions, deductibles, and limitations.

Also check into your insurance coverage for your primary residence when you are away for more than 30 consecutive days, and no one else is staying at your home. Again, policies vary, but most state that the insurance risk is greater when there is no one home for an extended period of time. They require certain protections in order for your coverage to protect you if there is a claim. Confirm the requirements in writing after your conversation.

You should go through an insurance broker who can compare rates of all relevant companies for you, so that you can short-list the companies that could meet your needs, and compare policy coverage and premium rates. It is normal to receive a pro-rata refund of the balance of any insurance policy if you have prepaid it for the year and cancel it before expiry. For more detail on insurance options, refer to Chapter 6, Insurance Needs and Options.

Some exchange companies have an exchange cancellation insurance option. It normally is a fund for the purpose of compensating members who suffer last-minute exchange cancellations, due to illness, personal crisis, etc., by their exchange partners. If you have already made financial commitments, such as booking flights, and your exchange arrangement is cancelled, you will consequently require accommodation at your destination. If you pay a set amount into a fund, the funds are pooled and available to members during that calendar/membership year, on a pro-rated basis, depending on the number and amount of claims in that time period. There is normally a maximum limit on the amount of compensation (e.g., up to $4,000), which could be total or partial. There are various conditions associated with these types of compensation funds, so make sure you obtain specific details in advance.

DOCUMENTATION TO SIGN WITH EXCHANGERS

Several of the major home-exchange websites have template documentation for you to print off and use if desired. Some examples are a home exchange agreement setting out the key terms, and an automobile exchange agreement, and what happens if there is an insurance claim. These documents would include issues such as responsibility for breakage, payment of the insurance claim deductible, or the minimum amount before an insurance claim would be made, etc. More examples are highlighted in the last section of this chapter.

LONG-TERM EXCHANGES

You might want to exchange for several months or much longer in a particular area. Possibly a specific location is required by the exchanging party for business or personal reasons. You could give a potential exchanger the option of using your primary residence as well as vacation home. For example, there could be artists or writers who might welcome the opportunity to stay in a relaxing resort or metropolitan area for creative stimulation.

If you are exchanging for an extended stay, discuss in advance how to deal with expenses such as utilities. It is not uncommon in this scenario for the exchange parties to reimburse each other for the utility expenses, especially if they might be disproportional. For example, air conditioning or other utility usage such as propane or natural gas might be more expensive in one country than another.

PREPARING FOR YOUR EXCHANGE GUESTS

Once you have your exchange arranged, you want to ensure that your home is ready for your new guests. If you frequently rent your vacation home, you are probably prepared for this routine. However, the common protocol for home-exchange guests tends to be a bit more personal. Here are some basic tips to maximize the enjoyment of your guests. Chances are that you will receive a reciprocal welcome procedure, especially if your exchange guests are experienced with the exchange lifestyle.

- Describe your home accurately in your listing and in all correspondence. You want your home-exchange partners to be pleasantly surprised, not disappointed, when they arrive. Always be upfront about the existence of pets, and whether they will be removed and cared for by others, or whether you would like your exchange guests to care for them.

- Leave your home clean. You probably do anyway. Standards of cleanliness vary and people's expectations can vary, but at a minimum you should make sure that floors are vacuumed and mopped, refrigerator emptied, stove and oven free from grease, shower and bath free of mould and grime, and surfaces dust-free.

- Leave sufficient clean sheets and towels, toilet paper, tissues, soap, shampoo, etc.

- Don't leave paperwork or bills hanging around. Clear away enough of your personal belongings to leave space on shelves, in closets, and in drawers that your guests can easily empty their suitcases, arrange their things in bedrooms and bathrooms, and feel at home. Any items that are precious or breakable, which might cause you worry, should be stored in a locked "no go" area of your house.

- Compile a clear and useful "Guide to Your Home and Surroundings." Include local tourist information and maps, your favourite restaurants and prices and maybe menus, and household notices about the use of electrical appliances, pool maintenance, pet and plant care (if applicable), and when the rubbish is put out.

- Compile an emergency phone number list, including a local contact number for a family member, relative, friend or friendly neighbour for the guest to contact if there are any questions or problems.

- Have an exchange contract to avoid any misunderstandings and to clarify who pays for what in terms of telephone; electric bills; insurance deductibles in case of accidents; replacement of staples like flour, sugar, and seasonings; and payment for a cleaning service at end of the stay. (Normally, you make arrangements for your own clean-up after the guests have gone to meet your own high standards of cleanliness.)

- Leave sufficient food for a first meal—just a snack to keep them going until they have time to go shopping. Leaving a fresh bouquet of flowers is always appreciated and sets a welcoming environment. It is a nice touch to leave a small gift of welcome, such as a bottle of local wine or local maple syrup. It is always a pleasant surprise to experience the thoughtfulness of the home exchanger, especially at the end of a long journey.

- Before leaving your exchange residence, remember to put things back where you found them, and leave the house organized and clean. This will be a welcome sight when your exchange partners arrive back home. Leaving a thank you card, along with a small gift, is also a thoughtful gesture.

Tips Before Leaving Canada

If you are considering a short- or long-term home exchange outside of Canada, here are some tips:

√ If you are exchanging cars, make sure that you car insurance will cover an approved third party driving the car. Speak to your insurance agent, and get that confirmed in writing in advance. Find out from the home exchange people the exact name and ages of the people who will be driving the car.

√ Sign an agreement in advance with the home exchange guest that clearly covers their responsibility to pay your insurance claim deductible in the event of any accident. Also find out from your insurance company the effect of you future premiums as a result of an accident, so that you can cover that aspect in your agreement as well.

√ Also, do the reverse to the above process. Check with the people whose home you are staying in and possibly whose car you are using to get confirmed in writing from them what coverage protection they have in the event that an accident or incident occurs while you are using their property or car, and what deductible would need to be paid. Confirm all these issues in writing so that there is no misunderstanding, and both parties to the home exchange are protected.

√ Check with your home insurance company that you will be fully covered in the event that any incident occurs while you are away, but while others will be staying at your home. Get that confirmation clarified in writing.

√ If you are having a long-term stay, clarify in writing what expenses you will be responsible for, and vice-versa, and an average of what those expenses have been historically.

√ Check with your home insurance company as well as car insurance company, to see if there is extended coverage that protects you while you are using someone else's car or home and an accident or incident occurs.

CHAPTER 3

Financial Planning and Money Management

INTRODUCTION

In order to achieve and maintain the Snowbird lifestyle, you need to have a realistic understanding of your present and future financial resources so that you can budget accordingly. This chapter covers the typical risk areas, the financial planning process, types of federal and provincial government pensions, employer-funded pension plans, your own tax-sheltered plans, the safety of your retirement plans and deposits, and your home as a source of additional income.

Numerous Canadian books are available on financial planning and money management issues and options. Books on these topics are becoming a Canadian growth industry. Many of these books are objective, balanced, informative, and relevant. Others are written to market the writer or his or her company or services and products and thus may be biased. It therefore pays to read selectively and to assess the credentials, credibility, and motivation of the writer. It also helps to read several books to get different perspectives and become familiar with the concepts involved.

Various educational seminars are available to further inform you about topical matters relating to retirement and Snowbird issues. The same cautions noted above relating to books apply to seminars.

In any event, you should obtain objective professional advice before you embark on any particular course of action. How to select professional advisors is covered in Chapter 9. The quality of the advice you rely on will profoundly affect your financial well-being, peace of mind, and quality of lifestyle.

POTENTIAL FINANCIAL AND OTHER RISK AREAS

There are 15 risk areas that could affect your financial net worth, cash flow, and lifestyle. In many cases, you can eliminate, minimize, or control each of these risk areas by knowing about them, doing research, and making prudent decisions. If you are retired, are planning retirement, or wish to become a Snowbird, these 15 key risk areas are particularly important to know. Statistically, if you

retire at 55 years of age, you can expect to live to 85 and have 30 years of retirement—almost as long as your working life. Planning to have enough funds to
meet your lifestyle needs is obviously critically important. Some of the potential risk areas are interrelated, but they are considered separately because they
should be identified specifically as risk. By obtaining customized financial
planning advice relevant to your own situation, you should be able to anticipate and neutralize many of the key financial risks.

1. Currency Risk

This is a particularly important issue for Canadian Snowbirds. If the Canadian
dollar drops in value relative to the U.S. dollar, you will notice an increase in the
cost of living due to the reduced purchasing power of your Canadian money
when you convert it to U.S. currency. If it goes down 5 percent, you have lost 5
percent of purchasing power in the United States. Conversely, an increase in the
Canadian dollar will enhance your purchasing power.

2. Inflation Risk

This is one of the most serious financial risks to those in retirement. Although
both Canada and the United States currently enjoy very low inflation rates, that
can change quickly. As you are probably aware, inflation eats away at your purchasing power. Inflation at 5 percent will reduce your purchasing power by 50
percent in less than 15 years. If you have investments that have interest rates or
value that is keeping up with the rate of inflation, or if you have annuities or
RRIFs indexed for inflation, then your purchasing power would at least remain
constant. If you have a fixed income, the inflation issue is especially critical.

   For example, with Canada Savings Bonds, inflation would erode the purchasing power of the bond as well as the interest. You also have to look at the
real rate of return on your money, after tax and inflation is factored in. If you
were earning 7 percent interest and were taxed at 35 percent, your net return
would be 4.5 percent. If inflation were 3 percent, in real terms, your purchasing
power would only be 1.5 percent.

3. Deflation Risk

If there is a severe or prolonged economic downturn or recession, the value of
your assets could drop accordingly.

4. Interest Rate Risk

Interest rates in Canada and the United States have been very volatile in the past 15 to 20 years on any type of interest-sensitive financial investment. In the early 1980s the prime rate was in the double digits, up to 22 percent. This was of course attractive for people with interest income from term deposits, mortgages, or bonds. By the mid-1990s, rates had plunged to the low single digits, down to 5 percent. Interest rate risk can cut both ways, however. For example, if you set your lifestyle needs based on high interest rate returns, your lifestyle will be negatively affected when rates fall. Or if you lock yourself into a fixed-rate bond when rates are low and then interest rates increase, the value of the bond investment will go down when you try to sell it. Another example is if you have a locked-in annuity bought at a low interest rate. If rates go up and there is inflation along with it, your purchasing power and lifestyle will be affected.

5. Government Policy Risk

The Canadian and U.S. governments are constantly changing the tax or pension laws, depending on the political philosophy of the party in power and on economic pressures. For example, Old Age Security pension payments are reduced if the recipient's income exceeds a certain amount. This amount could become lower and lower over time. The Guaranteed Income Supplement could be reduced or the eligibility criteria tightened up. Federal and/or provincial income taxes could be increased. The $100,000 personal capital gains deduction was removed many years ago. Provincial governments could reduce out-of-country medical coverage, resulting in increased out-of-country supplemental insurance premiums. The U.S. government could bring in legislation to increase taxes paid by non-U.S. residents, or a state could increase an estate tax on death on real estate or U.S. assets that you own.

6. Repayment Risk

This type of risk comes in several forms. One form of risk is not being repaid what you are owed when it is due or when you want your money. For example, if you buy a bond, the issuer's ability to repay you determines whether you are going to get your money back. Although bonds issued by municipalities, corporations, or governments rarely default, several levels of credit risk are normally involved. Agencies such as Standard & Poor's, Moody's Investors Service, and

Dominion Bond Rating Service rate the credit risk of various bonds, which generally ranges from AAA to D. These ratings indicate the repayment risk you are taking with a particular bond issue.

Insurance companies are also rated by different agencies. Considering that insurance companies go under from time to time, you don't want to risk losing money you might be expecting from insurance proceeds, cash surrender value funds, disability insurance payments, or annuities.

If you place money in an institution by means of a term deposit, for example, you want to feel confident that you will get your money back, including all principal plus interest, if the institution fails.

A discussion of certain types of money protection you should be aware of is covered on pages 55 to 58 in this chapter.

Another form of repayment risk is receiving your invested money back sooner than you expect or want it. For example, if you lock in a bond with an 8 percent yield and the rate falls to 4 percent, you will not be able to replace that bond with a new one at the same yield if the bond issuer redeems or calls the bond earlier than anticipated. Many corporate bond issuers have this right after a certain number of years after the bond was issued. Most government bonds cannot be called.

7. Market Cycle Risk

Many markets, such as the real estate market, stock market, and bond market, are cyclic. Depending on where your investment is at any point in the cycle, it could slowly or rapidly diminish in value. If you wanted or needed to sell it, you could lose money. Generally, the longer you hold an investment, the less the risk. The shorter the term you intend to keep the investment, the higher the risk that a market correction could impair your investment return.

8. Economic Risk

The economy obviously has an effect on such assets or investments as real estate or stocks. The more buoyant the economy, the more buoyant the price of real estate and stocks, and vice versa.

9. Lack of Diversification Risk

The risk here is having all your assets in one specific kind of investment, like real estate or bonds or stocks. You are not protected if that asset drops in value and you do not have alternative assets to buffer the loss. If you spread the risk, you lower the risk. To spread the risk, you could have different types of assets as well as different kinds of investments within each type of asset.

10. Lack of Liquidity Risk

Liquidity means the speed at which you can sell your asset, either at all, or at a fair price. For example, if you need to sell your home or stocks and the market has dropped, you could still sell, but it could take much longer and you will obtain a lower price. Negative publicity about stocks and real estate can have a dramatic short-term effect on the market, as potential buyers become nervous. Less demand means lower prices.

11. Taxation Risk

This risk affects your lifestyle if increased taxation reduces your anticipated retirement income. This form of risk could come from higher levels of income tax, the taxing of part or all of your income currently exempt from taxation (e.g., Guaranteed Income Supplement), or the taxing of RRSPs or RRIFs in some fashion, other than when you take the money out. Naturally, all the above possible initiatives would result in a strong public demand to rescind them. Economic pressure on federal or provincial governments to reduce their respective debts, however, could result in all areas of personal income being subject to review for additional tax.

12. Pension Risk

This type of risk takes various forms. One form is for federal or provincial governments to reduce the net amount of pension you receive through Old Age Security (OAS), Canada Pension Plan (CPP), or Guaranteed Income Supplement (GIS), through taxation, increased taxation, clawbacks based on your other income, reduction in amount of money, or more restrictive eligibility criteria. As you may know, if your taxable income is currently over $63,511, your OAS is "clawed back," or reduced by the amount of your income over $63,511. This amount could change at any time. Another form of risk is that a pension fund manager may not invest money prudently and the return to the pension fund may be less than expected. Or an employer may not make any profit in a particular year and therefore does not contribute anything to the pension fund. Or possibly an employer reduces or eliminates some pension plan collateral benefits, such as life insurance or health and dental plan coverage, for cost-saving reasons. Types of employer-funded pension plans are covered in this chapter on pages 46 to 49.

13. Acts of God Risk

When selecting your Sunbelt retirement location, it is important to assess the risk from natural disasters or "acts of God." These could include hurricanes, floods, fires, or earthquakes. For example, certain areas of California are prone to brush fires and earthquakes. Parts of Florida are prone to hurricanes or floods. Not only do these disasters pose a risk for your home or health and for the resale potential or value of your home, many insurance policies exclude any coverage of acts of God or specifically exclude potential risks of that nature that may be endemic to the area you are considering. Make sure you know what risks are partially or fully excluded. If you make a claim, an insurance company may require you to pay a deductible amount you cannot afford. Check with local insurance companies, real estate agents, and the local, state, or federal weather bureaus for seasonal statistics and risks in the geographic area you are considering.

14. Weather Risk

Apart from acts of God risks, when selecting your Sunbelt or retirement home consider such weather issues as average snowfall (if applicable), rainfall, and temperature at various times of the year. A very hot climate may hinder your comfort and outdoor activities (and increase your air conditioning costs). Conversely, a cold, rainy climate could reduce your physical comfort and safety, as well as increase your heating bills, augment the amount of home maintenance required, and reduce outside activity. Check with the weather bureau for seasonal statistics in the area you are considering. If the weather conditions are not attractive, the resale value of a home there could be affected.

15. Crime Risk

Certain Sunbelt states have areas of higher crime than others. Clearly this is an important area to clarify. Apart from your own peace of mind and health, local crime could result in break-ins, theft, vandalism, muggings, or other criminal activities. It would also affect the insurance premiums you pay (based on risk and claims experience) or increase the deductibles you might have to pay on any claim. The resale value of your home would obviously be affected. Check with the local police department for crime statistics in the area you are considering.

THE FINANCIAL PLANNING PROCESS

Financial planning is very individual and personal. It should take into account all the psychological and financial factors that may have an impact on your financial goals and objectives. In short, comprehensive financial planning provides you with a long-term strategy for your financial future, taking into consideration every aspect of your financial situation and how each one affects your ability to achieve your goals and objectives. A financial plan can help you construct the foundation on which to build a secure financial future.

1. How a Financial Advisor Helps You

Through six distinct steps in the comprehensive financial planning process, a financial advisor helps you:

- Clarify your present situation
- Decide where you want to be by identifying both financial and personal goals and objectives
- Identify financial problem areas
- Provide a written financial plan with recommendations
- Implement the agreed-upon recommendations and
- Periodically review and revise your plan.

2. What a Comprehensive Financial Plan Contains

Your financial plan is the strategy for achieving your goals and objectives. A comprehensive financial plan should address all pertinent areas relating to your situation. Those areas that the planner does not personally address in the development of the plan should be coordinated by the planner.

You may want your plan to cover only a specific area, such as estate or investment planning. Although a plan for such a goal or objective may be appropriate for the areas covered, you should be aware that it is not a comprehensive plan.

Your financial plan document should contain not only the plan strategies but also all pertinent data relating to the development of the plan. Although the order and style of presentation may vary, the plan document should include at least the 13 essential elements described below. This does not necessarily mean that your plan will be long, since each area should be addressed so that it suits your personal situation.

Completing the form in Appendix C will provide a lot of the background data for dealing with the following areas:

- Personal data

- Your goals and objectives

- Identification of issues and problems

- Assumptions used in plan preparation

- Balance sheet/net worth

- Cash flow management (e.g., income and expenses)

- Income tax strategies

- Risk management (e.g., different types of insurance)

- Investments

- Special needs, such as retirement planning

- Estate planning

- Recommendations

- Implementation.

If any area of the financial plan is not within the range of the financial planner's expertise, the planner has the responsibility to coordinate with other professionals and document such coordination in the financial plan report. Documentation of such areas can include the professional's name and when the review will be completed.

The analysis that is called for in all the elements of the plan should consist of a review of pertinent facts, a consideration of the advantage(s) and/or disadvantage(s) of the current situation, and a determination of what, if any, further action is required. The plan should include a summary statement providing the planner's comments on the analysis and his or her recommendations, where appropriate, for each element of the plan.

Once you have a plan in place, you should have it reviewed and revised from time to time to make sure you are on track and the current strategies are still appropriate for your needs.

As noted earlier, how to select a professional financial planner is covered in Chapter 9.

GOVERNMENT PENSION PLANS

There are many forms of federal and provincial government pension or financial assistance programs. Following is a brief overview of the key programs and guidelines that you should be familiar with. They are periodically modified, of course, so obtain a current update of regulations and criteria relevant to your circumstances. In addition, there could be exceptions in your case to the general guidelines outlined. For more information and assistance, including eligibility benefits, indexing, and payment outside of Canada, contact the Income Security Programs Branch of the Human Resources Development Canada (HRDC) office closest to you. Look in the Blue Pages of the phone book under Government of Canada. The HRDC covers all the programs described below, except for number 4 (covered by provincial governments) and number 10 (covered by Veterans Affairs Canada). Also contact your closest Health Canada office, found in the same Government of Canada section of the phone book (Blue Pages). Ask for their free publications, including the *Seniors Guide to Federal Programs and Services,* which will provide you with information about other government-subsidized services for seniors.

Keep in mind that the OAS, GIS, SPA, and CPP benefits are *not* paid automatically. You have to apply for them. You can arrange to have these funds automatically deposited into your bank account, a convenient option for Snowbirds. A brief discussion of these pension plans follows.

1. Old Age Security Pension (OAS)

The OAS pension is a monthly benefit available, if applied for, to anyone 65 years of age or over. OAS residence requirements must also be met. An applicant's employment history is not a factor in determining eligibility, nor does the applicant need to be retired. You have to pay federal and provincial income tax on your OAS pension.

Higher-income pensioners also repay part or all of their benefit through the tax system, referred to as a clawback. Contact your local HRDC office or Health Canada for the current amount of the clawback. This amount could be increased by the government over time. At present, there is a clawback if you earn more than $63,511. The government takes off the clawback amount in advance, based on your previous year's tax return. This rate is subject to change.

All benefits payable under the *Old Age Security Act* are increased in January, April, July, and October of each year based on increases in the cost of living as measured by the Consumer Price Index (CPI).

Once a full or partial OAS pension has been approved, it may be paid indefinitely outside Canada, if the pensioner has lived in Canada for at least 20 years after reaching 18 years of age. Otherwise, payment may be made only for the month of a pensioner's departure from Canada and for six additional months, after which payment is suspended. The benefit may be reinstated if the pensioner returns to live in Canada.

2. Guaranteed Income Supplement (GIS)

The GIS is a monthly benefit paid to residents of Canada who receive a basic, full, or partial OAS pension and who have little or no other income. GIS payments may begin in the same month as OAS pension payments. Recipients must reapply annually for the GIS benefit. Thus, the amount of monthly payments may increase or decrease according to reported changes in a recipient's yearly income. Unlike the basic OAS pension, the GIS is not subject to income tax.

The GIS may be paid outside Canada for only six months following the month of departure from Canada, regardless of how long the person lived in Canada.

3. Spouse's/Widowed Spouse's Allowance (SPA)

The SPA is paid monthly. It is designed to recognize the difficult circumstances faced by many widowed persons and by couples living on the pension of only one spouse. Recipients must reapply annually. Benefits are not considered as income for income tax purposes.

The SPA is not payable outside Canada beyond a period of six months following the month of departure, regardless of how long the person lived in Canada.

4. Provincial Social Security Supplement Programs

Some provinces have guaranteed annual income systems. If you are 65 years of age or older and you receive the federal Guaranteed Income Supplement, you might qualify for additional benefits from your province. These benefits will ensure that your income does not fall below the province's guaranteed income level.

To apply for provincial assistance, contact your provincial government.

5. Canada Pension Plan (CPP)/Quebec Pension Plan (QPP)

The CPP is a contributory, earnings-related social insurance program. It ensures a measure of protection to a contributor and his or her family against the loss of income due to retirement, disability, or death. The plan operates throughout Canada. Quebec has its own similar program, the Quebec Pension Plan (QPP), which is closely associated with the CPP. The operation of the two plans is coordinated through a series of agreements between the federal and Quebec governments. Benefits from either plan are based on pension credits accumulated under both, as if only one plan existed.

Benefits paid by the CPP are considered income for federal and provincial income tax purposes. You must apply for all CPP benefits, and you should apply for your retirement pension at least six months before you want to receive it.

A CPP retirement pension may be paid at age 60 with a penalty for starting before age 65. However, the contributor must have wholly or substantially ceased pensionable employment. Contributors are considered to have substantially ceased pensionable employment if their annual earnings from employment or self-employment do not exceed the maximum retirement pension payable at age 65 for the year the pension is claimed. After turning 65, a pensioner is not required to stop work to receive a retirement pension.

All CPP benefits are adjusted in January each year to reflect increases in the cost of living as measured by the Consumer Price Index.

All benefits under the CPP are payable no matter where the beneficiary lives, whether in Canada, in the United States, or abroad.

6. CPP Disability Pension

To receive a disability pension, a contributor must have been disabled according to the terms of the CPP legislation, must have made sufficient contributions to the plan, must be under the age of 65, and must apply in writing.

A contributor is considered to be disabled under CPP if he or she has a physical or mental disability that is both severe and prolonged. "Severe" means that the person cannot regularly pursue any substantially gainful occupation. "Prolonged" means that the disability is likely to be continued for a long time or indefinitely, or could result in death.

A disability pension begins in the fourth month after the month a person is considered disabled. It is payable until the beneficiary turns 65 or recovers from the disability (if this occurs before age 65), or until the beneficiary dies.

When the recipient of a disability pension reaches age 65, the pension is automatically converted to a retirement pension.

7. CPP Surviving Spouse's Pension

A spouse of a deceased contributor or a person of the opposite sex who lived in a marital relationship with a contributor before his or her death may be eligible for a survivor's pension. To qualify, the deceased must have contributed to the CPP during at least one-third of the number of calendar years in his or her contributory period. If the deceased's contributory period was less than nine years, then at least three years' worth of CPP contributions are needed. If the contributory period was more than 30 years, at least 10 years' worth of contributions are required.

To qualify for a benefit, the surviving spouse must be 45 or older. There are some exceptions for those younger than 45 years of age.

8. CPP Death Benefit

A death benefit may be paid to the estate of a deceased contributor, if contributions to the CPP were made for the minimum qualifying period, the same as for a surviving spouse's pension. The death benefit is also paid if there is no will or estate. In this case, the benefit is usually paid to the person or agency responsible for funeral costs.

The death benefit is a lump-sum payment equal to six times the monthly retirement pension of the deceased contributor or roughly 10 percent of the year's maximum pensionable earnings, whichever is less.

9. Reciprocal Social Security Agreements with the United States

Reciprocal social security agreements allow for the coordination of two countries' social security programs and make social security benefits portable between countries. The United States is party to this agreement with Canada on the items discussed below:

a) Old Age Security

The OAS program is included in reciprocal social security agreements. Such agreements enable people who live or who have lived in the other contracting country—for example, the United States—to add those periods of residence abroad to periods of residence in Canada to satisfy the minimum eligibility requirements for the basic OAS pension and the SPA. For example, someone who has lived in Canada for less than the 10 years required to receive a partial OAS pension in Canada would be able to use periods of residence in the other country to meet the 10-year requirement. A similar provision would apply for someone who has lived in Canada for less than the 20 years needed to receive a partial OAS pension outside the country.

Under some agreements, benefits may be based only on periods of residence or contributions after specific dates. Residents who have little or no other income may receive the GIS. As noted earlier, the GIS is not payable outside Canada beyond a period of six months, regardless of how long the person lived in Canada. Refer to Chapter 7 and to changes to the Canada/U.S. tax treaty that affect taxation of social security benefits.

b) Canada Pension Plan

Agreements are designed to avoid duplicate coverage—that is, the need to contribute to both the CPP and the comparable program of the other country for the same work.

Agreements may help people to qualify for disability, survivor's, and death benefits under the CPP. Each of the benefits has minimum qualifying conditions. An agreement may allow periods of contribution to the other country's social security system (or in some cases periods of residence abroad) to be added to periods of contribution to the CPP in order to meet these conditions. Once eligibility has been established, the amount of benefits is based on actual contributions to the CPP.

The CPP retirement pension is not included in agreements, since it is payable to anyone who has made at least one valid contribution. It is not necessary, therefore, to use periods of contribution in the other country to establish eligibility for the retirement benefit. Refer to Chapter 7 and to changes to the Canada/U.S. tax treaty that affect taxation of social security payments.

c) Provincial Social Security Programs

Canada's reciprocal social security agreements contain a provision that allows provinces to conclude understandings with other countries concerning social security programs under their jurisdiction—for example, the workers' compensation plans.

d) U.S. Social Security Programs

In many countries, nationality is an important criterion in determining eligibility for social security benefits. Non-citizens may be required to meet special conditions before they can receive a pension, and the payment of benefits to non-citizens living abroad may be severely restricted or even prohibited. Through the social security agreement between Canada and selected countries, including the United States, citizens and non-citizens become entitled to those benefits on the same conditions as the citizens of the other country. Most important, Canadian residents may start to receive benefits from the other country.

Most social security programs require contributions during a minimum number of years before a benefit can be paid. There may also be requirements for contributions in the period just before application for a benefit. People who have contributed to the programs of another country may not have enough periods of contributions to meet such requirements. Under the Canada-U.S. agreement, periods of residence in Canada and/or periods of contributions to the CPP may be used to satisfy the eligibility conditions of the other country's social security system. Refer to Chapter 7 and to changes to the Canada/U.S. tax treaty that affect taxation of social security payments.

10. Veterans' Pension

Veterans Affairs Canada provides a wide range of services and benefits to war veterans and former members of the Canadian Armed Forces in the form of disability pensions, survivors' pensions, and help with funeral and burial expenses. For more information, contact the nearest Veterans Affairs district office, listed in the Blue Pages of your telephone directory under Government of Canada. You must apply for all pensions or services provided by Veterans Affairs Canada. They do not start automatically.

EMPLOYER-FUNDED PENSION PLANS

You should be aware of the types of retirement plans sponsored by employers. You can make enquiries as to what exact benefits you will receive, how they will be structured, and how soon you could receive them. Some employers have more than one plan. Some employers will also include extended health and dental plan coverage as well as life insurance coverage after you retire.

1. Registered Pension Plans (RPPs)

These are the most heavily regulated by the government. The two main types of plans are defined benefit and defined contribution. The plan could be "contributory," in which you and the employer contribute payments, or "non-contributory," in which the employer pays the full amount due each year.

a) Defined Benefit Plan

This type of plan promises you a pension of a specific amount of money, based on your years of service and/or salary. There is no risk that your pension funding could be affected by economic or market fluctuations, since the employer must set aside, by law, enough money, separate from other employer funds, to capitalize the specific pension that has been promised to you. The pension fund will therefore exist even if the employer ceases to operate, though future benefits could then be restricted. If the pension fund investments do poorly, the employer must compensate by putting extra money into the fund.

There are two forms of defined benefit plans:

- **Accruing benefits plan**

This plan can vary considerably, depending on the employer. Some offer a pension based on a percentage (e.g., 2 percent) of your average salary over your final three or five years of employment. This amount is then multiplied by your years of employment with the company. Other plans average all your earnings during your employment with the firm. This is not as attractive an arrangement as the previous one, which is based on your tax-earning years.

Some employers offer a supplemental pension plan to extend the amount of pension from the RPP pension ceiling set by Canada Revenue Agency.

- **Flat benefit plan**

This type of plan bases the calculation of the pension on a flat amount per month for each year of employment—for example, $30 per month.

Some of these two types of plans include partial or full indexing for inflation. If this is your situation, you should verify that this provision is guaranteed, or possibly required by provincial legislation, rather than optional on the part of the company.

b) Defined Contribution Plan

These plans are sometimes referred to as "money purchase plans." The employer promises to contribute a certain amount to your pension account annually— for example, 3 to 6 percent of your annual salary. The amount of the pension, however, is not specified. You may be able to make your own contributions. In this type of plan, your employer invests the contribution on your behalf. The amount of your pension will vary, depending on the value of your pension account on retirement. If your employer invests well, you will receive a greater retirement income benefit. If not, you will get a lower amount. Your risk is related to the success of the pension fund manager and the level of interest rates when you retire.

- **Vesting**

    Vesting means that the pension credits you have earned are locked in, so you won't lose these benefits if you change your job. Ask your employer or the federal or provincial pension authorities responsible for your plan. Depending on the regulations, you might have to participate in the plan for two to five years or more before it can be vested.

    If you quit your job, you can let your vested credits remain with your employer rather than taking out the amount you are entitled to in a lump sum, which would, of course, be taxable income. If the vested credits remain, you could receive a retirement pension that could net you more than you otherwise could have earned. It all depends on your needs and circumstances and what you want to do with the money. Alternatively, you could transfer the money into a locked-in RRSP. Although you can't withdraw it until your normal retirement age, you would control how it is invested. You must use the funds to provide retirement income, which would normally require you to buy a life annuity or a Life Income Fund (LIF). An LIF could allow you to wait until the age of 80, if you want, before buying a life annuity. Check what regulations and options apply in your case.

2. Deferred Profit Sharing Plans (DPSPs)

These plans are also regulated by government but are less restrictive than RPPs. They are similar to a defined contribution RPP in the sense that the amount you receive relates to the amount of the employer contribution and how effectively the money was invested.

There are some significant differences, however, from RPPs. The employer is only permitted to contribute half the amount of a defined contribution plan. If there is an annual profit, the employer is obligated to make a minimum contribution. No contribution is required if the company shows a loss that year. Another difference is that you may not have to wait until retirement to withdraw money from the plan.

3. Group RRSPs

Some employers prefer not to have the regulatory controls of an RPP or a DPSP but still provide an employer-sponsored pension plan. A common approach is for the employer to contract with a professional money manager to establish an RRSP for each employee, with the administration fee normally borne by the employer. The employer could then increase your salary and deduct the increase from your salary to put into the individual RRSP. The benefit to you is that you have a form of forced savings plan, and you will receive more net pay each month, since the employer can withhold less for tax deductions as a result of the RRSP offset. The disadvantage is that you do not normally have the freedom to select your RRSP investments. The phrase "group RRSP" is a misnomer; although it is set up for a group of employees, each RRSP is individual.

YOUR OWN TAX-SHELTERED PENSION PLANS

1. Registered Retirement Savings Plans (RRSPs)

a) Types of RRSPs

There are three main types of RRSPs:

- **Deposit plans**

  These are offered by banks, trust companies, credit unions, and life insurance companies, and they include term deposits or Guaranteed Investment Certificates (GICs). Terms generally range from one to five years. It is prudent to vary the dates that your money comes due to average out changes in interest rates.

- **Managed plans**

In this type of plan, which includes mutual funds, your money is pooled with that of others in a diversified portfolio of stocks, bonds, real estate, and other assets. Alternatively, you may have a singular plan managed just for your investments. The value of the assets can vary, of course, depending on the market.

- **Self-directed plans**

With these plans, you are responsible for managing your own portfolio, subject to various restrictions. The funds are held by a trust company. You can buy and place in your plan a wide variety of assets, such as stocks, bonds, or mortgages.

Many retired people prefer to opt for the deposit plan or managed plan in conservative investments so that preservation of capital is foremost.

b) Types of RRSP Withdrawal Options

At some point you will have to decide what to do with the money you have built up in an RRSP—in other words, turn retirement savings into retirement income. If you have RRSP funds transferred from a pension plan, you may be subject to pension legislation. For example, you may be required to purchase only life annuities with your funds. Some provinces have approved various alternatives to life annuities. They are called Life Income Funds (LIFs) and/or Locked-in Retirement Income Funds (LRIFs). You basically have three RRSP withdrawal options:

- **Lump-sum withdrawal**

Since all the money you withdraw is taxable in the year you receive it, most people don't choose this option unless there is an urgent need. Depending on the amount you take out, the tax liability could be high.

- **Registered Retirement Income Fund (RRIF)**

This option is covered in more detail on the next page. It means you can keep deferring tax on your money, as with an RRSP.

- **Annuities**

Annuities provide regular income for life or for a specific period. This option is covered in more detail in Section 3.

2. Registered Retirement Income Funds (RRIFs)

An RRIF has become a very popular retirement income option because it pro-vides the flexibility to control your retirement income and investments. It is like an RRSP in that you can select the investments you want, adjust your income payments, or take lump-sum withdrawals at your pleasure. You can have a self-directed RRIF if you want. Like an RRSP, an RRIF can grow tax-free, if you have income or growth types of investments. An RRIF is like an RRSP in reverse. Instead of putting in a certain amount of money each year, you withdraw money that is taxable. You have to draw a minimum mandatory amount, but there is no maximum amount. (Obviously, the higher the payments you make to yourself, the sooner your funds will be depleted.) RRIFs can continue for the lifetime of the holder or the spouse. You have to make a conversion from an RRSP to an RRIF by the end of your 71st year, although you can do it earlier if you prefer—for example, if you need to qualify for the Pension Income Credit.

Your choice of RRIF will have an important impact on meeting your retirement needs. The key factors to consider include the amount of income you anticipate you will require in the short term and long term, and how long your savings will last.

a) Types of RRIF Withdrawal Options

Since you are permitted to have more than one RRIF, you might want to com-bine your withdrawal options to suit your needs. Not all institutions provide the options listed below. Obtain professional advice in advance.

- **Level payout**

Payments are the same each month, over, for example, a 25-year period. Although it is similar in some aspects to an annuity, you have control at all times.

- **Fixed-term payout**

This is used by people who want to use up the funds in a shorter period of time—for example, 10 to 15 years—frequently because of ill health.

- **Minimum payout**

This option maximizes your investment by allowing the funds to grow in a compounding tax-free environment. You can set up your RRIF at the end of your 71st year, but, for example, with payments to commence at the end of your 72nd year. You don't have to take any payments in the same calendar year you set up your RRIF. If your spouse is younger, you can set the formula based on his or her age, since there are advantages to this. Obtain further information for your situation.

- **Interest-only payout**

In this case, you would receive interest only until the deadline arrives for minimum withdrawals. At this point your capital will start eroding, and therefore growth will not occur. In the meantime, though, you would have preserved your capital.

- **Indexed payout**

Payments are increased annually based on a projected inflation rate—for example, 5 percent.

- **Smoothed payout**

Payments are adjusted so that you receive higher payments in the early years and lower payments in the later years. The schedule of payments is calculated according to actuarial projections.

b) Factors to Consider When Making Your RRSP or RRIF Selection

You can continue making RRSP payments up to your 71st year if you want, when you have to convert to an RRIF or an annuity or to take a lump-sum withdrawal. With both RRSPs and RRIFs, you can place your funds in different types of investments, from no-risk to high-risk. In choosing the type of investment you want, take into account the following considerations:

- **Safety**

Since you are retired or nearing retirement, preservation of capital is a primary consideration, followed by income or growth strategies that will at least neutralize inflation. You don't want to speculate. Spread any risk by diversifying your portfolio, unless you simply want to have money market funds such as GICs, Canada Savings Bonds, or term deposits. Don't invest in any product that could result in your losing money, which you can ill afford. Such an occurrence would negatively affect your retirement lifestyle or impair your peace of mind.

- **Diversification**

As you mature, you want to move into more stable and secure investments. Equity-based mutual funds or actual stocks tend to be too risky for most people. Either they don't understand the market or feel anxious about the potential risk of eroding their capital, with little time for recovery.

Conversely, if you have some "extra" money, you may wish to place some of it in more growth-oriented investments. There are many issues to consider, however.

- **Rate of return**

There is a direct correlation between risk and potential return. The lower the risk, the lower the return; the higher the risk, the higher the potential return. Since you want to preserve your capital, you will probably opt for safety and certainty. By actively considering your options and thoroughly checking out the competition, however, you could still get 1 to 4 percent more money without any risk of impairing your capital. Over time, this extra percentage could make a considerable difference, as it is compounded tax-free in your RRSP or RRIF.

- **Liquidity**

This refers to how quickly you can access your money. You want to have access to a certain amount of money when you need it. Or, if interest rates start increasing considerably, you want to be able to take advantage of that opportunity.

- **Fees**

Normally fees are not an issue for people with deposit funds, such as GICs and term deposits. However, if you have a self-directed RRSP or RRIF, a managed plan such as a mutual fund, or a personally managed portfolio, the issue of fees for management is a consideration.

3. Annuities

An annuity involves putting a lump sum of money into a plan that provides a regular income for life or for a specified period. There are some limitations to be aware of related to RRIFs. With an annuity, you have no income payment flexibility or opportunity to manage investment options so that you might increase your retirement income. You may also have little or no inflation protection unless the annuity is indexed for inflation. Some policies permit this. The amount an annuity pays is determined by your age and the interest rates at the time of purchase. For some, annuities are a viable option if they cannot (or prefer not to) manage their own money, as you can with an RRIF. There are other considerations and potential benefits as well.

Term certain annuities are sold by various institutions, including banks, trust companies, credit unions, and insurance companies. Life annuities are sold only by life insurance companies. Ask about deposit insurance protection, estate preservation, and fees on any RRIF or annuity before you invest.

Here are the two main types of annuities:

a) Term Certain Annuity to Age 90 (TCA90)

This annuity provides regular periodic payments, which can continue until your 90th year. Payments are normally level but can usually be indexed for inflation. If your spouse is younger than you are, you can purchase the TCA90 to continue after your death until your spouse's 90th year. If you die before 90 and do not have a spouse, you can make arrangements for the payments to go to your estate. Some issuers offer a TCA90 with an alternative to a fixed rate of return. In this option, the yield and payments are adjusted periodically to interest rates. You can obtain a TCA100 if you want.

b) Life Annuity

A life annuity provides regular payments that will continue for the rest of your life, no matter how long you live. When you die, however, any money left in the annuity goes to the issuer, not your estate. The exception is if you arrange an annuity that has a guaranteed payment period.

There are various types of life annuities:

- **Straight life annuity**

  This type of annuity is for an individual only and provides you with the highest amount of income for each dollar of premium in monthly or annual payments. However, it only lasts for your lifetime, unless you have a guaranteed period. This type of plan might be suitable for people who have no dependants.

- **Life annuity with a guaranteed period**

  This provides a guarantee that you or your beneficiary will receive back all of your investments, plus full interest if you wish, even if you only live for a short time. Alternatively, you may have the guarantee period set up to provide income payments for a fixed time frame, such as 5, 10, or 15 years from the start of payments to you, or until you or your spouse reach a certain age, such as 90. The longer the guaranteed period, the lower the payments.

- **Joint and last survivor annuity**

  This annuity provides a regular income as long as either spouse is living.

Payments can continue at the full amount to the surviving spouse, or they can be reduced by any stipulated percentage on the death of either spouse or specifically at your death. If you select the reduction option, this will result in higher payments while both spouses are alive, since it is necessary to have a higher income stream for two people than one. Although this type of plan results in less income for each dollar invested in the annuity, to many people the additional benefits are worth it.

- **Instalment refund annuity**

If you die before you have receive as much money as you paid for the annuity, this annuity will continue income payments to your beneficiary until they equal the amount you originally paid.

- **Cash refund annuity**

With this plan, instead of receiving continued income payments, as in the above example, your beneficiary receives a lump-sum payout.

- **Indexed life annuity**

This provides for annuity payments that automatically increase each year, from 1 to 5 percent, for example, based on the return of a specified group of assets. Although this plan provides you with some protection against rising living costs due to inflation, it will also reduce your payments in the early years.

- **Integrated life annuity**

If you wish, you can integrate your Old Age Security (OAS) payments with your annuity. With this plan, you would receive substantially increased annuity payments until age 65, at which time the payments would be reduced by the maximum OAS entitlement at the time you purchased the annuity.

ARE YOUR DEPOSIT MONIES, RRSPS, RRIFS, AND ANNUITIES PROTECTED AGAINST DEFAULT?

Depending on how and where you invest your money, it may or may not be partially or fully protected. Making sure your retirement investments and insurance benefits are protected is naturally a matter of concern. Some banks, trust companies, credit unions, and savings and loans institutions in the United States, and insurance companies in Canada and the United States, have ceased to operate. Verify all the information in this overview section to ensure that it is current, accurate, and relevant to your situation.

1. Protection of Deposit Monies, RRSPs, RRIFs, and Annuities in Canada

- **Deposits in a bank or trust company**

These are protected by the Canada Deposit Insurance Corp. (CDIC) up to a certain amount. In Quebec, the plans are protected by the Quebec Deposit Insurance Board. Your RRSP deposit or RRIF, regular savings or chequing funds on deposit, or term deposits are automatically insured for up to $100,000 for each separate account. Each deposit (in the form of an RRSP or otherwise) must mature in five years or less. If you have more than $100,000, you can divide your funds among several CDIC members who are separate financial institutions. Some banks and trust companies have subsidiaries that are separate CDIC members, resulting in a ceiling of $100,000 each. For information and confirmation, contact CDIC at 1-800-461-2342. The CDIC has an interactive deposit insurance calculator on its website www.cdic.ca. You can determine the extent of your coverage by answering the questions posed.

- **Deposits in a credit union**

These are protected by a provincial deposit insurance plan. Each province varies in its protection for deposits—savings, chequing, or term deposit, or RRSP or RRIF with term deposits or GICs less than five years. Depending on the province, the protection can range from $100,000 to unlimited protection—that is, 100 percent. Contact a credit union in your province to enquire, or phone CDIC at 1-800-461-2342 to obtain contact numbers for the credit union deposit insurance head office in your province. The CDIC website is: www.cdic.ca.

- **Deposits in a life insurance company**

These are covered by an industry-operated protection plan up to certain limits and in certain situations, depending on the nature of the investment. The limit for policies registered under the *Income Tax Act,* such as RRSPs, RRIFs, and pension policies, is $100,000. The limit is also $100,000 for non-registered policies, such as cash value of a life insurance policy. For information and confirmation, contact the Life and Health Insurance Ombudservice directly at 1-800-268-8099. The website is: www.clhio.ca. Also contact www.assuris.ca.

- **Managed funds**

Generally, these funds are protected if they are in an RRSP in the form of deposit funds—for example, term deposits or GICs under five years.

Mutual funds have no protection as such, because of the nature of the pooled investment. The funds' investments are segregated from the assets of the fund manager, however, in case the fund manager ceases to operate.

- **Self-directed plans**

These plans are not protected as such against the default of the institution holding them. Certain investments in the plan, however, such as term deposits or GICs under five years, could be protected. The amount of the protection depends on whether the institution is a bank, trust company, credit union, or brokerage firm. Refer to the deposit ceilings discussed earlier for these types of institutions.

If a brokerage firm ceases to operate, there could be protection for certain investments in your self-directed plan up to $1 million under an industry plan called the Canadian Investor Protection Fund. Only members, such as a Canadian stock exchange, and members of the Investment Dealers Association of Canada, are covered by this fund. No mutual fund companies or investment advisors not associated with a member broker are covered by this particular fund. For further information and confirmation, contact your broker or the CIPF office in Toronto at (416) 866-8366. The website is: www.cipf.ca.

- **Life insurance companies**

If a company that is a member of the insurance company protection plan makes promises in a life insurance, health insurance, money-accumulation, or annuity policy to pay either a fixed or a minimum amount of money to a person or on a person's death, and that company goes under, you could be protected up to a certain amount. If you have life insurance protection, the limit is $200,000; for life annuity and disability income policies with no options of a lump-sum withdrawal, the limit is $2,000 a month; and for health benefits other than disability income annuities, the limit is $60,000 in total payments.

For further information and confirmation, contact clhio at 1-800-268-8099, or www.clhio.ca, or assuris at www.assuris.ca or 1-866-878-1225.

- **Creditor-proofing**

If you have personally guaranteed loans for an incorporated company, or if you operate an unincorporated business, you could be exposed to claims from potential creditors. Funds placed with certain types of products from life insurance companies or with trust companies in Quebec could be protected from creditors. Obtain advice from the institution involved and verify it with your lawyer.

2. Protection for Deposit Monies in the United States

- **Deposits in U.S. federal or state banks, trust companies, and savings and loans institutions**

These are covered by the Federal Deposit Insurance Corporation (FDIC) up to $100,000 for each individual depositor.

If you want further information, consumer brochures on deposit insurance, or confirmation that the institution is covered by FDIC, contact FDIC at www.fdic.gov or 1-877-275-3342.

- **Deposits in U.S. credit unions**

These are covered up to $100,000 by the National Credit Union Share Insurance Fund (NCUSIF) for each individual depositor. Website: www.ncua.gov.

For further information, a consumer brochure on deposit insurance, or confirmation that the credit union is covered by NCUSIF, contact the fund at www.ncua.gov or 703-518-6300.

USING YOUR HOME AS A SOURCE OF ADDITIONAL INCOME

Many Canadian seniors prefer to remain in their own homes as long as possible for a variety of reasons, including the support network they have built up over the years, through neighbours, friends, church, or other regular social activities. Many seniors are unable to pay to remain at home, however. It is not uncommon for seniors to be house-rich and cash-poor.

There are many reasons why a senior may need extra cash or income to supplement existing financial resources. Even if contributions have been made to several savings programs, such as private pension plans, government pensions, or RRSPs, there could still be insufficient financial resources for the senior's needs or wants. Being a Snowbird and living in the U.S. Sunbelt states for up to six months a year could be one reason for lack of financial resources. Other seniors may not have the savings income mentioned and may rely only on federal Old Age Security (OAS) income, perhaps along with a federal Guaranteed Income Supplement (GIS). Some of these federal or provincial programs involve a means test, with the government setting a maximum income level for eligibility. If you exceed this income, you do not get the funding. Many seniors who have fixed savings have had their purchasing power eroded by inflation. The home is the single largest form of "savings" for seniors, especially if they can tap into the equity that has accumulated, for lump-sum and/or continuous income, without having to make monthly payments.

Many seniors think that a home cannot readily be converted into a source of income unless the home is sold. This can be a very stressful scenario to some. In contrast, there are seniors who, by circumstance or choice, sell their homes, buy a condominium (in many cases in a retirement area) and have a considerable amount of cash left over. For information about housing and real estate for Snowbirds, see Chapter 5.

There are options for seniors who want to stay in their own homes but need or wish to supplement their income. One option is to rent out a self-contained basement suite to provide income. Another option is to rent out spare rooms in the house, taking in boarders who share common kitchen facilities and washrooms. In many cases the income is not taxable, either because the income can be offset against a percentage of the house expenses or because of the low amount of income involved. These options may provide additional benefits in the form of companionship and the feeling of security. This latter benefit could be particularly attractive, especially if the owner is a Snowbird, or often away on trips. For other seniors, these options may not be attractive because of the loss of privacy. There could also be municipal bylaw regulations that could technically restrict having tenants. In many cases these regulations are flexible, depending on various factors, current municipal policy regarding enforcement, and extenuating circumstances of the owner.

Keep in mind that the following plans vary from province to province and are constantly changing. Obtain a current update. Also contact your local Canada Mortgage and Housing Corporation (CMHC) office for information about their wide range of programs and publications for seniors. Look for the local contact phone number for CMHC in the Blue Pages of your phone book under Government of Canada. Their website is: www.cmhc.ca.

1. Deferred Payment Plans

This type of plan involves the postponement of certain expenses until a fixed time in the future or until the house is sold. Generally, the expenses, along with any interest applicable, constitute a debt, with the equity in the home as security. This is the simplest form of equity conversion. Under these plans, you maintain ownership and possession of the home, as well as any equity appreciation. Here are some examples of deferred payment plans:

a) Deferment of Property Taxes

There are many people who are mortgage-free but who spend a significant amount of their net income on property taxes, even after a provincial home-owners' property tax grant is deducted. In addition to property taxes, there are other recurring expenses that further erode disposable income, including costs of maintenance, lighting, heating, water, or garbage removal.

Although property taxes are collected by and for the municipality, in most cases some provincial governments have established property tax deferment plans. Under this arrangement, a senior is entitled to delay payment of property taxes and accrued interest until the home is sold or the senior's estate is settled. Check with your local property tax department to see if such a program is available or is being considered.

b) Deferment or Subsidy of Home Rehabilitation Expenses

This arrangement is similar to the previous example in that any loans approved for improvement or rehabilitation of the home may be deferred until your home is sold, until your estate is settled, or until a fixed date in the future. In some cases, there is an outright subsidy that does not have to be repaid. There are several variations of this type of program, depending on whether funds are obtained through a federal CMHC or provincial government program. Find out what current programs are available. The advantage of this type of home rehabilitation expense deferment is that it allows you to improve your standard of living without eroding your income.

If you are considering either of the above deferred payment plan programs, there are several key questions that you should ask:

- Is there a limit on the income of applicants to be eligible?
- Is there a subsidy of the deferral plan?
- Is there a limit on the amount of payment due (e.g., property taxes) that can be deferred?
- Is there a limit on the time that an amount will be deferred?
- What is the interest charge on the amount deferred?

- How often is the interest rate adjusted, if at all, on the deferred payment?
- What is the formula used for determining the interest rate and how frequently is it compounded?
- If the amount of payment deferred and accrued interest eventually exceeds the value of the home, will you be obligated to sell the home?

Keep in mind that although property taxes can increase every year and that interest rates over time, especially compounded rates, can eat away the equity in the home, these effects should be partially offset by an increase in the value of the home as a result of inflation and market demand.

2. Reverse Mortgages

Reverse mortgages, reverse annuity mortgages (RAMs), and home equity plans are similar concepts that are becoming increasingly popular among seniors or early retirees across Canada. Over the years, many people can build up considerable equity in their houses, townhouses, or condominiums. Many Canadians have decided to turn their largest asset into immediate cash and/or regular revenue and still remain in the home.

The basic concept behind these various plans is simple. You take out a mortgage on part of the equity of your home (the debt-free portion of your home), and in exchange receive a lump-sum amount of money and/or a monthly income for a fixed period, for your life, or for the life of the surviving spouse. When you sell the home, when you die, or when your surviving spouse dies, the mortgage and accrued interest must be repaid. You do not have to make any payments in the meantime. If there is any balance left in residual equity in the home after the sale, it belongs to the senior or his or her estate. The various reverse mortgage options have different features. Here are some of the main ones:

- Reverse mortgages, RAMs, and other home equity programs are readily available through a variety of agents and brokers. This permits you to compare and contrast in a competitive marketplace and end up with a plan that has features customized for your specific needs. Research online, or look in the Yellow Pages under Financial Planning Consultants and Mortgages for companies that offer these home equity plans.
- The main home equity type of plans that are available have obtained an opinion from Canada Revenue Agency that the lump-sum payment

and monthly annuity payments are tax-free, as long as you live in your home. If you have selected a monthly income annuity that continues after you have moved out of your home, the income from the sale may be subject to favourable prescribed annuity taxation rules. The current ruling on the various means-tested programs, such as the federal Guaranteed Income Supplement (GIS), is that receiving the annuity will not interfere with your eligibility for, or cause a reduction in, the GIS. As tax laws and regulations change, make sure you obtain current independent advice from a tax accountant and Canada Revenue Agency on this issue.

- Since you retain ownership, you benefit from an appreciation in the value of your home over time—that is, you get an increase in equity. For example, if your property goes up 10 percent a year in value, and you locked in the mortgage on your property for the reverse mortgage or RAM at 8 percent, then you are technically ahead in the interest differential. In reality, because you are not making regular payments on your mortgage, the interest on it is being compounded and therefore, in practical terms, is ultimately eroding the increasing equity. The reduction could be substantially offset by an attractive average annual appreciation in property value.

Although many of the reverse mortgages, RAMs, and related plans operate in similar ways among various companies, interest rates and other specific conditions vary. Here are some of the points to consider in choosing a plan:

- What are the age requirements to be eligible for the lump-sum or annuity plan?

- Do you need to be mortgage-free on your home?

- Can you transfer the mortgage to another property if you move?

- What percentage of your home equity is used to determine the reverse mortgage or RAM, and what percentage of that is available for a lump-sum payment and annuity?

- Is the interest rate on the mortgage fixed for your lifetime or duration of the annuity, or is it adjusted, and if so, how regularly and using what criteria?

- If the reverse mortgage and lump sum is for a term period, what are the various terms available?

- What if the equity of the home on sale is insufficient to pay the mortgage and accrued interest? Are you or your estate liable for the shortfall?

- Can the agreement of the term be extended if the home has appreciated in value?

- Can you move out of the house, rent it, and still maintain the home equity plan?

- What if you already have a mortgage on the house?

- If the annuity is for life, is there a minimum guaranteed period of payment, or will payments stop immediately upon the death of the recipient and/or the surviving spouse?

- How will the income received under the proposed plan be taxed, if at all?

- Will the income received affect your eligibility under any federal or provincial housing or social programs?

The process of obtaining a reverse mortgage or RAM takes about four to six weeks on average, including home appraisal, annuity calculations, and other matters. It is essential that you obtain independent legal and tax advice in advance and thoroughly compare the features and benefits.

3. Renting Out Part of Your Home in Canada or the United States

If you choose to rent out a basement suite, you are entitled to offset the rental income you receive against a portion of your house-related expenses. For example, if you received rent of $300/month ($3,600 a year) from the rented area and the total house-related expenses were $14,400 a year, and the rented area comprised 25 percent of the total square footage of the home or $3,600 of the total expenses ($14,400 X 25 percent), then the income would be off-set by expense, leaving a zero taxable income. House-related expenses would include a portion of any mortgage interest, property tax, utilities (hydro, water, telephone, etc.), insurance, and maintenance costs. In all instances you should obtain tax advice from a professional accountant to make sure you are doing the calculations correctly.

If you are renting out part of your home, check with your provincial government to obtain information about your obligations and rights as a landlord; you will be governed and regulated by that legislation. For example, some provinces have rent control, and others do not. Ideally, you want to have a tenancy agreement that supplements the provincial legislation and deals with such issues as your policy on smoking, pets, noise, and the number of people living in the suite.

Your municipality has the authority to regulate zoning and determines whether a residence is zoned for single families. Technically, therefore, you could contravene a municipal zoning bylaw by renting out a part of your home to a non-relative. In effect, you would be operating as if your home were multi-family, which it wouldn't be zoned for. If you hear the term "illegal suite," it simply means it technically contravenes the existing municipal bylaw on the issue. The contravention has nothing to do with provincial legislation (dealing with landlord-tenant matters) or federal legislation (dealing with income tax). Each level of government is independent of the other.

Check with your local municipality. It could be that certain areas in the municipality are encouraged to have rental suites. Alternatively, the municipality may have the technical restriction but does not actively enforce it unless there is a complaint by a neighbour. If a municipal inspector does investigate, you normally have a right to appeal. One of the grounds of appeal is economic hardship for you, the owner, and serious inconvenience for the tenant. Some municipalities have a moratorium (temporary freeze) on enforcing the bylaw because of a shortage of rental accommodation and/or general recessionary hardship of property owners, who need a "mortgage helper" to meet payments.

Some provincial governments have programs to encourage home renovation in order to create rental suites. In addition, the CMHC (www.cmhc.ca) has some programs for renovation to accommodate handicapped or elderly people.

Make enquiries. The tax aspects of renting your U.S. Sunbelt home are covered in Chapter 7.

4. Operating a Business Out of Your Home

Many people, at some point, intend to start part-time or full-time businesses out of their homes. There is a growing trend to do this for various reasons, including eliminating daily commuting to work, fulfilling a lifestyle choice, creating retirement opportunity, supplementing salaried income, testing a business idea, or saving on business overhead and thereby reducing financial risk by writing off house-related expenses. There are many different types of home-based businesses. You need competent tax and legal advice before you start up. The last thing you want is potential risk, since that could deplete your retirement funds and hamper your lifestyle. You need a GST number if you have over $30,000 in income in your business or are paying GST on items you purchase and want to offset it against GST you are charging. Check with your accountant and closest GST office (Canada Revenue Agency—CRA): www.cra.gc.ca.

Expenses may be claimed for the business use of a work space in your home if:

- The work space is your principal place of business for the part-time or full-time self-employed aspect of your career (you could have a salaried job elsewhere; it is not required that you meet people at your home) or

- You only use the work space to earn income from your business and it is used regularly for meeting clients, customers, or patients—in which case you could also deduct expenses from an office outside the home.

Basically, you write off a portion of all your home expenses based on the portion of the home you use for business-related purposes (e.g., office; storage). Refer to the previous discussion of renting out your home. It is the same type of formula.

You may be able to claim 100 percent of the cost of business purchases or a depreciated amount over time, depending on the item. To clarify what you can deduct and how to do it, as well as other home business tax issues, speak to your accountant. You should also speak with your lawyer about the various types of legal issues when starting a business. See Chapter 9 for information about selecting advisors.

The tax and legal aspects of working in the United States are covered in the chapters on tax and immigration.

5. Keeping Records

If you are going to be renting out part of your principal residence or Sunbelt condo to a tenant, or if you intend to have a home-based business, make sure that you keep detailed records of all money collected and paid out. Purchases and operating expenses must be supported by invoices, receipts, contracts, or other supporting documents.

You do not need to submit these records when you file your return, but you need to have them in case you are ever audited.

Tips Before Leaving Canada

√ Investigate and evaluate the various potential financial and other risks discussed on pages 33 to 39 in this chapter and make the appropriate decisions before your departure.

√ Review your government, employer, or personal pension plans and make arrangements to have your pension or other income (e.g., dividends, tax refunds) deposited directly into your bank account during your absence.

√ Make sure that your funds will receive the best interest rate, depending on your liquidity and safety of principal needs. For example, if your direct deposit goes into a low-interest or chequing account, arrange to have a regular transfer of the funds into an investment that provides you with a higher return (e.g., GIC, term deposit, Treasury bill). Always make sure your Canadian account funds are receiving interest.

√ If you foresee that you will need some of your Canadian funds during your absence, have your financial institution forward the desired funds directly to your Sunbelt bank. Always confirm your instructions in writing and keep a copy.

√ Keep an accurate record of when any GICs, term deposits, or Treasury bills come due during your absence so that appropriate arrangements can be made.

√ Estimate how much money you will need while you are away and how to readily access it. Check your credit card and line of credit limits. If they are not high enough for possible emergencies, arrange to have them increased.

√ With Automated Banking Machines (ABMs), you do not need to carry a lot of cash. But check on your bank cash card withdrawal limit. For example, you may be limited to $100 a day, so arrange to have that increased before you leave, if you want to access a higher amount.

√ You can arrange to have your monthly bank statements forwarded to your Sunbelt address.

√ You can pay your Canadian bills personally, on your Canadian chequing account, by having your mail forwarded to your Sunbelt address. It can be more convenient and efficient, however, to arrange for automatic debiting of your Canadian bank account. Alternatively, you can arrange to have the bills sent to your financial institution to pay on your behalf. If you choose this alternative, put your instructions in writing. Bills that can be paid this way include utility bills, cable, house taxes, condominium maintenance fees, and quarterly income tax instalments.

√ You may have other investments your financial institution can deal with in your absence—for example, reinvestment of income, deposit of coupons, rollover of maturing deposits, or purchase and sale of securities. Make sure your instructions are in writing and any required documentation is signed in advance. Ask for copies of all transactions dealt with on your behalf to be sent to you at your Sunbelt address.

√ If you plan to purchase real estate in the United States, many American financial institutions and some Canadian ones will lend you money. Find out whether your Canadian financial institution will lend you money for a Sunbelt property based on your Canadian or U.S. assets. If you have sufficient equity in your Canadian property, can debt-service the mortgage for the U.S. property, and your credit rating is good, you should have no problem getting financing in Canada.

√ Take enough money in traveller's cheques to meet your needs for the first month. Many American financial institutions put a hold on a cheque from a Canadian account until it has cleared. This could take over three weeks. After you have established a relationship, however, many U.S. financial institutions will credit your U.S. account the same day you deposit your Canadian cheque.

√ If you do not already have an existing U.S. bank account, you can facilitate "no hold" chequing privileges by planning before you leave Canada. Ask the manager of your Canadian financial institution whether it has a correspondent banking relationship with a U.S. financial institution or what special Snowbird features are available. This will facilitate a "no hold" policy.

√ Ask your bank manager to provide you with a letter of introduction to give to a U.S. bank. Such a letter confirms your good banking track record and creditworthiness and personalizes you. If you have any hassles, there are many other financial institutions that would be delighted to have your business.

√ Consider the benefits of having a U.S. dollar chequing and/or savings account at a Canadian financial institution. These cheques are generally designed to clear through the U.S. clearing system. Also, consider a U.S. dollar credit card from a Canadian financial institution.

√ Most major Canadian financial institutions have a special toll-free telephone number for you to pay bills in Canada or the United States (in Canadian or U.S. dollar funds), as well as to make balance enquiries.

√ Always arrange to have a trusted friend or relative know how to contact you quickly in case of an emergency or to advise you of economic conditions that could affect your investments during your absence.

√ Subscribe to local publications in the Snowbird area that you are staying at.

CHAPTER 4

Immigration and Customs

INTRODUCTION

Few people really know which regulations apply when they are visiting in the United States for an extended stay each year. Every country has different regulations that will affect visitors, and you need to know what they are. Under the *Canada-U.S. Free Trade Agreement* (FTA), and its successor, the *North American Free Trade Agreement* (NAFTA), there is reciprocity of goods that are exempt from duty or have reduced duty when crossing the border, if the goods were made in the United States, Canada, or Mexico. Some provisions of NAFTA permit Canadians to stay in the United States longer for business or employment reasons.

This chapter provides an overview of the information about immigration and customs that you need to know, including documentation options, being prepared before you enter the U.S., working part-time in the U.S., and implications of being a U.S. citizen but having a Canadian primary residence.

PERSONAL DOCUMENTATION OPTIONS

When travelling outside Canada, make sure that you have appropriate documentation to be allowed entry into other countries. The U.S. has been tightening up its entry procedures for goods, services, or visits, and you could be refused entry if you don't have the appropriate ID, such as a passport, driver's licence, and evidence of a confirming residence in Canada. This would include such things as employment payroll records, registration of home ownership, or proof of bank accounts in Canada. You don't need the inconvenience of being turned away when heading down south. The request of a DHS (Department of Homeland Security) officer for specific documentation may be discretionary, but it is recommended that you have more rather than less documentation than you think you might require. As a basic caution, whether you are travelling by air or land, always take your passport with you. However, as rules and regulations change from time to time, check to get a current update of the required protocols before you depart.

If you are going to Mexico or other countries, or taking a cruise to a foreign country, a passport is a necessity. If you are a naturalized Canadian citizen, it could be wise to present a Canadian passport. Assume that you will be asked for one.

It's a good idea to carry an extra copy of your birth certificate, as well as to keep a record of your passport number. Make two photocopies of your passport identification page, tourist card (if travelling to Mexico), and other personal documents before leaving home. Leave one set with a relative or friend back home, whom you could contact in case of a loss. Carry the other set with you in a separate place from your actual documents. It will be easier to replace any lost or stolen passports if you have this documentation.

Here is an outline of the key types of personal documentation available.

1. Birth Certificate

You should have an official wallet-size version of this certificate. If you were born in Canada but outside Quebec, contact your provincial department of vital statistics. The contact number would be in the Blue Pages of your telephone book. If you were born in Quebec, you should get a wallet-size baptismal certificate or a small-size birth certificate.

2. Passport

Your passport is valid for five years. Make sure that it does not expire during your absence from Canada. If that does happen, you can contact the closest Canadian consular office in the country you are in. Refer to Appendix A for contact addresses. The consular office can arrange for issuance of a passport in an emergency situation. However, backlogs can affect how long it will take.

Otherwise, you can get a passport from the federal government passport office. Look in the Blue Pages of your phone book for the closest office. Alternatively, you can send away for it. You can pick up a Canadian passport application form from a post office, many travel agents, etc. The cost is approximately $85 (this can change at any time), and it takes several weeks or more to process. If you need it more urgently, it can be done in a number of days. You can also apply online at www.ppt.gc.ca.

To obtain your passport, you need to have proof of citizenship, such as a birth certificate or baptismal certificate (Quebec). You will need a Canadian citizenship card (either the actual certificate or laminated card) if you were born outside Canada. You will also need two recent passport photos taken by someone familiar with the format required. These must be verified by a guarantor who meets certain requirements. Photo requirements have become much stricter post-9/11, involving issues like whether you're smiling in the photo, whether your mouth is open a little, whether you're wearing glasses. Many people have passport applications rejected on the basis of now-unsuitable photographs, even when taken by a professional photographer. Allow extra time in case this should happen to you.

3. Citizenship Card

If you were born outside Canada and became a naturalized Canadian, you might want to obtain a wallet-size laminated citizenship card. It costs $75 and is good for life. You would need to return the original large certificate you received before the government would process the wallet-size card.

Contact your closest federal government citizenship office. Look in the Blue Pages of your phone book. You will need two other acceptable pieces of personal identification, such as a passport, driver's licence, health card, social insurance card, etc. You will also need two passport-type photos. You have to book an appointment with the citizenship office. Expect a delay of from four to six months before you receive the card, so plan ahead.

4. Driver's Licence

This is frequently useful to security officials, especially if you are involved in an accident in the U.S. If may also be required if you want to cash cheques there. Remember to renew your licence before you depart if it expires while you are away. Also make sure that you have proper vehicle registration documentation. You also want to check that your auto licence plates do not expire while you are away.

5. Provincial ID Card

Many people have not heard of this card. It is issued by provincial motor vehicle departments. Look in the Blue Pages of your telephone directory to make enquiries. Basically, you would go through the same photo process and end up with a laminated wallet card that looks like a driver's licence, but is called a provincial ID card.

The card is available for the many people who do not drive, but are frequently asked for ID to do any financial transactions. Fees vary depending on the province.

6. International Driver's Licence

You can obtain this document, which has your photo on it, from various sources, including your local CAA auto club. All you need to do to obtain one is show your current licence and another piece of ID. The cost is nominal.

You do not need this licence for the U.S., but it is advisable for Mexico and other countries. It is considered acceptable evidence of your right to drive in most countries of the world. Your provincial driver's licence would not be acceptable in most countries, as they are not familiar with it.

BE PREPARED WHEN ENTERING THE U.S.

Due to the U.S. war on terrorism, and the post-9/11 regulations and changes, increased security restrictions have resulted.

Entering the U.S. has particular steps and protocols you need to know. Here are the key ones to avoid frustration and delay.

1. Identification

The most important formality on entering the United States is giving proof of citizenship. In the past, U.S. officials have been willing to accept anything from a driver's licence or birth certificate to a Canadian Tire credit card. However, the climate has changed. Canadians are being required to show identification that includes a photo and proves their right to re-enter Canada. In practical terms, a passport is a necessity to avoid hassles or being legally blocked from entering the U.S.

2. Dual Nationality

Some Canadians may have U.S. as well as Canadian citizenship through birth in the United States or through naturalization or descent. Although this is not likely to create immigration problems—and in fact may solve some—it is wise for you to understand your status under U.S. law.

Canadians who are also U.S. citizens should always identify themselves as U.S. citizens when entering the United States. For information on dual nationality and a range of other relevant issues for U.S. citizens, contact a U.S.

immigration lawyer to get a current update specific to your situation. It is recommended travelling with both passports and showing the Canadian passport
when entering Canada, and the U.S. passport when entering the U.S.

3. Criminal Records

If you have a criminal record, no matter how minor or how long ago, you likely
will be ineligible to enter the United States. There may also be problems in
transit through U.S. airports.

Admitting you have committed a criminal offence may also make you
ineligible to enter the United States. Under U.S. law, a Canadian pardon does
not cancel a criminal conviction.

If you have ever been refused entry to the United States, regardless of the
reason, you are most likely ineligible to enter without special permission.

It is strongly recommended that if you have a criminal conviction, or previously have been denied entry, you should contact one of the U.S. Customs
and Border Protection (USCBP) offices at a port of entry well in advance of
your travel to the United States. If you are ineligible to enter the United States
and wish to apply for a waiver of ineligibility, you will be asked to complete
Form I-192, Application for Advance Permission to Enter as a Non-Immigrant.
It may take several months or longer to process your application. A Canadian
citizen convicted of an impaired driving violation need not file Form I-192.

If you left the United States to avoid military service during the Vietnam
War and have not since regularized your status, there might be an outstanding
warrant for your arrest or you might be ineligible for U.S. entry. If you are in
doubt, check with the nearest USCBP office at a port of entry.

4. Travel with/by Children

U.S. and Canadian authorities and transportation companies are increasingly
vigilant in questioning persons travelling with children. If you are planning to
travel to the United States with a child, for example, a grandchild, you should
carry documentation such as a custody order or a notarized letter certifying
that you have the legal right to bring the child with you. Also, persons under the
age of 18 who are travelling on their own should carry documentation showing
that they have the permission of custodial parents.

As well, if there is a possibility of a custody dispute developing while you
are away with your child, you should talk to a Canadian lawyer before leaving home. A special publication, *International Child Abductions: A Manual for*

Parents, is available from the Department of Foreign Affairs and International Trade. Also refer to the Canada Border Services Agency website (www.cbsa. gc.ca) for publications on travelling with children.

5. Drugs

The U.S. Government *Zero Tolerance Policy* legislation imposes severe penalties for the possession of even a small amount of an illegal drug. Even prescription drugs and syringes used for legitimate medical purposes come under intense scrutiny.

- Never carry a package or luggage for someone else unless you have been able to verify the contents completely.

- Choose your travelling companions wisely. Never cross the border with a hitchhiker. Though you may not be carrying anything illegal, your companions might be and you could be implicated.

- Be equally careful about whom and what you carry in your vehicle. As the driver, you could be held responsible for the misdeeds of your passengers, even if they were committed without your knowledge or involvement. Check all rental vehicles very carefully to make sure there is not hidden contraband.

6. Admissibility and Entry

As soon as you stop at the U.S. border or at an inland port of entry, you are subject to U.S. law. U.S. Immigration can refuse entry to persons with criminal records that render them inadmissable, or persons who cannot demonstrate that they have a legitimate reason to enter the United States.

Generally, the criteria for admissibility include citizenship, residence (permanent home abroad or significant reason to return abroad), purpose of the trip (legitimate reasons for entry), intended length of stay (against the backdrop of the individual's situation at home), and proof of financial support while in the United States. In a nutshell, this "test" helps tell whether you are travelling for legitimate reasons, have the financial resources for your travel and living expenses, and intend to return to a home abroad. The American official at the point of entry is the sole judge of your admissibility. Under U.S. law, as an alien detained at the border by Customs or Immigration, you do not have the right to representation by your lawyer.

The permanent U.S. record created when a Canadian has been refused entry to the United States becomes part of a computerized database readily available at all pre-clearance operations offices in Canada, and border and inland ports of entry.

At a pre-clearance facility in Canada, you may be given an option to withdraw your request to enter the United States, if border officials are questioning your application. This step can be taken before you are interviewed further, or your belongings searched. Despite your taking this approach, U.S. officials may, nonetheless, make a record of your attempted entry on the U.S. Immigration database.

What you say in answer to questions by Immigration or Customs officers can be used against you if you are considered to be inadmissible. Many persons have had their vehicles or vessels seized and eventually sold, because they pretended to be Canadian citizens when they were actually landed immigrants or visitors to Canada. Others have had their vehicles or vessels confiscated because they carried passengers who pretended to be Canadian citizens, or who did not admit to having a criminal record (no matter how long ago the conviction or how minor the offence) or who pretended to be visitors while planning to look for work in the United States. As a driver, you can be held responsible for the wrongdoings of your passengers regardless of knowledge or association. Assume the worst-case scenario, and govern your conduct accordingly by being prudent and cautious.

7. Expedited Removal

Canadians travelling to the United States should take note of a U.S. Immigration procedure called "expedited removal." The process allows an Immigration agent, with the concurrence of a supervisor, to bar non-citizens who are not U.S. permanent residents from the United States for five years if, in their judgment, the individuals presented false documentation or misrepresented themselves. Canadians should be aware that lying to a border official is a serious offence. Expedited removal can also be used against someone trying to return to an illegal residence, or coming to the U.S. to work without authorization.

Expedited removal is part of comprehensive reforms intended to control illegal immigration. There is no formal appeal process under expedited removal. If you believe the law has been misapplied in your case, you can request a supervisory review by writing to the BCIS (Bureau of Citizenship and Inspection Services) district director responsible for the port of entry where the decision was made. Cases of possible misapplication should also be brought to the attention of the Consular Affairs Bureau of the Department of

Foreign Affairs and International Trade in Ottawa, at 1-800-387-3124 or (613) 943-1055 or at the nearest Canadian consulate.

Expedited removal occurs at land borders or inland ports of entry only, not at Pre-Clearance Operational posts.

8. Pre-clearance

Under a Canada-U.S. agreement, U.S. Immigration has pre-clearance facilities at seven Canadian airports: Vancouver, Calgary, Edmonton, Winnipeg, Toronto, Montréal (Trudeau), and Ottawa. To allow sufficient time for the pre-clearance process when you are travelling to the United States from these airports, you should be at the U.S. Immigration desk at least two hours before your flight. Pre-clearance facilities are also available at the Victoria, British Columbia, ferry terminal for travel to Port Angeles in Washington State. Again, you should allow extra time for this process.

As a Canadian using American pre-clearance facilities, you are still required to meet American entry requirements. American officials here are authorized to inspect your luggage with your permission, and can refuse your entry into the United States. While you are on Canadian soil, you have rights under the *Charter of Rights and Freedoms,* subject to Canadian law, including those laws governing drugs and guns. Refusal to co-operate with American officials may result in your being refused entry to the United States.

9. American Border Fees

American border officials collect a nominal per-person fee, payable only in American dollars, to issue an Arrival/Departure Document, Form I-94. This form is distributed to Canadian citizens who are entering the United States to study or work and to visitors from other countries. The fee does not apply to Canadian citizens who are entering the United States on temporary visits for business or pleasure. Travellers arriving in the United States by air have already paid the fee as a part of their airline ticket expenses.

IMMIGRATION REGULATIONS

The following is a summary of the immigration regulations for people travelling or living in the United States.

1. Moving to the United States Part-time

Many Canadian Snowbirds live in the U.S. Sunbelt states for up to six months a year, during Canada's coldest months. There are tax and other considerations if you wish to stay longer. If you intend to stay only up to six months and you are a Canadian citizen, you will have no difficulty with U.S. immigration regulations as long as you have the proper documentation. You simply declare your intention at a U.S. point of entry. Remember to bring your passport, of course, as well as other photo ID, and proof of sufficient funds.

As a separate issue, you could be considered a U.S. resident for tax purposes only, even though you are still a Canadian citizen, if you stay in the United States for more than a set number of days a year over several years. This topic is discussed in Chapter 7. See Closer Connection discussion.

2. Moving to the United States Full-time

There are many implications of moving to the United States full-time. You have to consider issues such as tax, estate planning, financial planning, pensions, housing and health costs, cost of living, as well as possibly leaving friends and family. There are different implications, depending on whether you are living full-time in the United States permanently or temporarily, and the nature of your stay—for example, whether you are retired, working, or investing in the country. There are also distinct societal and governmental differences between Canada and the United States that become more apparent if you are living in the United States full-time.

Refer to Chapter 11 for a detailed discussion of the factors to consider when retiring outside Canada full-time.

Here are the steps to take if you want to explore the process of emigrating to the United States, remaining there over six months, working as a business visitor or professional, or entering under a trader or investor category:

- Contact a U.S. immigration attorney to obtain independent objective advice specific to your situation. Keep in mind that the USCBP is an enforcement agency, not an agency designed to provide helpful information. Additionally, the officers may know little about the best categories (i.e., H-1B, E-1, or E-2) for an individual, as they have no adjudicatory responsibilities.

- Review the website of the U.S. Consulate in Toronto for eastern Canada, or in Vancouver, for western Canada, if you wish to enter the United States under a trader or investor category.

- Contact a U.S. cross-border tax specialist to determine the tax implications of living full-time in the United States.

- Contact the Canada Revenue Agency (CRA) to determine the tax implications if you are leaving Canada to live full-time in the United States.

- Contact Health Canada and your provincial office for seniors to determine the implications for federal pensions or federal and provincial medicare coverage.

- Contact your employer/union/association retirement benefit plan to determine the implications of living full-time in the United States.

- Contact a lawyer who specializes in immigration law relating to emigrating to the United States or living there full-time. Contact your local lawyer referral service or look in the Yellow Pages of your phone book or check on the Internet under Lawyers. Ask your lawyer to give you a referral for U.S. lawyers who are experts on wills and estate issues, real estate, immigration (who are members of the AILA— American Immigration Lawyers Association) and so on, so that you can have your interests looked after for continuity before departure and after your arrival in the United States. Refer to Chapter 9 for information about selecting professional advisors in both Canada and the United States.

- Contact a professional accountant in Canada who specializes in cross-border tax issues to obtain customized advice for your situation. Most major international chartered accountancy firms have experts on the tax issues of Canadians living part-time or full-time in the United States. You may also want to have a second opinion from a U.S. Certified Public Accountant (CPA) who is an expert on cross-border tax issues. Arrange to have a referral to a U.S. accountant in the area where you will be living who is a tax expert. You want to have continuity of advice before leaving Canada. Refer to Chapter 9 for further information.

- Contact an objective, professional financial planner to give you customized assessment and advice before you move to the United States full-time. Again, refer to Chapter 9 for further information about selecting a financial planner. If you are staying in the United States full-time on a temporary basis—in other words, if you still have a cross-border connection with Canada—you will want to maintain a relationship with a professional financial planner in Canada.

- Read the booklets on the tax implications for Canadians working or doing business in the United States that are available free from international accountancy firms.

- Subscribe to the newsletter published by Richard Brunton, CPA, called *Brunton's U.S. Tax Letter for Canadians*. For information, contact (561) 241-9991. Write to him at: 4710 N.W. Boca Raton Blvd. #101, Boca Raton, Florida, 33431, U.S.A. The newsletter contains a lot of helpful information and analysis. Brunton is an expert on tax issues and filing issues for Canadians living part-time in the U.S. You can view a sample of the newsletter online at: www.taxintl.com.

3. Different U.S. Immigration Categories

You can become a citizen or lawful permanent resident of the United States through derivative citizenship, family, employment, investment, or business. Immigration procedures are highly technical, so you should retain an immigration lawyer experienced in U.S. immigration to assist you. Do your homework by first consulting the website: www.uscis.gov.

a) Derivative U.S. Citizenship

This concept means that you are entitled to obtain U.S. citizenship through ancestry. Perhaps you have ancestors or distant relatives who were U.S. citizens before their death. If you think you do, research your family tree and archival documents and records. You can hire professionals who do this type of research. After you have all the documentation and facts available, speak to a U.S. immigration lawyer.

b) Family-based Immigration

There are various ways that U.S. citizens or lawful permanent residents can bring their relatives into the United States under the family category. Some of the categories have an annual numerical limit and others don't. Immigration laws are constantly changing.

- **Immediate relative**

There is no limit on the number of people who can be sponsored under this category. It includes the children, spouse, and parents of a U.S. citizen. The U.S. citizen must be at least 21 years of age. Children are defined as unmarried persons under 21 years of age who are legitimate or legally legitimized children, adopted, or stepchildren.

• **Nonimmediate relative**

This category has annual quotas, and members of this category are ranked in order of preference. There are four preference levels. First is an unmarried son or daughter, over the age of 21, of a U.S. citizen. Second is a spouse of a lawful permanent resident alien or an unmarried adult son or daughter of a lawful permanent resident alien. Third is a married adult son or daughter of a U.S. citizen. The fourth preference level is a brother or sister of a U.S. citizen who is over 21 years of age. Waiting periods vary extensively per category.

c) Employment-based Immigration

This form of immigrant visa has four levels of reference. There are annual quotas in each category except for returning U.S. legal permanent residents or former U.S. citizens seeking reinstatement of citizenship.

The first preference is for priority workers, that is, people of extraordinary ability, outstanding professors and researchers, and multinational executives and managers. The second preference is for a professional with an advanced degree or exceptional ability. The third preference is for a professional without an advanced degree, a skilled worker, or an unskilled worker. The last and fourth preference is for what is called special immigrants, including religious workers and returning U.S. legal permanent residents or former U.S. citizens seeking reinstatement of citizenship.

d) Investor Immigration

The U.S. government wants to attract investors from other countries and if the conditions are met, will grant them an immigrant visa. The reason is to stimulate economic activity and employment. Canada has the same type of foreign investor interest, as do most other countries. Canadians wishing to make a business investment in the United States may qualify for this immigrant visa. It is referred to as a fifth preference category (EB-5) and has an annual limit. In addition, the Canada-U.S. *Free Trade Agreement* (FTA), which has been superseded for the most part by the *North American Free Trade Agreement* (NAFTA), gives Treaty Trader (E-1) and Treaty Investor (E-2) status to Canadian nonimmigrant investors.

A Canadian may qualify under the EB-5 category of immigrant visa if certain criteria are met. These could include establishing and investing in a business and employing at least 10 new U.S. workers full-time. Depending on the location and need, the financial investment required could range from $500,000 to $1 million. Some are regionally approved programs.

e) Business Travellers Under the Canada-U.S. *Free Trade Agreement* (FTA) and the *North American Free Trade Agreement* (NAFTA)

The FTA became effective on January 1, 1989, and was designed to facilitate trade and travel between the two countries. The agreement respecting various categories of business travellers is designed for non-immigrants who could be living full-time in the United States. The FTA affects only temporary entrants into the United States. It is possible, however, that a history of operating under one of these categories could facilitate a subsequent application for an immigrant visa under another category. Spouses and children accompanying business travellers must satisfy normal admission requirements and cannot work in the United States without prior authorization.

NAFTA became effective on January 1, 1994, and was designed to facilitate trade and travel between Canada, the U.S., and Mexico. It incorporated, for the most part, the provisions of the previous FTA.

There are several categories, the four main ones being:

- **Business visitor (B-1 status)**

Canadian citizens who visit the United States on business for their Canadian company and receive remuneration from their Canadian employer.

- **Intra-company transfer (L-1 status)**

A person who has been employed continuously for at least one year in the last three years by a Canadian firm, as executive, manager, or specialist. This person can render services temporarily to the same firm (or its subsidiary or affiliate) in the United States. The position has to be in an executive or managerial capacity, or in a position of special knowledge. Spouses can apply for employment authorization.

- **Professionals (TN status)**

A Canadian or Mexican professional, with an approved occupation, travelling to the United States to work temporarily in the profession for which they are qualified for one-year increments.

- **Traders and Investors (E-1 and E-2 visas)**

A trader who works in a Canadian-owned or -controlled firm in the United States that carries on substantial trade in goods or services, and its international trade is principally between Canada and the United States. The position must be supervisory or executive, or involve skill essential to the operation of the U.S. firm.

An investor who has invested, or is in the process of investing, a substantial amount of capital in a United States real, commercial operation, and must develop and direct the operation of the business in the United States.

4. Are You Unknowingly a U.S. Citizen?

U.S. citizens are taxed differently than citizens of other countries, and must file U.S. income tax returns regardless of where they live in the world, unless their income is below the minimum filing amount. Also, they are subject to U.S. gift and estate tax on their worldwide property regardless of where they live.

Many Canadians are U.S. citizens without knowing it. They may not realize they may have a birthright claim to citizenship. Refer to the previous discussion on derivative citizenship. Alternatively, some believe erroneously they have lost their U.S. citizenship. If you were a U.S. citizen and think you have lost your citizenship, here is what you need to know.

To lose U.S. citizenship, you must perform an "expatriating act" (for example, taking out Canadian citizenship with the intent to renounce U.S. citizenship), and as a result, obtain a Certificate of Loss of Nationality (CLN) from the U.S. Department of State. Therefore, even if you *think* you have lost U.S. citizenship, perhaps by becoming a Canadian citizen, you have not necessarily. You cannot be sure you have lost your U.S. citizenship unless you actually requested and received a CLN.

If you are a "former" U.S. citizen who took out Canadian citizenship and do not wish to be a U.S. citizen, make certain that you get a CLN, or you may be subject to unexpected U.S. income, gift, or estate tax. You can apply now for your CLN and it will be retroactive to the day you performed an "expatriating act."

On the other hand, if you were issued a CLN but now regret losing your U.S. citizenship, it may be possible for you to reclaim it. Prior to November 14, 1986, U.S. law did not allow dual citizenship, and a CLN may have been issued to you simply because you became a Canadian citizen, even though you had no desire to give up U.S. citizenship.

But the law was changed in 1986. Now dual citizenship is allowed and people do not automatically lose their U.S. citizenship unless they intentionally give up U.S. citizenship. If you previously lost your U.S. citizenship, you can apply to have it restored on the basis you did not intend to give up U.S. citizenship when you performed the expatriating act. If your application is allowed, your citizenship is restored retroactively, and you are considered to have been a U.S. citizen from your date of birth or original naturalization.

However, in the above case, you would want to thoroughly check out the U.S. tax implications of having your citizenship restored, before you commence the process. For example, would you need to retroactively file U.S. tax returns for all those prior years? Obtain expert professional tax advice on the effects, in advance.

5. Renouncing U.S. Citizenship

Occasionally a U.S. citizen residing outside the United States with no plans to return to live there may decide that renouncing U.S. citizenship is preferable to the continuing tax and other regulatory obligations. A person may voluntarily give up U.S. citizenship by performing one of the following "expatriating acts" with the *intention* of relinquishing U.S. nationality:

- Becoming naturalized in another country
- Formally declaring allegiance to another country
- Serving in a foreign army
- Serving in certain types of foreign government employment
- Making a formal renunciation of nationality before a U.S. diplomatic or consular officer in a foreign country
- Making a formal renunciation of nationality in the United States during a time of war
- Committing an act of treason.

If you wish to formally renounce U.S. citizenship you must execute an oath of renunciation before a consular officer, and your citizenship is nullified, effective on the date the oath is executed. In all other cases, your citizenship is revoked effective on the date the expatriating act was committed, even though it may not be documented until later. The U.S. State Department will document loss of citizenship in such cases when you acknowledge to a consular officer that the expatriating act was taken with the requisite intent.

To officially document your loss of citizenship you must apply for a Certificate of Loss of Nationality (CLN), and the consular officer will submit it to the State Department in Washington for approval. Before issuing the CLN the State Department will review the file to confirm:

- You were a U.S. citizen
- An expatriating act was committed
- The act was undertaken voluntarily
- You had the intent of relinquishing citizenship when the expatriating act was committed.

If your purpose in renouncing U.S. citizenship is to avoid tax liability, you may incur special tax liability by renouncing, and your act of renunciation may make you inadmissible to the U.S. You may require special permission to enter the U.S. in the future.

6. Working Part-time in the U.S.

If you want to earn some income while you are enjoying your Snowbird lifestyle, be wary. To work in the U.S., you need to have a Green Card or employment authorization. There are various ways that you may be eligible to apply for it—for example, if your spouse or one of your parents is a U.S. citizen. Another way of being able to work in the U.S. is under provisions of NAFTA, which may allow Canadians to work in the U.S. (for example, if you have a business in Canada and want to start a U.S. division).

If you work in the U.S. illegally, that is, work there without conforming to the above requirements, the penalties are heavy and not worth the risk. The U.S. Department of Homeland Security (DHS) or DCIS can turf you out of the country and, depending on how seriously they view the infraction, they could deny entry for 1 to 10 years.

If you wish to explore the work option, even part-time, the best thing to do is to speak to a U.S. immigration attorney about your wishes. Most initial consultations are free or at a nominal cost, but ask in advance. Simply look in the Yellow Pages of your local telephone directory for lawyers specializing in immigration matters. Make sure that you receive at least three opinions from these experts before you decide on your next step. You want to ensure that the customized advice that you are getting is consistent. In addition, there are potential tax implications, so you would need to speak to a cross-border tax specialist as well.

CUSTOMS REGULATIONS

1. Travelling to the United States

If you are a resident of Canada on a visit to the United States as a Snowbird for up to six months, your U.S. Customs status is that of a nonresident. There are various regulations involved, exemptions permitted, and privileges allowed.

If you are arriving in the United States by land, air, or sea, a simple oral declaration that the allowed exemptions from duty apply to you is generally sufficient. In certain situations you might be requested to fill out a written declaration. Make sure you bring your passport with you.

The following is a discussion of the main areas you need to know. Contact the U.S. DHS—Customs Service for further information and free explanatory brochures. Since regulations can change, make sure you have current information from the U.S. Customs Service.

a) Exemptions

Here are some of the main federal exemptions for nonresidents of the United States:

- *Personal effects* are exempt from duty if they are for your personal use, are owned by you, and accompany you to the United States.
- *Alcoholic beverages* are free of duty and internal revenue tax if they are for personal use and do not exceed one litre. Some state alcoholic beverage laws may be more restrictive than federal liquor laws.
- *Vehicles* can be temporarily imported to the United States for one year or less if they are used for transportation for you, your family, or your guests.
- *Household effects* are free from duty if they are for your personal use and not for another person or for sale.

b) Gifts

There are several exemptions under this category:

- *Gifts you bring with you* are free of duty or tax if you are remaining in the United States for at least 72 hours and if the gifts do not exceed US$100 in retail value. This exemption can be claimed once every six months. Alcoholic beverages are not included. Articles bought in so-called duty-free shops are subject to U.S. Customs duty and restrictions if they exceed your exemption.

- *Gifts sent by mail* are free of duty if they are mailed from Canada to the United States and do not exceed US$60 in retail value. You may send as many gifts as you wish, but if they are all sent to the same U.S. addressee, there will be duty payable if the daily receipt of gifts exceeds US$60. Packages should be marked "unsolicited gift" with the name of donor, nature of the gift, and fair retail value of the gift clearly written on the outside of the package.

c) Items Subject to Duty

If you import items to the United States that cannot be claimed under the allowed exemptions, they will be subject to applicable duty and tax. After deducting your exemptions and the value of any duty-free articles, a flat rate of duty of 10 percent will be applied to the next US$1,000 worth (fair retail value) of merchandise. If you exceed $1,000 worth, you will be charged duty at various rates, depending on the item. The flat rate of duty applies only if the items are for personal use or for gifts.

d) Shipping Goods

You do not need to accompany personal and household effects to the United States that are entitled to free entry. You can have them shipped to your United States address at a later time if it is more convenient. You do not need to use a Customs broker to clear your shipment through Customs. You may do this yourself after you arrive in the United States or designate a friend or relative to represent you in Customs matters. If you take the latter route, you must give your representative a letter addressed to the Officer in Charge of Customs authorizing that person to represent you as your agent on a one-time basis in clearing your shipment through Customs. You have five working days to clear your shipment through Customs after its arrival in the United States; otherwise, it will be sent, at your expense and risk, to a storage warehouse.

e) Money

There is no limit on the total amount of money you can bring into or take out of the United States. If you are carrying more than US$10,000 into or out of the country at any one time, however, you must file a report with U.S.

Customs. This rule applies to currency, traveller's cheques, money orders, ordinary cheques, and so on.

f) Prohibited and Restricted Items

Because U.S. Customs inspectors are stationed at ports of entry, they are frequently required to enforce laws and requirements of other U.S. government agencies in order to protect community health, to preserve domestic plant and animal life, and for other reasons.

There are several prohibited or restricted categories that you should be aware of. Here are a few of them:

- **Medicine and narcotics**

Narcotics are normally prohibited entry and are tightly regulated. However, if you require medicines containing habit-forming drugs or narcotics (e.g., cough medicine, diuretics, heart drugs, tranquillizers, sleeping pills, depressants, stimulants), you should:

a. have all drugs, medicines, and similar products properly identified;

b. carry only the quantity that might normally be used for the length of your stay in the United States for health problems requiring such drugs or medicine; and

c. have either a prescription or a written statement from your personal physician that the medicine is being used under a doctor's direction and is necessary for your physical well-being while travelling or staying in the United States.

- **Pets**

Cats and dogs can be brought in, but they must be free of evidence of communicable diseases. If you plan to bring your pet, obtain a copy of the leaflet explaining your rights and obligations. Check out the Canada Border Services Agency website at: www.cbsa.gc.ca.

- **Wildlife and fish**

These are subject to certain import and export restrictions, prohibitions, permits, and so on. Any part of certain types of wildlife or fish, or products and articles manufactured from them, could be affected, especially endangered species, which are prohibited from being imported or exported. If you are in doubt as to whether certain leather goods, skins, or furs are governed by the regulations, contact the U.S. Fish and Wildlife Service.

- **Food products**

Certain food products might be restricted. If you are in doubt, contact the U.S. Department of Agriculture Animal and Plant Inspection Service.

- **Fruits, vegetables, plants**

Every fruit, vegetable, or plant brought into the United States is supposed to be declared to the Customs officer in case it is a restricted item.

2. Returning to Canada

When you return to Canada after your U.S. Snowbird stay, there are various regulations that you must comply with. As far as the Canadian government is concerned, if you have not been out of the country for more than six months, you are still a resident Canadian citizen. If you have been out of the country more than six months or you are a U.S. citizen resident in Canada, other Customs regulations could apply. These Customs regulations cover such matters as bringing back goods and vehicles. For vehicles, Transport Canada's regulations also must be considered. Obtain current information, since regulations can change.

Here is a summary of the key regulations:

a) Bringing Back Goods Purchased in the United States

The *North American Free Trade Agreement* (NAFTA) eliminates the duty that applies to goods you acquire in the United States. Your goods qualify for the lower U.S. duty rate under NAFTA if they are:

- for personal use; and
- marked as made in the U.S. or Canada; or
- not marked or labelled to indicate that they were made anywhere other than in the U.S. or Canada.

If the goods you acquire in the U.S. are marked "Made in Mexico," the Mexican duty rate will apply. Refer to Chapter 10 on Snowbirding in Mexico. If you do not qualify for a personal exemption or if you exceed that limit, you will have to pay the goods and services tax (GST) over and above any duty or other taxes that may apply on the portion not eligible under your personal exemption.

- **Personal exemptions**

You are entitled to your basic duty-free and tax-free exemptions of CDN$750 after a seven-day absence outside Canada, and CDN$400 after 48 hours. In addition, you can also benefit from the low special duty rate which applies to the next CDN$300 worth of goods beyond your personal exemption, as long as these goods accompany you and are not alcohol or tobacco products. Because it is constantly changing, check the current duty rate. Pick up a copy of the Canada Revenue Agency brochure called *I Declare* for more information on personal exemptions. Also contact the Canada Border Services Agency. They have many helpful brochures on their website at: www.cbsa.gc.ca.

• **Prohibited, restricted, or controlled goods**

Canada limits or prohibits the importation of certain things. These can include cultural property that has historical significance in its country of origin, animals on the endangered species list (and any products made from them), certain food and agricultural products, and goods considered harmful to the environment.

There are also limits on the amounts of certain food products you can bring into Canada at the low duty rates or that you can include in your personal exemption. If you bring back quantities of these products above the set limits, you will have to pay a very high rate of duty (from 150 to 350 percent), and may also need an agricultural inspection certificate. The following are some examples of the limits that apply:

a. two dozen eggs;

b. CDN $20 worth of dairy products, such as milk, cheese, and butter;

c. three kilograms of margarine; and

d. 20 kilograms of meat and meat products, including turkey and chicken. Within the 20-kilogram limit, further restrictions apply as follows: a maximum of one whole turkey or 10 kilograms of turkey products; and a maximum of 10 kilograms of chicken. All meat and meat products have to be identified as products of the United States.

• **Alcohol and tobacco**

You can import alcohol and tobacco products if the quantity is within the limits set by the province or territory. You cannot import alcohol products duty-free and tax-free unless you have been outside Canada for at least 48 hours and qualify for a personal exemption. If you do not qualify for a personal exemption, or if you exceed the limit, you will have to pay the import duties and the provincial or territorial taxes that apply on the portion not eligible under your personal exemption.

- **Making your declaration**

Prepare a list of all the goods you bought in the United States, and keep sales receipts. This will make it easier and faster to declare all these goods when you return to Canada. You will also find it easier to claim any personal exemption to which you are entitled. When you present your list and receipts, the customs officer may then work out your personal exemption and any duties you owe in the way that benefits you most. Don't forget to have your identification ready, showing your name and address.

- **Paying duties**

You can pay by cash, travellers' cheque, VISA, MasterCard, or by personal cheque if the amount is not more than $500. In some cases, Canada Revenue Agency may accept a personal cheque for up to $2,500 as long as you can produce adequate identification.

- **Value of goods**

Canada Revenue Agency will include any state taxes you have paid on your goods when determining their value, and will use the prevailing exchange rate to convert the total to Canadian funds. The Customs officer will calculate duty on this Canadian value.

- **Goods and services tax (GST)**

If you buy goods beyond your personal exemption, GST applies to them, just as if you had purchased them in Canada. GST is payable on the "value for tax," which is made up of the value (see previous explanation), plus the duty, plus any excise tax that applies.

- **General Agreement on Tariffs and Trade (GATT)**

NAFTA goods also qualify for the GATT rate, so if the rate of duty payable on the goods you are importing is lower under GATT than under NAFTA, customs officers will automatically assess the lower rate.

For more information on GATT and its impact on duty rates, contact the nearest Canada Revenue Agency Customs office.

- **Provincial sales tax (PST)**

Depending on the agreements between the provinces and Ottawa, Canada Revenue Agency may collect any PST for goods you import that do not qualify under your duty-free and tax-free exemption. In addition, in most provinces and territories across Canada, Canada Revenue Agency collects special provincial or territorial assessments on alcohol and tobacco products that do not qualify under your duty-free and tax-free exemption. You should check on whether PST applies or HST (combined PST and GST).

- **Duty-free items**

Check with the Canada Border Services Agency (www.cbsa.gc.ca) for a current list of duty-free items, as these can change from time to time.

b) Bringing Back Cars, RVs, Trucks, and Other Vehicles Purchased in the United States

Special restrictions and import procedures apply to motor vehicles. For more information, see the Canada Revenue Agency brochure *Importing a Motor Vehicle into Canada.*

If you bought a new or used car, truck, trailer, or motor home in the United States, you will have to pay import assessments when you return to Canada. These include duty and excise tax if the vehicle is air-conditioned, or if it is a passenger vehicle in excess of a certain amount of weight. In addition, you would have to pay the federal goods and services tax (GST) and any applicable provincial sales or other taxes. Check with your provincial government.

The duty rate for eligible vehicles imported from the United States that fall under the Canada-U.S. *Free Trade Agreement* (NAFTA), that is, vehicles made in the United States or Canada, is low or non-existent, depending on the vehicle and applicable policy. If the vehicle was not made in the United States or Canada and therefore does not fall under NAFTA, then the duty is higher. Check on the current rates.

To determine the value of the vehicle for duty purposes, the original U.S. purchase price, including state sales tax and other applicable costs, will be converted into Canadian funds. That amount will vary, of course, depending on the exchange rate at the time. If you import a new vehicle within 30 days of the date it was delivered to you, the above formula applies, with no deduction for depreciation. If you purchased a new vehicle and imported it within one year of the date of delivery to you in the U.S., however, you can deduct an amount for depreciation of the value of the car before you actually imported it. Make enquiries for the current policies. You can't obtain depreciation for a car that was purchased used. For a used car, the fair market value will be set according to vehicle values from a neutral source—for example, the U.S. or Canadian *Automobile Red Book.* If you have traded your old car in for a different car, the value of the new car will be a used value.

Make sure you have all receipts with you and any bill of sale. Ideally, have a current fair market value done on dealership letterhead, if you bought the vehicle from a dealership. You do not want to declare an artificially low value for the vehicle or have receipts that are clearly way below market value. The reason: if you underestimate the vehicle value, Canada Border Services Agency can seize the vehicle and impound it until you pay a penalty of 40 percent of the correct value of the vehicle. In that event, you have a 30-day period to make a written appeal, but it could take up to a year or more to adjudicate, and in the meantime you are out your car or penalty money. To avoid any stress or uncertainty, contact Canada Border Services Agency beforehand if you have any questions or doubts in your particular circumstances. For further information about determining vehicle value for Customs purposes, contact the Canada Border Services Agency office closest to your expected point of entry. Their website is: www.cbsa.gc.ca.

c) Transport Canada Vehicle Prohibitions

There are no longer any Customs prohibitions on bringing a vehicle into Canada from the United States. There are restrictive importation rules for vehicles under Transport Canada regulations, however. Because of strict Canadian safety emission standards, you may be prohibited from importing a vehicle that only meets U.S. standards, unless it is brought up to full Canadian compliance standards.

To satisfy yourself that the vehicle you want to import is eligible and to find out what documents you need to do so, make enquiries before you buy the vehicle. Check with the Canada Border Services Agency. Their website is: www.cbsa.gc.ca.

Tips Before Leaving Canada

√ Take your passport and birth certificate with you if you are having an extended stay in the United States.

√ If you are considering staying in the United States more than six months in the year, check with the U.S. DHS, and with a U.S. Immigration attorney, as well as an experienced cross-border tax accountant on the tax implications before you depart. Refer to Chapter 9 on selecting professional advisors.

√ Check with U.S. Customs for the current policy on items you think might be prohibited or restricted in the United States. Ask about exemptions, shipping goods, and items that could be subject to duty.

√ If you are considering buying a vehicle in the United States, check Customs and Transport Canada regulations for returning to Canada with the vehicle. Do this before you buy the vehicle. Also check with the Registrar of Imported Vehicles.

√ Check with Canada Border Services Agency on the current policy for bringing back goods purchased in the United States. What items are duty-free and what items are not?

√ Take receipts for items that have a high dollar value, in case you are challenged on your return to Canada. It is good to have proof that you bought a camera or expensive jewellery in Canada.

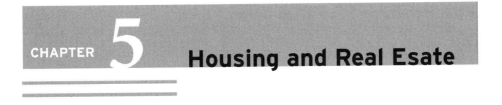

INTRODUCTION

There are many towns and RV or mobile home parks built specifically for retired people and Snowbirds in selected locations in the United States. Some of the advantages include the opportunity to live and socialize in a homogeneous community; planned social activities like bingo, dancing, crafts, card games, trips, and educational programs; recreational facilities, such as tennis courts, exercise rooms, a swimming pool, and golf and shuffle-board areas; maintenance services and shopping and transportation facilities; and religious services. Security is another reason for the popularity of retirement communities. Many have 24-hour security services, which keep watch on the residences and check all visitors when they enter or leave. Refer to page 286 in Appendix A for a schedule of activities of a sample mobile home/RV park.

Retirement communities have some drawbacks, however. For example, some communities are becoming crowded and increasingly costly. Some people don't enjoy planned activities and lessons. Others feel too isolated in communities that are far away from urban centres.

By identifying your own needs and wants, speaking to others, and doing your research, you will quickly determine which option is right for you.

This chapter provides an overview of the considerations you should keep in mind when buying a house, apartment, condominium, townhouse, time-share, mobile home, or recreational vehicle in the United States. Also covered is an overview of the home purchase process in the U.S., including terminology, types of property ownership, and obtaining a U.S. mortgage. The perils of selling your home yourself are also discussed. Refer to Chapter 7 for a discussion of the tax consequences of renting or selling your house or condo and of owning real estate in the United States when you die. In addition, refer to Chapter 9 for how to select a realtor.

THE PURCHASE PROCESS

1. Overview

When a potential buyer and seller wish to conclude a transaction, they will normally finalize the agreement by jointly signing a "contract for sale and purchase." In Canada, this document is often referred to as an "agreement of purchase and sale." Whatever terminology is used, the document describes the details and terms of the transaction, such as which party will pay the various expenses involved and when the contract will be finalized.

The transaction is usually finalized at the closing, when both parties normally approve and sign the settlement statement prepared by the closing agent. The settlement or closing statement (often referred to as the statement of adjustments in Canada) summarizes the financial aspects of the transaction. It lists the sale price, the expenses included, the pro-rations, and the net amount of money due from the buyer to the seller.

The closing agent, sometimes referred to as an escrow agent, is the individual or business, usually a lawyer (or attorney in the U.S.) or frequently a title insurance agent (not a lawyer), who organizes and conducts the closing. Closings are often conducted entirely by mail.

The expenses of the transaction include the documentary stamps (a government land transfer tax), intangible tax (a tax on any mortgages involved), title insurance or abstract fees, as applicable; legal fees, real estate commission, fees to record documents; and other expenses. The buyer often receives title insurance to ensure clear title to the property. In some counties and states, as an alternative to title insurance, the chain of title (abstract of title) will be examined to ensure the title is clear.

The pro-rations are the apportioning of direct property expenses between the buyer and seller for the portion of time the property is owned by each. This includes expenses such as the current year's property taxes and the current period's condominium or homeowner's association maintenance fees, where applicable. At the closing the seller will also sign a deed to formally transfer the property to the buyer. The closing agent will then send the new deed to the county for recording, after which it is sent on to the buyer.

If you are thinking of selling your home, the individual you engage to sell your real estate is generally referred to as a real estate agent or broker or, if he or she belongs to the National Association of Realtors, may also be referred to as a Realtor. There are brokers for both sellers and buyers. It can be helpful to be aware which type is assisting you so you can better evaluate their objectivity.

If you wish to offer your real estate for sale through a broker, you will likely sign some form of listing agreement. It will state the terms under which your property will be offered for sale, including the rate of the commission.

2. U.S. Terminology for Real Estate Transactions

Here is more detail on the process and jargon used in the U.S. Although there may be different terms used in some states, the concepts are similar.

a) Escrow Agent

The escrow agent's function is to serve as the depository of both funds and documents. Escrow agents are responsible for processing and coordinating those funds and documents, as well as for obtaining approvals from both parties, as required. They secure title insurance, and pro-rate and adjust for taxes, insurance, and rents. They record the deed and loan documents and are accountable for collecting and disbursing the monies to the appropriate parties.

b) Title Insurance

When a property is conveyed from one party to another, title insurance will be required. Two types of title insurance are generally issued, for the owner and the buyer. The owner's policy, which is paid for by the seller, ensures the buyer is receiving clear or "marketable" title to the property. A marketable title is one reasonably free of encumbrances and from risk of legal dispute over defects. The buyer's policy ensures the lender's loan position.

One of the first things an escrow agent will do after escrow instructions are completed is begin searching the title, to assure that there are no claims or liens, and to check for restrictions, or reconveyances on the property, that have not been disclosed by the seller. A thorough evaluation and search of public records will be conducted by the title company to ensure that no future claims arise.

Once all of the information is collected and examined, a preliminary title report will be prepared for both the buyer and seller, along with a copy of the legal description of the property. The search continues through escrow, and prior to closing a commitment of title will be issued.

c) Seller's Disclosure

In some states, the law requires that sellers complete a property disclosure and deliver it to the buyer for review and approval within a set number of days after contract acceptance. It is on this document that the seller must disclose any known defaults of the property and indicate any work that has been done on it. Many provinces in Canada have a similar type of disclosure statement. The buyer has a set period from receipt of the disclosure to accept or disapprove it. Should you find any problems or have concerns about the information presented, address the matter immediately with the seller, their agent, or your lawyer.

d) Appraisal

The lender will demand an appraisal of the property by a certified appraiser to prove that the sales price of the home is reasonable. The appraisal fee may be paid by either the buyer or seller, or split. Should the appraisal show that the sales price is too high, the buyer will have to either come up with the difference in cash or renegotiate with the seller. The appraisal will be sent directly to the lender for review, during their underwriting and loan processing.

e) Identity Statements

During the escrow process in some states, both the buyer(s) and seller(s) will be asked to complete a confidential identity statement. The purpose of this is to eliminate inaccurate data involving parties with the same or similar names. A name search will be run on both parties with state and federal authorities for tax liens, judgments, and bankruptcies.

f) Settlement Charges

The escrow agent will prepare a settlement statement of charges and send a copy to both the buyer and seller about a week before closing. This important financial statement summarizes the costs for both the buyer and seller, accounts for funds to be deposited and disbursed, makes adjustments, and indicates the amounts necessary to close escrow. Included within this statement are the pro-rations for taxes, interest, and insurance. The total adjusted amounts to be paid by the borrower and the seller are shown, along with the amount of the net proceeds to be disbursed to the seller, after costs are paid.

g) Insurance

Prior to closing, you will need to make arrangements for homeowner insurance coverage and have proof of coverage sent to the escrow agent or lender. The escrow agent will generally collect for at least one year's premium in advance. If your down payment is less than 20 percent, you will need another type of insurance, called mortgage insurance. We have the same concept in Canada if you are putting less than 25 percent as a down payment. The lender requires mortgage insurance for protection against your defaulting on the loan (if you did, the insurance would cover the lender for any shortfall). The lender will instruct the escrow agent to collect the premium for this insurance through the escrow.

h) Final Inspection

Prior to close of escrow, you will be asked to conduct a final walk-through to ensure that the property is in the same condition as when purchased and that everything is in good working order. If it was agreed that something was to be repaired or added and you find that the work has not been done, advise your agent immediately so that it can be corrected *before* you close escrow and take occupancy. In Canada this concept is not common. You don't customarily have the opportunity to approve the condition of the home before funds are released and possession occurs.

i) Closing Documentation

The date of closing is set in your contract, but may change due to a number of factors. For example, there can be delays due to title problems, the loan, the appraisal, inspections, insufficient funds in escrow, and missing signatures or documents. The final step in the escrow process is the recording of the documents, copies of which are sent to both the buyer and seller.

j) Trust Deeds

The principal instrument used to secure real property in many states is the trust deed, which is similar to a mortgage. The escrow agent will prepare the deeds, according to escrow instructions or the purchase contract. Signatures will be required by the parties at, or prior to, closing. Copies of the recorded documents will be sent to the seller, buyer, and lender.

k) Closing

All documents must be signed by the parties, proof of appropriate insurance provided, all inspections satisfactorily completed, and all funds deposited into escrow to finalize a closing. Once everything is complete, the escrow agent will take the paperwork to the county registry office for recording, and the funds will be disbursed to the proper parties.

3. Types of Property Ownership

When a sales contract is written, the buyer is asked to choose how he or she wishes to take title to the property (or elect to determine this in escrow). In either case, the buyer must tell the escrow agent, and the information will be in all final escrow documents.

It's helpful to have an understanding of the forms of ownership available to you as an owner of real estate property. Depending on the state, there can be different terminology, but the concepts are similar. Ask about the options in the state where you are purchasing property.

Select the type of ownership that best meets your needs. Consult your lawyer and professional accountant prior to making your selection, as there may be tax and estate consequences associated with each.

a) Severalty

This is an individual ownership by a person or a corporation.

b) Community Property

Not all states have community property laws, but Arizona and California, for example, do. There, if a husband and wife do not specify otherwise, it will be assumed that they are taking title as community property. This form of ownership is available only for a husband and wife, with each as equal partners with a half-interest in the property.

c) Joint Tenants with Right of Survivorship

This type of ownership is between two or more persons who take title with the right of survivorship. A single title is issued including all of the tenants' names, and each has equal ownership shares of the property. In the event that one party dies, his or her interest automatically goes to the other joint tenant(s). It therefore does not become an asset of the deceased's estate.

d) Tenants in Common

This form of ownership is for two or more individuals or entities, who take title without right of survivorship. The difference is that they do not have to have equal shares and that each party has its own separate title showing their portion of ownership. In the event that someone dies, his or her property interest becomes an asset of the estate; the will sets out what is to happen to that asset. If there is no will, the legislation of the state or province sets out the formula for dealing with assets of the deceased's estate.

4. Obtaining a U.S. Mortgage

Many mortgage companies provide loans for Canadians on the same basis as for U.S. citizens. Canadians receive "special" consideration because of the quality of the documentation that can be provided on the borrower's income and credit standing. Canadian tax returns are relatively easy for U.S. lenders to understand and analyse. Also, a credit history of any Canadian is readily available through computerized current credit reports to those authorized to make credit enquiries.

In many cases, Canadians can borrow up to 80 percent of the purchase price, at the same rates available to U.S. citizens. Canadian borrowers must provide the lender with their two most recent tax returns and evidence that they have sufficient cash on hand to complete the purchase. With some lenders, alternative documentation is acceptable. For example, a Canadian—particularly a self-employed individual—has the option of confirming his or her income with an accountant's letter, indicating taxable income for each of the last two years. Also, sometimes an employed individual can provide an employer's letter. In some cases, a letter of credit from your Canadian bank is acceptable.

The process of applying for a loan is quite simple. You are required to provide copies of the appropriate income confirmation discussed above, the contract to purchase the property, and two months' bank statements showing where the needed funds are deposited. If you want a smaller amount of money, you could be eligible for a no-income-verification loan, which does not require you to provide documentation. Obviously, excellent credit and substantial assets would need to be shown.

You do not have to be present in the U.S. to close. The deed and loan documents can be sent to you in Canada and executed in the presence of an appropriate notary or lawyer, and then returned to the U.S. for funding and recording.

BUYING A HOUSE

You may wish to buy a house in the U.S. Sunbelt that you intend to live in while you are there and leave vacant or possibly rent out the rest of the time. Maybe you hope to move to the United States at some point to live there full-time. Whatever your motivation, there are some key steps to follow. You have probably already owned a house at some point, but the following tips and cautions bear repeating as a reminder. Many of these are equally applicable when selecting a condo.

For more information, refer to my book, *101 Streetsmart Condo Buying Tips for Canadians*. The contents have crossover relevance to condo cautions when buying in the U.S. and Mexico. Also refer to my book, *The Complete Guide to Buying and Owning Recreational Property in Canada* if you are considering buying a resort condo or property. In addition, refer to my website: www.homebuyer.ca.

1. Where to Find a Home for Sale

There are some preliminary considerations you need to work through before starting your search:

- Be clearly focused on what type of real estate you want in order to save time and stress.

- Target specific geographic area or areas. This means restricting your choices to specific communities or areas within a community. This makes your selection much easier and gives you an opportunity to get to know specific areas thoroughly. Obtain street maps of the areas.

- Know the price range that you want based on your funds and real estate needs.

- Determine the type of ideal purchase package that you want (e.g., price and terms) as well as your bottom-line fallback position. What is the maximum you are willing to pay?

- Make comparisons and shortlist choices. That way you can ensure that you get the best deal.

There are various methods of finding out about what real estate is for sale. The most common methods are word-of-mouth, using a real estate agent, reading local or real estate newspaper ads, or driving through the preferred neighbourhood and looking for For Sale signs.

2. General Tips When Looking for a Home

a) Location

One of the prime considerations is the location. How close is the property to cultural attractions, shopping centres, recreational facilities, community and religious facilities, and transportation? How attractive is the present development of the area surrounding the property? What is likely to happen in the future? Is there ample access to parking? Heavy traffic can be a noise nuisance as well as a hazard.

b) Pricing

The pricing of the property you are considering should be competitive with that of other, similar offerings. This can be difficult to determine unless you are comparing identical homes in a subdivision or condos in the same complex. If you are purchasing a condominium unit, for example, it is sometimes difficult to compare prices accurately without taking into account the different amenities that may be available in one condominium complex that are not available in the other—for example, tennis courts, swimming pool, and recreation centre. You may decide that you do not want these extra facilities, in which case paying an extra price for the unit because it has these features would not be attractive. At the same time, you have to look at the resale potential.

c) Knowledge of the Home and Neighbourhood

Surveys have shown that the average home buyer spends 17 minutes looking at the home before making the purchase decision, often making a decision on an emotional basis. Seventeen minutes is not enough time for anything other than a superficial look. Look at the property on several occasions to obtain a fresh perspective. Look at it in the day and evening. Look at the house when the owner is not present so that you can examine it thoroughly and at a leisurely pace. Bring a friend or relative with you. Take pictures outside and inside, if necessary, to enhance your recall if you are serious about buying the place. Drive around the neighbourhood to get a feeling for the appearance and conditions of other homes in the vicinity. If you wish to place an offer, remember to include a condition relating to inspection by a professional home inspector.

d) Reasons for Sale

An important factor to determine is why the property is for sale. Maybe the vendor knows something you don't that will have a bearing on your future interest. Or maybe the vendor is selling the home because of a desire to move to a larger or smaller home or a condo, because of loss of employment, or because of a serious illness or disability.

e) Property Taxes

Compare the costs of property taxes in the area that you are considering with those of other, equally attractive areas. Different municipalities have different tax rates, and there could be a considerable cost saving or expense. Also enquire as to whether there is any anticipated tax increase and why. For example, if the area is relatively new, there could be future property taxes or special levies to establish schools or other community support services.

f) Transportation

If you drive a car, how much traffic is there and how long would the commute take at various times of the day? Is public transportation available within walking distance? How reliable and frequent is it? Whether it is a bus, subway, rapid transit, freeway, ferry, or other mode of transportation, the quality of transportation will affect the quality of your life, as well as the resale price.

g) Crime Rate

Naturally this is an important issue. Check with the local police department for crime statistics in your area, and talk with neighbours on the street. Ask if there is a block watch or neighbourhood watch program in the area.

h) Services in the Community

Depending on your needs, you will want to check on the different services available in the community. A community will often be characterized by the local services. Is there adequate police, fire, and ambulance protection? Is there a hospital in the area? Are there doctors and dentists located in the vicinity? How often is garbage collected and are streets maintained? Is mail delivered to your door or to a central mailbox on your street or in your neighbourhood? If you wish to join an organization or club, is it close? Does the area cater to seniors or Snowbirds? Are there community centres or public parks nearby? Is there a place of worship of your faith in the neighbourhood? If the house or condo is near a commercial development, are noise and traffic a problem? What types of businesses, stores, or services are nearby?

i) Climate

If you are buying for personal use, the issue of climate is important. Certain areas of your city or community may have more rain and wind than others, depending on climate patterns. Check with a local, state, or national weather bureau.

j) Parking

Is parking outdoors, in a garage, in an open carport, or underground? Is there sufficient lighting for security protection? Is it a long walk from the parking spot to your home? Is there parking space available for a recreational vehicle or second car? Is there ample parking for visitors in the lot or on the street? Is there a private driveway or back lane connected to the garage or carport? Is street parking restricted in any fashion (e.g., residents' parking only)? Is the restriction enforced? Do you need to buy a permit?

k) Topography

The layout of the land is an important consideration. If there is a hill along the property, water could collect around the base of the house, causing drainage problems. If water collects under the foundation of the house and there is only soil under the foundation, the house could settle.

l) Condition of Building and Property

Obtain an objective and accurate assessment of the condition of the property. Have an independent building inspector look at it. You can find a building inspector in the Yellow Pages of the phone book. In addition, the vendor should answer specific questions, posed by either the building inspector or you. You also want to make sure you include appropriate conditions in your agreement of purchase and sale for obtaining or confirming information.

m) Type of Construction

Is the building constructed of wood, brick, concrete, stone, or other material? Is this important for fire safety concerns you might have?

n) Common Elements and Facilities

If you are buying a condominium unit, review all the common elements that make up the condominium development. Consider whether these elements are relevant to your needs as well as what maintenance or operational costs might be required to service these features.

o) Noise

Thoroughly check the levels of noise. Consider location of highways, driveways, parking lots, playgrounds, and businesses. If you are buying a condominium, also consider the location of the garage doors, elevators, and garbage chutes, as well as the heating and air-conditioning plant or equipment.

p) Privacy

Privacy is an important consideration and has to be thoroughly explored. For example, you want to make sure that the sound insulation between the walls, floors, and ceilings of your property is sufficient to enable you to live comfortably without annoying your neighbours or having your neighbours annoy you. If you have a condominium or townhouse unit, such factors as the distance between your unit and other common areas (including walkways, parking lot, and fences) are important.

q) Storage Space

Is there enough closet and storage space? Is the location and size suitable? Are the kitchen, hall, and bedroom closets big enough for your needs? Are the basement or other storage areas large enough for sports and other equipment, tools, and outdoor furniture?

r) Heating/Cooling

How is the house heated or cooled—directly and indirectly? Is the system efficient for your needs (e.g., does it use natural gas, oil, forced air, hot water, radiators, electric baseboards, wood-burning stove, or fireplace)? How old is the furnace? Has it been serviced regularly and is it still covered by warranty? Do you have any air-conditioning or ceiling fans? Is there a heat exchanger system in the fireplace? What are the annual heating/cooling bills?

3. Questions to Ask

Address these common questions to your lawyer, real estate agent, vendor, and building inspector.

a) Questions of a General Nature

- Does the property contain unauthorized accommodation?
- Are you aware of any registered or unregistered encroachments, easements, or rights of way?
- Have you received any notice or claim affecting the property from any person or public body?
- Are the premises connected to a public water system?
- Are the premises connected to a private or a community water system?

b) Questions About the Structure of the Dwelling

- Are you aware of any infestation by insects or rodents?
- Are you aware of any damage due to wind, fire, or water?
- Are you aware of any moisture and/or water problems in the basement or crawl space?
- Are you aware of any problems with the heating and/or central air-conditioning system?
- Are you aware of any problems with the electrical system?
- Are you aware of any problems with the plumbing system?
- Are you aware of any problems with the swimming pool and/or hot tub?
- Are you aware of any roof leakage or unrepaired damage?
- How old is the roof?
- Are you aware of any structural problems with the premises or other buildings on the property?
- Are you aware of any problems related to the building's settling?
- Are you aware of any additions or alterations made without a required permit?

- Has the wood stove or fireplace been approved by local authorities?
- To the best of your knowledge, have the premises ever contained urea formaldehyde foam insulation (UFFI)?
- To the best of your knowledge, have the premises ever contained asbestos insulation?
- To the best of your knowledge, is the ceiling insulated?
- To the best of your knowledge, are the exterior walls insulated?

c) Questions Regarding a Condominium Property

- Are there any restrictions on pets, children, or rentals?
- Are there any pending rules or condominium bylaw amendments that may alter the uses of the property?
- Are there any special assessments voted on or proposed?

BUYING A CONDOMINIUM OR TOWNHOUSE

Living in a condominium is not right for everyone since it involves not only individual ownership of the unit and shared ownership of other property but also adherence to rules and regulations, along with shared decision making. But many people prefer condominium living over the alternatives, especially since many condominiums are adult-oriented and don't permit children unless they are just visiting. Other condominium projects are geared specifically to retired people, providing security and social activities.

Condominiums may be detached, semi-detached, row houses, stack townhouses, duplexes, or apartments. They can even be building lots, subdivisions, or mobile home parks. The most familiar format for a condominium is an apartment condominium (one level) or a townhouse condominium (two or more levels). Whatever the style, a residential unit is specified and is owned by an individual in a freehold (owning the land) or leasehold (leasing rights to the land only) format. The rest of the property, including land, which is called "the common elements" in most provinces and states, is owned with the other owners. Common elements generally include walkways, driveways, lawns and gardens, lobbies, elevators, parking areas, recreational facilities, storage areas, laundry rooms, stairways, plumbing, electrical systems and portions of walls, ceilings and floors, and other items. If there are 50 condominium owners, then each individual owner would own one-fiftieth of the common elements as tenants in common. The legislation of each province or state can vary, but it is always designed to provide the legal and structural framework for the efficient management and administration of each condominium project.

The part of the condominium that you own outright is referred to as the unit in most provinces and states. You have full and clear title to this unit when you purchase it (assuming you are buying a freehold, not a leasehold, property), and the property is legally registered in your name in the land registry office in the province or state. The precise description of the common elements, and exactly what you own as part of your unit, may differ from development to development, but it is stipulated in the documents prepared and registered for each condominium. Part of the common elements may be designated for the exclusive use of one or more of the individual unit owners, in which case they are called limited common elements. In other words, they are limited only for the use of specific owners. Examples include parking spaces, storage lockers, roof gardens, balconies, patios, and front and back yards.

A condominium development is administered by various legal structures set out in provincial or state legislation. Snowbirds who purchase a recreational or resort condominium tend to own it outright and leave it empty when not in use. They may also rent it by using the condominium corporation or management company as an agent, a real estate agent, or they may rent it independently.

In any situation of shared ownership and community living there are advantages and disadvantages. An overview of these follows:

1. Advantages

- Ready availability of financing, similar to a single-family home
- Range of prices, locations, types of structures, sizes, and architectural features available
- Availability of amenities such as swimming pool, tennis courts, health clubs, community centre, saunas, hot tubs, exercise rooms, and sun decks
- Benefits of home ownership in ability to participate in the real estate market and potential growth in equity
- Freedom to decorate interior of unit to suit personal tastes
- Enhancement of security by permanence of neighbours and, in many cases, controlled entrances

- Elimination of many of the problems of upkeep and maintenance often associated with home ownership, since maintenance is usually the responsibility of a professional management company or manager
- Often considerably cheaper than buying a single-family home because of more efficient use of land and economy of scale
- Reduction of costs due to sharing of responsibilities for repair and maintenance
- Enhancement of social activities and sense of neighbourhood community by relative permanence of residents
- In many cases, the residents are other Snowbirds
- Elected council that is responsible for many business and management decisions
- Participation of owners in the operation of the development, which involves playing a role in setting and approval of budget, decision making, determination of rules, regulations, and bylaws, and other matters affecting the democratic operation of the condominium community.

2. Disadvantages

- May be difficult to assess accurately the quality of construction of the project
- A loss of freedom may be experienced through restrictions contained in the rules and bylaws (e.g., restriction on the right to rent, on pets, on duration of stay of visitors, or on use of a barbecue on the patio)
- People live closer together, creating problems from time to time; problem areas include the five Ps: pets, parking, personality, parties, and people
- One could be paying for maintenance and operation of amenities that one has no desire or intention to use
- Management of the condominium council is by volunteers, who may or may not have the appropriate abilities and skills.

Condominiums are a popular form of housing, especially for older or retired Canadians. The many benefits will ensure that the demand for this type of housing will grow. Make sure you obtain objective legal advice from a real estate lawyer before you make a final decision to purchase a condominium.

3. Know the Real Reasons Behind the Sale

An important factor to know is why a condo is up for sale. Perhaps the vendor knows something you don't, which will have a bearing on your further interest.

If you can, try to determine the real motivation for the owner to sell the condo. Try to dig below the surface. This will assist you in knowing how to negotiate in terms of your offer price and terms and general strategies. The motivation for sale could be a positive or negative one.

Some of the frequent reasons for sale of a principal residence include the following:

- Separation or divorce
- Death of owner or co-owner
- Job loss
- Job relocation
- Ill health
- Retirement and therefore relocation or downsizing house size needs, or desire to take some of the equity out of the condo for retirement purposes
- Owner lost money in a business or other investment venture and needs to sell the condo to pay off the debt
- Owner has not made payments on the mortgage due to personal or financial problems, so the lender has started court proceedings to have the condo sold
- Owner wants to sell in a seller's market
- Owner is concerned that the market is changing and could become a buyer's market
- Owner is testing the market to see what the market will pay without making any serious attempt to sell
- Children are leaving the home and therefore the owner's housing needs are changing
- Owner wants to buy a larger home due to increasing family size or needs. This could also be due to having an extended family, e.g., in-law suite or extra space for parents or relatives, or blended family due to a second marriage or common-law relationship, etc.
- Owner wants to trade up to a nicer home or better neighbourhood

- Owner wants to buy a house with a rental suite in basement for revenue purposes
- Owner is trying to avoid an upcoming expensive special assessment for condo repairs (e.g., roof, leaking buildings) and/or major amenity upgrades and maintenance (e.g., pool)
- Owner is concerned the mix of renters and owner-occupiers is too high, and causing a negative impact on the condo community
- Owner has a noisy neighbour or is facing a noisy street
- Owner knows that a building development has been approved that will block the view from the condo.

4. Where to Look for Your Condo

There are some preliminary considerations you need to work through before starting your search.

General Guidelines

- Clearly define your needs and wants and why.
- Be clearly focused on what type of condominium you want and its location, in order to save time and stress.
- Do your preliminary research on the Internet through MLS (www.mls. ca) and Google using keyword searches.
- Target a specific geographic area or areas. This means restricting your choices to specific communities or areas within a community. This makes your selection much easier and gives you an opportunity to get to know specific areas thoroughly. Obtain street maps of the area as well as a zoning map from city hall. You can also access detailed maps on the Internet through Google and Mapquest.
- Know the price range that you want based on your available financing and real estate needs. Obtain a pre-approved mortgage so that you have that reality check.
- Determine the type of ideal purchase package that you want (e.g., price and terms) as well as your "bottom line" fallback position. You want to know the maximum you are willing to pay and the most restrictive terms that you can live with. Make sure that you don't compromise your own position.

- Do comparisons and short-list choices. That way you can ensure you get the best deal, in comparative terms.

- Be realistic in terms of your purchase conditions in light of the current market situation. Many people fantasize about buying real estate for less than the fair market value and keep searching for this elusive purchase. The reality is, that situation could be very difficult to find.

- Don't necessarily wait for mortgage rates to go down before looking. Higher mortgage rates generally mean less demand in the market and therefore lower prices and more negotiating leverage for the purchaser. Conversely, lower mortgage rates generally mean more demand in the market, and therefore higher prices and less negotiating leverage for the purchaser. These are guidelines only. The key factor is to buy at the right price, taking all the factors outlined in this chapter and other chapters into consideration. If mortgage rates come down, you can renegotiate a lower mortgage rate with or without a penalty, depending on the mortgage you originally negotiated.

- Remember, the location of a property is very important, especially for a principal residence. Location is, of course, also important for investment property, but it has to be balanced against overall investment goals such as tax benefits, appreciation, resale potential, net revenue, and risk assessment.

5. Where to Find Real Estate for Sale

There are various methods of finding out about real estate for sale. Here are some of the most common approaches in the Canadian context. Modify the guidelines for the U.S. market.

a) Internet

As noted earlier, this is the primary research tool for over 70 percent of Canadians in locating a property of interest. There are many websites available. The MLS site is a comprehensive listing at www.mls.ca. All the major real estate companies have their own websites with listings. Also do a key word search on Google.ca.

b) Multiple Listing Service (MLS)

MLS is an excellent tool for obtaining condo listing information. If you are looking at an MLS book or online at www.mls.ca, look for specific factors that will give you clues as to vendor motivation. This could assist you in negotiating a lower price. For example, look for the exact area, when the property was listed (how long), if it has been re-listed, whether the property is vacant, if any price reductions have occurred (for how much and when), and whether there has been a previous collapsed sale. Also look in the remarks/comments section in the MLS listing book. For example, it could say why the property is for sale, such as foreclosure action, order for sale, relocation, bought another property, etc. All this information is important research for you. If you can't readily access any of the above information, ask your realtor for it.

c) Real Estate Agent

A good real estate agent is an invaluable asset for buying or selling real estate. He or she can save you time, expense, and frustration, and provide advice and expertise. Remember that the vendor pays the real estate commission whether the agent is a listing or selling broker.

There are many advantages to using realtors, which are discussed throughout this book. You can use their services to source out property listed on multiple or exclusive listings, or for property "for sale by owner." You can also use them to contact owners of property who do not currently have the property for sale. The advantage of using realtors with non-listed property is that they can possibly negotiate a better deal for you than you may be able to get yourself. There are strategic benefits to having an agent present the offer and negotiate on your behalf. Frequently, the owner will agree to pay a commission to the realtor if you buy, although the commission in a non-listed sale would generally be less. This is because the realtor has not had the expense of time or advertising in actively promoting the listing. Alternatively, you could arrange to pay the realtor a negotiated fee if he or she arranged a sale at a price attractive to you.

If you use a realtor to assist your search, be loyal if you purchase the property. On the other hand, if the realtor is turning out to be unmotivated, then find another. Make sure you give your agent a list of your requirements so he or she can be precise in conducting your search for you.

d) Newspaper Ads

Look in the classified section of your daily or community newspaper. The weekend section tends to have the most listings. The Monday classified section has the fewest listings. Because fewer people look in the Monday section, that could mean fewer potential buyers are paying attention and leaving more opportunity for you. Ignore the sales puffery. Many ads are designed to entice you with the impression the owner is anxious and therefore imply that you may be able to get a better price. This may or may not be the case. Pay particular attention to ads that may imply that an owner is under time pressure, such as "estate sale," "owner transferred," or "foreclosure sale." Also, look in the special real estate newspapers that are available free and come out weekly in many major Canadian cities.

e) Drive Through Neighbourhoods

As mentioned earlier, it is important to develop a familiarity with the area in which you are interested. Drive through the area on a regular basis and look for For Sale signs, both property listed with a realtor and For Sale by Owner. Take down addresses, names, and telephone numbers.

f) Through Word of Mouth

You could let your friends, neighbours, relatives, or business associates know that you are looking to buy property, the type of property, and the location, in case they hear of someone who is thinking of selling or see a property for sale in their neighbourhood that might interest you.

6. Pros and Cons of Different Types of Condos

There are different cautions and approaches when dealing with different types of condo sales. Here is a very brief overview. This book emphasizes the wide range of ways that you can protect yourself through knowledge and due diligence research before you sign on the dotted line. In all cases, you want to have the assistance of a real estate lawyer to review all the documents and give you advice. It can frequently be a challenge for a layperson to interpret the implications of the fine print.

a) Buying a Resale Condo

When you buy a previously owned condo, you need to ensure you obtain all the necessary documents and information. Depending on your province and your condo corporation, there could be additional documents. You want to make your offer to purchase subject to your lawyer obtaining all the relevant documents to review and being satisfied with them. Make sure you give yourself and your lawyer sufficient time to review and understand the documents—a week to 10 days. There will be a lot to review, as there is a history to the condo. You also want to ensure you obtain a home inspection on the unit and the building to check on construction quality. Talk to the people who own condos in the complex. Speak to a condo corporation director and the property management company about any problems and the governance of the condo corporation.

You want to ask detailed questions about the reserve/contingency fund, and what major expenses could be anticipated and when. You also want to review the annual report and read the last 24 months of condo corporation minutes to owners, to see if there are any matters of concern—leaking roofs, break-ins of cars and units, litigation pending. If you are serious about buying a unit, it would be prudent to hire a competing condo property management company to the one used by your condo corporation, e.g., one of the larger and more experienced companies, to review the documentation and give you their candid feedback. They may have heard information that would either affirm it is a good location and complex, or one to stay away from. It would be inexpensive to obtain this third-party feedback—probably only $200 or so. That is money well spent. You want to see in the documents what the restrictions are on the total number of rental units that can be permitted in the complex.

Some of the advantages of buying a resale condo include:

- No lengthy wait time before you can move in.
- You can see what you are buying.
- There is a history to the complex in terms of operation and structure and any problems.
- You can speak to people who live in the complex to see if the community is a good fit for your lifestyle, needs, and wants.
- Condo developments that are older may have larger-sized units.
- There is no GST.
- Deposits tend to be lower.

Some of the disadvantages include:

- Major repairs could soon be required or planned for. If the reserve/contingency fund is insufficient, a special assessment could be charged to the owners to fund the repairs.
- Different construction standards could create problems with leaks, squeaks, noise, or heat loss.
- Older condo complexes tend to require more maintenance and therefore costs.

- The New Home Warranty coverage would likely have expired.
- Limited choice in types of units or upgrade potential.
- May lack in the amenities that are important to you.

b) Buying a Conversion Condo

This format means that the building was originally used for some other purpose, but has been renovated for residential use. It could have been a rental apartment block before. Or if it is a loft-style condo, it could have been converted from a former industrial or commercial building. You would normally be buying this type of condo from the developer if it has just been converted. The same cautions and suggestions outlined for resale and new condos apply.

Some of the advantages of a conversion condo include:

- Possible creative and unique designs and layout.
- Tend to be less expensive than a new completed unit due to lower core construction costs.
- Tend to be located in downtown areas of a city.

Some of the disadvantages include:

- As in a new-construction condo, the dates you have planned for occupancy could be delayed due to construction delays.
- If the core building is old, that could mean potential costly repair or maintenance costs in the future. Without an adequate contingency/reserve fund, that would mean that special assessments would be raised from condo owners.
- New Home Warranty coverage may not apply. For example, in a new construction the warranty company knows the quality of the construction and the builder. Dealing with a conversion of an older building has inherent risks for any New Home Warranty insurer. The developer could provide warranty coverage, but that is highly risky, as the developer could go under, or could have set up a corporation for the conversion that has no extra assets in it once the units have all been sold.

c) Buying a New Condo

If you are buying a new condo, there are additional cautions, as there is no history. That is, no history in terms of problems with the project. The term "new" refers to condo buildings that are under construction or recently completed.

You want to make sure you obtain a home inspection anyway, even though it is new. You also want to check into New Home Warranty protection coverage. Do your due diligence on the reputation and experience of the developer. What other projects have they done? How long have they been in business? Can you check out a project they did in the past, by speaking with the president of the condo corporation board or council to obtain their candid comments? Are there any complaints against them with the Better Business Bureau?

Have a lawyer check all the documents, including the disclosure statement, thoroughly before you ever make a purchase decision. Is there a time period within which you can get out of the deal and get your deposit money back? Make sure you pay your deposit only into a lawyer's trust account—your lawyer or the developer's lawyer. If there is a realtor involved, it could go into the realtor's trust account. In all cases, you want interest to be credited to you up till the day of completion. If you are buying into a phased development, you want to review all the documents to see what is intended to occur and when and where. You want to know, in writing, what the restrictions are on the total number of rental units permitted in the complex. Be cautious about construction warranties by the developer. They are only as strong as the developer. Many developers incorporate a new company for each development, so that each risk is self-contained.

Some of the advantages of buying a new condo include:

- Flexibility in types of units available.
- Ability to upgrade features at the outset with customized change options.
- Ability to change the interior decorating to suit personal needs and wants.
- Built by current building code standards, which could be of higher quality.
- New Home Warranty coverage for financial protection.

Some of the disadvantages include:

- Your deposit funds will be held up until completion is complete. However, if you make sure that you are getting interest on those funds to your credit, that reduces the discomfort.
- Construction delays are common for a variety of reasons. This could be inconvenient for you, especially if you are selling your present

home and are relying on moving on the proposed completion date of the condo. You can try to negotiate a penalty clause into the offer agreement to buffer the risk, with X amount of money deducted from the purchase price for each week of delay in completion. However, depending on circumstances and the developer, they may or may not go for it. Seek the advice of a lawyer to assist you in this area.

- If construction is not completed in other parts of the condo complex, other than your building, there could be noise and disruptive inconvenience for a period of time.

- As the project is conceptual in nature, rather than tangible, you will have to rely on artist renderings and floor plans. You will not be able to assess the quality of construction until the building is completed.

d) Buying a Pre-sale Condo

In order for developers to test the market and obtain lender financing, they need to go through the stages of attempting to pre-sell the condo units before construction can start. This process is normally done by having a sales office on the site of the future condo building, with artist renderings, architectural plans, scale models of the proposed development, etc. There would also probably be a sample showroom set up, showing the typical condo layout, showing carpets, cabinets, appliances, paint, fireplace, and so on.

Many people like the idea of locking in a condo at the current price, paying a 5 percent or 10 percent down payment but not having to pay the full amount until the project is completed, which could be one to three years later. The length of time will depend on the nature of the project, the size of the developer, and availability of construction trades. Also, the lender generally wants to see at least 75 percent or more in pre-sales before funding will be approved. A buyer of a pre-sale condo in an escalating market could hope to obtain an attractive increase in equity before the project is even completed.

If you are seriously interested in buying a pre-sale condo, you want to make sure that you read all the documents carefully and understand them and have a real estate lawyer advise you before you sign any contract or pay any down payment. You want to know the fine print, e.g., can you get out of the deal with or without getting your deposit back and without any further legal commitment or liability? Can the developer adjust the price upward before closing due to market demand? You want to ensure that the funds are kept in a lawyer's trust account and that interest will accrue to your credit. You also want to know if there is a period of time in a pre-sale condo situation when you can back out of the deal and get all your deposit money back—within 30 days, for example.

The same general cautions as outlined for new condos also apply to pre-sale condos.

7. Know the Typical Costs of Owning a Condo

As an owner of a condo, you must be prepared to pay costs that reflect belonging to a community. You must factor these in to your purchase decision. As an owner of a condominium unit, there are ongoing monthly or annual expenses and potential expenses that you have to plan for. The most common expenses are as follows:

a) Mortgage Payments

Unless you paid cash for your unit, you will be making monthly payments for principal, interest, and probably taxes.

b) Property Taxes

Each individual condominium unit is assessed by the municipality and has to make an annual payment for the property taxes. If you have a mortgage, the lender may or may not have required you to include extra monthly payments along with your mortgage. These are held in a property tax account so that the lender can pay your municipal property taxes annually. If you do not have a mortgage, you will have to pay property tax separately. The common elements have a property tax as well, but that tax is covered in your monthly maintenance payments.

c) Maintenance Payments

Naturally, you are responsible for your own personal condo unit costs. This section just relates to common expenses. Maintenance payments or "assessments for common expenses" cover all the operating costs of the common elements and are adjusted accordingly for any increase or decrease in expenses. You are responsible for a portion of the development's total operating cost. The formula for determining your portion will be discussed shortly. The payments for common expenses are made directly to the condominium corporation and generally cover the following items:

- **Maintenance and Repair of Common Property**

  This includes costs for maintenance, landscaping, building repairs, recreational facilities, equipment, and other expenses.

- **Operating and Service Costs**

  These include expenses relating to garbage removal, electricity, and municipal water use.

- **Contingency Reserve Fund**

  This is a fund for unforeseen problems and expenses. For example, unexpectedly the roof needs repair/replacement or the heating/cooling system breaks down. This fund is for expenses that have not been included in the annual budgeted expense calculations for the common property and other assets of the condominium corporation. Owners contribute monthly to this fund, on the basis of a portion of the monthly maintenance fee. The condominium legislation in most provinces requires a minimum amount to be contributed by owners to the contingency reserve fund (e.g., 10 percent of the annual budget). If you are buying an older condominium, you should check to see what percentage of the monthly payments is being allocated toward this fund, as there is a higher risk of needing to use the fund in older buildings than in new developments. In older buildings, the fund should likely be 25 percent or more, depending on the circumstances.

  In most cases you are not entitled to a refund of your contribution to the reserve fund when you sell your unit, or have it calculated on the purchase and sale statement of adjustments.

d) Management Costs

These are the costs associated with hiring private individuals or professional management firms to administer all or part of the daily functions of the condominium development.

e) Condo Corporation Insurance

Condominium legislation requires that the development carry sufficient fire and related insurance to replace the common property in the event of fire or other damage. Condominium corporations generally obtain further insurance to cover other payables and liabilities. The insurance does not cover the damage done to the interior of an individual unit. The cost of condo insurance for the corporation is included in your monthly maintenance fees.

f) Special Assessment

There may be situations in which 75 percent or more of the condominium members wish to raise funds for special purposes. These funds would not be able to come from the contingency reserve fund or from the regular monthly assessments. For example, there could be an interest in building a swimming pool or tennis courts, or it may be necessary to cover costs of repairs beyond the contingency reserve fund. Once the decision is made to assess members, you cannot refuse to pay the special assessment if it has been properly approved, even though you might not agree with its purpose.

g) Lease Payments

If you have a leasehold condominium, you will be required to make monthly lease payments in addition to many of the other costs outlined in this section.

h) Condominium Owner Insurance

As mentioned earlier, the insurance on the building that is covered by the condominium development *does not* include the interior of your unit. Therefore, you will need to get separate insurance to cover the contents as well as damage to the inside of your unit, including walls, windows, and doors. There are several types of insurance, including replacement-cost, all-risk comprehensive, and personal liability. It is also wise to get insurance to cover deficiencies in the condominium corporation's insurance coverage in the event of fire so that any damage to your unit could be repaired in full; otherwise the unit owners would have to pay on a proportional basis any deficiency by means of a special assessment. You should also carry sufficient liability insurance.

Many insurance companies have developed a specialized program referred to as condominium homeowner's package insurance. Check in the Yellow Pages or on the Internet, under "Insurance Brokers" and compare coverage and costs. Refer to Chapter 6 for a more detailed discussion of insurance protection.

i) Unit Repair and Maintenance Costs

You will have to allocate a certain amount of your personal financial budget to repair and maintenance needs relating to the inside of your unit. Your monthly assessment fee would cover common elements outside your unit only. Your portion of this cost is usually determined by means of a unit entitlement.

Unit entitlement is the basis on which the owner's contribution to the common expenses or maintenance fees of the condominium corporation are calculated. Various formulas are used for the calculation. In some developments, the percentage calculated for the unit's share is determined by the original purchase price of each unit in relation to the value of the total property. Another method is to apportion costs on the basis of the number of units in equal proportion, regardless of unit size. But the most common formula is to calculate the unit entitlement by dividing the number of square feet in an owner's unit by the number of square feet in all the units.

For example, let's say a condominium development contains 15 condominium units, the total square feet of all units is 15,680, your individual unit is 784 square feet, and the annual cost to maintain the common elements and other related expenses is $60,000. Then to calculate your monthly financial commitment you would go through the following steps:

- Calculate your unit entitlement (784 ÷ 15,680 = ¹⁄₂₀ share in the common property)

- Calculate the annual share of maintenance costs (¹⁄₂₀ x $60,000 = $3,000 per year)

- Calculate the monthly share of maintenance costs (¹⁄₁₂ x $3,000 = $250 per month)

j) Utilities

You are responsible for your own utilities that you use in your unit, including hydro, water, and heat. In apartment condominiums, these expenses are usually included in the maintenance fee, whereas townhouse condominiums tend to be separately metered and you are billed directly and individually by the utility companies.

BUYING A TIMESHARE

Resort time-sharing originated in Europe in the 1960s, when high costs and demand for limited resort space created the need for a way to ensure accommodation for a certain period of time each year. Timeshares are usually sold by the week and include fully furnished accommodation with maintenance and maid service. The concept was adopted in Florida in the 1970s to revive the sluggish condominium industry. Since then, timeshares have grown rapidly, with thousands of this type of resort throughout the world. These resorts range

from Ontario cottage country resorts to Florida condos to Mexican beach vil-
las. Hundreds of thousands of people have purchased timeshares. At some time
or another you have probably seen the ads: "Luxury Lifestyle at Affordable
Prices!" "Vacation the World!" "Trade for Exotic Climes!"

Other frequently used terms that are synonymous with time-sharing
include resort time-sharing, vacation ownership, multiownership, interval
ownership, and shared vacation plan. The timeshare concept has been applied
to numerous other areas, such as recreational vehicle and mobile home parks.

There are two main categories of timeshares: fee simple ownership and
right-to-use.

1. Fee Simple Ownership

There are different formats. One option is to own a portion of the condominium, such as one-fiftieth of the property. Each one-fiftieth portion entitles you
to one week's use of the premises per year. Other people also buy into the property. Frequently you are allocated a fixed week every year. In other instances,
you could have a floating time, with the exact dates to be agreed upon according to availability. In some cases, you might purchase a quarter- or half-interest.
These are sometimes referred to as fractional interest purchases. If the complete
property is sold, you would receive your proportional share of any increase in
net after-sale proceeds for the increase in equity since you originally purchased
your percentage interest. You would also normally be able to rent, sell, or give
your ownership portion to anyone you wished.

2. Right-to-Use

This concept is much like having a long-term lease, but with use for just a one-
week period every year. This arrangement is similar to prepaying for a hotel
room for a fixed period every year for 20 years in advance. In other words, you
don't have any portion of ownership in the property; you only have a right to
use it for a fixed or floating time period every year. Condominiums, recreational
vehicle parks, and other types of properties offer right-to-use timeshares.

The opportunity for return on your money in a right-to-use timeshare
is limited or nonexistent. This is because there is generally very little demand
in the after-sale market, as well as other restrictions on resale or pricing of the
resale.

In practical terms, time-sharing is primarily a lifestyle choice. Here are some of the disadvantages and cautions to be aware of:

- You may tire of going to the same location every year, since your needs may change over time.

- The timeshare programs that include an exchange option (e.g., switching a week in a different location) are not always as anticipated in availability, flexibility, convenience, or upgrade fee.

- Make sure you know what you are getting. Some people who purchase the right-to-use type think they are buying a fee simple ownership portion.

- Be wary of hard-sell marketing. In most instances, the dream fantasy is heavily reinforced, and "free" inducements, such as a buffet dinner or an evening dinner cruise with a large group of other people, are used to entice you to hear a sales pitch first. High-pressure sales pitches, with teams of salespeople, can go on for hours. The sales representatives can be very persuasive, if not aggressive, and often use very manipulative techniques to get you to sign a credit card slip as a deposit. The "freebies" would generally cost you from $10 to $25. It is an illusion to think you are going to get something for nothing. At best, you will be subjected to an intense one-on-one sales approach. At worst, you will be out your deposit money if you change your mind, unless there is a time period during which you may cancel. Trying to get your money back if you suffer from buyer's remorse is extremely difficult, if not impossible, especially if the timeshare is outside Canada.

- Timeshare sales in Canada and some U.S. states are sometimes covered by consumer protection, ensuring your right to get your money back by rescinding (cancelling) the contract within a certain time period.

- There is usually a regular management fee for maintaining the premises.

Timeshares are a dream for some but a nightmare for others. Speak to at least three other timeshare owners in the project you are considering to get their candid opinion before you decide to buy. Never give out your credit card as a deposit, and don't sign any documents requested of you without first speaking with a local real estate lawyer. You can obtain a lawyer's name from the local lawyer referral service or provincial or state bar association; refer to Chapter 9. You might also want to check with the local Better Business Bureau before you make a decision. Don't let yourself be pressured. Sleep on the idea for a while, and if the deal seems too good to be true, it probably is.

If you want more details on timeshares in Canada, contact the Canadian Resort Development Association (CRDA), in Toronto at 1-800-646-9205 . Also ask if a particular development is a member of CRDA and if there have been any complaints. Their website is: www.crda.com.

If you are buying in the United States, contact the American Resort Development Association (ARDA) in Washington, DC, at (202) 371-6700. Ask for their free consumer publications. Most RV or timeshare companies will permit you to stay at their locations for a nominal fee, without obligation, to see if you like them. The ARDA website is: www.arda.org.

BUYING A MOBILE HOME/MANUFACTURED HOME

Mobile homes, now frequently referred to as manufactured homes, are a very popular form of housing for Canadian Snowbirds. Some people live in a mobile home in Canada as well as one in the United States. The term mobile home can be confusing. It is not an RV and has no wheels, though it is manufactured to be moved by a large truck and set up on a permanent foundation, referred to as a pad. It is meant to be like any other house, except that it can be readily moved to a new location if desired. In some cases, a basement is built and the mobile home is set on top.

Mobile homes generally come in two widths. The single width is about 10 to 16 feet (3 to 5 m) wide and sometimes as long as 64 feet (19.5 m). The double homes are built in two sections and when combined are approximately twice as wide as a single. This type of unit can be very spacious and in many respects have the rooms, features, and appliances of a regular house. You can either buy a mobile home and have it put on the location of your choice or buy one already on a site. When selecting a mobile home, you must make sure it meets safety standards. Some older mobile homes contain flammable materials or are poorly designed and may not even be insurable, so check with your insurance company beforehand. Most mobile homes are in parks that are set up as permanent communities, even though many of the residents may be Snowbirds who only live there for six months a year. These private parks provide water, sewer, and electricity hook-ups and frequently have other features, such as a recreation and social centre, a swimming pool, tennis courts, a golf course, and security personnel. Some parks may have from 200 to 1,000 or more mobile homes.

Some parks are restricted to retired people, others to Snowbirds; some combine seasonal and permanent residents. RVs are permitted in some parks and not in others. There is a variety of different formats for these parks, which are regulated by local and/or state bylaws. In some rural locations there are few restrictions; in urban settings separate parks are established specifically for mobile homes. Some have communities that are independent and include their own facilities, whereas others use the facilities of the closest community.

Before deciding to buy a mobile home, you may want to rent one for a season to see if you like the concept and the area. Talk to other mobile home-owners to get their advice on makes and models. Do an Internet search, for example, a google.com search, for an association of mobile home owners in the state of interest to you. Simply type in those "keywords" and the state. These associations can provide you with invaluable information, insurance, and the names of mobile home parks in their state. They also lobby for the interests of mobile homeowners in their respective states. In addition, check with the Association of Retired Persons (www.aarp.org) for any recent surveys or reports on mobile homes that could assist you.

Finally, before you sign any documents to buy a mobile home or rent a park location, check with a real estate lawyer in the area for your protection. Your lot lease and mobile home warranty and contract can be reviewed for clauses or exclusions that you might not understand or want.

BUYING A RECREATIONAL VEHICLE (RV)

Owning an RV is a growing trend, especially among people aged 55 and up. Nearly half of the 12 million RVs on the road in the United States are owned by people over 55. People in this age group have the time, discretionary income, and desire to see and experience the small towns, big cities, popular attractions, and natural beauty of North America. RVs provide an enjoyable, comfortable, and economical way to take it all in and provide an opportunity to meet new people on the road. RVs can be kept packed with essentials and ready to travel at a moment's notice. Comfort is another factor. RVs can have complete living, dining, sleeping, and bathroom facilities to provide travellers with all the amenities of home while on the road, as well as slide-out rooms for expansion.

An RV is defined as a motorized or towable vehicle that combines transportation and temporary living quarters for travel, recreation, and camping. RVs do not include mobile homes. There are many types of RVs, with a wide range of prices for new RVs, from CDN $2,000 for the least expensive folding camping trailer to over CDN $200,000 for a customized motor home. Used RVs of course cost less, and if you buy off-season, you can get better deals. Here is a description of some of the specific types of RVs and the current average retail price in Canadian dollars.

1. Types of RVs

There are two main categories of RVs—towables and motorized:

a) Towable RVs

A towable RV is designed to be towed by a motorized vehicle (auto, van, or pick-up truck) and is of such size and weight as not to require a special highway movement permit. It is designed to provide temporary living quarters for recreational, camping, or travel use and does not require permanent on-site hook-up. The following are types of towable RVs:

- **Folding camping trailer (average price, CDN $7,500)**

  This is a recreational camping unit, designed for temporary living quarters, mounted on wheels and connected with collapsible sidewalls that fold for towing by a motorized vehicle. It provides kitchen, dining, and sleeping facilities for up to eight people. Some larger models come with full bathroom and heating/air-conditioning options.

- **Truck camper (average price, CDN $20,000)**

  This recreational camping unit is designed to be loaded onto or affixed to the bed or chassis of a truck and is constructed to provide temporary living quarters for recreational camping or travel use. Most provide kitchen, sleeping, and bathroom facilities for two to six people, heat, air conditioning, and running water. The unit can be easily loaded onto a truck bed in a few minutes.

- **Conventional travel trailer (average price, CDN $25,000)**

  This unit typically ranges from 12 to 35 feet (3.6 to 10.6 m) in length and is towed by means of a bumper or frame hitch attached to the towing vehicle. It provides temporary living quarters for four to eight people, with kitchen, toilet, sleeping and dining facilities, electrical and water systems, and modern appliances. The unit is available in conventional and two-level fifth-wheel models.

- **Fifth-wheel travel trailer (average price, CDN $36,600)**

This unit can be equipped the same as the conventional travel trailer but is constructed with a raised forward section that allows a bi-level floor plan. This style is designed to be towed by a vehicle equipped with a device known as a fifth-wheel hitch.

b) Motorized RVs

- **Custom van conversion (average price, CDN $45,000)**

This refers to a complete or incomplete automotive van chassis that has been modified by the RV manufacturer to be used for transportation and recreation. Modifications may include the addition of windows, carpeting, panelling, seats, sofas, reclining captain's chairs, closets, stereo systems, and accessories.

- **Van camper (average price, CDN $65,000)**

This is a panel-type truck to which the RV manufacturer has added any two of the following conveniences: sleeping, kitchen, or toilet facilities. The truck also includes 100-volt hook-up, fresh water storage, city water hook-up, and a top extension to provide more head room.

- **Motor home (compact) (average price, CDN $52,000)**

This unit is built on an automotive manufactured cab and chassis having a gross vehicle weight ratio (GVWR) of less than 6,500 pounds (3,000 kg). It may provide any or all of the conveniences of the larger units.

- **Motor home (mini-low profile) (average price, CDN $69,000)**

This unit is built on an automotive manufactured van frame with an attached cab section having a GVWR of 6,500 pounds (3,000 kg) or more, with an overall height of more than 8 feet (2.4 m) (low profile is less than 8 feet). The RV manufacturer completes the body section containing the living area and attaches it to the cab section.

- **Motor home (high profile) (average price, CDN $100,000)**

The living unit has been entirely constructed on a bare, specially designed motor vehicle chassis. Kitchen, sleeping, bathroom, and dining facilities are easily accessible to the driver's area from inside. Three types—conventional motor homes, mini-motor homes, and van-campers—range from 17 to 40 feet (5 to 12 m) long. Motor homes sleep up to eight people.

2. Where to Get Further Information

If you are buying an RV in the United States, check to make sure that it is endorsed by the Recreational Vehicle Industry Association (RVIA). Their website is: www.rvia.com. This endorsement shows that the RV has complied with applicable national safety standards, such as those of the American National Standards Institute. If you are buying an RV in Canada, make sure that it is endorsed by the Canadian Recreational Vehicle Association (CRVA), showing that it has received Canadian Standards Association (CSA) safety approval. Ask about warranty coverage in the United States and Canada. The CRVA is based in Toronto and can be contacted at (416) 971-7800. Their website is: www.crva. ca. Also contact the state or provincial RV dealers' association.

You should also check on various Canadian government regulations or legal implications if you buy an RV or car in the United States and wish to take it home with you to Canada.

You may not be sure if you want to buy an RV right away, so consider renting one to see if you like it. If you have some friends with RVs, ask to go along on a short trip with them. Also ask them about their RV experiences and tips they could give you. Check with your local RV dealer in Canada about rentals in Canada.

PERILS OF SELLING YOUR OWN HOME YOURSELF

Whatever type of accommodation you eventually select, at some point you will want to sell it. If you own a house or a condo, there are particular cautions to keep in mind for the sale process.

When the time comes to sell your U.S. or Canadian home, you may be tempted to sell it yourself. Aside from a personal challenge or learning experience, there is primarily only one reason for doing so—to save on a real estate commission. You may indeed save money. On the other hand, the saving could be an expensive illusion.

There are some general disadvantages of selling a home yourself, as opposed to using a carefully selected and experienced realtor. The following remarks are not intended to dissuade you from attempting to sell your own home, but to place the process in realistic perspective. You will have to balance the benefits and disadvantages, and decide what is best. The comments apply whether you are selling your own home or an investment property, but the examples given relate primarily to a house or condo.

1. Inexperience

If you don't know all the steps involved, from the pre-sale procedures and strategies to completing the deal and receiving the money, you could and probably would make mistakes that could be costly to you.

2. Emotional Roller Coaster

Many people, especially with their own home, tend to get emotionally involved in the sale process because of the direct interaction with the prospective purchasers. For example, frustration can be experienced due to rejection of the house, negative comments or fault-finding people whose personality you don't like, or people who negotiate toughly on the price. These one-on-one direct dynamics or comments can sometimes be taken personally, and therefore be a cause of stress.

3. Time Commitment

You have to have open houses as well as show your property at times that may not necessarily be convenient to you. In addition, you are going to be spending time preparing the ad copy and staying at home to respond to telephone calls or people knocking on the door.

4. Expense, Nature, and Content of Advertising

Costs include all the daily or weekly newspaper classified and/or box ads, as well as a lawn sign. In addition, you may not know what specific types of advertising would be appropriate for your type of property; how to write ad copy that would grab the attention of a reader and prospective purchaser; or how to identify and emphasize the key selling features of your property.

5. Limited Market Exposure

There are considerable differences in market exposure in terms of advertising by yourself and the types of advertising and promotion a realtor could do for you. There is obviously a direct correlation between the nature and degree of market exposure and the end price. Clearly, limited market exposure means limited prospective buyers.

6. Potential Legal Problems

The prospective purchaser may supply you with his own agreement of purchase and sale. This contract may have clauses and other terms in it that could be legally risky, unenforceable, unfair, or otherwise not beneficial to you. You may not recognize these potential problems or risks. In addition, you could end up agreeing to take back a mortgage (vendor-back mortgage) when it would not be necessary or wise, or to accept a long-term option or other legal arrangement that could be risky.

7. Lack of Familiarity with Market

You may not have a clear or objective idea of exactly what a similar property in your market is selling for, or the state of the real estate market at that time. This can place you at a distinct disadvantage. For example, if you are being unrealistic in your pricing, along with limited advertising exposure, you could virtually price yourself out of the market. Prospective purchasers may not even look, let alone make an offer. You may eventually sell your property, but only after several price reductions and after a long period of time. Naturally, of course, this depends on the market and the nature of your property. Conversely, you could have a property with unique features or potential that could justify a higher sale price than you might realize.

8. No Pre-screening of Prospective Purchasers

You would not generally know the art of pre-screening prospects in terms of questions to ask them over the phone. The end result is that you could waste your time talking to people over the phone or showing them through the house, who are not and never will be serious prospects. You could also end up accepting an offer from someone who does not realistically have a chance of financing the house, or who asks for unrealistic time periods for removing purchaser conditions, which effectively would tie up your property during that time.

9. Offer Price Not Necessarily the Best

You may think the offer is the best offer from that prospective purchaser, or any purchaser, and therefore may accept it. That price may not be the best price at all. You may have started too low or too high for your initial asking price, based on emotion or needs, not on reality; you may have received a low-ball offer from a prospective purchaser that was never intended to be accepted but was designed to reduce your expectations; or you may be subjected to effective closing skills on the part of the prospective purchaser.

10. Lack of Negotiating Skills

You may lack essential negotiating or sales skills and feel very uncomfortable or anxious in a negotiating context. As a consequence, the price and terms you eventually settle for may not be as attractive as they otherwise could be.

11. Purchaser Wanting Discount in Price Equal to Commission Saved

It is not uncommon for the prospective purchaser to determine what the fair market value is and then ask to have an additional discount equal to the real estate commission you are saving. The primary reason why prospective purchasers are attracted to a For Sale by Owner is the prospect of getting a better deal than a property listed with a realtor, due to the commission otherwise built into the sale price. The primary reason why you are selling the property yourself is to save the full amount of any commission otherwise payable. Hence the problem. A compromise may be possible whereby the price is further reduced by a percentage of the commission saved. Again, in practical terms, it is normally an illusion to think that you will save the full or even a substantial amount of the commission. You may have netted more by listing with a Realtor.

12. Tough to Sell in a Buyer's Market

Buyers in this type of market are very price sensitive, negotiate strenuously because they want the best deal, and have the time to be selective after comparing what is available in the market. You are at a disadvantage if you don't receive all the exposure possible and use all the negotiating and selling skills available. You could wait a long time before finally selling, and the market could go down further by that time in a declining sale market, due to an oversupply of homes, limited demand, and reduced exposure.

As you can see, there are distinct advantages to utilizing the services and skills of a professionally trained and experienced realtor. Of course, there are exceptions in certain situations where you may choose to sell yourself, but you have to be very aware of the potential disadvantages. The vast majority of homeowners realize the benefits of using a realtor and do so, whether for buying or selling real estate.

Tips Before Leaving Canada

√ If you are thinking of purchasing U.S. real estate, speak to your financial institution before you leave regarding their policy on financing U.S. property.

√ Be wary about buying timeshares before leaving Canada without knowing their advantages and disadvantages. Always check out the resort you are thinking of using, without further financial obligation. Speak to others who have bought timeshares from the company.

√ Always seek legal advice to review any legal documents before you purchase a home or RV.

√ If you are thinking of buying a house or condo or mobile home in a specific location, have a real estate professional, or owner send material to you to review before you depart. The more research you do before you leave, the more objective and realistic your final decision will be.

√ If you want to be certain you like a particular area or type of housing, consider renting a house, condo, or mobile/manufactured home or RV in your first Snowbird season. This is a low-risk and highly effective way of making your decision. You can make all your enquiries, thoroughly review information, and speak to references before you leave.

CHAPTER 6

Insurance Needs and Options

INTRODUCTION

Adequate insurance is necessary for your peace of mind and financial health. As a Snowbird, you need to be familiar with all the options, benefits, features, and rates, as well as the exclusions, exemptions, and deductibles; it is very important to understand the terms and concepts. Take the time to do your research so that you can make the right decisions to meet your needs and protect yourself from potential risks.

It is also important to shop around for comparable rates and coverage. The insurance market is highly competitive, and you will find considerable differences in price and in the quality of coverage offered by different insurance companies. Obtain a minimum of three competitive quotes. For out-of-country insurance coverage, you need more of a comparison than that. You want to check out as many Canadian insurance programs as you can that offer the type of coverage you are seeking to evaluate their relative strengths and weaknesses. These comparisons will make the process much less stressful. To eliminate misunderstanding, get confirmation in writing of any requests made by you to your insurer or insurance company, or of representations made by an insurance company representative to you. Keep copies of all correspondence between you and your insurance company, as well as any receipts for items to be claimed for reimbursement.

This chapter covers the various types of insurance you should consider, depending on your circumstances: out-of-country medical insurance, homeowner insurance, home office insurance, mobile/manufactured home insurance, automobile insurance, RV insurance, automobile roadside assistance, and life insurance.

OUT-OF-COUNTRY EMERGENCY MEDICAL INSURANCE

If you have a serious injury or illness in the United States and require emergency medical attention, you will be financially devastated unless you have out-of-country medical insurance. Provincial health insurance plans vary by province, but each provides you with the necessary protection when travelling within Canada. Coverage by provincial plans outside Canada is nominal, however—maybe $75 to $400+ Canadian funds per day for hospital care. Payments for doctors' services outside Canada, in Canadian funds, will not exceed the amount payable had you been treated in your own province. This is a very low amount compared with U.S. rates. This would generally represent less than 10 percent of the hospitalization cost in the U.S.

Health coverage in the United States is very different from the medicare coverage we are accustomed to in Canada. We are not accustomed to being personally billed, so we don't appreciate the real cost of treatment, which is paid by the government. In the U.S. system, private hospitals and doctors operate in a profit-oriented environment, and costs are much greater. The average hospital stay often exceeds US$1,500 a day and can run as high as US$10,000 a day for intensive care. Certain emergency surgical operations can cost $100,000 or more. So who pays the shortfall if you have a medical emergency in the United States? You do. Unless, of course, you have wisely purchased supplemental health insurance *before* you leave Canada, for the duration of your U.S. stay, be it a day or six months. Keep in mind that this supplemental insurance covers emergency treatment for injury or illness only. It does not cover non-emergency treatment or services. It is not a substitute for Canadian medicare.

Premium rates vary greatly between insurers. The rate depends on factors such as the nature of the coverage, your age and existing medical condition, policy exclusions and limitations, the deductible portion of your policy, whether you have a preferred (for healthy people) or standard rate plan, and the duration of your stay in the United States. The premium range for a six-month extended-stay plan could range per person from $500 to $3,000 or more, depending on the above variables. Rates are normally set by the insurer between June and September each year for extended-stay Snowbird coverage. For competitive reasons, the insurer might drop the market rates after you have taken the policy out, but such a reduction should be passed on to you. Do not choose a plan based on price alone; consider benefits, limitations, exclusions, and deductibles.

Claiming Tax Credits

On the positive side, some financial relief might be available from the tax credits you can earn when you purchase medical insurance. Many people overlook this substantial saving, which could effectively reduce your premium by up to one-quarter. You earn credits of approximately 27 cents for each dollar of medical expenses (i.e., 27 percent) in any consecutive 12-month period that exceed either 3 percent of income or $1,614, whichever is less. This is a good reason to make sure you keep receipts of all your medical expenses.

For example, let's say a retired couple, through careful professional financial and tax planning, have split their retirement income so that they are both earning $20,000 a year. By doing this, they have lowered their marginal tax rates (rather than one spouse having a higher taxed income) and minimized the risk of reaching the clawback threshold on their Old Age Security (OAS) pension, which occurs after approximately $53,215 of individual net income. They can each claim credits for medical expenses exceeding $600 (calculated by taking 3 percent of $20,000) in any consecutive 12-month period, at the rate of approximately 27 percent. To clarify, this 27 percent figure consists of a combined federal and provincial tax credit benefit. The federal tax credit is 17 percent, but this results in a reduction and, therefore, a savings in provincial tax payable, since provincial tax is a portion of federal tax. Provincial tax rates vary.

Returning to the retired couple, if they are each paying, for example, $1,400 in insurance premiums, they would be eligible to claim credits of $216 each for a total savings of $432 ($1,400 - $600 = $800 x 27 percent). If the couple were earning a lower income than $20,000 a year each, they would have a larger credit and save even more money. Other eligible medical expenses, such as prescription drugs, dental work, or eyeglasses, may also be claimed, as well as:

- Twenty percent of the cost to adapt a van for transporting an individual using a wheelchair—up to a maximum of $5,000

- A maximum allowance of $2,000 to cover expenses incurred when moving to accessible housing

- Fifty percent of the cost of an air conditioner prescribed by a medical practitioner as being necessary to assist an individual in coping with a chronic illness or disorder—to a maximum of $1,000

- The amount eligible for the tax credit for part-time attendant care of $10,000

- No limit on the deduction from income for attendant care expenses that are necessary to allow the disabled individual to work.

Understanding Insurance Options

Many insurance plans are available, and it can be very confusing and frustrating trying to understand which plan is right for you. Keep in mind that one plan can't be all things to all people. You want to determine your needs and then shortlist two or three plans that meet your needs. Only then do you consider the issue of premium cost.

It is helpful to understand how the insurance system works, since several parties are involved. Insurers are the people you deal with directly. They are the companies or organizations that package a plan and arrange for an insurance company to underwrite it, or pay the claims. The companies that pay the claims are called underwriters. Sometimes the underwriters sell directly themselves or through travel agents. Sometimes underwriters insure plans for various insurers, which could be competing with each other. In that case, each plan tends to be customized for each insurer, so they are slightly different from each other. In a medical emergency, the underwriter or insurer contracts with an emergency medical assistance company to provide information, guidance, and coordination of your medical care. In other words, the company helps deal with your emergency medical needs, telling you which hospital or doctor to go to and so on. Such companies have a 24-hour, 7-day hotline, generally toll-free, or they accept collect calls from anywhere in the United States. They also monitor your treatment and make other arrangements as required. Always keep a record of whom you spoke with when phoning this emergency medical number.

To keep costs down, many underwriters have negotiated reduced rates with specific hospitals and doctors, and therefore you might be referred specifically to them. If your condition is safely stabilized, they will likely send you back to Canada by air ambulance to save themselves money, since your treatment would then be covered by Canadian medicare.

Here are the main issues and options you need to know about:

a) Full Disclosure of Personal Health Information

The issue of full disclosure of health information in your initial policy application cannot be overemphasized. If the insurer denies your claim, your explanation that you made a mistake, misunderstood, or didn't know will bear no weight. As far as the insurer is concerned, you could have been deliberately misleading the company in order to save money on premiums or to get the coverage in the first place. So don't be tempted to play with the facts. Insurers are entitled to see all your past medical history records, and they know what to look for.

Money is money, and the fine print of the policy governs. No insurer is going to pay out a lot of money if it technically and legally doesn't have to.

b) Extended-Stay and Multi-trip Plans

An *extended-stay plan* is intended to cover you for the duration of your Snowbird stay in the United States for a continuous period. The premium is based on the duration of your stay—for example, up to six months. You pay for the exact number of days you need.

A *multi-trip plan* is designed for shorter-term stays in the United States. You arrange coverage for a packaged number of days—for example, a maximum single-duration stay not exceeding 90 days. This means you can travel and stay in the United States as many times as you like within the length of your policy coverage (say, up to six months), as long as any one trip does not exceed your maximum number of days per trip (e.g., 15, 30, or 90 days). As soon as you return to Canada for at least a day, the cycle starts again. For example, some people purchase a plan for 90-day periods and stay in the United States for six months but break up the stay by flying back to Canada before the first 90-day period expires—for example, at Christmas. A few weeks later they return to the United States for another period not exceeding 90 days. There could be some savings on insurance premium if this type of arrangement suits your lifestyle, even after taking the airfare into account. However, there could be a risk of loss of coverage if your medical condition changes or if you need to take new medication after you return to Canada and before you return to the United States. Check this out thoroughly.

These multi-trip plans are usually based on an annual premium, for example, covering a calendar year or 12 months from the time you take it out. If the plan is based on a calendar year, some companies pro-rate the premium; others don't. One of the main benefits of a multi-trip plan is that it covers spontaneous trips any time you go back and forth across the Canada-U.S. border. You can obtain multi-trip plans through travel agents, banks, and some credit card companies or insurers directly. Many of these companies do not provide multi-trip plans but only offer extended-stay plans.

c) Top-up Insurance

This concept means that you acquire additional supplemental emergency medical coverage to "top up" an existing out-of-country medical plan. This existing plan could be coverage you get as a retiree from a government plan, other employer plan, union or association plan, or credit card plan. There are risks, however, with the top-up approach. Some plans don't permit top-ups. There can be great differences in plan policies. There could be a lapse in time periods or amounts between coverage, or disputes between different insurers on the issue of coverage. For example, if your basic medical plan coverage has a ceiling cap of $50,000 and lasts for a maximum number of days, and your top-up plan kicks in at the end of that time period, what happens if you have a catastrophic injury before the first plan lapses? You are only covered for $50,000, and your expenses could be $200,000. You would be out the difference. Another example is if the top-up company decides that your illness was pre-existing if you make a claim with your first insurer first. An alternative is to coordinate a basic plan and top-up plan from the same insurer.

The other reality is that generally it is less expensive and less risky to have just one plan cover everything. It certainly eliminates the uncertainty. It also saves the inconvenience and frustration of having to deal with two different claims procedures.

d) Add-on Insurance

If you want to stay longer outside Canada than your current insurance policy covers, you can, in many cases, request an extension while still outside the country. You need to make these arrangements *before* the expiry of your current coverage. You can charge the extra premium to your credit card. Always ask for a confirmation number and particulars of whom you spoke to and when. Ideally, have the confirmation faxed to you or sent to you for your records. Check out the terms of the policy as well. For example, if you have developed any medical conditions while outside the country, ask whether that will be excluded from coverage under the extension plan. Get it in writing.

e) Subrogation Clause

If you take out Snowbird insurance with one insurer, and the company finds out that you have existing insurance coverage through an employer or pension health plan, the Snowbird insurer can, in some cases, make a claim against that plan. This process is called subrogation. Most insurance policies state the right to do this. You may not want that to happen, since such a claim could dilute your fixed health benefits under your employer/union/association pension plan coverage.

If this is an issue to you, make sure you discuss the matter with your prospective Snowbird insurer. Get an agreement in writing to avoid any misunderstanding. Some insurers will waive any claim, some will do so for a premium surcharge (e.g., 10 to 15 percent), and others will limit their subrogation claim to a certain ceiling (e.g., $3,000).

Ask if the insurer is a member of the Canadian Life and Health Insurance Ombudservice (CLHIO). CLHIO has adopted a member policy that members will not claim against your pension plan coverage, by means of subrogation, under a certain amount of money. Check with your insurer (get it in writing) and with CLHIO at 1-800-268-8099. Website: www.clhio.ca.

f) Payment of Deductibles

To reduce the risk, many insurance companies will offer you premium discounts if you agree to pay a deductible up to a certain amount—for example, from $100 to $10,000. The larger the deductible, the larger the saving in premiums, perhaps 25 to 40 percent. You have to determine your own financial comfort level and the risk you are willing to take. Check to see if the deductibles are paid in U.S. or Canadian dollars. When comparing premium rates, take into account your net deductible outlay. If you have an employee retirement health benefit plan, check to see if it covers any deductibles.

g) What Is Included in Your Insurance Policy Coverage?

You want to make sure you know what protection you are getting for your money, so compare the same types of benefits when you are comparing policies. The main types of emergency-related (injury or illness) coverage paid for by the insurer in many policies include ambulance, hospital care, special nursing care, doctor and dental services, and necessary medication. In addition, reimbursement of emergency-related expenses that you have incurred, payment for transportation of a relative to your hospital, return of your car or RV to Canada, and return of your body to Canada if you die are frequently included. If you require further treatment but can safely be returned to Canada, the insurer will normally cover the cost of an air ambulance (medically equipped jet) or regular airline to take you back home.

h) What Is Excluded From Your Insurance Coverage?

Certain medical or surgical treatment or diagnostic expenses are not covered by your medical emergency insurance in the United States. Some of the common expenses are pre-existing conditions (refer to the next item); unnecessary diagnostic procedures; treatment that can safely wait until you return to Canada; rehabilitative or continuing care treatment for substance abuse (e.g., drugs or alcohol); chronic conditions (e.g., diabetes, emphysema); cancer that was diagnosed before you left Canada; and elective non-emergency treatment, such as treatment by a chiropractor, podiatrist, optometrist, or physiotherapist.

i) Pre-existing Conditions

This issue is an important one for insurers, since it relates to risk. For example, if you had previous signs of angina, you might already be on medication. The risk to an insurer is that you could have a heart attack in the United States, resulting in medical treatment that could cost the insurer $100,000 or more. It's a calculated risk for the insurer, and different insurers deal with the risk in different ways. For example, some insurers will simply refuse to cover you. Others would cover you except for any emergency medical condition relating to your pre-existing condition. Some offer a co-payment plan. This means if emergency medical treatment is required in the United States for a pre-existing condition, then the insurer will share the expense. For example, the insurer might pay 70 percent of the cost and you would pay the remaining 30 percent. Another variation is that the insurer agrees to pay up to a maximum amount in the event of such a claim—for example, $50,000. You would pay the rest. This could be a crippling expense financially. Some insurers will accept a pre-existing condition if it has been stabilized, with or without medication, for 3, 6, or 12 months. Ask your insurer if seeing your doctor for monitoring a condition is considered treatment and has to be disclosed on your application or before you leave Canada. Find out from your doctor if changes in medication are really necessary for your health, since they could impair your Sunbelt insurance coverage. For example, some insurance companies will not insure you if you are on medication before you depart, unless that was approved before your departure. Obviously, you don't want to risk your health. Also find out whether you have to notify your insurance company if you pay for non-emergency medical treatment in the United States.

j) Reasons for Rejection of a Medical Emergency Expense Claim

There are situations in which your insurance company could refuse to pay your claim. You could be stuck with the bill, which could be massive. The reasons for rejecting a claim include pre-existing conditions that you have not disclosed; medical exclusions set out in the policy; failure to make a formal claim before a deadline; failure to notify the insurer by calling the medical emergency number within the policy time period (e.g., before entering the hospital or within 24 to 48 hours afterwards); refusal to go to a hospital or doctor of the insured's choice; refusal to be returned to Canada for continuing treatment after your condition was medically stabilized; lapse of your policy coverage period; or dispute with an insurance company if you are using two companies for coverage.

If you are treated for an illness during a short trip home to Canada, and you subsequently have emergency medical treatment for that ailment in the United States, you could be deemed to have a pre-existing illness that the insurer was never advised about. As a result, the insurer could deny the claim. Before you decide on an insurer and before you leave Canada, check out all these issues and get answers to your questions in writing to avoid any misunderstanding.

Key Questions to Ask

Here is a checklist of key questions to ask before deciding on the insurance coverage. Not all of them are necessarily applicable in your situation, but you should have them all answered to determine whether you can be covered adequately as well as to determine the benefits or drawbacks of the coverage.

- What are the age restrictions?
- What pre-existing conditions are permitted, and for how long must they be stable?
- Are there different policy plans and options available and what are they?
- What restrictions and limitations does the policy have?
- Are there any sports activities I cannot participate in, such as scuba diving or mountain climbing?
- What exactly does the policy cover in detail?
- What is the amount of the policy coverage limit (e.g., $1 million, $2 million, or unlimited)?
- Is the insurance paid out in U.S. or Canadian dollars?
- May I select the doctor and hospital of my choice or does the insurance company choose?
- If I wish to select my own hospital and doctor despite restrictions, will

the insurance company still pay a portion of the bills, and if so, what percentage?

- Do I (or a spouse or family member) have to notify the insurance company within a certain time of my illness or injury to be eligible for coverage (e.g., before I enter a hospital, or within 24 or 48 hours), and if so, what is the time period? Is this position waived if I am unconscious or incapacitated?

- If I forget to comply with the above deadline but could have complied with it, what is the penalty? Does the insurance company only pay a portion of the cost, or a certain maximum dollar amount?

- Does the insurance company have a toll-free or collect telephone number to coordinate my emergency treatment and care that can be reached from anywhere in the United States? Do the representatives speak English, French, and other languages (depending on your needs)?

- Does the insurance company submit the claim directly to my provincial health insurance plan, or do I have to do it myself?

- Is there a limited time period for submitting claims after the emergency treatment has been completed, after which the claim could be denied? What is that deadline for claims with respect to the insurer? What is the claim submission deadline with respect to your provincial health department? What documentation is required, and what invoices or receipts for expenses am I required to keep and submit?

- Do I have to pay up front for any hospital and medical treatment and then seek reimbursement from my provincial health plan and insurance company later, or do the U.S. hospitals and doctors bill my provincial health insurance plan and/or insurance company directly? If I have to cover minor expenses, up to how much and what types of expenses?

- Do I have to notify the insurer of any monitoring of my existing condition, treatment for illness, or change in medication after I have been approved for coverage but before I leave Canada? Will these circumstances affect my coverage? What if I pay for such non-emergency treatment or medication change after I leave Canada for the United States? If I see my doctor during a short visit home to Canada at Christmas, do I need to notify the insurer before I return to the United States about any existing condition, monitoring, medication change, or treatment for an illness? Will that affect my coverage?

- Does the insurer offer full payment for emergency expenses for a stabilized medical condition, or only a part of the expense (e.g., co-insurance), and would I have to pay the rest? What percentage or maximum dollar amount would the insurer pay in this instance (e.g., 50 to 90 percent, or $25,000 to $100,000)?

- If coverage is from an employer, government, or union pension health plan, who is the contact person to determine my benefits? Can coverage details be obtained in writing?

- Does my existing out-of-country medical emergency plan from a past employer, union, or other source permit me to top it up with other insurance? Does the top-up insurer immediately take over after the basic policy reaches the maximum number of days or amount of coverage? Is there a subrogation clause, and if so, what does it say?

- Will a basic out-of-country emergency medical plan allow secondary top-up insurance coverage, if required?

- Will the use of a basic plan mean that the top-up plan will consider the treated condition a pre-existing one and refuse to pay?

- Does my existing retiree/government/union health plan restrict the amount of coverage (e.g., $100,000 maximum) or days (e.g., 30 days)?

- Will the insurance company completely waive any claim for subrogation against my retiree/employee/union health benefit plan and put that in writing? If not, will the insurer waive a subrogation claim for a premium surcharge and what is that surcharge (e.g., 10 to 15 percent), or will the insurer limit a subrogation claim to a certain ceiling (e.g., $3,000)?

- If I have extended-stay coverage rather than a multi-trip plan, will it impair my coverage in any way if I return to Canada for short periods during my six-month stay in the United States?

- If credit card medical coverage is being obtained, does it start on the day of departure and how long is the maximum coverage? Can I obtain all the plan benefits in writing?

- If I die, does my coverage include the expense of returning my body to Canada? My RV or car? My spouse?

- Am I reimbursed for certain additional medical/travel-related expenses, such as accommodation, meals, or transportation of my automobile back to Canada, if I have an accident or illness that is deemed by the insurer to be an emergency?

- If I am ill or injured, will the insurance company pay the air fare for an immediate family member, relative, or friend to visit me?

- Does the insurance company restrict the nature of the relationship of the person to visit me—for example, immediate family only?

- If I have to return to Canada because of my illness or injury, will the insurance company pay to have a person of my choice accompany me?

- If I am being treated for an injury or illness and the insurance company deems it safe for me to travel, can the insurance company arbitrarily arrange for me to fly back to Canada in a commercial plane or air ambulance jet so that medicare can take over?

- Will I have to pay a deductible if I have a claim? How much? In U.S. or Canadian dollars? And under what circumstances?

- Will I have to join an organization to access the medical insurance coverage, and how much will the annual dues be?

- Does the insurance policy cover any trip cancellation costs, baggage loss, or other losses?

Before You Leave Canada

- Take your provincial health care card.

- Take your out-of-country medical insurance policy and number and related documents.

- Take your emergency assistance phone number for your out-of-country medical insurance and carry it in your wallet or purse at all times.

- Take two photocopies of all your important papers before you go, leaving a copy with a relative and keeping a copy yourself. These papers include such items as your current prescriptions, medical history, birth certificate, passport, driver's licence, credit cards, provincial health care card, out-of-province emergency assistance policy, and emergency assistance phone number.

- See your doctor for a thorough examination before you leave Canada. Apart from having a current assessment of your condition, you then also have a reference date for verifying that you did not have a pre-existing illness in case you have a later dispute with your insurance company.

- You should maintain a record of medical and personal data, which will be helpful if you have a medical emergency in the United States. Include your name, address, home phone number, spouse's name, and doctor's name and phone number; the person to be notified in case of an emergency and that person's phone number; and your birth date, social insurance number, provincial health insurance number, out-of-province supplementary insurance plan number, blood type, drug allergies, immunization details, existing conditions, and current medications.

- If you are currently taking medication covered by your provincial health plan, supplemental health plan, or previous employer health plan, ask your doctor to prescribe enough medication before you leave Canada so that you won't run out while you are in the United States.

- If you have friends or relatives who are going to visit you in the United States, make sure you caution them to obtain out-of-country medical insurance to cover them while they are in the United States. Many people going there for only a day or even for several weeks don't think of getting additional insurance protection. A medical emergency could therefore turn into an economic nightmare. A single or multi-trip type of plan coverage might be appropriate.

- Check to see what potential health risks you should be aware of before you go to a specific area—for example, intense sunlight, air pollution, strong water currents, or infectious or poisonous insects, reptiles, or plants.

HOMEOWNER INSURANCE

If you own a house or condominium in Canada, or in the United States as well, you should have a comprehensive homeowner policy that covers you for replacement cost if your home burns down. Your policy should also cover a range of potential risks, such as theft; vandalism; water damage due to frozen pipes, sewer back-up, or snow and ice build-up; or acts of God such as floods, earthquakes, tornadoes, or hurricanes. Check with your insurance company about the types of optional coverage available. The lower the deductible amount, the higher the insurance premium, so you can save some money by increasing your deductible. Deductibles can range from $200 to $2,500. Or you may prefer to have a lower deductible and pay a slightly higher premium for it.

It all depends on how much you can afford to pay if you have to make a claim. Some insurance companies give premium discounts to people over 50, or if smoke detectors and/or fire or burglar alarms are installed in the home. Make enquiries.

Ensuring That You Are Fully Covered

If you are going to live in the United States for up to six months, check with your insurance company beforehand to ensure that you are fully covered during your absence. Different insurance companies have different policies. For example, your coverage might require you to notify the company in writing that you will be gone and who your local contact person is, turn off and empty all your water taps before you go, have the house maintained at a certain temperature so that freezing won't occur, and have your home checked once a week (or more often, depending on your policy) by a friend or neighbour or someone else you select. That person should have your house key, information on how to contact you in case of a home emergency, and the name and contact person of your homeowner insurance company.

Home Security Tips

Here are some home security tips to consider before you leave Canada. Many of these are equally applicable if you have a home in a Sunbelt state:

- Keep a current inventory list of your belongings and other personal possessions.
- Keep receipts for valuable articles, such as cameras, jewellery, art, stereo equipment, and furniture.
- Take photographs or a video of your rooms and belongings for additional support if you have to make a claim.
- Mark your valuable assets for identification in case they are stolen. You can generally borrow a marker from your local police department.
- Keep a copy of your inventory list, receipts, and photographs in your safety deposit box in case your home burns down.
- Get extra coverage for expensive items such as jewellery, since the limit may be $2,000 for any claim.
- Don't leave a message on your answering machine that you are out of the country for six months.

- Cancel newspaper delivery while you are away.

- Arrange with Canada Post to forward your mail or hold it until your return.

- Arrange for a neighbourhood friend or student to clear away advertising flyers.

- Have a reliable neighbourhood friend or student clear the snow from your sidewalk or at least tramp it down.

- Store small valuables in a safety deposit box. Store expensive items (e.g., TV or stereo) with a friend or relative while you are away, or move them out of sight if they can be seen from a window.

- Use clock timers to activate lights and radios.

- Keep garage doors locked and windows covered.

- Secure air conditioners and other openings into your home.

- Change your locks if keys are lost or stolen.

- Make sure door hinge bolts are inside the house; hinges can easily be removed if they are on the outside.

- Install one-inch deadbolt locks on exterior doors. Doorknob locks are unreliable and easily forced.

- Insert a metal piece or fitted wood into sliding glass-door tracks.

- Reinforce basement windows with bars.

Selecting an Insurance Broker

Although it is possible to buy too much insurance, many people don't purchase enough or the right type of insurance. You want to minimize the risks you face on property from fire or theft, for example, by making sure you have adequate insurance protection.

Regular reviews of risk exposure can help avoid overlaps and gaps in coverage, and thereby keep your risk and premiums lower. This is especially important if you are investing in recreational real estate. Reviews can also help you keep current with inflation.

Types of Property Coverage

When you are buying real estate for personal use, investment, or rental purposes, it is important to understand the jargon of the property insurance trade, and how premiums are determined and risk assessed. This will enhance your negotiating skills, save you money, and ensure you get the right protection for your needs. It will also protect you from having inadequate insurance coverage or running the risk that a claim could be denied. Here is an overview of the key concepts.

Inflation Allowance

This coverage protects you against inflation by automatically increasing the amount of your insurance during the term of your policy without increasing your premium. On renewal, the insurance company will automatically adjust the amount of your insurance to reflect the annual inflation rate. The premium you pay for your renewal will be based on those adjusted amounts of insurance.

Inflation allowance coverage will not fully protect you if you make an addition to your building or if you acquire additional personal property. This is why you need to review the amount of your insurance every year to make sure it is adequate.

Special Limits of Insurance

The contents of your dwelling are referred to as "Personal Property." Some types of personal property insurance, such as jewellery, furs, and money, have "Special Limits of Insurance." This is the maximum the insurer will pay for those types of property. If these limits are not sufficient for your needs, you can purchase additional insurance.

Your policy automatically includes some additional coverage to provide you with more complete protection. The individual types of coverage that are included are listed in the section "Additional Coverage."

Insured Perils

A peril is an occurrence such as fire or theft. Some policies protect you against only those perils that are listed in your policy. Other policies protect you against "all risks" ("risk" is another word for peril). This means you are protected against most perils.

All insurance policies have exclusions. Even if you have selected "all risks" coverage, this does not mean that *everything* is covered. It is important that you read the exclusions carefully in order to understand the types of losses that are not covered by your policy. For example, floods and earthquakes may not be covered if you reside in a high-risk location for these types of perils.

Loss or Damage Not Insured

This is the "fine print," the section that tells you what is not covered. They are also known as "exclusions." Exclusions are necessary to make sure that the insurance company does not pay for the types of losses that are inevitable (e.g., wear and tear), uninsurable (e.g., war), or for which other specific policy forms are available to provide coverage (e.g., automobiles).

Basis of Claim Settlement

This section describes how the insurer will settle your loss. It's the real test of the value of your policy and the reason why you purchased insurance.

Replacement Cost

You should purchase replacement-cost coverage for your property. This is particularly important for your personal property (e.g., the contents of your dwelling and personal effects). Otherwise the basis of settlement will be "actual cash value," which means that depreciation is applied to the damaged property when establishing the values. You therefore would get less money, possibly considerably less, than what you originally paid for your property or what it would cost you to replace the property at current prices.

"New for old" coverage is available. All you have to do is ask for "replacement-cost coverage" and then make sure that your amounts of insurance are sufficient to replace your property at today's prices.

Guaranteed Replacement Cost

This is one of the most important types of coverage available to a homeowner. You can qualify for this coverage by insuring your home to 100% of its full replacement value. If you do, then the insurance company will pay the full claim, even if it is more than the amount of insurance on the building. Make sure this is shown on your policy.

The guaranteed replacement cost coverage applies only to your building, not your personal property.

There is usually an important exclusion. Many insurance companies won't pay more than the amount of insurance if the reason the claim exceeds that amount is the result of any law regulating the construction of buildings. Check this out.

Bylaws

Some municipalities have laws that govern the height of a house, what materials you have to use, or even where you can build it. These are known as bylaws.

If the insurance company has to rebuild your house to different standards, this can increase the amount of your claim significantly.

Your policy doesn't cover this increased cost because the insurance company has no way of knowing which laws may apply in your municipality, but you can find out. Then make sure that your amounts of insurance are high enough to cover the increased cost, or increase them if necessary, and ask for a bylaws coverage endorsement. It'll cost a bit more now, but it can save you a lot later.

Deductible

There is a deductible and the amount is shown on the coverage summary page of your policy. It means that you pay that amount for most claims—for example, $250 or $1,000. The insurance company pays the rest.

As you can imagine, the cost to investigate and settle a claim can be considerable, often out of proportion when the size of the claim is relatively small. These expenses are reflected in the premiums you pay. By using deductibles to eliminate small claims, the insurance company can save on expenses and therefore offer insurance at lower premiums.

Conditions

This is a very important part of your policy. It sets out the mutual rights and obligations of the insurer and the insured. This section governs how and when a policy may be cancelled, as well as your obligations after a loss has occurred.

Purchasing Adequate Amounts of Insurance

Purchasing adequate amounts of insurance that reflect the full replacement value of everything you own is without a doubt the single most important thing you can do to protect yourself. The penalty is that insurance companies will not pay more than the amounts of insurance you have purchased, so it is up to you to make sure the coverage is adequate and realistic. Review your coverage before the annual policy renewal date.

Establish how much it would cost to rebuild your vacation home from scratch. This is the amount for which you should insure the house or condo, in order to make sure that you are fully covered.

If you put an addition onto the house or carry out major renovations, you should recalculate the replacement value, as your current amount of insurance will not have taken this into consideration. Notify your insurance company representative. The inflation allowance feature of your policy does protect you against normal inflation, but is not sufficient to cover major changes.

You may also want to check with municipal authorities to see whether there are any bylaws that govern the construction of houses in your area, as you may need a higher amount of insurance so that the reconstruction expense of your home will be fully covered.

Contents Coverage

If you are using the home personally, the following discussion relates to personal use. Your policy provides coverage for your contents. You should make sure that this amount is enough to replace all your possessions at today's prices. If the home is rented to tenants, they are responsible for obtaining tenant's insurance. You should make that a condition of any rental agreement.

If you have a claim, the insurance company will ask you to compile a complete list of everything that you have lost. Ideally, you should maintain an inventory of everything—furniture, appliances, clothes, and other possessions. Estimating what it would cost you to replace them is a good way to check on whether the amount of insurance you carry is enough.

At the very least you should keep the receipts for all major purchases in a safe place. Another good idea is to take pictures of your contents or make a video of everything by walking from room to room. In addition, most insurance companies will provide you with a checklist, so you can compile a list of your contents. This may seem like a chore right now, but it can really save time and aggravation if you do have a claim.

As you could lose your inventory or photographic evidence in a major loss, you should store your records away from your house. The best place is a safety deposit box. Whatever method you use, remember that you should update it periodically (ideally annually) to make sure that it remains accurate.

How Insurance Companies Calculate the Premium

The pricing of insurance is governed by a principle known as the "spread of risk." This means that the premiums paid by many people pay for the losses of the few.

When more dollars in claims are paid out than taken in as premiums, then the premium paid by everyone goes up.

The premium you pay therefore represents the amount of money needed by the insurance company to pay for all losses, plus their expenses in providing the service, plus a profit factor divided by the number of policyholders.

The potential for loss assessment is based upon a number of risk factors. Most of these risk factors are based upon where your recreational property is located. Here are the three most important ones:

Fire

Although theft losses occur more often, fire still accounts for most of the dollars insurance companies pay out in claims. The potential damage due to fire is therefore based upon a municipality's ability to respond to, and put out, a fire.

If you own recreational property in an area with fire hydrants, your premium will be lower because the fire department will have access to a large water supply. Fires in hydrant-protected areas can be extinguished at an earlier stage than those in less well-protected areas. If you own recreational property in an area without hydrants or even a fire department close by, or just a volunteer fire department, the premium will be even higher, due to the obvious higher risk.

Theft

Insurance companies track the claims loss experience caused by theft in all geographic areas. High or low loss experiences (e.g., the claims that an insurance company has to pay out) are reflected in the premium you pay.

Weather

If the location of your recreational property has a history of severe weather storms, such as windstorms, snowstorms, hail, or flooding, insurance companies obviously look at and rate these risks as well. They will exclude coverage for those risks, limit it, increase the deductible or increase the premium.

Ways to Reduce Your Premiums

Higher Deductible

Many people don't realize there are ways to reduce the premium payment significantly. What exactly do you want protection for? What you are really concerned with is the possibility of a catastrophe or a total loss. If so, you can save money by increasing your deductible. By doing so, you save the insurance company the expense of investigating and settling small claims. That saving is passed back to you in the form of a reduced premium.

You should never reduce your amount of insurance so that you pay a lower premium. If you ever do have a claim, it could cost you a lot more than any amount you might save.

Use Discounts

Always ask what discounts are available and see if you are eligible. Generally, discounts recognize a lower category of risk. Listed below are the most common types of discounts available. They could range from a 5 to 10 percent premium discount for each, depending on the category. You could utilize several of them. However, most insurance companies have a limit on the aggregate amount of discounts not being more than a total of about 50 to 70 percent of the base premium. Otherwise, you could end up getting free insurance!

- Mortgage-free discount
- Loyalty discount (e.g., a customer for more than three years)
- Community Watch discount (e.g., your community is a member of Block Watch or Neighbourhood Watch)
- Mature discount (over 50 years of age)
- Senior discount (over 60 or 65 years of age)
- New home (up to 10 years old) discount (with a depreciated premium discount for each year the house is older than new)
- Monitored fire and burglary alarm (through a central station)
- Local alarm discount (alarm built into the home that will go off when motion or fire is detected)
- Multi-line discount (if you have different types of insurance products with the same insurance company or broker, e.g., house, boat, car, etc.)
- Claims-free discount (you don't usually have to ask for this)

Most insurance companies will reduce your premium automatically if you have been claims-free for three or more years, but don't assume this. Ask in advance.

Personal Liability Protection

This is the part of the policy that protects you if you are sued. If someone injures himself or herself on your vacation property (falls on your stairs; slips on your driveway or dock) and a court determines that you are responsible and therefore liable, your insurance company should defend you in court and pay all legal expenses and the amount up to the limit of the policy. The normal minimum limit is $1 million. However, you can and should increase this amount. It is recommended that you increase your coverage up to $5 million minimum. The extra premium is normally very reasonable, and it is money well spent for peace of mind.

There are specific exclusions that apply to this section of the policy. They are listed under the heading "Loss or Damage Not Insured." Make sure you read this carefully.

How to Avoid Being Sued

Every year, many people are injured while visiting the premises of others. The last thing you want is to be sued. The process is stressful, negative, uncertain, time-consuming, and often protracted. Here are some suggestions to avoid problems. If you are renting to a tenant, your contract should cover hazard reduction and require the tenants to have tenant insurance coverage as a condition of your tenancy agreement. You should receive a copy of the policy.

Maintain Your Premises
Most injuries are caused by "slip and fall." They are usually the result of a lack of maintenance. In winter, you should clear ice and snow from all walkways on your premises. Exterior steps should be kept in good repair and a handrail provided.

Inside your house, carpets should be secured to stairs.

Alcohol and Guests
If you serve alcohol to guests, you could be found responsible, to some extent, for their subsequent actions. Some courts have gone to extraordinary lengths to assign responsibility to a host. Good judgment is required. In particular, never allow an intoxicated guest to drive a car or boat.

Other Hazards
You are potentially responsible for everything that happens on your premises. If you have a swimming pool, you are responsible for the safe use of the pool. If you have a dog, you are responsible for the actions of the dog. The list is almost endless. If you are renting to a tenant, you want to pass on the responsibility and liability as much as possible to your tenant. As mentioned earlier, you should make it a condition of tenancy that the tenant obtain tenant insurance prior to moving in and provide you with a copy of it.

The good news is that most injuries can be avoided by using nothing more than common sense. All you have to do is be alert to the potential hazards on your own premises.

Additional Types of Insurance to Consider

Mortgage Insurance

If you owe money on your mortgage and die, the bank insurance offered by your lender will pay off the outstanding mortgage. However, there are drawbacks and other options available to this type of insurance. The good news about mortgage insurance is that almost everyone is considered insurable. The drawbacks are that the premiums are high and the insurance is not portable. In other words, it is only for the purpose of paying off your mortgage. A better alternative is to get your own private term life insurance coverage. The premiums will be lower, and you can keep the insurance coverage long after the mortgage has been paid off. It gives you that flexibility. Also, if you become uninsurable in the future due to health reasons, at least you will have your own portable life insurance protection.

Life Insurance

Term life insurance insures a person for a specific period of time or term, and then stops. Term life does not have a cash-surrender value or loan value as with a whole-life plan. Term premiums are less expensive than whole-life premiums. If you have a bank loan or personal or business obligations, consider term life coverage. If you could be hit with a capital gains tax on your death, you should consider the benefits of your estate or beneficiaries being protected from that expense with term life insurance. All insurance proceeds are tax-free.

Rental Insurance

If you are renting your vacation home out for nightly or weekly rentals full-time, seasonally, or periodically, you need to extend your basic homeowner coverage to include this risk. If a problem and claim occurs and the insurance company does their investigation, and finds out that you were insured for personal use only, your claim will be denied. Premiums are based on insurance risk. The more you rent out the property during the year, the more likely the insurance company will rate your property under their commercial coverage. This would entail higher premiums, due to the higher risk as a consequence of higher turnover and use by renters.

Have your insurance broker get competitive quotes from different companies. You want to make sure you understand the fine print, and know the limitations and exclusions, etc. You want to make sure you have high third-party liability coverage in case anyone is seriously injured. You don't want to be faced with a shortfall. If your recreational property is a full-time or significant rental property, make sure you get protection to cover you for lost revenue while your home is being rebuilt. Sometimes it takes a year or so for a house to be rebuilt, and that could constitute considerable lost revenue.

Title Insurance

Your lawyer or lender could also recommend the benefits of obtaining title insurance for your peace of mind. Sometimes lenders require it. This insurance protects you in the event that pre-existing property defects show up after you buy the property. You would be covered up to the amount of your policy for as long as you are still the property owner.

The types of risks that are usually covered include: claims due to fraud, forgery, or work orders not complied with; zoning and setback non-compliance or deficiencies; survey irregularities; forced removal of existing structures, unregistered rights of way or easements; and lack of vehicular or pedestrian access to the property. Do your comparison-shopping of policy rates, features, and coverage.

HOME OFFICE INSURANCE

It is important to recognize the potential risks of working from home and the policies available for protection against them. If you don't have home office insurance protection, your claim could be denied; that is, you could be personally liable for all financial losses. Always advise your insurance agent that you are operating a business from your home. You will need extra coverage for any risk areas involved directly or indirectly with your business operation. The home office coverage is normally an extension endorsement of your regular homeowner insurance policy coverage. Almost all basic homeowner policies exclude home businesses.

If you have a part-time or full-time home-based business in Canada, you want to make sure you are protected in case you have to make a claim for a loss or injury that is related to your business use. Otherwise, your current policy would likely not cover any such claims. Most basic homeowner policies specifically exclude business use of the home without additional coverage. For example, if a business-related computer or other business equipment were stolen, or if someone visiting you on business were injured on your property or in your home, your basic insurance policy would not cover you.

MOBILE/MANUFACTURED HOME INSURANCE

If you have this type of dwelling, either in the United States or Canada, you can get insurance to cover the risks that are unique to these types of homes—for example, damage caused by faulty blocks or jack, damage to tie-down equipment, damage to adjacent structures (e.g., storage area), or damage from falling objects, such as tree branches. You also want to consider replacement cost coverage in case the whole dwelling is destroyed. Deal with an insurance company that specializes in this type of insurance protection. In the United States, check with a state association of mobile/manufactured homeowners to get names of recommended companies.

AUTOMOBILE INSURANCE

This type of insurance covers you for losses you might suffer due to damage to your car, car theft, vandalism, or fire. It also covers claims made against you if you have a car accident and damage someone else's car or property or injure other people.

As previously mentioned, you can reduce your insurance premiums by increasing the deductible portion of your policy. That is the portion you pay first if you make a claim with your insurance company. This amount ranges from $100 to $2,500. The lower the deductible amount, of course, the higher the premium. Another way of reducing your insurance premium is to have an accident-free claims history.

Here are some further points:

- It is prudent to carry a minimum of $1 million third-party liability coverage, and ideally more (e.g., $5 million). Third-party coverage means that you are covered if you cause an accident to a third party who then makes a claim against you. The premium difference between $1 million and $3 million is relatively small. If one or two people are seriously injured or die as a consequence of an accident that you were responsible for, the award against you could be millions of dollars, especially in the United States. You should have adequate insurance coverage for your peace of mind.

- Obtain underinsured motorist coverage (UMP). This type of coverage protects you in case you or your car is hit by a driver of a car with inadequate or nonexistent insurance coverage. You or a passenger could be seriously injured or permanently disabled or killed. In that event, you are covered for any claim up to the limit of your own third-party liability insurance coverage (e.g., $5 million), subject to any state or provincial ceilings. If someone with inadequate or nonexistent insurance hit you and you didn't have the UMP coverage, you would have no protection. You could sue the driver of the other car, but most likely that person would have no assets and you would be totally out of luck. The premium for underinsured motorist coverage is low, perhaps $20 to $100 a year. That's cheap for the peace of mind.

- If you bought your car in Canada, you would obtain your insurance in Canada. This insurance covers you against any claims you make as a consequence of car accidents, damage, or theft in the United States. If you buy a car in the United States, however, you need U.S. insurance, which you would cancel and replace with Canadian insurance when you arrive back in Canada. You can get this U.S. insurance through your local automobile travel club in the United States (for instance, AAA) or through other private carriers.

- If any personal possessions are stolen from your car, other than a car radio, for example, your car insurance would not cover it. You would have to make a claim under your homeowner insurance policy, which normally has a deductible that you have to pay first. This deductible could be from $100 to $500 or more, depending on your policy.

- If you are travelling to Mexico, your Canadian auto insurance will not cover you. You need to obtain a separate insurance policy for the duration of the trip. This policy can be obtained from a local auto club (AAA) branch close to the Mexican border. This is covered in more detail in Chapter 10.

- If you were the cause of a car accident and your car is damaged so badly that it is considered a write-off, the insurance company can pay you either the depreciated or book value of the car or the replacement cost. Clarify with your insurance company the type of coverage you have. Generally, it is optional coverage with an additional premium if you want to receive replacement market value of the vehicle. The older the vehicle, the higher the replacement cost premium.

- If you have a part-time or full-time home-based or small business in Canada, make sure you have additional insurance coverage for business use of your personal car. It doesn't cost much extra. Otherwise, if there is an accident and the car was being used for business-related purposes, the insurance company will reject the claim.

RECREATIONAL VEHICLE (RV) INSURANCE

If you have an RV of any type, make sure you have adequate coverage. Check with your current auto insurance company, RV dealers, and your local CAA auto club for names of insurance companies that specialize in this type of coverage. You want to consider coverage for such occurrences as hitch failure and collision with a low-hanging tree, as well as coverage for replacement of the RV.

AUTOMOBILE ROADSIDE ASSISTANCE AND OTHER COVERAGE

This is an essential type of coverage, especially if you are travelling in the United States. Most people have auto coverage with a local branch of the CAA (Canadian Automobile Association). Refer to item 36 in Appendix A for contact numbers. There are many benefits of membership, including roadside assistance if your car won't start or if you are locked out of your car, for example. The plan also covers towing your car to a service station for repair if necessary, paying for hotel accommodation for a reportable accident up to a maximum amount, and paying a court bond up to a maximum amount if you have committed a traffic offence that requires a bond.

There is a toll-free 24-hour CAA and AAA emergency phone number you can phone from anywhere in the United States or Canada for roadside assistance. You can also obtain free travel books, maps, and customized route destination guides by being a member of a CAA club. Your membership is recognized by all AAA club members in the United States. Ask for a free U.S. AAA club directory with contact numbers. Most CAA auto clubs have optional coverage packages over and above the basic membership benefits.

LIFE INSURANCE

You may not require any life insurance if you have sufficient life savings, investments, and pensions to meet your needs and your spouse's needs. Depending on your age and medical condition, you may not be eligible for life insurance in any event, or if you are, it could be at a very high premium rate with a low amount of coverage. Insurance companies base premiums on risk—the higher the age, the greater the risk.

As previously mentioned, the most common type of insurance for those over 55 is term insurance. This insures a person for a specific period of time or term and then stops. If you are a nonsmoker, the premium is lower. There are several companies that specialize in insuring those over 60 years of age, regardless of medical condition. The coverage tends to be low—for example, a maximum of $10,000—with an annual premium that is generally increased every year. If you require additional money to meet financial obligations on death, such as funeral expenses, you may want to consider that option. Most auto clubs provide coverage for accidental death from motor vehicle accidents. These premiums are generally very low.

You may already be covered by an insurance policy you had with your previous employer, even in retirement. In addition, your estate does receive death benefits from your government CPP, OAS, and Veterans' pension plans.

TRAVEL INSURANCE

Consider obtaining insurance to cover you for travel-related risks. For example, loss or damage of luggage or personal possessions; missed flights due to weather, delay, illness or death; repatriation (return) of your body to your home city in the event of your death; and other protections.

Tips Before Leaving Canada

√ Refer again to the tips in the lower sections on pages 146 and 148, in this chapter.

√ Thoroughly compare the premiums of at least three insurance companies in each area for which you want coverage. Check on exclusions, limitations, deductibles, and coverage.

√ Make sure that you fully understand the nature of your coverage and that it is confirmed in writing before you depart.

√ Make sure you have left your United States forwarding address with family or friends and a telephone contact number in case you need to be reached in an emergency.

√ If you do not have a fixed address because you have a transient RV lifestyle, set up a routine of phoning home the first or middle of the month, or more frequently. This way, your key contact people in Canada know when you will be communicating.

Tax Issues and Options

INTRODUCTION

Tax issues can be confusing to many Canadians. When you also live in the United States part-time and own property or other investments there, it can become quite complex because you can be affected by the tax laws of both countries. In the United States, for example, you could be liable under certain circumstances for income tax, capital gains tax, estate tax, gift tax, excise tax, and even substantial penalties for failure to report property you have in Canada.

This chapter attempts to answer the common questions about tax that arise out of being a Snowbird. The following overview provides general guidelines only; competent professional tax advice is essential. Topics covered include determining if U.S. tax laws affect you, types of U.S. residency, renting U.S. property, selling U.S. property, U.S. gift tax, paying U.S. and Canadian taxes on death, and the *Canada-U.S. Tax Convention* ("the tax treaty"). Also covered are strategies for reducing taxes on U.S. vacation property, filing deadlines with the IRS, the tax impact of cross-border marriages, tax information exchange between the U.S. and Canada, tax credit for out-of-country medical insurance, where to get tax advice and information, tips before leaving Canada, and other topics.

Pages 163 to 176 cover U.S. income tax. Pages 176 to 179 cover U.S. estate and gift tax.

DO U.S. INCOME TAX LAWS APPLY?

Even though you are a Canadian citizen, not a U.S. citizen, and only living in the United States part-time, you could still be subject to U.S. taxation. Even if you are not required to pay U.S. tax, you could be subject to various U.S. filing requirements and U.S. reporting requirements, many with substantial penalties for noncompliance. On the other hand, the tax treaty includes many provisions that may benefit you, if you are aware of them and properly claim them. Some of these provisions are discussed on pages 176 to 183. Since changes to the laws and the treaty can occur at any time, be sure to obtain updated professional tax advice before taking any action.

If you are a U.S. citizen you are subject to U.S. tax filing requirements, U.S. reporting requirements, and U.S. income tax, regardless of where you live in the world. Much of the discussion that follows is not relevant for you; contact the Internal Revenue Service (IRS) in Ottawa (refer to item 11 in Appendix A), or, if you are in the United States, the IRS office in your area. If you are in the United States on business or for employment, contact Canada Revenue Agency and obtain a copy of the pamphlet *Canadian Residents Abroad.*

The comments in the balance of this chapter apply only to individuals who are not U.S. citizens.

1. Resident vs. Nonresident Alien Tax Status

The United States tax code uses the expression "alien" to define an individual who is not a United States citizen. Hence the income tax rules define a "nonresident alien" as an individual who is neither a U.S. citizen nor a resident of the U.S., for U.S. income tax purposes. If you are a Canadian resident who spends part of the year in the United States, the IRS considers you either a resident alien or a nonresident alien for income tax purposes. It is important to know which category you fall into, since there are considerable tax implications. For example, resident aliens generally must file annual United States income tax returns and disclose their income from all sources throughout the world, including, of course, Canadian income. Nonresident aliens are generally taxed only on income from U.S. sources and income connected with a U.S. business. Not all nonresident aliens have to file a U.S. income tax return.

2. Definition of Resident Alien

The IRS considers you a resident alien of the United States if you meet either one of two tests:

- The Green Card test, or
- The substantial presence test (and do not file a valid "Closer Connection Exception Statement" by the deadline).

The Green Card Test. If you obtain a Green Card (become a "lawful permanent resident of the United States" under the immigration laws), you are considered a resident alien once you enter the U.S. Thus you must file a U.S. income tax return annually, provided your income is above the filing threshold.

The Substantial Presence Test. The substantial presence test is a count of the number of days you are present in the United States over a three-year period.

You add up the following:

- The number of days present in the U.S. in the "current" year (i.e., the year about which you are checking your residency status), plus

- One-third of the number of days present in the U.S. in the preceding year, plus

- One-sixth of the number of days present in the U.S. in the year before that.

When totalling all the days for each of the above three years, remember that the days don't have to be consecutive, and a part of a day constitutes a full day. Certain days present can be ignored, such as days you were present as an "exempt person," days you could not leave because of a medical condition that arose in the United States, or certain days commuting to work or traveling in transit to another country. In some cases you must make a U.S. filing to obtain the exclusion.

If the total equals or exceeds 183 days, and you were present at least 31 days in the current year, you have met the substantial presence test and are considered a resident alien for tax purposes for the current year unless you file a valid Closer Connection Exception Statement (IRS Form 8840) by the deadine.

Closer Connection Exception Statement (IRS Form 8840). Even if you meet the substantial presence test you may still qualify as a nonresident alien if you file a valid Closer Connection Exception Statement by the deadline. Green Card holders are not eligible for the Closer Connection Exception. You are only eligible to file the Closer Connection Exception Statement if you:

- Spend less than 183 days in the U.S. in the "current" year

- Do not hold, and have not applied for, a Green Card

- Have a "tax home" in Canada, or another foreign country

- Can demonstrate a "closer connection" to Canada (or other foreign country above), and

- File IRS Form 8840 (Closer Connection Exception Statement) by the deadline.

Generally, your "tax home" is where you work. If you are not employed or self-employed, your tax home is where you have your "regular abode."

Some of the factors to demonstrate that you had a "closer connection" to Canada than the United States are the location of:

- Your permanent residence
- Your family
- Your personal belongings, such as cars, furniture, clothing, and jewelry
- Your bank
- Where you carry on business (if applicable)
- The jurisdiction where you vote
- The jurisdiction where you hold a driver's licence
- The jurisdiction where you acquire medical insurance.

The deadline to file the Closer Connection Exception Statement (IRS Form 8840) is the 15th day of the 6th month after the end of your tax year (15th day of the 4th month if you have wages subject to U.S. withholding). Thus the deadline is generally June 15, unless you obtain an extension. Form 8840 must be filed for each year you meet the substantial presence test. If you are not eligible to file Form 8840, or if you miss the deadline, you are considered a resident alien.

To obtain Form 8840, contact the closest IRS office in your area, if you are in the United States. In Canada, contact the closest U.S. consulate office in your area. Check out the IRS web site at: www.irs.ustreas.gov.

3. Residency Benefit Under the Tax Treaty

If you meet the Green Card test, or if you meet the substantial presence test and are not eligible to file IRS Form 8840 (or you miss the filing deadline), you are a resident alien. However, under certain circumstances described in the tax treaty, you may nonetheless be able to compute your U.S. income tax as if you were a nonresident alien. This does not change your status to nonresident alien. For the significance of remaining to be considered a resident alien please see page 164. (See The Concept of "Nonresident" Under the Tax Treaty on page 167.)

If you are simultaneously a resident of Canada and a resident alien of the United States, you are a "dual resident" and (for purposes of computing your U.S. income tax) you may have your residency determined under the so-called residency tie-breaker rules contained in Article IV of the tax treaty. Under those rules you are treated as a resident of the country where you have a "permanent home." If you have a permanent home in both countries (or in neither), you are treated as a resident of the country where you have the strongest personal and economic relations (your centre of vital interests). If the latter cannot be determined, you will be a resident of the country where you have an habitual abode. If you have an habitual abode in both, or in neither, you will be a resident of the country where you are a citizen. If you are a citizen of both or neither, the two governments will decide by mutual agreement.

To determine whether the above exemption applies to you, you can contact any Canada Revenue Agency income tax office or the International Taxation Office. Also contact the closest IRS office if you are in the United States or the other IRS sources noted in the previous section.

4. The Concept of "Nonresident" Under the Tax Treaty

Once you are a resident alien (i.e., meet either the Green Card test or the substantial presence test and fail to file a valid IRS Form 8840 by the filing deadline), you are a resident alien and you must file a U.S. income tax return. Normally the income tax return is IRS Form 1040, which is used by U.S. citizens and U.S. residents. On this form you must report, and you are taxed on, your worldwide income. Of course if you pay tax in Canada, you may get a tax credit for that tax on your U.S. income tax return.

However, if you exercise the benefits of the tax treaty residency tie-breaker rules to claim the right to compute your U.S. income tax as if you were a nonresident alien, you file IRS tax Form 1040NR (nonresident) instead of Form 1040. On the body of Form 1040NR you are only required to report U.S. source income and income effectively connected with a U.S. trade or business. The balance of your worldwide income is simply listed on a statement attached to the back of the tax return. You are not taxed in the U.S. on this other income. If you are a Green Card holder, this claim may jeopardize your Green Card.

If you make this residency claim under the tax treaty to compute your U.S. tax as if you were a nonresident alien, it does not actually make you a nonresident alien. You are still considered a resident alien for all other purposes of the U.S. Internal Revenue Code and are subject to all the reporting rules of the tax code. This may include reporting Canadian partnerships, corporations, or trusts with which you are involved. Failure to comply with these reporting requirements can result in penalties of $10,000 or more.

5. Summary of Guidelines for Filing a U.S. Income Tax Return

a) Resident Alien Not Claiming a Tax Treaty Residency Benefit

Resident aliens not claiming a tax treaty residency benefit must file a U.S. tax return (Form 1040) reporting worldwide income for the year if their income is above the filing threshold.

b) Resident Alien Claiming a Tax Treaty Residency Benefit

A resident alien claiming a tax treaty residency benefit must still file a U.S. income tax return but files IRS Form 1040NR. The body of the return contains all your U.S. source income and income effectively connected with a U.S. trade or business. A statement attached to the back of the return discloses the balance of your worldwide income.

c) Nonresident Alien

If you are a nonresident alien, you file IRS Form 1040NR. The income that is reported, and is subject to U.S. income tax, is divided into two categories:

- Income that is effectively connected with a trade or business in the United States, including income from the sale or exchange of U.S. real estate property and, in some cases, real estate rental income. This income, after allowable deductions, is generally taxed at the same rates that apply to U.S. citizens and resident aliens. As a nonresident alien, you must file a U.S. tax return if you have income that is effectively connected with a U.S. trade or business even if there is a loss.

- Income that is not effectively connected with a trade or business in the United States but is from U.S. sources, such as dividends, annuities, certain interest, and sometimes rental income from real estate. This income is taxed at a flat rate of 30 percent or lower tax treaty rate where applicable.

If you only have income that is not effectively connected with a U.S. trade or business, you must file a U.S. income tax return only if insufficient tax was withheld at source (or if excess tax was withheld and you wish to claim a refund).

TYPES OF U.S. RESIDENCY

A discussion of U.S. rules and regulations is often made more complicated because of a misunderstanding of the words that are used. One such word that often causes confusion is the word "resident."

The word "resident" is used in many different contexts and may have a different meaning and definition in each context. A few examples of the use of the word "resident" are as follows:

- To describe whether a person has the legal right to live in a country
- To compute an individual's income tax liability
- To compute an individual's estate (death) tax liability
- To determine what jurisdiction's laws apply to a contract agreement
- To determine an individual's rights to certain health benefits
- To determine what jurisdiction's divorce laws apply and
- To determine whether certain assets of an individual are exempt from attack by creditors.

The most relevant types of "resident" are the first three types mentioned above—U.S. residency for U.S. immigration purposes, U.S. residency for U.S. income tax purposes, and U.S. residency for U.S. estate tax purposes.

1. Immigration

A non-U.S. individual can be a U.S. "resident" for immigration purposes, and thus acquire the right to live in the United States, only if that person obtains that right under U.S. immigration laws from the U.S. Bureau of Citizenship Immigration Services (BCIS). The BCIS has its own criteria, entirely separate from tax law, to determine if you will be permitted to live in the United States. Further, the fact you have the right to live in the United States does not mean you are a resident of the United States for income tax or estate tax purposes. (For example, see pages 165 to 166.)

The possession of a Green Card denotes "permanent resident" status under the immigration laws. This is the only permanent visa. Examples of other U.S. visas that permit you to live temporarily in the U.S. are E-2 (Investor), L-1 (Corporate Transferee), and H-1B (Work Permit) visas.

2. Income Tax

As discussed in the previous section, the U.S. has two separate tests to determine whether an individual is a U.S. resident for income tax purposes, the Green Card test and the substantial presence test. Except for individuals who have Green Cards, the immigration status of an individual does not affect his or her status for income tax purposes. In other words, you may be considered a resident of the U.S. for income tax purposes even though you do not have the right to live in the United States. Conversely you may have an E-2, L-1,or H1B visa (and thus the right to live in the U.S.), but not be a resident for income tax if you do not meet the substantial presence test, or if you meet the substantial presence test but file a valid Form 8840 by the deadline.

3. Estate Tax

Individuals who are nonresidents of the U.S. (as defined for estate tax purposes) are subject to U.S. estate tax only on their U.S. situs property. Individuals who are residents of the U.S. for estate tax purposes are subject to U.S. estate tax of their worldwide property.

The rules that apply to determine U.S. residency for income tax purposes do not apply to determine residency for estate tax purposes. Determining residency for estate tax, often referred to as your place of "domicile," is not as clearly defined as determining residency for income tax. Also it appears you can have only one domicile at a time, whereas you can be a resident of two countries simultaneously for income tax. It is possible to be a resident of the U.S. for income tax purposes without being domiciled in the United States.

The U.S. tax regulations state, "A person acquires a domicile in a place by living there, for even a brief period of time, with no definite present intention of later removing therefrom."

CROSS-BORDER MARRIAGES CREATE NEW ISSUES RELATING TO RESIDENCY

Suppose you are a retired Canadian who has always lived in Canada and you marry a retired U.S. citizen who has always lived in the United States. The two of you then spend approximately six months annually in Canada and approximately six months in the United States. Of which country are you resident for income tax purposes? Are you resident in both? Is one spouse resident in one country and the other spouse resident in the other country?

It appears likely these questions will arise with increasing frequency in the years ahead and the answers may be complex.

Canada and the United States each have their own domestic tax law to determine residency of an individual in their country for income tax purposes. The rules are completely different in each country, and each country initially makes its determination under its domestic law without regard to whether the individual is a resident of another country. As indicated in Section B, the U.S. determination of residency involves application of the two tests—the Green Card test and the substantial presence test. In Canada, an individual can either be "ordinarily" resident in Canada (a factual resident) or a "deemed" resident of Canada. Consult your Canadian tax advisor for the Canadian rules.

In the example of a hypothetical cross-border marriage, suppose the Canadian spouse wishes to remain a resident of Canada for medical insurance purposes, but the U.S. spouse does not wish to be a resident of Canada because of a potentially higher Canadian tax liability. Can the spouses each consider themselves a resident of different countries even though they live together throughout the year?

1. Domestic Law Rules

Although each country's rules are different, it appears that if an individual spends more than 182 days in either country he or she will generally be a resident of that country for income tax purposes under the domestic law of that country. (But see 2 below.)

Therefore if the Canadian spouse wishes to qualify for Canadian medical insurance and the spouses wish to live together throughout the year, the U.S. spouse might be considered a resident of Canada.

Of course, the U.S. spouse could live apart from the Canadian spouse for a few days to reduce the number of days present in Canada and thus attempt to avoid being classified as a "deemed resident" of Canada. However, since the U.S. individual is married to a Canadian resident who spends more than 182 days in Canada, and since they live together almost the entire year, it is possible the U.S. spouse would be considered to be a factual resident of Canada. Canada appears to have an informal "couples in tandem" guideline, whereby both spouses may tentatively be considered residents of Canada if either one is resident in Canada.

2. Tax Treaty Rules

Each country's domestic law, as noted above, can be overridden by the tax treaty. Under the tax treaty's residency "tie-breaker" rules it is possible to pay your taxes in one of the countries as if you were a nonresident of that country even though you would be classified as a resident of that country under its domestic law. Thus the U.S. spouse, in this example, may be entitled to pay Canadian taxes as a nonresident of Canada even though he or she spends more than 182 days annually in Canada, and despite Canada's "couples in tandem" guideline. In cases where a U.S. spouse is a deemed resident of Canada but wishes, and is eligible, to be taxed in Canada as a nonresident of Canada, pursuant to the tax treaty residency "tie-breaker" rules, it may be possible for the U.S. spouse to file a "protective" tax return in Canada. This protective return can perhaps be used to commence the statute of limitations in Canada and thus limit the time period in which the U.S. spouse is exposed to attack from the Canada Revenue Agency.

U.S. TAX NUMBERING SYSTEM FOR CANADIANS

Individuals who are U.S. citizens or Green Card holders, and individuals who possess a visa to live and work in the United States, obtain a Social Security number by filing IRS Form SS-5 with the U.S. Social Security Administration.

All other individuals obtain an "individual taxpayer identification number" (ITIN) by filing IRS Form W-7 with the U.S. Internal Revenue Service.

When Do You Require an ITIN?

- If you are filing a U.S. tax return for yourself. For example, if you sell U.S. real estate, you want to claim a tax refund, or you have U.S. real estate rental income you must obtain an ITIN.

- If you are claiming your spouse as a dependant for deduction purposes on your U.S. tax return, an ITIN must be obtained for your spouse, even if your spouse has no connection with the U.S.

- If you are claiming children (or others) as dependants on your U.S. tax return, an ITIN must be obtained for each dependant. For example, if you are a nonresident alien filing a U.S. tax return for U.S. real estate rental income and you wish to claim a deduction for your children, you must obtain an ITIN for each child, even if they are all minors living in Canada. Similarly, if you are a U.S. citizen or Green Card holder living in Canada, the same requirement exists when you file your U.S. tax return.

- If you are the spouse of a U.S. person and you elect to file a joint U.S. tax return with that person, you must obtain an ITIN.

You can also obtain an ITIN in the case of four different "exceptions" as set out in the instructions to Form W-7. An example is the situation in which a U.S. financial institution is requiring a number from you.

How to Obtain an ITIN

You apply for an ITIN on IRS Form W-7, which you can obtain by contacting the IRS in the U.S., or, by calling a U.S. Consular Office in Canada. It would be helpful to get professional advice on this process. Check out Richard Brunton's website for tax assistance for Canadian residents. He is an expert on the topic area: www.taxintl.com.

IRS Shares Information with the Canada Revenue Agency

The ability of the IRS and the Canada Revenue Agency (CRA) to exchange data on Canadian and U.S. taxpayers by computer has been increased dramatically as a result of the requirements for certain Canadians to have a U.S. individual taxpayer identification number (ITIN).

As mentioned, you apply for your ITIN on IRS Form W-7, at which time you must provide some brief but very personal information to the IRS. Of course you must provide your name, and your name at birth, if it was different. In addition, Form W-7 requires you to provide your address in Canada. Post office boxes and care-of addresses are not allowed. Your date and place of birth, passport number, and U.S. visa number are also needed.

You are also asked for your Canadian social insurance number. You can imagine the potential cooperation between the IRS and CRA this would facilitate. The IRS could have a fast, computerized cross-referencing capability between your U.S. and Canadian taxpayer numbers. Information on certain U.S. tax-related activities in which you are involved, such as the sale or rental of U.S. real estate, or your claim for a U.S. tax refund on U.S. investment or pension income, can be transmitted to the CRA by computer, giving the CRA your name, your Canadian address, and your Canadian social insurance number.

RENTAL INCOME FROM U.S. REAL ESTATE

You may be renting out your U.S. property part-time or full-time. As a nonresident alien, you are subject to U.S. income tax on the rental income. The rental income is taxed in one of two different ways.

Tax on Gross Rental Income

If the level of activity of a real estate rental does not rise to the level of a trade or business, you can be subject to U.S. income tax at a flat rate of 30 percent on the gross rents without the benefit of deductions. Your tenant, property management agent, or Realtor is required to deduct the tax and remit it to the IRS. It doesn't matter if the tenants are Canadians or other nonresidents of the United States, or if the rent was paid to you while you were in Canada. Your tenant or property management agent must complete Form 1042, Annual Withholding Tax Return for U.S. Source Income of Foreign Persons, as well as Form 1042-S, Foreign Persons' U.S. Source Income Subject to Withholding. For more information, contact the IRS and request publication 515, *Withholding of Tax on Non-Resident Aliens and Foreign Corporations,* and publication 527, *Residential Rental Property.*

If the tax has not been collected and remitted to the IRS by the tenant, property management agent, or Realtor you must file Form 1040NR, U.S. Non-Resident Alien Income Tax Return, report the income, and pay the 30 percent tax (subject to paragraph 2, below).

Tax on Net Rental Income

If the level of activity of your rental activity rises to the level of a trade or business, you must file a U.S. income tax return (Form 1040NR) even if there is a loss. You then pay tax on the net profit from the rental activity (if any). You are subject to the same graduated tax rates as a U.S. citizen or U.S. resident on the net profit after deducting your expenses.

If your rental activity does not rise to the level of a trade or business and you do not wish to pay the tax rate of 30 percent of gross income (see above section), you can elect under the U.S. tax rules to compute your tax instead as if the level of activity rose to the level of a trade or business. In this case, as above, you must file Form 1040NR and report your income and expenses and pay tax at graduated rates on the net profit, if any.

To make this election you attach a statement to your tax return stating that you are making the election. You also need to include the following information:

- A list of all of your real estate located in the United States
- The extent (percentage) of your ownership in the property
- The location of the property
- Any major improvements in the property and
- Any previous applications you have made of the real estate net income election.

After you have made the election, it is valid for all subsequent years, unless approval to revoke it is requested and received from the IRS.

Unlike in Canada, on the U.S. income tax return you must compute depreciation expense (capital cost allowance).

You can deduct interest on a mortgage on the property, but not interest on a mortgage on a Canadian property even if the funds from the mortgage were used to purchase the U.S. property. Obtain strategic tax planning advice on this issue.

If you want to be exempt from the nonresident withholding tax and are making that election, you should give your tenant or property management agent IRS Form W-8ECI, Exemption from Withholding Tax on Income Effectively Connected with the Conduct of a Trade or Business in the U.S. Contact the IRS for further information and request the publications 515 and 527.

When you file your annual return, show the income and the tax withheld. If you end up with a loss, after deducting expenses from income, you are entitled to a refund of the taxes withheld. The due date of your return is June 15 of the following year (April 15 if you also had wages subject to U.S. withholding).

SELLING OF U.S. REAL ESTATE

If you are a nonresident alien, any gain that results from a sale or disposition of your U.S. real estate is considered to be effectively connected with a U.S. trade or business. The purchaser or agent of the purchaser is generally required to withhold 10 percent of the gross sale price at the time the sale transaction is completed and the balance of payment is made, unless an exception applies. The 10 percent holdback is only a prepayment of whatever U.S. income tax (capital gains tax) you may owe. The holdback is to be forwarded to the IRS unless you apply to the IRS for a withholding certificate by the day of closing, in which case it is still withheld but not sent to the IRS until a response to the withholding certificate application is received from the IRS.

Waiver of Withholding Tax

You may be exempt from withholding tax if the selling price of your property does not exceed US$300,000 and the buyer and his or her family intend to use the property as a residence at least half of the time it is used by any persons during each of the first two 12-month periods following the date of sale. The buyer does not have to be a U.S. citizen or resident or use the property as a principal residence. To obtain this type of exemption, the buyer must sign an affidavit setting out the facts related above. If the purchase price is over US$300,000 or the buyer is unwilling or unable to sign the affidavit, it may be practical to file a with-holding certificate application discussed in the next paragraph.

Withholding Certificate Application

If your maximum U.S. tax will be less than the 10 percent to be withheld, you can apply to the IRS in advance to have the withholding tax reduced or elimi-nated by completing a withholding certificate application (IRS Form 8288-B). If the 10 percent has already been paid, you would still be entitled to a refund after you filed your U.S. tax return if the 10 percent was greater than the amount due. You can also make an application for an early refund.

Filing Requirements

You are required to report the gain or loss on sale by filing Form 1040NR, the U.S. Non-Resident Alien Income Tax Return. You would have to pay U.S. fed-eral tax on any gain. Depending upon the individual state in which the property is located you may also owe state income tax. If you own the real estate jointly with another person, such as your spouse, each of you must file the above form. For more information, contact the IRS and ask for publication 519, *U.S. Tax Guide for Aliens.*

In addition, you must report any capital gain on the sale of your U.S. property in your next annual personal tax return filing with the Canada Rev-enue Agency. Remember, you must report your worldwide income and gains and pay tax on 50 percent of any capital gain, translated to the equivalent in Canadian dollars at the time of sale.

U.S. GIFT TAX

One might think that as a nonresident alien of the U.S. you could give anything to your spouse, children, or other family members, and the IRS would not have any jurisdiction. The laws, however, are not that simple. You may have U.S. gift tax to pay if you give real property or tangible personal property located in the United States to another person.

There is a $12,000 annual exemption per recipient. In other words, you can give $12,000 per year (indexed for inflation) to as many different people as you wish, without being subject to gift tax. If the recipient is your spouse, the annual exemption is $125,000 (indexed for inflation). If the recipient spouse is a U.S. citizen, as a general rule you can give unlimited amounts without gift tax, but exceptions apply for both exemptions. Do not proceed without consulting your tax advisor.

The gift tax rates are the same as the estate tax rates, but the actual amount of the gift tax may be higher than estate tax because there generally are no tax credits or deductions for gift tax purposes.

Subject to the foregoing exemptions, the rules are as follows:

Real Estate

If you own U.S. real estate directly and give it to another person, U.S. gift tax will generally be payable. Alternatively if you buy real estate jointly with another person (other than your spouse) and the two of you make unequal contributions to the purchase price, gift tax may be payable.

If you purchase real estate jointly with your spouse and make unequal contributions, you must beware when you sell the property. If the sales proceeds are not distributed to the two of you in proportion to your original contributions, gift tax may apply.

Suppose, at the time of purchase, the title to the property is placed entirely in the name of your spouse (or other family member) but the funds to make the purchase come solely from you. Gift tax may apply since you bought the property for the other person.

Personal property (as distinguished from real property such as real estate) can be classified into one of two types: tangible or intangible.

Tangible Personal Property

Tangible personal property includes things such as residence furnishings, paintings, cars, boats, and jewellry.

You are subject to U.S. gift tax on your gifts of tangible personal property located in the United States. However, in this case, as a general rule your property is only considered located in the U.S. if its normal location or domicile is the United States. For example, if you give a car to a family member while both you and the car are in the U.S., the gift tax position may depend upon whether the car was normally based in Canada or the United States.

Intangible Personal Property

Normally a nonresident alien is not subject to U.S. gift tax on the gift of intangible property (e.g., stocks and bonds) regardless of where the property is located. In other words, as a general rule, you can give U.S. stocks or bonds to another person regardless of whether the securities are located in a U.S. or Canadian brokerage firm. However, an exception applies if you are subject to the expatriation rules (exit tax rules). For example, those rules apply to certain U.S. citizens renouncing U.S. citizenship and certain "long-term residents" giving up their Green Cards. Check with an accountant.

U.S. AND CANADIAN TAXES ON DEATH

If you are a nonresident alien (as defined in the estate tax rules), you are subject to U.S. estate tax at your death on any U.S. situs assets. Assets might include U.S. real estate and furnishings, stock in U.S. corporations, golf equity memberships, and vehicles or boats that remain in the United States.

You may also be subject to a "deemed disposition" tax in Canada if your assets do not pass to your surviving spouse. Please consult your tax advisor.

U.S. Estate Tax

U.S. federal estate tax is based on the fair market value of your U.S. situs assets on the date of death (or six months later). There may be individual state estate taxes as well, depending on the state.

All nonresident aliens (as defined in estate tax law) are entitled to a tax credit of $13,000 against the tentative estate tax liability. However, the tax treaty, as discussed in the next section on the Canada-U.S. Tax Treaty (see page 179), may provide a larger tax credit if you are willing to disclose your worldwide assets.

Canadian Capital Gains Tax

Canada does not have an estate or death tax as such. But the Canada Revenue Agency considers that you have disposed of your assets at the time of your death and taxes you on any capital gains on your assets, whether they are in Canada or the United States. Exceptions apply, including cases in which the property passes to your surviving spouse.

If Canadian tax does apply (either because of the deemed disposition or an actual disposition the property), U.S. estate tax may offset part or all of the Canadian capital gains tax. The benefit of this should be kept in perspective, however. Canada only taxes on 50 percent of the capital gains of the U.S. property; that is, on 50 percent of the difference between your "adjusted cost base" and the deemed value of the property or asset at the time of the sale or death.

With proper tax planning, Canadian residents can defer Canadian capital gains tax on death by leaving the property to a spouse or spousal trust. Please consult your tax advisor.

THE CANADA-U.S. TAX TREATY

Under the Canada-U.S. Tax Convention (the tax treaty) there are significant U.S. estate tax savings (and other benefits) for Canadians who are nonresident aliens of the U.S., as well as estate planning opportunities. Make sure you obtain advice about the most current status of the tax treaty from a professional tax expert familiar with cross-border tax issues. The following discussion is intended to raise your awareness of key issues that may affect you.

U.S. Estate Tax Eligible for Canadian Foreign Tax Credit

As indicated above, Canada will provide a full or partial tax credit for a U.S. tax paid that can be applied against Canadian capital gains tax on U.S. source gains.

U.S. "Unified Tax Credit" Against U.S. Estate Tax

Canadians who are nonresident aliens of the U.S. are generally entitled to a "unified tax credit" in the amount of $13,000. By contrast, U.S. citizens are entitled to a much larger "unified tax credit." The amount depends upon the year of death. For deaths in 2007 the amount is $780,800. This amount will likely change; remain in contact with your tax advisor.

If you are willing to disclose your worldwide assets (your worldwide estate) on the U.S. estate tax return, you are entitled to a proportion of the unified tax credit available to U.S. citizens. The proportion is the same proportion that your U.S. assets bear to your worldwide assets. Your worldwide estate includes assets in the United States, Canada, and elsewhere, including the value of RRIFs, RRSPs, and certain life insurance proceeds.

For example, let's say a person has a U.S. condominium worth US $300,000 (U.S. estate) and a worldwide estate of US $1,000,000. Applying the above rule, the "unified tax credit" for 2007 would be

$$\frac{\$300,000}{\$1,000,000} \times \$780,800 = \$234,240$$

In addition to the "unified tax credit" you are entitled to a "marital tax credit" to the extent your U.S. property passes to your surviving spouse.

Marital Tax Credit

If U.S. property is left to a spouse who is not a U.S. citizen, a second tax credit may be available. A "marital tax credit" in the maximum amount of the "unified tax credit" is available to the extent the property passes to your surviving spouse. Thus the tax credit is potentially doubled if all of the U.S. property is left to the surviving spouse. In this scenario, it is assumed that both spouses are citizens and residents of Canada and are seasonal residents in the United States. Of course if the surviving spouse is a U.S. citizen, there will generally be no U.S. estate tax at all on assets that pass to him/her.

Social Security Benefits

If you are a Snowbird, you are still considered a permanent Canadian resident as far as Canada is concerned, so no withholding tax is deducted for social security payments sent to you in the United States during your Snowbird stay. If you intend to eventually live full-time in the U.S. or another country, refer to Chapter 11 for a discussion of the impact on social security payments.

Withholding Tax on Interest

The general rule of withholding tax on interest income from U.S. sources is 10 percent for individuals as well as corporations. However, bank interest and certain "portfolio interest" are exempt from U.S. tax provided the interest is not connected with your U.S. business. The U.S. withholding tax on most cross-border direct dividends is 15 percent (5 percent in the case of a Canadian corporate recipient owning 10 percent or more of the U.S. payor).

Gambling Winnings

If you have ever bet on a horse race, gambled in a casino, or entered a lottery in the United States, a U.S. withholding may have been deducted from your winnings. Winnings are subject to a 30 percent withholding tax, except for blackjack, baccarat, craps, roulette, and big-six wheel, referred to as exempt games.

Under the Canada-U.S. tax treaty, you can offset your losses against winnings in all other types of U.S. gambling and pay U.S. tax only on your net winnings. You can only offset U.S. losses. You cannot offset losses from exempt games. To obtain your refund you must file a U.S. tax return.

On the tax return you must be able to substantiate the losses you are off-setting. Therefore you should keep an accurate record of your bets or other gambles, including the date, type, location, other persons present, and, of course, details of the actual amount bet and the results.

Some specific documents you should retain are:

a) Horse Racing and Dog Racing

A record of the actual races, numbers, date and times, the details and results of each bet, and payment records from the racetrack.

b) Lotteries

The lottery name, ticket dates, unredeemed tickets, and details of each ticket, including the amount paid and the result.

c) Slot Machines

Record the slot machine number, and keep a record of winnings by date and time.

d) Poker and Other Table Games

Record the table number where you played, and casino credit card data, if applicable, indicating whether credit was issued in the pit or at the cashier's cage.

In the case of slots, poker, and other games, you can get a gambling card for the asking from most casinos. You insert this card in the slot machines or give it to the casino staff prior to a table game. Minimum bet limits could be required to record the bet, depending on the house policy. This card automatically records your wins and losses on a computerized data bank. You can obtain a printout of your gambling history at the end of the year from the locations you gambled. This could be used for tax filing purposes.

Do not destroy or throw away your tickets from losing bets. These tickets may be required to document your loss to the IRS to obtain your refund. You should attach proof of the U.S. tax withheld to the back of your U.S. tax return.

Tax Information Exchange Between the U.S. and Canada

The purpose of an exchange of information is to ensure a correct and speedy application of domestic tax legislation, to assist in the application of tax treaties, and to prevent tax avoidance and evasion.

There are three main types of information exchange between countries:

a) On Request

For example, the Canada Revenue Agency (CRA) could request from the IRS specific information about a U.S. real estate sale by a particular Canadian resident.

b) Automatic

For example, all information available to the IRS on U.S. rental income received by Canadians or U.S. real estate sales by Canadians could be sent automatically to the CRA by the IRS.

c) Spontaneous

For example, in the course of an IRS tax audit of a Canadian for a U.S. real estate sale, the IRS might spontaneously decide to send the information to the CRA if it believes the information may be of interest to the CRA.

What Does the IRS Know About You?

The IRS potentially has a wide variety of information available on individuals having U.S. income, U.S. property, or involved in a U.S. financial transaction. For example:

- If you purchase U.S. real estate, your name and address are recorded in the local county property records. When you sell your U.S. real estate, another entry is made in the county records. Information on both of these transactions is readily available to the IRS if it wishes to obtain it.

- If you sell U.S. real estate, the closing agent (e.g., the lawyer or title insurance agent) must complete IRS Form 1099-S and submit it to the Internal Revenue Service, along with a copy to you. This form includes your name, address, and the sale price of your property. The IRS can use the form to determine whether you have filed a U.S. tax return.

- If you sell U.S. real estate to a U.S. person and take back a mortgage, a notation of the interest paid to you must be made on the U.S. person's tax return.

- If you rent out your U.S. real estate, another IRS form may be generated. The rental agent is required to complete IRS form 1042-S and submit it to the Internal Revenue Service along with a copy to you. The form lists your name, Canadian address, and the rental income you received. Again, the IRS can use this form to determine if you have made the proper U.S. filing.

- If you receive certain types of interest or dividends from U.S. sources, IRS Form 1042-S is also filed with the IRS.

- If you receive pension income from U.S. sources, similar IRS forms may also be generated and sent to the IRS.

As mentioned, all the information available to the IRS can also be given to the Canada Revenue Agency.

Mutual Assistance in Collection Efforts

The tax treaty includes a provision that Canada and the United States will assist each other (in certain cases) in collecting revenue owing for taxes, interest, penalties, and costs. In practical terms, it will be much easier for the other country to collect taxes owing and harder for the taxpayer to avoid collection efforts from the other country. This issue has been covered in other sections of this chapter.

YOUR U.S. BANK INTEREST WILL BE REPORTED TO CANADA REVENUE AGENCY

If you receive U.S. bank interest, your bank will be required to advise the IRS of your name and address and the amount of interest paid to you. The bank will be able to identify you as a Canadian from IRS Form W-8BEN, which you must file with the bank. Normally, you must file IRS Form W-8BEN at the bank when the account is opened, and every three years thereafter. If you do not do so, the bank is required to deduct U.S. withholding tax on your interest.

You should expect that the IRS will automatically send the information of revenue you are making in the U.S. to the Canada Revenue Agency. There is a frequent exchange of information between the two taxing authorities on matters such as this.

STRATEGIES FOR REDUCING U.S. ESTATE TAX ON U.S. VACATION PROPERTY

The section beginning on page 179 summarized some provisions in the tax treaty with respect to U.S. estate tax. These provisions may eliminate the U.S. estate tax problem for many Snowbirds. However, if you are a high net worth individual, the estate tax provisions in the tax treaty may be of little or no benefit to you. If you think this is your situation, you should consider some estate planning options to reduce any estate tax liability. Obtain expert professional tax advice customized to your situation, since the best solution may be complex.

To lower your Canadian deemed disposition tax liability on your death (if any), you may be able to claim the principal residence exemption on the U.S. property. This is assuming you were eligible to claim it—in other words, that it was a principal residence at least for part of the year. Of course this will affect your ability to make the principal residence claim on your Canadian residence. Therefore make sure that you obtain tax advice from an expert familiar with both U.S. and Canadian taxes.

Joint Ownership of Property with Spouse or Family Members

If you die while jointly owning U.S. property with one or more other individuals, the entire value of the property is subject to U.S. estate tax except to the extent your estate can prove that the other joint owner(s) contributed to the purchase price and improvements to the property. An exception applies if the property is owned in the relatively unusual type of joint ownership referred to as "tenants in common." With the most usual type of joint ownership (joint ownership with right of survivorship) your estate is only subject to estate tax on your proportionate interest if contribution by other joint owners can be proven. However, please refer to the gift tax rules above (see pages 176 to 178). There is an annual U.S. exemption of $125,000 for gifts to non-U.S. citizen spouses (adjusted for inflation). When used with the "tenants in common" deed, such gifts may reduce future estate liability in the United States.

Canadian capital gains tax (CGT) would apply, however, to any gift of your U.S. second property (non-principal residence) to someone other than your spouse. The CGT is based on 50 percent of the proportional amount of the gain in current fair market value from your "adjusted cost base." The gift would be considered by the Canada Revenue agency as a "deemed disposition" of part of your U.S. property. For example, if the home went up in value by $100,000 in Canadian funds, and you were making a gift of half of the property, that would be a gain of $50,000 (half of the total gain). You would have to include 50 percent of that gain, or $25,000, in your tax filing for income in that taxation year. You would be paying Canadian tax on an artificial income from your second property.

In addition, if you decided to sell part of your U.S. property to friends or relatives, the U.S. capital gains tax would apply to that sale at fair market value. As mentioned in Section G, at the time of sale, the buyer is required to remit 10 percent of the fair market value or purchase price to the IRS as a credit towards any U.S. capital gains tax that you may be required to pay when you file a U.S. tax return. Any excess amount paid would be refunded to you on your U.S. income tax return. If you receive payments on the installment basis (over a number of years) you want to synchronize the payment structure to minimize the capital gains paid in both countries. There are foreign tax credits available for U.S. capital gains tax paid, to enable you to apply them against your Canadian tax payable.

Sale and Leaseback

If you want to avoid estate tax but continue living in your U.S. residence, you can sell the property at fair market value and then lease it back for a certain number of years with options for renewal. This may minimize or reduce taxes, such as Canadian and U.S. capital gains tax on a profit from the sale, U.S. estate tax on the value of a mortgage received from the purchaser as part of the purchase price package, and (with proper planning) U.S. withholding tax for future U.S. income tax liability on any interest income you receive from a mortgage you accepted as part of the purchase price. Since everyone's situation is unique, make sure you get specific tax advice from a professional accountant.

Disposing of U.S. Property Prior to Your Death

This strategy may be desired if you want to defer selling the property right now, and thereby defer any U.S. and Canadian capital gains tax until a future time. At the same time, you could avoid any U.S. estate tax by having an option to purchase your U.S. property exercised before your death, if possible.

For example, you may wish to grant an option, for a fee, to a family member to purchase the U.S. property before or on a certain date. The price could be fixed at the time of the written option or a price formula could be included in the option document. You can include in the option that you have the power to nullify the deal if you wish. You need to have legal advice to ensure that the option is considered valid, including the payment of money for the granting of the option—for example, a nominal sum such as $100—from the person receiving the option. You should also grant a power of attorney (PA) to the person who has the option to purchase or to another party, depending on the circumstances. The PA would be specific to the sale and transfer of the property, pursuant to the terms of the option. You need to be in good mental health when you grant the PA. Make sure you see a local U.S. lawyer experienced in these matters. If you suddenly become ill or incapacitated, prompt action could be taken by the option holder to transfer the real estate out of your name to the option holder's name, thereby avoiding U.S. estate tax.

The exercise of the option prior to your death subjects you to U.S. and Canadian capital gains tax (CGT). You pay Canadian CGT whether your property is transferred before your death or triggered by your death (deemed disposition). However, the U.S. CGT would most likely be creditable against Canadian CGT. Therefore, the combined amount of U.S. and Canadian capital gains taxes could be significantly less, if the property is transferred before your death by the exercising of the option, than the combined amount of U.S. estate tax and Canadian capital gains tax that would arise on your death, if it wasn't transferred out beforehand.

If you suddenly die, however, no action could be taken under the option agreement and PA. There could therefore be estate tax payable on the value of your U.S. real estate property in your name, subject to any of the changes to the Canada-U.S. tax treaty discussed on pages 179 to 183. Refer to Chapter 8 for more discussion on PAs.

Buying Term Life Insurance

This is an option to help pay for any future estate tax liability shortfall. For many Snowbirds, however, it is not a realistic option, because it is either impossible to acquire or too expensive. Even if you could afford to acquire enough coverage, you would need to increase the face value, since the value of your estate goes up every year, along with the cost of your insurance premium. You should attempt to buy a policy that enables you to increase the face value up to a certain amount, without having to undergo a medical exam each time. If you can't obtain term life insurance, you may want to consider the cheaper accidental death insurance.

There are other strategies that may or may not be beneficial or necessary in your individual situation to reduce or eliminate U.S. estate taxes. For example, selling the U.S. property outright and renting; renting but not buying any U.S. property in the first place; holding the U.S. property in a Canadian corporation (but this may create Canadian tax problems—please consult your tax advisor); taking out a non-recourse U.S. mortgage on the U.S. home; purchasing the property through a Canadian partnership with a "check the box" election in the United States; or (in certain very limited cases) using a Canadian trust. A non-recourse mortgage means a lender can only take legal action against the property. They have no recourse against you personally.

Also, your U.S. estate tax can be deferred (but not necessarily forgiven) to the extent the property passes to your surviving spouse via a U.S. "Qualified Domestic Trust."

Each option has advantages and disadvantages. Make sure you obtain tax advice from a tax expert skilled in U.S.-Canada tax strategies.

DEADLINES FOR FILING WITH THE IRS

Here is a summary of some key deadlines you should be aware of. Depending on your situation, there could be other forms to complete and file with the IRS.

Closer Connection Exception Statement (IRS Form 8840)

Form 8840 must be filed within five and a half months after the end of your tax year (within three and a half months if you received wages subject to U.S. withholding) unless you received an extension. Thus, it is generally due June 15 for the previous tax year. Failure to file a required 8840 will likely result in your being considered a U.S. resident for U.S. income purposes unless you can demonstrate you tried to comply.

Qualified Domestic Trust Election

Canadian estates wishing to defer U.S. estate tax on U.S. property through the use of a Qualified Domestic Trust must generally make an election no later than one year after the normal due date for the return (including extensions). The due date (without extensions) is normally nine months after the date of death. If the election is not made in time, the trust could not be used in most cases, and hence the tax deferral is forfeited.

Estate Marital Tax Credit Claim

Canadian estates desiring to reduce their U.S. estate tax liability by claiming a marital tax credit under the Canada-U.S. tax treaty have an important deadline to meet. The estate will generally be disqualified from obtaining this important tax reduction if the proper waiver and claim are not made by the same deadline described above for the Qualified Domestic Trust election.

TAX CREDIT FOR OUT-OF-COUNTRY EMERGENCY MEDICAL INSURANCE PREMIUMS

The Canada Revenue Agency will permit you to claim, as a tax credit, a percentage of the amount of your insurance premium, as long as it is deemed to be a qualifying medical expense. Refer to Chapter 6, page 136 for a more detailed discussion.

WHERE TO GET TAX ADVICE AND INFORMATION

Many sources of information and assistance are available to help you understand the tax issues and improve your decision making.

- **Canada Revenue Agency (CRA)** has many free guides, pamphlets, and interpretation bulletins covering a wide range of issues. They will also provide you with assistance on your tax return questions and on international tax issues, such as being a Snowbird in the United States. However, never rely on the opinion of an employee of CRA in your decision-making. It is just general information, and may not be accurate in the facts of your situation. You need to obtain independent tax advice from a qualified professional. Also, refer to the CRA website for tax information: www.cra-arc.gc.ca.

- **Canada Border Services Agency (CBSA)** has information brochures and will answer your enquiries relating to any taxes, such as duties and so on when you are bringing goods back to Canada. Their website is: www.cbsa-asfc.gc.ca. Refer to item 4 in Appendix A and Chapter 4.

- **The U.S. Internal Revenue Service (IRS)** has many free publications and a toll-free enquiry number for assistance with the tax implications and filing requirements of being a Canadian nonresident alien of the United States or another category of temporary resident.

- **Independent professional advisors** such as chartered accountants (Canada) or certified public accountants (United States) and lawyers who specialize in tax matters and are familiar with cross-border Canada/U.S. tax issues. Refer to the IRS Internet site. See item 11 in Appendix A. As mentioned before, it is prudent to obtain at least one opinion from a Canadian expert and one from a U.S. expert. The more extensive and complex your investments or assets in the United States, the more important it is to satisfy yourself that the advice you are getting is consistent. If you are considering moving to the United States permanently, it is imperative that you receive opinions from tax experts on both sides of the border. For suggestions on what to look for in a professional tax accountant or lawyer, refer to Chapter 9.

- *Brunton's U.S. Tax Letter for Canadians* is available by subscription. It contains a lot of helpful information and analysis. Richard Brunton is an expert on tax issues and filing issues for Canadians living part-time in the U.S. Contact Richard Brunton, CPA, at (561) 241-9991 or you can view a sample online at: www.taxintl.com.

Tips Before Leaving Canada

Here are some reminders of tax-related steps you should take before leaving on your extended vacation in the United States. Or make arrangements for these matters to be dealt with while you are away. There are significant deadlines that have negative tax or financial consequences if they are not met.

√ If you pay the current year's income tax in quarterly installments, make arrangements to have your December 15 and March 15 installments paid on time.

√ If Canada Revenue Agency (CRA) has not yet notified you of acceptance of your previous year's income tax return self-assessment, make sure you are notified of any ruling while you are gone. You only have 90 days to file a notice of objection if CRA rejects your return and does a reassessment. If you are staying in one place for the duration of your snowbird vacation, you probably have mail forwarded to you regularly. If you have no fixed address because you are an RV nomad, have someone monitor your mail and notify you when you next communicate with that person.

√ Remember some key deadlines that may occur while you are away. For example, December 31 is the deadline for an annual withdrawal from Registered Retirement Savings Plan (RRIF); March 2 is the deadline for any contributions to a Registered Retirement Savings Plan (RRSP).

√ If you turn 69 in the current calendar year, make your RRSP contribution by December 31 of the current year, rather than by 60 days after the end of the year. The government has recently announced it is extending the RRIF deadline to 71 years of age.

√ Pay safety deposit fees, RRSP administration fees, accounting fees, investment council fees, charitable donations, and moving expenses by December 31 if you intend to claim them as deductions or credits in the tax return for the current year.

√ If you have spent at least 31 days in the United States in the current calendar year and have spent substantial periods in the U.S. in the previous two years, you may be required to fill a treaty disclosure return or a Closer Connection statement before April 15 or June 15, respectively, of the following year, to avoid significant penalties.

√ Before you leave Canada, select a professional accountant who can assist you, before you depart, on the cross-border tax issues you need to know. Leave your U.S. contact address and phone number with the accountant before the end of December to see if there are any tax-related matters that have to be dealt with before the end of that month, or the next quarter of the following year.

CHAPTER 8 — Wills, Trusts, and Estate Planning

INTRODUCTION

Over the course of your life you will sign many documents. Your will is the most important one you will ever sign. With very few exceptions, everybody should have a will. A will is the only legal document that can ensure that your assets will be distributed to the beneficiaries of your choice, in the way that you wish, instead of by a government formula in the absence of a will. A will also ensures that your estate will be settled in a timely and efficient manner, rather than in a delayed fashion that will be a burden for your family. Combined with effective estate planning, a will can ensure that the least amount of tax is payable. There are no estate taxes or succession duties in Canada at this time. There are tax implications for dying in the United States, however, if you own property there; this is discussed in Chapter 7. As a Snowbird living in the United States for an extended period, you should deal with your will, power of attorney, and estate planning matters before your departure.

It is estimated that only one out of three adults has a will, meaning that two-thirds of the time when people die their wishes are not met and the government has to become involved. There are various reasons for the failure of people to prepare a will. Some people just procrastinate by nature or have busy lives and simply never make writing a will a priority. Others do not appreciate the full implications of dying without a will or even put their minds to the issue. And some people simply resist the reality that they are mortal. The contemplation of the finality of death is discomfiting to many people, and therefore they resist dealing with issues connected to death. Preparing a will and dealing with estate planning means facing the issue of mortality in a direct way.

Of those who do have a will, many do not review it regularly or modify it according to changing circumstances. Typically, people first think of their will at predictable stages of their lives, such as when they get married, when their first child is born, the first time they fly without their children, or upon news of the sudden death of a friend or relative. After the will has been completed, they forget about it. Not updating it can be as bad as not having a will at all. It can cause the beneficiaries a lot of grief, stress, time, and expense when these problems are easily avoided by regular review and updating of the will. Other people do their own will, with potentially serious implications if it is not done properly.

Your will comes into effect only after your death and is strictly confidential until that time. You can rewrite or amend the will at any time. In fact, the need to keep your will up to date cannot be overemphasized, since circumstances can change at any time. A will should be reviewed every year, ideally at the same time—for example, on the first day of the new year or on some other special event or another set date. For example, your family needs or marital status may have changed; your assets may have increased or decreased; you may have moved to a new province, or bought a U.S. Sunbelt condo or house; or new government tax or other legislation may have been introduced that should prompt you to look at your estate plan again.

As a caution, this chapter provides general guidelines only. The laws and terminology relating to will preparation or estate planning can vary from province to province and state to state—and can change. Federal and provincial income tax legislation continually changes. Seek professional advice. Refer to Appendix C for assistance in planning.

For a more detailed explanation of will and estate planning, refer to the book I co-authored with John Budd. It is called *The Canadian Guide to Will and Estate Planning*. Also refer to my book: *The Complete Guide to Buying and Owning Recreational Property in Canada*, and the website: www.estateplanning.ca and www.homebuyer.ca.

WHAT'S IN A WILL?

Depending on the complexity of your estate, your finances and personal affairs, your will can be short and simple, or long and complex. Here is an outline of the main contents of a basic will:

- Identification of person making the will
- Statement that the current will revokes all former wills and codicils (a codicil is a supplementary document to a will that may change, add to, or subtract from the original will)
- Appointment of an executor and trustee (this is discussed in more detail later)

- Authorization to pay outstanding debts, including funeral expenses, taxes, fees, and other administrative expenses, before any gift of property can be made
- Disposition of property
- Special provisions (such as trusts or alternative beneficiaries)
- Funeral instructions.

WHAT HAPPENS IF THERE IS NO WILL?

If you don't have a will, or don't have a valid will, the outcome could be a legal and financial nightmare and an emotionally devastating ordeal for your loved ones. Not having a will at the time of death is called being intestate. It means you have not left instructions for how you want your assets to be dealt with on your death and you have not appointed anyone to be legally in charge of your estate. Accordingly, provincial and state (if you are a Snowbird with assets in the United States) legislation covers that situation. The court eventually appoints an administrator. If no family member applies to act as administrator, the public trustee or official administrator is appointed. Your estate will be distributed in accordance with the formulas of the laws of your province or state, which are inflexible and may not reflect either your personal wishes or the needs of your family or loved ones. Although the law attempts to be fair and equitable, it does not provide for special needs. For example, a home or other assets could be sold under unfavourable market conditions in order to effect the necessary distribution of assets that the law requires. In addition, the settling of your estate could be a long and expensive matter.

If you have assets in both Canada and the United States, you will have two separate probates governed by the laws of the province and state where you had assets. Your heirs could end up paying taxes that might easily have been deferred or reduced. There may not be enough assets in the estate to pay the taxes. Your family could be left without enough cash for an extended period of time. During this period, your assets may suffer a loss because of a lack of proper safeguards. There may be a delay in the administration of your estate and added costs such as an administrator bond. (A bond is similar to an insurance policy in case the administrator makes a mistake.)

The consequences of not having a will are not the the memory or legacy most people would choose to leave to their children, spouse, or relatives. At the time of a death and during the natural grieving process, the survivors do not want the stress and uncertainty of there not being a will. You should leave them cherished memories, including the foresight, consideration, and love shown by having a valid will that reflects current realities and your wishes.

WHAT IS A LIVING WILL?

A living will is designed for those who are concerned about their quality of life when they are near death. It is a written statement of your intentions to the people who are most likely to have control over your care, such as your family and your doctor. Have a copy of the living will where it can be readily obtained—for example, in your wallet or purse. Give a copy to your spouse and family doctor. You should also review your living will from time to time. The purpose of a living will is to convey your wishes in the event that there is no reasonable expectation of recovery from physical or mental disability. Such a will requests that you be allowed to die naturally, with dignity, and not be kept alive by artificial means or "heroic medical measures." In some provinces, a living will is merely an expression of your wishes only and is not legally binding on your doctor or the hospital in charge of your care in Canada. However, other provinces have legislation on the issue of living wills. These provinces officially endorse the concept, if your written instructions are correctly done. Contact the Centre for Bioethics below for further information.

1. Canada

To obtain a sample living will with instructional booklet and/or videotape, you can download information from the website below, or contact them directly.

> *Centre for Bioethics*
> *University of Toronto*
> *88 College Street*
> *Toronto, ON M5G IL4*
> *Tel: (416) 978-2709*
> *Web site: www.utoronto.ca/jcb.*

2. U.S.

In the United States, most states recognize a properly drawn living will. Except for Michigan, New York, and Massachusetts, all the U.S. states, including the Sunbelt states, have some form of legislation dealing with living wills. For further information and to obtain a living will and health care proxy form customized for the Sunbelt state you reside in, contact:

National Hospice and Palliative Care Hotline
Tel: (202) 338-9790
Toll-free: 1-800-989-9455
Web site: www.caringinfo.org

If you are a Snowbird, you should consider two living wills. One should be recognized in Canada and comply with any provincial legislation; it should also be generic enough for provinces in Canada without legislation. The other living will would be prepared for your extended stay in the United States and comply with appropriate U.S. state legislation or be generic enough to express your wishes for states that do not have specific living will legislation. You may also wish to consult a lawyer in Canada and, if you are living in the United States as a Snowbird, a U.S. lawyer as well, if you desire further information on this issue.

PREPARING A WILL AND SELECTING A LAWYER

There are basically three ways to have your will prepared: write it yourself, have a lawyer do it for you, or have a trust company arrange a lawyer to do it for you. A brief overview follows. When you read the section on the reasons for seeing a lawyer, you will see the compelling need to protect your estate and personal wishes by doing so.

Writing Your Own Will

This is the poorest choice, because it could have many defects and inadequacies that could result in legal, financial, and administrative grief for your family, relatives, and beneficiaries. How you expressed your wishes may very well be legally interpreted differently from what you intended because of ambiguity. Worse still, any ambiguous clause in the will could be deemed void or the whole will could be considered void for various technical reasons. Some people do their own will by drafting it from scratch or by using a standard form for a will purchased in a bookstore or stationery store. The risk is very high when you try to save money and do it yourself rather than using a skilled professional. It is false economy, and depending on your situation, you could have a lot to lose. Many people assume that a simple will that they complete will suffice. What may appear to be simple to a layperson, however, could require more complex decisions and wording. Each person's situation is unique. There are better and inexpensive alternatives to provide you with peace of mind, as outlined in the next two subsections.

Hiring a Lawyer and Other Specialists

Wills, in almost all cases, should be prepared by a lawyer who is familiar with them and is qualified to provide legal advice and is knowledgeable about how to complete the legal work required in drafting a will. If your will is properly and professionally drafted, it will be valid in the United States and will cover your U.S. assets. If you have assets in both the United States and Canada, there will be a probate in both countries on your death. Your estate will require a lawyer in each country. Probate is governed by the laws and taxes of the province and state in which you have assets.

Depending on the complexity of the estate, however, a lawyer may not have the expertise to advise you on other, non-legal issues, such as tax, investments, and retirement. If that is your situation, you should enlist the expertise of the other specialists, such as a professionally qualified accountant who specializes in tax, specifically a chartered accountant (CA) or certified general accountant (CGA). A lawyer specializing in wills could recommend a tax expert. You can also look in the Yellow Pages of the telephone book for accountants with these designations. Ask to speak to a tax specialist.

If you are selecting a financial planner as well, make sure that you check that person's credentials, expertise, and reputation. Ask for referrals from your lawyer or accountant and have any advice verified for the tax, legal, and administrative implications by your lawyer, accountant, and trust company.

For a discussion of how to select a lawyer, accountant, or financial planner, see Chapter 9.

The legal fee for preparing a basic will is very modest, generally between $100 and $200 per person. If your estate is complex, of course, this fee could be higher because of the additional time and expertise required. A "back-to-back" will is a duplicate reverse one for husband and wife and is generally a reduced price.

Main Reasons for Consulting a Lawyer When Preparing a Will

To reinforce the necessity of obtaining a legal consultation before completing or redoing a will, just look at some of the many situations in which legal advice is specifically required because of the complex legal issues and options involved. Not dealing with these issues could create serious legal and financial problems upon your death.

- You want to live in the United States or elsewhere for extended periods of time—for example, to retire and travel south in the winter months. The issue of your technical domicile, or permanent residence, at the time of your death has legal and tax implications for your will. This is discussed in detail in Chapter 7.

- You own or plan to own foreign real estate, in the United States or elsewhere.

- You have a will that was signed outside Canada or plan to do so.

- You are separated from your spouse but not divorced.

- You are divorced and want to remarry.

- You are divorced and paying for the support of your former spouse and your children.

- You are living common-law, will be entering a common-law relationship, or are leaving an existing one.

- You are in a blended family relationship, with children of each spouse from previous relationships.

- You have children from a previous relationship and an existing one.

- You own your own business or partly own a business with other partners.

- Your estate is large and you need assistance with estate planning long before your death to reduce, delay, or eliminate taxes on your death.

- You have a history of medical problems and so someone could attack the validity of your will on the basis that you did not know what you were doing when you signed the will or were not capable of understanding the financial matters covered in the will.

- You want to have objective, unbiased, and professional advice rather than making choices in a vacuum or possibly being in an environment where you could be influenced by others who have a vested interest in the contents of the will, or you do not want to feel under duress or pressure from relatives or family members when preparing your will.

- You want to forgive certain people for debts they owe you, or make special arrangements for the repaying of debts or mortgages to your estate should you die before the debt or mortgage is paid back to you.

- You want certain events to occur that are complicated and have to be carefully worded, such as having a spouse or friend receive a certain income or use a home until he or she remarries or dies, at which time the balance of the money or the house would go to someone else.

- You want to set up a trust arrangement to cover various possibilities. Trusts are discussed later in this chapter.

- You want to make special arrangements to care for someone who is incapable of looking after himself or herself, or who is unable to apply sound financial or other relevant judgment—for example, a child, an immature adolescent, a gambler, an alcoholic, a spendthrift, or someone who has emotional, physical, or mental disabilities or limitations or who is ill.

- You wish to disinherit a spouse, relative, or child. There are several reasons for disinheriting someone. For example, you may have lent a lot of money to one child out of several, the money was not repaid, promises were broken, and a serious estrangement occurred. The unpaid money substantially reduced your estate, and to keep peace with the rest of the family you may want to remove the debtor child from sharing in the proceeds of your estate or reduce that child's portion by the amount of the debt. Another, more positive reason might be that all your children are now wealthy on their own and don't need your money at all. You may therefore want to give the majority of your estate to charitable causes that interest you.

- You wish to appoint a guardian to look after any children you are responsible for, in case you and your spouse die together.

- You have several children and you want to provide the opportunity for one specific child to buy, have an option to buy, or receive in the will the house, business, or farm or a specific possession or asset of your estate, and you want to set up the appropriate procedures and wording to enable your wishes to occur.

When viewing your own situation at this point, or where you project your circumstances might be in the near future, there could be at least one, if not many different reasons to consult with a legal expert on the topic of wills customized for your needs and wishes.

Using a Trust Company

A trust company can offer extensive services related to wills and estate planning, generally in conjunction with a lawyer of your choice or one recommended by the trust company. Always make sure that you obtain independent legal advice. A trust company can administer a trust set up as part of your estate planning or act as your executor. Everyone's needs vary and after obtaining advice you may not require a trust company. Compare a minimum of three trust companies before deciding whom to deal with. The decision is a critically important one, and you want to feel confident in your choice. Look in the Yellow Pages of your phone book under Trust Companies.

Make Sure Your Canadian Will Is Valid in Your Snowbird State

The following explanation is general in nature. You should seek professional advice customized to your specific situation, from a U.S. and a Canadian lawyer skilled in wills, to ensure that there is no conflict of wills. In particular, when you are dealing with the issue of more than one will, the situation is fraught with potential perils, unless your U.S. and Canadian lawyers coordinate the contents of each will and any amendments to them.

In general terms, if you have a valid will which is legally enforceable in your province, it would probably also be valid in the U.S. state in which you have assets.

There could be a serious problem if you have two wills. Because there are different legal jurisdictions between Canada and the U.S., there could be, in theory, a challenge about the contents of the will by a beneficiary (or someone who would like to be one), in one will jurisdiction but not in the other one. Another point is that standard boilerplate clauses in wills state that the most recent will automatically revokes any and all previous wills. You can imagine the problem in that case, if you inadvertently included that clause in a U.S. will. It would automatically nullify your Canadian will!

There are other options to consider for your Snowbird assets that might be more appropriate for your needs. One option is for your Canadian lawyer to include specific terms in your Canadian will relating to your U.S. Snowbird property, and have affidavit attestation of the witnesses of your will at the same time. All this must be done in conjunction with feedback from a U.S. lawyer expert in will matters in your Snowbird state. Another option is to have a U.S. lawyer transfer your U.S. property and other assets into joint names, with right of survivorship, so that your assets in your Snowbird state would automatically go to your surviving spouse and bypass probate. A further option to consider is to have your Snowbird property in a living trust or revocable trust. This bypasses your estate, and therefore probate procedures, as the trust is not in the deceased's name, but a trustee's name. Check into the pros and cons of these options in your personal situation.

As mentioned earlier, if your will has been correctly executed in your provincial jurisdiction and has the appropriate clauses, then it should be valid for your assets under the laws of your Snowbird state. It could then be admitted to probate, once the court has been satisfied that the will has been properly witnessed. If you do not have any assets in the U.S. because you are renting, the issue of a valid U.S. will is not applicable, as there would be no U.S. probate procedures on death.

GRANTING POWER OF ATTORNEY

Many lawyers draft a power of attorney at the same time that they prepare a will. The purpose of a power of attorney is to designate a person or a trust company to take over your affairs if you can no longer handle them (because of illness or incapacitation, for example). This is normally referred to as an "enduring power of attorney." Another reason is that you may be away for extended periods on personal or business matters or on a vacation. You may want to give someone the authority to sign documents on your behalf regarding the sale of your home while you are away. This is normally referred to as a "specific power of attorney," which is limited in scope and time. Considering the benefits of a power of attorney is important if you have substantial assets that require active management. You can revoke the power of attorney at any time in writing.

If you do not have a power of attorney and are unable to manage your financial affairs because of illness, accident, or mental infirmity, an application has to be made to the court by the party who wishes permission to manage your affairs. This party is referred to as a committee. If another family member does not wish to take on this responsibility, a trust company can be appointed, with court approval. Committee duties include filing with the court a summary of assets, liabilities, and income sources, along with a description of the person's needs and an outline of how the committee proposes to manage the accounts or structure the estate to serve those needs. In addition, continuing asset management is required to meet any changes in circumstances or needs, as well as record-keeping and accounting functions, all subject to the direction of the court.

Make Sure Your Power of Attorney Is Valid in Your Snowbird State

How valid your Canadian power of attorney (PA) is in your Snowbird state, if you suffer a stroke or are otherwise incapacitated, depends on the terminology of the PA. There are two main types of PAs. One type would not be recognized in Florida, for example, and the other one might be. If you have a PA that gives someone a specific right to act on your behalf within a certain time period (e.g., selling a house in Canada for you), that is one type of PA. If you have a PA that gives someone authority to look after all your affairs if you are incapacitated, that is another type of PA. It is the second type that you have to be careful of, in terms of the terminology in any Snowbird states.

If it is a contingent (or non-enduring) PA, that is, it only takes effect when and if you become incapacitated, it is *not* recognized in Florida. If you have a "durable" PA, sometimes referred to in Canada as an "enduring" PA, then that type of PA *could* be valid in Florida. In that type of PA, you are appointing someone to be an attorney now, but it survives incapacity or disability—the premise being that if you give someone the right to act on your behalf, you have to have the right to revoke that if you are mentally capable, unless the specific terminology in the PA deals with the issue of incapacity (e.g., enduring or durable). Naturally, all PAs terminate at death, when your will takes over.

Even if your Canadian PA is technically acceptable in Florida it may not be functionally useable. That is because the people who are being asked to accept the PA (e.g., transfer or sell property) will be naturally concerned and cautious about its validity and could refuse to recognize it because they are not familiar with the terminology or the content of the document. The more remote the area, the greater the chance of rejection. For example, if you have a Florida PA, dealing specifically with your Florida property and assets, and it is on a statutory form, accepted and approved by the Florida government (the standard form came out in 1995), then naturally that will make a huge difference in acceptance. It costs approximately CDN$200–$300 to have a Florida PA drawn up by a lawyer.

Although this example referred to Florida, the guidelines and cautions would be pertinent to consider for other popular Snowbird states, such as Arizona, Texas, or California. You can see why you need to get legal advice from a lawyer in the U.S. state in which you have assets. You also want to check with your Canadian lawyer to make sure there is no conflict between your PAs in each country.

SELECTING AN EXECUTOR OR TRUSTEE

One of the most important decisions you will make is your choice of executor to fulfill your instructions in your will. Your executor acts as your personal representative and deals with all the financial, tax, administrative, and other aspects of your estate, including assembling and protecting assets, projecting future cash needs, handling all tax requirements, distributing the assets of the estate, and acting as a trustee for the continuing management of the assets of your estate. As you can see, it would be difficult to find a layperson or family member who would have the range of skills and expertise needed to adequately fulfill all the functions that might be required. An executor should either be an expert or retain specialists in potentially diverse areas such as law, income tax, real estate, asset evaluation and management, accounting, financial administration, and insurance. Not only can the process be time-consuming and complicated, it can also expose the executor to personal legal liability if errors are made. The executor is accountable to all beneficiaries.

Selecting an Executor

A will takes estate planning only so far. It is up to the executor to settle the estate to the satisfaction of the beneficiaries. Generally, there are two kinds of executors. One type is the professional executor, such as a lawyer, accountant, or trust company. The other type is the inexperienced layperson, generally a relative or family friend familiar with your personal life.

Many people consider being asked to be an executor an honour, a reflection of the trust and respect in the relationship. Unfortunately, in the emotional context of a death, conflicts can and do occur between executors and beneficiaries. The conflicts can arise if the executor is perceived as being overzealous or indifferent, being authoritarian or showing favouritism, lacking necessary knowledge, making decisions too hastily, or lacking tact, sensitivity, or insight in dealing with people.

An executor can retain the services of a lawyer, of course, and use a trust company as an agent. Another possibility is to appoint a co-executor. If the will names more than one person to administer the estate, they are referred to as co-executors. They have equal rights and responsibilities in administering the estate. For example, you could consider having a spouse and a trust company as co-executors. In addition, if you are naming an individual as an executor or a co-executor, make sure you have an alternative executor in the event the first one is unwilling or unable to act.

Selecting a Trustee

You may want to set up trusts that are operable during your lifetime. These are generally called *inter-vivos* trusts. You need to have a trustee manage the trust. Another type of trust is one that is operable upon your death, as outlined in your will. This is generally referred to as a testamentary trust.

Through your will, you can appoint an individual or trust company to administer assets of your estate that you identify for later distribution. For example, you may wish to appoint a trustee to manage a portion of your assets for an extended period of time. If you are selecting a layperson to be the executor, you may not want the same person to be the trustee. There could be a potential conflict of interest for various reasons, and different skills could be required.

You can also set up trust funds in a variety of ways, depending on your objectives. You may want the beneficiaries to have regular monthly payments of the income generated from the original capital of trust money. This could be the situation if you are leaving money to an educational or charitable organization. Or you could have that monthly payment provision in favour of a surviving spouse, with the stipulation that payments cease if he or she remarries. The remaining capital goes elsewhere.

If you are setting up a trust for young children, payments are usually made to parents or guardians for the maintenance and education of the child. For such a trust, there should be a provision allowing the trustee to deplete the capital of the trust fund, as required, to meet the needs set out in the trust provisions. Another option is to invest the trust funds until a specified time and then release the total funds. For example, if a child has been financially irresponsible, you may wish to have the funds held until he or she is more mature, say, 35 or 40 years old. If you wish to keep a gift in your will secret, there are various ways of doing that. Speak to a lawyer who is experienced in dealing with trusts.

Trustees are normally given the power in the will to undertake many duties, including taking in money, investing money, selling assets, and distributing the estate proceeds in accordance with the trust terms.

It is important the trustee maintain a balance between the interests of income beneficiaries and beneficiaries subsequently entitled to the capital. In addition, a trustee should maintain accounts and regularly issue accounting statements and income tax receipts to beneficiaries, make income payments to beneficiaries, and exercise discretion on early withdrawal of capital where permitted, to meet special needs of beneficiaries. Finally, the trustee makes the final distribution of the trust fund to beneficiaries on the death of the income beneficiary and/or when beneficiaries reach a certain age designated in the terms of the will, or based on other conditions in the will.

You can see why trust companies perform a vital role. An individual may not have the long continuity required, because of death or lack of interest or ability, for the 10, 15, 20, 25 or more years required. It is an onerous role to place on an individual. The benefits of using a trust company are discussed in the next section of this chapter (see page 206).

Fees and Expenses

There are various fees associated with probating a will, settling an estate, or dealing with a trust. If you die in the United States and have assets there, such as a condo, you would have probate in both countries with a duplication in costs. The main costs are as follows:

a) Compensation for Executors/Administrators

In most cases an executor or administrator is entitled to a fee for his or her time and services provided. The maximum fee is normally 3 to 5 percent of the value of the estate. The beneficiaries or the court must approve the accounts prepared for compensation, and the amount comes out of the estate. An executor who is also a beneficiary could be denied a fee unless the will makes it clear that the gift to the executor is given in addition to, not instead of, executor's fees.

b) Legal Fees

A lawyer can assist in locating and collecting assets, make any necessary application to court and prepare related documents, get the assets transferred into the name of the executor or administrator, prepare accounts, distribute funds, obtain releases, and file tax returns.

Legal fees are considered a proper expense and may be paid out of estate funds, subject to approval of the court or the beneficiaries. A lawyer may charge a fee for itemized services rendered or a lump-sum fee of generally up to 2 percent of the value of the estate for certain basic services. This is a maximum percentage, not a standard rate. If any legal issue arises, such as the validity or meaning of a will, or if an application to the court is made, legal fees will be extra and are normally billed out at the lawyer's hourly rate. This could be over $200 an hour.

c) Probate Fees

These are also known as court fees. They are established by provincial or state legislation. They do not form part of the executor's compensation, nor do they include legal fees associated with administering the estate. The probate fees can range from low to high, depending on the province or state. Check with a Canadian and a U.S. lawyer. The value of the estate is used as a base when determining the probate fee. It is paid to the provincial and/or state government.

d) Trustee Fees

These would generally be negotiated separately, especially if a trust company is involved, and confirmed in writing.

e) Additional Fees and Costs

Naturally, income-tax-related costs and financial costs are extra.

If a beneficiary of the estate thinks that the administration fee charged by an executor is excessive, he or she can ask the executor to "pass accounts" in a court of law. The executor must present an accounting of the work done to the court and ask a judge to set the fees. The final fee may be higher or lower than the fee that the executor initially requested. When beneficiaries are infants or children, the executor may be required to pass accounts because minors cannot give their approval for the actions of the executor. If the executor or beneficiary believes that the legal fees are excessive, they can be challenged. This is called "taxing" a lawyer's account. The account is generally taxed before the registrar at the courthouse. Procedures may differ in your community.

Selecting the right executor for your needs will enhance the smooth disposition of your assets and the administration of your estate. It will also reduce the stress your family will be under. Selecting the wrong executor for your needs will result in the opposite outcome. To be on the safe side, use a professional to act as an executor or trustee, or appoint a family member to be a co-executor or co-trustee if the circumstances warrant it or you wish that to occur. Remember to shortlist three prospects and/or trust companies before you decide who will act as your executor and/or trustee.

BENEFITS OF USING A TRUST COMPANY AS EXECUTOR OR TRUSTEE

Many people prefer to name a trust company in the will as their executor for a variety of reasons. Compare these benefits to the capabilities of a personal friend, relative, or family member acting as an executor in your situation.

1. Experience and Expertise in Will and Estate Planning

A large portion of any trust company's operation involves acting as an executor. A trust company's staff can regularly advise you about coordinating the contents of your will with the other financial affairs, needs and personal changes in your life, since they are closely interrelated, and in conjunction with your legal and tax advisors. This broad expertise should enable the trust company to administer the estate economically and efficiently. Part of estate planning involves establishing objectives for estate distribution, taking into consideration any legislation concerning provision for dependants. In addition, planning involves determining what taxes would be payable by the estate or beneficiaries and considering procedures for minimizing or providing for these taxes.

2. Continuity of Service

The appointment of a trust company ensures continuity of service during the full period of administration of the estate. This is particularly important if the estate involves a trust responsibility that might have to be administered for many years (e.g., if young children are the beneficiaries). A trust company will designate only their most experienced staff to deal with the administration of estates. The staff must combine both business ability and capacity for human understanding and empathy. These qualities enable them to deal tactfully and fairly with each beneficiary.

3. Accessibility

A trust officer is assigned a specific estate and is personally responsible for providing customized and responsive service.

4. Full Attention to the Needs of Your Estate

With a trust company as executor, the operation of estate administration is smooth, since infrastructure and continuity exists. If a layperson is an executor, that person's attention to the executor duties may be influenced by other personal interests, age, ill health, procrastination, or excessive stress due to the demands of fulfilling expectations in an area where he or she has no experience, expertise, or interest.

5. Portfolio Management

A trust company can provide expertise for your estate's investment needs, such as cash management or operating a business.

6. Ensuring Control When That Is Important

There could be instances when a professional, neutral, and experienced executor or trustee must deal with issues in the will that require an element of control—for example, releasing funds over time to a child who is an adult but lacks financial responsibility. Another example is managing a business until the appropriate time to market and sell it. Trust companies have access to this type of expertise and can competently deal with any situation that might come up.

7. Confidentiality

Trust company staff are trained to treat the estate administration and related client business in the strictest confidence.

8. Sharing of Responsibility

If you decide to name a friend or relative as joint executor, the trust company assumes the burden of the administration but works together with your other executor to make joint decisions.

9. Financial Responsibility and Security

Most trust companies in Canada are well established and are backed by substantial capital and reserve accounts. Reputable trust companies also strictly segregate estate assets from general funds. In addition, a trust company is covered by insurance if there is a mistake or oversight due to negligence or inadvertence.

10. Funding Capacity

A trust company can work with your family to provide for their immediate financial requirements and needs immediately after your death.

11. Specialized Knowledge

Because of the increasingly complex nature of an estate, as well as a wide variety of options available, a trust company employs a staff of experts to review and advise on matters that arise. Specialists offer expertise in tax, legal, insurance, investment, and other areas.

12. Ability to Act as a Trustee

This means that the trust company protects your interests after you die. For example, the company might manage your investments or capital and make payments to designated beneficiaries as required over time. If there are minor children, children from a previous marriage, or situations in which the estate assets have to be controlled for an extended period of time, for example, a trustee could be giving out necessary funds from your estate over a period of 20 years or more.

13. Group Decisions

If vital matters come up that involve a major decision, a trust company will use the collective expertise of a variety of senior staff and specialists to arrive at a decision.

14. Fees and Savings

Most trust companies will enter into a fee agreement at the time your will is prepared. Trust company fees are determined by legislative guidelines and the courts, in most provinces. The same guidelines also apply to a private executor. There can also be savings due to efficiency by having an experienced trust company perform the executor duties. This would not, of course, include fees involved in regular estate management or the maintenance of trusts set up during the will planning process and included in the will. Obtain quotes from the trust company.

15. Avoidance of Family Conflict

In any family situation there could be personality or ego conflicts, or friction due to issues dealing with control, power, money, distribution of family possessions or assets, resentment due to past financial favours to certain children or forgiveness of loans to others, unequal distribution of the estate to family members, or a multitude of other potential conflict areas. A trust company acts as a neutral, objective, and professional catalyst in resolving potential disagreements affecting the estate. Based on practical experience, a trust company understands and anticipates the many personal, financial, and emotional dynamics at work following a death and during the administration of the wishes set out in the will.

16. Peace of Mind

It eliminates stress to know that your estate will be administered competently, professionally, promptly, and in accord with your stated wishes. An experienced trust company can provide this peace of mind and feeling of security.

There are clear advantages to using the services of a trust company in many situations, not only to act as an executor, but also to act as a trustee. As mentioned earlier, you may wish to appoint a spouse or family member as a co-executor or co-trustee in certain situations. Always have your own lawyer, from whom you can obtain independent legal advice on will or trust matters. Make sure your lawyer has expertise in this area.

ESTATE PLANNING AND TRUSTS

Reasons for Estate Planning

Estate planning refers to the process required to transfer and preserve your wealth in an orderly and effective manner. Trusts are often at the centre of the strategic planning process. There are many types of trusts. A living trust, referred to as an *inter-vivos* trust, is established while the creator of the trust is still alive; these are very common. Trusts are set up with various instructions and conditions that the trustee must follow. There are tax and non-tax reasons for setting up a trust. A trust enables you to set aside money for a specific person or beneficiary under specific conditions. It is a powerful instrument, and great care must be taken in setting one up, since it enables you to exercise "control from the grave." Trusts vary widely. Some give the trustee wide discretion; others are rigid. Once again, a properly drafted will is the foundation of a strategic estate plan.

From a tax perspective, your estate planning objectives include:

- Minimizing taxes on your death so that most of your estate can be preserved for your heirs and

- Moving any tax burden to your heirs to be paid only upon the future sale of the assets.

There are various techniques for attaining the above objectives. Some of these are:

- Arranging for assets to be transferred to family members in a lower tax bracket

- Establishing trusts for your children to maximize future tax savings

- Setting up estate freezes, generally for your children, meaning that you reduce the tax they pay in the future on the increased value of selected assets

- Making optimal use of the benefit of charitable donations, tax shelters, holding companies, or dividend tax credits and

- Taking advantage of special income tax options to minimize tax or payments on your present assets.

Federal and provincial governments are always looking for ways of increasing revenue. One way is to tax what has been exempted before. Proper estate planning can anticipate these events and therefore reduce, delay, or save tax.

Stages of Estate Planning

Estate planning is a continuing process, as your circumstances, needs, and wishes change. Regardless of your age, the issue of estate planning, in conjunction with your will, is an essential element of life planning. There are different stages in a person's life, though, when certain issues may arise that require different estate planning strategies.

In the later stages of life, you could be approaching retirement or already be retired. As you get older, there could be health concerns or medical needs that you or your spouse have. Your assets are probably at their peak. Your children may be married and may or may not need your financial support. Alternatively, you may have a child who is out of work, divorced or separated and requires financial support. Here are the basic steps you want to consider:

a) Assess your financial status and your personal needs, goals, priorities, and wishes

If you are reading this book, you are probably already a Snowbird or plan to become one. You may also want to do a lot of travelling by car, RV, or other means. You may wish to sell your existing home and move to a condominium in a quiet, retirement-oriented community in Canada or the United States with activities that challenge and stimulate as well as provide a socializing dimension. Many people "cash out" by doing this; in other words, they have so much equity in their home that after their new purchase they still have lots of money left. If you are considering any of the above real estate options, refer to Chapter 5. Complete Appendix C, a checklist for retirement, financial, and estate planning.

b) Review your will

You need to balance the needs of your spouse against those of your children. You may wish to enjoy your lifestyle and retirement fully and leave whatever is left to your children. Alternatively, you may wish to leave a trust for your grandchildren or give additional money to a favourite charity or other worthwhile cause. If your children are already financially independent, these options may be attractive to consider. You may want to completely disinherit a child for other reasons. Make sure your lawyer words the will carefully to minimize the chance that it could be contested.

c) Reconsider your executor and trustee

Make sure that your executor will completely fulfill your needs. For a variety of reasons, an immediate family member or relative may not be the best choice as executor or trustee. For example, there could be personality conflicts between someone chosen as executor or trustee and other members of the family. You may therefore wish to retain a trust company to act as your executor and trustee. You could name a responsible family member as a co-executor and co-trustee.

d) Obtain professional advice on minimizing taxes

The issue of tax is always an important one, and the size of your estate can have considerable tax consequences. Federal and provincial income taxes are due when you die. There are tax consequences of having U.S. assets, but there are steps you can take in advance to minimize or eliminate them; refer to Chapter 7. Unless you have taken steps to minimize taxes on your death, taxes could seriously deplete your estate. Obtain advice from your lawyer, professional tax accountant, and trust company.

Reducing Probate Fees and Taxes

Assets of your estate that are passed on through your will and go through the probate process are subject to probate fees. Some provinces have a ceiling, whereas other provinces do not. As a reminder, whenever an executor asks the court to confirm or validate the executor's right to deal with an estate, the executor applies for what is referred to as a Grant of Probate. This permits the executor to deal with the assets of the estate. At the time that this formal confirmation is made, the probate fees are due. If the executor did not go through this legal confirmation process, many people, regulatory or government agencies, or banks could become concerned that the will is invalid or that there could be a later will, and thus they refuse to recognize the executor's authority. Even if no will exists, the courts must formally and legally confirm the authority of an administrator to administer the estate, and a probate fee must still be paid.

You can minimize the amount of probate tax paid by removing assets from your estate. Clearly, if after professional consultation you choose to do this, you must be sure to leave enough assets or funds in your estate to pay the tax. These strategies have to be viewed, though, in the context of your overall estate plan. For example, if you have a business, part of your estate plan could be to place most of your assets beyond the reach of potential creditors.

In addition, you may not want certain assets to remain in the estate, since these could be frozen pending the probate of the estate. Obtain professional advice from your lawyer, accountant, and trust company on the various issues that concern you, such as relinquishing control, your marital situation (particularly if you are separated or living common-law), whether you have children, tax consequences, legal or creditor considerations, and many other issues. There are some key techniques to move assets out of an estate before death or to automatically transfer them directly to a beneficiary at the time of death, thereby avoiding going through the will and probate. For example:

- Register property jointly so that it automatically passes to the survivor and not through the estate. In other words the asset is not affected by the will. Examples are a joint tenancy in real estate or a joint bank account.

- Designate beneficiaries on your life insurance policies, RRSPs, RRIFs, annuity programs, and employee pension plans. If you are designating beneficiaries, check to see if you can easily change the beneficiary during your lifetime (without the consent of the beneficiary). This could be relevant in case of a marital estrangement. Some provinces don't allow you to name a beneficiary of an RRSP.

- Establish trusts during your lifetime to transfer title to property before your death.

The main financial purpose of an estate plan is to keep taxes and expenses as low as possible and pay as much as possible to your beneficiaries. You don't want to automatically make decisions as described just to reduce probate fees when other strategies could better suit your overall estate planning objectives:

- Using a testamentary trust to split income among your beneficiaries. This type of trust operates through the provisions of your will at the time of your death.

- Using the $500,000 capital gains deduction for the sale of shares in a privately held Canadian business by selling the asset to family members and thereby crystallizing the tax-free gain while you are still alive. This is assuming you have not already used $100,000 of it as your personal tax exemption in the past. Collateral documentation for you to retain control of the operation or management of the business could be negotiated and signed, including the remuneration package. This deduction is still available, but could be changed in any federal budget.

- Using strategies to protect certain family assets, in a marital breakdown, from being deemed to be marital property. This is relevant if you have married a second time and wish to protect the interests of the children of the first marriage, as well as the rights of your second spouse.

Death Benefits Available Through the Canada Pension Plan

A surviving spouse will probably be entitled to two benefits under the CPP. One is called a death benefit and comes in a lump-sum payment, with a ceiling. The second benefit is called the survivor's benefit and depends on the age of the surviving spouse. There is a ceiling per month for a person over 65, and the survivor receives it for life. The survivor is also entitled to his or her own CPP benefits, but the two benefits have a ceiling. Check with your local CPP office for more information. Refer to Chapter 3.

Tips Before Leaving Canada

√ Make sure that your will is current and reflects your wishes.

√ Keep a copy of your will in your safety deposit box, as well as with your lawyer and/or trust company. Tell a close, trusted family member where your safety deposit box is located and who your lawyer is.

√ Review your selection of executor and trustee, and consider the benefits of a trust company for those roles, as sole executor and trustee or co-executor and co-trustee.

√ Have your Canadian lawyer confirm, or confirm with a lawyer in the Sunbelt state you live in, that according to the laws of the state your Canadian will covers any U.S. real estate assets.

√ Consider the benefits of a power of attorney, either to handle specific matters during your absence or to deal with any incapacity on your part.

√ Consider the benefits of a living will. Make sure you have left copies of such a will with key relatives, your spouse, and your doctor. Carry a copy in your purse or wallet and in the glove compartment of your car. It you are seriously ill or in an accident, you want the document to be accessible.

√ Ensure that you have adequately arranged your estate planning needs to reduce probate fees and other taxes.

√ If you do not already have a will or power of attorney, select a lawyer skilled in those areas and have the documents completed before you leave.

√ If you do not already have a professional accountant who is skilled in cross-border tax issues, select one and obtain advice before you depart.

CHAPTER 9

Selecting Professional Advisors

INTRODUCTION

Professional advisors are essential to protect your interests. They can provide knowledge, expertise, and objective advice in areas in which you have little experience. It is important to recognize when it is necessary to call in an expert to assist you. Because of the costs associated with hiring a lawyer, accountant, or financial planner, some people are inclined to try the do-it-yourself approach, but this decision can be short-sighted.

For instance, the person who processes his or her own income tax return may miss out on tax exemptions that could save much more than the cost of an accountant's time. Or a person who does his or her own will or power of attorney could end up having the will or power of attorney deemed invalid because of a technicality. Lack of professional tax and estate planning could mean owing a lot more tax during your lifetime and after your death than is necessary.

Professional advisors you may need include lawyers, accountants, and financial planners. They serve different functions, and you have to be very selective in your screening process.

GENERAL FACTORS TO CONSIDER

There are many factors you should consider when selecting a professional advisor. The person's professional qualifications, experience in your specific area of need, and fee for services are factors you will want to consider. It is helpful to prepare a list of questions about these factors, plus others relating to your specific needs. List the questions in order of priority in case you run out of time. You want to control the agenda. You also want to see if the advisor is proactive—that is, asks you questions rather than being strictly reactive—that is, expecting you to ask all the questions. Some people may feel awkward discussing fees and areas of expertise with a lawyer, for instance, but it is important to establish these matters from the outset, before you make a decision to use that person's services. Some of the most common general selection criteria include the following:

Qualifications

Before you entrust an advisor with your affairs, you will want to know that he or she has the necessary qualifications to do the job. These may include a lawyer's or accountant's professional degree, or if you are looking for a financial planner, professional training accreditation and experience in the person's professed area of expertise. The fact that the person is an active member of a professional association or institute usually means a continuing interest in seminars and courses to keep his or her professional training current.

Experience

It is very important to take a look at the advisor's experience in the area in which you need assistance. Such factors as the degree of expertise, the number of years' experience as an advisor, and percentage of time spent practising in that area are critically important. The amount of reliance you are going to place on someone's advice and insights is obviously related to the degree of experience he or she has in the area. The fact that a lawyer might have been practising law for 10 years does not necessarily mean that the lawyer has a high degree of expertise in the area in which you are seeking advice—for example, real estate law dealing with houses, condominiums, timeshare properties, or immigration. Perhaps only 10 percent of the practice has been spent in that specific area. An accountant who has had 15 years' experience in small business accounting is not likely to have expertise in providing advice on tax planning strategies for individuals living part-time in Canada and the United States. It cannot be overemphasized how important it is to enquire about the degree of expertise and length of experience in the specific area you are interested in. If you don't ask the question, you won't be given the answer that may make a difference between satisfaction and dissatisfaction.

Compatible Personality

When choosing an advisor, make certain that you feel comfortable with the individual's personality. If you are going to have a long-term relationship with the advisor, it is important that you feel comfortable with the degree of communication between the two of you. You should also find out about the advisor's attitude, approach, degree of candour, and commitment to meet your needs. A healthy respect and rapport will increase your comfort level when discussing your needs and will thereby enhance further understanding of the issues. If you don't feel that there is the chemistry you want, don't continue the relationship. It is only human nature to resist contacting someone you don't like, and that could compromise your best interests.

Objectivity

This is an essential quality for a professional advisor. If advice is tainted in any way by bias or personal financial benefit, that advice is unreliable and self-serving. That is why you want to get a minimum of three opinions on your personal situation before carefully deciding which professional to select.

Trustworthiness

Trust is a vital element of your relationship with the person you select to advise you. Whether the person is a lawyer, accountant, financial planner, or other investment advisor, if you don't intuitively trust the advice as being solely in your best interests, do not use that person again. You have far too much to lose in financial security and peace of mind to have any doubts whatsoever. By having a better understanding of how to cautiously select an advisor, you will increase the odds of selecting wisely and developing a relationship with a professional you know will be guided by your needs at all times. You cannot risk the chance that advice is governed primarily by the financial self-interest of the advisor, with your interests as a secondary consideration.

Confidence

You must have confidence in your advisor if you are going to rely on his or her advice to improve your decision making and minimize your risk. After considering the person's qualifications, experience, personality, and style, you may feel a strong degree of confidence and trust that he or she will be totally objective. If you do not, don't use the person as an advisor; seek someone else as soon as possible.

Fees

It is important to feel comfortable with the fee being charged and the terms of payment. Is the fee fair, competitive, and affordable? Does it match the person's qualifications and experience? The saying "You get what you pay for" can be true of fees charged by lawyers, accountants, and financial planners. For instance, if you need a good tax accountant to advise you on minimizing taxes, you may have to pay a high hourly rate for the quality of advice that will save you thousands of dollars.

Most initial meetings with a lawyer, accountant, or financial planner are free or carry a nominal fee. Ask in advance. This meeting provides an opportunity for both parties to see if the advisory relationship would be a good fit.

Comparison

It is important that you not make a decision about which advisor to use without first checking around. See a minimum of three advisors before deciding which one is right for you. You need that qualitative comparison to know which one, if any, of the three you want to rely on. Seeing how they each respond to your list of prepared questions is a good comparison. The more exacting you are in your selection criteria, the more likely it will be that a good match is made and the more beneficial that advisor will be for you.

SELECTING A LAWYER

There are many situations in which you might require a lawyer in Canada or the United States—for example, having to do with wills, living wills, powers of attorney, trusts, estates, buying or selling of real estate, timeshares, leases, contracts, insurance or accident claims, legal disputes, or immigration matters. If you have a business, you will need a lawyer to assist you.

For the most part, you will deal with a lawyer in Canada for the above needs. There are situations, however, in which you would require a U.S. lawyer—for example, if you are buying a condo or timeshare in the United States, or if you are signing legal documents there. In certain situations, your lawyer in Canada would coordinate services with your U.S. lawyer.

Although your lawyer is trained to give legal advice about your rights, remedies, and options, it is you who must decide on the action to be taken.

1. Qualifications

a) Canada

Lawyers in Canada generally have a Bachelor of Laws degree (LL.B.) from a recognized Canadian university and must be licensed to practise by the provincial law society in the province where they are practising.

b) United States

Lawyers in the United States (sometimes referred to as attorneys) have a Juris Doctorate degree (JD) and must be licensed by the state bar association in the state they are practising.

2. How to Find a Lawyer

Methods of finding lawyers include referrals by a friend, a banker, or an accountant, or through the Yellow Pages. There is also an excellent system called a lawyer referral service you should consider.

In Canada, most provinces have a lawyer referral program that is usually coordinated through the Canadian Bar Association. Simply look in the telephone directory under Lawyer Referral Service or contact the Law Society or Canadian Bar Association branch in your province. The initial meeting is usually free or carries a nominal fee (perhaps $10).

In the United States, similar lawyer referral systems are available, operated by the state or local bar association. Look in the telephone directory.

3. Understanding Fees and Costs

Whatever costs a lawyer incurs on your behalf and at your request will be passed on to you as an expense.

There are various types of fee arrangements, depending on the nature of the services provided. To avoid any misunderstanding, always ask about fees at the outset, as well as any applicable federal or provincial or state taxes that are added to those fees.

The main fee options include hourly fee, fixed fee (e.g., for routine services), percentage fee (e.g., for probating an estate up to a certain maximum), or contingency fee (e.g., for a personal injury claim in a car accident; if the lawyer attains a settlement, he or she receives a percentage of that, but if no settlement is made, there is no fee). Only some provinces allow contingency fees.

SELECTING AN ACCOUNTANT

You should speak with a tax accountant to advise you on matters dealing with tax and estate planning, including the possible use of trusts, in order to minimize taxes during your life and tax consequences on your death. Depending on the size and nature of your estate, there could be numerous tax issues and consequences involved.

A Canadian tax accountant will probably meet your needs, if he or she is familiar with the Canadian and U.S. tax consequences of holding U.S. real estate or other investments and dying in the United States. Many large chartered accountancy (CA) firms in Canada have tax experts who are familiar with cross-border tax and estate planning issues. They also have associate offices in the United States. However, you may wish to get a second opinion from a certified public accountant (CPA) in the United States who is a tax expert familiar with U.S. and Canadian tax consequences. To locate such a professional, as well as a CPA who is also an expert on financial planning, refer to the next section in this chapter.

1. Qualifications

a) Canada

In Canada, anyone can call himself or herself an accountant, and even use the title "public accountant" without any qualifications, experience, regulations, or accountability to a professional association. That is why you have to be very careful when selecting the appropriate accountant for your needs. There are two main designations of qualified professional accountants in Canada that could provide tax and estate planning advice: Chartered Accountant (CA), and Certified General Accountant (CGA). Accountants with the above designations are governed by provincial statutes.

b) United States

In the United States, contact a Certified Public Accountant (CPA) for tax and estate planning advice if you have assets in the United States. A CPA is similar to a Chartered Accountant (CA) in Canada. Some CPAs also have a specialty designation in financial planning, for example a Certified Financial Planner (CFP), which could include knowledge of U.S. and Canadian tax and estate planning issues. This is important; otherwise decisions could be made in a vacuum, with adverse tax consequences.

2. How to Find an Accountant

One of the main purposes of having an accountant is to tailor strategic tax and estate planning to your needs. It is therefore prudent to seek advice from a professional accountant who specializes in tax matters exclusively, since tax and estate planning are highly specialized areas. Again, be sure to speak to three different tax experts before choosing an accountant. When you are phoning an accounting firm, ask which accountant specializes in tax and estate planning matters. Most initial meetings are free, without any further obligation. Keep in mind that all professional tax experts do not have the same mindset. Some are very conservative in their advice, whereas others are very bullish. Some enjoy the professional and intellectual challenge of knowing where the fine line is and adopt an aggressive approach to tax planning strategies. Others are more reluctant to do this. In all instances, we are talking about using accredited professional accountants. They have too much to lose to advise you improperly. But you will definitely find differences in style and attitude. The quality and nature of the advice could make a profound difference in the tax and estate savings you enjoy. That is why you need to compare accountants. You will have a much better idea who will meet your needs after you have interviewed three or more accountants.

You can obtain names of accountants and their specialties from their professional associations. Ask for referrals from friends, a lawyer, or a banker. Look in the Yellow Pages. Whatever sources you use, apply the preceding selection criteria.

3. Understanding Fees and Costs

Accountants' fees vary depending on experience, specialty, type of service provided, size of firm, and other considerations. The fee can range between $100 and $200 or more per hour for tax and estate planning advice.

SELECTING A FINANCIAL PLANNER

Some people may wonder if they need to use a U.S. financial planner as well as a Canadian one. It really depends on the circumstances. For the most part, a Canadian financial planner will meet your needs, since you are a resident of Canada and most, if not all, of your assets and investments are in Canada. If you are a U.S. citizen or plan to live in the United States full-time, however, or if you have assets or investments in the United States, then there are cross-border tax and estate planning considerations, and you should obtain tax and legal advice in those areas. There are chartered accountants and lawyers in Canada who have expertise on these issues; refer to pages 219 to 221 amd pages 218 to 219. Also, many Canadian financial planners have a network of tax and legal professionals who are experts in U.S. tax implications and can advise you. The hourly rates for equivalent expertise would be comparable. Getting a second opinion can be reassuring if you get consistent advice. If not, you want to find out why not.

Qualifications

When you are choosing a financial planner, keep in mind that anyone can call himself or herself a planner; no federal, provincial (except for Quebec), state, or local laws require qualifications like those imposed on other professionals, such as lawyers. Several associations and organizations grant credentials that signify a planner's level of education; since criteria can change from time to time, however, check with the association involved. The most common designation in both Canada and the U.S. is the Certified Financial Planner (designation):

Canada

• Certified Financial Planner (CFP)

CFP is an internationally recognized designation used in the U.S., United Kingdom, Australia, New Zealand, and Japan. It was first introduced into Canada in November 1995 by the Financial Planners Standards Council of Canada (FPSCC), a nonprofit organization with the objective of increasing consumer understanding and enhancing the reputation of the financial planning industry.

Obtaining a CFP requires taking various comprehensive financial planning courses. The program takes an average of two years to complete. A six-hour, two-part exam is written. Candidates must also satisfy a work requirement of at least two years in the industry. After the licence is granted, it is renewed annually, as long as the planner follows the code of ethics and completes 30 hours of continuing education each year. If complaints are received by the FPSCC about a planner, and if they prove to be valid and serious, FPSCC has the authority to revoke the CFP designation. The website is: www.cfp-ca.org.

United States

• Certified Financial Planner (CFP)

This designation is earned by people who have been licensed by the International Board of Standards and Practices for Certified Financial Planners, Inc. (IBCFP). The majority of these licensees have taken a self-study program administered by the Denver-based College for Financial Planning. These people must then pass a certification exam over several months to prove their expertise in financial planning, insurance, investing, taxes, retirement planning, employee benefits, and estate planning. In addition to passing the tests, a CFP must possess a certain amount of work experience in the financial services industry, have a defined amount of college education, participate in a continuing education program, and abide by a strict code of ethics. The website is: www.cfp.net.

• Registry of Financial Planning Practitioners (Registered Financial Planner)

The Atlanta-based International Association for Financial Planning (IAFP) has established the Registry of Financial Planning Practitioners. To become a member of the registry, a planner must hold a CFA, CFP, CHFC, or CPA or a degree that has a strong emphasis on financial services, complete a minimum number of hours of continuing education credits every two years, possess three years of experience, and obtain letters of recommendations from clients, among other requirements. Website: www.iafp.org.

• Personal Financial Specialist (PFS)

The PFS is awarded only to people who are already Certified Public Accountants (CPAs). Within the American Institute of Certified Public Accountants (AICPA), those with a PFS concentrate on financial planning. They must be members in good standing of the AICPA, possess at least three years of personal financial planning experience, and demonstrate special expertise by passing a comprehensive financial planning exam. Website: www.aicpa.org.

How to Find a Financial Planner

There are several ways of locating a financial planner. A referral by a friend, accountant, or lawyer is one way. Looking in the Yellow Pages or doing an Internet search is another. One of the most effective ways is to contact a financial planning professional association.

There are several financial planning associations in Canada and the United States that will provide you with names and other educational information.

a) Canada

The Financial Advisors Association of Canada (Advocis)
Tel: (416) 444-5251 or 1-800-563-5822
Website: www.advocis.ca

The association will give you the contact phone number for the chapter in your province, plus consumer information.

b) United States

The Institute of Certified Financial Planners
Tel: (303) 759-4900 or 1-800-282-7526
Website: www.cfp.net

The ICFP represents financial planners who have passed the CFP test. They will refer you to several planners in your area as well as send you free information brochures.

National Association of Personal Financial Advisors (NAPFA)
Tel: (847) 537-7722 or 1-888-333-6659
Website: www.napfa.org

The NAPFA represents financial planners who work for fees only and collect no commissions from the sale of products. They will refer you to planners in your area as well as send you free informational brochures.

American Institute of Certified Public Accountants
Tel: (201) 938-3000 or 1-888-777-7077
Website: www.aicpa.org

The AICPA represents and maintains standards for CPAs. They can help you find a local tax-oriented accountant or an accountant who provides financial planning services and who has a personal financial specialist (PFS) designation. The AICPA will also send you a free copy of various information brochures.

How to Select a Financial Planner

After you've decided to seek the services of a financial planner, you may have other questions: Which professional is right for me? How do I identify a competent financial planner who can coordinate all aspects of my financial life? Just as you select a doctor or lawyer, you should base your decision on a number of factors: education, qualifications, experience, and reputation.

When selecting your financial planner, choose one you can work with confidently. You are asking this person to help shape your financial future, and you are paying him or her to do so. It is your responsibility and right to fully enquire about the planner's background, numbers of years in practice, credentials, client references, and other relevant information.

Once again, it is recommended that you meet with at least three planners before you make your final selection. To work effectively with a planner, you will need to reveal your personal financial information, so it's important to find someone with whom you feel completely comfortable. Research shows that consumers rate "trust" and "ethics" as the most important elements in their relationship with financial advisors. In fact, survey respondents gave this response twice as often as they mentioned good advice and expertise. By asking the following questions, you should get the information you need to make your decision on which financial planner to hire. As you think of others, add them to your list. Keep in mind how the answers fit your personal needs.

Questions to Ask a Financial Planner

- *How long has the planner been working with clients in the comprehensive financial planning process?*
- *What did the planner do before becoming a financial planner?*

Most planners come from fields related to financial services. If he or she started out as a lawyer, accountant, insurance agent, or other specialist, that background will most likely affect the advice the planner gives.

- *What are the planner's areas of expertise?*

Ideally, these should include investments, insurance, estate planning, retirement planning, and/or tax strategies.

- *What services does the planner provide?*

Most planners will help you assemble a comprehensive plan, but some specialize in particular areas of finance. The services you should expect include cash management and budgeting; estate planning; investment review and planning; life, health, and property/casualty insurance review; retirement planning; goal and objective setting; and tax planning. Ask about each service specifically.

- *Who will you deal with regularly?*

You might see the planner only at the beginning and end of the planning process and work with associates in between. Ask if this will be the arrangement, and ask to meet the personnel involved. Also enquire about their qualifications.

- *What type of clientele does the planner serve?*

Some planners specialize by age, income category, or professional group.

- *Will the planner show you a sample financial plan he or she has done?*

The planner should be pleased to show you the kind of plan you can expect when the data-gathering and planning process is complete. Naturally, any plan you are shown would not reveal client names or confidential information.

- *Does the planner have access to other professionals if the planning process requires expertise beyond the scope of the planner?*

Most financial planners are generalists and frequently consult with other professionals from related fields for added expertise in specialty areas. A good planner has a network of lawyers, accountants, investment professionals, and insurance specialists to consult if questions arise.

- *Does the planner just give financial advice, or does he or she also sell financial products?*

As discussed earlier, there are several different types of advisors.

- *Will the planner's advice include only generic product categories or specific product recommendations?*

Some planners will name a particular mutual fund or stock, for example. Others will advise that you keep a certain percentage of your assets in stocks, bonds, and cash, leaving you to assess which bonds, stocks, and money market funds are appropriate.

- *Will the planner spend the time explaining his or her reasons for recommending a specific product and how it suits your goals, circumstances, and tolerance for risk?*

Ask how the planner will monitor a recommended mutual fund or investment product after you've bought it. You should feel comfortable that the planner will ensure that you understand the strategy and products.

- *Will the planner do independent analysis on the products or become dependent on another company's research? Does the practitioner have any vested interest in the products recommended?*

- *How will you follow up after the plan is completed to ensure that it is implemented?*

A good planner makes sure that you take steps to follow your plan. The plan should be reviewed and revised as conditions in your life, tax laws, or the investment environment changes.

- *How is the planner compensated?*

Some planners charge for the advice they give. Others collect commissions from the sale of products they recommend. Some charge both a planning fee and a sales commission. Ask for a written estimate of any fees. An explanation of compensation is covered in the subsection below.

- *Will the planner have direct access to your money?*

Some planners want discretionary control of their clients' funds, which permits the planners to invest at their discretion. You have to be extremely careful, since there is a high degree of potential risk. If you do agree to it, make sure that the planner has an impeccable track record, is bonded by insurance, and is covered by professional liability insurance. Also, limit the amount so that it is within your financial comfort zone and have it confirmed in writing.

- *Are there any potential conflicts of interest in the investments the planner recommends?*

A planner must advise you, for example, if he or she or the planner's firm earns fees as a general partner in a limited partnership that the planner recommends. If the planner receives some form of payment, frequently called a referral fee, when he or she refers you to another firm, you want to know.

- *What professional licences and designations has the planner earned?*

Enquire whether the planner holds an RFP, CFP, CHFC, CA, CGA, CPA, PFS, LL.B., or CFA. Also find out the planner's educational background.

- *Has the planner ever been cited by a professional or governmental organization for disciplinary reasons?*

Even if the planner says that he or she has an impeccable professional track record, you can check with the provincial or state securities office, and the provincial or state financial planning associations.

How a Financial Planner Is Compensated

Generally, financial advisors are compensated in one of four ways: solely by fees, by a combination of fees and commissions, solely by commissions, or through a salary paid by an organization that receives fees. It is important to understand, and be comfortable with, the way your financial planner gets paid—and ensure the planner's compensation method is suited to your particular needs. In some cases, financial advisors may offer more than one payment option. Compensation is just one among many important elements that should figure into your decision about hiring a financial advisor.

Here's how these different methods work:

a) Fee-Only

Many lawyers, accountants, and fee-only financial planners charge an hourly rate, and your fee will depend on how much time the advisor spends on your situation, including time in research, reviewing the plan with you, and discussing implementation options. Others just charge a flat amount. Such planners usually offer a no-cost, no-obligation initial consultation to explore your financial needs. Some ask you to complete a detailed questionnaire and then provide a computerized profile and assessment of your situation and options for a nominal fee that can range from $200 to $500 or more.

Fee-only financial advisors typically advise you on investments, insurance, and other financial vehicles but do not benefit from commissions if you take their suggestions. The advantage of this type of arrangement is that the planner has no vested interest in having you buy one product over another, since there is no financial gain to be made personally from any specific recommendation. Some fee-only financial planners will help you follow through on their recommendations using mutual funds and other investments, if you wish.

b) Commission-Only

Some financial advisors charge no fee for a consultation but are compensated solely by commissions earned by selling investments and insurance plus services necessary to implement their recommendations—for example, a life insurance policy, annuity, or mutual fund. A commission-only advisor will develop recommendations for your situation and goals, review the recommendations with you, and discuss ways to implement these recommendations.

In some cases, the commissions are clearly disclosed—for example, a percentage front-end-load commission on a mutual fund. In other cases, the fees are lumped into the general expenses of the product, as with life insurance, so you won't know how much your planner makes unless you ask him or her. When you interview such a planner, ask him or her approximately what percentage of his or her firm's commission revenue comes from annuities, insurance products, mutual funds, stocks and bonds, and other products. The planner's answers will give you a sense of the kind of advice his or her firm usually gives.

Not only do you pay fees in the form of an upfront charge, but you could also pay regular charges that apply as long as you hold an investment. For example, some insurance companies pay planners trailing fees for each year a client pays the premiums on an insurance policy. In addition, some mutual funds levy fees, which are annual charges of your assets designed to reward brokers and financial planners for keeping clients in a fund.

Some companies reward commission-motivated planners with prizes of free travel or merchandise if their sales of a particular product reach a target level. Other arrangements award planners who attain certain target sales goals with noncash goods and services, such as assistance in paying for investment research.

Your planner might not like your questioning his or her cash payment and other perks. It is your right to know, however, whether the products you buy generate direct fees and indirect benefits for the planner. By knowing the full extent of your planner's compensation, you will be better able to decide whether his or her advice is self-serving or objective.

c) Fee Plus Commission

Some planners charge a fee for assessing your financial situation and making recommendations and may help you implement their recommendations by offering certain investments or insurance for sale. They typically earn a commission on the sale of some of those products.

In some cases, planners are actually captives of one company, so they recommend only its product line. They may have a comprehensive product line or a small one. Other planners are independent and therefore recommend the mutual funds or insurance policies of any company with which they affiliate.

Like fee-only planners, fee-plus-commission advisors may charge a flat fee or bill you based on the amount of time they spend on your situation. Others use a fee scale, varying their fees according to the complexity of your financial situation.

Another form of compensation is called fee offset, meaning that any commission revenue your planner earns from selling you products reduces his or her fee for planning. If you buy so many products that your entire fee is covered, you should request a refund of the fee you paid for your basic plan.

d) Salary

Many banks, trust companies, credit unions, and other companies offer financial planning services. In most instances, the financial advisors on their staffs are paid by salary and earn neither fees nor commissions. There could be other incentives, however, based on the volume and value of the business done, including a raise in salary or a promotion given at an annual performance review. Alternatively, there could be quotas to be met.

All four compensation methods discussed have their advantages. You must choose the method that, combined with the other qualities of the advisor you select, best meets your needs. If you don't understand how your financial advisor is compensated, it's your responsibility and your right to ask.

An advisor who is honest and straightforward about compensation gives you the information you need to make smart financial decisions. Do not consider hiring a financial planner who will not disclose how he or she is compensated.

SELECTING A REALTOR

There are distinct advantages to having a Realtor acting for you in buying a home. As with any profession, you can minimize the risks and benefits greatly by choosing a knowledgeable, experienced, and sincere Realtor. The terms agent, broker, and Realtor are often used interchangeably. You do not pay a commission fee to a Realtor for assisting your purchase. Only the vendor pays the commission.

1. Qualifications

a) Canada

Real estate agents are required to be licensed by their respective provincial governments.

b) U.S.

Real estate agents are required to be licensed by their respective states.

2. Where to Find a Realtor

- Open houses provide an opportunity to meet Realtors.
- Newspaper ads list the names and phone numbers of agents who are active in your area.
- For Sale signs provide an agent's name and phone number.
- Real estate firms in your area can be contacted. Speak to an agent who specializes in the type of property you want and is an experienced salesperson.

3. Selection Criteria

After you have met several agents who could potentially meet your needs, there are a number of guidelines to assist you with your selection:

- Favour an agent familiar with the neighbourhood you are interested in. Such an agent will be on top of the available listings, will know comparable market prices, and can target the types of property that meet your needs.
- Favour an agent who is particularly familiar with the buying and selling of residential and revenue properties.
- Look for an agent who is prepared to pre-screen properties so that for viewing purposes, you are informed only of those that conform to your guidelines.
- Look for an agent who is familiar with the various conventional and creative methods of financing, including the effective use of mortgage brokers.
- Look for an agent to be thorough on properties you are keen on, in terms of background information such as length of time on the market, reason for sale, and price comparisons among similar properties.
- Look for an agent who will be candid with you in suggesting a real estate offer price and explain the reasons for the recommendation.
- Look for an agent who has effective negotiating skills to ensure that your wishes are presented as clearly and persuasively as possible.

- Favour an agent who is working on a full-time basis, not dabbling part-time.

- Look for an agent who attempts to upgrade professional skills and expertise.

- Look for an agent who is good with numbers—in other words, is familiar with the use of financial calculations.

Because of the time expenditure by the agent, you should give the agent your exclusive business if you have confidence in him or her. Keep the agent informed of any open houses in which you are interested. Advise any other agents that you have one working for you. Focus clearly on your needs and provide the agent with a written outline of your criteria to assist in shortlisting potential prospects. If for any reason you are dissatisfied with your agent, find another agent as quickly as possible.

In addition to the MLS, which can provide instant, thorough, and accurate information on properties, an agent could use the Internet as a research tool to assist your search. Without an agent searching for you, you seriously minimize your range of selection and the prospect of concluding the deal at a price that is attractive to you. In many cases, Realtors can refer you to a lender or mortgage broker to assist you in arranging mortgage financing.

4. Types of Realtors

In Canada, there is a structure for the relationship between real estate agents and home buyers and sellers across Canada. In the U.S., this type of option has been in existence for some time. The reason for the clarification of expectations had to do with public confusion as to the roles of a Realtor representing the buyer or the vendor. Many people assumed that if they found a Realtor and the house was listed on the MLS (Multiple Listing System) that Realtor would represent their interests exclusively when an offer was presented and candid financial and negotiating information was shared by the buyer with that Realtor.

The law, however, took a different view, related to the issue of principal and agent. The agent (e.g., Realtor) owed a duty of trust to the seller. Legally, the agent was bound to be completely loyal to the seller, not disclose any information to the prospective purchaser that could compromise the seller's interests, take reasonable care in his actions, etc. Any subagent, e.g., another Realtor involved, was considered to be bound completely to the seller by an extension of the principal/agent law. Hence the confusion. Litigation issues could result because of this confusion, by either the buyer or the seller, against the selling or listing Realtor.

The real estate broker system sets out the respective roles and responsibilities of each Realtor involved. The seller still pays the real estate commission, which is shared with any other Realtor involved. All disclosures of who is acting for whom are spelled out in the agreement of purchase and sale. In some cases, an agent working with the buyer may also enter into a Buyer Agency Contract. In other words, each Realtor is acting exclusively for the benefit of the buyer or seller. There is no confusing perceived overlap. However, if the listing Realtor is also the selling Realtor (double-end deal), the agent has to enter into a Limited Dual Agency Agreement. This is agreed upon and signed by both the buyer and the seller. The agent modifies his or her exclusive obligations to both the buyer and the seller by limiting it primarily to confidentiality as to each party's motivation and personal information.

You can get more information from any Canadian or U.S. real estate agent, real estate company, or your local real estate board.

5. Understanding Fees and Costs

In both Canada and the U.S., it is the seller who customarily pays the real estate commission. The buyer does not. If you are selling, the amount of the commission could vary, as it is negotiable in various circumstances and jurisdictions. It could range from 5 to 7 percent on the first $100,000 purchase price and 2.5 percent thereafter. It could be lower or you could negotiate a flat rate.

OTHER PEOPLE PROVIDING FINANCIAL AND INVESTMENT ADVICE OR INFORMATION

Your first step is to have an objective financial planner assess your current financial situation and needs and give advice on fulfilling your long-term objectives and needs with an integrated and comprehensive financial plan. In many cases, a professional financial planner tries to perform this integration in conjunction with your lawyer and professional accountant, so that all decisions are made in context of the implications it has on legal and tax considerations.

There are other people in the financial and investment area, however, whom you might have dealings with or hear about at some point. Here is a brief summary.

1. Retirement Counsellor

A retirement counsellor specializes in clients who are generally over 50 years of age, that is, nearing retirement or actually retired. Types of investments sold include RRSPs, RRIFs, LIF annuities, GICs, and mutual funds. The main thrust of these investments should be preservation of capital and low or moderate risk.

2. Company Human Resource Personnel

If you have a pension plan from your employer, you should ask the people administering it to provide you with details. Also ask them to assist you in projecting the income you will receive from the plan and, after you retire, what additional benefits, other than pension income, you will be entitled to. Also ask if these benefits are guaranteed or if the employer can withdraw them at any time. Refer to the discussion of company pension plans in Chapter 3.

3. Government Pension Plan Personnel

Check with the federal and provincial governments to see what pension or financial assistance plans you may be currently eligible for, such as OAS, CPP, QPP, or GIS. Refer to Chapter 3 for more detail.

4. Bank, Trust Company, or Credit Union Personnel

These financial institutions have an extensive range of investment products, including mutual funds, GICs, term deposits, Canada Savings Bonds, and so on. With mutual funds, there is generally a wide selection of money market funds, growth funds, income funds, and balanced funds to accommodate people's investment needs and risk tolerance.

The range of training and expertise of bank, trust company, or credit union personnel can vary. Staff members licensed to sell mutual funds can give very helpful advice about the nature and benefits of their particular products. Expect to get general advice, however, not comprehensive advice dealing with all your present and future needs. Many of these institutions have instructive pamphlets to give you a better understanding of general money management strategies.

Many major financial institutions in Canada are expanding into collateral financial services beyond their traditional scope. This is being done through subsidiary companies in areas such as discount stock brokerages, investment portfolio management, estate planning, trusts, and asset management and insurance.

One service provided by most major financial institutions is called private banking services, or something similar. It involves giving customized, personalized, and integrated advice about a mixture of services and products for example, straight banking, investment, wealth management, and trust and estate planning. To be eligible, you have to meet certain criteria, such as having a minimum of net worth and/or liquid assets available for investing. The criteria vary considerably, depending on the institution involved.

5. Insurance Agent or Broker

The primary goal of these advisors is to sell life insurance and other insurance company products such as annuities or segregated mutual funds. As a consequence, you may be limited to building a financial plan around an insurance policy. An agent is a person who sells the products of only one company, whereas a broker can sell the products of any company. Thus, while the recommended solutions offered by an agent could be restricted to a small range of products, an independent insurance broker could offer a wide range of different insurance-related products.

6. Mutual Fund Broker

Since a broker makes a commission on any product sold to you, you have to satisfy yourself that it is the right type of product and the best choice of that product for your needs. A high degree of trust is necessary, as you don't want to feel a broker's recommendation is based on the size of the commission or other special incentives. Be cautious, as a broker may only have a mutual fund licence but promote himself or herself as a professional financial planner.

7. Stockbroker/Investment Advisor

Sometimes stockbrokers refer to themselves as "investment advisors." Although the advice is free, the client pays for it through commissions that his or her accounts generate. Some full-service brokers offer investment advice on a broad range of financial products, such as stocks, bonds, mutual funds, and mortgage-backed securities. Some stockbrokers don't want to deal actively with small investor accounts because of the time involved, but would probably recommend a mutual fund to serve your needs instead.

Many brokerage firms offer "managed" accounts, referred to as "wrap" accounts in the industry. With these accounts, your money is invested in several pooled portfolios, depending on your risk profile, and managed generally by an outside money manager rather than a broker. You normally pay a fixed annual fee, based on a percentage of the value of the money invested.

8. Discount Broker

Although these brokers charge significantly lower commissions than do full-service stockbrokers, they only buy and sell based on your instructions. They do not give advice. Using discount brokers is only a realistic investment option if you know the stock and bond market thoroughly and can take the time to make prudent decisions by understanding and researching the market.

9. Deposit Broker

These individuals generally sell term deposits, GICs, annuities, and RRIFs; in some cases, they are licensed to sell mutual funds.

10. Investment Counsellor

This type of financial advisor generally only deals with wealthy clients wishing to invest a minimum of $250,000 to $1 million. This restriction is due to the time involved to customize and monitor an investment portfolio. (Some investment counsellors will take on a lower investment portfolio.) A management fee is generally a percentage, normally 1 to 2 percent, of the value of the assets in the portfolio. If the management skill results in an increase in value of the client's portfolio, the fee obtained increases accordingly.

Tips Before Leaving Canada

√ Make sure your financial affairs are in good order before you depart.

√ Select objective professional tax, legal, and financial planning advice as your situation and needs dictate before you depart.

√ Seek advice on the various cross-border implications of being a Canadian citizen living part-time in the United States for up to six months.

√ Obtain advice on your various retirement, pension, and investment needs before you head South.

Snowbirding in Mexico

INTRODUCTION

Mexico is a very popular tourist destination and increasingly popular with Snowbirds. Naturally, there are considerable differences between being a seasonal resident in the U.S. and being one in Mexico. But it is precisely these differences that attract those who choose Mexico.

There are many issues to consider when selecting any foreign country as a part-time residence, including language, culture, and regulatory differences. If you don't speak Spanish, you can pick up key words and phrases very quickly. Also, in the popular Snowbird retirement areas, English is frequently spoken. Residing in a foreign country is not for everyone of course; spend some time there as a tourist, investigate the various locations where other Canadian and American Snowbirds reside, and make an assessment. The next step is to try it for part of a season, say a month or so, and rent housing while you are there, or you might have an RV or mobile home.

This chapter is merely the starting point in your extensive research. It includes some popular Snowbird destinations, preliminary factors to consider, entering Mexico, insurance matters, and some other information.

An excellent book to read if you are considering being a Snowbird in Mexico is *Mexico: The Trick Is Living Here*, second edition, by an expat American, Julie Taylor. The book can be downloaded from her website: www.home-sweet-mexico.com.

POPULAR SNOWBIRD DESTINATIONS

The four most prominent areas for Canadian/American Snowbirds in Mexico are:

- Guadalajara (residential areas of Las Fuentes, Chapalita, and Ciudad Buganvilias)
- Lake Chapala (villages of Chapala, Chula Vista, and Ajijic)
- San Miguel de Allende
- Cuemavaca

In addition, there are a few other retirement areas for Snowbirds.

Cuemavaca

Located south of Mexico City, it can be reached over a four-lane mountain highway. Its population is approximately 350,000 At an altitude of 1524m (5,000 feet), the climate of Cuemavaca is ideal. Usual average temperature is 20.5°C (69°F). Nights and early mornings are crisp and cool in December and January—24 to 28 degrees in May. In December and January it gets down to 15 degrees. Northern Cuemavaca is cooler and recieves more rain than the southern area. (Urban growth is causing a noticeble change in the climate—it is getting hotter in the summer and cooler in the winter.) There is a large enclave of retired North Americans who lead active social lives.

Guadalajara

The second-largest city in Mexico, with a population of over 4 million people, Guadalajara has a benign climate, along with a slower pace, but almost as many attractions as Mexico City for the retiree. Flowering trees and shrubs, lovely old churches and residential areas contribute to its beauty. It is in the centre of the breadbasket of Mexico, so food is plentiful and inexpensive. There is a large Canadian/American colony, and living costs are substantially lower than in Mexico City.

Guadalajara has many modern supermarkets, pharmacies, and small shops with a wide variety of American and Mexican products.

Lake Chapala

Chapala is about 40 minutes by car from Guadalajara on a paved highway on the shores of Lake Chapala, the largest lake in Mexico. Originally a lakeshore resort popular among Mexicans, it has also become the locale of a large Canadian/American settlement.

Ajijic, also on Lake Chapala, is a well-known Canadian/American retirement locale. The beauty of this area has spurred the development of many retirement homes.

Oaxaca

The capital city of the state of Oaxaca is one of the least expensive retirement centres in Mexico. It is far from the hustle and bustle of the big cities, but has a population of approximately 130,000, at an altitude of 1524m (5,000 feet) with an average temperature of 20°C (68°F).

San Miguel de Allende

About a three-hour drive north from Mexico City, in the state of Guanajuato, San Miguel has a population of approximately 25,000, with a large number of tourists and retired people during the winter. It is the outstanding model of Spanish colonial architecture in Mexico and is located in a mountain setting. At an altitude of 1950m (6,400 feet), it is colder than Mexico City, with an average temperature of 17.5°C (64°F). There is a fairly active artists' colony with frequent exhibits by local painters. Living costs are considerably lower than in Mexico City.

PRELIMINARY FACTORS TO CONSIDER

Travelling to Mexico

There are direct flights to the most popular Snowbird areas from several points in the United States, or connecting flights from anywhere in the U.S. or Canada through Los Angeles, Dallas, or Houston. The only documents you need to go to Mexico are a valid passport; photo ID, such as a driver's licence; and a tourist visa, which you can fill out on the plane or at the border. You can obtain a tourist visa at your entry point, at the airport, or before your departure. This visa will be valid for the length of your stay in Mexico, up to 180 days, if requested.

Should you decide to drive, there are excellent, modern toll roads. The older thoroughfares can be more time-consuming.

Residential Status

If you decide you want to stay in Mexico for a longer time than permitted by a tourist visa, you have two choices. You can apply for an FM3 permit, which is a temporary residence permit that must be renewed every year, or an FM2 permit, which is a permanent residence permit and allows you to work in the country. You can work with some FM3s, e.g., "non-immigrant with lucrative activities." With both, you are required to have a certain amount of income from the U.S. or Canada, or to have a sufficient amount of investments in Mexico to provide this amount of income. If you own a home in Mexico, the amount is reduced by half for the main applicant. You need to check on the current status of these amounts, as they can change at any time.

Cost of Living

In general, the cost of living in Mexico is much less than in Canada or the U.S., even after devaluation and inflation. Notable items that are much cheaper are medicine (which often can be purchased over the counter without a prescription); medical and home insurance; fresh fruits and vegetables; and wine, beer, and liquor. Foreign residents do not pay any taxes on their income in Mexico. The only tax you would pay is a modest property tax (perhaps CDN$50 to $150 per year), if you buy a home. You need to find out the current rates, as they can change at any time.

Utility costs are also much lower. Electricity will be about CDN$30 per month, because heating and air conditioning are not necessary due to the comfortable weather all year round. The tap water is used for washing and gardening. For drinking purposes, most residents prefer to buy bottled water, delivered in 20-litre (five gallon) containers right to your home. Even Canadian bottled water is available in some stores.

If you bring your Canadian or U.S. car and apply for FM2 or FM3 status, which allows you to keep your foreign-plated car legally in Mexico as long as your residence status is up-to-date, your insurance will cost you CDN$300 to $600 per year. You are not allowed to sell your foreign-plated car in Mexico.

Health Care

You may have wondered about the quality of health care in Mexico. This is a common concern of U.S. and Canadian citizens considering a move south. Snowbirds in Guadalajara, Lake Chapala, and other popular areas can choose from a variety of health care options. For example, there is private medical care, which is very personalized. Another option is enrolling in a medical group that gives access to English-speaking doctors in several specialties. As Canadians are accustomed to a full medicare system in Canada with high standards, you don't want to be disappointed or put your health at risk by using inadequate health services; you should check into the benefits of the private care option thoroughly.

Not only are costs lower, but the risk factor has decreased considerably with the influx of modern equipment and local doctors learning about new treatments and medications. Many doctors have also trained in the United States and speak English well.

Mexico has a nationalized health care system, and almost every town and city in Mexico now has either a national hospital or medical clinic. Before you leave home, check with your health insurance carrier to make sure that your insurance plan will cover you in Mexico. Refer to the medical insurance subsection on page 247. Currently no vaccinations are needed to enter Mexico from the United States or Canada.

In the event of a major medical emergency, medical jet evacuation services are available. Do a Google.com search under the keywords "Air Ambulance." Here are several companies that perform this service (always get competitive quotes):

- American Air Ambulance (www.americanairambulance.com) 1-800-863-0312 or (941) 536-2002.
- Aerocare (www.aerocare.com) 1-800-823-1911 or (630) 466-0900.

However, you want to arrange for out-of-country emergency medical insurance before you leave Canada.

Staying Healthy

You may find that your eating and drinking habits are initially different from the way they were back home. Altitude, climate, and time zone changes also throw your system off during your first few days.

Here are some tips to smooth the transition:

- Take it easy for the first few days.
- Ease into local eating and drinking habits.
- Always wash your hands before eating.
- Drink bottled water.
- Take yogurt or papaya enzyme tablets throughout your stay to act as a buffer for stomach upset.
- When eating from open-air food stands, use discretion.
- Drink plenty of nonalcoholic fluids and do not become dehydrated.
- Take a siesta (nap) each afternoon.

If you have a problem, Mexico has pharmacies (*farmacias*) which dispense prescription drugs at a fraction of their cost back home. Anti-diarrhea drugs like Lomotil are readily available. Obviously, you should consult your physician before taking any prescription drugs.

If you require medicines containing habit-forming drugs or narcotics, take precautions to avoid any misunderstanding. Under Mexican law, possession of illegal drugs is a federal offence. Properly identify all drugs, carry only the necessary quantity, and have with you a prescription or written statement from a physician. These safeguards will also help to avoid potential Customs problems upon return to Canada.

Consular Aid

If, for any reason, you require the aid of a lawyer or consul, there are many bilingual legal aids in Guadalajara, Chapala, and other popular Snowbird areas. As well, both Canada and the United States have consulates in or near key Snowbird areas. Refer to Appendix A.

Money Matters

All the major Mexican banks are represented in the major retirement areas. In most cases, accounts can easily be opened and deposit investments made, at generally higher rates than in Canada or the U.S. Transfers of funds or money exchange can be done fairly efficiently. Mexican bank hours are normally from 9 A.M. to 2:30 P.M., weekdays only. Some branches are open in the afternoon from 4 to 6 P.M. and on weekends. However, banks in Mexico are inconvenient, and you often have to spend at least 45 minutes in line. That is why many Canadians prefer to deal with the same international bank that they deal with in Canada, if possible.

Money is often exchanged at *casas de cambio* (currency exchange houses) that are open longer hours than banks and offer quicker service. The worst exchange rates are at hotels, the best at exchange houses. Expect a slightly lower rate for traveller's cheques. Exchange fees are generally not charged.

You can also access ATMs. For example, Bancomer ATMs are now in the Cirrus and PLUS systems, and offer Spanish/English menus. Many Snowbirds prefer to use bank ATMs for their money needs. Some machines will dispense pesos or dollars. Credit cards are widely accepted, including VISA, MasterCard, and American Express. There is a sales tax of 15 percent applied to the purchase of most items and paid by everyone, residents and visitors alike. Often this tax is included in the purchase price.

ENTERING MEXICO

Mexican Customs

Tourists normally are subject to a brief and informal baggage inspection when entering Mexico. There are limitations and restrictions on what you can bring into the country. Check with your nearest Mexican Consulate. You are allowed to bring in any of the following, but check on the current policy before you depart, as the regulations can change at any time:

- Personal items, such as clothing, footwear, toiletries, all in reasonable quantities according to trip duration
- Medicine for personal use, with a medical prescription in the case of psychotropic substances
- Books and magazines
- One portable TV set, and one computer
- Used or second-hand sporting equipment
- A musical instrument
- Up to 20 CDs
- One camera
- Fishing equipment, a pair of skis, and two tennis racquets
- Three litres of alcohol or wine
- 400 cigarettes or 50 cigars.

Customs declaration forms can be obtained from airlines or at border crossings. Here is how the Customs inspection system works:

- Visitors complete a Customs declaration form provided by the personnel on the airline, in the language preferred by the traveler.
- Visitors declare whether they are importing items beyond their allowance.
- Those declaring items have their belongings searched, and duty is collected.
- Those not declaring items are asked to push a button on a street traffic light that is mounted on a post inside the Customs area. A green light allows you to pass without inspection. A red light will signal an inspection is requested.

In the event that items are found that were not declared, heavy fines and penalties apply.

Documents Required

Your first stop is at Mexican Immigration *(Migración)* where proof of citizenship is inspected, and tourist cards are validated.

Visitors need three items to enter Mexico:

- A photo ID such as a driver's licence
- A valid proof of citizenship, such as a passport and
- A tourist card.

Tourist Card

This two-part document is your "permission" from the Mexican government to visit Mexico. It is available free of charge, and is provided by the personnel on the airline. Here are some tips:

- Do not lose the blue copy handed back to you after the Immigration inspection, as it must be returned on departure. Write down your tourist card number and keep it with your travel documents. If the card is lost, having the number will help greatly.
- Keep your tourist card and travel documents in a secure place.
- You can ask to have your card validated for up to 180 days.

Proof of Citizenship

You will need:

- A valid Canadian passport, which, of course, includes your photo. This is the most recommended document.
- Canadian naturalization papers, showing that you are a naturalized Canadian. It can be the original certificate or laminated card with your photo on it. Photocopies are not acceptable.

Refer to Chapter 4 for more information on the above documents.

Minors

Any person under 18 years of age is considered a minor. Very strict regulations govern travel by minors into Mexico. This may not be relevant to your own children, but could be to your grandchildren or visiting friends with minor children.

- If travelling alone, the minor must have a notarized consent form signed by both parents.
- If travelling with only one parent, the minor must have a notarized letter of consent signed by the absent parent. If a couple is divorced, getting the consent of the former spouse may be difficult.
- If travelling with only one parent and the other parent is deceased or the child has only one legal parent, a notarized statement must be obtained as proof.

INSURANCE MATTERS

There are various important types of insurance to consider, such as auto, out-of-country emergency medical, and legal insurance.

Auto Insurance

Canadian automobile insurance is not valid in Mexico. Only a Mexican automobile liability policy is acceptable as evidence of financial responsibility if you have an accident in that country. Compare the features and limitations of various competitive insurance coverages. Arrange for a policy with full coverage issued through a reliable Mexican insurance company with complete adjusting facilities in cities throughout the country. You can get Mexican auto insurance coverage from various sources, including AAA club offices in U.S. border states. You also need permission to bring the car itself. You leave your credit card number or a deposit as a guarantee that you will remove the car from Mexico at the time that your tourist card expires.

Unlike the U.S. and Canada, Mexican law is based on the Napoleonic Code, which presumes guilt until innocence is proven. As a result, all parties (operators of vehicles) involved in an accident involving injury are detained for assessing responsibility. A Mexican insurance policy is recognized by the authorities as a guarantee of proper payment for damages according to the policy terms. When presented, it can significantly reduce red tape and help to bring about an early release. When you choose an insurance company, choose one that can send an insurer out to the scene of your accident. Make sure that they cover the areas you expect to be travelling in, so that they can smooth things over with the police for you.

All accidents or claims must be reported before leaving Mexico. Only obtain assistance in a claim from an authorized agent or adjuster of the insurance company that issued the policy. Official release papers should be kept as evidence that the case is closed, especially if the car shows obvious damage from the accident.

The Mexican government has no minimum requirement for insurance, but you should get the maximum available, as a precaution.

Legal Insurance for Motor Vehicle Accidents

If detained or arrested for involvement in a traffic accident that involves injury, you should immediately contact the closest Canadian consulate, in Mexico. Refer to Appendix A. Most insurance companies do not cover lawyer's fees to defend the driver against criminal charges, so it is important that you also have legal coverage. Get that phone number when you take out the policy, and keep it with you at all times.

Here are the types of legal coverage and insurance protection services that you would want:

- Legal assistance and defence before any authority until the case is closed
- Release of the driver when arrested or detained due to a traffic accident
- Bail bond provision integrated into your vehicle's liability insurance policy
- Release of your vehicle if impounded
- Your defence in case of a traffic accident in which a third party is involved
- Assistance in case of theft of your vehicle
- Court costs covered and lawyer fees without monetary limit
- Towing and roadside assistance
- 24-hour toll-free telephone number with assistance available in English.

There are several companies that provide auto, RV, and legal insurance coverage.

CAA members can obtain various types of Mexican car or RV insurance coverage from AAA border state offices. You can contact your local CAA office for further information. There are also many other companies providing Mexican insurance coverage that you will see along the border routes. However, it is critical that you scrutinize any coverage closely to know exactly what the features and benefits are, and that you understand them fully. If you do not, ask. As with other important types of insurance, the limitations, deductibles, and exclusions are the determining factors. If you buy based merely on low price, it could be that there are some key elements of protection missing. Do your research thoroughly before you depart, so you can make a decision without time pressure.

Out-of-Country Emergency Medical Insurance Coverage

This is very important coverage. In fact, don't leave home without it. Inadequate coverage could cause you massive financial loss in the event of an emergency, such as a major surgery or hospitalization outside Canada. If you are medically stabilized, it is common for your insurance company to transport you back to Canada by medical jet. The Canadian medicare system then takes over your treatment and care, and the insurance company saves on that expense. Refer to Chapter 6 on Insurance Needs and Options for a detailed discussion of all the issues that you need to know.

In terms of insurance coverage for Mexico, you have a number of options:

a) Worldwide Insurance Coverage, including Mexico

You would purchase this coverage in Canada before your departure. It would cover you in Mexico as well as the U.S. if you had a stopover there and had serious medical problems requiring treatment in the U.S.

b) Mexico Insurance Plus Transit Insurance Through the U.S.

In this case, you would have two separate insurance policies. One would cover you while you are in Mexico, the other while you are travelling in the U.S.

c) Air Ambulance Insurance

Both of the above options have advantages and disadvantages. The most suitable option depends on your research and needs, and an objective comparison of the features, benefits, limitations, exclusions, and deductibles. However, some people prefer to get insurance for air ambulance coverage, in case they may wish to return to Canada that way. This would normally be the route that your insurance company would take, for cost saving. It would be risky for you to attempt to "save" on a regular out-of-country emergency medical insurance premium, on the premise that if you were seriously ill or injured, you would coordinate your own air ambulance return to Canada.

TRANSPORTATION TIPS

Gasoline

Gasoline is available at stations throughout Mexico. As in Canada, gas is sold in litres (3.78 litres = 1 gallon). *Sin* (green pump) is unleaded, and *premium* (red pump) is also unleaded. *Nova* (blue pump) is leaded. Prices are generally cheaper than in Canada. You can pay with a credit card. You sign a receipt that the attendant gives you and must have ID. All PennMex gas stations are open 24 hours all over Mexico.

Roadside Assistance

Major highways are patrolled by Green Angels (*Los Angeles Verdes*). These government-operated green pick-up trucks are driven by mechanics. The service is free, except for parts and gas. Make sure that your auto insurance includes roadside assistance in case the Green Angels are off duty (generally after 8 P.M.).

Road Travel Guidebooks

Due to the variety of highways and terrain throughout Mexico, a guidebook will maximize your trip enjoyment. Contact your CAA branch for AAA guidebooks on Mexico (free to members).

Travel by Bus

Bus trips in Mexico are inexpensive and convenient. It's so much easier just to take buses and taxis when you get to Mexico. Some Canadians might assume that they will need a car and not even consider the buses. With buses you just get on and relax. You don't have to worry about car-related insurance, costs, or stress. You reduce risks and you see more of Mexico because you travel with Mexicans. Most good travel guides will have the bus information included in them. Of course, it all depends on your lifestyle and what option is most comfortable for you.

Just go to the bus station. In larger towns there may be more than one, so you can ask at your hotel or look in a travel guide to learn the name of the one you want. Tell the taxi driver to take you to the station. When you get there look on the boards behind the ticket counter for the destination you want. The times of depature are listed too. From city to city there are departures every 30 minutes to one hour. For closer destinations there may be one or two buses per day, but so many people use the buses that they can tell you when the bus leaves.

BUYING MEXICAN REAL ESTATE

New Regulations

Under the Mexican constitution, foreigners may not hold title to property within the restricted zone—that is, within 50 kilometres of any coastline. To circumvent this limitation, the Mexican Congress has implemented a system whereby Mexican banks acquire the property and place it in trust for the sole "use and enjoyment" of a beneficiary. This includes the right to resell the property at fair market value any time during the trust. Terms of the trust usually extend to 50 years, renewable in 50-year increments.

Mortgages for Mexican Real Estate

Mortgage capital is now being made available to Canadians and Americans acquiring property in Mexican resort destinations. Canadian and U.S. banks have traditionally been reluctant to provide mortgage financing on trust property because of their inability to obtain title, along with potential difficulties with foreclosing in a foreign country. And Mexican banks have not entered the field due to a lack of available capital. Purchases have therefore been limited to investors with sufficient resources to buy real estate without financing.

This situation has changed recently. There are several American mortgage firms offering financing for up to 70 percent of the appraised trust amount. Interest rates vary, yet most are between 2 and 3 percent above the prevailing Canadian rate, for amortization terms up to 15 years. The trust is itself sufficient collateral and a simple notation is made on the Mexican trust to protect the lender. Always check on the current market options, as laws and regulations can change at any time.

Some mortgage firms require an application fee of 1.5 percent while others ask for a flat US$250 registration. Mortgage documents are signed in Canada or the U.S. and the promise to pay is considered to have originated in Canada or the U.S. for legal purposes. Documentation is in English, but all Mexican transactions must be done in Spanish.

Getting Legal Advice

You should use the services of a Mexican lawyer skilled in real estate matters before signing any documents or paying any money. This is wise even in Canada, but especially so in a foreign country with different laws and procedures.

To obtain the name of a lawyer, contact the Canadian Consulate or Mexican Tourism Office in the city you are thinking of buying real estate. Refer to Appendix A for contact information.

BRINGING BACK GOODS FROM MEXICO

The *North American Free Trade Agreement* (NAFTA) continues to gradually eliminate the duty that applies to goods you acquire in Mexico. Your goods qualify for the lower Mexican duty rate under NAFTA if they are for personal use and marked as made in Mexico or Canada or not marked or labelled to indicate that they were made anywhere other than in Mexico or Canada.

If you do not qualify for a personal exemption or if you exceed your limit, you will have to pay the goods and services tax (GST) over and above any duty or other taxes that may apply on the portion not eligible under your personal exemption.

Personal exemptions

You are entitled to the basic duty- and tax-free exemptions of CDN$750 for absence outside Canada a minimum of seven days. In addition, you can benefit from the low special duty rate if you exceed your personal exemption limit. This special duty rate applies to the next CDN$300 worth of goods when you exceed your $750 exemption, as long as these goods accompany you and are not alcohol or tobacco products. Pick up a copy of the Canada Revenue Agency brochure called *I Declare* for more information.

Prohibited, restricted, or controlled goods

Canada limits or prohibits the importation of certain goods. These can include cultural property which has historical significance in its country of origin, animals on the endangered species list (and any products made from them), certain foodstuffs and agricultural products, and goods considered harmful to the environment.

There are also limits and restrictions on the amount of meat and other products you can bring into Canada from Mexico. For more information, contact your Canada Revenue Agency Customs office.

Alcohol and tobacco

You can import alcohol and tobacco products only if you meet the minimum age requirements of the province or territory of entry, and if the quantity is within the limits the province or territory sets.

You cannot import alcohol or tobacco products duty-free and tax-free unless you have been outside Canada for at least 48 hours and qualify for a personal exemption. If you do not qualify, or if you exceed your limit, you will have to pay not only the import duties, but also the provincial or territorial taxes and levies that apply on the portion not eligible under your personal exemption.

Making your declaration

By preparing a list of all the goods you have acquired in Mexico, and by keeping sales receipts, you will find it easier and faster to fully declare all these goods when you return to Canada. You will also find it easier to claim any personal exemption to which you are entitled. When you present your list and receipts, the Customs officer can then work out your personal exemption and any duties you owe in the way that benefits you most.

Paying duties

You can pay by cash, traveller's cheque, VISA, MasterCard, or personal cheque if the amount is not more than $500. In some cases, Canada Revenue Agency may accept a personal cheque for up to $2,500 as long as you can produce adequate identification.

Value of goods

Canada Revenue Agency will include any taxes you have paid on your goods when determining their value, and will use the prevailing exchange rate to convert the total to Canadian funds. The Customs officer will calculate this duty.

Goods and services tax (GST)

With the exception of goods you include in your personal exemption, GST applies to your goods as if you had purchased them in Canada. GST is payable on the "value for tax," which is made up of the value (discussed above), plus the duty, and any applicable excise tax.

General Agreement on Tariffs and Trade (GATT)

Mexico is part of the *North American Free Trade Agreement* (NAFTA). Goods from Mexico also qualify for the GATT rate, so if the rate of duty payable on the goods you are importing is lower under GATT than under NAFTA, Customs officers will automatically assess the lower rate. For more information on GATT and the current laws and regulations, contact the Canadian Customs office.

Provincial sales tax (PST)

In some provinces, Canada Revenue Agency collects any PST that applies to goods you import that do not qualify under your duty-free and tax-free exemption. In addition, in most provinces and territories, the department collects special provincial or territorial assessments on alcohol and tobacco products that do not qualify under your duty-free and tax-free exemption.

WHERE TO GET FURTHER INFORMATION

Whether it is for a short trip or longer Snowbird season stay, there is a tremendous amount of helpful information available.

Books

An excellent book to read if you are considering being a Snowbird in Mexico is *Mexico: The Trick Is Living Here*, second edition, by an expat American, Julie Taylor. The book can be downloaded from her website: www.home-sweet-mexico.com.

Your local public library and bookstores in your community offer many other books on Mexico that will fascinate and inform you. Also check out the publications on Mexico published by the AAA Auto Club and available free to members through your local CAA branch.

Newsletters

Many travel agencies specializing in travel to Mexico have free regular newsletters on Mexico.

DVDs and Videos

DVDs and videos give you a colourful sense of Mexico in its various forms; check with your local library.

Mexican Government Tourism Offices in Canada

These offices will be very helpful in answering any questions that you have. You can also visit them in person. Check for your local office in the phone book or online.
For websites on Mexico, refer to Appendix B.

Mexican Government Consulates in Canada

You could have questions relating to obtaining tourist cards, applying to retire in Mexico under various categories, or about government policy that might affect you.

Mexican State Tourism Offices in Mexico

Do a www.google.ca search to find the various state tourism offices in Mexico.

Canadian Consulates in Mexico

Canada has numerous federal government consulates throughout the world to represent the interests of Canadians. There are several Canadian consulate offices throughout Mexico. Check the Canadian government websites for more information: www.voyage.gc.ca and www.dfait-maeci.gc.ca.

Foreign Affairs and International Trade Canada

You can obtain information about current conditions and "risk assessments" that might affect you if you are travelling in any country in the world, through various Canadian government websites. These include crime, political instability, weather conditions (e.g., hurricanes), natural disasters (e.g., earthquakes), general or specific tourist advisory warnings, health issues, and so on. You can speak to someone on the phone, or listen to their "voice prompt" recorded messages on various countries. In addition, this government department has an excellent website, which is linked to other relevant government sites. Here are two of them: www.voyage.gc.ca and www.dfait-maeci.gc.ca.

Internet

Refer to Appendix B for a list of key websites dealing with Mexico. Many of these have links to other key information sites.

Travel Agents

Travel agents familiar with travel in Mexico can be of great assistance.

Tips Before Leaving Canada

√ The sections "Tips Before Leaving Canada" at the ends of Chapters 1 through 8 contain a lot of information relevant to Mexico.

√ Research the various sources of information discussed on pages 252 to 254.

√ Speak to other Canadians and Americans who have been seasonal residents of Mexico and ask for their opinions and suggestions. Participating in an online forum can help get you in touch with other expats who know the area that you are considering. Some online forums are free and others have a nominal charge to join. A popular one is: www.mexconnect.com.

√ If you are considering being a Snowbird in Mexico, you may wish to read the book *Mexico: The Trick Is Living Here*, second edition, by an expat American, Julie Taylor. The book can be downloaded from her website: www.home-sweet-mexico.com.

√ Contact the various social associations of Canadian and American Snowbirds or full-time retirees in Mexico. The Canadian Consulate offices throughout Mexico that have Canadian/American retirement communities will be able to provide you with that information.

√ Have sufficient auto, legal, and out-of-country emergency medical insurance coverage to protect you before you leave Canada.

CHAPTER 11

Permanent Retirement Outside of Canada

INITIAL CONSIDERATIONS

There are many implications of moving to another country full-time and becoming an official nonresident of Canada. Permanently severing ties with Canada can be a difficult decision. You have to consider issues such as tax, estate planning, financial planning, pensions, housing, health costs, and the cost of living. You also need to look at the citizenship, cultural, societal, government, and language issues. There are considerations if you are leaving family, relatives, and friends behind.

This chapter gives an overview of the practical issues to consider, including documentation requirements, immigration, citizenship, taxation, health, and housing issues, and a list of tips before you leave Canada. Careful research is essential, and the Internet makes it more practical than ever to carry out a detailed evaluation before you leave.

Reasons for Retiring Outside Canada

Retiring permanently outside of Canada holds many potential pitfalls for those who choose a destination on the basis of a dream rather than on sound planning. In general, those who consider only the financial benefits of moving south or overseas are more likely to experience disappointment than those who retire abroad for lifestyle or cultural reasons.

If you are retiring as part of a couple, do your research together; both of you should understand what your choices involve. Recognizing and preparing for potential difficulties ahead of time is much easier than dealing with disappointment, or even a crisis, later.

Many Canadians who retire outside Canada full-time are surprised at the cultural isolation that they experience. This can make the normal adjustments from a career to full-time leisure even more stressful. Before you go, make sure you understand the social environment where you will be living. Are you prepared to be in a minority and to be treated as a foreigner? Do you make new friends easily? Are you open to different ways of doing things? Can you handle a much slower or faster pace of life and a varying level of bureaucracy? You need to think about all these are questions before deciding to retire permanently south or abroad.

Destination

Spend significant time in the country or countries where you are thinking of retiring before you make any major commitment. Go in the off-season to see if you are prepared to live there all year round.

If climate is one of your considerations, you can obtain reliable weather statistics on the Internet. Be sure to consider the situation year-round. Many countries with warm winters are hot and humid in the summer and the cost of air-conditioning is often high.

Immigration regulations vary greatly from one country to another. Before you leave, make sure you understand all the regulations of the country you have chosen for retirement. Always consult qualified legal counsel.

Finances

Taxation and the cost of living are related issues. Many developing countries lack the resources to collect taxes on foreign source income, so they compensate by imposing high consumption taxes or import duties. Take into account all taxes, duties and fees, as well as the withholding taxes you will pay on income originating in Canada.

Withholding tax is the money that the Canadian government requires to be held back from income being received by Canadians who are no longer residents of Canada. In the case of money paid out by the federal government, such as OAS and CPP, the amount of withholding tax can vary from zero to 25 percent depending on the country involved. The amount of holdback for other money being generated in Canada and paid out to a nonresident can vary depending on the type of income (rental income, RRSP, RRIF, or employer or private pension payments).

You also need to consider how much it will cost you in communications and travel to stay in touch with your family and friends in Canada.

Medical Advice

It is a good idea to have a medical checkup before you go and to plan carefully for your health needs before you have left Canada. Many nations have health care systems that most Canadians would consider inadequate. The cost of medical care outside Canada can be extremely high. Arrange for adequate private health care coverage before you leave Canada. Take copies of your prescriptions and an initial supply of non-prescription medicines. Plan for emergency contingencies.

Remember, there is a considerable difference between health care coverage for a seasonal absence and that for a permanent absence from Canada. Snowbird insurance acts as a supplement to your provincial medicare coverage and only covers you for emergency medical treatment that can't wait until you return to Canada. If you are severing your ties to Canada and living permanently outside the country, you will need to obtain full health insurance. There is a big difference in premium rates as well, as you can understand, since the latter insurance replaces the Canadian medicare program administered by your current home province.

Find out well before your departure date if you need any special vaccinations or preventive medications for such illnesses as yellow fever, typhoid, meningitis, Japanese encephalitis, hepatitis, or malaria. An International Certificate of Vaccination may be a legal requirement to enter certain countries. You can obtain this information from your doctor, from the Canadian Society for International Health at (613) 241-5785, from the website of Health Canada's Laboratory Centre for Disease Control (LCDC) (www.hc-sc.gc.ca) or from the LCDC FAXlink service at (613) 941-3900.

Documentation

Once you have chosen a destination, make sure your passport, any visas you require, and other travel documents are in order, including those concerning your status in your new country. Demand for such documentation is high, so plan well in advance.

A valid passport is essential. It will expedite immigration procedures and is useful for other purposes, such as opening bank accounts and cashing traveller's cheques. If your passport will expire while you are abroad, make plans to renew it on time.

Even though you may be resident in another country full-time, you may wish to retain your Canadian citizenship and current passport. Many countries will permit you to retire permanently without taking out the citizenship of that country. Some countries permit you to have dual citizenship, such as the U.S. There are many reasons why you may want to maintain your Canadian citizenship and keep your passport current. For example, some countries, due to political differences, will not permit you to enter if you have a passport from certain countries. However, Canadians citizens are looked on very favourably internationally, so if you intend to do a lot of travelling a Canadian passport will open many doors.

Be sure that, when you leave, you have copies of all essential records. You may need these later to clarify your tax status. And keep in mind that you may come home sooner than you planned. Prepare a three-ring binder with transparency pages for all key documents.

Make sure that you know how to contact the nearest Canadian diplomatic or consular mission in your new country in case you run into difficulties. Your rights to Canadian consulate assistance are based on your citizenship. As long as you remain a Canadian citizen, you will always have those rights anywhere in the world that you might be. However, if you relinquish Canadian citizenship through an act of renunciation, you would lose all the rights of a Canadian citizen in a foreign country.

Travel Arrangements

The relatively low cost of travel to popular vacation destinations usually involves charter flights that originate in Canada and are available only on a seasonal basis. In addition, direct flights to Canada are not available from many popular destinations on a year-round basis.

Many countries require foreign visitors to have a valid return ticket pending formal confirmation that you have been accepted as a full-time resident. The paid ticket has to show a return date within the time limits allowed by the country's immigration authorities. A full-fare return ticket with an "open" travel date is generally acceptable, but an unused return portion of a charter flight ticket is not. You may need to purchase expensive one-way open tickets connecting through other countries to satisfy immigration authorities, even if your application for residency is pending. If you have to make an unplanned trip home for family or personal reasons, be prepared to pay several times the charter rate.

If you have special needs when travelling, make sure that before you go, you research the attitudes and facilities that you may encounter. You may have to make special arrangements to obtain amenities that you expect as a matter of right in Canada. While most developed countries can provide for many special needs, few places, can offer as sophisticated arrangements as Canada. And in some countries, disabled people are not expected to access travel facilities and other public places at all.

ISSUES TO CONSIDER

Retiring permanently to another country is an option for Canadians who are seeking a lower tax jurisdiction, do not intend to return regularly to Canada, and can obtain adequate health care protection.

The most popular destination for permanent retirement is the U.S. The popularity of other destinations depends on the motivation. For example, if you are concerned about the tax advantages elsewhere, you might be attracted to a country which is a tax haven or has low taxes. Many small countries in Europe or in the Caribbean fall into this category. They want to attract people with money to invest. Possibly you have family ties to the country where you were born or have an extensive network of relatives. Maybe climate or recreational opportunities are considerations.

Taking up permanent residence in another country involves establishing a legal status there that goes well beyond that of an annual tourist. You may seek either permanent residency or citizenship status, or both. Either may impose a variety of conditions and requirements, and you should be very clear about their implications. Among other consequences, Canadian consular officials in your new country may not be able to help you if you run into difficulties.

As mentioned before, most Canadians would not choose to give up their Canadian citizenship.

1. Immigration and Citizenship Issues

a) Country of Destination Regulations for Immigrants

Immigration regulations vary greatly from country to country, and it is essential that you understand them before you go.

Most countries base their immigration system on three fundamental principles: employment; investment; family connections.

Some countries also recognize retirees or people with a guaranteed minimum income as potential immigrants, but this is far from universal. For example, Mexico has a special category for retirees called *immigrante rentista*, but the United States does not recognize retirement as a valid reason for establishing permanent residency.

Countries that do recognize retirement as an immigrant category generally require proof of sufficient guaranteed income to support the retiree and any dependants. Mexico requires an income of 10,000 pesos per month, and half as much for each dependant.

Regardless of your country of destination, you will need proof of Canadian citizenship. A valid Canadian passport is the best form of proof, and is often required for entry. Many countries require prospective immigrants to apply before they leave Canada; others allow individuals to enter as tourists and then apply to immigrate. Carefully research these aspects of any destination you are considering for retirement.

b) Canadian Citizenship

Canadian citizenship can be relinquished only through a specific act of renunciation. An individual has to apply to Citizenship and Immigration Canada and complete a specific form to begin the process of terminating Canadian citizenship.

One reason for relinquishing your Canadian citizenship could be because your newly adopted country requires you to be a citizen to live full-time and/or own property and does not permit dual citizenship. Alternatively, maybe you no longer have ties to Canada in any way, and see no practical benefit in your circumstances. Possibly there could be tax or pension benefits in certain situations in relinquishing your Canadian citizenship. Countries tend to tax based on residency.

c) Dual Nationality

Many countries do not recognize a person's right to have more than one nationality (citizenship). If you were born outside Canada, or, in some instances, if your parents were born outside Canada, you may be regarded as a citizen of the other country. In some cases, the laws of your country of origin may provide for the revocation of your citizenship if you become a citizen of Canada, but this is not necessarily automatic. You may have to take overt action, such as living on a permanent basis in Canada, consistently using a Canadian passport, and obtaining a visa when you travel to your country of origin. In some countries, you can formally renounce citizenship.

Canadian law permits a Canadian to have more than one nationality. The Canadian government encourages Canadians to use a Canadian passport when travelling abroad and to always present themselves as Canadians to foreign authorities. Canadian officials abroad will offer consular assistance to Canadian citizens wherever they can. However, local authorities may not assist Canadians who have not specified their Canadian citizenship when entering the country.

2. Taxation Issues

a) Severing Canadian Residency

You cannot terminate your Canadian citizenship or residency simply by living in another country. Moreover, becoming a legal resident of another country does not establish nonresidence in Canada for tax purposes. You must demonstrate your intention to leave the country permanently. Revenue Canada determines nonresident status on a case-by-case basis, so you should consult a tax advisor about the necessary steps you should take. Retaining Canadian residency does not necessarily put you at a disadvantage.

Depending on your situation, your actual tax liability could be lower than the nonresident withholding taxes imposed on your Canadian pensions and investment income. For example, if you have a modest income and would not have to pay much tax under Canadian tax laws, you could be further ahead tax-wise than if you relinquished your residency. (If you are a nonresident, there is a flat rate withholding tax that could be more than you otherwise would need to pay.)

In general, absence from Canada for two years or longer is considered evidence of nonresidence, provided that you relinquish or terminate other key connections:

- Residences
- Bank accounts
- Credit cards
- Driver's licences
- Health-plan memberships
- Club or professional memberships.

If you return to Canada to live within two years, you will probably be taxed on the income you earned while you were gone. Regular visits to Canada or stays for extended time periods, such as several months at a time, can be regarded as evidence of continued residency. This is especially a risk if you have family connections in the country. If you retain ownership of your home, you should lease it on a non-revocable basis; if you have ongoing access to it, it may still be regarded as your residence.

Although you are not obliged to do so, as a taxpayer you may submit an NR73 Residency Determination Form to Revenue Canada to see if you are regarded as a nonresident. Further information is available from Revenue Canada's Interpretation Bulletin IT-221, Determination of an Individual's Residence Status, and its special release.

In order to determine what would be best for your situation, consider the following questions:

- Have you allowed for Canadian withholding taxes on your pension income?
- Will you be subject to double taxation in your country of destination?
- Have you arranged to file required tax returns in Canada?
- Have you made allowances for additional communications and travel costs, and import duties?

b) Nonresident Tax Returns

Once you have become a nonresident of Canada as defined by Canada Revenue Agency (CRA), you are no longer required to file income tax returns. It may be in your interest to do so, however, if you have income subject to Canadian withholding tax. Withholding taxes are considered final if you do not file a return, but you may be entitled to a refund if you file a return and your taxable income is low enough.

c) Canadian Departure Taxes

Taxpayers who emigrate from Canada are generally deemed to have disposed of their assets at fair market value on the date they leave. Capital gains taxes, if any, are assessed at this time. Assets affected by this provision include shares in Canadian corporations, but not real estate. Deemed disposition is triggered by your declaration that you have left the country, which you make on your final income tax return, filed by April 30 of the year following your departure. Those with assets valued at more than $25,000 must file a special return.

d) Receiving Canadian Public Pensions Abroad

Canada Pension Plan/Quebec Pension Plan (CPP/QPP) and Old Age Security (OAS) benefits can be paid to you when you are living outside the country, subject to certain conditions. If you have lived or worked in a country with which Canada has concluded a reciprocal social security agreement, you may qualify for social security benefits from both countries for the duration of your lifetime.

Canada's OAS system is intended to guarantee a minimum income to retirees, and it is subject to an income test. You can receive OAS benefits outside Canada for the duration of your lifetime, but you must file an annual return reporting your worldwide income.

Refer to Chapter 3 for a more detailed discussion of pension availability and criteria.

e) Canadian Nonresident Withholding Taxes

Canada imposes a withholding tax on "passive" income paid to nonresidents from Canadian sources, including annuity payments and pension plans. As of January 1, 1996, this tax applies to CPP/QPP and OAS benefits. You are eligible for OAS payments for your lifetime, as long as you were resident in Canada for at least 20 years before you leave Canada. You are eligible for CPP payments for your lifetime as well, without a minimum residency requirement. The amount varies depending on the type of income, but it is 25 percent for pension payments. This tax may be reduced or waived according to the terms of tax treaties between Canada and other countries. For example, the withholding rate on pensions is waived for residents of the U.S. and is 15 percent for residents of Mexico. Rates vary for other countries.

f) Tax Treaties

The tax situation of Canadians living abroad is complicated to some extent by the fact that each country bases its income tax system on different principles. Canada and the United States both tax factual residents on their worldwide income, and also tax nonresidents on some types of domestic income. Many other countries tax only income from local sources, partly because they lack the resources to assess worldwide income. A few countries do not tax income at all, relying instead on consumption taxes and import duties.

Fortunately, the situation is simplified if you move to a country with which Canada has a tax agreement. Canada has tax conventions or agreements (commonly referred to as tax treaties) with more than 60 countries. These tax treaties often eliminate double taxation for those who would otherwise have to pay tax on the same income in two countries. Generally, tax treaties determine how much each country can tax income such as salaries, wages, pensions, and accrued interest.

If you move to a country that does not have a tax treaty with Canada, you may be subject to double taxation. You should carefully research the tax laws of your intended country of destination. If you will be taxed on your Canadian source income, find out if the withholding taxes you pay in Canada will be credited against your tax liability in your country of destination.

g) Estate Tax

Canada does not levy an estate tax, but many other countries, including the United States federal government, as well as various states in the U.S. do so. (See Chapter 7 for more information.) In the United States, this tax can reach 55 percent for large estates. If you are going to become a resident of a country with an estate tax and you have substantial assets, you should consult a tax advisor in your country of destination. You may need to draw up a new will or make other strategic arrangements, such as establishing trusts.

3. Health Care Issues

a) Canadian Provincial Health Care Programs

Canadian provincial health care programs provide limited coverage during temporary periods of absence from Canada, typically six months. The level of benefits, however, may be inadequate to cover costs in some locations, especially the United States. The reason for this is that the payments allowed for out-of-country treatment are comparable to the fees paid by the provincial plans to health care providers in Canada. A foreign hospital may charge several times as much as your provincial program will allow. It is therefore essential that you arrange for private health care insurance for when you are resident outside Canada. The seasonal resident aspect has been covered in some detail in Chapter 6 on insurance. Health insurance coverage for permanent residents outside Canada is a different matter. This is discussed in the next sub-section.

In most cases, you must be physically present in your Canadian province of residence for 183 days of each calendar year to maintain your provincial health care coverage. The rationale for this is that, when you are out of the country, you are not paying provincial sales tax or the Goods and Services Tax, both of which help to pay for medical care.

If you lose your provincial health care coverage, there is a waiting period to re-qualify after you return. In most provinces, this period is three months. Supplementary private insurance sold in Canada generally will not cover you during this period, because such policies are usually issued on the condition that you maintain eligibility under provincial plans.

In some provinces, you can avoid the re-qualification period by waiving your right to coverage while you are out of the country. This way, you will be covered immediately upon your return, even though you were out of the country for more than six months. Before leaving Canada, you should check with your provincial health care authorities to make sure you fully understand how your health care coverage will be affected, and consider the following questions:

- What will you do if you have an accident or become ill?
- Are you prepared for emergency repatriation?
- Have you checked the provisions of your provincial health care plan?

b) Health Care Programs in Your Country of Destination

Health care is a serious issue for Canadian expatriates, because few countries have systems that are as comprehensive or as inexpensive for the user as Canada's. Some developed countries have comprehensive health care plans that will cover you, after a waiting period, if you immigrate. But the countries that are the major destinations for Canadian retirees generally do not offer comparable programs. Private health care in the United States presents particular problems because the Health Management Organization (HMO) system that covers the majority of Americans is generally restricted to U.S. residents with a social security number. Even then, unrestricted coverage usually ceases at age 65, when the Medicare system begins its coverage.

Many developing countries provide free universal medical care to citizens and permanent residents. Mexico, for example, has a national health care program. But most Canadians living in these countries seek private medical care, which many consider to be of a higher quality and which involves shorter waiting periods. Private health care facilities are fairly advanced in most countries, and a private hospital or clinic will usually see you immediately, for a fee approaching the cost of similar services in the United States. Faced with these trade-offs, most Canadians choose the private alternative and make sure they are well covered by insurance.

c) Private Health Care Insurance

There are two types of private health care insurance. Supplementary insurance provides supplementary benefits for people who are covered by a Canadian provincial health care plan and who are seasonal residents only in another country for up to six months a year, e.g., Snowbirds. This type of coverage has been discussed at some length in Chapter 6. Replacement insurance provides coverage for those who are ineligible for provincial plans.

d) Replacement Insurance

If you will be living outside Canada long enough to lose your provincial health care coverage, you will need full replacement coverage and not just supplementary benefits. You may elect to waive your temporary out-of-country coverage if your provincial plan allows it, since you will need replacement coverage from the date of departure anyway.

Full replacement insurance is less readily available than supplementary insurance, but there are a number of companies that provide insurance specifically designed for expatriates. An Internet search on the keywords "global expatriate health insurance" produces the names of several alternative providers. You should arrange for replacement insurance before you leave, but be aware that you may not be able to obtain appropriate coverage from a Canadian company.

Most of these policies reserve the right to repatriate you to a country for which you hold a passport in the event of serious illness or injury, and they may not pay for treatment in Canada. This is another reason for waiving your out-of-country coverage when you leave.

All such policies place some limitations on pre-existing medical conditions and have age restrictions. It is possible, however, to obtain coverage from an international provider with no forced repatriation provision that will cover you up to age 75, with limited coverage for pre-existing medical conditions.

After age 75, the coverage could lapse because of the risks of illness. The premiums for such a policy are in the neighbourhood of CDN$15,000 per year for each covered person at the higher end of the age range. This would be for coverage in the U.S. However, it is important to comparison-shop.

4. Real Estate Issues

For many Canadians, owning their own home is part of their dream of an ideal retirement. This is also a practical issue, since good rental accommodation is expensive in many popular destinations, especially as furnished homes are often the norm for expatriates. While it is prudent to rent for a time before you decide on a particular location, purchasing a condominium or a house is an option you may want to consider.

a) Property Ownership

Purchasing property in some countries can be risky because of the difficulty in obtaining clear title. Careful research and professional legal representation are essential to prevent you from falling victim to unscrupulous operators. In some countries, you can also buy title insurance.

The right of foreigners to buy certain property is restricted in some countries. In Mexico, for example, Canadians and other foreigners require special permits to buy land. They cannot own land within a 100-kilometre band along the borders or a 50-kilometre zone along the coasts. In addition, they cannot own mineral or water rights. They may, however, set up trusts to hold restricted property for them. In the U.S. there is no restriction on property ownership.

It is difficult for foreigners who are not locally employed to obtain conventional mortgage financing in most countries. If you still have Canadian residency status, your Canadian bank may extend a personal loan based on your Canadian assets and your credit rating at home, but in general the terms are not nearly as favourable as they are for mortgages. So depending on your circumstances, you might just need to pay for the property outright with your own financial resources.

b) Condominiums

In principle, condominiums offer many advantages to retirees. External maintenance is handled on a shared basis, and it is relatively safe to leave units unoccupied for extended periods. On the other hand, condominiums can entail serious risks in countries with little experience in administering the relevant laws. You cannot assume that condominium bylaws drafted by property developers will actually be enforceable. Indeed, some restrictions, such as those prohibiting occupancy by pets or children, may contravene local laws.

Condominiums in developing countries tend to be occupied by foreigners from many parts of the world, who may have very different ideas from yours about the use of common property. Many condominiums have rental units available, and leasing one before buying is a good way to check out not only the property, but also the community.

c) Real Estate Agents and Lawyers

Few developing countries regulate real estate agents and lawyers as rigorously as Canada. In most parts of Latin America and the Caribbean, for example, real estate agents require no formal qualifications or training and are not prevented from promoting sales in which they have an undisclosed personal interest. Similarly, regulations governing conflicts of interest by lawyers may be much less stringent than they are in Canada. Moreover, the authorities may not take complaints from foreigners seriously, especially if the agent or lawyer is an established member of the local community.

You should therefore be very careful about accepting claims regarding property that you have not checked out yourself. Such claims as "beach access" may turn out to be fictitious and you could find yourself without any recourse. Do not sign anything that has not been carefully examined by your own lawyer. If possible, try to retain a Canadian lawyer with expertise in the laws of your country of destination. If you have trouble locating an English- or French-speaking local lawyer, the nearest Canadian diplomatic or consular mission can provide you with a list of reputable lawyers who speak English or French. You can also seek out other Canadians in the area and ask for a recommendation.

A lot of the key areas that you need to consider when looking at retiring outside of Canada on a permanent basis have been highlighted. These would involve tax, pensions, safety, security, citizenship, health, housing, cost of living, and cultural considerations. Separation from family and friends is another factor to evaluate.

Your peace of mind, health, quality of life, and financial security are key factors when weighing your options. A feeling of well-being and balance is so important. Statistics have shown that some Canadians who do sever their ties to Canada to live permanently elsewhere get homesick and return.

Tips Before Leaving Canada

√ Do a thorough self-evaluation of the reasons why you want to leave Canada permanently. Put the reasons in writing and include the pros and cons and implications. This list would include tax, pensions, housing, cost of living, health care, and quality of life. Also include the language; societal, cultural, and government differences; and the implications of missing family, relatives, and friends.

√ Contact the consular office of the country that you are moving to and obtain information about eligibility for full-time residence and the tax and pension implications.

√ Make sure that you are familiar with the country that you intend to move to permanently. Visit it often in advance and stay for extended periods, as a visitor, to satisfy yourself that your intended decision is the right one.

√ Contact Canada Revenue Agency to determine the tax implications if you are leaving Canada permanently. Speak to the International Tax Services office at 1-800-267-5177. You can obtain numerous free publications that will be helpful, including *Emigrants and Income Tax*. Website: www.cra-arc.gc.ca.

√ Contact Human Resources and Social Development Canada to determine the implications on federal government pensions if you leave permanently. Website: www.hrsdc.gc.ca.

√ Contact Health Canada to determine any necessary health precautions that you should consider before departure. Look in the Blue Pages of your phone directory. Website: www.hc-sc.gc.ca.

√ Contact Foreign Affairs and International Trade Canada for information on the country that you are considering for permanent residence. They also have many excellent publications and helpful information on health, safety, and political issues for any country in the world. Website: www.dfait-maeci.gc.ca.

√ Contact your provincial office for seniors to determine the implications on any provincial pension plans that you have.

√ Contact a professional tax accountant in Canada who specializes in international tax to obtain customized advice for your situation. Most major international chartered accountancy firms have experts on the tax issues of Canadians living full-time in another country.

√ If you are intending to move permanently to the U.S., refer to the sub-section Moving to the U.S. Full-time, on page 77 of Chapter 4, Immigration and Customs.

√ Contact the providers of your employer/union/association retirement benefit plan to determine the implications of living full-time outside of Canada.

√ Read the book by immigration attorney Larry Behar, *How to Immigrate to the USA*, and visit his website: www.immigrationflorida.com.

12 Answers to the Most Commonly Asked Snowbird Questions

Whether you are an experienced or novice Snowbird, there are always lots of questions involved in being a seasonal resident of the U.S., Mexico, or elsewhere. Laws and regulations that might affect you, whether Canadian or foreign, are always in a state of flux. Here is a sampling of some common questions gleaned from my past bi-weekly *Snowbird Q & A* columns in *Canada News*, and from radio or TV interviews and educational seminars.

RELATING TO HEALTH INSURANCE

Q: If you had a pre-existing condition such as diabetes and got sick in the States, how adequately would your insurance cover you?
A: It depends on the insurance company and its policy. Some policies will cover a pre-existing illness such as diabetes if it has been under control for at least three months with no change in the type or dosage of medication. If the medication changes frequently (say, monthly) and the condition is therefore not stabilized, most policies will exclude coverage for it, but will cover you for everything else.

Q: I'm a retiree with a $25,000 extended health benefits plan. I'd like to protect that plan. Where can I obtain that type of insurance that waives subrogation?
A: A subrogation clause gives the insurance company the right to collect on any other insurance coverage you have (e.g., provincial government health programs or your retiree insurance plans). Ask your insurance company if it is a member of the Canadian Life and Health Insurance OmbudService (CLHIO). If so, CLHIO has adopted a policy that its member companies will not use subrogation clauses unless the claim is over a certain amount. To get the current figure, check it out. Call CLHIO at 1-800-268-8099. Website: www.clhio.ca.

Q: As a senior who intends to go to the States for five months, should I get insurance coverage in Canada or the States?

A: You want to get insurance in Canada. The companies here are familiar with insuring Canadian travelers and with the protocol of getting partial reimbursement from your provincial government and other issues. In addition, coverage is less costly in Canada.

Q: *I have a credit card that grants me 22 days of free out-of-country medical coverage. Can I buy eight more days to make it a month?*
A: Yes. It is easier to get it from the same credit-card insurer. Some credit-card companies require you to deal with them for extended coverage or it voids the underlying policy. Others don't care who you use, as long as that insurer knows who the primary out-of-country carrier is. It is best, though, in this type of situation to try to deal with the same company.

Q: *What insurance pitfalls should I be aware of?*
A: Be sure to disclose any pre-existing conditions and understand the terms of coverage, including deductibles, limitations, exclusions, and claim deadlines. Thoroughly comparison-shop and look at features and benefits. Price should be the last consideration. Always make sure you fully understand the terms of the coverage, or ask questions until you do. You don't want to take chances, because there is so much at stake if you have a claim.

RELATING TO TRAVEL

Q: *Which planning tips should I keep in mind if I am considering the Snowbird option for the first time?*
A: You should start cautiously and step by step. Do your research thoroughly. Read up as much as you can on the areas that interest you. Look at Snowbird newspapers. Speak to other Snowbirds and ask about their experiences and what they would recommend and why. Rent a mobile home in a Snowbird retirement park or a condo in a retirement complex, or rent an RV. Just spend a month or so outside the country for a couple of years until you get a good feeling for what place is right for you. Ask lots of questions of other Snowbirds whenever you can when you are renting. Make sure you feel good about your decision before you buy any housing.

Also, set out your goals, expectations, needs, and wants. Put them in writing. You want to make sure that your spouse is on the same wavelength. Take your time in decision-making.

Q: Is there a place you recommend for novice Snowbirds?
A: No. It is very much an individual decision. Most Western Canadians prefer Arizona (Phoenix area) first, California (Palm Springs area) second, and southern Florida last. The first two Sunbelt states have a dry climate, whereas Florida tends to be more humid. Most Eastern Canadians prefer Florida first followed by Arizona and then California or Texas. Proximity of travel is a primary factor. Try it step by step.

Q: What is the cheapest way to snowbird in the States?
A: It depends. Travelling and living in an RV can be very inexpensive. Buying a used mobile home in a mobile home park can be very reasonable, and if you buy at the end of the Snowbird season (April), you can get good deals. At that time you could buy a mobile home for CDN$5,000 to $8,000, for example. Fees for pad rental could range from CDN$250 to $350 and more per month based on a one-year contract. Another option is to rent a mobile home, RV, or apartment.

Q: I bought my car in Canada but use it for my Snowbird stay. Is there any additional car insurance coverage I should have to protect myself in the U.S.?
A: It depends on the coverage you currently have. Wherever possible, obtain competitive quotes from car insurance companies in your province.

It is prudent to carry a minimum of $1 million third-party liability coverage, and ideally more (e.g., $5 million). Third-party coverage means that you are covered if you cause an accident and the other person makes a claim against you. The premium difference between $1 million and $5 million is relatively small. If one or two people are seriously injured or die as a consequence of an accident that you were responsible for, the award against you could be millions of dollars, especially in the United States.

Obtain under-insured motorists' coverage (UMP). This type of coverage protects you in case you or your car should get hit by someone with inadequate or no insurance coverage. In that event, you are covered for any claim up to the limit of your own third-party liability insurance coverage (e.g., $1–5 million), subject to any state or provincial ceilings. Without the UMP coverage, you would have no protection. You could sue the driver of the other car, but most likely they would have few assets and you would be totally out of luck. The premium for under-insured motorist coverage is low.

If you are travelling to Mexico, your Canadian auto insurance will not cover you. You need to obtain a separate insurance policy for the duration of that trip from a Mexican insurance company. This policy can be obtained from a local auto club (AAA) branch close to the Mexican border, or other companies.

Q: I have a question about insurance on a rented vehicle. If I have the correct coverage in Canada, will it cover everything the same in the U.S.? Is getting a letter from my insurance company enough? Also, if I don't have out-of-country medical coverage, will I be covered for all health care costs due to an auto accident?
A: First, check with the rental company and its insurance company. It depends on the policy of each individual company. However, most rental car companies continue all coverage whether an accident occurs in Canada or the U.S., even though you rented the car in Canada.

Second, check to make sure the auto insurance policy is very clear on the above point. If it is not, make sure you do get a letter from the rental company confirming coverage. Never rely on a verbal confirmation. Also make sure there is no limitation on the number of days you can stay in the U.S.

Finally, you again want to check the coverage of the policy and obtain a separate letter from the rental company if the coverage is not completely clear. You want to check on the dollar limit of the injury coverage (in Canadian or U.S. funds), any exceptions or exclusions in the coverage, and coverage for the costs of sending you back home.

Make sure that you have out-of-country emergency medical coverage for trips to the U.S., no matter how short. You could have medical problems other than auto injuries, or as side effects of the accident (such as a heart attack or stroke) that would not necessarily be covered by the rental car insurance. In that case, only your out-of-country coverage would protect you from a potentially massive financial outlay.

Q: This is my first year as a Snowbird. I am renting an RV and travelling to various Sunbelt states but would like to eventually settle in one place. Where can I get information on the safety and security aspects?
A: There are various free resources about home security, travelling precautions, and special areas of risks. By planning ahead, you will minimize the chance of a bad experience.

- **Foreign Affairs and International Trade Canada.** This service continually monitors and assesses potential risks to Canadians in all countries outside Canada. For example, a travel information report is available on Florida, including specific precautions to take to avoid being a victim of crime. Contact the Travel Information Service for Canadians abroad before your departure date. It contains cautions on countries and cities throughout the world. They can be reached 24 hours a day, 7 days a week, at 1-800-267-6788 The website is: www. dfait-maeci.gc.ca.

- **Local police department.** You could contact the police in the place you are planning to stay to obtain crime statistics on the area and precautions to follow.

- **State tourism offices.** These offices can provide you with travel safety tips and advice about specific areas.

- **Travel agencies.** Various travel agencies have free booklets and pamphlets giving general safety tips and specific ones for certain areas.

- **Travel guides.** Your auto club (CAA or AAA affiliate offices) produces travel guides that include travel safety tips and warnings.

Q: What about the timeshare option?
A: Time-sharing is primarily a lifestyle choice. Your needs may change, you may tire of the same place, and exchange options may not be as flexible as claimed. Beware of free dinners or evening cruises that expose you to high-pressure sales tactics. The freebie is seldom worth the hassle. If you're tempted, always seek candid opinions from at least three other timeshare owners in the project, and never put a deposit on your credit card. Don't sign any documents without speaking to a real estate lawyer. You may also want to speak with the local Better Business Bureau. Then sleep on the idea for a while.

Q: What about security for my home in Canada while I am away?
A: Check with your insurance company, which probably sets stringent requirements to maintain full homeowner coverage during your absence. You may need to name a contact person who will check the home at least once a week to pick up flyers and provide other security measures. And don't leave a message on your answering machine that you're out of the country for six months!

RELATING TO CUSTOMS

Q: What are the current regulations in terms of bringing back goods from the U.S.? I am interested for myself and also for various relatives and friends who will be visiting me in the U.S. for short periods.

A: When you re-enter Canada you must declare everything you acquired abroad, whether you purchased goods for yourself or gifts for others. This includes anything you bought at Canadian or U.S. duty-free shops. Remember to keep all receipts and have them readily available for inspection by a Canada Customs officer.

Here are the regulations relating to the time spent outside Canada and the value of goods that are duty-free. If someone is away from Canada for only 24 hours, they can bring in CDN$50 worth of goods, excluding alcohol and tobacco, duty-free. After a 48-hour absence, the duty-free exemption is extended to CDN$400. A person may bring back CDN$750 worth of goods duty-free without restriction (including alcohol or tobacco) after an absence of seven full days. This includes up to 1.5 litres of liquor or wine, or a case of 24 bottles/cans of beer, each containing 340 ml (12 ounces). In addition, a person can bring back 50 cigars, one carton of cigarettes, or 400 grams of tobacco.

Other goods subject to restrictions include meat or dairy products, plants, vehicles, or exotic animals or products made from their skins, feathers, or bones.

If you have specific questions concerning imports, contact the closest Canadian Border Services office. These can be contacted 24 hours a day from inside Canada at 1-800-461-9999, or from outside Canada at (613) 993-0534.

Q: What if I want to buy a vehicle and return it to Canada?
A: Determine if your vehicle meets Canadian safety and emission standards first. Before you arrive at the border, contact Canada Border Services Agency (CBSA) at your expected point of entry to find out what you will owe in import duties. You will also be required to pay GST plus provincial sales taxes. Check out their website for further information: www.cbsa.gc.ca.

Q: What do you need to do to take a cat or dog across the border?
A: Get a certificate signed by your vet confirming that the cat or dog has been vaccinated against rabies in the past three years. Make sure this protection doesn't lapse while you are away. This policy is required by both U.S. and Canadian Customs.

RELATING TO FINANCIAL TRANSACTIONS

Q: What are my options for dealing with my various financial transactions while I am in the U.S.?

A: You have lots of options available. Here are some of the main ones to consider.

- Check to make sure your funds will receive the best interest rate, depending on your liquidity and safety of principal needs. For example, if your direct deposit goes into a low-interest or chequing account, arrange to have a regular transfer of the funds into an investment that provides you with a higher return (GIC, term deposit, Treasury bill). Always make sure your Canadian account funds are receiving interest.

- You may have other investments your financial institution can handle in your absence—for example, reinvestment of income, deposit of coupons, rollover of maturing deposits, or purchase and sale of securities. Make sure your instructions are in writing and any required documentation is signed in advance. Ask for copies of all transactions to be sent to you at your Sunbelt address.

- You can arrange to have your monthly bank statements forwarded to your Sunbelt address.

- You can pay your Canadian bills personally, on your Canadian chequing account, by having your mail forwarded to your Sunbelt address. However, it can be more convenient and efficient to arrange for automatic debiting of your Canadian bank account. Alternatively, you can arrange to have the bills sent to your financial institution to pay on your behalf. In that event, put your instructions in writing. Many bills can be paid this way—utility bills, cable, house taxes, condominium maintenance fees, quarterly income tax installments.

- All Canadian financial institutions offer 24-hour, 7-day toll-free automatic access to your account, which you can manage online.

- Consider the benefits of having a U.S. fund chequing account at your Canadian bank, with cheques encoded for the U.S. clearing system.

- If you do not already have an existing U.S. bank account, you can facilitate "no hold" chequing privileges by planning for it before you leave Canada. Some banks will hold an out-of-country cheque for up to three weeks for processing and clearing before they will release the funds. Ask the manager of your Canadian financial institution whether they have a correspondent banking relationship with a U.S. financial institution. If they do, this will facilitate a "no-hold" policy.

- Before you leave Canada, check to see what special Snowbird features are available from Canadian and American financial institutions.

Q: I have read about various financial institutions in Canada and the U.S. having problems or going under. How do I find out what protections I have for savings or chequing deposits in a U.S. bank or savings and loans?

A: You have good reason to feel cautious. Many people assume that their deposit funds are protected, and they may be—to a certain amount. Here is an overview of deposit money protection in the U.S. and where to get further information:

- Deposits in U.S. federal or state banks, trust companies, and savings and loans are covered by the Federal Deposit Insurance Corporation (FDIC) up to $100,000 for each individual account. For further information, consumer brochures on deposit insurance, and confirmation that the institution is covered by the FDIC, contact the FDIC Their website is: www.fdic.gov.

- Deposits in U.S. credit unions are covered for up to $100,000 by the National Credit Union Share Insurance Fund (NCUSIF) for each individual account. For further information, consumer brochures on deposit insurance, and confirmation that the credit union is covered by NCUSIF, contact the National Credit Union Administration at (703) 518-6300. Their website is: www.ncua.gov.

Q: How can I stretch my dollar as a Snowbird?

A: You can open up a U.S. dollar chequing and savings account at your financial institution in Canada. You can also obtain a U.S. dollar credit card so you can make payments from your U.S. dollar account. This savings account also acts as a buffer to average out the currency exchange rate fluctuations. Ask your financial institution for any discount programs.

Also get into the habit of looking at special discount coupons in Snowbird community newspapers. Look for seniors' specials or promotions.

One of the many benefits of the Snowbird lifestyle is that fruit and vegetables tend to be much cheaper and fresher than in Canada during the winter months. Most Snowbird states are in the breadbasket areas of the U.S., so the cost of living is lower in that respect, even with the exchange rate.

RELATING TO TAXATION

Q: Can I write off part of my out-of-country medical insurance premium from my annual income to reduce my income tax, and if so, how do I go about it?

A: Some financial relief might be available from the tax credits you can earn when you purchase medical insurance. Many people overlook this substantial saving, which could effectively reduce your premium by up to one quarter. You could earn total credits of approximately 27 for each dollar of medical expenses (e.g., 27 percent) in any consecutive 12-month period, which exceeds the lesser of 3 percent of income or $1,614. For example, if you were earning $20,000 a year, 3 percent of that is $600. If your out-of-country emergency insurance premium were $1,400 for a six-month stay in the U.S., you would be eligible to claim a tax credit of $216 ($1,400 minus $600 = $800 X 27 percent).

Don't forget to claim other eligible medical expenses, such as prescription drugs, dental work, or eyeglasses. If you have further questions, contact your accountant or closest CRA office.

Q: Must I file a U.S. tax return?
A: Cross-border tax issues can be confusing, especially if you have property or other investments in the U.S. Even if you are not required to pay tax, you could be subject to U.S. filing requirements if your visits to the U.S. exceed 182 days over three years, based on a formula counting the current year visits in full, the previous year as one-third days, and one-sixth of days for the year preceding that. Contact a professional accountant familiar with cross-border tax issues as well as the U.S. Internal Revenue Service.

Q: What if I want to rent out or sell my U.S. property?
A: Rents are subject to a 30 percent withholding tax, but owners can claim rental expenses including mortgage interest and property tax, and deduct depreciation by filing an annual U.S. tax return. If you sell, the purchaser is required to forward 10 percent of the gross sale price to the U.S. Internal Revenue Service at the time of the transaction. You would be entitled to a refund at tax time if the amount were greater than the tax due. You can request a waiver from the withholding tax if the purchase price of your U.S. property is less than US$300,000 and the buyer intends to use it as a residence for at least half of the subsequent two years.

Q: How do I find the right professional advisor?
A: If you already have a trusted lawyer, accountant, or financial planner, he or she should be able to recommend a specialist in cross-border issues. If you are starting from scratch, various professional associations will offer names as well as advice on qualifications, experience, compatibility, and fees. Trying to do it all yourself could cost you more than you have saved, and give you an ulcer in the bargain!

Q: I am currently a Snowbird, but am seriously considering living in the U.S. full-time if I can. What information do I need?

A: There are many implications of moving to the U.S. full-time. You have to consider issues such as tax, estate planning, pensions, housing and health costs, cost of living, and the problem of leaving behind friends and relatives. Taxes and pensions will vary, depending on whether you are living full-time in the U.S., permanently or temporarily, and the nature of your stay (e.g., retired, working, or investing). There are also distinct societal and governmental differences between Canada and the U.S., which would become more apparent if you were living in the U.S. full-time. Here are the steps to take if you want to explore the process of emigrating to the U.S., remaining in the U.S. over six months, working in the U.S. as a business visitor or professional, or entering the U.S. under the category of trader or investor:

- Contact the nearest U.S. Immigration and Naturalization Service (INS) to find out if you are eligible and the procedures to follow.

- Contact the closest U.S. Consulate or Embassy if you wish to enter the U.S. under the trader or investor category. They will advise you of your eligibility and what the current rules are. Refer to Chapter 4 on Immigration and Customs.

- Contact the U.S. Internal Revenue Service (IRS) to determine the tax implications of living full-time in the U.S.

- Contact Canada Revenue Agency to determine the tax implications if you are leaving Canada to live full-time in the U.S.

- Contact Health Canada and your provincial office for seniors to determine how it will affect your federal pension and medicare coverage.

- Contact your employer/union/association retirement benefit plan to determine the implications of living full-time in the U.S.

- Contact a lawyer in Canada who specializes in immigration law as it relates to emigrating to the U.S. or living there full-time.

- Contact a professional accountant in Canada who specializes in cross-border tax issues to obtain customized advice in your situation.

RELATING TO WILLS AND ESTATES

Q: What are the implications if I die owning U.S. property?

A: Under changes to the Canada-U.S. tax treaty, your estate can offset the U.S.

taxes against capital gains tax owed in Canada. Also, there are exemptions up to a certain amount and you can defer estate tax if your spouse is a beneficiary. With proper tax planning, Canadians can also defer Canadian capital gains tax on death by leaving the property to a spouse or a spousal trust.

Q: *Is my Canadian will valid in the U.S. if I own property there?*
A: Since laws relating to wills can change and can vary from place to place, it is essential to seek professional advice. If you have a valid and enforceable will in your province, it would usually be deemed valid in the state where you have property. For a comprehensive discussion of estate planning, refer to *The Canadian Guide to Wills and Estate Planning* (Gray and Budd), published by McGraw-Hill Ryerson. The second edition was released in 2002. Also www. estateplanning.ca.

RELATING TO A PERMANENT MOVE OUTSIDE CANADA

Q: *What are the tax implications of permanent residence in another country?*
A: There are numerous implications depending on how you go about departing. If you decide to be officially designated by Canada Revenue Agency as a nonresident of Canada, you will have to pay a departure tax on your capital gains calculated as of the date of departure. You may also have tax withheld from any income that you continue receiving from Canada (for example, CPS, RRSP, or real estate rental revenue). There are various amounts of tax taken off at source, depending on the nature of the income. Depending on your personal financial circumstances, you could be further ahead to remain a technical resident of Canada for tax purposes.

There are many issues for consideration. You need professional tax advice based on where you plan to move. You need to look at the strategic pros and cons of your tax options. As your decisions make such a difference in the tax outcome, it is ideal to obtain three opinions from tax experts.

Sources of Further Information

One of the challenges of gathering information is knowing where to start. This Appendix can save you a great deal of time, energy, money, and hassle by providing you with contact numbers you may wish to phone.

1. Federal Government Information

If you can't locate the phone number for a federal government office and services available in Canada, phone Service Canada at 1-800-667-3355.The website is: www.servicecanada.gc.ca. Its representatives are very resourceful in providing information.

2. Provincial Government Information

If you would like information about any provincial or territorial government departments and services, check in the Blue Pages of your telephone directory. Alternatively, you can go to the following website (www.canada.gc.ca) to locate the main websites for each province and territory. On the left you will see a category called "Resource Centre." Scroll down to "Provinces and Territories."

3. Canada Revenue Agency (CRA)

There could be tax implications of living, working, investing, or owning assets in the United States. Contact your closest CRA office. Also, check out their website for all the latest pamphlets, brochures and consumer information.

Website: cra-arc.gc.ca

4. Canada Border Services Agency (CBSA)

It is important to know your rights and obligations when coming back from a trip to the United States. To save frustration and expense, check with the CBSA before you leave. Check their website for the latest list of publications and pamphlets—www.cbsa.gc.ca.

5. Transport Canada

There are technical requirements to consider if bringing a U.S.-purchased car or RV back to Canada (for example, emission control). Enquire before you go to the U.S., or before you buy a vehicle in the U.S. For information, contact CRA and the CBSA. The Transport Canada website is: www.tc.gc.ca.

6. Health Canada

There are many forms of federal government assistance and free educational material for seniors. Contact your local office (see the Blue Pages in your telephone directory). Their website is: www.hc-sc.gc.ca.

7. Travel Health

For information on a wide range of issues dealing with travel health, refer to: www.phac-aspc.gc.ca.

8. Human Resources and Social Development Canada

For information on old age security, retirement pensions, spousal allowance, survivor benefits, and other services for seniors, refer to the website: www.hrsdc.gc.ca.

9. Foreign Affairs and International Trade Canada

The consular service of this Canadian government department provides invaluable services throughout the world to all Canadians. If any unexpected problems occur, you can contact the closest office to you in the U.S., Mexico, or Costa Rica. If you cannot reach the local office promptly and there is an emergency, you can phone the headquarters in Ottawa collect at (613) 996-8885. It is open 24 hours, 7 days a week.

There are many publications available as well as current updates on safety and travel concerns and tips for Canadians throughout the world. This service constantly monitors and assesses potential risks to Canadians outside Canada. Contact them before you depart. They can be reached 24 hours a day, 7 days a week. For other information, contact the numbers listed on the next page.

Website: www.dfait-maeci.gc.ca

InfoCentre

235 Sussex Drive
Ottawa, ON K1A 0G2
Tel: 1-800-267-8376 (Canada only)
or 1-800-267-6788 (Canada only)
(613) 944-6788

Free Publications

Here is a sampling of the types of free publications available. Check for a current list.

* *Crossing the 49th: A Compendium of the Bumps on the Road for Canadians Going South*
* *Bon Voyage, But: Tips for Canadians Travelling Abroad*
* *Retirement Abroad—Seeking the Sunsets*
* *Her Own Way: Advice for Woman Traveller*
* *A Guide for Canadians Imprisoned Abroad*
* *Working Abroad: Unravelling the Maze*
* *Mexico Qué Pasa? A Guide for Canadian Visitors*
* *Country Travel Reports*—These reports offer travellers current information on conditions in over 170 countries, including safety, health, and passport requirements. Services are available 24 hours a day, 7 days a week.

If you have any problems (for example, you lose your passport) that require Canadian government assistance, contact the closest Canadian consulate in the United States. In cases of emergency when you cannot contact the local office quickly, you can phone the Ottawa office of the Department of Foreign Affairs and International Trade. The number is: (613) 996-8885 (24 hours, 7 days a week). You can phone collect.

10. Canadian Consulates

There are many Canadian government consular offices in the U.S., Mexico, and around the world to assist you in any way that you might require, especially in the case of an emergency or some other difficulty. If you are unable to contact a Canadian consulate in the case of an emergency, you can phone collect to the

Foreign Affairs and International Trade Canada office in Ottawa, at (613) 996-8885, 24 hours, 7 days a week.

Websites: www.dfait-maeci.gc.ca and www.voyage.gc.ca.

11. U.S. Internal Revenue Service (IRS)

The IRS is equivalent to Canada Revenue Agency. As there could be various tax implications to your stay in the United States, income derived in the United States, or assets owned in the United States, you need to check things out beforehand. Their website is: www.irs.ustreas.gov.

12. News for Canadian Snowbirds on Sunbelt Radio Stations

There are various radio programs containing news specifically for Canadian Snowbirds. The news program with the greatest coverage is called *Canadian News with Prior Smith* and is heard in Florida, Arizona, and the Bahamas each weekday. Website: www.canadacalling.com.

13. Two-day Activity Schedule of a Sample Mobile Home/RV Park

Day/Time	Activity	Location
SUNDAY		
11:00 am	Chapel—nondenominational	Activity Hall
1:00 pm	Solo Potluck (1st Sunday)	All Purpose Room
5:30 pm	Organ Music	Activity Hall
6:00 pm	Ice Cream	Activity Hall
7:00 pm	Entertainment	Activity Hall
7:00 pm	Euchre	All Purpose Room

MONDAY		
7:00 am	Richard Simmons Coed Aerobics	Social Hall
7:50 am	Bend & Stretch (Coed)	Social Hall
8:00 am	Aqua Trims	Pool
8:00 am	Oil Painting	Paint Room

Continued

Day/Time	Activity	Location
MONDAY (cont)		
8:00 am	Golf	Golf Course
8:00 am	Line Dancing—Country & Western	Activity Hall
8:30 am	Jackpot Shuffleboard	Court
8:45 am	Coffee	Patio
8:45 am	Piano Practice	Social Hall
9:00 am	Woodworking (9 to 12, 1 to 4)	Shop
9:00 am	Lapidary (closed 12 to 1)	Shop
9:00 am	Silversmithing (closed 11 to 1)	Shop
10:00 am	Round Dance (Phase 3 to 4 workshop)	Activity Hall
10:00 am	Ceramics	Ceramics Room
10:00 am	Friendship Bible Studies	All Purpose Room
10:15 am	Jackpot Shuffleboard	Court
1:00 pm	Craft Class	Paint Room
1:00 pm	Square Dance (A-2 workshop)	Activity Hall
1:00 pm	Round Dance (basic beginners)	Social Hall
3:00 pm	Little Theatre	Activity Hall
3:15 pm	Ladies Barbershop	Social Hall
4:00 pm	Cabaret Meeting (1st Monday)	All Purpose Room
5:30 pm	Potluck	Activity Hall
6:00 pm	Ladies' Pool	Pool Room
6:30 pm	Water Aerobics	East Pool
7:00 pm	Jackpot Nickel	Social Hall
7:00 pm	Cribbage	All Purpose Room
7:00 pm	Chapel Committee (2nd Monday)	Paint Room

NAME OF SITE	WEBSITE
Snowbird General Information	
Canadian Snowbird Institute Inc.	www.snowbird.ca
Canada Calling (With Prior Smith)	www.canadacalling.com
Tax Information	
Canada Revenue Agency	www.cra-arc.gc.ca
Internal Revenue Service (IRS)—U.S.	www.irs.ustreas.gov
Deloitte Touche Accounting Firm	www.deloitte.ca
Mintz & Partners Accounting Firm	www.mintzca.com
KPMG Accounting Firm	www.kpmg.ca
Financial and Stock Market Information	
MSN Money Central	www.msn.ca
Bloomberg Financial News	www.bloomberg.com
Moneysense magazine	www.moneysense.ca
Canadian Business Magazine	www.canadianbusiness.com
Sedar (database information filled with regulatory agencies by public companies and mutual funds)	www.sedar.com
Financial Institutions	
Bank of Montreal	www.bmo.com
Bank of Nova Scotia	www.scotiabank.ca
Canada Trust	www.canadatrust.com
Canadian Imperial Bank of Commerce	www.cibc.com
Royal Bank of Canada	www.royalbank.com
Toronto-Dominion Bank	www.tdbank.ca

Federal Government Programs for Seniors

Human Resources and Social
  Development Canada   www.hrdc-drhc.gc.ca
Canadian Government Information   www.canada.gc.ca

Federal Government Pensions and Benefits Information

Human Resources and Social
  Development Canada   www.hrdc-drhc.gc.ca
Veterans' Affairs   www.vac-acc.gc.ca

News Publications

Canwest   www.canada.com
The Globe and Mail   www.globeandmail.ca
National Post   www.nationalpost.com
Toronto Star   www.torontostar.com

Health Information

Canadian Health Network   www.canadian-health-network.ca
Centre for Disease Control   www.cdc.gov/travel/travel.html
New England Journal of Medicine   www.nejm.org
CNN Health   www.cnn.com
National Library of Medicine   www.nlm.nih.gov

Information on Travel, Health, Visa, and Safety Tips

Foreign Affairs and International
  Trade Canada   www.dfait-maeci.gc.ca
Weather Info   www.weather.com
Centre for Disease Control   www.cdc.gov/travel/travel.html
World Travel Guide   www.wtgonline.com
Lonely Planet   www.lonelyplanet.com
CNN Weather News   www.cnn.com
Canadian Automobile Association   www.caa.ca

Information for those 50+

Canadian Estate Planning Institute Inc. www.estateplanning.ca
Canadian Association of Retired Persons www.fifty-plus.net
American Association of Retired Persons   www.aarp.org

Canadian Retirement Planning Institute Inc.	www.retirementplanning.ca
Elderhostel	www.elderhostel.org

Financial Planning

The Financial Advisors Association of Canada	www.advacis.ca
Financial Planners Standards Council of Canada	www.cfp-ca.org
Canadian Snowbird Institute Inc.	www.snowbird.ca
Canadian Estate Planning Institute Inc.	www.estateplanning.ca
Canadian Retirement Planning Institute Inc.	www.retirementplanning.ca

Estate Planning

Canadian Snowbird Institute Inc.	www.snowbird.ca
Canadian Estate Planning Institute Inc.	www.estateplanning.ca

Life and Health Insurance

Canadian Life and Health Insurance Association	www.clhia.ca
Insurance Bureau of Canada	www.ibc.ca

Living Wills

Joint Centre for Bioethics (Canada)	www.utoronto.ca/jcb
Partnership for Caring (U.S.)	www.parttenershipforcaring.org

Charitable Giving

Canadian Centre for Philanthropy	www.ccp.ca

Small Business/Home Business

Canadian Enterprise Development Group Inc.	www.smallbiz.ca

Real Estate

National Real Estate Institute Inc.	www.homebuyer.ca
Canada Mortgage and Housing Corporation	www.cmhc.ca

Mexico Information

Mexican Government Tourism	www.mexico-travel.com
Home Sweet Mexico	www.home-sweet-mexico.com
Virtual Mexico	www.virtualmex.com
Mexico Online	www.mexonline.com
Mexico Connect	www.mexconnect.com
Mexico Travel Guide	www.go2mexico.com
Information Mexico	www.mexicosi.com

Vacation Rental Websites
(many also have vacation/home exchange option)

www.whistlerchalet.ca
www.resortac.com
www.alluradirect.com
www.cyberrentals.com
www.greatrentals.com
www.holiday-rentals.com
www.vacationrentals.com
www.vacationvillas.net
www.vrbo.com
www.perfectplaces.com
www.craigslist.com
www.cottageportal.com
www.greatrentals.com
www.holiday-rentals.uk.com
www.lakerentals.com
www.ownerdirect.com
www.shorevacations.com
www.srbo.com
www.digsville.com

Vacation/Home Exchange Websites
(many also have vacation rental option)

www.whistlerchalet.ca
www.exchangehomes.com

Continued

www.homeexchange.com
www.homeinvite.com
www.homelink.ca
www.intervac.ca
www.trading-homes.com
www.sunswap.com
www.seniorshomeexchange.com
www.craigslist.com

Retirement, Financial, and Estate Planning Checklist

By completing this extensive checklist, you will focus on key points and issues as well as assemble information, all of which will assist you in developing a financial and estate plan. It will help clarify your wishes when you discuss your needs with your lawyer, tax accountant, financial planner, or financial institution. It will also enhance your peace of mind to know your affairs are in order when you leave Canada for an extended stay. This checklist should be dated, and reviewed and updated annually. Keep a copy in your safety deposit box. Some items may not apply to everyone. Although this checklist highlights many key areas, your advisors can suggest additional issues for you to detail in your specific situation.

Topic Headings:

A. Personal Information
B. Current Financial Net Worth
C. Current and Projected Retirement or Snowbird Monthly Income and Expenses
D. Projected/Potential Financial Needs
E. Where Your Retirement Income Will Come From
F. Retirement Planning Goals

A. PERSONAL INFORMATION

	You	Your Spouse
1. Name (full)		
Address (Canadian)		
City/Province		
Postal Code		
Phone Numbers residence		
work		
Fax Numbers residence		
work		

	You	**Your Spouse**
Address (U.S.)	_____	_____
City/State	_____	_____
Zip Code	_____	_____
Phone Numbers residence	_____	_____
work	_____	_____
Fax Numbers residence	_____	_____
work	_____	_____
Email Address	_____	_____
Date of Birth	_____	_____
Place of Birth	_____	_____
Citizenship	_____	_____
Social Insurance Number	_____	_____
Place of Marriage*	_____	_____
(if applicable)		
(*Specify whether legal or common-law)		
Name of Doctor (Canada)	_____	_____
Name of Doctor (U.S.)	_____	_____

2. **Children** (indicate if by your or your spouse's previous marriage, adopted, or born in a common-law relationship)

Name	Date of Birth	Married?	Telephone Number(s)	Dependent On You?
_____	_____	_____	_____	_____
_____	_____	_____	_____	_____
_____	_____	_____	_____	_____

3. **Grandchildren**

Name	Date of Birth
_____	_____
_____	_____
_____	_____
_____	_____

4. Other Dependants

Name	Date of Birth	Telephone Number(s)	Relationship to You
_____	_____	_____	_____
_____	_____	_____	_____
_____	_____	_____	_____
_____	_____	_____	_____

5. Have you entered into a prenuptial or other marriage contract with your spouse? If so, outline a summary of the contract's terms. Where is the document located?

6. If you or your spouse were previously married, describe any remaining financial obligations (e.g., child support, alimony).

Obligations	You	Your Spouse
Name of former spouse	_____	_____
Address	_____	_____
City/Province or State	_____	_____
Postal or Zip Code	_____	_____
Social Insurance Number	_____	_____
Phone Numbers residence	_____	_____
work	_____	_____

7. If you or your spouse have any prospective inheritances, detail sources, approximate amounts, and possible dates of receipt.

8. Explain any present or potential special support needs (e.g., for a disabled child, spouse, or parent).

9. Location of Documents and Other Information

Item	Location

1) Birth certificates _____

2) Marriage certificate _____

3) Children's birth certificates _____

4) Prenuptial agreements or marriage contracts _____

5) Maintenance, alimony, or custody orders _____

6) Divorce decrees or separation agreements _____

7) Husband's latest will and any codicils _____

8) Wife's latest will and any codicils _____

9) Husband's Power of Attorney _____

10) Wife's Power of Attorney _____

11) Wills of family members, if pertinent _____

12) Passports _____

13) Citizenship papers _____

14) Cemetery deeds _____

15) Directions regarding burial _____

16) List of heirs _____

17) Medical records _____

18) Insurance policies _____

      – Life _____

      – Disability _____

      – Out-of-country medical _____

      – Property _____

      – Automobile _____

      – Home _____

      – Other _____

19) Stocks _____

20) Bonds _____

21) Term deposits _____

22) Investment certificates _____

23) Notes or mortgages receivable _____

24) Real estate documents _____

25) Leases _____

26) Inventory of assets of estate _____

27) Appraisals _____

28) Bankbooks _____

29) Financial records _____

30) Income tax returns (personal and business) _____

31) Valuation day documents (value of asset as of 1972, if applicable, for taxation value base purposes) _____

32) If you own a business, balance sheets and profit/loss statements for last 5 years _____

33) Business agreements _____

34) Employment contracts _____

35) Employee benefit plan documents _____

36) Buy-sell agreements if a shareholder in a business _____

37) Partnership or shareholder agreements if in a business _____

38) Trust agreements _____

39) Promissory notes (personal and business) _____

40) Loan documents (personal and business) _____

41) Automobile ownership documents (personal and business) _____

42) RRSP/RRIF records _____

43) Pension plan documentation (government and/or employer) _____

44) List of bank accounts _____

45) List of credit card/charge accounts _____

46) Miscellaneous documents _____

47) Other (name) _____

10. Advisors

Lawyer	Name	_____
	Address	_____
	Phone	_____
Accountant	Name	_____
	Address	_____
	Phone	_____
Financial Planner	Name	_____
	Address	_____
	Phone	_____
Life and Other Insurance Agents		
	Name	_____
	Address	_____
	Phone	_____

Financial Institution

	Name	_____
	Address	_____
	Phone	_____

Banker

	Name	_____
	Address	_____
	Phone	_____

Investment Dealer

	Name	_____
	Address	_____
	Phone	_____

Other (name)

	Name	_____
	Address	_____
	Phone	_____

B. CURRENT FINANCIAL NET WORTH

Liquid Assets	**You**	**Your Spouse**
(Can be relatively quickly converted into cash)		
Term deposits/GICs	$ _____	$ _____
Chequing accounts	_____	_____
Savings accounts	_____	_____
Stocks	_____	_____
Bonds	_____	_____
Term deposits (savings)	_____	_____
Pensions (government or employer)	_____	_____
Annuities	_____	_____
RRSPs/RRIFs/LIFs		
Life insurance cash surrender value	_____	_____
Demand loans		
– family	_____	_____
– other	_____	_____
Automobile	_____	_____
Tax installments made/withheld	_____	_____

Other (specify)	_____	_____
Subtotal	$ _____	$ _____

Non-Liquid Assets	**You**	**Your Spouse**
(Take longer to convert into cash or to accrue total financial benefit)		
Business interests	$ _____	$ _____
Long-term receivables, loans	_____	_____
Deferred income plans	_____	_____
Interest in trusts	_____	_____
Tax shelters	_____	_____
Principal residence	_____	_____
Other real estate	_____	_____
(e.g., second home, or revenue or investment property)		
U.S./foreign assets	_____	_____
(e.g., Snowbird mobile home, condo)		
Personal property	_____	_____
Valuable assets	_____	_____
(e.g., art, antiques, jewellery)		
Other (specify)	_____	_____
Subtotal	$ _____	$ _____
Total Assets (A)	$ _____	$ _____

Current Liabilities	**You**	**Your Spouse**
(Currently due within 1 year, or on demand)		
Bank loans	$ _____	$ _____
(Currently due or on line of credit demand, or within 1 year)		
Credit cards/ charge accounts	_____	_____
Income tax owing	_____	_____
Alimony	_____	_____
Child support	_____	_____
Monthly rent	_____	_____

Other		
Subtotal	$ _____	$ _____

Long-Term Liabilities	**You**	**Your Spouse**
(Generally not due for over 1 year)		
Term loan	$ _____	$ _____
Mortgages		
– principal residence	_____	_____
– other property	_____	_____
(investment, revenue, recreational, or commercial)		
Other	_____	_____
Subtotal	$ _____	$ _____
Total Liabilities (B)	$ _____	$ _____
Net worth before tax (A minus B)	$ _____	$ _____
Tax cost if assets liquidated (if any)	$ _____	$ _____
Net worth after tax	$ _____	$ _____

C. CURRENT AND PROJECTED RETIREMENT OR SNOWBIRD MONTHLY INCOME AND EXPENSES

	Current	**Projected at Retirement**
I. **Income** (Average monthly income, actual or estimated)		
Salary, bonuses, and commissions	$ _____	$ _____
Dividends	$ _____	$ _____
Interest income	$ _____	$ _____
Pension income	$ _____	$ _____
Other (name)	$ _____	$ _____
Total Monthly Income	(A) _____	(X) _____

	Current	Projected at Retirement
II. **Expenses** (In Canada and the United States)		
Regular monthly payments on:		
Rent or mortgage	$ _____	$ _____
Automobile(s)	$ _____	$ _____
Appliances/TV	$ _____	$ _____
Home improvement loan	$ _____	$ _____
Credit cards/charge accounts (not covered elsewhere)	$ _____	$ _____
Personal loans	$ _____	$ _____
Medical plan	$ _____	$ _____
Installment and other loans	$ _____	$ _____
Life insurance premiums	$ _____	$ _____
House insurance premiums	$ _____	$ _____
Other insurance premiums (auto, extended out-of-country medical, etc.)	$ _____	$ _____
RRSP deductions	$ _____	$ _____
Pension fund (employer)	$ _____	$ _____
Investment plan(s)	$ _____	$ _____
Miscellaneous	$ _____	$ _____
Other (name)	$ _____	$ _____
Total Regular Monthly Payments	$ _____	$ _____
Household operating expenses:	$ _____	$ _____
Telephone	$ _____	$ _____
Gas and electricity	$ _____	$ _____
Heat	$ _____	$ _____
Water and garbage	$ _____	$ _____
Other household expenses (repairs, maintenance, etc.)	$ _____	$ _____
Cable	$ _____	$ _____

	Current	Projected at Retirement
Other (name)	$ _____	$ _____
Total Household Operating Expenses	$ _____	$ _____
Food expenses:	$ _____	$ _____
At home	$ _____	$ _____
Away from home	$ _____	$ _____
Total Food Expenses	$ _____	$ _____
Personal expenses:	$ _____	$ _____
Clothing, cleaning, laundry	$ _____	$ _____
Drugs	$ _____	$ _____
Transportation (other than auto)	$ _____	$ _____
Medical/dental	$ _____	$ _____
Day care	$ _____	$ _____
Education (self)	$ _____	$ _____
Education (children)	$ _____	$ _____
Dues (e.g., union or association)	$ _____	$ _____
Gifts, donations	$ _____	$ _____
Travel	$ _____	$ _____
Recreation	$ _____	$ _____
Newspapers, magazines, books	$ _____	$ _____
Automobile maintenance, gas, and parking	$ _____	$ _____
Spending money, allowances	$ _____	$ _____
Other (name)	$ _____	$ _____
Total Personal Expenses	$ _____	$ _____
Tax expenses:	$ _____	$ _____
Federal and provincial income taxes	$ _____	$ _____
Home property taxes	$ _____	$ _____
Other (name)	$ _____	$ _____
Total Tax Expenses	$ _____	$ _____

III. Summary of Expenses	Current	Projected at Retirement
Regular monthly payments	$ _____	$ _____
Household operating expenses	$ _____	$ _____
Food expenses	$ _____	$ _____
Personal expenses	$ _____	$ _____
Tax expenses	$ _____	$ _____
Total Monthly Expenses	$(B) _____	$(Y) _____
Total Monthly Disposable	$(A-B)	$(X-Y)
Income Available	$ _____	$ _____
(subtract total monthly expenses from total monthly income)		
Total Annual Disposal Income Available (multiply monthly figures above by 12)	$ _____	$ _____

D. PROJECTED/POTENTIAL FINANCIAL NEEDS

1. At what age do you plan to retire?
2. At what age does your spouse plan to retire?
3. Are you a citizen, or a resident, of another country?
   Yes   No   If so, what country?
4. Is your spouse a citizen, or a resident, of another country?
   Yes   No
5. Do you and your spouse plan to become nonresidents of Canada?
   Yes   No   If so, when?
6. Are you planning to reside or are you currently residing three to six months a year in the United States?
   Yes   No   In another country?
   Yes   No   If so, which?
7. Have you thoroughly checked out the implications for your pension plan or health plan eligibility by being away an extended period?
   Yes   No

8. Do you or your spouse expect to receive any lump-sum retirement benefits?
Yes No   If so, how much?

	You	Your Spouse
	$	$

From what source?

9. Do you or your spouse anticipate any employment after retirement (part-time or full-time) or income from part-time or full-time self-employment in a home-based or small business?
Yes No

	You	Your Spouse
Estimated annual earnings	$	$

10. Do you or your spouse anticipate any major changes in your financial situation in the:

– short term (less than 2 years)?	Yes	No
– medium term (2 to 5 years)?	Yes	No
– long term (more than 5 years)?	Yes	No

11. What combined level of income will you require in retirement (current-year dollars)?
12. How many years of retirement have you projected?
13. If you or your spouse died or became disabled, what income would be required to maintain your family's current standard of living (current dollars)?

	You	Your Spouse
Until youngest child no longer financially dependent	$	$
Until age 60	$	$
Until age 65	$	$
Over age 65	$	$

14. What level of inflation do you anticipate will prevail during the time periods in #12?
Have you factored that into your projected future financial needs?
Yes No

E. WHERE YOUR RETIREMENT INCOME WILL COME FROM

	Estimated Monthly Retirement Income	
	You	**Your Spouse**
Employer's pension plan	$_____	$_____
Canada Pension Plan	$_____	$_____
Old Age Security	$_____	$_____
Guaranteed Income Supplement	$_____	$_____
RRSP/RRIF retirement income	$_____	$_____
LIF income	$_____	$_____
Annuity income	$_____	$_____
Profit-sharing fund payout	$_____	$_____
Salary expected from any earned income in retirement	$_____	$_____
Any other fees, payments for services	$_____	$_____
Disability insurance payments	$_____	$_____
Income expected from a business (part-time or full-time, home-based or small business)	$_____	$_____
Income expected from real estate investments or revenue property	$_____	$_____
Income from renting out part of the house (e.g., basement suite/boarders)	$_____	$_____
Savings account interest (credit union, bank, trust company, other)	$_____	$_____
Federal or provincial savings bonds interest, term deposit interest, guaranteed investment certificate interest, other	$_____	$_____
Other investments: stocks, bonds, mutual funds, etc.	$_____	$_____
Investment income from any expected inheritance	$_____	$_____
Income from other investments you expect to create income	$_____	$_____
Other income sources: alimony, social assistance, UIC, etc.	$_____	$_____
Total Expected Monthly Income:	$_____	$_____
Total Annual Income of you and your spouse (Multiply monthly incomes by 12)	$_____	$_____

F. RETIREMENT PLANNING GOALS

	You	Your Spouse

A. Financial Goal

√ Have you determined when your children will finish their schooling?   _____   _____

√ Have you determined when any other dependants you have will no longer require your financial support?   _____   _____

√ Have you determined when your mortgage will be paid off?   _____   _____

√ Have you checked up on the company pension you will receive in retirement, when it will be at the maximum, and when you are eligible to commence receiving benefits?   _____   _____

√ Have you determined when you can get the maximum income from your RRSPs?   _____   _____

√ Have you determined when you will become eligible for Canada Pension Plan and Old Age Security payments?   _____   _____

√ Are you working towards supplementing your pension?   _____   _____

√ Have you checked out discounts for seniors on transportation, entertainment, prescription drugs, banking services, etc. (in Canada and the U.S.)?   _____   _____

√ Have you explored the kind of work you would like to do and where to find it?   _____   _____

√ Are you investigating retirement income plans to convert your RRSP into (such as an RRIF or annuity)?   _____   _____

√ Have you found out whether your hobby can earn extra cash for you?   _____   _____

√ Are you checking out "tax breaks" for seniors and organizing your income to take maximum advantage of them?   _____   _____

B. Residence Goal	You	Your Spouse
√ Have you decided whether to live with, or close to, your family?	_____	_____
√ Have you decided where you want to live in retirement?	_____	_____
√ Have you checked out the adequacy of transportation facilities?	_____	_____
√ Have you checked out how to make your home safe from break-ins or accidents?	_____	_____
√ Have you decided whether to sell your house or condominium and move to a smaller one, rent an apartment, or live in a retirement community or recreational vehicle park?	_____	_____

C. Activity/Recreational Goal

√ Have you determined what you want to do in retirement?	_____	_____
√ Have you researched interesting volunteer work that you might do?	_____	_____
√ Have you checked out travel, cruises, or other tours that you might enjoy?	_____	_____
√ Have you found out how you can become more active in community affairs?	_____	_____
√ Have you checked out educational courses of interest to you?	_____	_____
√ Have you assessed your skills, attributes, talents, interests, values, strengths, and weaknesses?	_____	_____
√ Have you checked out social activities for yourself and your partner?	_____	_____

D. Health Goal

√ Are you doing everything possible to stay in good physical and mental condition?	_____	_____
√ Have you investigated the medical facilities available in the community you intend to retire in?	_____	_____
√ Have you researched the provincial medical coverage you obtain if you are travelling outside your province	_____	_____

	You	Your Spouse

within Canada, or travelling outside Canada
(U.S. or elsewhere)?

√ Are you working out a retirement plan with the _____ _____
active participation of your partner?

√ Are you working at maintaining good relationships _____ _____
with family and friends?

√ Have you obtained adequate travel medical _____ _____
insurance coverage to supplement your provincial
coverage?

E. Estate Goal

√ Have you recorded the location of your _____ _____
family assets (property, bank accounts, stocks,
bonds, etc.), including documents and related
information, and left one copy with your executor
and another copy in your safety deposit box?

√ Have you made or updated your will and power of _____ _____
attorney, and confirmed the availability, willingness,
and suitability of the executor, trustee, and/or guardian?

√ Have you checked out the tax implications of _____ _____
transferring specific personal or business assets to
your beneficiaries?

√ Have you told your family, a trusted friend, and _____ _____
your executor where your records are located?

√ Have you consulted a lawyer, tax accountant, _____ _____
and financial advisor?

Appendix D — Property Assessment Checklist

This assessment checklist has many of the essential features to look when evaluating an apartment condominium or townhouse condominium (100% owned, fractional interest, timeshare, etc.), or a vacation house.

Not all the categories are necessarily applicable in your case. Terminology in some instances can vary from province to province or state to state.

On the line provided, indicate your rating of the listed factor—excellent, good, poor, available, not available, not applicable, further information required—to help you in your research and provide objective clarity for each property you are seriously considering.

A. General Information

Location of property _____

Condition of neighbourhood _____

Condition of property _____

Upkeep required of property _____

Age of property _____

Type of property _____

Zoning of property _____

Zoning of surrounding areas _____

Nightly rentals permitted in property _____

Nightly rentals permitted in surrounding areas _____

Prospect for future increase in value _____

Prospect for future change of zoning _____

Traffic density in area _____

Proximity and number of neighbouring properties _____

Land boundaries clearly marked and surveyed _____

Crime stats and nature of crime in area _____

Risk of forest fire or other natural disaster _____

Full-time or volunteer fire department and proximity of
   firehalls and hydrants _____

Annual weather patterns (sun, snow, rain, etc.) _____

Special Features:

Lakefront   _____

Riverfront (risk of flooding?)   _____

Oceanfront   _____

Lakeview   _____

Riverview   _____

Oceanview   _____

Mountainview   _____

Proximity to body of water   _____

Recreational Amenities:

Nature of amenities   _____

Private and cost of use if applicable   _____

Public and cost of use if applicable   _____

Proximity of:

Schools   _____

Churches   _____

Shopping   _____

Recreation   _____

Entertainment   _____

Parks   _____

Children's playgrounds   _____

Public transportation   _____

Highways   _____

Hospital   _____

Police department   _____

Fire department   _____

Ambulance   _____

Neighbours   _____

Access, Water, and Sewage:

Accessibility of property—drive, fly, boat, ferry, etc.   _____

Availability for use—year-round or seasonal _____

Municipal sewage piping system   _____

Sewage holding tank (pump-out required and cost)   _____

Septic field   _____

Municipal water supply   _____

Well water—quality and supply   _____
Cost to drill well   _____
Other forms of water supply   _____
Garbage removal or other forms of disposal   _____

Taxes:
Provincial   _____
Municipal/Local   _____
How taxes assessed and primary revenue source   _____
Maintenance fees/assessments (if condominium)   _____

Property Restrictions:
Easements   _____
Rights of way   _____
Restrictive covenants of builder or developer   _____
Restrictive covenants of local government   _____
Local zoning bylaw restrictions (e.g., nightly rentals not
  permitted, no mobile homes on property, no other
  buildings to be constructed, seasonal use only, etc.)   _____
Condo bylaw restrictions   _____
Condo property management restrictions   _____
Condo rental pool restrictions   _____
Pending local tax or development changes and impact   _____
Other   _____

Quietness of:
Neighbourhood   _____
Condo complex   _____
Individual condominium unit   _____
House   _____

Condominium Development:
Percentage of units that are owner-occupied (if
condominium)   _____
Percentage of units that are rented out (if condominium)   _____
If next to commercial or tourist centre, is access to
  residential section well controlled?   _____

Is adjacent commercial/tourist development being
  planned?   _____

Size of development related to your needs (small,
  medium, large)   _____

Development compatible with your lifestyle   _____

Style of development—adult-oriented, children,
  retirees, etc.   _____

Age of development, in years   _____

Rental of Your Recreational Property:

Seasonal nightly renters permitted?   _____

Are you required to put your condo in rental pool when
  not in use?   _____

Are you required to use a specific property management
  company for any rentals and what is their
  commission/fee?   _____

If you are relying on rental revenue and you are required
  to use a specific property management company, what
  marketing program do they have, and what is their
  historical track record of net revenue for your unit? _____

If you are required to be in a rental pool, are the expenses
  fair and fairly apportioned?   _____

If you are not required to be in a rental pool for your
  condo, and not required to use a specified property
  management company, how do you propose to market
  your condo or other property, e.g., through owner-direct
  Internet sites, etc.?   _____

B. Exterior Factors

Privacy:

Roadway (public street, private street, safety for children) _____

Sidewalks (adequacy of drainage)   _____

Driveway (public, private, semi-private)   _____

Privacy   _____

Garage:

Reserved space (one or two cars)   _____

Underground garage   _____

Automatic garage doors _____

Security _____

Adequate visitor parking _____

Housing Construction:

Construction material (brick, wood, stone) _____

Siding (aluminum, vinyl, wood, other) _____

Condition of paint _____

Other _____

Roof:

Type of material _____

Age _____

Condition _____

Balcony or Patios:

Location (view, etc.) _____

Privacy _____

Size _____

Open or enclosed _____

Landscaping:

Trees _____

Shrubbery, flowers _____

Lawns _____

Automatic sprinklers _____

Condition and upkeep of exterior _____

C. Interior Factors

Security:

Intercom system _____

Medical alert system _____

Fire safety system (fire alarms, smoke detectors, sprinklers) _____

Burglar alarm system _____

General Safety:

TV surveillance _____

Controlled access _____

Pre-wired for television and telephone cable   _____

Lobby:
Cleanliness   _____
Decor   _____
Security guard   _____

Public Corridors:
Material used   _____
Condition   _____
Plaster (free of cracks, stains)   _____
Decor   _____

Access:
General accessibility   _____
Number of stairwells   _____
Elevators   _____
Wheelchair accessibility   _____

Storage Facilities:
Location   _____
Size   _____
Cost   _____
Adequacy (if you have lots of toys, e.g., boats, skidoos,
   snowmobiles, kayaks, canoes, dirt bikes, quads, etc.)   _____

Heating and Insulation:
Insulation: (The R factor is the measure of heating and
cooling efficiency; the higher the R factor, the more efficient)
R rating in walls (minimum of R-19; depends
   on geographic location)   _____
R rating in ceiling (minimum of R-30; depends
   on geographic location)   _____
Heat pumps   _____
Windows (insulated, storm, screen)   _____
Air conditioning   _____
Heating (gas, electric, hot water, oil)   _____

Temperature Controls:

Individually controlled _____

Convenient location _____

Plumbing:

Functions well _____

Convenient fixtures _____

Quietness of plumbing _____

Suitable water pressure _____

Utility Costs:

Gas _____

Electric _____

Other _____

Other:

Laundry facilities (private or public) _____

Soundproofing features _____

D. Management of Condominium

Condominium management company _____

Owner-managed _____

Resident manager _____

Management Personnel:

Front desk _____

Maintenance _____

Gardener _____

Trash removal _____

Snow removal _____

Security (number of guards, hours, location, patrol) _____

E. Condominium Corporation

Experience of directors of corporation _____

Positive or negative relationship between owners and

   condo council or board of directors, and other owners _____

Any litigation history of condo corporation? _____

Any upcoming special assessments or other anticipated
   maintenance/repair expenses in near future? _____

Average age of other owners _____

Percentage of renters vs. owner-occupiers _____

Is condo still covered by a New Home Warranty program? _____

Condo unit monthly maintenance fees _____

Condo contingency/reserve fund balance _____

F. Recreation Facilities (if condominium)
Clubhouse
Club membership fees (included, not included) _____

Sports:
Courts (tennis, squash, racquetball, handball, basketball) _____
Games room (ping-pong, billiards) _____
Exercise room _____
Bicycle path/jogging track _____
Organized sports and activities _____

Children's Playground:
Location (accessibility) _____
Noise factor _____
Organized sports and activities (supervised) _____

Swimming Pool:
Location (outdoor, indoor) _____
Children's pool _____
Noise factor _____

Visitors' Accommodation: _____

G. Individual Unit (if condominium)
Location in complex _____
Size of unit _____
Is the floor plan and layout suitable? _____
Will your furnishings fit in? _____
Is the unit exposed to the sunlight? _____

Does the unit have a scenic view? _____

Is the unit in a quiet location (away from
   garbage unit, elevator noise, playgrounds, etc.)? _____

Accessibility (stairs, elevators, fire exits) _____

Closets:

Number _____

Location _____

Carpet:

Colour _____

Quality/texture _____

Hardwood floors, condition: _____

Living Room:

Size/shape _____

Windows/view _____

Sunlight (morning, afternoon) _____

Fireplace _____

Privacy (from outside, from rest of condo) _____

Dining Room:

Size _____

Accessibility to kitchen _____

Windows/view _____

Den or Family Room:

Size/shape _____

Windows/view _____

Sunlight (morning or afternoon) _____

Fireplace _____

Privacy (from outside, from rest of condo) _____

Laundry Room:

Work space available _____

Washer and dryer _____

Size/capacity _____

Warranty coverage _____

Kitchen:

Size   _____

Eating facility (table, nook, no seating)   _____

Floors (linoleum, tile, wood)   _____

Exhaust system   _____

Countertop built in   _____

Countertop material   _____

Work space   _____

Kitchen cabinets (number, accessibility)   _____

Cabinet material   _____

Sink (size, single, double)   _____

Sink material   _____

Built-in cutting boards   _____

Oven (single, double, self-cleaning)   _____

Gas or electric oven   _____

Age of oven   _____

Microwave (size)   _____

Age of microwave   _____

Refrigerator/freezer (size/capacity)   _____

Refrigerator (frost-free, ice maker, single/double door)   _____

Age of refrigerator   _____

Dishwasher (age)   _____

Trash compactor/garbage disposal   _____

Pantry or storage area   _____

Is there warranty coverage on all appliances?   _____

Bedrooms:

Total number of bedrooms   _____

Master Bedroom:

Size/shape   _____

Privacy (from outside, from rest of condo)   _____

Closets/storage space   _____

Fireplace   _____

Floor and wall covering   _____

Master Bathroom (En Suite):

Size　　　　　　　　　　　　　　　　　　_____

Bathtub　　　　　　　　　　　　　　　　_____

Whirlpool tub/Jacuzzi　　　　　　　　　　_____

Shower　　　　　　　　　　　　　　　　_____

Steam room　　　　　　　　　　　　　　_____

Vanity　　　　　　　　　　　　　　　　_____

Sink (single, double, integrated sink bowls)　_____

Medicine cabinet　　　　　　　　　　　　_____

Bathrooms:

Total number of bathrooms　　　　　　　　_____

Complete, or sink and toilet only?　　　　　_____

Fractional Ownership of Condo:

What are conditions of personal use and rentals?　_____

What are monthly maintenance costs?　　　　_____

H. Legal and Financial Matters

Project documents (e.g., disclosure/declaration)
　received and read (if new condominium)　_____

Bylaws received and read (if condominium)　_____

Rules and regulations received and read
　(if condominium)　　　　　　　　　　_____

Financial statements received and read
　(if condominium or revenue-generating property)　_____

Condo council minutes, and annual general
　meeting and special general meeting minutes
　over past two years received and read
　(if condominium or revenue-generating property)　_____

No litigation or pending litigation　　　　　_____

No outstanding or pending special assessments　_____

No pending repairs, or leaky condo problems　_____

Other documents (list):

_____　　　_____

_____　　　_____

_____　　　_____

All above documentation (as applicable) reviewed
by your lawyer and legal advice on potential
purchase obtained

_____

Financial statements reviewed by your accountant
and tax advice on investment obtained

_____

All assessments, maintenance fees, and taxes detailed _____

Condominium corporation insurance coverage
adequate

_____

Restrictions acceptable (e.g., pets, renting of unit,
number of people living in suite, children, etc.) for
rental condo

_____

All verbal promises or representations of sales
representative or vendor's agent that you are relying
on written into the offer to purchase

_____

If you are buying a property with other parties, agreement
on use, repairs, expenses, and sale, etc., prepared and/or
reviewed by your lawyer in advance of any purchase
and acceptable to you

_____

If you are buying a property for rental purposes,
periodically or full-time, rental documents prepared
by your lawyer, along with security deposits, etc.

_____

If you are buying a property you would like to pass
on to your children on your death, tax planning
strategic advice obtained in advance from a qualified
tax expert (lawyer or accountant, i.e., CGA or CA) as
to the best tax-saving options available to you
(e.g., trusts, etc.)

_____

Your will is current and prepared by a lawyer (don't do a
"do-it-yourself" will)

_____

Other

_____   _____

_____   _____

_____   _____

_____   _____

Index

Further Information, Seminars, and Reader Feedback

Further Information:

If you would like further information on the snowbird lifestyle and will and estate planning, retirement planning, tax planning, and other related issues, please check out the website www.snowbird.ca.

Feedback:

If you would like to provide any feedback for improvement in the next edition of this book, please use the "contact us" section of the website www.snowbird.ca.

Seminars or Presentations

If you are interested in having the author give a seminar or presentation to your group or association, anywhere in Canada or the United States, please write to:

Canadian Retirement Planning Institute Inc.
#300 – 3665 Kingsway
Vancouver, BC
V5R 5W2
Tel: (604) 436-9311
Website: www.snowbird.ca

Associated Websites:

Please also refer to our associated websites:

www.estateplanning.ca
www.retirementplanning.ca
www.homebuyer.ca
www.smallbiz.ca

About the Author

Douglas Gray, B.A., LL.B., formerly a practicing lawyer, is now a consultant, columnist, and Canada's most published business author, with 24 bestselling business and personal finance books. He retired from his practice of law to concentrate on his educational interests of writing and public speaking.

He is an internationally recognized expert on financial and retirement planning and has given seminars to over 250,000 people nationally and internationally in his various areas of expertise.

Mr. Gray is frequently interviewed as an expert on financial matters by the media in Canada.

He is the president of the Canadian Retirement Planning Institute Inc. This organization offers objective educational programs nationally on a wide range of issues related to personal finance, tax, estate planning, and retirement planning which are of interest to those planning for or in retirement, and snowbirds.

Mr. Gray lives in Vancouver, British Columbia.

He has a family of associated websites relating to his books and expertise:

www.snowbird.ca
www.retirementplanning.ca
www.estateplanning.ca
www.homebuyer.ca
www.smallbiz.ca

Better Homes and Gardens

365

30-minute
meals

inspiring meals for every day of the year

WILEY

John Wiley & Sons, Inc.

Library of Congress Cataloging-in-Publication Data:

Better Homes and Gardens 365 30-minute meals.

    p. cm.

  Includes index.

  ISBN 978-1-118-00003-8 (pbk.); 978-1-118-11953-2 (ebk.); 978-1-118-11954-9 (ebk.); 978-1-118-11955-6 (ebk.)

  1. Quick and easy cooking. 2. Cookbooks. I. Better Homes and Gardens Books (Firm) II. Title: 365 30-minute meals. III. Title: Three hundred sixty five thirty-minute meals.

  TX833.5.B4878 2012

  641.5'55--dc23

                2011017538

Printed in the United States of America

10 9 8 7 6 5 4 3 2 1

Meredith Corporation
Editor: Jan Miller

Contributing Editor: Jeanne Ambrose

Recipe Development and Testing: Better Homes and Gardens® Test Kitchen

John Wiley & Sons, Inc.
Publisher: Natalie Chapman

Associate Publisher: Jessica Goodman

Executive Editor: Anne Ficklen

Editor: Meaghan McDonnell

Production Editor: Abby Saul

Production Manager: Diana Cisek

Interior Design: Jill Budden

Layout: Indianapolis Composition Services

Manufacturing Manager: Tom Hyland

Our seal assures you that every recipe in *365 30-Minute Meals* has been tested in the Better Homes and Gardens® Test Kitchen. This means that each recipe is practical and reliable and meets our high standards of taste appeal. We guarantee your satisfaction with this book for as long as you own it.

Table of Contents

Ready, Set, Cook

Be forewarned. These 30-minute dishes will banish blandness and feed cravings. They'll help you avoid the breakfast sprint, the lunchtime rush, and the dinner dash. Even in crunch time, these go-to meals provide plates full of big flavor, all homemade in half an hour. Look for these icons throughout the book when choosing recipes.

 Healthful

 Kid-Friendly

 Quick and Special

Power Up the Pantry

Keeping a pantry stocked with basic ingredients gives you a head start on creating quick meals. When you do need to go to the store for fresh meat or produce, you'll be able to dash in and out, knowing you have a pantry full of staples at home. These lists show ingredients often used in recipes in this book to quicken your prep and cooking time. Tailor your pantry according to foods you love, including must-have spices and condiments.

FOR THE SHELF

Beans, canned (kidney, black, cannellini)

Bread (baguette, ciabatta, focaccia, country Italian)

Broth, canned (chicken, beef, vegetable)

Couscous

Flour

Garlic

Mandarin oranges

Nuts (almonds, peanuts, pecans, walnuts)

Oils (canola, olive, vegetable)

Onions

Pasta, dried (small shapes including orzo, macaroni, and shells cook quickly)

Pouches of cooked rice (brown, white, blends)

Roasted red sweet peppers

Salsa

Salt, pepper, herbs, and spices

Soy sauce

Sugar (granulated, brown)

Tomatoes, canned and diced or stewed (plain, Mexican-style, Italian)

Tuna, canned

Vinegar (cider, red and white wine, balsamic)

FOR THE REFRIGERATOR

Bacon

Butter or margarine

Cheese (cheddar, feta, Parmesan, Swiss)

Cooked chicken (grilled or roasted)

Cream cheese and flavored cream cheese sauces and spreads

Eggs

Fresh ginger

Lemons

Mayonnaise

Milk

Pesto

Polenta, cooked (plain, flavored)

Potatoes (including sweet), cooked and refrigerated (diced, hash browns, mashed, wedges)

Precut vegetables

Salad dressing (Asian-style, Italian, vinaigrettes)

Salad greens

Shredded cabbage with carrot (coleslaw mix)

Smoked sausage

Spinach

Sour cream

Tortillas (corn, flour)

Yogurt

Embrace Convenience

When time is tight, reach for no-fuss convenience foods to trim prep and cooking time. Here are some options for serving up flavor—fast.

Shop the refrigerated section and the produce area. Look for ready-to-serve crepes; steamed black-eyed peas, lentils, and red kidney beans; peeled and cooked baby beets; ready-to-eat edamame (soybeans); and peeled garlic and shallots.

Take advantage of the salad bar. Pick up chopped celery, carrots, olives, onions, or other fresh vegetables.

Reach for deli-roasted chicken. Grilled chicken breasts or strips means cooking time is eliminated.

Pick up quick-cooking refrigerated pastas, including fettuccine, linguine, tortellini, and ravioli.

Check out refrigerated cooked beef roasts au jus, meatloaf, beef tips, and cooked pork roasts.

Try shelf-stable cooked polenta, plain and flavored.

Use refrigerated potatoes that are peeled, sliced, diced, mashed, and/or flavored for you.

Play with purchased pesto. Heat it up and drizzle it in an omelet, stir it into mashed potatoes, add it to cooked vegetables or pasta, or use it as a sandwich spread.

Serve Simple Sides

Plump up your plate by adding quick-to-the-table side dishes, including salads, fruits, and vegetables. Try these options.

- Fresh breads from the supermarket bakery—great for dipping in soups or stews or toasting on the grill.
- Refrigerated mashed potatoes—stir in fresh chopped herbs or sprinkle on shredded cheese.
- Prewashed salad greens—top with berries and pecans or almonds and toss with a vinaigrette.
- Deli salads—choose from coleslaw, broccoli, pasta, bean, and potato salads. Boost the flavor with a bit of finely chopped jalapeño peppers, dried cranberries, or a handful of fresh chopped herbs.
- Quick-cooking rice or refrigerated pastas can be simply served or dressed up with a splash of coconut milk, orange juice, or a flavored olive oil. And just about everything is better with basil, especially fresh and chopped.

Canned or Frozen?

Canned and frozen vegetable and fruit options make the goal of eating the recommended five servings a day easily attainable. Both options have nutritional value and are often less expensive than fresh produce. Before purchasing, consider these tips.

1 Rinse and drain canned fruits and vegetables before using.

2 Buy no-salt-added canned vegetables

3 Opt for canned fruits in light syrup or in natural juices.

4 Pick frozen vegetables that have no salt or sodium added.

5 Choose frozen vegetable packs that do not have sauces, butter, or flavorings added.

6 Buy frozen fruit without added sugar.

Seek Out Shortcuts

• Purchase precut fresh vegetables, presliced mushrooms, bagged salad, and slaw mixes, or prepared salsas and sauces. Jars of roasted red peppers also shave prep time (no more roasting and peeling your own).

• Choose ready-made sauces and cheese blends, allowing you to use fewer ingredients to achieve saucy results. Global-inspired sauces offer worldly flavors. Simmer sauces, available in a variety of flavors, make easy work for weeknight meals. Just brown chicken or meat and/or vegetables, pour on the sauce, and heat until the poultry, meat, or vegetables are cooked through. Simmer sauces also perk up pasta or rice dishes.

• Shake seasoning blends over almost any dish to enhance its flavor.

• Go for ingredients with built-in flavor such as seasoned pork tenderloin. Some options include lemon-pepper, Italian, chipotle, and herb and garlic. Roast them whole or cut up or cubed for kabobs or stir-fries.

• Start with purchased precooked beef, pork, or chicken. It's a great way to speed up a traditionally slow-cooking dish. All you need is a few minutes of reheating time. Or, if you'd rather cook your own meat, make a bonus batch, such as extra chicken breasts or a roast, which can be tossed into a main-dish salad or added to quesadillas the next day.

• Jazz up an everyday sauce, such as marinara, for a quick meal. Stir any of the following into the sauce and serve over pasta: chopped olives, shredded mozzarella or Parmesan cheese, sautéed zucchini slices, crisp-cooked bacon, or slivers of prosciutto.

Cook with Timesaving Appliances

Microwave oven It's an easy, no-mess way to melt butter, thaw meats and poultry, steam fresh or frozen veggies, or reheat precooked rice or pasta.

Food processor This chopping, mincing, and pureeing machine comes in handy during prep time. Prepare extra ingredients, such as chopped onion or sweet pepper, to freeze for later meals.

Necessities

Colander Use this stainless-steel or enamel-coated steel perforated bowl to drain boiled vegetables or pasta and hold foods while rinsing.

Silicone scrapers Get the last bits of whatever's in your bowl, jar, or pan with a heatproof scraper. They also work well for folding ingredients together and spreading.

Measuring spoons Use to measure both dry and liquid ingredients. These nested spoons commonly come in sets that include a tablespoon, teaspoon, ½ teaspoon, and ¼ teaspoon.

Graduated measuring cups Also called dry measuring cups, use these for only dry ingredients, such as sugar, and soft solids, such as shortening. Most sets come with a cup, ½ cup, ⅓ cup, and ¼ cup.

Liquid measuring cups Place this clear glass or plastic measuring cup on a level surface to ensure you measure all of your liquid ingredients accurately. The 1-cup and 2-cup measurers are a must for any kitchen.

Wooden spoons Stirring thick batter and dough is an easy task using these sturdy spoons. And because they're made of wood, they stay cool and don't scratch nonstick cookware.

Vegetable peeler Its obvious function is to remove the skin from vegetables, but it can also be used to create chocolate shavings or cheese shavings from chunks of aged cheese.

Egg separator Separating the yolk from the white by tossing the yolk from shell to shell can spread harmful bacteria. This handy gadget cradles the yolk over a cup that catches the white.

Bottle/can opener A sharp, round, rotating blade cuts into the edges of the can as you turn the handle. After opening, handle the lid with caution; it can be as sharp as a knife.

Box grater Sharp-edged holes or slits are used to grate or shred foods into finer pieces. The smaller the hole or slit, the finer the food.

Turner/spatula Flip and serve anything you've grilled, broiled, baked, or panfried.

Tongs Toss a salad, flip cutlets in a frying pan, or snag pickles out of the jar with this handy tool. Some have a locking mechanism for easy storage.

Whisk This tool is a must for beating eggs and other ingredients, but can also be used for making smooth sauces.

Useful Extras

Rolling pin Whether wood, ceramic, metal, silicone, or marble, use it to roll out piecrust, pizza dough, or puff pastry. Rolling pins come in classic roller style or a French-style, an elongated rod with tapered ends.

Slotted spoon Useful for removing solids from liquids, such as ground beef from its grease. Use this for stirring too.

Fine-mesh sieve Instead of a colander, use this when handling fine foods. It can also be used for sifting.

Pastry brush Brush on glazes, oils, pan juices, and drippings to the meat you cook. These brushes are also great for greasing pans before baking.

Pastry blender If you like to bake biscuits or pies, this is a helpful tool for cutting cold butter or shortening into flour.

Citrus juicer Make juicing lemons, limes, and oranges a cinch with this handy gadget. A juicer often comes with a sieve that strains the pulp and seeds and a spout for easy pouring.

Potato masher For fluffy mashed potatoes, try this low-tech tool. Easily mash bananas for baking.

Kitchen timer Avoid overdone or underdone with a kitchen timer. Digital timers can help you time cooking steps down to the second.

Pizza cutter Slices or squares, cut your pizza the way you want it.

Microplane Depending on the size of the hole or slit in the metal tool, this handheld grater can grate, shave, zest, or shred.

Cheese slicer Slicing cheese is easier with the right tool. Most have an adjustable wire to slice thinner or thicker pieces. Don't have a slicer? A paring knife is a good substitute.

Mortar and pestle Crush herbs and spices to boost the fresh flavors in your cooking.

Meat mallet This is a tool that doesn't belong in the basement workbench. The smooth side flattens, while the spiked side tenderizes and flattens.

Emergency Substitutions

IF YOU DON'T HAVE:	SUBSTITUTE:
Bacon, 1 slice, crisp-cooked, crumbled	1 tablespoon cooked bacon pieces
Baking powder, 1 teaspoon	$\frac{1}{2}$ teaspoon cream of tartar plus $\frac{1}{4}$ teaspoon baking soda
Balsamic vinegar, 1 tablespoon	1 tablespoon cider vinegar or red wine vinegar plus $\frac{1}{2}$ teaspoon sugar
Bread crumbs, fine dry, $\frac{1}{4}$ cup	$\frac{3}{4}$ cup soft bread crumbs, or $\frac{1}{4}$ cup cracker crumbs, or $\frac{1}{4}$ cup cornflake crumbs
Broth, beef or chicken, 1 cup	1 teaspoon or 1 cube instant beef or chicken bouillon plus 1 cup hot water
Buttermilk, 1 cup	1 tablespoon lemon juice or vinegar plus enough milk to make 1 cup (let stand 5 minutes before using) or 1 cup plain yogurt
Cornstarch, 1 tablespoon (for thickening)	2 tablespoons all-purpose flour
Egg, 1 whole	$\frac{1}{4}$ cup refrigerated or frozen egg product, thawed
Garlic, 1 clove	$\frac{1}{2}$ teaspoon bottled minced garlic or $\frac{1}{8}$ teaspoon garlic powder
Ginger, grated fresh, 1 teaspoon	$\frac{1}{4}$ teaspoon ground ginger
Half-and-half or light cream, 1 cup	1 tablespoon melted butter or margarine plus enough whole milk to make 1 cup
Mustard, dry, 1 teaspoon	1 tablespoon prepared (in cooked mixtures)
Mustard, yellow, 1 tablespoon	$\frac{1}{2}$ teaspoon dry mustard plus 2 teaspoons vinegar
Onion, chopped, $\frac{1}{2}$ cup	2 tablespoons dried minced onion or $\frac{1}{2}$ teaspoon onion powder
Sour cream, dairy, 1 cup	1 cup plain yogurt or 1 cup light sour cream
Sugar, brown, 1 cup packed	1 cup granulated sugar plus 2 tablespoons molasses
Sugar, granulated, 1 cup	1 cup packed brown sugar or 2 cups sifted powdered sugar
Tomato juice, 1 cup	$\frac{1}{2}$ cup tomato sauce plus $\frac{1}{2}$ cup water
Tomato sauce, 2 cups	$\frac{3}{4}$ cup tomato paste plus 1 cup water
Wine, red, 1 cup	1 cup beef or chicken broth or cranberry juice in savory recipes; cranberry juice in desserts
Wine, white, 1 cup	1 cup chicken broth in savory recipes; apple juice or white grape juice in desserts

Seasonings

Apple pie spice, 1 teaspoon	$\frac{1}{2}$ teaspoon ground cinnamon, $\frac{1}{4}$ teaspoon ground nutmeg, $\frac{1}{8}$ teaspoon ground allspice, and dash ground cloves or ginger
Cajun seasoning, 1 tablespoon	$\frac{1}{2}$ teaspoon white pepper, $\frac{1}{2}$ teaspoon garlic powder, $\frac{1}{2}$ teaspoon onion powder, $\frac{1}{2}$ teaspoon cayenne pepper, $\frac{1}{2}$ teaspoon paprika, and $\frac{1}{2}$ teaspoon black pepper
Fajita seasoning, 1 tablespoon	$1\frac{1}{2}$ teaspoons ground cumin, $\frac{1}{2}$ teaspoon dried oregano, crushed; $\frac{1}{4}$ teaspoon salt; $\frac{1}{4}$ teaspoon cayenne pepper; $\frac{1}{4}$ teaspoon black pepper; $\frac{1}{8}$ teaspoon garlic powder; and $\frac{1}{8}$ teaspoon onion powder
Herbs, snipped fresh, 1 tablespoon	$\frac{1}{2}$ to 1 teaspoon dried herb, crushed, or $\frac{1}{2}$ teaspoon ground herb
Thai seasoning, 1 tablespoon	1 teaspoon ground coriander, 1 teaspoon crushed red pepper, $\frac{1}{4}$ teaspoon salt, $\frac{1}{4}$ teaspoon ground ginger, $\frac{1}{4}$ teaspoon garlic powder, and $\frac{1}{4}$ teaspoon onion powder

Breakfast

Start the day sunny-side up with hearty egg dishes, fruit-topped pancakes, stuffed French toast, or oatmeal loaded with extras. Or enjoy breakfast any time of the day.

Apple Pie Pancakes

START TO FINISH 30 minutes MAKES 10 to 12 pancakes

$1\frac{1}{2}$ cups all-purpose flour

2 tablespoons sugar

1 tablespoon baking powder

$\frac{1}{2}$ teaspoon apple pie spice or ground cinnamon

$\frac{1}{4}$ teaspoon salt

2 eggs, lightly beaten

1 cup apple juice or $\frac{1}{2}$ cup apple juice and $\frac{1}{2}$ cup milk

3 tablespoons butter, melted, or vegetable oil

2 teaspoons vanilla

$\frac{1}{4}$ cup snipped dried apple or $\frac{1}{2}$ cup chopped fresh apple

   Maple syrup

   Coarsely chopped walnuts or pecans, toasted (optional)

1 In a medium bowl stir together flour, sugar, baking powder, apple pie spice, and salt. Make a well in center of flour mixture; set aside.

2 In a small bowl combine eggs, apple juice, melted butter, and vanilla. Add egg mixture all at once to flour mixture. Stir just until moistened (batter should be slightly lumpy). Stir in apple.

3 For each pancake, pour about $\frac{1}{4}$ cup batter onto a hot, lightly greased griddle or heavy skillet. Spread batter to a 4-inch circle. Cook over medium heat for 1 to 2 minutes on each side or until pancakes are golden brown. Turn over when surfaces are bubbly and edges are slightly dry.

4 Serve warm with maple syrup. If desired, top with toasted walnuts.

NUTRITION FACTS PER PANCAKE:
143 cal., 5 g total fat (3 g sat. fat), 51 mg chol., 209 mg sodium, 22 g carb., 1 g dietary fiber, 2 g protein.

tip

Keep pancakes warm while cooking the remaining batter by placing the cooked pancakes on an ovenproof plate in a 200°F oven.

Puffed Oven Pancake with Brown Sugar–Banana Sauce

START TO FINISH **30 minutes**   OVEN **400°F**   MAKES **8 servings**

2   tablespoons butter
4   eggs, lightly beaten
2/3 cup all-purpose flour
2/3 cup fat-free milk
1/4 teaspoon salt
1/2 cup butter
1/3 cup packed brown sugar
3   medium bananas, sliced
2   tablespoons light rum or
     apple juice
     Powdered sugar (optional)
     Whipped cream (optional)

1 Preheat oven to 400°F. Place 2 tablespoons butter in a 12-inch ovenproof skillet. Place skillet in oven for 3 to 5 minutes or until butter is melted.

2 Meanwhile, in a medium bowl using a wire whisk or rotary beater beat eggs. Add flour, milk, and salt; beat until smooth. Immediately pour batter into the hot skillet. Bake for 20 to 25 minutes or until puffed and well browned.

3 For sauce, in a small saucepan combine 1/2 cup butter and brown sugar. Cook and stir over medium heat until melted. Add bananas; cook about 2 minutes or until heated through, stirring gently. Carefully stir in rum; heat through.

4 Spoon sauce over pancake. If desired, sprinkle lightly with powdered sugar and serve with whipped cream. Cut into wedges. Serve warm.

NUTRITION FACTS PER SERVING:
290 cal., 17 g total fat (10 g sat. fat), 144 mg chol., 222 mg sodium, 28 g carb., 1 g dietary fiber, 6 g protein.

An oven-baked pancake means there's no need to stand over the skillet flipping individual flapjacks. Instead, create one big pancake that rises like a popover in the oven. Instead of the Brown Sugar Banana Sauce, consider these topping options:
• Sliced fresh peaches or nectarines and maple syrup
• Heated strawberry jam and sliced fresh strawberries
• Honey butter made by combining 1/4 cup softened butter with 2 tablespoons honey
• Fresh chopped mangoes and lemon yogurt

Blackberry-Ricotta Pancake Wraps

START TO FINISH 30 minutes   MAKES 8 wraps (4 servings)

1¼   cups all-purpose flour
1   tablespoon granulated sugar
2   teaspoons baking powder
¼   teaspoon salt
1   egg, lightly beaten
1   cup milk
2   tablespoons vegetable oil
1   cup ricotta cheese
¼   cup powdered sugar
½   teaspoon finely shredded lemon peel
¼   teaspoon vanilla
1   cup fresh blackberries, raspberries, and/or blueberries
   Powdered sugar

1 In a medium bowl stir together flour, granulated sugar, baking powder, and salt. Make a well in center of flour mixture; set aside. In a small bowl combine egg, milk, and oil. Add egg mixture all at once to flour mixture. Stir just until moistened (batter should be slightly lumpy).

2 For each pancake, pour about ¼ cup batter onto a hot, lightly greased griddle or heavy skillet. Spread batter to a 5-inch circle. Cook over medium heat for 1 to 2 minutes on each side or until pancakes are golden brown. Turn over when surfaces are bubbly and edges are slightly dry.

3 Meanwhile, for filling, in a small bowl combine ricotta cheese, ¼ cup powdered sugar, lemon peel, and vanilla.

4 Spread filling over pancakes. Top with berries; roll up pancakes. Sprinkle with additional powdered sugar.

NUTRITION FACTS PER SERVING: 424 cal., 18 g total fat (7 g sat. fat), 89 mg chol., 422 mg sodium, 51 g carb., 3 g dietary fiber, 15 g protein.

Fruit-Filled Crepes

START TO FINISH 30 minutes MAKES 9 servings

1 egg, lightly beaten
¾ cup fat-free milk
½ cup all-purpose flour
1 teaspoon vegetable oil
⅛ teaspoon salt
1 recipe Creamy Fruit Dip
   (use 1 cup)

1 In a medium bowl combine egg, milk, flour, oil, and salt; beat until smooth.

2 Heat a lightly greased 6-inch nonstick skillet over medium-high heat. Remove from heat. Spoon in 2 tablespoons batter; lift and tilt skillet to spread batter evenly. Return to heat; cook for 1 to 2 minutes or until brown on one side only. (Or cook on a crepe maker according to the manufacturer's directions.) Invert skillet over paper towels; remove crepe. Repeat with the remaining batter, greasing skillet occasionally. If crepes are browning too quickly, reduce heat to medium.

3 Spread 1 well-rounded tablespoon of the Creamy Fruit Dip across center of unbrowned side of each crepe. Fold opposite edges of crepe up and over filling toward center.

NUTRITION FACTS PER SERVING:
91 cal., 5 g total fat (2 g sat. fat), 36 mg chol., 93 mg sodium, 8 g carb., 0 g dietary fiber, 4 g protein.

Creamy Fruit Dip

START TO FINISH 15 minutes MAKES about 2⅓ cups

1 cup assorted fruit, such as sliced peeled peaches, strawberries, mandarin orange sections, and cubed pineapple
1 8-ounce carton light sour cream
1 8-ounce package reduced-fat cream cheese (Neufchâtel)
1 teaspoon vanilla
½ teaspoon finely shredded orange peel

1 Place fruit in a blender or food processor. Cover and blend or process until smooth. Add sour cream, cream cheese, vanilla, and orange peel; cover and blend or process until smooth.

NUTRITION FACTS PER 1 TABLESPOON DIP: *26 cal., 2 g total fat (1 g sat. fat), 7 mg chol., 25 mg sodium, 1 g carb., 0 g dietary fiber, 1 g protein.*

Make-Ahead Directions: Prepare as directed. Cover and chill for up to 24 hours. If dip is too thick after chilling, stir in a little milk, 1 tablespoon at a time, to reach desired consistency.

Ham-and-Cheese-Stuffed French Toast

START TO FINISH 30 minutes MAKES 6 servings

2 **eggs, lightly beaten**

1 **cup half-and-half, light cream, or milk**

1 **teaspoon vanilla**

½ **teaspoon ground cinnamon**

6 **ounces Gruyère or Swiss cheese, sliced**

12 **slices firm-texture white, whole wheat, or rye bread**

8 **ounces very thinly sliced cooked ham**

1 **medium carambola (star fruit), sliced (optional)**

1 **medium kiwifruit, peeled and sliced (optional)**

1 In a shallow dish combine eggs, half-and-half, vanilla, and cinnamon; set aside.

2 Divide cheese slices among six of the bread slices. Top with ham and the remaining bread slices. Dip sandwiches into egg mixture, turning to coat both sides and allowing excess egg mixture to drip off.

3 Cook sandwiches, half at a time if necessary, on a hot, lightly greased griddle or nonstick skillet over medium heat for 6 to 8 minutes or until golden brown, turning once. Serve warm. If desired, garnish with carambola and kiwifruit slices.

NUTRITION FACTS PER SERVING:
449 cal., 28 g total fat (14 g sat. fat), 153 mg chol., 968 mg sodium, 29 g carb., 0 g dietary fiber, 23 g protein.

Stuffed Croissant French Toast

START TO FINISH **30 minutes**   MAKES **4 servings**

- 1   8-ounce package cream cheese, softened
- $\frac{1}{4}$ cup maple syrup
- $\frac{1}{2}$ cup chopped fresh strawberries
- 4   large croissants
- 2   eggs, lightly beaten
- $\frac{1}{2}$ cup half-and-half or light cream
- 1   tablespoon packed brown sugar
- $\frac{1}{2}$ teaspoon ground cinnamon
- $\frac{1}{2}$ teaspoon ground nutmeg
-     Fresh strawberries, halved
-     Maple syrup

1 For filling, in a medium bowl combine cream cheese and $\frac{1}{4}$ cup maple syrup. Beat with an electric mixer on medium speed until smooth. Stir in chopped strawberries. Using a serrated knife, carefully cut each croissant in half horizontally, leaving one side attached. Spoon filling into croissants.

2 In another medium bowl combine eggs, half-and-half, brown sugar, cinnamon, and nutmeg. Carefully dip filled croissants into egg mixture, turning to coat both sides and being careful not to squeeze filling out.

3 On a lightly greased griddle or 12-inch skillet cook filled croissants, two at a time if necessary, over medium heat for 2 to 4 minutes or until golden brown, turning once. (If necessary use a spatula and a fork to help turn the croissants. Some of the filling may leak out onto the pan. If necessary wipe the pan and lightly grease it again before cooking the remaining croissants.)

4 Serve warm with halved strawberries and additional maple syrup.

NUTRITION FACTS PER SERVING: *843 cal., 46 g total fat (28 g sat. fat), 253 mg chol., 641 mg sodium, 94 g carb., 2 g dietary fiber, 13 g protein.*

To vary the filling, substitute one of the following for the chopped strawberries in Step 1:
- Soak $\frac{1}{2}$ cup raisins in $\frac{1}{4}$ cup orange juice for 30 minutes; drain. Stir soaked raisins and $\frac{1}{2}$ teaspoon finely shredded orange peel into filling.
- Stir $\frac{1}{2}$ cup chopped tart apple and $\frac{1}{4}$ cup shredded sharp cheddar cheese (2 ounces) into filling.
- Stir $\frac{1}{4}$ cup chopped pitted whole dates or dried pineapple and $\frac{1}{4}$ cup shredded coconut into filling.

Poached Eggs

START TO FINISH **10 minutes** MAKES **3 or 4 poached eggs**

4 **cups water**
1 **tablespoon vinegar**
3 **or 4 eggs**
  Salt
  Ground black pepper

1 In a large skillet combine the water and vinegar. Bring to boiling; reduce heat to simmering (bubbles should begin to break the surface of the water).

2 Break 1 egg into a cup; slip egg into the simmering water. Repeat with the remaining eggs, allowing each egg an equal amount of space.

3 Simmer eggs, uncovered, for 3 to 5 minutes or until whites are completely set and yolks begin to thicken but are not hard. Using a slotted spoon, remove eggs from skillet, letting the water drain away. Season to taste with salt and pepper.

NUTRITION FACTS PER EGG: *73 cal., 5 g total fat (2 g sat. fat), 212 mg chol., 273 mg sodium, 1 g carb., 0 g dietary fiber, 6 g protein.*

Poaching Pan Directions: Lightly grease each cup of an egg-poaching pan. Place poaching cups into bottom pan over boiling water according to the manufacturer's directions (water should not touch bottoms of cups); reduce heat to simmering. Break an egg into a measuring cup and slip egg into a poaching cup. Repeat with the remaining eggs. Cook, covered, for 4 to 6 minutes or until whites are completely set and yolks begin to thicken but are not hard. Run a knife around edges to loosen eggs. Invert poaching cups to remove eggs.

Make-Ahead Directions: Prepare as directed, except place cooked eggs in a bowl of cold water. Cover and chill for up to 1 hour. To reheat eggs, in a saucepan bring water to simmering. Using a slotted spoon, slip eggs into the simmering water and heat about 2 minutes. Remove with slotted spoon.

Eggs Benedict, 4 Ways

START TO FINISH **25 minutes** MAKES **4 servings**

4   **Poached Eggs**
2   **English muffin halves, split**
4   **slices Canadian-style bacon**
1   **recipe Mock Hollandaise Sauce**
    Cracked black pepper
    (optional)

1 Preheat broiler. Prepare Poached Eggs.

2 Meanwhile, place muffin halves, cut sides up, on a baking sheet. Broil 3 to 4 inches from the heat about 2 minutes or until toasted. Top muffin halves with Canadian-style bacon; broil about 1 minute more or until bacon is heated through.

3 Using a slotted spoon, place cooked eggs on bacon-topped muffin halves. Spoon Mock Hollandaise Sauce over eggs. If desired, sprinkle with pepper.

NUTRITION FACTS PER SERVING: *346 cal., 25 g total fat (7 g sat. fat), 240 mg chol., 885 mg sodium, 14 g carb., 1 g dietary fiber, 14 g protein.*

Mock Hollandaise Sauce

In a small saucepan combine $1/3$ cup sour cream, $1/3$ cup mayonnaise or salad dressing, 2 teaspoons lemon juice, and 1 teaspoon yellow mustard. Cook and stir over medium-low heat until warm. If desired, thin with a little milk. Makes about $2/3$ cup.

Portobello Mushroom Benedict:

Prepare as directed, except before poaching eggs, in a large skillet cook four $3 1/2$- to 4-inch diameter stemmed fresh portobello mushroom caps in 1 tablespoon hot olive oil over medium-high heat about 6 minutes or until tender, turning once. Blot mushrooms with a paper towel. Slice mushrooms; lightly sprinkle with salt and ground black pepper. Cover with foil and keep warm. Continue as directed, except substitute the mushroom slices for the Canadian-style bacon. Sprinkle with chopped seeded tomato.

NUTRITION FACTS PER SERVING: *same as main recipe*

Salmon Benedict:

Prepare as directed, except spread 1 tablespoon tub-style cream cheese spread with chive and onion on each toasted muffin half and substitute 4 ounces thinly sliced, smoked salmon (lox-style) for the Canadian-style bacon. If desired, stir 1 tablespoon drained capers and $1/2$ teaspoon dried dill into the Mock Hollandaise Sauce. If desired, sprinkle with additional dried dill.

NUTRITION FACTS PER SERVING: *391 cal., 30 g total fat (10 g sat. fat), 248 mg chol., 1,161 mg sodium, 15 mg carb., 1 g dietary fiber, 15 g protein.*

Reuben Benedict:

Prepare as directed, except substitute 4 slices marble rye or rye bread for the English muffins and 4 ounces thinly sliced corned beef for the Canadian-style bacon. Spoon $1/2$ cup rinsed and drained sauerkraut over the corned beef. Stir $1/2$ cup shredded Swiss cheese (2 ounces) into the Mock Hollandaise Sauce.

NUTRITION FACTS PER SERVING: *461 cal., 34 g total fat (11 g sat. fat), 269 mg chol., 1,160 mg sodium, 19 mg carb., 3 g dietary fiber, 19 g protein.*

Eggs over Steaks and Mushroom Hash

START TO FINISH 30 minutes   MAKES 4 servings

2   tablespoons vegetable oil

3   cups sliced fresh mushrooms
    (8 ounces)

2   cups frozen diced hash brown
    potatoes with onions and
    peppers

4   3- to 4-ounce thin breakfast
    steaks
    Salt
    Ground black pepper

4   to 6 cloves garlic, thinly sliced

4   eggs
    Fresh tarragon sprigs
    (optional)

1 In a 12-inch skillet heat 1 tablespoon of the oil over medium-high heat. Add mushrooms and potatoes; cook, covered, for 10 minutes, stirring occasionally. Remove from skillet; cover and keep warm.

2 Sprinkle steaks with salt and pepper. In same skillet heat the remaining 1 tablespoon oil. Add steaks and garlic; cook for 3 to 4 minutes or until steaks are desired doneness, turning once. Remove from skillet; cover and keep warm.

3 Break eggs into hot skillet; sprinkle with additional salt and pepper. Cook until desired doneness. Remove from heat.

4 Divide potato mixture, steaks, and eggs among plates. Garnish with tarragon sprigs, if desired.

NUTRITION FACTS PER SERVING:
324 cal., 15 g total fat (3 g sat. fat), 258 mg chol., 397 mg sodium, 17 g carb., 2 g dietary fiber, 29 g protein.

tip

If you like, stir snipped fresh herbs such as tarragon, rosemary, or oregano into the cooked potato mixture.

Denver Scrambled Eggs

START TO FINISH **15 minutes** MAKES **3 servings**

6 eggs, lightly beaten
⅓ cup milk, half-and-half, or light cream
  Dash ground black pepper
2 tablespoons butter or margarine
1 cup sliced fresh mushrooms
⅓ cup diced cooked ham
¼ cup chopped onion
2 tablespoons finely chopped green sweet pepper

1 In a medium bowl combine eggs, milk, and pepper. In a large skillet heat butter over medium heat until melted. Add mushrooms, ham, onion, and sweet pepper; cook for 2 minutes, stirring occasionally.

2 Pour egg mixture over vegetables. Cook over medium heat, without stirring, until egg mixture begins to set on bottom and around edge. Using a spatula or large spoon, lift and fold the partially cooked egg mixture so the uncooked portion flows underneath. Continue cooking for 2 to 3 minutes or until egg mixture is cooked through but is still glossy and moist. Immediately remove from heat.

NUTRITION FACTS PER SERVING:
263 cal., 20 g total fat (9 g sat. fat), 454 mg chol., 404 mg sodium, 5 g carb., 1 g dietary fiber, 17 g protein.

Salmon-Potato Scramble

START TO FINISH 25 minutes MAKES 6 servings

- 1 pound fresh or frozen skinless salmon fillets, about ¾ inch thick
- 2 tablespoons butter or margarine
- 2 cups frozen diced hash brown potatoes, thawed
- ¾ cup chopped green sweet pepper (1 medium)
- 2 to 3 teaspoons Old Bay seasoning
- 6 eggs, lightly beaten
- ⅓ cup water

1 Thaw fish, if frozen. Rinse fish; pat dry with paper towels. In a covered 12-inch skillet cook fish in a small amount of boiling water for 6 to 9 minutes or until fish flakes easily when tested with a fork. Remove fish from skillet; discard liquid. Using a fork, break fish into large chunks.

2 Wipe skillet with a paper towel. In the skillet heat butter over medium-high heat until melted. Add potatoes, sweet pepper, and Old Bay seasoning; cook for 5 to 10 minutes or until potatoes start to brown, stirring occasionally.

3 In a medium bowl combine eggs and the water; pour over potato mixture. Cook over medium heat, without stirring, until egg mixture begins to set on bottom and around edge. Using a spatula or large spoon, lift and fold the partially cooked egg mixture so the uncooked portion flows underneath. Continue cooking for 2 to 3 minutes or until egg mixture is cooked through but is still glossy and moist. Gently stir in cooked fish; heat through. Immediately remove from heat.

NUTRITION FACTS PER SERVING: 294 cal., 17 g total fat (6 g sat. fat), 266 mg chol., 396 mg sodium, 12 g carb., 1 g dietary fiber, 23 g protein.

Scrambled Egg Waffle Stacks

START TO FINISH 25 minutes   MAKES 6 servings

2   tablespoons butter
1   tablespoon all-purpose flour
    Dash ground black pepper
¾   cup milk
¾   cup shredded American
    cheese (3 ounces)
6   eggs, lightly beaten
⅓   cup milk
¼   teaspoon salt
6   frozen waffles
6   slices bacon, crisp-cooked,
    drained, and halved crosswise

1 For sauce, in a medium saucepan heat 1 tablespoon of the butter over medium heat until melted. Stir in flour and pepper. Gradually stir in ¾ cup milk. Cook and stir until thickened and bubbly. Gradually add cheese, stirring until melted. Remove from heat; cover and keep warm.

2 In a medium bowl combine eggs, ⅓ cup milk, and salt. In a large skillet heat the remaining 1 tablespoon butter over medium heat until melted. Pour in egg mixture. Cook over medium heat, without stirring, until egg mixture begins to set on bottom and around edge. Using a spatula or large spoon, lift and fold the partially cooked egg mixture so the uncooked portion flows underneath. Continue cooking for 2 to 3 minutes or until egg mixture is cooked through but is still glossy and moist. Immediately remove from heat.

3 Heat waffles according to package directions. To serve, divide cooked eggs among waffles. Spoon sauce over eggs and top with bacon.

NUTRITION FACTS PER SERVING:
424 cal., 28 g total fat (28 g sat. fat), 285 mg chol., 774 mg sodium, 24 g carb., 1 g dietary fiber, 18 g protein.

Brown Rice Scramble with Tomatoes

START TO FINISH **20 minutes** MAKES **2 servings**

- 4 eggs, lightly beaten
- ½ cup cooked brown rice
- ⅛ teaspoon salt
- ⅛ teaspoon cracked black pepper
- Nonstick cooking spray
- ¾ cup seeded and chopped tomato
- 1 tablespoon snipped fresh basil

1 In a medium bowl combine eggs, cooked rice, salt, and pepper. Coat a medium skillet with cooking spray; heat skillet over medium heat. Pour in egg mixture. Cook over medium heat, without stirring, until egg mixture begins to set on bottom and around edge. Using a spatula or large spoon, lift and fold the partially cooked egg mixture so the uncooked portion flows underneath.

2 Sprinkle with tomato. Continue cooking about 2 minutes or until egg mixture is cooked through but is still glossy and moist. Immediately remove from heat. Sprinkle each serving with basil.

NUTRITION FACTS PER SERVING:
210 cal., 11 g total fat (3 g sat. fat), 423 mg chol., 292 mg sodium, 15 g carb., 2 g dietary fiber, 15 g protein.

Tex-Mex Baked Eggs

START TO FINISH **25 minutes** OVEN **400°F** MAKES **2 servings**

Nonstick cooking spray

4 **eggs**

2 **tablespoons fat-free milk**

¼ **teaspoon ground white or black pepper**

⅛ **teaspoon salt**

½ **cup canned black beans, rinsed and drained**

¼ **cup chunky salsa**

⅓ **cup chopped tomato (1 small)**

2 **tablespoons plain yogurt**

1 **tablespoon snipped fresh cilantro**

Fresh cilantro sprigs (optional)

¼ **cup crumbled queso fresco or shredded Monterey Jack cheese (1 ounce)**

Lime wedges (optional)

1 Preheat oven to 400°F. Lightly coat a 2-quart square baking dish with cooking spray; set aside. In a medium bowl beat together eggs, milk, pepper, and salt with a fork or whisk until combined but not frothy.

2 Place the prepared baking dish on an oven rack. Carefully pour egg mixture into dish. Bake about 10 minutes or until egg mixture is set but is still glossy.

3 Meanwhile, in a small saucepan combine beans and salsa. Cook over low heat until heated through, stirring occasionally.

4 Cut baked egg mixture into four squares. On each plate overlap two egg squares. Top with bean mixture, tomato, yogurt, and snipped cilantro. If desired, garnish with cilantro sprigs. Serve with cheese and, if desired, lime wedges.

NUTRITION FACTS PER SERVING:
244 cal., 12 g total fat (4 g sat. fat), 429 mg chol., 696 mg sodium, 16 g carb., 3 g dietary fiber, 19 g protein.

Pepper-Avocado Omelet

START TO FINISH **30 minutes** MAKES **2 servings**

2 tablespoons butter

2 eggs, lightly beaten

1/2 cup chopped roasted red sweet pepper

1/2 of a medium avocado, seeded, peeled, and coarsely chopped

1/4 of a medium fresh jalapeño chile pepper, thinly sliced* (optional)

1/4 cup shredded Manchego cheese (1 ounce)

Freshly ground black pepper

Crushed red pepper (optional)

1 recipe Fresh Tomato Compote

1 In a 10-inch nonstick skillet heat butter over medium-high heat until melted. Add eggs; lift and tilt skillet to spread eggs evenly.

2 Cook over medium-high heat. When eggs begin to bubble, sprinkle with roasted sweet pepper, avocado, and, if desired, jalapeño chile pepper. Cook until edge of omelet is very light brown. Sprinkle with cheese.

3 Using a plastic spatula, loosen eggs from side of skillet; fold omelet in half. Sprinkle with black pepper and, if desired, crushed red pepper. Serve with Fresh Tomato Compote.

NUTRITION FACTS PER SERVING: *379 cal., 32 g total fat (13 g sat. fat), 252 mg chol., 504 mg sodium, 15 g carb., 5 g dietary fiber, 11 g protein.*

Fresh Tomato Compote

In a medium skillet heat 1 tablespoon olive oil over medium heat. Add 1/2 cup thinly sliced onion; cook about 5 minutes or until tender, stirring occasionally. Stir in 1 cup halved red and/or yellow cherry tomatoes, 1 tablespoon snipped fresh parsley, 1/8 teaspoon salt, and 1/8 teaspoon ground black pepper; heat through.

*tip

Because chile peppers contain volatile oils that can burn your skin and eyes, avoid direct contact with them as much as possible. When working with chile peppers, wear plastic or rubber gloves. If your bare hands do touch the peppers, wash your hands and nails well with soap and warm water.

6   eggs, lightly beaten
$\frac{1}{3}$ cup water
$\frac{1}{8}$ teaspoon salt
$\frac{1}{8}$ teaspoon ground black pepper
2   tablespoons butter or margarine
$1\frac{1}{4}$ cups diced cooked ham (about 6 ounces)
$\frac{1}{2}$ cup chopped green and/or red sweet pepper
$\frac{1}{4}$ cup chopped onion
$\frac{1}{2}$ cup shredded cheddar cheese (2 ounces)
8   6-inch ready-to-use crepes*
     Salsa

1 In a medium bowl combine eggs, the water, salt, and black pepper; set aside. In a large nonstick skillet heat butter over medium heat until melted. Add ham, sweet pepper, and onion; cook for 3 to 4 minutes or until vegetables are tender, stirring occasionally.

2 Pour egg mixture over ham mixture. Cook over medium heat, without stirring, until egg mixture begins to set on bottom and around edge. Using a spatula or large spoon, lift and fold the partially cooked egg mixture so the uncooked portion flows underneath. Continue cooking for 2 to 3 minutes or until egg mixture is cooked through but is still glossy and moist. Immediately remove from heat. Sprinkle with cheese. Cover and let stand about 2 minutes or until cheese is melted.

3 In an 8-inch skillet heat crepes over medium heat for a few seconds or until warm. On each plate overlap two crepes, browned sides down. Divide cooked egg mixture among overlapped crepes. Roll up crepes. Serve with salsa.

NUTRITION FACTS PER SERVING:
351 cal., 21 g total fat (10 g sat. fat), 377 mg chol., 1,121 mg sodium, 14 g carb., 1 g dietary fiber, 25 g protein.

*tip
If purchased crepes are larger than 6 inches, use only 1 crepe per serving.

Mushroom, Artichoke, and Basil Egg White Omelet 🥕

START TO FINISH **20 minutes** MAKES **1 serving**

1 teaspoon olive oil

½ cup sliced fresh cremini mushrooms

⅛ teaspoon garlic salt or sea salt

¼ cup coarsely chopped canned artichoke hearts

3 egg whites, or 1 whole egg and 2 egg whites

Nonstick cooking spray

2 tablespoons coarsely snipped fresh basil

3 tablespoons shredded Italian cheese blend

¼ cup chopped red sweet pepper or tomato

Cracked black pepper

1 In an 8-inch nonstick skillet with flared sides heat oil over medium heat. Add mushrooms and garlic salt; cook about 5 minutes or until mushrooms are tender, stirring occasionally. Stir in artichoke hearts. Transfer mushroom mixture to a small bowl; set aside. Cool skillet slightly; wipe with a paper towel.

2 In a small bowl beat egg whites with a fork or whisk just until frothy. Coat skillet with cooking spray. Sprinkle basil in center of skillet to within 1 inch of the edge. Slowly pour egg whites around edge of skillet, then over top of basil. Cook over medium heat. As egg whites begin to set, use a heatproof silicone spatula to gently lift edges of set egg whites toward the center, tilting pan to let liquid egg whites run under set egg whites. Continue cooking until egg whites are set but are still shiny.

3 Sprinkle 2 tablespoons of the cheese across center of omelet; top with mushroom mixture. Using the spatula, lift and fold one edge of omelet about one-third of the way toward center. Fold the opposite edge toward center. Transfer omelet to a plate. Top with sweet pepper and the remaining 1 tablespoon cheese; sprinkle with black pepper.

NUTRITION FACTS PER SERVING:
196 cal., 10 g total fat (4 g sat. fat), 15 mg chol., 692 mg sodium, 8 g carb., 3 g dietary fiber, 19 g protein.

tip
Carefully handle egg white omelets because they are so light that they tear easily. Or, make the omelets a little stronger by using the option of 1 whole egg and 2 whites.

Spinach and Feta Omelet

START TO FINISH **20 minutes** MAKES **2 servings**

1 **cup refrigerated or frozen egg product, thawed, or 4 eggs, lightly beaten**

1/8 **teaspoon salt**

   Dash ground black pepper

   Nonstick cooking spray

1 **cup sliced fresh mushrooms**

1/2 **cup chopped onion (1 medium)**

2 **teaspoons olive oil or canola oil**

2 **cups lightly packed fresh baby spinach**

1/4 **cup crumbled feta cheese (1 ounce)**

1 In a small bowl combine egg product, salt, and pepper; set aside. Lightly coat an 8-inch nonstick skillet with flared sides with cooking spray; heat skillet over medium heat. Add mushrooms and onion; cook until onion is tender, stirring occasionally. Remove vegetables from skillet.

2 Add 1 teaspoon of the oil to skillet; heat over medium heat. Add half of the egg mixture to skillet. Immediately begin stirring egg mixture gently but continuously with a wooden or plastic spatula until mixture resembles small pieces of cooked egg surrounded by liquid egg. Stop stirring. Cook for 30 to 60 seconds more or until egg mixture is set.

3 Spoon half of the mushroom mixture onto half of the omelet. Top with 1 cup of the spinach and 1 tablespoon of the cheese. Using the spatula, lift and fold unfilled half of omelet up and over filling. Cook about 1 minute more or just until spinach starts to wilt. Transfer omelet to a warm plate; cover and keep warm. Repeat to make a second omelet.

4 Before serving, sprinkle omelets with the remaining 2 tablespoons cheese.

NUTRITION FACTS PER SERVING:
178 cal., 8 g total fat (3 g sat. fat), 13 mg chol., 562 mg sodium, 11 g carb., 2 g dietary fiber, 17 g protein.

Polenta with Sausage and Eggs

START TO FINISH **30 minutes** MAKES **4 servings**

- ½ of a 16-ounce tube refrigerated cooked polenta
  Nonstick cooking spray
- 1 7-ounce package low-fat, reduced-sodium cooked smoked sausage links
- 1 medium red sweet pepper, seeded and cut into bite-size strips
- 8 eggs
- 1 to 2 teaspoons water
- ¼ cup basil pesto

1 Slice or mash polenta and cook according to package directions.

2 Meanwhile, coat a large skillet with cooking spray; heat skillet over medium-high heat. Add sausage and sweet pepper; cook about 4 minutes or until sausage is light brown and sweet pepper is tender, stirring occasionally. Remove from skillet; cover and keep warm.

3 Break eggs into skillet; reduce heat to medium. When edges of eggs turn white, add the water to skillet. Cook, covered, for 3 to 4 minutes or until yolks begin to thicken but are not hard.

4 Divide eggs among plates. Serve with sausage mixture, polenta, and pesto.

NUTRITION FACTS PER SERVING: *376 cal., 24 g total fat (7 g sat. fat), 449 mg chol., 852 mg sodium, 16 g carb., 3 g dietary fiber, 24 g protein.*

Rosemary-Potato Frittata

START TO FINISH **25 minutes** MAKES **2 servings**

1 cup tiny new potatoes cut into $\frac{1}{4}$-inch slices (4 ounces)

$\frac{1}{4}$ cup chopped red onion or yellow onion

$\frac{1}{4}$ cup chopped red, green, and/or yellow sweet pepper

Nonstick cooking spray

4 eggs, lightly beaten

$\frac{1}{2}$ teaspoon snipped fresh rosemary or $\frac{1}{4}$ teaspoon dried rosemary, crushed

$\frac{1}{8}$ teaspoon salt

$\frac{1}{8}$ teaspoon ground black pepper

$\frac{1}{4}$ cup shredded Swiss cheese (1 ounce)

1 In a covered 6- to 7-inch nonstick skillet with flared sides cook potatoes and red onion in a small amount of boiling water for 7 minutes. Add sweet pepper; cook, covered, for 3 to 5 minutes more or until vegetables are tender. Drain vegetables in a colander. Cool skillet slightly; wipe with a paper towel. Lightly coat skillet with cooking spray; return vegetables to skillet.

2 In a small bowl combine eggs, rosemary, salt, and black pepper. Pour egg mixture over vegetables. Cook over medium heat, without stirring, until egg mixture begins to set on bottom and around edges. Using a spatula or large spoon, lift and fold the partially cooked egg mixture so the uncooked portion flows underneath. Continue cooking and lifting edges until egg mixture is nearly set (surface will be moist). Remove from heat.

3 Sprinkle with cheese. Let stand, covered, for 3 to 4 minutes or until surface is set and cheese is melted. Cut into wedges.

NUTRITION FACTS PER SERVING:
271 cal., 14 g total fat (6 g sat. fat), 436 mg chol., 320 mg sodium, 17 g carb., 2 g dietary fiber, 18 g protein.

Bacon and Egg Breakfast Wraps

START TO FINISH 25 minutes MAKES 4 wraps

4 slices bacon, chopped

1 cup chopped fresh mushrooms

½ cup chopped green sweet pepper (1 small)

¼ teaspoon chili powder

¼ teaspoon ground black pepper

⅛ teaspoon salt

1 cup refrigerated or frozen egg product, thawed, or 4 eggs, lightly beaten

¼ cup seeded and chopped tomato

Few drops bottled hot pepper sauce

4 8-inch flour tortillas, warmed*

1 In a large nonstick skillet cook bacon over medium heat until crisp. Using a slotted spoon, remove bacon and drain on paper towels; reserve 1 tablespoon drippings in skillet.

2 Add mushrooms, sweet pepper, chili powder, black pepper, and salt to the reserved drippings; cook about 3 minutes or until vegetables are tender, stirring occasionally.

3 Pour egg product over mushroom mixture. Cook over medium heat, without stirring, until egg begins to set on bottom and around edge. Using a spatula or large spoon, lift and fold the partially cooked egg so the uncooked portion flows underneath. Continue cooking about 2 minutes or until egg is cooked through but is still glossy and moist. Immediately remove from heat.

4 Stir in cooked bacon, tomato, and hot pepper sauce. Divide egg mixture among tortillas; roll up tortillas.

NUTRITION FACTS PER WRAP:
195 cal., 9 g total fat (3 g sat. fat), 11 mg chol., 462 mg sodium, 18 g carb., 1 g dietary fiber, 11 g protein.

*tip

To warm tortillas, wrap in microwave-safe paper towels. Microwave on 100 percent power (high) about 30 seconds or until heated through.

Breakfast Burritos

START TO FINISH 25 minutes   MAKES 4 burritos

- 4   eggs, lightly beaten
- ¼   cup milk
- ¼   teaspoon salt
-     Dash ground black pepper
- 1   tablespoon butter or vegetable oil
- 4   slices bacon, crisp-cooked, drained, and crumbled
- ¼   cup chopped onion
- 4   8-inch flour tortillas, warmed*
- ½   cup shredded Monterey Jack cheese (2 ounces)
-     Salsa (optional)

1 In a medium bowl combine eggs, milk, salt, and pepper. In a large skillet heat butter over medium heat until melted. Pour in egg mixture. Cook over medium heat, without stirring, until egg mixture begins to set on bottom and around edge. Using a spatula or large spoon, lift and fold the partially cooked egg mixture so the uncooked portion flows underneath. Stir in bacon and onion. Continue cooking for 2 to 3 minutes or until egg mixture is cooked through but is still glossy and moist. Immediately remove from heat.

2 Divide egg mixture among tortillas, spooning it down the center of each tortilla. Sprinkle with cheese. If desired, top with salsa; roll up tortillas.

NUTRITION FACTS PER BURRITO:
325 cal., 11 g total fat (3 g sat. fat), 37 mg chol., 1,038 mg sodium, 30 g carb., 3 g dietary fiber, 26 g protein.

*tip
To warm tortillas, wrap tortillas in microwave-safe paper towels. Microwave on 100 percent power (high) about 30 seconds or until heated through.

Breakfast

Super Simple Sausage Skillet

START TO FINISH 20 minutes MAKES 2 servings

- 1 teaspoon canola oil
- 2 ounces smoked turkey sausage links, cut diagonally into $\frac{1}{2}$-inch slices
- 1 cup frozen diced hash brown potatoes
- $\frac{1}{2}$ of a small zucchini, halved lengthwise and cut into $\frac{1}{2}$-inch pieces
- $\frac{1}{2}$ of a medium red sweet pepper, seeded and coarsely chopped
- 1 wedge red onion, thinly sliced (about $\frac{1}{3}$ cup)
- 1 clove garlic, minced
- $\frac{1}{4}$ teaspoon chili powder
- $\frac{1}{8}$ teaspoon ground black pepper
- $\frac{1}{4}$ cup salsa (optional)

1 In a large nonstick skillet heat oil over medium heat. Add sausage, potatoes, zucchini, sweet pepper, red onion, garlic, chili powder, and black pepper; cook for 4 to 5 minutes or until sausage is light brown and vegetables are tender, stirring occasionally. If desired, spoon salsa over sausage mixture.

NUTRITION FACTS PER SERVING:
176 cal., 6 g total fat (1 g sat. fat), 19 mg chol., 281 mg sodium, 25 g carb., 3 g dietary fiber, 8 g protein.

Bacon-Cheddar Scones

START TO FINISH **30 minutes**   OVEN **400°F**   MAKES **8 scones**

1¾   **cups all-purpose flour**

2   **tablespoons sugar**

1   **tablespoon baking powder**

¼   **teaspoon salt**

1   **cup whipping cream**

½   **cup shredded cheddar cheese
(2 ounces)**

4   **slices packaged ready-to-
serve cooked bacon, chopped**

1   **egg, lightly beaten**

1   **tablespoon water**

½   **teaspoon dried thyme,
crushed**

1 Preheat oven to 400°F. In a medium bowl stir together flour, sugar, baking powder, and salt. Make a well in center of flour mixture; set aside. In another medium bowl combine cream, cheese, and bacon. Add cream mixture all at once to flour mixture. Stir just until moistened with a fork.

2 Turn dough out onto a floured surface. Knead dough by folding and gently pressing it for 10 to 12 strokes or until nearly smooth. Pat or lightly roll into an 8-inch circle. Cut into 8 wedges. Place 1 inch apart on an ungreased baking sheet.

3 In a small bowl combine egg and the water. Brush tops of wedges with egg mixture and sprinkle with thyme. Bake about 15 minutes or until golden brown. Remove scones from baking sheet. Serve warm.

NUTRITION FACTS PER SCONE:
265 cal., 15 g total fat (9 g sat. fat),
77 mg chol., 318 mg sodium, 25 g carb.,
1 g dietary fiber, 7 g protein.

Mango Breakfast Trifles

START TO FINISH 25 minutes MAKES 4 servings

- 2 cups plain Greek yogurt
- ¼ cup orange juice
- 1 cup lightly sweetened multigrain clusters cereal with almonds and flax or granola
- 3 cups coarsely chopped mango and/or papaya
- ¼ cup toasted coconut
- ¼ cup honey

1 In a medium bowl combine yogurt and orange juice.

2 In four 8-ounce glasses layer ingredients in the following order: cereal, yogurt mixture, and mango and/or papaya. Sprinkle each serving with coconut and drizzle with honey.

NUTRITION FACTS PER SERVING: 323 cal., 7 g total fat (4 g sat. fat), 7 mg chol., 102 mg sodium, 57 g carb., 5 g dietary fiber, 15 g protein.

Fruit Bowls with Coconut Yogurt and Granola

START TO FINISH **25 minutes** MAKES **8 servings**

2 tablespoons sugar

4 teaspoons finely shredded lime peel

3 6-ounce cartons plain low-fat yogurt

$\frac{1}{2}$ cup canned cream of coconut

$\frac{1}{2}$ of a medium pineapple, peeled, cored, and chopped, or 2 cups canned pineapple tidbits

1 small red papaya, seeded, peeled, and chopped

2 oranges, peeled and chopped

2 kiwifruits, peeled and cut up

1 cup granola

$\frac{1}{2}$ cup chopped macadamia nuts or sliced almonds, toasted

1 In a large bowl combine sugar and lime peel. Using the back of a metal spoon, grind and mash mixture until sugar looks wet and sandy. Stir in yogurt and cream of coconut.

2 Add pineapple, papaya, oranges, and kiwifruits to sugar mixture; toss gently to combine. Top each serving with granola and toasted nuts.

NUTRITION FACTS PER SERVING:
285 cal., 14 g total fat (6 g sat. fat), 4 mg chol., 100 mg sodium, 39 g carb., 4 g dietary fiber, 6 g protein.

Breakfast

Pumpkin-Apple Quick Oatmeal

START TO FINISH 15 minutes   MAKES 4 servings

1⅓   cups water
2⁄3   cup apple juice
½   cup canned pumpkin
⅓   cup chopped dried apples
1¼   cups quick-cooking rolled oats
1   tablespoon packed brown sugar
1   teaspoon ground cinnamon
¼   teaspoon ground nutmeg
½   cup vanilla fat-free yogurt
    Ground cinnamon or stick cinnamon (optional)

1 In a medium saucepan combine the water, apple juice, pumpkin, and dried apples. Bring to boiling. In a small bowl combine oats, brown sugar, 1 teaspoon cinnamon, and nutmeg. Stir oat mixture into boiling pumpkin mixture. Cook for 1 minute, stirring occasionally.

2 Spoon among bowls. Top each serving with yogurt and, if desired, garnish with additional cinnamon.

NUTRITION FACTS PER SERVING:
168 cal., 2 g total fat (0 g sat. fat), 1 mg chol., 30 mg sodium, 35 g carb., 4 g dietary fiber, 5 g protein.

Sandwiches and Pizzas

The flavor-packed combos in these handheld meals offer a collection of "greatest hits" from cheesy classics to wrap-and-roll to modern-day spicy numbers.

Apple-Bacon Burgers

START TO FINISH 30 minutes MAKES 4 servings

6 slices bacon

2 small green apples

8 ounces bulk Italian sausage

8 ounces ground beef

2 tablespoons mayonnaise

1 tablespoon Dijon-style mustard

1 teaspoon honey

4 kaiser rolls, split and toasted

1 In a 12-inch skillet cook bacon over medium heat until crisp. Remove bacon and drain on paper towels. Halve bacon crosswise; set aside.

2 Core and finely chop one of the apples. In a large bowl combine chopped apple, sausage, and ground beef; mix well. Shape meat mixture into four $\frac{1}{2}$-inch-thick patties.

3 For a charcoal grill, grill patties on the rack of an uncovered grill directly over medium-hot coals for 8 to 10 minutes or until done (160°F), turning once halfway through grilling. (For a gas grill, preheat grill. Reduce heat to medium-high. Place patties on grill rack over heat. Cover and grill as above.)

4 Meanwhile, in a small bowl combine mayonnaise, mustard, and honey. Core and slice the remaining apple.

5 On bottoms of rolls layer apple slices, burgers, and bacon. Generously spread tops of rolls with mayonnaise mixture; add tops of rolls.

NUTRITION FACTS PER SERVING:
659 cal., 42 g total fat (14 g sat. fat), 99 mg chol., 1,164 mg sodium, 40 g carb., 3 g dietary fiber, 28 g protein.

★ BBQ Chicken Burgers and Sweet Potato Fries

START TO FINISH **30 minutes** OVEN **425°F** MAKES **4 servings**

⅓ cup barbecue sauce

⅓ cup grape jelly or seedless raspberry jam

4 cups frozen french-fried sweet potatoes

2 tablespoons fine dry bread crumbs

2 tablespoons finely chopped honey-roasted peanuts or almonds

1 tablespoon barbecue sauce

½ teaspoon poultry seasoning

8 ounces uncooked ground chicken or turkey

8 dinner rolls, split

Small roma tomato slices, small lettuce leaves, and/or pickle slices (optional)

1 Preheat oven to 425°F. Line a 9×9×2-inch baking pan with foil; set aside. In a small bowl whisk together ⅓ cup barbecue sauce and jelly until nearly smooth; set aside.

2 Arrange french-fried sweet potatoes in a single layer in an ungreased 15×10×1-inch baking pan. Bake for 10 minutes.

3 Meanwhile, in a medium bowl combine bread crumbs, peanuts, 1 tablespoon barbecue sauce, and poultry seasoning. Add ground chicken; mix well. Shape chicken mixture into eight balls; place 2 inches apart in the prepared baking pan. Flatten until about ¼ inch thick.

4 Place pan of patties in oven on a separate oven rack from the potatoes. Bake patties and french-fried sweet potatoes for 5 minutes. Turn patties; stir french-fried sweet potatoes. Bake about 5 minutes more or until patties are no longer pink and french-fried sweet potatoes are golden brown, brushing patties with 2 tablespoons of the jelly mixture during the last 2 minutes of baking.

5 Serve burgers in rolls with the remaining jelly mixture and, if desired, tomato, lettuce, and/or pickles. Serve with french-fried sweet potatoes.

NUTRITION FACTS PER SERVING:
598 cal., 18 g total fat (3 g sat. fat), 73 mg chol., 855 mg sodium, 94 g carb., 5 g dietary fiber, 29 g sugar, 19 g protein.

Bruschetta Burgers

4 frozen tomato-, basil-, and Parmesan cheese-flavor meatless burger patties

4 slices mozzarella cheese (about 3 ounces)

2 thin multigrain sandwich rounds or 4 slices whole wheat bread

8 to 12 fresh basil leaves

4 slices tomato

Shredded fresh basil (optional)

1 Prepare frozen patties according to package directions. Meanwhile, preheat broiler. Arrange patties on one side of a large baking sheet; top with cheese. Separate sandwich rounds and place, cut sides up, beside patties on baking sheet.

2 Broil 4 to 5 inches from the heat for 1 to 2 minutes or until cheese is melted and sandwich rounds are toasted. Divide basil leaves among sandwich rounds. Top with burgers, tomato, and, if desired, shredded basil.

NUTRITION FACTS PER SERVING:
178 cal., 5 g total fat (3 g sat. fat), 16 mg chol., 538 mg sodium, 21 g carb., 6 g dietary fiber, 17 g protein.

★ Chicken Dinner Burgers

START TO FINISH **30 minutes**   MAKES **4 servings**

- 1 egg, lightly beaten
- ¼ cup fine dry bread crumbs
- ½ teaspoon salt
- ¼ teaspoon ground black pepper
- 1 pound uncooked lean ground chicken or turkey
- 1 tablespoon olive oil
- ¼ cup barbecue sauce
- 4 slices Texas toast or other thick-sliced bread
  Deli coleslaw or grated jicama (optional)
  Pickle slices (optional)

1 In a medium bowl combine egg, bread crumbs, salt, and pepper. Add ground chicken; mix well. Shape chicken mixture into four ¾-inch-thick patties.

2 In a large nonstick skillet heat oil over medium heat. Add patties; cook about 10 minutes or until no longer pink (165°F), turning once halfway through cooking. Brush both sides of patties with barbecue sauce. Cook for 2 minutes more, turning once.

3 Place burgers on toast. If desired, top with coleslaw and pickles.

NUTRITION FACTS PER SERVING:
371 cal., 17 g total fat (1 g sat. fat), 103 mg chol., 912 mg sodium, 27 g carb., 0 g dietary fiber, 28 g protein.

Broiling Directions: Preheat broiler. Place patties on the unheated rack of a broiler pan. Broil 4 to 5 inches from the heat about 10 minutes or until no longer pink (165°F), turning once halfway through broiling. Brush both sides of patties with barbecue sauce. Broil for 2 minutes more, turning once halfway through broiling.

Rosemary Chicken and Brie Burgers

START TO FINISH **30 minutes** MAKES **4 servings**

⅓ cup fine dry bread crumbs

¼ cup finely shredded Parmesan cheese (1 ounce)

2 tablespoons snipped fresh parsley

2 teaspoons snipped fresh rosemary

¼ teaspoon salt

¼ teaspoon ground black pepper

1¼ pounds uncooked ground chicken

Nonstick cooking spray

3 ounces Brie cheese, rind removed and thinly sliced

4 kaiser rolls, split and toasted

2 tablespoons mayonnaise

4 lettuce leaves

1 recipe Tomato Kabobs (optional)

1 In a large bowl combine bread crumbs, Parmesan cheese, parsley, rosemary, salt, and pepper. Add ground chicken; mix well. Shape chicken mixture into four ½-inch-thick patties.

2 Lightly coat a grill pan or large skillet with cooking spray; heat grill pan over medium heat. Add patties; cook for 10 to 12 minutes or until no longer pink (165°F), turning once halfway through cooking and topping with Brie cheese for the last 1 minute of cooking.

3 Spread bottoms of rolls with mayonnaise; top with lettuce and burgers. Add tops of rolls. If desired, serve with Tomato Kabobs.

NUTRITION FACTS PER SERVING:
623 cal., 35 g total fat (6 g sat. fat), 28 mg chol., 871 mg sodium, 38 g carb., 2 g dietary fiber, 38 g protein.

Tomato Kabobs

Measure four 6-inch sprigs of fresh rosemary. Leaving ½ inch of leaves intact at the top of each sprig, use your fingers to pull the remaining leaves down and away, exposing stems. Using a bamboo skewer, make a hole through the stem ends of 16 cherry tomatoes. Thread four tomatoes onto each rosemary sprig.

Salmon Burgers

START TO FINISH **30 minutes** MAKES **4 servings**

1 **1-pound fresh or frozen skinless salmon fillet**

¼ **cup light mayonnaise**

2 **tablespoons snipped fresh dill**

⅓ **cup fine dry bread crumbs**

¼ **cup thinly sliced green onions (2)**

¼ **teaspoon salt**

¼ **teaspoon ground black pepper**

 Nonstick cooking spray

4 **whole wheat hamburger buns, split and toasted**

1 Thaw fish, if frozen. In a small bowl combine mayonnaise and 1 tablespoon of the dill; set aside.

2 Rinse fish; pat dry with paper towels. Cut fish into pieces. In a food processor combine the remaining 1 tablespoon dill, fish pieces, bread crumbs, green onions, salt, and pepper. Cover and process with on/off pulses until fish is finely chopped. Shape fish mixture into four 3-inch-diameter patties. Lightly coat both sides of patties with cooking spray.

3 For a charcoal grill, grill patties on the rack of an uncovered grill directly over medium-hot coals about 10 minutes or until fish flakes easily when tested with a fork, turning once halfway through grilling. (For a gas grill, preheat grill. Reduce heat to medium-high. Place patties on grill rack over heat. Cover and grill as above.)

4 Serve burgers in toasted buns with mayonnaise mixture.

NUTRITION FACTS PER SERVING:
406 cal., 19 g total fat (3 g sat. fat), 72 mg chol., 609 mg sodium, 29 g carb., 3 g dietary fiber, 28 g protein.

Tomato-Basil Turkey Burgers

2 pounds uncooked ground turkey breast

2 tablespoons finely chopped oil-packed dried tomato

2 tablespoons snipped fresh basil

1 teaspoon sea salt

½ teaspoon freshly ground black pepper

4 ounces smoked or fresh mozzarella cheese, thinly sliced

2 cups lightly packed arugula or watercress

8 sourdough or other hamburger buns, split and toasted

1 large yellow sweet pepper, roasted* and cut into strips, or ¾ cup roasted red sweet pepper strips (optional)

1 recipe Pesto Mayonnaise (optional)

1 In a large bowl combine ground turkey, dried tomato, basil, salt, and black pepper; mix well. Shape mixture into eight ½-inch-thick patties.

2 For a charcoal grill, grill patties on the rack of an uncovered grill directly over medium coals for 10 to 13 minutes or until no longer pink (165°F), turning once halfway through grilling and adding cheese for the last 1 to 2 minutes of grilling. (For a gas grill, preheat grill. Reduce heat to medium. Place patties on grill rack over heat. Cover and grill as above.)

Pesto Mayonnaise

In a small bowl stir together ⅓ cup fat-free mayonnaise and ¼ cup basil pesto. Season to taste with salt, ground black pepper, and bottled hot pepper sauce.

3 Place arugula on bottoms of toasted buns; add burgers. If desired, top with pepper strips and Pesto Mayonnaise. Add tops of buns.

NUTRITION FACTS PER SERVING:
328 cal., 5 g total fat (2 g sat. fat), 65 mg chol., 700 mg sodium, 33 g carb., 2 g dietary fiber, 35 g protein.

*tip

To roast the sweet pepper on the grill, quarter pepper lengthwise; remove stem, seeds, and membranes. For a charcoal grill, grill pepper pieces, skin sides down, on the rack of an uncovered grill directly over medium coals about 10 minutes or until blistered and dark. (For a gas grill, preheat grill. Reduce heat to medium. Place pepper pieces, skin sides down, on grill rack over heat. Cover and grill as above.) Wrap pepper pieces in foil; let stand about 15 minutes or until cool enough to handle. Using a sharp knife, loosen edges of skins; gently pull off skins in strips and discard.

Turkey Pizza Burgers

1   **egg, lightly beaten**

¼   **cup quick-cooking rolled oats**

4   **teaspoons snipped fresh oregano**

⅛   **teaspoon salt**

⅛   **teaspoon ground black pepper**

1   **pound uncooked ground turkey breast**

4   **slices provolone cheese (2 ounces)**

½   **cup reduced-sodium red pasta sauce**

4   **whole wheat hamburger buns, split and toasted**

1 In a medium bowl combine egg, oats, 2 teaspoons of the oregano, the salt, and pepper. Add ground turkey; mix well. Shape turkey mixture into four ¾-inch-thick patties.

2 For a charcoal grill, grill patties on the rack of an uncovered grill directly over medium coals for 14 to 18 minutes or until no longer pink (165°F), turning once halfway through grilling and adding cheese for the last 1 minute of grilling. (For a gas grill, preheat grill. Reduce heat to medium. Place patties on grill rack over heat. Cover and grill as above.)

3 Meanwhile, in a small saucepan cook pasta sauce until heated through.

4 Place burgers on bottoms of buns. Top with pasta sauce and the remaining 2 teaspoons oregano. Add tops of buns.

NUTRITION FACTS PER SERVING:
354 cal., 9 g total fat (3 g sat. fat), 133 mg chol., 487 mg sodium, 28 g carb., 3 g dietary fiber, 38 g protein.

Italian Sausage Burgers ★

START TO FINISH 30 minutes MAKES 4 servings

- 1 **cup marinara sauce**
- ¼ **cup finely shredded Parmesan cheese (1 ounce)**
- 2 **tablespoons snipped fresh basil or 2 teaspoons dried basil, crushed**
- 1 **pound ground beef**
- 4 **ounces bulk pork sausage**
- 4 **slices Italian bread, toasted**
- ¼ **to ½ cup shredded provolone or mozzarella cheese (1 to 2 ounces)**
  Shredded fresh basil (optional)

1 In a large bowl combine 2 tablespoons of the marinara sauce, the Parmesan cheese, and snipped basil. Add ground beef and sausage; mix well. Shape meat mixture into four ¾-inch-thick patties.

2 For a charcoal grill, grill patties on the rack of an uncovered grill directly over medium coals for 14 to 18 minutes or until done (160°F), turning once halfway through grilling. (For a gas grill, preheat grill. Reduce heat to medium. Place patties on grill rack over heat. Cover and grill as above.)

3 Place burgers on toasted bread slices. Heat the remaining marinara sauce; spoon over burgers. Sprinkle with provolone cheese and, if desired, top with shredded basil.

NUTRITION FACTS PER SERVING:
548 cal., 34 g total fat (14 g sat. fat), 109 mg chol., 796 mg sodium, 24 g carb., 2 g dietary fiber, 31 g protein.

Greek-Style Sloppy Joes

START TO FINISH 20 minutes MAKES 6 sandwiches

- 1 **pound lean ground lamb or beef**
- ½ **cup chopped onion (1 medium)**
- 1 **15-ounce can tomato sauce**
- ⅓ **cup bulgur**
- 1 **teaspoon dried oregano, crushed**
- ½ **teaspoon salt**
- ¼ **teaspoon ground black pepper**
- 2 **cups shredded romaine lettuce**
- 6 **kaiser rolls, split and toasted**
- 1 **cup crumbled feta cheese with tomato and basil or plain feta cheese (4 ounces)**

1 In a large skillet cook ground meat and onion over medium-high heat until meat is brown, using a wooden spoon to break up meat as it cooks. Drain off fat. Stir in tomato sauce, bulgur, oregano, salt, and pepper. Bring to boiling; reduce heat. Simmer, uncovered, about 5 minutes or to desired consistency, stirring occasionally.

2 Divide lettuce among bottoms of rolls. Spoon meat mixture onto lettuce and sprinkle with cheese. Add tops of rolls.

NUTRITION FACTS PER SANDWICH:
418 cal., 17 g total fat (7 g sat. fat), 67 mg chol., 1,086 mg sodium, 42 g carb., 4 g dietary fiber, 23 g protein.

Anytime Egg Sandwich

START TO FINISH **30 minutes** OVEN **400°F** MAKES **4 sandwiches**

⅔   **cup chopped roma tomatoes (2 medium)**

2   **green onions, finely chopped***

¼   **cup fresh cilantro leaves**

1   **medium fresh jalapeño chile pepper, finely chopped****

    Salt

    Ground black pepper

¼   **cup butter, melted**

1   **teaspoon ground ancho chile pepper or chili powder**

4   **ciabatta buns or other hearty rolls, split**

1   **cup shredded Monterey Jack cheese (4 ounces)**

4   **eggs**

8   **slices bacon, crisp-cooked and drained**

1   **avocado, seeded, peeled, and mashed**

    Lime wedges (optional)

1 Preheat oven to 400°F. For pico de gallo, in a medium bowl combine tomatoes, the chopped white parts of the green onions (reserve the chopped green parts), cilantro, and jalapeño chile pepper. Season to taste with salt and black pepper; set aside.

2 In a small bowl stir together melted butter and ancho chile pepper. Brush the uncut side of tops of buns with some of the butter mixture (reserve the remaining butter mixture). Place tops of buns, cut sides down, on a baking sheet. Sprinkle cut sides of bottoms of buns with cheese; place on baking sheet. Bake about 5 minutes or until buns are golden brown and cheese is melted.

3 Meanwhile, beat eggs with a whisk until pale yellow in color. Season with additional salt and black pepper. Stir in the reserved green parts of the green onions. Brush a 12-inch nonstick skillet with the remaining butter mixture. Add egg mixture to skillet. Cook over medium heat, stirring eggs gently but continuously with a spatula until mixture resembles small pieces of cooked egg surrounded by liquid egg. Stop stirring. Cook for 30 to 60 seconds more or until egg mixture is set but shiny. Turn out onto a baking sheet. Cut into 4 portions.

4 Place egg portions on bottoms of buns, folding to fit. Layer bacon, avocado, and pico de gallo. Add tops of buns. If desired, serve with lime wedges.

NUTRITION FACTS PER SANDWICH:
590 cal., 39 g total fat (18 g sat. fat), 285 mg chol., 1165 mg sodium, 35 g carb., 5 g dietary fiber, 26 g protein.

*tip

Use the white parts of the green onions in the pico de gallo and the green parts in the eggs.

**tip

Because chile peppers contain volatile oils that can burn your skin and eyes, avoid direct contact with them as much as possible. When working with chile peppers, wear plastic or rubber gloves. If your bare hands do touch the peppers, wash your hands and nails well with soap and warm water.

Chicken-Apple Crunch Salad Sandwich

START TO FINISH 25 minutes MAKES 4 sandwiches

1½ cups shredded purchased roasted chicken

1½ cups chopped Granny Smith apple

½ cup chopped celery (1 stalk)

⅓ cup dried cranberries

2 tablespoons sliced green onion (1)

⅓ cup light mayonnaise

⅓ cup light sour cream

1 tablespoon lemon juice

⅛ teaspoon salt

⅛ teaspoon ground cinnamon

⅛ teaspoon ground black pepper

4 8-inch multigrain flour tortillas or 4 whole wheat pita bread rounds, halved crosswise

1 In a large bowl combine chicken, apple, celery, dried cranberries, and green onion.

2 In a small bowl stir together mayonnaise, sour cream, lemon juice, salt, cinnamon, and pepper. Add sour cream mixture to chicken mixture; stir to coat.

3 Spoon chicken mixture onto tortillas; roll up or fold tortillas.

NUTRITION FACTS PER SANDWICH:
408 cal., 21 g total fat (6 g sat. fat), 69 mg chol., 1,080 mg sodium, 42 g carb., 7 g dietary fiber, 18 g protein.

Double Pork–Cuban Sandwiches

START TO FINISH 30 minutes   MAKES 4 sandwiches

2   tablespoons Dijon-style mustard

2   tablespoons mayonnaise or salad dressing

1   teaspoon lime juice

1/8 teaspoon ground cumin

4   English muffins or ciabatta buns, split

8   ounces thinly sliced cooked ham

8   slices packaged ready-to-serve cooked bacon

8   lengthwise sandwich pickle slices

4   slices provolone or Swiss cheese (about 4 ounces)

1   tablespoon butter, softened

1 In a small bowl combine mustard, mayonnaise, lime juice, and cumin. Spread cut sides of muffins with mayonnaise mixture. Layer ham, bacon, pickle slices, and cheese. Replace tops of muffins, spread sides down. Spread outsides of sandwiches with butter.

2 Preheat a covered indoor grill, panini press, grill pan, or large skillet. Place sandwiches, two at a time if necessary, in grill or panini press. Cover and cook for 6 to 8 minutes or until golden brown and cheese is melted. (If using a grill pan or skillet, place sandwiches on grill pan or skillet. Weight sandwiches down with a heavy skillet [add food cans for more weight] and cook for 2 minutes. Turn sandwiches over, weight down, and cook for 2 to 3 minutes more or until golden brown and cheese is melted.)

NUTRITION FACTS PER SANDWICH:
426 cal., 22 g total fat (10 g sat. fat), 65 mg chol., 1,755 mg sodium, 29 g carb., 2 g dietary fiber, 24 g protein.

Grilled Turkey–Apricot Sandwiches

START TO FINISH 20 minutes   MAKES 4 sandwiches

- 3   tablespoons apricot preserves
- 2   tablespoons Dijon-style mustard
- 8   slices whole grain bread
- 8   ounces sliced cooked turkey breast
- 4   slices Muenster cheese
- ¼   cup butter, softened

1 In a small bowl combine preserves and mustard. Spread one side of bread slices with mustard mixture. On four of the bread slices layer turkey and cheese. Top with the remaining four bread slices, spread sides down. Spread outsides of sandwiches with butter.

2 Heat a griddle or large skillet over medium heat. Add sandwiches, two at a time if necessary, and cook for 4 to 6 minutes or until golden brown and cheese is melted, turning once.

NUTRITION FACTS PER SANDWICH:
471 cal., 21 g total fat (11 g sat. fat), 75 mg chol., 1,238 mg sodium, 42 g carb., 8 g dietary fiber, 26 g protein.

Open-Face Chicken and Basil Sandwiches

START TO FINISH 30 minutes   MAKES 8 sandwiches

- 1   8-ounce container whipped cream cheese
- ½   cup snipped fresh basil
- 3   tablespoons bottled ranch salad dressing
- 2   6-ounce packages refrigerated chopped cooked chicken breast
- 1   cup chopped roma tomatoes (3 medium)
- 2   tablespoons snipped fresh basil
- 8   ½-inch slices French or Italian bread, toasted
- ½   cup finely shredded Parmesan cheese (2 ounces)

1 Preheat broiler. In a small bowl combine cream cheese, ½ cup basil, and salad dressing; set aside. In a medium bowl combine chicken, tomatoes, and 2 tablespoons basil.

2 Spread one side of bread slices with cream cheese mixture; place on a baking sheet. Top with chicken mixture; sprinkle with cheese. Broil 3 to 4 inches from the heat for 1 to 2 minutes or until heated through and cheese is melted.

NUTRITION FACTS PER SANDWICH:
268 cal., 15 g total fat (7 g sat. fat), 62 mg chol., 795 mg sodium, 17 g carb., 1 g dietary fiber, 17 g protein.

Cajun-Spiced Turkey Sandwiches

START TO FINISH **20 minutes** MAKES **4 sandwiches**

- ⅓ cup light mayonnaise or salad dressing
- 1 teaspoon purchased salt-free Cajun seasoning or Homemade Salt-Free Cajun Seasoning
- 1 clove garlic, minced
- 8 thin slices firm-texture whole wheat bread, toasted if desired
- 1 cup fresh spinach leaves
- 8 ounces reduced-sodium cooked turkey breast, sliced
- 4 slices tomato
- 1 small green sweet pepper or poblano chile pepper*, seeded and sliced

1 In a small bowl stir together mayonnaise, Cajun seasoning, and garlic. Spread one side of bread slices with mayonnaise mixture.

2 Arrange spinach on four of the bread slices. Layer with turkey, tomato, and sweet pepper. Top with the remaining four bread slices, spread sides down.

NUTRITION FACTS PER SANDWICH:
210 cal., 9 g total fat (1 g sat. fat), 37 mg chol., 635 mg sodium, 19 g carb., 3 g dietary fiber, 16 g protein.

Homemade Salt-Free Cajun Seasoning

In a small bowl stir together ¼ teaspoon ground white pepper, ¼ teaspoon garlic powder, ¼ teaspoon onion powder, ¼ teaspoon paprika, ¼ teaspoon ground black pepper, and ⅛ to ¼ teaspoon cayenne pepper.

*tip
Because chile peppers contain volatile oils that can burn your skin and eyes, avoid direct contact with them as much as possible. When working with chile peppers, wear plastic or rubber gloves. If your bare hands do touch the peppers, wash your hands and nails well with soap and warm water.

Garlic-Mustard Steak Sandwiches

START TO FINISH **30 minutes** MAKES **4 sandwiches**

8   ½-inch slices French bread
1   tablespoon honey mustard
2   cloves garlic, minced
½   teaspoon dried marjoram or thyme, crushed
¼   teaspoon coarse ground black pepper
12 ounces beef flank steak
1   large red onion, cut into ½-inch slices
2   tablespoons light sour cream
2   ounces thinly sliced reduced-fat Swiss cheese

1 Preheat broiler. Place bread slices on the unheated rack of a broiler pan. Broil 4 to 5 inches from the heat for 2 to 4 minutes or until toasted, turning once halfway through broiling. Transfer to a wire rack; set aside. In a small bowl stir together honey mustard, garlic, marjoram, and pepper; set aside.

2 Trim fat from meat. Score both sides of meat in a diamond pattern by making shallow diagonal cuts at 1-inch intervals. Place meat on one side of the broiler pan. Divide the mustard mixture in half. Spread half of the mustard mixture over meat. Place onion slices beside meat on broiler pan.

3 Broil 4 to 5 inches from the heat for 15 to 18 minutes or until meat is medium (160°F) and onion is crisp-tender, turning onion slices once halfway through broiling (do not turn meat). Thinly slice meat diagonally across the grain. Separate onion slices into rings.

4 In a small bowl stir together sour cream and the remaining mustard mixture. Spread sour cream mixture on half of the bread slices. Layer with meat, red onion, and cheese. Return to the broiler pan. Broil about 1 minute or until cheese is melted. Top with the remaining bread slices.

NUTRITION FACTS PER SANDWICH:
334 cal., 9 g total fat (4 g sat. fat), 38 mg chol., 425 mg sodium, 35 g carb., 2 g dietary fiber, 30 g protein.

Tote-and-Slice Salami and Cheese Loaf

¾ cup dried tomatoes (not oil pack)

1 16-ounce loaf unsliced Italian or French bread

½ of an 8-ounce package cream cheese, softened

⅓ cup basil pesto

8 ounces thinly sliced provolone cheese

8 ounces thinly sliced peppered or regular salami

1 medium fresh banana chile pepper or 8 bottled banana chile peppers, stemmed, seeded, and sliced

½ of a medium red onion, thinly sliced

Small bottled pepperoncini salad peppers and/or pimiento-stuffed green olives (optional)

1 In a small bowl combine dried tomatoes and enough boiling water to cover. Let stand for 10 minutes; drain. Place tomatoes in a food processor. Cover and process until finely chopped. (Or finely chop drained tomatoes by hand.)

2 Using a serrated knife, cut bread in half horizontally. Remove some of the soft bread from bottom half of loaf, leaving a ½-inch shell.

3 Spread cream cheese on cut sides of bread. Spread top half with finely chopped tomatoes and bottom half with pesto. On the bottom half layer half of the provolone cheese, the salami, banana chile pepper, red onion, and the remaining provolone cheese. Add top half of bread, cream cheese side down.

4 If toting, tightly wrap loaf in plastic wrap. Tote in an insulated cooler with ice packs.

5 To serve, slice loaf crosswise into six sandwiches. If desired, secure with long wooden picks threaded with pepperoncini peppers and/or olives.

NUTRITION FACTS PER SANDWICH:
588 cal., 34 g total fat (14 g sat. fat), 69 mg chol., 1,645 mg sodium, 46 g carb., 4 g dietary fiber, 24 g protein.

Chicken Club Sandwiches with Avocado Spread

START TO FINISH **15 minutes**   MAKES **4 sandwiches**

1   **medium ripe avocado**

1   **tablespoon lime juice**

   Salt

   Ground black pepper

4   **potato rolls, ciabatta buns, or hamburger buns, split and toasted**

1   **6-ounce package refrigerated Southwestern cooked chicken breast strips***

8   **slices packaged ready-to-serve cooked bacon**

1   **small tomato, thinly sliced**

1 Seed and peel avocado. In a medium bowl mash avocado with a fork or the back of a wooden spoon; stir in lime juice. Season to taste with salt and pepper. Set aside.

2 On bottoms of rolls layer chicken, bacon, and tomato. Spread tops of rolls with avocado mixture; add tops of rolls, spread sides down.

NUTRITION FACTS PER SANDWICH: *280 cal., 12 g total fat (3 g sat. fat), 38 mg chol., 892 mg sodium, 27 g carb., 5 g dietary fiber, 17 g protein.*

*tip

For a warm sandwich, heat chicken strips according to package directions. Assemble as directed.

Grilled Chicken–Mole Sandwiches

START TO FINISH **30 minutes**   MAKES **4 sandwiches**

1   **small avocado, seeded, peeled, and mashed**

2   **tablespoons mayonnaise**

¼   **teaspoon salt**

¼   **teaspoon cayenne pepper**

4   **skinless, boneless chicken breast halves (about 1¼ pounds total)**

Salt

Ground black pepper

⅓   **cup mole sauce**

4   **4- to 6-inch ciabata buns, split and toasted**

Tomato slices

Baby romaine lettuce or other lettuce leaves

1 In a small bowl stir together avocado, mayonnaise, ¼ teaspoon salt, and cayenne pepper. Cover and chill until ready to serve.

2 Sprinkle chicken with additional salt and black pepper. Using a sharp knife, cut a horizontal slit two-thirds of the way through each chicken piece. Open each piece and spread with 1 tablespoon of the mole sauce; fold closed.

3 For a charcoal grill, grill chicken on the rack of an uncovered grill directly over medium coals for 12 to 15 minutes or until chicken is no longer pink (170°F), turning once halfway through grilling and brushing with the remaining mole sauce during the last 3 minutes of grilling. (For a gas grill, preheat grill. Reduce heat to medium. Place chicken on grill rack over heat. Cover and grill as above.)

4 Cut chicken diagonally into ¼- to ½-inch slices. Spread avocado mixture on bottoms of buns. Layer with chicken, tomato, and lettuce. Add tops of buns.

NUTRITION FACTS PER SANDWICH:
624 cal., 18 g total fat (3 g sat. fat), 85 mg chol., 1,101 mg sodium, 67 g carb., 7 g dietary fiber, 46 g protein.

Mole (pronounced MO-lay) is the Spanish word for mixture. Traditionally, the Mexican sauce includes roasted and ground pumpkin seeds, onions, herbs, and two or more types of chiles.

Avocado BLT Sandwiches

START TO FINISH 25 minutes MAKES 4 sandwiches

- 1 large ripe avocado
- 2 tablespoons light mayonnaise
- 1 teaspoon lemon juice
- 1 clove garlic, minced
- 8 slices whole wheat bread, toasted
- 4 slices bacon, crisp-cooked, drained, and halved crosswise
- 4 leaves romaine lettuce
- 1 large tomato, thinly sliced

1 Seed and peel avocado. Transfer one-half of the avocado to a small bowl; mash with a fork or the back of a wooden spoon. Stir in mayonnaise, lemon juice, and garlic; set aside. Thinly slice the remaining avocado half.

2 On four of the bread slices layer avocado slices, bacon, lettuce, and tomato. Spread the remaining four bread slices with mayonnaise mixture; place over tomato, spread sides down.

NUTRITION FACTS PER SANDWICH:
257 cal., 14 g total fat (2 g sat. fat), 10 mg chol., 432 mg sodium, 27 g carb., 7 g dietary fiber, 9 g protein.

Ham and Swiss Grilled Sandwiches ★

START TO FINISH 15 minutes MAKES 2 sandwiches

- 4 slices firm-texture whole wheat, white, or sourdough bread
- 2 to 3 teaspoons Dijon-style mustard
- 2 ounces thinly sliced cooked ham
- 2 slices Swiss cheese (2 ounces)
- 1 egg white
- ¼ cup milk
  Nonstick cooking spray

1 Spread one side of two of the bread slices with mustard. Layer ham and cheese; top with the remaining two bread slices. In a shallow dish combine egg white and milk.

2 Coat a nonstick griddle or large skillet with cooking spray; heat griddle over medium heat. Dip each sandwich into egg mixture, turning to coat. Place sandwiches on griddle; cook for 2 to 4 minutes or until golden brown and cheese is melted, turning once.

NUTRITION FACTS PER SANDWICH:
317 cal., 13 g total fat (6 g sat. fat), 43 mg chol., 855 mg sodium, 31 g carb., 0 g dietary fiber, 20 g protein.

★ Veggie-Cheese Sandwich and Tomato Soup

START TO FINISH **25 minutes** MAKES **4 servings**

8 ½-inch slices crusty country white or whole wheat French bread

2 tablespoons honey mustard or bottled ranch salad dressing

4 ounces thinly sliced farmer cheese or cheddar cheese

½ cup thinly sliced cucumber or roma tomatoes

½ cup fresh spinach leaves or packaged shredded broccoli (broccoli slaw mix)

¼ cup thinly sliced red onion or red sweet pepper strips

1 tablespoon olive oil or vegetable oil

2 10.75-ounce cans condensed tomato soup

2½ cups water

1 cup chopped roma tomatoes (3 medium)

1 tablespoon balsamic vinegar

¼ cup plain low-fat yogurt or light sour cream (optional)

1 tablespoon snipped fresh chives

1 Spread one side of bread slices with honey mustard. On four of the bread slices layer cheese, cucumber, spinach, and red onion. Top with the remaining four bread slices, mustard sides down. Brush outsides of sandwiches with oil.

2 Preheat a covered indoor grill, panini press, grill pan, or large skillet. Place sandwiches, two at a time if necessary, in grill or panini press. Cover and cook about 6 minutes or until golden brown and cheese is melted. (If using a grill pan or skillet, place sandwiches on grill pan or skillet. Weight sandwiches down with a heavy skillet [add food cans for more weight] and cook for 2 minutes. Turn sandwiches over, weight down, and cook about 2 minutes more or until golden brown and cheese is melted.)

3 Meanwhile, in a medium saucepan stir together soup, the water, tomatoes, and vinegar; heat through. If desired, top each serving with yogurt; swirl slightly. Sprinkle with chives. Serve sandwiches with soup.

NUTRITION FACTS PER SERVING:
413 cal., 13 g total fat (3 g sat. fat), 9 mg chol., 1,380 mg sodium, 60 g carb., 4 g dietary fiber, 11 g protein.

Open-Face Italian Beef Sandwiches

START TO FINISH 20 minutes MAKES 4 sandwiches

¼ cup white wine vinegar or cider vinegar

1 teaspoon sugar

½ teaspoon salt

½ teaspoon ground black pepper

1 17-ounce package refrigerated cooked Italian-style beef roast au jus, undrained

1 cup sliced baby or regular red and/or yellow sweet peppers

2 square whole grain ciabatta buns, split

4 slices provolone cheese (4 ounces)

2 tablespoons snipped fresh Italian (flat-leaf) parsley

Snipped fresh Italian (flat-leaf) parsley (optional)

1 Preheat broiler. In a large microwave-safe bowl combine vinegar, sugar, salt, and pepper. Stir in meat with juices and sweet peppers. Microwave, covered, on 100 percent power (high) for 4 minutes.

2 Meanwhile, place buns, cut sides up, on a baking sheet. Broil 3 to 4 inches from the heat about 1 minute or until lightly toasted. Top with cheese. Broil for 1 to 2 minutes more or until cheese is melted.

3 Using a fork, coarsely shred meat. Stir in 2 tablespoons parsley. Using a slotted spoon, mound meat mixture onto toasted bun halves. If desired, sprinkle with additional parsley. Serve with any remaining juices.

NUTRITION FACTS PER SANDWICH:
341 cal., 15 g total fat (8 g sat. fat), 78 mg chol., 774 mg sodium, 22 g carb., 2 g dietary fiber, 31 g protein.

Antipasto Panini

- 1 9- to 10-inch Italian flatbread (focaccia)
- ¼ cup olive tapenade and/or pesto
- 4 ounces sliced provolone cheese
- 3 ounces sliced salami
- 3 ounces sliced capicola
- 4 pepperoncini salad peppers
- 6 large fresh basil leaves
- 2 tablespoons butter, softened

1 Using a serrated knife, cut focaccia in half horizontally. If necessary, trim off tops or bottoms of focaccia halves to make each about ¾ inch thick. Spread cut sides of focaccia with tapenade.

2 On one of the focaccia halves layer half of the cheese, salami, capicola, pepperoncini peppers, and basil. Top with the remaining cheese and the remaining focaccia half, tapenade side down. Spread outside of sandwich with butter.

3 For a charcoal grill, arrange medium-hot coals around edge of grill. Test for medium heat above center of grill. Place sandwich on grill rack over center of grill. Weight sandwich down with a baking sheet topped with 2 bricks. Cover and grill for 6 to 8 minutes or until golden brown. Turn sandwich over and weight down. Cover and grill for 6 to 8 minutes more or until golden brown and cheese is melted. (For a gas grill, preheat grill. Reduce heat to medium. Adjust for indirect cooking. Grill as above.)

NUTRITION FACTS PER SERVING:
604 cal., 35 g total fat (13 g sat. fat), 78 mg chol., 1,912 mg sodium, 51 g carb., 3 g dietary fiber, 25 g protein.

Chicken Panini Sandwiches 🥕

⅓   cup fat-free mayonnaise or salad dressing

2   cloves garlic, minced

1   teaspoon dried Italian seasoning, crushed

8   ½-inch slices crusty country multigrain bread

1½ cups sliced or shredded cooked chicken breast

½   cup roasted red sweet pepper strips

1   cup lightly packed fresh basil leaves

4   teaspoons olive oil

1 In a small bowl stir together mayonnaise, garlic, and Italian seasoning. Spread one side of bread slices with mayonnaise mixture. On four of the bread slices layer chicken, roasted pepper, and basil. Top with the remaining four bread slices, spread sides down. Lightly brush outsides of sandwiches with oil.

2 Preheat a covered indoor grill, panini press, grill pan, or large skillet. Place sandwiches, two at a time if necessary, in grill or panini press. Cover and cook about 6 minutes or until golden brown and heated through. (If using a grill pan or skillet, place sandwiches on grill pan or skillet. Weight sandwiches down with a heavy skillet [add food cans for more weight] and cook for 2 minutes. Turn sandwiches over, weight down, and cook about 2 minutes more or until golden brown and heated through.)

NUTRITION FACTS PER SANDWICH:
312 cal., 9 g total fat (1 g sat. fat), 47 mg chol., 390 mg sodium, 35 g carb., 9 g dietary fiber, 25 g protein.

Tuna and White Bean Panini

START TO FINISH **30 minutes** MAKES **4 sandwiches**

1 15-ounce can cannellini beans (white kidney beans), rinsed, drained, and slightly mashed

2 7.1-ounce packages albacore tuna (water pack), drained and slightly flaked

¼ cup finely chopped red onion

2 cloves garlic, minced

¼ cup mayonnaise

8 ½-inch slices crusty country Italian or sourdough bread, or white or whole wheat sandwich bread

3 tablespoons butter, softened

Garlic-flavor oil (optional)

2 medium tomatoes, thinly sliced

1 cup lightly packed large fresh basil leaves

4 ounces sliced provolone cheese

Cherry tomatoes (optional)

1 In a medium bowl combine beans, tuna, red onion, and garlic. Stir in mayonnaise; set aside.

2 Spread one side of bread slices with butter. If desired, brush the remaining sides with garlic-flavor oil. Spread tuna mixture on the unbuttered sides of four of the bread slices. Layer with tomatoes, basil, and cheese. Top with the remaining bread slices, buttered sides up.

3 Preheat a covered indoor grill, panini press, grill pan, or large skillet. Place sandwiches, two at a time if necessary, in grill or panini press. Cover and cook about 6 minutes or until golden brown and cheese is melted. (If using a grill pan or skillet, place sandwiches on grill pan or skillet. Weight sandwiches down with a heavy skillet [add food cans for more weight] and cook for 2 minutes. Turn sandwiches over, weight down, and cook about 2 minutes more or until golden brown and cheese is melted.)

4 If desired, garnish each sandwich with a wooden pick threaded with a cherry tomato.

NUTRITION FACTS PER SANDWICH:
630 cal., 33 g total fat (8 g sat. fat), 93 mg chol., 1,090 mg sodium, 45 g carb., 8 g dietary fiber, 43 g protein.

Apple, Ham, and Brie Panini

START TO FINISH 20 minutes MAKES 4 sandwiches

- 8   ½-inch slices sourdough bread
- 2   ounces low-fat, reduced-sodium sliced cooked ham, cut into bite-size strips
- 1½ ounces brie cheese, sliced
- 2   medium tart apples, cored and thinly sliced
- ½   cup whole cranberry sauce
- 2   tablespoons olive oil

1 On four of the bread slices layer ham, cheese, and apples. Spread the remaining four bread slices with cranberry sauce; place on sandwiches, cranberry sides down. Brush outsides of sandwiches with oil.

2 Preheat a covered indoor grill, panini press, grill pan, or large skillet. Place sandwiches, two at a time if necessary, in grill or panini press. Cover and cook about 6 minutes or until golden brown and cheese is melted. (If using a grill pan or skillet, place sandwiches on grill pan or skillet. Weight sandwiches down with a heavy skillet [add food cans for more weight] and cook for 2 minutes. Turn sandwiches over, weight down, and cook about 2 minutes more or until golden brown and cheese is melted.)

NUTRITION FACTS PER SANDWICH:
333 cal., 11 g total fat (3 g sat. fat), 18 mg chol., 505 mg sodium, 49 g carb., 3 g dietary fiber, 10 g protein.

Turkey Panini with Basil Aioli

START TO FINISH **30 minutes** MAKES **4 sandwiches**

2 **tablespoons mayonnaise or salad dressing**

1 **tablespoon basil pesto**

4 **ciabatta buns, split, or 8 slices sourdough bread**

8 **ounces thinly sliced cooked turkey breast**

1 **3.5-ounce package thinly sliced pepperoni**

½ **cup sliced roasted red sweet pepper**

4 **ounces sliced provolone cheese**

1 **to 2 tablespoons olive oil**

1 In a small bowl combine mayonnaise and pesto. Spread cut sides of buns with pesto mixture. On bottoms of buns layer turkey, pepperoni, and roasted pepper, and cheese. Add tops of buns. Lightly brush outsides of sandwiches with oil.

2 Preheat a covered indoor grill, panini press, grill pan, or large skillet. Place sandwiches, two at a time if necessary, in grill or panini press. Cover and cook for 6 to 8 minutes or until golden brown and cheese is melted. (If using a grill pan or skillet, place sandwiches on grill pan or skillet. Weight sandwiches down with a heavy skillet [add food cans for more weight] and cook for 2 minutes. Turn sandwiches over, weight down, and cook for 2 to 3 minutes more or until golden brown and cheese is melted.)

NUTRITION FACTS PER SANDWICH:
506 cal., 30 g total fat (11 g sat. fat), 80 mg chol., 1,534 mg sodium, 30 g carb., 2 g dietary fiber, 29 g protein.

Cheesy Ham and Pesto Panini

START TO FINISH **30 minutes** MAKES **6 sandwiches**

¼ **cup mayonnaise**

1 **tablespoon basil pesto**

1 **16-ounce loaf unsliced ciabatta bread or Italian bread**

6 **ounces thinly sliced provolone cheese**

6 **ounces thinly sliced cooked ham and/or salami**

2 **cups fresh spinach or arugula**

2 **tablespoons olive oil**

1 In a small bowl stir together mayonnaise and pesto; set aside.

2 Using a serrated knife, cut bread in half horizontally. Place half of the cheese on bottom half of bread. Spread cheese with mayonnaise mixture. Layer with ham, spinach, and the remaining cheese. Add top half of bread. Brush outside of bread with oil. Cut crosswise into six sandwiches.

3 Preheat a covered indoor grill, panini press, grill pan, or large skillet. Place sandwiches, three at a time if necessary, in grill or panini press. Cover and cook about 6 minutes or until golden brown and cheese is melted. (If using a grill pan or skillet, place sandwiches on grill pan or skillet. Weight sandwiches down with a heavy skillet [add food cans for more weight] and cook for 3 minutes. Turn sandwiches over, weight down, and cook about 3 minutes more or until golden brown and cheese is melted.)

NUTRITION FACTS PER SANDWICH:
429 cal., 23 g total fat (8 g sat. fat), 39 mg chol., 954 mg sodium, 37 g carb., 2 g dietary fiber, 19 g protein.

Customize a grilled sandwich or panini by altering the fillings to fit your taste. Try these options:
- **Camembert with apples and pancetta**
- **Brie with turkey and cranberries**
- **Fontina with caramelized onions and pears**
- **Blue cheese and crumbled walnuts**

Turkey-Mango Quesadillas

START TO FINISH **30 minutes**   MAKES **4 servings**

4   **8-inch flour tortillas**

1   **tablespoon vegetable oil**

1½ **cups chopped cooked or
    smoked turkey or chicken
    (about 8 ounces)**

6   **ounces Gouda or smoked
    Gouda cheese, thinly sliced or
    shredded**

1   **cup mango salsa or mango-
    peach salsa**

½   **cup sliced roasted red sweet
    pepper**

¼   **cup snipped fresh cilantro
    (optional)**

1 Brush one side of tortillas with oil.
Place tortillas, oiled sides down,
on a work surface or waxed paper.
On half of each tortilla layer turkey,
cheese, ½ cup of the salsa, the roasted
pepper, and, if desired, cilantro. Fold
tortillas in half, pressing gently.

2 Heat a 12-inch skillet over
medium heat. Add quesadillas,
two at a time, and cook about
6 minutes or until light brown and
heated through, turning once.

3 Cut quesadillas into wedges.
Serve warm with the remaining
½ cup salsa.

NUTRITION FACTS PER SERVING:
*392 cal., 18 g total fat (9 g sat. fat),
96 mg chol., 778 mg sodium, 27 g carb.,
5 g dietary fiber, 32 g protein.*

Salmon and Asparagus Wraps

START TO FINISH 25 minutes MAKES 4 wraps

12 thin fresh asparagus spears (about 4 ounces)

½ cup cream cheese spread with chive and onion

2 teaspoons finely shredded lemon peel

2 tablespoons lemon juice

⅛ teaspoon cayenne pepper

6 ounces smoked salmon, flaked, with skin and bones removed

2 tablespoons snipped fresh basil or 1 teaspoon dried basil, crushed

4 6- to 7-inch whole wheat flour tortillas

½ of a medium red sweet pepper, seeded and cut into thin bite-size strips

1 Snap off and discard woody bases from asparagus. In a covered medium saucepan cook asparagus in a small amount of boiling, lightly salted water for 2 to 3 minutes or until crisp-tender; drain. Plunge into ice water to cool quickly; drain again. Pat dry with paper towels.

2 In a medium bowl stir together cream cheese spread, lemon peel, lemon juice, and cayenne pepper. Fold in salmon and basil.

3 Spread salmon mixture on tortillas. Top with asparagus and sweet pepper. Roll up tortillas. If necessary, secure with toothpicks.

NUTRITION FACTS PER WRAP: *254 cal., 14 g total fat (8 g sat. fat), 40 mg chol., 697 mg sodium, 17 g carb., 10 g dietary fiber, 13 g protein.*

Make-Ahead Directions: Prepare as directed. Wrap in plastic wrap and chill for up to 6 hours.

Chicken Lettuce Wraps

START TO FINISH **15 minutes**   MAKES **8 wraps (4 servings)**

2 **6-ounce packages refrigerated cooked chicken breast strips**

2 **cups shredded cabbage with carrot (coleslaw mix)**

1 **medium red sweet pepper, seeded and cut into bite-size strips**

$\frac{1}{4}$ **cup sliced green onions (2)**

2 **tablespoons snipped fresh cilantro**

2 **tablespoons teriyaki sauce or $\frac{1}{3}$ cup peanut stir-fry sauce**

8 **leaves butterhead (Boston or bibb) lettuce or leaf lettuce**

Fresh cilantro leaves (optional)

1 In a large skillet cook and stir chicken over medium heat until heated through. Remove from heat. Stir in coleslaw mix, sweet pepper, green onions, snipped cilantro, and teriyaki sauce.

2 Divide chicken mixture among lettuce leaves. If desired, sprinkle with cilantro leaves. Roll up lettuce.

NUTRITION FACTS PER SERVING:
131 cal., 2 g total fat (1 g sat. fat), 55 mg chol., 748 mg sodium, 9 g carb., 2 g dietary fiber, 21 g protein.

Tuna and Hummus Wrap 🥕 ★

START TO FINISH 20 minutes   MAKES 4 wraps

1	6-ounce can low-sodium chunk white tuna (water pack), drained
1¼	cups peeled, seeded, and finely chopped cucumber (1 small)
⅓	cup seeded and chopped tomato (1 small)
2	tablespoons olive oil
1	tablespoon snipped fresh dill or 1 teaspoon dried dill, crushed
¼	teaspoon ground black pepper
4	cups torn baby romaine lettuce or mixed lettuces
4	8-inch whole wheat tortillas
⅓	cup refrigerated cucumber and dill hummus

1 In a medium bowl stir together tuna, cucumber, tomato, oil, dill, and pepper. Add lettuce; toss gently to combine.

2 Spread one side of tortillas with hummus. Divide tuna mixture among tortillas; roll up tortillas.

NUTRITION FACTS PER WRAP:
280 cal., 11 g total fat (1 g sat. fat), 19 mg chol., 482 mg sodium, 32 g carb., 4 g dietary fiber, 16 g protein.

Mexican Tuna Melt

START TO FINISH 20 minutes   MAKES 4 sandwiches

2	6-ounce cans chunk white tuna (water pack), drained
¼	cup mayonnaise or salad dressing
2	tablespoons toasted pumpkin seeds (pepitas)* or dry roasted sunflower kernels
1	tablespoon finely chopped red onion
½	teaspoon finely shredded lime peel
1	tablespoon lime juice
1	teaspoon finely chopped chipotle pepper in adobo sauce (optional)
8	slices whole wheat bread
1	cup shredded Monterey Jack cheese with jalapeño peppers (4 ounces)
1	small tomato, thinly sliced
1	cup shredded iceberg lettuce

1 Preheat broiler. In a medium bowl combine tuna, mayonnaise, pumpkin seeds, red onion, lime peel, lime juice, and, if desired, chipotle pepper. Place four of the bread slices on a baking sheet. Spread tuna mixture on bread slices; top with cheese.

2 Broil 4 to 5 inches from the heat for 1½ to 3 minutes or until cheese is melted. Top with tomato, lettuce, and the remaining four bread slices.

NUTRITION FACTS PER SANDWICH:
467 cal., 26 g total fat (9 g sat. fat), 73 mg chol., 883 mg sodium, 24 g carb., 4 g dietary fiber, 36 g protein.

*tip

To toast pumpkin seeds, spread seeds in a shallow baking pan. Bake in a 350°F oven for 7 to 10 minutes or until light brown. Cool.

Cucumber and Chicken Pitas

START TO FINISH **30 minutes** MAKES **6 servings**

2 cups shredded purchased roasted chicken

2 cups cubed honeydew melon

1 cup finely chopped cucumber

1 cup finely chopped zucchini (1 small)

¼ cup thinly sliced green onions (2)

⅓ cup lime juice

2 tablespoons canola oil

2 tablespoons water

2 tablespoons snipped fresh mint

1 tablespoon sugar

⅛ teaspoon ground black pepper

6 whole grain pita bread rounds, halved crosswise

1 In a large bowl toss together chicken, honeydew melon, cucumber, zucchini, and green onions.

2 For dressing, in a screw-top jar combine lime juice, oil, the water, mint, sugar, and pepper. Cover and shake well.

3 Drizzle dressing over chicken mixture; toss gently to coat. Spoon chicken mixture into pita halves.

NUTRITION FACTS PER SERVING:
339 cal., 12 g total fat (3 g sat. fat), 42 mg chol., 627 mg sodium, 46 g carb., 6 g dietary fiber, 16 g protein.

Stuffed Focaccia

START TO FINISH 20 minutes   MAKES 3 servings

½ of a 9- to 10-inch garlic, onion, or plain Italian flatbread (focaccia)

½ of an 8-ounce carton mascarpone cheese

1 6-ounce jar marinated artichoke hearts, drained and chopped

1 tablespoon drained capers (optional)

4 ounces thinly sliced Genoa salami

1 cup arugula leaves

1 Using a serrated knife, cut focaccia in half horizontally. Spread cut sides of focaccia with mascarpone cheese. Sprinkle bottom half of focaccia with artichoke hearts and, if desired, capers; top with salami and arugula. Add top half of focaccia.

Make-Ahead Directions: Prepare as directed. Wrap in plastic wrap and chill for up to 4 hours.

NUTRITION FACTS PER SERVING:
545 cal., 36 g total fat (16 g sat. fat), 83 mg chol., 970 mg sodium, 43 g carb., 3 g dietary fiber, 23 g protein.

Fontina Cheese and Artichoke Pizza

START TO FINISH **30 minutes**   OVEN **450°F**   MAKES **6 servings**

1   tablespoon olive oil or
    vegetable oil

1   medium red onion, thinly
    sliced

2   cloves garlic, minced

1   12-inch Italian bread shell,
    such as Boboli brand

1½ cups shredded fontina or
    Swiss cheese (6 ounces)

½   of a 9-ounce package frozen
    artichoke hearts, thawed and
    cut up

½   cup pitted kalamata olives,
    halved or quartered

    Coarse ground black pepper

    Alfredo pasta sauce, warmed
    (optional)

1 Preheat oven to 450°F. In a medium skillet heat oil over medium heat. Add red onion and garlic; cook until onion is tender and golden brown, stirring occasionally.

2 Place bread shell on a lightly greased baking sheet. Bake for 5 minutes. Sprinkle with ½ cup of the cheese. Top with onion mixture, artichokes, and olives. Sprinkle with the remaining 1 cup cheese. Sprinkle lightly with pepper.

3 Bake for 8 to 10 minutes more or until heated through and cheese is melted. If desired, serve pizza with warm Alfredo sauce.

NUTRITION FACTS PER SERVING:
368 cal., 18 g total fat (6 g sat. fat), 38 mg chol., 780 mg sodium, 38 g carb., 2 g dietary fiber, 16 g protein.

Olive and Arugula Flatbread

START TO FINISH **25 minutes** MAKES **4 servings**

- 2 cups baby arugula or fresh spinach
- 2 to 3 tablespoons olive oil
- 1 teaspoon lemon juice
- 1 teaspoon red wine vinegar
- ¼ teaspoon salt
- ⅛ teaspoon cracked black pepper
- 1 14×12-inch Italian flatbread (focaccia) or one 12-inch thin Italian bread shell
- 2 teaspoons olive oil
- ¼ cup olive pesto or tapenade
- 18 to 20 pimiento-stuffed green olives
- ¼ cup shaved Parmesan cheese (1 ounce)*

1 Place arugula in a medium bowl. For dressing, in a screw-top jar combine 2 to 3 tablespoons oil, lemon juice, vinegar, salt, and pepper. Cover and shake well. Drizzle dressing over arugula; toss gently to coat.

2 Brush focaccia with 2 teaspoons oil. For a charcoal grill, grill focaccia on the rack of an uncovered grill directly over medium coals for 1 to 2 minutes or just until golden brown, turning once halfway through grilling. (For a gas grill, preheat grill. Reduce heat to medium. Place focaccia on grill rack over heat. Cover and grill as above.)

3 Spread focaccia with pesto. Top each with dressed arugula, olives, and cheese.

NUTRITION FACTS PER SERVING:
472 cal., 26 g total fat (6 g sat. fat), 4 mg chol., 879 mg sodium, 50 g carb., 5 g dietary fiber, 12 g protein.

*tip
To shave the cheese, use a vegetable peeler or a grater with large holes.

Easy Barbecued Pork Pizza

START TO FINISH **30 minutes** OVEN **425°F** MAKES **8 servings**

1 **17- to 18-ounce tub refrigerated barbecue sauce with shredded pork**

1 **tablespoon vegetable oil**

2 **cups thin red and/or yellow sweet pepper strips (2 medium)**

1 **medium onion, cut into thin wedges**

1 **12-inch packaged prebaked pizza crust**

1 **cup shredded Monterey Jack cheese (4 ounces)**

1 Preheat oven to 425°F. Heat barbecue sauce with pork according to package directions. Meanwhile, in a large skillet heat oil over medium-high heat. Add sweet peppers and onion; cook about 5 minutes or until crisp-tender.

2 Place pizza crust on a baking sheet. Spoon barbecue sauce with pork over crust, spreading evenly. Top with sweet pepper mixture; sprinkle with cheese. Bake about 12 minutes or until crust is light brown and cheese is melted.

NUTRITION FACTS PER SERVING:
319 cal., 11 g total fat (3 g sat. fat), 33 mg chol., 862 mg sodium, 39 g carb., 1 g dietary fiber, 17 g protein.

Individual Turkey Pizzas

START TO FINISH **25 minutes** MAKES **4 pizzas**

4 cups mesclun mix or other mixed baby greens

$\frac{1}{4}$ cup bottled peppercorn ranch salad dressing

1 tablespoon olive oil

1 clove garlic, minced

4 8-inch Italian bread shells, such as Boboli brand

3 cups chopped cooked turkey (about 1 pound)

$\frac{3}{4}$ cup chopped roasted red sweet pepper

$1\frac{1}{2}$ cups shredded mozzarella cheese (6 ounces)

Bottled peppercorn ranch salad dressing (optional)

1 Preheat broiler. In a large bowl combine mesclun mix and $\frac{1}{4}$ cup salad dressing; toss gently to coat. Set aside.

2 In a small bowl combine oil and garlic. Lightly brush tops of bread shells with oil mixture. Place bread shells, oiled sides up, on an extra-large baking sheet or two large baking sheets. Broil 4 to 5 inches from the heat for 2 to 3 minutes or until bread shells are light brown (if using two sheets, broil one sheet at a time).

3 Top bread shells with turkey and roasted pepper. Sprinkle with cheese. Broil about 2 minutes more or until cheese is melted. Top with dressed mesclun mix. If desired, serve with additional salad dressing.

NUTRITION FACTS PER PIZZA:
827 cal., 36 g total fat (13 g sat. fat), 116 mg chol., 1,287 mg sodium, 70 g carb., 3 g dietary fiber, 55 g protein.

Grilled Vegetable Pizzas

START TO FINISH **30 minutes** MAKES **4 pizzas**

75

1 medium zucchini, quartered lengthwise

1 small yellow summer squash, quartered lengthwise

1 small red sweet pepper, seeded and quartered lengthwise

2 tablespoons olive oil

¼ teaspoon salt

⅛ teaspoon ground black pepper

1 large ripe tomato, seeded and chopped

¼ cup mayonnaise or salad dressing

3 tablespoons basil pesto

4 6- to 7-inch pita bread rounds or Italian bread shells, such as Boboli brand

1 cup shredded mozzarella or smoked provolone cheese (4 ounces)

1 Brush zucchini, yellow squash, and sweet pepper with oil; sprinkle with salt and black pepper. For a charcoal grill with a cover, grill vegetables, uncovered, on the grill rack directly over medium coals until crisp-tender, turning once halfway through grilling. Allow 5 to 6 minutes for zucchini and yellow squash and 8 to 10 minutes for sweet pepper. (For a gas grill, preheat grill. Reduce heat to medium. Place vegetables on grill rack over heat. Cover and grill as above.) Remove vegetables from grill.

2 Chop grilled vegetables. In a medium bowl combine chopped vegetables, tomato, mayonnaise, and pesto. Spread vegetable mixture over pita rounds. Sprinkle with cheese.

3 Return vegetable-topped pita rounds to grill. Cover and grill for 2 to 3 minutes or until pita rounds are light brown, vegetables are heated through, and cheese is melted.

NUTRITION FACTS PER PIZZA: *513 cal., 33 g total fat (6 g sat. fat), 34 mg chol., 821 mg sodium, 41 g carb., 3 g dietary fiber, 14 g protein.*

Grilled Seafood Pizzas:

Prepare as directed, except add 5 ounces smoked salmon, slightly flaked, with skin and bones removed; one 9.25-ounce can tuna, well drained and slightly flaked; or 5 ounces chopped cooked shrimp to the vegetable mixture.

NUTRITION FACTS PER SERVING: *555 cal., 34 g total fat (7 g sat. fat), 42 mg chol., 1,099 mg sodium, 41 g carb., 3 g fiber, 21 g protein.*

Grilled Chicken Pizzas:

Prepare as directed, except add 5 ounces chopped cooked chicken to the vegetable mixture.

NUTRITION FACTS PER SERVING: *581 cal., 35 g total fat (7 g sat. fat), 65 mg chol., 851 mg sodium, 41 g carb., 3 g fiber, 25 g protein.*

tip

For a crispier crust, grill untopped pita rounds on the grill rack directly over medium coals for 1 to 2 minutes or until light brown. Turn pita rounds over and spread with vegetable mixture. Continue as directed.

Meatball Pizza ★

1 **12-inch Italian bread shell, such as Boboli brand**

1 **8-ounce can pizza sauce**

2 **cups shredded fontina cheese (8 ounces)**

½ **of a 16-ounce package (16) frozen cooked Italian-style meatballs, thawed and halved**

¼ **cup finely shredded fresh basil**

¼ **cup finely shredded Parmesan cheese (1 ounce)**

1 Preheat oven to 425°F. Place bread shell on a baking sheet. Spread with sauce; sprinkle with 1 cup of the fontina cheese. Top with meatballs and basil. Sprinkle with the remaining 1 cup fontina cheese and the Parmesan cheese.

2 Bake about 10 minutes or until heated through and cheese is melted.

NUTRITION FACTS PER SERVING: *698 cal., 38 g total fat (18 g sat. fat), 110 mg chol., 1,801 mg sodium, 53 g carb., 5 g dietary fiber, 38 g protein.*

Alfredo and Sweet Pepper Pizza:

Prepare as directed, except substitute a mixture of ¾ cup Alfredo pasta sauce and ½ teaspoon dried Italian seasoning, crushed, for the pizza sauce; Italian 4-cheese blend for the fontina cheese; and one 16-ounce package frozen sweet pepper and onion stir-fry vegetables, thawed and well drained, for the meatballs. Omit basil and Parmesan cheese.

NUTRITION FACTS PER SERVING: *590 cal., 29 g total fat (12 g sat. fat), 86 mg chol., 1,273 mg sodium, 58 g carb., 1 g dietary fiber, 30 g protein.*

Buffalo Chicken Pizza:

Prepare as directed, except substitute a mixture of ⅓ cup bottled ranch or blue cheese salad dressing and 1 to 2 teaspoons bottled hot pepper sauce for the pizza sauce; mozzarella cheese for the fontina cheese; one 6-ounce package refrigerated cooked Southwestern chicken breast strips, coarsely chopped, for the meatballs; and ¼ cup sliced green onions (2) for the basil. Omit Parmesan cheese. If desired, drizzle pizza with ⅓ cup warmed barbecue sauce before serving.

NUTRITION FACTS PER SERVING: *611 cal., 30 g total fat (9 g sat. fat), 73 mg chol., 1,552 mg sodium, 53 g carb., 0 g dietary fiber, 37 g protein.*

3

Soups and Stews

These bowls full of bliss show off down-home

goodness perfect for sit-down dinners or

casual-but-sublime suppers.

Garden Vegetable Gazpacho

START TO FINISH **30 minutes** MAKES **3 servings**

3 cups chopped red and/or partially green tomatoes

2 11.5-ounce cans (about 3 cups) tomato juice

1/2 cup chopped cucumber

1/2 cup chopped tomatillos (2 medium; optional)

1/4 cup finely chopped green onions (2)

1/4 cup finely snipped fresh cilantro

1 large fresh jalapeño chile pepper, seeded and finely chopped*

1 tablespoon olive oil

1 tablespoon lime juice

1 clove garlic, minced

1/4 teaspoon salt

1/4 teaspoon bottled hot pepper sauce

1 avocado, seeded, peeled, and chopped (optional)

Snipped fresh cilantro (optional)

Bottled hot pepper sauce (optional)

1 In a large bowl combine tomatoes, tomato juice, cucumber, tomatillos (if desired), green onions, 1/4 cup cilantro, jalapeño pepper, oil, lime juice, garlic, salt, and 1/4 teaspoon hot pepper sauce.**

2 If desired, serve with avocado and additional cilantro. If desired, pass additional hot pepper sauce.

NUTRITION FACTS PER SERVING: *120 cal., 6 g total fat (0 g sat. fat), 0 mg chol., 796 mg sodium, 18 g carb., 4 g dietary fiber, 4 g protein.*

Shrimp Gazpacho:

Prepare as directed through Step 1. Using 8 ounces peeled and deveined cooked shrimp, set aside a few shrimp for garnish. Chop the remaining shrimp. Before serving, stir chopped shrimp into gazpacho. If desired, garnish each serving with some of the reserved shrimp.

NUTRITION FACTS PER SERVING: *196 cal., 6 g total fat (0 g sat. fat), 148 mg chol., 966 mg sodium, 18 g carb., 4 g dietary fiber, 20 g protein.*

*tip

Because chile peppers contain volatile oils that can burn your skin and eyes, avoid direct contact with them as much as possible. When working with chile peppers, wear plastic or rubber gloves. If your bare hands do touch the peppers, wash your hands and nails well with soap and warm water.

**tip

If time permits, cover and chill for up to 24 hours to allow flavors to blend.

Shrimp Cocktail Soup

START TO FINISH **30 minutes** MAKES **6 servings**

3 cups peeled, seeded, and chopped ripe tomatoes

1¾ cups peeled, seeded, and chopped cucumber (1 medium)

½ cup finely chopped green sweet pepper (1 small)

⅓ cup finely chopped red onion (1 small)

2 cloves garlic, minced

2 cups tomato juice

1 14-ounce can reduced-sodium chicken broth

¼ cup red wine vinegar

2 tablespoons snipped fresh basil or 2 teaspoons dried basil, crushed

½ teaspoon salt

¼ to ½ teaspoon bottled hot pepper sauce

¼ teaspoon ground black pepper

12 ounces chopped, peeled and deveined cooked shrimp

Lime wedges (optional)

 1 In an extra-large bowl combine tomatoes, cucumber, sweet pepper, red onion, and garlic. Stir in tomato juice, broth, vinegar, basil, salt, hot pepper sauce, and black pepper.* Stir in shrimp.

2 If desired, serve with lime wedges.

NUTRITION FACTS PER SERVING:
109 cal., 1 g total fat (0 g sat. fat), 111 mg chol., 734 mg sodium, 11 g carb., 2 g dietary fiber, 16 g protein.

*tip
If time permits, cover and chill for up to 24 hours to allow flavors to blend. Before serving, stir in shrimp.

Asparagus-Basil Soup

START TO FINISH 30 minutes   MAKES 2 servings

1   pound fresh asparagus spears
1   14-ounce can vegetable broth
1½ cups frozen diced hash
    brown potatoes
½   cup snipped fresh basil
1   cup water
1   cup plain soy milk or milk
    Salt
    Ground black pepper
    Fresh basil leaves (optional)

1 Snap off and discard woody bases from asparagus. Cut off tips; set aside. Chop asparagus spears. In a medium saucepan combine chopped asparagus, broth, and frozen potatoes. Bring to boiling; reduce heat. Simmer, covered, about 5 minutes or just until asparagus is tender. Remove from heat; cool slightly. Stir in snipped basil.

2 Pour potato mixture into a blender. Cover and blend until smooth. Return to saucepan. (Or use an immersion blender to blend potato mixture in the saucepan until smooth.)

3 Meanwhile, in a small saucepan combine the water and reserved asparagus tips. Bring to boiling; reduce heat. Simmer, uncovered, for 3 minutes; drain.

4 Stir milk into potato mixture; heat through. Stir in asparagus tips. Season to taste with salt and pepper. If desired, garnish each serving with basil leaves.

NUTRITION FACTS PER SERVING:
238 cal., 4 g total fat (0 g sat. fat), 0 mg chol., 1,030 mg sodium, 42 g carb., 8 g dietary fiber, 12 g protein.

Broccoli-Potato Soup with Greens

START TO FINISH **20 minutes**   MAKES **4 servings**

2 **cups chopped round red potatoes (2 medium)**

1 **14-ounce can vegetable broth**

3 **cups small broccoli florets**

2 **cups milk**

2 **cups shredded smoked Gouda cheese (8 ounces)**

3 **tablespoons all-purpose flour**

Freshly ground black pepper

2 **cups torn winter greens, such as curly endive, chicory, romaine lettuce, escarole, and/or spinach**

Shredded smoked Gouda cheese (optional)

1 In a large saucepan combine potatoes and broth. Bring to boiling; reduce heat. Simmer, covered, for 8 minutes. Slightly mash potatoes with a potato masher or fork. Add broccoli and milk; bring just to simmering.

2 Meanwhile, in a medium bowl combine 2 cups cheese and flour; toss gently to coat. Gradually add to potato mixture, stirring until cheese is melted. Season to taste with pepper. Top each serving with greens and, if desired, additional cheese.

NUTRITION FACTS PER SERVING:
334 cal., 17 g total fat (11 g sat. fat), 55 mg chol., 1,254 mg sodium, 30 g carb., 4 g dietary fiber, 19 g protein.

Ham and Vegetable Soup

2 teaspoons canola oil

1 cup cubed low-fat, reduced-sodium cooked ham (5 ounces)

2 cups water

1 14-ounce can reduced-sodium chicken broth

12 ounces fresh peas or one 10-ounce package frozen baby peas

1 cup sliced carrots (2 medium)

1 cup sliced celery (2 stalks)

$1/3$ cup diagonally sliced green onion

1 tablespoon snipped fresh tarragon or $1/2$ teaspoon dried tarragon, crushed

Lemon wedges

$1/2$ of a 6-ounce carton plain fat-free yogurt

1 In a large saucepan heat oil over medium heat. Add ham; cook, without stirring, for 3 minutes. Stir ham; cook for 2 to 3 minutes more or until brown.

2 Add the water, broth, peas, carrots, celery, green onion, and tarragon. Bring to boiling; reduce heat. Simmer, covered, for 5 to 10 minutes or until peas and carrots are tender. Serve with lemon wedges and yogurt.

NUTRITION FACTS PER SERVING: 176 cal., 4 g total fat (1 g sat. fat), 19 mg chol., 586 mg sodium, 21 g carb., 6 g dietary fiber, 14 g protein.

Hearty Garlic and Snap Pea Soup

START TO FINISH **30 minutes** MAKES **4 servings**

2 tablespoons olive oil

¼ cup chopped onion

4 cloves garlic, minced

2 14-ounce cans reduced-sodium chicken broth

1 pound Yukon gold potatoes, sliced

1¾ cups water

1½ cups thinly sliced fennel

1½ cups fresh sugar snap pea pods, trimmed

½ teaspoon salt

¼ teaspoon ground black pepper

Olive oil (optional)

Plain low-fat yogurt (optional)

Snipped fennel leaves (optional)

1 In a large saucepan heat 2 tablespoons oil over medium heat. Add onion and garlic; cook for 3 to 5 minutes or until onion is tender, stirring occasionally. Add broth, potatoes, and the water. Bring to boiling; reduce heat. Simmer, covered, for 10 to 15 minutes or until potatoes are tender. Remove from heat.

2 Using an immersion blender, blend potato mixture in saucepan until smooth.* Stir in 1½ cups fennel, sugar snap peas, salt, and pepper. Bring to boiling; reduce heat. Simmer, uncovered, for 3 minutes.

3 If desired, drizzle each serving with additional oil and top with yogurt and fennel leaves.

NUTRITION FACTS PER SERVING:
204 cal., 6 g total fat (0 g sat. fat), 0 mg chol., 806 mg sodium, 30 g carb., 6 g dietary fiber, 6 g protein.

83

*tip
If you don't have an immersion blender, transfer the potato mixture, one-third at a time, to a blender or food processor. Cover and blend or process until smooth. Return to saucepan.

Tortellini Florentine Soup

START TO FINISH 30 minutes MAKES 6 servings

- 1 9-ounce package refrigerated 3-cheese tortellini
- 2 14-ounce cans reduced-sodium chicken broth
- 1 10-ounce container refrigerated light Alfredo pasta sauce
- 2 cups shredded purchased roasted chicken
- ½ cup oil-pack dried tomato strips, drained
- ½ of a 5-ounce package (about 3 cups) fresh baby spinach
  Shaved or shredded Parmesan cheese (optional)

1 In a 4-quart Dutch oven cook tortellini according to package directions; drain. Set aside.

2 In the same Dutch oven combine broth and pasta sauce. Stir in chicken and dried tomatoes. Bring just to boiling; reduce heat. Simmer, uncovered, for 5 minutes.

3 Stir in cooked tortellini and spinach. Cook for 1 to 2 minutes or just until tortellini is heated through and spinach is wilted. If desired, top each serving with cheese.

NUTRITION FACTS PER SERVING:
286 cal., 15 g total fat (6 g sat. fat), 77 mg chol., 1,094 mg sodium, 21 g carb., 1 g dietary fiber, 20 g protein.

Creamy Tortellini Tomato Soup ☆

START TO FINISH 20 minutes MAKES 4 servings

- 2 14-ounce cans reduced-sodium chicken broth or vegetable broth
- 1 9-ounce package refrigerated tortellini
- ½ of an 8-ounce tub-style cream cheese spread with chive and onion
- 1 10.75- or 11-ounce can condensed tomato or tomato bisque soup
  Snipped fresh chives (optional)

1 In a medium saucepan bring broth to boiling. Stir in tortellini; reduce heat. Simmer, uncovered, for 5 minutes.

2 In a small bowl whisk ⅓ cup of the hot broth into cream cheese spread until smooth. Return cream cheese mixture to saucepan. Stir in tomato soup; heat through. If desired, sprinkle each serving with chives.

NUTRITION FACTS PER SERVING:
363 cal., 14 g total fat (8 g sat. fat), 57 mg chol., 1,264 mg sodium, 44 g carb., 1 g dietary fiber, 14 g protein.

Chicken Soup with Spinach and Orzo

START TO FINISH **25 minutes** MAKES **6 servings**

4   14-ounce cans reduced-sodium chicken broth

1   cup dried orzo pasta (rosamarina)

12   ounces fresh asparagus spears, trimmed and cut diagonally into 1½-inch pieces

3   cups chopped fresh spinach, Swiss chard, or kale or one 10-ounce package frozen chopped spinach, thawed and well drained

1½   cups chopped tomatoes (3 medium)

1½   cups shredded cooked chicken

⅓   cup cubed cooked ham

     Salt

     Ground black pepper

     Snipped fresh chives and/or parsley (optional)

1 In a covered 5- to 6-quart Dutch oven bring broth to boiling. Stir in pasta. Return to boiling; reduce heat. Simmer, uncovered, for 6 minutes. Stir in asparagus. Simmer, uncovered, about 2 minutes more or until pasta is tender and asparagus is crisp-tender.

2 Stir in spinach, tomatoes, chicken, and ham; heat through. Season to taste with salt and pepper. If desired, sprinkle each serving with chives and/or parsley.

NUTRITION FACTS PER SERVING: *221 cal., 4 g total fat (1 g sat. fat), 35 mg chol., 837 mg sodium, 28 g carb., 3 g dietary fiber, 20 g protein.*

85

Chunky Vegetable and Turkey Soup

START TO FINISH 30 minutes MAKES 6 servings

2   14-ounce cans reduced-
     sodium chicken broth

1½   cups water

½   cup thinly sliced carrot
     (1 medium)

½   cup thinly sliced celery
     (1 stalk)

⅓   cup thinly sliced onion
     (1 small)

1   teaspoon snipped fresh
     rosemary or ¼ teaspoon
     dried rosemary, crushed

¼   teaspoon ground black pepper

1   cup instant brown rice

1   cup frozen cut green beans

2   cups chopped cooked turkey
     or chicken breast (10 ounces)

1   14.5-ounce can no-added-salt
     diced tomatoes, undrained

     Fresh rosemary sprigs
     (optional)

1 In a large saucepan or Dutch oven combine broth, the water, carrot, celery, onion, rosemary, and pepper. Bring to boiling. Stir in uncooked rice and frozen beans. Return to boiling; reduce heat. Simmer, covered, for 10 to 12 minutes or until vegetables are tender.

2 Stir in turkey and tomatoes; heat through. If desired, garnish each serving with rosemary sprigs.

NUTRITION FACTS PER SERVING:
143 cal., 1 g total fat (0 g sat. fat), 39 mg chol., 384 mg sodium, 16 g carb., 3 g dietary fiber, 18 g protein.

86

★ Easy Chicken Noodle Soup

START TO FINISH **30 minutes** MAKES **6 servings**

3 14-ounce cans reduced-sodium chicken broth

1 cup chopped onion (1 large)

1 cup sliced carrots (2 medium)

1 cup sliced celery (2 stalks)

1 cup water

2 teaspoons dried Italian seasoning, crushed

$\frac{1}{2}$ teaspoon ground black pepper

1 bay leaf

1 16-ounce package frozen egg noodles

2 cups chopped cooked chicken or turkey (10 ounces)*

2 tablespoons snipped fresh parsley (optional)

1 In a large saucepan combine broth, onion, carrots, celery, the water, Italian seasoning, pepper, and bay leaf. Bring to boiling; reduce heat. Simmer, covered, for 5 minutes.

2 Stir in frozen noodles. Return to boiling; reduce heat. Simmer, covered, for 10 to 12 minutes more or until noodles are tender but still firm and vegetables are just tender. Stir in chicken; heat through.

3 Remove and discard bay leaf. If desired, sprinkle each serving with parsley.

NUTRITION FACTS PER SERVING: *339 cal., 6 g total fat (2 g sat. fat), 130 mg chol., 554 mg sodium, 46 g carb., 3 g dietary fiber, 23 g protein.*

*tip

If you don't have any leftover chicken or turkey, use about half of a 2- to 2¼-pound purchased roasted chicken from the supermarket deli, then skin, bone, and chop the meat. Or cook your own chicken. In a large skillet combine 12 ounces skinless, boneless chicken breast halves and 1½ cups water. Bring to boiling; reduce heat. Simmer, covered, for 12 to 14 minutes or until chicken is no longer pink (170°F). Drain and chop.

Creamy Asparagus and Bacon Soup

1¼ pounds fresh asparagus spears, trimmed

1 12-ounce can evaporated milk

1¼ cups water

1¼ pounds potatoes, peeled and cut into ½-inch pieces

½ teaspoon salt

½ teaspoon ground black pepper

6 slices bacon

1 tablespoon honey

Desired toppings, such as finely shredded lemon peel, snipped fresh Italian (flat-leaf) parsley, coarse salt, and/or freshly ground black pepper

88

1 Reserve about one-third of the asparagus; set aside. In a large saucepan combine the remaining asparagus, evaporated milk, the water, potatoes, salt, and pepper. Bring to boiling; reduce heat. Simmer, covered, about 10 minutes or until potatoes are tender. Cool slightly.

2 Transfer potato mixture, half at a time, to a blender or food processor. Cover and blend or process until smooth.

3 Meanwhile, in a large skillet cook bacon over medium heat until crisp. Remove bacon; drain on paper towels, reserving 1 tablespoon drippings in skillet. Crumble bacon; set aside. Add the reserved asparagus to the reserved drippings. Cook for 5 to 6 minutes or until asparagus is crisp-tender, stirring occasionally.

4 Before serving, place crumbled bacon in a microwave-safe pie plate. Drizzle with honey; cover with vented plastic wrap. Microwave on 100 percent power (high) for 30 seconds.

5 Top each serving with the reserved asparagus, honey-drizzled bacon, and your choice of toppings.

NUTRITION FACTS PER SERVING: *356 cal., 15 g total fat (7 g sat. fat), 41 mg chol., 673 mg sodium, 43 g carb., 4 g dietary fiber, 15 g protein.*

Tortellini Meatball Soup

START TO FINISH **30 minutes** MAKES **4 to 6 servings**

1   tablespoon olive oil or vegetable oil

1   cup chopped sweet onion (1 large)

1   cup coarsely chopped carrots (2 medium)

3   cloves garlic, minced

1   32-ounce carton reduced-sodium or regular chicken or beef broth

½   cup water

1   9-ounce package refrigerated 4-cheese tortellini

½   of a 16-ounce package (16) frozen cooked Italian-style meatballs

1   teaspoon dried Italian seasoning, crushed

3   cups chopped fresh spinach or half of a 10-ounce package frozen chopped spinach, thawed and drained

3   tablespoons chopped roasted red sweet pepper

1   tablespoon lemon juice (optional)

     Salt

     Ground black pepper

1   tablespoon snipped fresh basil

1 In a Dutch oven heat oil over medium heat. Add onion, carrots, and garlic; cook for 3 minutes, stirring occasionally. Add broth and the water. Bring to boiling. Stir in tortellini, meatballs, and Italian seasoning. Return to boiling; reduce heat. Simmer, uncovered, for 4 minutes.

2 Stir in spinach, roasted pepper, and, if desired, lemon juice. Simmer, uncovered, about 3 minutes more or until tortellini are tender. Season to taste with salt and black pepper. Before serving, stir in basil.

NUTRITION FACTS PER SERVING: *461 cal., 23 g total fat (9 g sat. fat), 68 mg chol., 1,443 mg sodium, 44 g carb., 5 g dietary fiber, 22 g protein.*

Make-Ahead Directions: Prepare soup as directed. Cover and chill for up to 4 hours; reheat in Dutch oven. For longer storage, prepare as directed, except do not add tortellini and basil and use the frozen spinach option. Cover and chill for up to 3 days. To reheat, bring soup just to boiling; stir in tortellini and simmer for 7 minutes. Before serving, stir in basil.

Chicken-Pasta Soup with Pesto

START TO FINISH **25 minutes** MAKES **4 to 6 servings**

2 **14-ounce cans reduced-sodium chicken broth**

1 **pound skinless, boneless chicken breast halves or thighs, cubed**

1 **14.5-ounce can diced tomatoes with basil, garlic, and oregano, undrained**

½ **cup dried orzo pasta (rosamarina)**

1 **cup chopped zucchini (1 small)**

1 **teaspoon finely shredded lemon peel**

1 **tablespoon lemon juice**
   Ground black pepper

4 **to 6 tablespoons basil pesto**

1 In a large saucepan combine broth, chicken, tomatoes, and pasta. Bring to boiling; reduce heat. Simmer, uncovered, for 6 minutes.

2 Stir in zucchini, lemon peel, and lemon juice. Return to boiling; reduce heat. Simmer, uncovered, for 3 to 4 minutes more or until chicken is no longer pink and pasta and zucchini are tender. Season to taste with pepper. Top each serving with pesto.

NUTRITION FACTS PER SERVING:
371 cal., 12 g total fat (0 g sat. fat), 68 mg chol., 1,180 mg sodium, 30 g carb., 1 g dietary fiber, 35 g protein.

Minestrone

1 tablespoon olive oil

$\frac{1}{2}$ cup chopped onion (1 medium)

2 cloves garlic, minced

2 14-ounce cans beef broth

2 cups water

$1\frac{1}{4}$ cups coarsely chopped zucchini (1 medium)

$1\frac{1}{4}$ cups coarsely chopped yellow sweet pepper (1 large)

1 15-ounce can cannellini beans (white kidney beans), rinsed and drained

8 ounces fresh green beans, trimmed and cut into $1\frac{1}{2}$-inch pieces ($1\frac{1}{2}$ cups)

1 cup dried mostaccioli pasta

$\frac{1}{4}$ cup coarsely snipped fresh basil or 2 teaspoons dried basil, crushed

2 cups fresh baby spinach

$1\frac{1}{2}$ cups coarsely chopped tomatoes or halved cherry tomatoes

Salt

Ground black pepper

Shaved Parmesan cheese (optional)

1 In a 5- to 6-quart Dutch oven heat oil over medium heat. Add onion and garlic; cook until tender, stirring occasionally. Add broth, the water, zucchini, and sweet pepper. Bring to boiling.

2 Stir in cannellini beans, green beans, pasta, and, if using, dried basil. Return to boiling; reduce heat. Simmer, covered, for 10 to 12 minutes or until pasta is tender, stirring occasionally. Stir in spinach, tomatoes, and, if using, fresh basil. Remove from heat.

3 Season to taste with salt and black pepper. If desired, top each serving with cheese.

NUTRITION FACTS PER SERVING: *186 cal., 3 g total fat (0 g sat. fat), 0 mg chol., 621 mg sodium, 34 g carb., 7 g dietary fiber, 10 g protein.*

91

Spring Greens Soup

START TO FINISH 30 minutes MAKES 3 servings

- 1 tablespoon vegetable oil
- 1 medium onion, halved and sliced
- 3 cups reduced-sodium chicken broth or vegetable broth
- ¼ to ½ teaspoon freshly ground black pepper
- 12 ounces Yukon gold potatoes, quartered
- 2 tablespoons butter
- 3 cups sliced fresh mushrooms (8 ounces, optional)
- 3 cups fresh spinach leaves
- 3 cups arugula leaves
- 2 cups fresh Italian (flat-leaf) parsley leaves and tender stems
  Salt
  Arugula

1 In a large saucepan heat oil over medium heat. Add onion; cook about 5 minutes or until tender, stirring occasionally. Add broth and pepper. Bring to boiling. Add potatoes. Return to boiling; reduce heat. Simmer, covered, for 10 minutes; remove from heat.

2 Meanwhile, in a large skillet heat butter over medium heat until melted. Add mushrooms; cook for 6 to 8 minutes or until tender and liquid has evaporated. Set aside.

3 Using an immersion blender, blend potato mixture in saucepan until nearly smooth. Stir in spinach, 3 cups arugula, and parsley. Bring to boiling; remove from heat. Using immersion blender, blend mixture again until nearly smooth and flecks of green remain. Season to taste with salt.

4 Top each serving with cooked mushrooms and additional arugula.

NUTRITION FACTS PER SERVING: *184 cal., 6 g total fat (0 g sat. fat), 0 mg chol., 824 mg sodium, 28 g carb., 6 g dietary fiber, 8 g protein.*

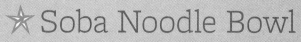

★ Soba Noodle Bowl

START TO FINISH **25 minutes**   MAKES **4 servings**

2   14-ounce cans reduced-sodium chicken broth

1   cup water

12 ounces skinless, boneless chicken breast halves, cut into very thin slices

6   ounces soba (buckwheat noodles)

1   cup thinly sliced carrots (2 medium)

2   tablespoons reduced-sodium soy sauce

1   fresh red or green jalapeño chile pepper, seeded and thinly sliced*

8   ounces fresh sugar snap pea pods, halved if desired

    Crushed red pepper (optional)

    Snipped fresh parsley (optional)

1 In a large saucepan combine broth and the water. Bring to boiling. Stir in chicken, soba, carrots, soy sauce, and jalapeño pepper. Return to boiling; reduce heat to medium. Cook, covered, about 7 minutes or until chicken is no longer pink and soba is tender.

2 Stir in sugar snap peas; cook, covered, about 3 minutes or just until snap peas are tender.

3 If desired, sprinkle each serving with crushed red pepper and parsley.

NUTRITION FACTS PER SERVING:
295 cal., 1 g total fat (0 g sat. fat), 49 mg chol., 1,172 mg sodium, 41 g carb., 4 g dietary fiber, 30 g protein.

93

*tip
Because chile peppers contain volatile oils that can burn your skin and eyes, avoid direct contact with them as much as possible. When working with chile peppers, wear plastic or rubber gloves. If your bare hands do touch the peppers, wash your hands and nails well with soap and warm water.

Country Chicken and Potato Soup ✦

START TO FINISH 25 minutes MAKES 4 servings

- 2 **14-ounce cans reduced-sodium chicken broth**
- 1 **20-ounce package refrigerated red-skinned potato wedges**
- ½ **cup chopped leek, white part only**
- 2 **to 3 cloves garlic, minced**
- 2 **cups chopped cooked chicken (10 ounces)**
- 1 **tablespoon snipped fresh chives**
- ⅛ **teaspoon freshly ground black pepper**
- 1 **cup half-and-half, light cream, or milk**
  Whole fresh chives
  Garlic-flavor olive oil* (optional)

1 In a large saucepan combine 1 can of the broth, the potatoes, leek, and garlic. Bring to boiling; reduce heat. Simmer, covered, for 5 minutes; remove from heat.

2 Using a potato masher slightly mash potatoes, leaving some unmashed potato pieces. Add chicken, snipped chives, and pepper. Stir in the remaining 1 can broth and half-and-half; heat through.

3 Top each serving with whole chives and, if desired, a few drops of garlic-flavor oil.

NUTRITION FACTS PER SERVING:
319 cal., 12 g total fat (6 g sat. fat), 85 mg chol., 707 mg sodium, 23 g carb., 4 g dietary fiber, 28 g protein.

*tip

If you prefer, make your own garlic-flavor olive oil. In a small skillet heat 2 tablespoons olive oil over medium heat. Add 1 clove minced garlic; cook and stir until garlic begins to brown. Remove from heat. Strain to remove garlic. Discard any unused oil (do not store).

Crab and Poblano Soup

START TO FINISH **30 minutes**   MAKES **4 servings**

¼   **cup butter**

2   **fresh poblano chile peppers, seeded and chopped***

¾   **cup chopped red sweet pepper (1 medium)**

½   **cup chopped onion (1 medium)**

2   **cloves garlic, minced**

¼   **cup all-purpose flour**

¼   **teaspoon salt**

¼   **teaspoon ground black pepper**

1   **14-ounce can chicken broth**

2   **cups milk**

1½ **cups shredded asadero cheese or Monterey Jack cheese (6 ounces)**

1   **6-ounce can crabmeat, drained, cut into bite-size pieces, and cartilage removed, or 1 cup cooked crabmeat, cut into bite-size pieces and cartilage removed**

1   **recipe Fresh Tomato Salsa**

1   **recipe Crisp Tortilla Strips (optional)**

1 In a large saucepan heat butter over medium heat until melted. Add chile peppers, sweet pepper, onion, and garlic; cook 4 to 5 minutes or until tender, stirring occasionally. Stir in flour, salt, and black pepper. Add broth all at once. Cook and stir until thickened and bubbly. Cook and stir for 1 minute more.

2 Reduce heat to medium-low. Stir in milk and cheese. Cook and stir for 3 to 5 minutes or until cheese is melted. Stir in crabmeat; heat through.

3 Top each serving with Fresh Tomato Salsa. If desired, serve with Crisp Tortilla Strips.

NUTRITION FACTS PER SERVING:
406 cal., 24 g total fat (16 g sat. fat), 120 mg chol., 1,328 mg sodium, 22 g carb., 2 g dietary fiber, 28 g protein.

95

Fresh Tomato Salsa

In a small bowl combine 1 cup seeded and chopped roma tomatoes (3 medium), 1 tablespoon thinly sliced green onion (1), 1 tablespoon snipped fresh cilantro, 2 teaspoons lime juice, and 1 teaspoon finely chopped fresh jalapeño chile pepper.* Season to taste with salt and ground black pepper.

Crisp Tortilla Strips

Preheat oven to 350°F. Roll up each of 3 flour tortillas; slice crosswise into long thin strips. Lightly coat tortilla strips with nonstick cooking spray and spread on a baking sheet. Bake about 5 minutes or until golden brown. Cool.

*tip

Because chile peppers contain volatile oils that can burn your skin and eyes, avoid direct contact with them as much as possible. When working with chile peppers, wear plastic or rubber gloves. If your bare hands do touch the peppers, wash your hands and nails well with soap and warm water.

O'Brien Potato Soup

START TO FINISH **30 minutes**   MAKES **4 servings**

1   28-ounce package frozen diced hash brown potatoes with onions and peppers

3   cups fat-free half-and-half

1   cup chopped miniature sweet peppers

1   cup water

½   teaspoon salt

½   teaspoon curry powder

⅛ to ¼ teaspoon cayenne pepper or ground black pepper

1½   cups shredded cheddar cheese (6 ounces)

Sliced miniature sweet peppers (optional)

Snipped fresh Italian (flat-leaf) parsley (optional)

1 In a 4-quart Dutch oven combine potatoes, half-and-half, 1 cup sweet peppers, ½ cup of the water, the salt, curry powder, and cayenne pepper. Bring just to boiling; reduce heat to medium. Cook, covered, for 10 minutes, stirring occasionally. Cool slightly.

2 Transfer 3 cups of the potato mixture to a blender; add the remaining ½ cup water. Cover and blend until nearly smooth. Return mixture to Dutch oven; cook and stir until mixture is heated through and potatoes are tender. Stir in cheese; cook and stir over low heat until cheese is melted.

3 If desired, top each serving with sliced sweet peppers and parsley.

NUTRITION FACTS PER SERVING: *438 cal., 17 g total fat (11 g sat. fat), 54 mg chol., 883 mg sodium, 53 g carb., 5 g dietary fiber, 19 g protein.*

Sausage, Beans, and Greens Soup

START TO FINISH **30 minutes** MAKES **4 servings**

- **12** ounces uncooked hot or sweet Italian sausage links, cut diagonally into $\frac{1}{2}$-inch slices
- **$\frac{1}{2}$** cup chopped onion (1 medium)
- **2** 15-ounce cans cannellini beans (white kidney beans), rinsed and drained
- **2** cups coarsely chopped escarole or fresh spinach
- **$1\frac{1}{2}$** cups reduced-sodium chicken broth
- **$\frac{1}{4}$** cup dry white wine or reduced-sodium chicken broth
- **2** tablespoons snipped fresh thyme or 1 teaspoon dried thyme, crushed
- **$\frac{1}{4}$** cup finely shredded Parmesan cheese (1 ounce)

1 In a large saucepan cook sausage and onion over medium heat about 10 minutes or until sausage is no longer pink, stirring occasionally. Drain off fat.

2 Add beans, escarole, broth, wine, and thyme. Bring to boiling; reduce heat. Simmer, covered, for 5 minutes. Sprinkle each serving with cheese.

NUTRITION FACTS PER SERVING:
470 cal., 26 g total fat (12 g sat. fat), 61 mg chol., 1,393 mg sodium, 35 g carb., 11 g dietary fiber, 34 g protein.

Escarole, a leafy green relative of endive, has a bold flavor with subtle hints of nuttiness. In addition to being used in soups and stews, escarole makes a delicious side dish when sautéed in olive oil and garlic. It also can be used raw in salads.

Turkey and Rice Soup

START TO FINISH **20 minutes** MAKES **6 servings**

4 **cups chicken broth**

¼ **teaspoon dried Italian seasoning, crushed**

¼ **teaspoon ground black pepper**

1 **10-ounce package frozen mixed vegetables**

1 **cup instant white or brown rice**

2 **cups chopped cooked turkey or chicken (10 ounces)**

1 **14.5-ounce can diced tomatoes, drained**

2 **tablespoons basil pesto**

1 In a large saucepan combine broth, Italian seasoning, and pepper. Bring to boiling. Stir in frozen vegetables and uncooked rice.

2 Return to boiling; reduce heat. Simmer, covered, for 8 to 10 minutes or until vegetables are tender. Stir in turkey, tomatoes, and pesto; heat through.

NUTRITION FACTS PER SERVING:
233 cal., 6 g total fat (1 g sat. fat), 38 mg chol., 847 mg sodium, 25 g carb., 2 g dietary fiber, 18 g protein.

Creamy Turkey and Rice Soup:

Prepare as directed. In a small bowl combine one 8-ounce carton sour cream and 2 tablespoons all-purpose flour. Stir sour cream mixture into hot soup; cook and stir until thickened and bubbly. Cook and stir for 1 minute more.

NUTRITION FACTS PER SERVING: *304 cal., 13 g total fat (6 g sat. fat), 58 mg chol., 884 mg sodium, 27 g carb., 2 g dietary fiber, 19 g protein.*

☆ Beefy Vegetable Soup

START TO FINISH **30 minutes** MAKES **6 servings**

1½ pounds ground beef sirloin

1 cup chopped onion (1 large)

1 cup sliced celery (2 stalks)

2 14-ounce cans lower-sodium beef broth

1 28-ounce can diced tomatoes, undrained

1 10-ounce package frozen mixed vegetables

2 tablespoons steak sauce

2 teaspoons Worcestershire sauce

¼ teaspoon salt

¼ teaspoon ground black pepper

¼ cup all-purpose flour

1 In a 4-quart Dutch oven cook ground beef, onion, and celery over medium-high heat until meat is brown, using a wooden spoon to break up meat as it cooks. Drain off fat.

2 Stir in 1 can of the broth, the tomatoes, frozen vegetables, steak sauce, Worcestershire sauce, salt, and pepper. Bring to boiling; reduce heat. Simmer, covered, for 15 to 20 minutes or until vegetables are tender.

3 In a medium bowl whisk together the remaining 1 can broth and flour; stir into meat mixture. Cook and stir until thickened and bubbly. Cook and stir for 1 minute more.

99

NUTRITION FACTS PER SERVING:
306 cal., 12 g total fat (5 g sat. fat), 74 mg chol., 747 mg sodium, 21 g carb., 4 g dietary fiber, 27 g protein.

Cuban Black Bean Soup

START TO FINISH 25 minutes   MAKES 4 servings

1   **16-ounce jar mild or medium thick and chunky salsa or salsa with lime and garlic**

1   **15-ounce can black beans, rinsed and drained**

1   **14-ounce can chicken broth**

1¾   **cups water**

1½   **cups cubed cooked ham (about 8 ounces)**

1   **teaspoon ground cumin**

½   **cup sour cream**

¼   **cup salsa verde (optional)**

     Crushed lime-flavor tortilla chips (optional)

1 In a large saucepan or Dutch oven combine salsa, beans, broth, the water, ham, and cumin. Bring to boiling; reduce heat. Simmer, covered, for 10 minutes.

2 Top each serving with sour cream and, if desired, salsa verde and tortilla chips.

NUTRITION FACTS PER SERVING: *175 cal., 6 g total fat (3 g sat. fat), 12 mg chol., 1,359 mg sodium, 26 g carb., 8 g dietary fiber, 10 g protein.*

Cuban Black Bean Soup with Peppers:

Prepare as directed, except substitute 2 cups frozen sweet pepper and onion stir-fry vegetables for the ham.

NUTRITION FACTS PER SERVING: *167 cal., 5 g total fat (3 g sat. fat), 14 mg chol., 1,365 mg sodium, 26 g carb., 7 g dietary fiber, 10 g protein.*

Mexican-Style Chicken Soup

START TO FINISH **30 minutes**   MAKES **6 servings**

1 **32-ounce carton reduced-sodium chicken broth**

1 **15.5-ounce can golden hominy, rinsed and drained**

1 **15-ounce can black beans, rinsed and drained**

1 **cup bottled nopalitos (cactus leaves), drained, or bite-size green sweet pepper strips**

1 **cup salsa**

1 **4-ounce can diced green chile peppers, undrained**

1 **tablespoon chili powder**

1 **teaspoon ground cumin**

2½ **cups chopped cooked chicken (about 12 ounces)**

Snipped fresh herbs (optional)

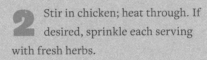 In a 4-quart Dutch oven combine broth, hominy, beans, nopalitos, salsa, chile peppers, chili powder, and cumin. Bring to boiling; reduce heat. Simmer, covered, for 20 minutes.

2 Stir in chicken; heat through. If desired, sprinkle each serving with fresh herbs.

NUTRITION FACTS PER SERVING:
240 cal., 6 g total fat (1 g sat. fat), 52 mg chol., 1,060 mg sodium, 25 g carb., 7 g dietary fiber, 25 g protein.

Macaroni and Cheese Chowder

START TO FINISH 25 minutes   MAKES 4 servings

- 2 cups water
- 1 14-ounce can reduced-sodium chicken broth
- 1 7.25-ounce package macaroni-and-cheese dinner mix
- 1 14.75-ounce can cream-style corn
- 1 cup diced cooked ham (5 ounces)
- 1 cup milk
- ½ cup frozen peas (optional)

1 In a large saucepan combine the water and broth. Bring to boiling. Gradually add macaroni from dinner mix; reduce heat. Simmer, covered, for 7 to 8 minutes or until macaroni is tender. Do not drain.

2 Stir contents of the cheese packet, corn, ham, milk, and, if desired, peas into broth mixture. Cook and stir over medium heat until heated through.

NUTRITION FACTS PER SERVING:
349 cal., 5 g total fat (2 g sat. fat), 28 mg chol., 1,571 mg sodium, 59 g carb., 3 g dietary fiber, 21 g protein.

Smoked Turkey and Corn Chowder

START TO FINISH 20 minutes   MAKES 4 servings

- 1 8-ounce tub-style cream cheese spread with chive and onion
- 2 cups milk
- 1 14.75-ounce can cream-style corn
- 1½ cups chopped smoked turkey breast (about 8 ounces)
- 1 cup frozen peas
-    Ground black pepper

1 In a medium saucepan heat cream cheese over medium heat until softened. Gradually stir in milk and corn until combined. Stir in turkey and peas; heat through. Season to taste with pepper.

NUTRITION FACTS PER SERVING:
397 cal., 23 g total fat (15 g sat. fat), 88 mg chol., 1,159 mg sodium, 27 g carb., 3 g dietary fiber, 19 g protein.

Pumpkin, Barley, and Sage Soup

START TO FINISH **30 minutes** MAKES **4 servings**

1 tablespoon vegetable oil

8 ounces cooked smoked andouille or other sausage links, chopped

$\frac{1}{3}$ cup chopped onion (1 small)

1 tablespoon snipped fresh sage or 1 teaspoon dried sage, crushed

4 cups water

1 cup quick-cooking barley

1 teaspoon instant chicken bouillon granules

1 15-ounce can pumpkin

2 tablespoons maple syrup

1 tablespoon cider vinegar

Salt

Ground black pepper

Thinly sliced apple (optional)

Small fresh sage leaves (optional)

1 In a 4-quart Dutch oven heat oil over medium heat. Add sausage, onion, and snipped sage; cook for 3 minutes, stirring frequently. Add the water, barley, and bouillon granules. Bring to boiling; reduce heat. Simmer, covered, for 12 minutes, stirring occasionally.

2 Stir in pumpkin, maple syrup, and vinegar; heat through. Season to taste with salt and pepper. If desired, garnish each serving with apple slices and sage leaves.

NUTRITION FACTS PER SERVING:
439 cal., 21 g total fat (6 g sat. fat), 35 mg chol., 832 mg sodium, 51 g carb., 11 g dietary fiber, 14 g protein.

103

Fast Paella

START TO FINISH **30 minutes** MAKES **6 servings**

- 1 **14.5-ounce can Mexican-style or Cajun-style stewed tomatoes, undrained and cut up**
- 1 **14-ounce can reduced-sodium chicken broth**
- 1 **cup chopped onion (1 large)**
- 2 **teaspoons dried oregano, crushed**
- 1 **teaspoon garlic salt**
- 1 **teaspoon ground turmeric**
- 1 **teaspoon paprika**
- 1/4 **teaspoon crushed red pepper or 1/8 teaspoon bottled hot pepper sauce**
- 1/4 **teaspoon ground black pepper**
- 1 **14- to 16-ounce package cooked smoked turkey or chicken sausage, halved lengthwise and cut into 1-inch pieces**
- 12 **ounces frozen peeled and deveined cooked shrimp**
- 1 **10-ounce package frozen peas**
- 1 **8.8-ounce pouch cooked long grain rice**
  Lemon slices or wedges
  Snipped fresh cilantro or Italian (flat-leaf) parsley

1 In a 12-inch skillet combine tomatoes, broth, onion, oregano, garlic salt, turmeric, paprika, crushed red pepper, and black pepper. Bring to boiling; reduce heat. Simmer, covered, for 10 minutes.

2 Stir in sausage, shrimp, peas, and cooked rice; heat through. Serve in shallow soup bowls. Garnish with lemon slices and sprinkle with cilantro.

NUTRITION FACTS PER SERVING:
303 cal., 9 g total fat (2 g sat. fat), 154 mg chol., 1,269 mg sodium, 29 g carb., 5 g dietary fiber, 27 g protein.

Hearty Italian Stew

START TO FINISH **20 minutes** MAKES **6 servings**

1 tablespoon olive oil

2 cloves garlic, minced

2 14.5-ounce cans diced tomatoes with basil, garlic, and oregano, undrained

1 14-ounce can beef broth

1¾ cups water

1 16-ounce package (32) frozen cooked Italian-style meatballs

½ of a 16-ounce package frozen sweet pepper and onion stir-fry vegetables

½ of a 10-ounce package (about 3 cups) shredded cabbage

1 9-ounce package refrigerated 3-cheese tortellini

Grated Parmesan cheese

1 In a 4- to 5-quart Dutch oven heat oil over medium heat. Add garlic; cook and stir for 30 seconds. Add tomatoes, broth, and the water. Stir in meatballs and frozen vegetables.

2 Bring to boiling over medium-high heat. Stir in cabbage and tortellini; cook, covered, about 5 minutes or until meatballs are heated through and vegetables are tender. Sprinkle each serving with cheese.

NUTRITION FACTS PER SERVING:
459 cal., 23 g total fat (10 g sat. fat), 71 mg chol., 1,705 mg sodium, 40 g carb., 4 g dietary fiber, 23 g protein.

Spring Chicken Stew

START TO FINISH **30 minutes** MAKES **4 servings**

1   **lemon**

1¼   **pounds skinless, boneless chicken thighs**

     Salt

     Ground black pepper

1   **tablespoon olive oil**

1   **12-ounce jar chicken gravy**

1½   **cups water**

8   **ounces baby carrots with tops, trimmed and halved lengthwise**

1   **tablespoon Dijon-style mustard**

2   **heads baby bok choy, quartered**

     Fresh lemon thyme sprigs (optional)

1 Finely shred peel from lemon; set peel aside. Cut lemon in half; squeeze juice; set juice aside. Lightly sprinkle chicken with salt and pepper.

2 In a Dutch oven heat oil over medium-high heat. Add chicken; cook for 2 to 3 minutes or until chicken is brown, turning occasionally to brown evenly.

3 Stir in gravy, the water, carrots, and mustard. Bring to boiling. Place bok choy on top of chicken and carrots; reduce heat. Simmer, covered, about 10 minutes or until chicken is no longer pink (180°F) and vegetables are just tender.

4 Stir in lemon juice to taste. Top each serving with lemon peel and, if desired, lemon thyme sprigs.

NUTRITION FACTS PER SERVING:
273 cal., 12 g total fat (2 g sat. fat), 117 mg chol., 909 mg sodium, 13 g carb., 3 g dietary fiber, 31 g protein.

Caribbean-Style Pork Stew

START TO FINISH **30 minutes** MAKES **6 servings**

1 **15-ounce can black beans, rinsed and drained**

1 **14-ounce can beef broth**

1¾ **cups water**

12 **ounces cooked lean boneless pork, cut into thin bite-size strips**

3 **plantains, peeled and cubed**

½ **of a 16-ounce package (2 cups) frozen sweet pepper and onion stir-fry vegetables**

1 **cup chopped tomatoes (2 medium)**

1 **tablespoon grated fresh ginger**

1 **teaspoon ground cumin**

¼ **teaspoon salt**

¼ **teaspoon crushed red pepper**

3 **cups hot cooked rice**

Crushed red pepper (optional)

Fresh pineapple slices (optional)

1 In a 4-quart Dutch oven combine beans, broth, and the water. Bring to boiling. Stir in meat, plantains, frozen vegetables, tomatoes, ginger, cumin, salt, and ¼ teaspoon crushed red pepper. Return to boiling; reduce heat. Simmer, covered, for 10 minutes or until plantains are tender.

2 To serve, divide rice among soup bowls. Top with meat mixture. If desired, sprinkle with additional crushed red pepper and garnish with pineapple.

NUTRITION FACTS PER SERVING:
367 cal., 5 g total fat (1 g sat. fat), 32 mg chol., 555 mg sodium, 64 g carb., 7 g dietary fiber, 22 g protein.

107

Italian Meatball Stew

START TO FINISH **25 minutes** MAKES **6 servings**

2 **14.5-ounce cans Italian-style stewed tomatoes, undrained and cut up**

1 **16-ounce package (32) frozen cooked Italian-style meatballs**

1 **15-ounce can cannellini beans (white kidney beans), rinsed and drained**

¾ **cup water**

¼ **cup basil pesto**

1 In a large saucepan combine tomatoes, meatballs, beans, the water, and pesto. Bring to boiling; reduce heat. Simmer, covered, about 15 minutes or until heated through.

Italian Sausage Stew:

Prepare as directed, except omit meatballs. In a large saucepan cook 1 pound bulk Italian sausage over medium-high heat until brown, using a wooden spoon to break up meat as it cooks. Drain off fat. Stir in the remaining ingredients; heat through.

NUTRITION FACTS PER SERVING: *same as main recipe*

NUTRITION FACTS PER SERVING:
391 cal., 25 g total fat (8 g sat. fat), 50 mg chol., 1,031 mg sodium, 25 g carb., 7 g dietary fiber, 19 g protein.

Easy Texas-Style Chili

START TO FINISH **20 minutes** MAKES **6 servings**

12 **ounces lean ground beef**

1 **15-ounce can pinto beans, undrained**

1 **cup salsa**

½ **cup beef broth**

1 **teaspoon chili powder**

½ **teaspoon ground cumin**
   Sour cream (optional)

1 In a large skillet cook ground beef over medium-high heat until brown, using a wooden spoon to break up meat as it cooks. Drain off fat.

2 Stir in beans, salsa, broth, chili powder, and cumin. Bring to boiling; reduce heat. Simmer, covered, for 10 minutes. If desired, top each serving with sour cream.

NUTRITION FACTS PER SERVING:
178 cal., 8 g total fat (3 g sat. fat), 36 mg chol., 442 mg sodium, 12 g carb., 4 g dietary fiber, 15 g protein.

Chipotle Chili with Beans

START TO FINISH **25 minutes** MAKES **4 servings**

Nonstick cooking spray

8 ounces ground beef sirloin, uncooked ground chicken breast, or uncooked ground turkey breast

1 cup chopped onion (1 large)

1½ teaspoons ground cumin

2 14.5-ounce cans stewed tomatoes, undrained and cut up

1 15-ounce can red beans, rinsed and drained

1½ cups coarsely chopped red and/or yellow sweet peppers (2 medium)

½ cup water

2 to 3 teaspoons chopped canned chipotle peppers in adobo sauce

1 tablespoon snipped fresh oregano

¼ cup shredded reduced-fat cheddar cheese (1 ounce)

Lime wedges (optional)

Baked tortilla chips (optional)

1 Lightly coat a large saucepan with cooking spray; heat saucepan over medium-high heat. Add ground beef and onion; cook until meat is brown, using a wooden spoon to break up meat as it cooks. If necessary, drain off fat.

2 Stir in cumin; cook and stir for 1 minute. Stir in tomatoes, beans, sweet peppers, the water, and chile peppers. Bring to boiling; reduce heat. Simmer, covered, for 5 minutes. Stir in oregano.

3 Sprinkle each serving with cheese. If desired, serve with lime wedges and tortilla chips.

NUTRITION FACTS PER SERVING: *398 cal., 14 g total fat (6 g sat. fat), 57 mg chol., 1,030 mg sodium, 40 g carb., 10 g dietary fiber, 27 g protein.*

tip
Chipotle chile peppers are dried, smoked jalapeño peppers. Canned in adobo sauce, they're often used to add a spicy heat to chilies, soups, and casseroles. Find them in the ethnic food aisle of your grocery or in Hispanic food markets.

Soups and Stews

Southwestern White Chili

START TO FINISH **30 minutes** MAKES **8 servings**

1 **tablespoon olive oil**

1 **cup chopped onion (1 large)**

4 **cloves garlic, minced**

2 **teaspoons ground cumin**

1 **teaspoon dried oregano, crushed**

1/4 **teaspoon cayenne pepper**

3 **15-ounce cans Great Northern beans, rinsed and drained**

4 **cups chicken broth or reduced-sodium chicken broth**

2 **4-ounce cans diced green chile peppers or jalapeño chile peppers, undrained**

3 **cups chopped cooked chicken (about 1 pound)**

2 **cups shredded Monterey Jack cheese (8 ounces)**

Sour cream (optional)

Canned diced green chile peppers or jalapeño chile peppers (optional)

1 In a large Dutch oven heat oil over medium heat. Add onion and garlic; cook until onion is tender, stirring occasionally. Stir in cumin, oregano, and cayenne pepper; cook and stir for 2 minutes more.

2 Add 1 can of the beans; mash with a potato masher or fork. Stir in the remaining 2 cans beans, broth, and 2 cans chile peppers. Bring to boiling; reduce heat. Simmer, uncovered, for 5 minutes. Stir in chicken; heat through.

3 Top each serving with 1/4 cup of the cheese. If desired, top with sour cream and additional chile peppers.

NUTRITION FACTS PER SERVING:
471 cal., 16 g total fat (7 g sat. fat), 76 mg chol., 468 mg sodium, 43 g carb., 9 g dietary fiber, 38 g protein.

Set up a buffet of tasty toppers for chili. In addition to corn chips, cheese, and sliced green onions, try these flavor boosters.
• **Cilantro Sour Cream:** Combine one 9-ounce carton sour cream and 1/4 cup snipped fresh cilantro. Add a squeeze of fresh lime juice, if desired.
• **Avocado-Tomato Salsa:** Combine 1 firm, ripe avocado, peeled, pitted, and chopped; 1 cup cherry tomatoes, quartered; 1 tablespoon lime juice; and 1 fresh jalapeño chile pepper, seeded and chopped.

Corn Bread–Crusted Chili

START TO FINISH **20 minutes**   MAKES **4 servings**

1   **pound lean ground beef**

1   **16-ounce jar salsa**

1   **15-ounce can chili beans in chili gravy, undrained**

1   **cup frozen whole kernel corn**

1¼ **cups packaged corn bread stuffing mix**

3   **tablespoons butter, melted**

1   **to 2 tablespoons snipped fresh parsley (optional)**

1 Preheat broiler. In a large broiler-proof skillet cook ground beef over medium-high heat until brown, using a wooden spoon to break up meat as it cooks. Drain off fat. Stir in salsa, beans in gravy, and frozen corn; heat through. Spread meat mixture into an even layer.

2 Meanwhile, in a small bowl combine stuffing mix, melted butter, and, if desired, parsley. Sprinkle evenly over meat mixture. Broil 3 to 4 inches from the heat about 2 minutes or until top is golden brown.

NUTRITION FACTS PER SERVING:
588 cal., 28 g total fat (12 g sat. fat), 100 mg chol., 1,249 mg sodium, 53 g carb., 9 g dietary fiber, 33 g protein.

White Bean–Chicken Chili

START TO FINISH 20 minutes MAKES 4 servings

1 tablespoon vegetable oil

½ cup chopped onion
(1 medium)

1 15.5-ounce can hominy,
drained

1 15-ounce can Great Northern
beans, rinsed and drained

1 14-ounce can reduced-sodium
chicken broth

1 9-ounce package frozen
cooked chicken breast strips

¼ cup lime juice

2 tablespoons snipped
fresh cilantro

¼ teaspoon ground cumin

¼ teaspoon ground black pepper

½ cup shredded Colby and
Monterey Jack cheese,
Monterey Jack cheese, or
cheddar cheese (2 ounces)

Salsa verde

White corn tortilla chips

Fresh cilantro leaves
(optional)

1 In a large saucepan heat oil over medium heat. Add onion; cook for 3 minutes, stirring occasionally. Stir in hominy, beans, broth, chicken, lime juice, snipped cilantro, cumin, and pepper. Cover and cook over medium heat until heated through, stirring occasionally.

2 Sprinkle each serving with 2 tablespoons of the cheese. Top with salsa, tortilla chips, and, if desired, cilantro leaves.

NUTRITION FACTS PER SERVING:
434 cal., 14 g total fat (5 g sat. fat), 58 mg chol., 1,001 mg sodium, 48 g carb., 9 g dietary fiber, 31 g protein.

4

Main-Dish Salads

Salad takes on a delicious new meaning as a
mealtime centerpiece, especially when it includes
dramatic bites of flavor and a dazzling dressing.

Superfoods Salad

⅓ cup raspberry vinegar

2 tablespoons snipped fresh mint

2 tablespoons honey

1 tablespoon canola oil

¼ teaspoon salt

6 cups fresh baby spinach

3 cups chopped cooked chicken breast or purchased roasted chicken (about 1 pound)

2 cups fresh strawberries, sliced

½ cup fresh blueberries

¼ cup walnuts, toasted and coarsely chopped

¼ cup crumbled goat cheese (chèvre) (1 ounce)

½ teaspoon freshly ground black pepper

1 For vinaigrette, in a screw-top jar combine vinegar, mint, honey, oil, and salt. Cover and shake well.

2 In an extra-large bowl combine spinach, chicken, strawberries, blueberries, walnuts, and cheese.

3 Shake vinaigrette. Pour over salad; toss gently to coat. Sprinkle with pepper.

NUTRITION FACTS PER SERVING:
243 cal., 9 g total fat (2 g sat. fat), 62 mg chol., 191 mg sodium, 15 g carb., 2 g dietary fiber, 25 g protein.

114

Chicken, Grapes, and Goat Cheese Salad

START TO FINISH **30 minutes** MAKES **4 servings**

¼ cup grape seed oil or olive oil

3 tablespoons balsamic vinegar

1 tablespoon dried dill

1 large clove garlic, minced

¼ teaspoon dried oregano, crushed

¼ teaspoon freshly ground black pepper

1¼ pounds skinless, boneless chicken breast halves

Montreal steak seasoning or Kansas City steak seasoning

8 cups mesclun mix, spring salad greens, or fresh spinach

¾ cup seedless red grapes, halved

⅓ cup crumbled goat cheese (chèvre)

¼ cup pine nuts, toasted

1 For vinaigrette, in a screw-top jar combine oil, vinegar, dill, garlic, oregano, and pepper. Cover and shake well.

2 Lightly sprinkle chicken with steak seasoning. For a charcoal grill, grill chicken on the rack of an uncovered grill directly over medium coals for 12 to 15 minutes or until chicken is no longer pink (170° F), turning once halfway through grilling. (For a gas grill, preheat grill. Reduce heat to medium. Place chicken on grill rack over heat. Cover and grill as above.)

3 Divide mesclun mix among dinner plates. Top with grapes, cheese, and pine nuts. Slice chicken; arrange on top of salads. Shake vinaigrette; drizzle over salads.

NUTRITION FACTS PER SERVING:
429 cal., 25 g total fat (5 g sat. fat), 92 mg chol., 186 mg sodium, 13 g carb., 2 g dietary fiber, 38 g protein.

115

Poached Lemon Chicken Salad 🥕

START TO FINISH **30 minutes** MAKES **4 servings**

1 **lemon**

1 **pound skinless, boneless chicken breast halves, cut into 2-inch pieces**

1 **cup chicken broth**

2 **cloves garlic, minced**

¼ **teaspoon ground black pepper**

4 **cups thinly sliced vegetables, such as cucumber, radishes, and/or carrots**

6 **cups torn mixed salad greens**

3 **tablespoons olive oil**

Salt

Ground black pepper

1 Using a vegetable peeler, remove yellow peel from lemon. Cut lemon in half; set aside. In a medium saucepan combine lemon peel, chicken, broth, garlic, and ¼ teaspoon pepper. Bring to boiling; reduce heat. Simmer, covered, about 7 minutes or until chicken is no longer pink. Drain, discarding cooking liquid and lemon peel. Cool chicken slightly. Using two forks, pull chicken apart into coarse shreds.

2 In a large bowl combine shredded chicken and vegetables. Divide chicken mixture among dinner plates. Top with salad greens; drizzle with oil.

3 Squeeze juice from lemon halves over salads. Season to taste with salt and additional pepper.

NUTRITION FACTS PER SERVING:
255 cal., 12 g total fat (2 g sat. fat), 66 mg chol., 495 mg sodium, 10 g carb., 4 g dietary fiber, 29 g protein.

Buffalo Chicken Salad

START TO FINISH 25 minutes OVEN per package directions MAKES 4 servings

1   25.5-ounce package frozen buffalo-style boneless chicken bites

2   hearts of romaine lettuce, cut up

$1\frac{1}{2}$ cups sliced celery (3 stalks) and/or carrot strips (3 medium)

$\frac{1}{2}$ cup light mayonnaise

$\frac{1}{4}$ cup crumbled blue cheese (1 ounce)

4   teaspoons lemon juice

$\frac{1}{4}$ teaspoon ground black pepper

    Lemon halves or wedges

1 Prepare chicken bites according to package directions.

2 Meanwhile, arrange lettuce on a serving platter or four dinner plates. Top with celery and/or carrots. For dressing, in a small bowl combine mayonnaise, cheese, lemon juice, and pepper.

3 Cut chicken bites in half. Arrange warm chicken on top of lettuce mixture. Serve salad with dressing and lemon halves.

NUTRITION FACTS PER SERVING:
389 cal., 16 g total fat (3 g sat. fat), 157 mg chol., 1,359 mg sodium, 14 g carb., 6 g dietary fiber, 48 g protein.

117

Pesto Chicken Salad

START TO FINISH 30 minutes MAKES 4 servings

1   2- to $2\frac{1}{4}$-pound purchased roasted chicken

2   tablespoons olive oil

1   pound sliced fresh mushrooms

$\frac{1}{2}$ cup dried tomato pesto

3   tablespoons balsamic vinegar

$\frac{1}{2}$ cup cherry tomatoes, halved

8   cups mixed salad greens

1 Remove and chop enough meat from the chicken to make 2 cups. Save any remaining chicken for another use.

2 In a large skillet heat oil over medium heat. Add mushrooms; cook about 10 minutes or until tender, stirring occasionally. Stir in pesto and vinegar. Bring to boiling. Stir in chopped chicken; heat through. Gently stir in tomatoes.

3 Arrange salad greens on a serving platter; top with chicken mixture. Serve warm.

NUTRITION FACTS PER SERVING:
419 cal., 24 g total fat (6 g sat. fat), 96 mg chol., 330 mg sodium, 14 g carb., 3 g dietary fiber, 38 g protein.

Pulled Chicken–Peanut Salad 🥕 ★

START TO FINISH 25 minutes MAKES 4 servings

2 tablespoons frozen orange juice concentrate, thawed

1 tablespoon water

2 teaspoons toasted sesame oil

¼ teaspoon salt

⅛ teaspoon coarse ground black pepper

6 cups torn mixed salad greens

2 cups coarsely shredded cooked chicken

1 11-ounce can mandarin orange sections, drained

¼ cup cocktail peanuts

1 For dressing, in a small bowl stir together juice concentrate, the water, sesame oil, salt, and pepper.

2 Divide salad greens among dinner plates. Arrange chicken, oranges, and peanuts on top of salad greens; drizzle with dressing.

NUTRITION FACTS PER SERVING:
263 cal., 12 g total fat (3 g sat. fat), 62 mg chol., 247 mg sodium, 15 g carb., 2 g dietary fiber, 24 g protein.

★ Almond Chicken Salad

START TO FINISH **15 minutes**   MAKES **4 servings**

12   ounces packaged refrigerated grilled chicken breast strips

1   6-ounce package fresh baby spinach

1   cup seedless red grapes, halved

1   11-ounce can mandarin orange sections, drained

¼   cup sliced almonds

½   cup orange juice

2   tablespoons balsamic vinegar

1   tablespoon toasted sesame oil

¼   teaspoon ground black pepper

1 In an extra-large bowl combine chicken, spinach, grapes, oranges, and almonds.

2 For dressing, in a screw-top jar combine orange juice, vinegar, sesame oil, and pepper. Cover and shake well. Pour dressing over spinach mixture; toss gently to coat.

NUTRITION FACTS PER SERVING:
249 cal., 8 g total fat (1 g sat. fat), 55 mg chol., 431 mg sodium, 25 g carb., 3 g dietary fiber, 22 g protein.

119

Warm Chicken-Spinach Salad

START TO FINISH **20 minutes**   MAKES **4 servings**

1¼   pounds skinless, boneless chicken breast halves

Salt

Ground black pepper

2   tablespoons vegetable oil

1½   cups sliced fresh mushrooms (4 ounces)

1   10-ounce package fresh spinach

½   cup broken walnuts, toasted if desired

2   tablespoons finely shredded Parmesan cheese

1 Sprinkle chicken with salt and pepper. In a 12-inch skillet heat oil over medium heat. Add chicken; cook for 8 to 12 minutes or until chicken is no longer pink (170°F), turning once. Remove chicken from skillet; cover and keep warm.

2 Add mushrooms to skillet. Cook and stir for 2 minutes. Add spinach to skillet. Cook, covered, for 1 to 2 minutes or just until spinach begins to wilt, stirring once. Remove from heat; stir in walnuts. Season to taste with additional salt and pepper.

3 Divide spinach mixture among dinner plates. Slice chicken; arrange on top of spinach mixture. Sprinkle with cheese.

NUTRITION FACTS PER SERVING:
347 cal., 19 g total fat (2 g sat. fat), 84 mg chol., 192 mg sodium, 6 g carb., 3 g dietary fiber, 39 g protein.

Main-Dish Salads

Chicken and Jicama Spinach Salad

START TO FINISH **30 minutes** MAKES **6 servings**

8   cups torn fresh spinach

3   cups chopped cooked chicken
    or turkey (about 1 pound)

½   of a small jicama, peeled and
    cut into thin strips (about
    2 cups)

1   medium red onion, thinly
    sliced and separated into
    rings

½   cup sliced radishes

¼   cup sliced almonds, toasted

3   tablespoons olive oil

2   tablespoons lemon juice

2   tablespoons maple syrup

1 In a large salad bowl combine
spinach, chicken, jicama, red
onion, radishes, and almonds.

2 For dressing, in a screw-top jar
combine oil, lemon juice, and
maple syrup. Cover and shake well.
Pour dressing over spinach mixture;
toss gently to coat.

NUTRITION FACTS PER SERVING:
*294 cal., 20 g total fat (5 g sat. fat),
75 mg chol., 528 mg sodium, 14 g carb.,
4 g dietary fiber, 18 g protein.*

⏱ Glazed Chicken with Wilted Spinach

START TO FINISH **30 minutes** MAKES **4 servings**

1   **recipe Ginger-Apple Glaze**

1¼   **pounds skinless, boneless chicken breast halves**

     Nonstick cooking spray

2   **cups sliced apples (2 medium)**

⅓   **cup sliced leek (1 medium) or chopped onion (1 small)**

2   **cloves garlic, minced**

2   **tablespoons apple juice, apple cider, or chicken broth**

1   **10-ounce package fresh spinach**

     Salt

     Ground black pepper

1 Prepare Ginger-Apple Glaze. Reserve ¼ cup of the glaze to use for apple mixture.

2 For a charcoal grill, grill chicken on the rack of an uncovered grill directly over medium coals for 12 to 15 minutes or until chicken is no longer pink (170°F), turning once halfway through grilling and brushing frequently with the remaining glaze during the last 5 minutes of grilling. (For a gas grill, preheat grill. Reduce heat to medium. Place chicken on grill rack over heat. Cover and grill as above.) Remove chicken from grill; cover and keep warm.

3 Lightly coat a Dutch oven with cooking spray; heat Dutch oven over medium heat. Add apples, leek, and garlic; cook for 3 minutes, stirring occasionally. Stir in the reserved ¼ cup glaze and apple juice. Bring to boiling. Add spinach; toss just until wilted. Remove from heat. Season to taste with salt and pepper.

4 Divide spinach mixture among dinner plates. Slice chicken; arrange on top of spinach mixture.

NUTRITION FACTS PER SERVING: *335 cal., 2 g total fat (1 g sat. fat), 82 mg chol., 673 mg sodium, 44 g carb., 4 g dietary fiber, 36 g protein.*

121

Ginger-Apple Glaze

In a small saucepan combine ½ cup apple jelly; 2 tablespoons soy sauce; 1 tablespoon snipped fresh thyme or 1 teaspoon dried thyme, crushed; 1 teaspoon finely shredded lemon peel; and 1 teaspoon grated fresh ginger. Cook and stir just until jelly is melted. Makes ⅔ cup.

Roasted Chicken, Focaccia, and Olive Salad ⏱

START TO FINISH 30 minutes MAKES 4 servings

5 tablespoons olive oil

¼ cup white wine vinegar or cider vinegar

2 teaspoons Mediterranean seasoning or spaghetti seasoning

1 teaspoon sugar

3 cups torn, day-old garlic Italian flatbread (focaccia) or Italian bread (6 ounces)

2 cups shredded purchased roasted chicken or cooked chicken breast

¾ cup pitted olives

3 hearts of romaine lettuce, cored and coarsely chopped

1 For dressing, in a small bowl whisk together 4 tablespoons of the oil, the vinegar, Mediterranean seasoning, and sugar; set aside.

2 In a 12-inch skillet heat the remaining 1 tablespoon oil over medium-high heat. Add bread. Cook and stir about 5 minutes or until lightly toasted. Remove from skillet. Add dressing, chicken, and olives to skillet. Cook and stir for 2 to 3 minutes or until chicken is heated through. Return bread to skillet; toss gently to coat.

3 Divide lettuce among dinner plates. Top with chicken mixture.

NUTRITION FACTS PER SERVING:
478 cal., 34 g total fat (8 g sat. fat), 83 mg chol., 998 mg sodium, 22 g carb., 3 g dietary fiber, 21 g protein.

122

Chicken and Broccoli Salad

START TO FINISH 20 minutes MAKES 4 servings

½ cup mayonnaise or salad dressing

2 tablespoons cider vinegar

4 cups packaged shredded broccoli (broccoli slaw mix)

2 cups chopped cooked chicken

2 cups chopped red apples

3 slices bacon, crisp-cooked, drained, and crumbled

Bacon, crisp-cooked, drained, and crumbled (optional)

1 For dressing, in a small bowl stir together mayonnaise and vinegar; set aside.

2 In a large bowl combine shredded broccoli, chicken, apples, and 3 slices crumbled bacon. Pour dressing over chicken mixture; toss gently to coat. If desired, sprinkle with additional crumbled bacon.

NUTRITION FACTS PER SERVING:
426 cal., 30 g total fat (6 g sat. fat), 79 mg chol., 382 mg sodium, 16 g carb., 4 g dietary fiber, 25 g protein.

Pork and Noodle Salad

START TO FINISH **25 minutes** MAKES **4 servings**

4 ounces dried Chinese egg noodles or fine egg noodles, broken in half

12 ounces fresh asparagus spears, trimmed and cut into 2-inch pieces, or one 10-ounce package frozen cut asparagus

8 ounces cooked lean boneless pork, cut into bite-size pieces

2 medium carrots, cut into thin bite-size strips

1 recipe Soy-Sesame Vinaigrette
Sesame seeds (optional)
Sliced green onions (optional)

1 Cook noodles according to package directions; drain. Rinse with cold water until cool; drain well.

2 Meanwhile, in a covered small saucepan cook fresh asparagus in a small amount of boiling, lightly salted water for 4 to 6 minutes or until crisp-tender; drain. (Or cook frozen asparagus according to package directions.) Rinse with cold water until cool; drain well.

3 In a large bowl combine noodles, asparagus, pork, and carrots. Shake Soy-Sesame Vinaigrette. Drizzle over noodle mixture; toss gently to coat. If desired, sprinkle with sesame seeds and green onions.

NUTRITION FACTS PER SERVING: *328 cal., 12 g total fat (3 g sat. fat), 76 mg chol., 974 mg sodium, 31 g carb., 2 g dietary fiber, 24 g protein.*

165

Soy-Sesame Vinaigrette

In a screw-top jar combine $\frac{1}{4}$ cup reduced-sodium soy sauce, 2 tablespoons rice vinegar or vinegar, 1 tablespoon vegetable oil, 1 tablespoon honey, and 1 teaspoon toasted sesame oil. Cover and shake well.

tip
Toasted sesame oil brings a deep-flavored smoky-nutty taste to this salad.
Find sesame oil in the Asian ingredients aisle of the supermarket.

Ravioli and Greens Salad

START TO FINISH 25 minutes MAKES 4 servings

1   9-ounce package refrigerated whole wheat 4-cheese ravioli

6   cups torn mixed salad greens

1   cup red sweet pepper strips (1 medium)

1   cup yellow and/or red tomato wedges

$\frac{1}{4}$ cup shredded carrot

$\frac{1}{4}$ cup snipped fresh basil, oregano, and/or dill

$\frac{1}{4}$ cup white wine vinegar or white vinegar

2   tablespoons water

2   tablespoons olive oil

2   teaspoons sugar

2   cloves garlic, minced

$\frac{1}{4}$ teaspoon ground black pepper

1 Cook ravioli according to package directions; drain. Rinse with cold water; drain well.

2 Divide salad greens among dinner plates. Top with cooked ravioli, sweet pepper, tomato, carrot, and herbs.

3 For dressing, in a screw-top jar combine vinegar, the water, oil, sugar, garlic, and black pepper. Cover and shake well. Drizzle dressing over salads.

NUTRITION FACTS PER SERVING:
302 cal., 14 g total fat (5 g sat. fat), 43 mg chol., 456 mg sodium, 33 g carb., 5 g dietary fiber, 11 g protein.

Money-Saving Tip

Use canned tomatoes rather than fresh, but make sure to rinse them well or get the no-salt-added kind to keep from adding any sodium to the salad.

Asian Chicken and Rice Salad

START TO FINISH **25 minutes**   MAKES **4 to 6 servings**

1   **6- to 7-ounce package rice pilaf mix**

2   **cups shredded or chopped cooked chicken**

1   **14-ounce can whole baby corn, drained**

½   **cup chopped red sweet pepper (1 small)**

½   **cup fresh snow pea pods, halved, or thinly sliced celery (1 stalk)**

¼   **cup sliced green onions (2)**

½   **cup bottled Asian salad dressing**

Toasted sesame seeds (optional)

1 Cook rice mix according to package directions.

2 Meanwhile, in a large bowl combine chicken, corn, sweet pepper, pea pods, and green onions. Stir in cooked rice. Add dressing; stir gently to combine.

3 If desired, sprinkle salad with sesame seeds.

NUTRITION FACTS PER SERVING: *429 cal., 14 g total fat (3 g sat. fat), 62 mg chol., 1,057 mg sodium, 46 g carb., 5 g dietary fiber, 26 g protein.*

167

Make-Ahead Directions: Prepare salad as directed through Step 2. Cover and chill for up to 24 hours. If desired, sprinkle with sesame seeds before serving.

Kielbasa, Rice, and Bean Salad

START TO FINISH 20 minutes MAKES 6 servings

12 ounces cooked smoked Polish
    sausage (kielbasa) links,
    halved lengthwise and cut
    into $\frac{1}{2}$-inch pieces

1   14.8-ounce pouch cooked long
    grain rice

3   cups fresh baby spinach

1   15-ounce can cannellini beans
    (white kidney beans), rinsed
    and drained

1   cup grape or cherry tomatoes,
    halved

$\frac{1}{2}$ cup chopped yellow sweet
    pepper (1 small)

$\frac{1}{3}$ cup chopped red onion
    (1 small)

$\frac{1}{2}$ cup bottled red wine
    vinaigrette salad dressing
    or Italian salad dressing
    with cheese

1 In a large skillet cook sausage over medium heat just until heated through, stirring occasionally. Meanwhile, heat rice in a microwave oven according to package directions.

2 In a large bowl combine spinach, beans, tomatoes, sweet pepper, and red onion. Stir in sausage and rice. Pour salad dressing over salad; toss gently to coat.

NUTRITION FACTS PER SERVING:
421 cal., 25 g total fat (8 g sat. fat), 25 mg chol., 904 mg sodium, 38 g carb., 5 g dietary fiber, 15 g protein.

Meatless

Warming up to meat-free meals takes little effort
with these options that are fully loaded with pasta,
grains, vegetables, fruits, herbs, and spices.

5

Fettuccine Alfredo with Veggies

START TO FINISH **30 minutes** MAKES **4 servings**

8 ounces dried fettuccine

¹⁄₂ cup dried tomatoes (not oil-pack), snipped

4 tablespoons butter

1 tablespoon olive oil

4 ounces asparagus spears, trimmed

4 ounces Brussels sprouts, trimmed and quartered

1¹⁄₂ cups broccoli florets

8 fresh mushrooms, sliced

2 tablespoons all-purpose flour

1¹⁄₄ cups milk

¹⁄₂ cup finely shredded Parmesan cheese

Milk (optional)

2 teaspoons finely shredded lemon peel

Finely shredded Parmesan cheese

1 Cook pasta according to package directions, adding dried tomatoes for the last 2 minutes of cooking; drain. Return to saucepan; keep warm.

2 Meanwhile, in a large skillet heat 1 tablespoon of the butter and the olive oil over medium heat. Add asparagus, Brussels sprouts, broccoli, and mushrooms. Cook about 8 minutes or until vegetables are tender, stirring frequently. Remove vegetables from skillet; set aside.

3 In the same skillet heat the remaining 3 tablespoons butter over medium heat until melted. Stir in flour. Cook and stir for 1 minute. Stir in 1¹⁄₄ cups milk. Cook and stir until thickened and bubbly. Stir in ¹⁄₂ cup Parmesan cheese. Gently stir in cooked pasta and vegetables. If necessary, stir in additional milk to reach desired consistency. Sprinkle with lemon peel and additional Parmesan cheese.

NUTRITION FACTS PER SERVING:
500 cal., 21 g total fat (11 g sat. fat), 46 mg chol., 491 mg sodium, 60 g carb., 5 g dietary fiber, 20 g protein.

Spinach and Bean Greek Pasta

START TO FINISH **30 minutes** MAKES **6 servings**

12 ounces dried cavatappi or farfalle pasta (bow ties)

1 15-ounce can Great Northern beans, rinsed and drained

1 5- to 6-ounce package fresh baby spinach

1 cup crumbled feta cheese (4 ounces)

¼ cup dried tomatoes (not oil-pack), snipped

2 green onions, chopped

2 cloves garlic, minced

1 teaspoon finely shredded lemon peel

2 tablespoons lemon juice

2 tablespoons olive oil

1 tablespoon snipped fresh oregano

1 tablespoon snipped fresh lemon thyme or regular thyme

½ teaspoon kosher salt or sea salt

½ teaspoon freshly ground black pepper

Shaved Parmesan or Pecorino Romano cheese

1 Cook pasta according to package directions; drain, reserving ¼ cup of the cooking water.

2 Meanwhile, in a large serving bowl combine beans, spinach, cheese, tomatoes, green onions, garlic, lemon peel, lemon juice, oil, oregano, thyme, salt, and pepper.

3 Toss pasta and the reserved cooking water with the spinach mixture. Serve warm or at room temperature. Top with shaved Parmesan cheese.

NUTRITION FACTS PER SERVING:
408 cal., 10 g total fat (4 g sat. fat), 19 mg chol., 487 mg sodium, 62 g carb., 6 g dietary fiber, 17 g protein.

171

tip

Cavatappi are sometimes called double macaroni. They look like corkscrew-shaped macaroni and often have small grooves on the outside. Most small pastas make good substitutes, including bow tie pasta or rotini.

Meatless

Noodle Bowls with Spinach and Tofu

START TO FINISH **20 minutes** MAKES **6 servings**

Nonstick cooking spray

1 **16-ounce package extra-firm or firm tofu (fresh bean curd), drained**

⅔ **cup hoisin sauce (7.25-ounce jar)**

4 **14-ounce cans chicken broth**

1 **tablespoon bottled minced roasted garlic**

12 **ounces dried udon noodles or linguine, broken**

2 **6-ounce packages fresh baby spinach**

1 Preheat broiler. Lightly coat the unheated rack of a broiler pan with cooking spray. Cut tofu crosswise into six slices; pat dry with paper towels. Arrange tofu slices in a single layer on the prepared rack of the broiler pan; brush tops of tofu slices with 3 tablespoons of the hoisin sauce. Broil 4 to 6 inches from heat for 8 to 10 minutes or until hoisin is bubbly (do not turn slices).

2 Meanwhile, in a 4- to 6-quart Dutch oven combine broth, roasted garlic, and the remaining hoisin sauce. Bring to boiling. Add noodles and cook according to package directions, adding spinach for the last 2 minutes of cooking. Divide mixture among four large, deep soup bowls.

3 Cut tofu into cubes or strips. Top noodle mixture with tofu.

NUTRITION FACTS PER SERVING:
340 cal., 6 g total fat (1 g sat. fat), 3 mg chol., 1,573 mg sodium, 55 g carb., 4 g dietary fiber, 16 g protein.

Ramen Noodles with Mushrooms and Shallots

START TO FINISH **25 minutes** MAKES **2 servings**

1 **3-ounce package ramen noodles (any flavor)**

2 **tablespoons butter or margarine**

6 **ounces assorted fresh mushrooms, stemmed if necessary, and sliced**

¼ **cup finely chopped shallots (2 medium)**

¼ **cup dry white wine or reduced-sodium chicken broth**

2 **tablespoons soy sauce**

1 Cook noodles according to package directions (discard seasoning packet); drain and keep warm.

2 Meanwhile, in a large skillet heat butter over medium heat until melted. Add mushrooms and shallots; cook about 4 minutes or until tender. Remove from heat. Stir in wine and soy sauce. Return to heat. Cook, uncovered, about 5 minutes or until most of the liquid evaporates. Add cooked noodles; toss to coat.

NUTRITION FACTS PER SERVING:
375 cal., 22 g total fat (8 g sat. fat), 31 mg chol., 1,010 mg sodium, 33 g carb., 1 g dietary fiber, 10 g protein.

Broccoli Spaghetti

6   **ounces dried spaghetti**

3   **cups broccoli florets**

1   **15- to 19-ounce can cannellini beans (white kidney beans), rinsed and drained**

1   **10-ounce container refrigerated light Alfredo sauce**

3   **cloves garlic, minced**

½   **cup croutons, coarsely crushed**

¼   **teaspoon crushed red pepper**
    Olive oil

1 Cook pasta according to package directions, adding broccoli for the last 3 to 4 minutes of cooking; drain, reserving ½ cup of the cooking water. Return pasta mixture to hot pan; keep warm.

2 Meanwhile, in a blender or food processor combine beans, Alfredo sauce, garlic, and the reserved cooking water. Cover and blend or process until nearly smooth. Transfer to a small saucepan; heat through over medium heat, stirring frequently.

3 Spoon sauce onto dinner plates. Top with pasta mixture, crushed croutons, and crushed red pepper; drizzle with oil.

NUTRITION FACTS PER SERVING:
402 cal., 12 g total fat (5 g sat. fat), 18 mg chol., 659 mg sodium, 60 g carb., 8 g dietary fiber, 19 g protein.

173

Farfalle with Mushrooms and Spinach

START TO FINISH **20 minutes** MAKES **2 servings**

6 **ounces dried farfalle pasta (bow ties)**

1 **tablespoon olive oil**

1 **cup sliced portobello or other fresh mushrooms**

½ **cup chopped onion (1 medium)**

2 **cloves garlic, minced**

4 **cups thinly sliced fresh spinach**

1 **teaspoon snipped fresh thyme**

⅛ **teaspoon ground black pepper**

2 **tablespoons shredded Parmesan cheese**

1 In a large saucepan cook pasta according to package directions; drain.

2 Meanwhile, in a large skillet heat oil over medium heat. Add mushrooms, onion, and garlic. Cook for 2 to 3 minutes or until mushrooms are nearly tender. Stir in spinach, thyme, and pepper; cook about 1 minute more or until heated through and spinach is slightly wilted. Stir in cooked pasta; toss gently to mix. Sprinkle with cheese.

NUTRITION FACTS PER SERVING: *451 cal., 11 g total fat (2 g sat. fat), 4 mg chol., 131 mg sodium, 74 g carb., 5 g dietary fiber, 17 g protein.*

174

Penne with Green Beans and Gorgonzola

START TO FINISH **30 minutes** MAKES **4 servings**

6 ounces dried penne or cut ziti pasta

8 ounces fresh green beans, trimmed and bias-sliced into 1-inch pieces (about $1\frac{1}{2}$ cups), or one 9-ounce package frozen cut green beans, thawed

$\frac{1}{3}$ cup bottled Italian salad dressing

1 tablespoon snipped fresh tarragon or $\frac{1}{2}$ teaspoon dried tarragon, crushed

$\frac{1}{4}$ teaspoon ground black pepper

1 cup shredded radicchio or red cabbage

1 6-ounce package fresh baby spinach

$\frac{1}{2}$ cup crumbled Gorgonzola cheese or blue cheese (2 ounces) or $\frac{1}{4}$ cup shaved Parmesan cheese (1 ounce)

1 Cook pasta according to package directions, adding fresh green beans for the last 5 to 7 minutes of cooking (if using frozen beans, add for the last 3 to 4 minutes); drain. Rinse with cold water; drain again.

2 In a large bowl combine Italian dressing, tarragon, and pepper. Add cooked pasta mixture and radicchio; toss gently to coat. Line a serving platter with spinach. Spoon pasta mixture on top of spinach. Sprinkle with cheese.

NUTRITION FACTS PER SERVING:
294 cal., 10 g total fat (4 g sat. fat), 10 mg chol., 560 mg sodium, 40 g carb., 4 g dietary fiber, 12 g protein.

Good and Healthy Macaroni and Cheese 🥕★

START TO FINISH **30 minutes** MAKES **5 servings**

8 **ounces dried multigrain elbow macaroni or penne pasta**

1 **cup chopped fresh or frozen mixed vegetables**

1 **12-ounce can evaporated fat-free milk**

2 **tablespoons all-purpose flour**

¼ **teaspoon salt**

⅛ **teaspoon ground black pepper**

1¼ **cups shredded reduced-fat cheddar cheese (5 ounces)**

1 **ounce American cheese, shredded**

Ground black pepper (optional)

1 Cook pasta according to package directions, adding the vegetables for the last 2 minutes of cooking; drain. Return pasta mixture to hot pan.

2 Meanwhile, in a medium saucepan whisk together milk, flour, salt, and ⅛ teaspoon pepper. Cook and stir over medium heat until thickened and bubbly. Add cheeses; cook and stir until melted.

3 Pour sauce over pasta mixture in pan; heat through. If desired, sprinkle with additional pepper.

NUTRITION FACTS PER SERVING:
344 cal., 9 g total fat (5 g sat. fat), 28 mg chol., 553 mg sodium, 46 g carb., 4 g dietary fiber, 23 g protein.

⭐ Ravioli with Tomatoes and Spinach

START TO FINISH **30 minutes** MAKES **4 servings**

1 **24- to 25-ounce package frozen cheese-filled ravioli**

4 **large tomatoes, cut into thin wedges and seeded (about 4 cups)**

¾ **cup small fresh basil leaves**

¼ **cup capers, drained**

½ **teaspoon salt**

¼ **teaspoon ground black pepper**

2 **tablespoons butter or margarine**

6 **cloves garlic, minced**

2 **cups fresh baby spinach**

½ **cup shredded Parmesan cheese (2 ounces)**

1 Cook pasta according to package directions; drain. Return pasta to hot pan; cover and keep warm.

2 Meanwhile, in a large bowl combine tomatoes, basil, capers, salt, and pepper; set aside.

3 For sauce, in a large skillet heat butter over medium heat until melted. Add garlic; cook for 30 seconds. Add tomato mixture; cook just until heated through. Remove from heat; gently stir in spinach.

4 To serve, place cooked pasta on a large serving platter. Spoon sauce over pasta. Sprinkle with Parmesan cheese.

NUTRITION FACTS PER SERVING: *480 cal., 18 g total fat (11 g sat. fat), 93 mg chol., 914 mg sodium, 57 g carb., 5 g dietary fiber, 22 g protein.*

Ravioli and Zucchini Skillet

START TO FINISH **20 minutes**   MAKES **4 servings**

1   **14.5-ounce can Italian-style stewed tomatoes, undrained**

½   **cup water**

2   **medium zucchini and/or yellow summer squash, halved lengthwise and cut into ½-inch pieces (about 2½ cups)**

1   **9-ounce package refrigerated whole wheat four-cheese ravioli**

1   **15-ounce can cannellini beans (white kidney beans) or navy beans, rinsed and drained**

2   **tablespoons finely shredded or grated Parmesan cheese**

2   **tablespoons snipped fresh basil or parsley**

1 In an extra large skillet combine tomatoes and the water. Bring to boiling. Stir in zucchini and ravioli. Return to boiling; reduce heat. Boil gently, covered, for 6 to 7 minutes or until ravioli are tender, stirring gently once or twice.

2 Stir beans into ravioli mixture; heat through. Sprinkle with cheese and basil.

NUTRITION FACTS PER SERVING:
305 cal., 8 g total fat (4 g sat. fat), 44 mg chol., 986 mg sodium, 49 g carb., 11 g dietary fiber, 18 g protein.

Ravioli with Garden Vegetables

START TO FINISH 25 minutes   MAKES 4 servings

- 1   9-ounce package refrigerated cheese-filled ravioli or tortellini
- 2   teaspoons olive oil or vegetable oil
- 2   cloves garlic, minced
- 1¼ cups thinly sliced yellow summer squash (1 medium)
- 1   15-ounce can garbanzo beans (chickpeas), rinsed and drained
- 4   roma tomatoes, quartered
- 2   teaspoons snipped fresh thyme or ½ teaspoon dried thyme, crushed
- ¼   teaspoon ground black pepper
- 4   cups shredded fresh spinach
    Olive oil or vegetable oil (optional)
    Grated Parmesan cheese (optional)

1 Cook ravioli according to package directions; drain.

2 Meanwhile, in a large skillet heat 2 teaspoons oil over medium-high heat. Add garlic; cook and stir for 30 seconds. Add squash, garbanzo beans, tomatoes, thyme, and pepper; cook and stir over medium-high heat for 4 to 5 minutes or until squash is crisp-tender and mixture is heated through.

3 Add ravioli to vegetable mixture; toss lightly. Arrange spinach on four dinner plates; top with ravioli mixture. If desired, drizzle with a little additional oil and/or sprinkle with Parmesan cheese.

NUTRITION FACTS PER SERVING:
304 cal., 7 g total fat (2 g sat. fat), 25 mg chol., 688 mg sodium, 48 g carb., 7 g dietary fiber, 15 g protein.

179

Stuffed Peppers ⏱ 🥕

START TO FINISH **30 minutes** MAKES **4 servings**

- 4 **large yellow, red, and/or green sweet peppers**
- 3 **tablespoons water**
- 1 **15-ounce can no-salt-added black beans, rinsed and drained**
- 1 **15-ounce can no-salt-added whole kernel corn, drained**
- 1 **14.5-ounce can diced tomatoes, undrained**
- 1 **8.8-ounce pouch cooked whole grain brown rice, heated according to package directions**
- ½ **cup salsa**
- ½ **teaspoon cumin or chili powder**

1 Cut off the top of each sweet pepper; remove cores and stems, hollowing out the peppers. Arrange peppers in a microwave-safe 2-quart square baking dish. Pour the water around peppers.

2 Microwave peppers, uncovered, on 100 percent power (high) about 8 minutes or just until peppers are starting to soften.

3 Meanwhile, in a medium bowl stir together black beans, corn, tomatoes, rice, salsa, and cumin.

4 Divide bean mixture evenly among the peppers. Microwave, uncovered, on 100 percent power (high) about 4 minutes or until filling is heated through and peppers are tender.

NUTRITION FACTS PER SERVING:
362 cal., 3 g total fat (0 g sat. fat), 0 mg chol., 327 mg sodium, 76 g carb., 12 g dietary fiber, 13 g protein.

Rice and Red Beans

START TO FINISH **25 minutes**   MAKES **8 servings**

1   **tablespoon olive oil or canola oil**

½   **cup chopped onion (1 medium)**

1   **14-ounce package instant brown rice (2 cups)**

1   **cup water**

2   **15-ounce cans kidney beans or black beans, rinsed and drained**

2   **14.5-ounce cans Italian-style stewed tomatoes, cut up**

¼   **teaspoon crushed red pepper (optional)**

1   **cup shredded Monterey Jack cheese or cheddar cheese (4 ounces)**

¼   **cup snipped fresh cilantro**

1 In a large saucepan heat oil over medium heat. Add onion; cook until tender. Add rice and the water. Stir in beans, tomatoes, and, if desired, crushed red pepper. Bring to boiling; reduce heat. Simmer, covered, for 10 minutes. Remove from heat.

2 Stir in ½ cup of the cheese and the cilantro. Let stand, covered, for 5 minutes. Top with the remaining ½ cup cheese.

NUTRITION FACTS PER SERVING:
376 cal., 8 g total fat (3 g sat. fat), 13 mg chol., 479 mg sodium, 67 g carb., 10 g dietary fiber, 17 g protein.

181

Couscous and Squash

START TO FINISH **30 minutes** MAKES **4 servings**

- 2 **limes**
- 1/3 **cup olive oil**
- 1/2 **teaspoon ground cumin**
- 1/2 **teaspoon salt**
- 1/2 **teaspoon ground black pepper**
- 2 **small zucchini and/or yellow summer squash**
- 1 **small head cauliflower, trimmed**
- 1 **small red onion**
- 1 1/2 **cups water**
- 1 **cup couscous**
- 1/2 **cup shredded Parmesan cheese**
  Snipped fresh parsley (optional)

1 Finely shred enough peel from 1 of the limes to make 1 teaspoon shredded peel; set aside. Juice limes to make 1/4 cup juice. In a small bowl whisk together the lime juice, oil, cumin, salt, and pepper.

2 Cut zucchini lengthwise into 1/2-inch slices. Cut cauliflower into six wedges. Cut red onion crosswise into 1/2-inch slices. Brush vegetable slices with some of the oil mixture.

3 For a charcoal grill, grill vegetable slices on the rack of an uncovered grill directly over medium coals until crisp-tender, carefully using a wide spatula to turn vegetables once. Allow 5 to 6 minutes for zucchini slices and 10 to 12 minutes for cauliflower and onion slices. (For a gas grill, preheat grill. Reduce heat to medium. Place vegetables on grill rack over heat. Cover and grill as above.) Remove vegetables from grill as they get done. Cut vegetables into 1- to 2-inch pieces.

4 Meanwhile, in a medium saucepan bring the water to boiling. Stir in couscous and the shredded lime peel. Remove from heat; cover and let stand for 5 minutes. Fluff with a fork.

5 To serve, drizzle vegetables and couscous with the remaining oil mixture. Top with some of the Parmesan cheese. If desired, sprinkle with parsley. Serve with the remaining Parmesan.

NUTRITION FACTS PER SERVING:
428 cal., 21 g total fat (4 g sat. fat), 7 mg chol., 505 mg sodium, 49 g carb., 7 g dietary fiber, 13 g protein.

Herbed Garden Couscous

START TO FINISH **30 minutes**   MAKES **6 servings**

1	cup whole wheat couscous
2	cups cherry tomatoes, halved
1½	cups coarsely chopped cucumber (1 medium)
¾	cup chopped green sweet pepper (1 medium)
½	cup snipped fresh chives
¼	cup snipped fresh Italian (flat-leaf) parsley
¼	cup snipped fresh mint
¼	cup snipped fresh oregano
⅓	cup balsamic vinegar
⅓	cup olive oil
2	teaspoons sugar
½	teaspoon salt
¼	teaspoon ground black pepper
½	cup crumbled feta cheese (2 ounces)
½	cup coarsely chopped walnuts, toasted

1 Cook couscous according to package directions. Fluff with fork.

2 Meanwhile, in a large bowl combine tomatoes, cucumber, sweet pepper, chives, parsley, mint, and oregano. Fold in couscous.

3 In a small bowl whisk together vinegar, oil, sugar, salt, and black pepper. Pour over couscous mixture; toss to combine. To serve, top with feta cheese and walnuts.

NUTRITION FACTS PER SERVING: *392 cal., 12 g total fat (4 g sat. fat), 12 mg chol., 344 mg sodium, 42 g carb., 6 g dietary fiber, 10 g protein.*

183

Quinoa Toss with Chickpeas and Herbs

START TO FINISH 30 minutes   MAKES 6 servings

1   cup quinoa

2   cups chicken broth or
     vegetable broth

¼   cup olive oil

2   tablespoons lemon juice

½   teaspoon salt

½   teaspoon ground black pepper

1   15-ounce can garbanzo beans
     (chickpeas), rinsed and
     drained

1   cup frozen corn, thawed

½   cup crumbled feta cheese
     (2 ounces)

¼   cup finely chopped sweet
     onion, such as Vidalia or Maui

3   tablespoons snipped fresh
     basil

2   tablespoons snipped fresh
     Italian (flat-leaf) parsley

1   cup canned diced beets,
     drained

     Romaine leaves

1 Rinse quinoa in a fine-mesh sieve under cold running water; drain. In a medium saucepan bring broth to boiling. Add quinoa. Return to boiling; reduce heat. Simmer, covered, about 15 minutes or until broth is absorbed. Remove from heat; set aside.

2 Meanwhile, for dressing, in a small bowl whisk together oil, lemon juice, salt, and pepper. In a large bowl combine cooked quinoa, garbanzo beans, corn, cheese, onion, basil, and parsley. Add dressing to quinoa mixture; toss to coat.

3 Stir in beets. Line salad bowls with lettuce; top with quinoa mixture.

NUTRITION FACTS PER SERVING:
349 cal., 14 g total fat (3 g sat. fat), 9 mg chol., 918 mg sodium, 46 g carb., 8 g dietary fiber, 12 g protein.

tip

Quinoa is a tiny protein-packed seed that is often treated as a grain. In fact, you can easily substitute quinoa for rice in many recipes. It's quick cooking—ready in 15 minutes—and has a mild, nutty flavor and an al dente crunch. Look for it in the pasta and rice section or the health food area of major grocery stores.

Garbanzo Bean Salad with Grilled Pita

START TO FINISH **20 minutes**   MAKES **4 servings**

2   15-ounce cans no-salt-added garbanzo beans (chickpeas) or regular garbanzo beans (chickpeas), rinsed and drained

6   roma tomatoes, sliced

1   cup crumbled feta cheese with tomato and basil (4 ounces)

¼   cup lightly packed small fresh mint leaves

⅓   cup white vinegar

¼   cup olive oil

1   tablespoon sugar

½   teaspoon ground black pepper

1   or 2 pita bread rounds

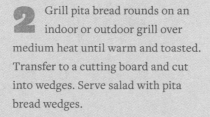

1 In a large bowl combine beans, tomatoes, feta, and mint. In a screw-top jar combine vinegar, oil, sugar, and pepper; shake to combine. Pour over bean mixture; set aside.

2 Grill pita bread rounds on an indoor or outdoor grill over medium heat until warm and toasted. Transfer to a cutting board and cut into wedges. Serve salad with pita bread wedges.

NUTRITION FACTS PER SERVING:
454 cal., 22 g total fat, 21 mg chol., 878 mg sodium, 49 g carb., 10 g dietary fiber, 17 g protein.

185

Beets and Greens with Cheesy Baguette Bites

START TO FINISH **30 minutes** MAKES **4 servings**

6	small golden and/or red beets
½	cup cider vinegar
2	tablespoons sugar
2	tablespoons water
1	small baguette, diagonally sliced
4	ounces semisoft cheese with garlic and herb
¼	cup olive oil
½	teaspoon salt
½	teaspoon ground black pepper
8	cups mixed salad greens
⅓	cup dried cranberries
	Shelled roasted pumpkin seeds (optional)

1 Preheat broiler. Place whole beets (greens trimmed) in a 1-quart microwave-safe casserole dish; add vinegar, sugar, and the water. Microwave, covered, on 100 percent power (high) for 9 to 12 minutes or until tender, stirring once. Trim stems and slip off skins. Slice beets; reserve cooking liquid.

2 While beets are in microwave, prepare toast. Spread baguette slices with cheese. Broil 4 inches from heat about 3 minutes or until cheese is melted and bread edges are toasted; set aside.

3 For dressing, add oil, salt, and pepper to reserved cooking liquid; whisk to combine. In a serving bowl combine beets, salad greens, and cranberries. Drizzle dressing over salad; toss to coat. Sprinkle with pumpkin seeds. Serve with toast.

NUTRITION FACTS PER SERVING:
581 cal., 24 g total fat (8 g sat. fat), 22 mg chol., 1,070 mg sodium, 74 g carb., 6 g dietary fiber, 19 g protein.

Apple-Brie Grilled Sandwiches

START TO FINISH **25 minutes**   MAKES **4 servings**

1   **tablespoon vegetable oil**

1   **medium sweet onion, such as Vidalia or Maui, cut into thin wedges**

2   **tablespoons apple jelly**

1   **5-ounce package soft-style spreadable Brie cheese***

8   **slices whole grain bread**

1   **medium Granny Smith apple, cored and thinly sliced**

¼   **cup butter, softened**

1 In a large skillet heat oil over medium heat. Add onion; cook about 5 minutes or until very tender and beginning to brown. Transfer onions to a small bowl; stir in apple jelly. If desired, snip onions into smaller pieces.

2 Spread Brie cheese on half of the bread slices. Top with apple slices and onion mixture. Top with the remaining bread slices.

3 Spread top slices of bread with half of the butter. In a very large skillet over medium heat place sandwiches, buttered sides down. Carefully spread unbuttered bread with the remaining butter. Cook for 4 to 6 minutes or until cheese melts and bread browns, turning once.

NUTRITION FACTS PER SERVING: *484 cal., 28 g total fat (14 g sat. fat), 66 mg chol., 529 mg sodium, 44 g carb., 9 g dietary fiber, 19 g protein.*

187

*tip

If you can't find soft-style spreadable Brie, thinly slice regular Brie and place on the bread slices; using a knife, carefully spread the Brie on the bread.

Meatless

Farmers' Market Grilled Cheese

START TO FINISH **30 minutes** MAKES **4 servings**

- 2 **cups fresh baby spinach**
- ¼ **cup mayonnaise or salad dressing**
- 1 **teaspoon bottled minced garlic**
- ¼ **teaspoon salt**
- ¼ **teaspoon ground black pepper**
- 8 **½-inch slices sourdough bread**
- 2 **tablespoons olive oil**
- ½ **of a 3.5- to 4-ounce package garlic-and-herb goat cheese, softened**
- 1 **small zucchini, thinly sliced lengthwise**
- 1 **tomato, sliced**

1 In a blender or food processor combine 1 cup of the spinach, the mayonnaise, garlic, salt, and pepper. Cover and blend or process until nearly smooth. Set aside.

2 Brush one side of each bread slice with oil; place bread, oiled sides down, on waxed paper. Spread goat cheese on half of the slices; layer zucchini, tomato, and the remaining 1 cup spinach on top. Spread some of the mayonnaise mixture on the remaining bread slices; place on top of the vegetables, spread sides down.

3 In a very large skillet cook sandwiches over medium-high heat for 6 to 8 minutes or until bread is golden, turning once. Pass any remaining mayonnaise mixture.

NUTRITION FACTS PER SERVING: *369 cal., 22 g total fat (6 g sat. fat), 15 mg chol., 636 mg sodium, 32 g carb., 3 g dietary fiber, 10 g protein.*

Grilled Vegetables on Ciabatta

3 tablespoons red wine vinegar

2 tablespoons water

1 tablespoon olive oil

1 teaspoon dried oregano, crushed

¼ teaspoon salt

¼ teaspoon ground black pepper

3 large red and/or orange sweet peppers

2 medium zucchini and/or yellow summer squash, halved crosswise and sliced lengthwise into ¼-inch slices

1 16-ounce loaf ciabatta bread

2 ounces soft goat cheese (chèvre)

2 ounces reduced-fat cream cheese (Neufchâtel), softened

Fresh oregano (optional)

1 In a small bowl whisk together vinegar, the water, oil, dried oregano, salt, and black pepper; set aside. Cut sweet peppers into quarters. Remove stems, membranes, and seeds. Brush sweet pepper quarters and zucchini slices with some of the vinegar mixture.

2 For a charcoal grill, grill vegetables on the rack of an uncovered grill directly over medium coals until crisp-tender, turning once halfway through grilling and brushing often with the vinegar mixture. Allow 8 to 10 minutes for sweet peppers and 5 to 6 minutes for zucchini. Remove vegetables from grill. (For a gas grill, preheat grill. Reduce heat to medium. Place vegetables on grill rack. Cover and grill as above.) Cut peppers into strips.

3 Halve ciabatta lengthwise. Place ciabatta halves, cut sides down, directly over medium coals for 1 to 2 minutes or until bread is lightly toasted. In a small bowl combine goat cheese and cream cheese, stirring until smooth.

4 To assemble, spread goat cheese mixture over bottom half of the ciabatta. Top with sweet peppers and zucchini. Drizzle with any remaining vinegar mixture. Place the top half of the ciabatta over vegetables. Slice to serve. If desired, garnish with fresh oregano.

189

NUTRITION FACTS PER SERVING:
312 cal., 9 g total fat (4 g sat. fat),
12 mg chol., 621 mg sodium, 45 g carb.,
5 g dietary fiber, 11 g protein.

Tomato-Avocado Grilled Cheese

START TO FINISH 25 minutes   MAKES 4 sandwiches

1   ripe avocado, halved, seeded, and peeled
1   tablespoon lemon juice
½   teaspoon ground cumin
¼   teaspoon salt
2   tablespoons snipped fresh Italian (flat-leaf) parsley
8   slices whole grain bread
6   ounces reduced-fat Monterey Jack cheese, sliced
1   large tomato, thinly sliced
2   tablespoons butter or margarine, softened

1 In a small bowl use a fork to mash together avocado, lemon juice, cumin, and salt until smooth. Stir in parsley; set aside.

2 Top four of the bread slices with the cheese; spread with the avocado mixture and top with tomato slices. Top with the remaining bread slices. Spread top of the bread slices lightly with some of the butter.

3 Heat a large nonstick griddle or 12-inch skillet over medium-high heat. Carefully add sandwiches, buttered sides down. Very carefully spread tops with the remaining butter. Cook for 4 to 6 minutes or until golden, turning once.

NUTRITION FACTS PER SANDWICH:
417 cal., 23 g total fat (10 g sat. fat), 45 mg chol., 772 mg sodium, 37 g carb., 11 g dietary fiber, 22 g protein.

Veggie Grilled Cheese

3 cups packed baby spinach leaves

2 cups bottled pickled mixed vegetables (giardiniera), rinsed and well drained

6 ounces fresh mozzarella cheese, chopped

½ cup oil-pack dried tomatoes, snipped

1 teaspoon bottled minced garlic

½ teaspoon ground black pepper

12 slices whole grain bread, toasted

1 In a large microwave-safe bowl combine spinach, mixed vegetables, cheese, dried tomatoes, garlic, and pepper. Microwave, uncovered, on 100 percent power (high), about 2 minutes or just until the mixture is warm, the spinach is wilted, and the cheese is beginning to melt.

2 To assemble sandwiches, layer half of the cheese and vegetable mixture on four slices of the bread. Top with four more slices of the bread and the remaining cheese mixture. Place the remaining four bread slices on top. Cut each sandwich diagonally in half.

NUTRITION FACTS PER SERVING:
359 cal., 14 g total fat (7 g sat. fat), 30 mg chol., 782 mg sodium, 42 g carb., 7 g dietary fiber, 17 g protein.

Falafel Patty Melt

START TO FINISH **25 minutes** OVEN **400°F** MAKES **4 servings**

½ cup frozen peas

1 **16-ounce can garbanzo beans (chickpeas), rinsed and drained**

½ cup shredded carrot (1 medium)

2 **tablespoons all-purpose flour**

2 **tablespoons olive oil**

½ teaspoon ground black pepper

¼ teaspoon salt

4 **flatbreads or pita bread rounds**

8 **slices dilled Havarti cheese (4 to 6 ounces total)**

Romaine leaves (optional)

Sliced tomato (optional)

1 Preheat oven to 400°F. Place peas in 1-quart microwave-safe dish. Microwave, covered, on 100 percent power (high) for 2 minutes. In a food processor bowl combine garbanzo beans, carrot, flour, 1 tablespoon of the olive oil, the pepper, and salt. Cover and process until finely chopped and mixture holds together. Stir in peas. Using clean hands, shape mixture into eight patties.

2 In a large nonstick skillet heat the remaining 1 tablespoon oil over medium-high heat. Add patties. Cook for 4 to 6 minutes or until browned and heated through, turning once.

3 Meanwhile, place flatbreads on baking sheet. Place two slices of cheese on top of each flatbread. Bake about 5 minutes or until cheese is melted. Place two patties on each flatbread; fold over. Cut into halves. If desired, serve with romaine and tomato.

NUTRITION FACTS PER SERVING: *508 cal., 17 g total fat (7 g sat. fat), 21 mg chol., 1,006 mg sodium, 66 g carb., 8 g dietary fiber, 18 g protein.*

Eggplant Muffaletta

START TO FINISH **30 minutes** OVEN **350°F** MAKES **6 to 8 servings**

½ cup all-purpose flour

1 egg, lightly beaten

½ cup milk

¾ cup seasoned fine dry bread crumbs

½ of a small eggplant, cut lengthwise into ¼-inch slices

  Salt

  Freshly ground black pepper

¼ cup vegetable oil

1 boule (round Italian bread loaf) or focaccia, cut in half horizontally

1 recipe Olive Dressing

1 cup bottled roasted red sweet peppers, cut into strips

4 ounces smoked fresh mozzarella cheese or fresh mozzarella cheese, sliced

1 Preheat oven to 350°F. Place flour in a shallow dish. In another shallow dish stir together egg and milk. Place bread crumbs in a third shallow dish. Sprinkle eggplant slices with salt and black pepper. Dip eggplant slices in flour, turning to coat. Dip in the egg-and-milk mixture, turning to coat. Dip in the bread crumbs, turning to coat.

2 In a very large skillet heat oil over medium-high heat. Add eggplant slices; cook about 3 minutes or until eggplant is golden, turning once. Drain on paper towels.

3 Place bread loaf halves on a large baking sheet, cut sides up. Generously brush cut sides of the bread with Olive Dressing. Top bottom half of the bread with fried eggplant and roasted red pepper strips. Top with cheese slices. Bake for 10 to 12 minutes or until cheese is bubbly. Add top half of bread over cheese; cut sandwich into wedges to serve.

NUTRITION FACTS PER SERVING:
544 cal., 30 g total fat (6 g sat. fat), 50 mg chol., 1,166 mg sodium, 54 g carb., 5 g dietary fiber, 14 g protein.

Olive Dressing

In a large bowl combine ¾ cup pitted and finely chopped kalamata olives, ½ cup chopped pimento-stuffed green olives, ¼ cup olive oil, ¼ cup snipped fresh parsley, 2 tablespoons finely chopped red onion, 1 tablespoon finely chopped capers, 2 teaspoons snipped fresh oregano, and 2 cloves garlic, minced. Mix well. Makes 1½ cups.

Eggplant Parmesan Heroes

START TO FINISH **30 minutes** OVEN **400°F** MAKES **4 servings**

Nonstick cooking spray
1 **medium eggplant (about 1 pound)**
1 **cup seasoned croutons**
1/3 **cup shredded Parmesan cheese**
1 **cup marinara sauce**
4 **bratwurst buns, split**
Fresh basil leaves (optional)

1 Preheat oven to 400°F. Lightly coat a baking sheet with cooking spray. Peel eggplant, if desired; slice eggplant lengthwise into about ¼-inch slices.

2 Crush croutons; in a shallow dish combine croutons and ¼ cup of the cheese. Place marinara sauce in another shallow dish. Dip eggplant slices in marinara sauce, turning to coat. Dip into crouton mixture, turning and pressing lightly to coat. Place on prepared baking sheet. Lightly coat with cooking spray.

3 Bake about 15 minutes or until breading is browned and eggplant is tender. If desired, place buns, cut sides up, on a baking sheet. Remove eggplant from oven and bake or broil buns about 2 minutes or until toasted.

4 Meanwhile, in a small microwave-safe bowl microwave the remaining marinara sauce on 100 percent power (high) for 30 seconds.

5 Place eggplant slices on buns; top with the warmed sauce and the remaining cheese. If desired, garnish with fresh basil.

NUTRITION FACTS PER SERVING:
423 cal., 9 g total fat (3 g sat. fat), 7 mg chol., 1,011 mg sodium, 73 g carb., 9 g dietary fiber, 13 g protein.

194

Grilled Portobello Fajitas

START TO FINISH **30 minutes** MAKES **4 servings**

2 tablespoons olive oil

¼ teaspoon salt

¼ teaspoon ground black pepper

3 medium portobello mushrooms

1 red or yellow sweet pepper, seeded and quartered

8 6- to 7-inch flour tortillas (soft taco or fajita-size)

2 medium avocados, halved, seeded, and peeled

¼ cup light mayonnaise or salad dressing

1 teaspoon chili powder

Salt

Ground black pepper

Salsa verde (optional)

Fresh cilantro sprigs (optional)

Lime wedges (optional)

1 In a small bowl combine oil, ¼ teaspoon salt, and ¼ teaspoon black pepper. Brush mushrooms and sweet pepper with the oil mixture. Stack tortillas and wrap in foil.

2 For a charcoal grill, place mushrooms, pepper quarters, and foil packet on the rack of an uncovered grill directly over medium coals. Grill for 8 to 10 minutes or until mushrooms and pepper quarters are tender, turning once halfway through grilling. (For a gas grill, preheat grill. Reduce heat to medium. Place mushrooms, pepper quarters, and foil packet on grill rack over heat. Cover and grill as above.)

3 Slice mushrooms and sweet pepper into strips. In a medium bowl use a fork to mash one avocado; stir in mayonnaise and chili powder. Season to taste with additional salt and black pepper. Slice the remaining avocado. Layer mushrooms, sweet pepper, and sliced avocado on tortillas. Top with mayonnaise mixture. If desired, serve with salsa verde, cilantro, and lime wedges.

NUTRITION FACTS PER SERVING: *479 cal., 30 g total fat (3 g sat. fat), 5 mg chol., 401 mg sodium, 40 g carb., 7 g dietary fiber, 10 g protein.*

195

Rice and Bean Tostadas ☆

1 cup water

1 cup quick-cooking brown rice

½ cup chopped onion
(1 medium)

1 15-ounce can chili beans with
chili gravy, undrained

1 8.75-ounce can whole kernel
corn, drained

8 tostada shells

3 cups shredded lettuce

½ cup shredded cheddar cheese
(2 ounces)

1 cup quartered cherry
tomatoes

Salsa

1 Preheat oven to 350°F. In a large saucepan bring the water to boiling. Stir in rice and onion. Return to boiling; reduce heat. Simmer, covered, for 5 minutes. Remove from heat; stir. Cover and let stand for 5 minutes. Stir chili beans and corn into rice mixture; heat through.

2 Meanwhile, place tostada shells on a baking sheet. Bake about 5 minutes or until heated through.

3 To assemble, place two of the tostada shells on each dinner plate. Top tostadas with shredded lettuce and the rice-bean mixture. Sprinkle with cheese; top with tomatoes and salsa.

NUTRITION FACTS PER SERVING: 417 cal., 14 g total fat (4 g sat. fat), 15 mg chol., 816 mg sodium, 63 g carb., 12 g dietary fiber, 15 g protein.

Two-Bean Burritos

START TO FINISH **30 minutes** MAKES **6 servings**

- 6 10-inch spinach flour tortillas
- 1 15-ounce can black beans, rinsed and drained
- 1 8.75-ounce can whole kernel corn, rinsed and drained
- 1 medium mango, seeded, peeled, and chopped (1 cup)
- 1/3 cup chopped red sweet pepper
- 1/4 cup snipped fresh cilantro
- 2 tablespoons lime juice
- 1 fresh jalapeño chile pepper, seeded and finely chopped*
- 2 teaspoons olive oil or vegetable oil
- 1/2 cup chopped onion (1 medium)
- 1 16-ounce can vegetarian refried beans
- 1/2 cup salsa

1 Preheat oven to 350°F. Wrap the tortillas in foil. Bake about 10 minutes or until warm.

2 Meanwhile, in a medium bowl combine half of the black beans, the corn, mango, sweet pepper, cilantro, lime juice, and chile pepper. Set aside.

3 In a large skillet heat oil over medium heat. Add onion. Cook about 5 minutes or until tender. Stir in the remaining black beans, the refried beans, and salsa; heat through.

4 Divide the refried bean mixture among the warm tortillas; roll up. Serve burritos with corn mixture.

NUTRITION FACTS PER SERVING: *503 cal., 9 g total fat (2 g sat. fat), 0 mg chol., 1,253 mg sodium, 88 g carb., 14 g dietary fiber, 19 g protein.*

*tip

Because chile peppers contain volatile oils that can burn your skin and eyes, avoid direct contact with them as much as possible. When working with chile peppers, wear plastic or rubber gloves. If your bare hands do touch the peppers, wash your hands and nails well with soap and warm water.

Meatless

Bean Burritos with Lime Mayonnaise

START TO FINISH **20 minutes** MAKES **4 servings**

- 4 **9- to 10-inch flour tortillas**
- 1 **16-ounce can refried beans**
- ¼ **cup salsa**
- ¼ **cup mayonnaise or salad dressing**
- ½ **teaspoon finely shredded lime peel**
- 1 **tablespoon lime juice**
- 2 **cups shredded lettuce**
- ½ **cup cherry tomatoes, quartered**
- 2 **ounces Monterey Jack cheese with jalapeño chile peppers, shredded (½ cup)**

1 Place tortillas between paper towels. Microwave on 100 percent power (high) for 20 to 30 seconds or until heated through.

2 Meanwhile, in a small saucepan combine refried beans and salsa. Cook over medium heat until heated through, stirring frequently.

3 In a medium bowl combine mayonnaise, lime peel, and lime juice. Add lettuce and tomatoes; toss to coat.

4 Spoon about ½ cup of the bean mixture onto each tortilla just below the center. Top each with 2 tablespoons of the cheese and about ⅓ cup of the lettuce mixture. Fold bottom edge of each tortilla up and over the filling. Fold opposite sides in and over filling. Roll up from the bottom.

NUTRITION FACTS PER SERVING: *414 cal., 19 g total fat (6 g sat. fat), 29 mg chol., 992 mg sodium, 47 g carb., 9 g dietary fiber, 15 g protein.*

Greek Spinach Veggie Burgers

START TO FINISH **30 minutes** MAKES **4 servings**

¼   cup olive oil

1   clove garlic, minced

1   teaspoon dried oregano, crushed

1   teaspoon dried dill

¼   teaspoon ground black pepper

1   cup herb-seasoned stuffing mix

2   eggs, lightly beaten

1   10-ounce package frozen chopped spinach, thawed and well drained

½   cup crumbled feta cheese (2 ounces)

4   whole wheat hamburger buns, split and toasted

   Assorted toppers, such as crumbled feta cheese, plain low-fat yogurt, sliced bottled roasted red sweet peppers, and/or sliced red onion (optional)

1 In a medium bowl combine oil, garlic, oregano, dill, and black pepper. Add stuffing mix, stirring to coat well. Stir in eggs, spinach, and the ½ cup crumbled feta. Using clean hands, shape into four ½-inch patties.

2 Heat a griddle or large nonstick skillet over medium heat. Add patties. Cook for 6 to 8 minutes or until browned and heated through, turning once. Serve in buns with assorted toppers.

NUTRITION FACTS PER SERVING: *367 cal., 18 g total fat (4 g sat. fat), 13 mg chol., 732 mg sodium, 36 g carb., 4 g dietary fiber, 13 g protein.*

Lemony Garbanzo Bean Sandwiches 🥕

START TO FINISH **20 minutes** MAKES **4 sandwiches**

1 **15-ounce can no-salt-added garbanzo beans (chickpeas), rinsed and drained***

3 **tablespoons snipped fresh parsley**

1 **teaspoon finely shredded lemon peel**

2 **tablespoons lemon juice**

1 **tablespoon finely chopped red onion**

1 **tablespoon olive oil**

¹⁄₈ **teaspoon ground black pepper**

¹⁄₂ **of a large cucumber, peeled, quartered, and sliced (about 1 cup)**

¹⁄₂ **cup watercress or arugula**

¹⁄₃ **cup bottled roasted red sweet pepper strips**

1 **1-pound loaf focaccia bread, quartered**

1 In a medium bowl combine garbanzo beans, parsley, lemon peel, lemon juice, red onion, oil, and black pepper. Using a potato masher or fork, mash the garbanzo bean mixture until the beans are in coarse chunks. Add cucumber, watercress, and sweet pepper strips. Toss to combine.

2 Split each focaccia portion. Spoon garbanzo bean mixture onto bottom portions; add tops.

NUTRITION FACTS PER SANDWICH: *401 cal., 8 g total fat (0 g sat. fat), 10 mg chol., 472 mg sodium, 71 g carb., 5 g dietary fiber, 16 g protein.*

*tip
If desired, substitute 1³⁄₄ cups cooked dried garbanzo beans for the canned beans.

Grilled Artichoke Flatbreads

START TO FINISH 20 minutes   MAKES 4 servings

4   whole wheat flatbreads
    (naan)

3   tablespoons olive oil

6   cups fresh spinach leaves

6   ounces garlic-and-herb-flavor
    goat cheese, crumbled

2   6-ounce jars marinated
    artichoke hearts, drained and
    cut up

½   cup chopped tomato

½   teaspoon salt

¼   teaspoon ground black pepper

    Pizza seasoning and/
    or snipped fresh herbs
    (optional)

1 Brush both sides of each flatbread lightly with some of the oil. For a charcoal grill, grill the flatbreads on the rack of an uncovered grill directly over medium coals about 2 minutes or until golden. (For a gas grill, preheat grill. Reduce heat to medium. Add flatbreads to grill rack. Cover and grill as above.) Remove from heat.

2 Top the grilled side of each flatbread with spinach, cheese, artichoke hearts, and tomato. Sprinkle with salt and pepper. Grill about 2 minutes more or until bottoms are browned and toppings are heated through. If desired, sprinkle with pizza seasoning and/or fresh herbs.

NUTRITION FACTS PER SERVING:
720 cal., 43 g total fat (15 g sat. fat), 44 mg chol., 1,559 mg sodium, 65 g carb., 7 g dietary fiber, 21 g protein.

Focaccia Topped with Vegetables and Goat Cheese ⏱

START TO FINISH 30 minutes   MAKES 4 servings

$\frac{1}{3}$ cup olive oil

1 medium yellow summer squash, quartered lengthwise and sliced (about 1$\frac{1}{4}$ cups)

$\frac{1}{2}$ cup chopped carrot (1 medium)

$\frac{1}{2}$ cup chopped green sweet pepper (1 small)

$\frac{1}{2}$ cup chopped red sweet pepper (1 small)

$\frac{1}{2}$ cup broccoli florets

$\frac{1}{2}$ of a small red onion, sliced

4 cloves garlic, minced

$\frac{2}{3}$ cup chopped roma tomatoes (2 medium)

12 pimiento-stuffed green olives, halved

1 tablespoon olive liquid from jar

4 6- to 7$\frac{1}{2}$-inch individual focaccia

2 cups crumbled goat cheese (chèvre) (8 ounces)

Sea salt

Freshly ground black pepper

1 Preheat broiler. In a 12-inch skillet heat 2 tablespoons of the oil over medium-high heat. Add squash, carrot, sweet peppers, broccoli, red onion, and garlic. Cook and stir for 3 minutes. Add tomatoes, olives, and olive liquid. Cook 2 minutes more or until vegetables are tender, stirring occasionally.

2 Lightly brush both sides of each focaccia with some of the remaining oil. Place on an extra-large baking sheet.* Broil about 4 inches from the heat for 2 to 4 minutes or until lightly browned, turning once halfway through broiling. Remove from broiler.

3 Using a slotted spoon, divide vegetable mixture among focaccia; sprinkle with cheese. Broil about 2 minutes more or until cheese is softened. Drizzle with any remaining oil and sprinkle with salt and black pepper.

NUTRITION FACTS PER SERVING:
611 cal., 40 g total fat (15 g sat. fat), 45 mg chol., 894 mg sodium, 45 g carb., 5 g dietary fiber, 20 g protein.

*tip
If necessary, divide focaccia between two baking sheets and broil in batches.

Tofu and Vegetable Stackups

START TO FINISH 30 minutes MAKES 4 servings

- 2 ears of corn, husks and silks removed
- 2 12- to 16-ounce packages firm or extra-firm tofu (fresh bean curd), drained
- 1/3 cup yellow cornmeal
- 2 teaspoons chili powder
- 1/2 teaspoon salt
- 3 to 4 tablespoons olive oil
- 1 medium red sweet pepper, seeded and sliced
- 2 medium green tomatoes, sliced
- Lime wedges
- Fresh cilantro leaves (optional)

1 In a covered large saucepan cook corn in a large amount of boiling salted water for 7 minutes; drain.

2 Meanwhile, slice each block of tofu horizontally into four slices. In a shallow dish combine cornmeal, chili powder, and salt; dip tofu slices into mixture, turning to coat.

3 In a 12-inch skillet heat 1 tablespoon of the oil over medium-high heat. Add tofu, in batches; cook for 4 to 6 minutes or until crisp and golden, turning once (add more of the oil as needed). Remove tofu from skillet. Add the remaining oil to the same skillet; cook sweet pepper and green tomatoes about 3 minutes or until tomatoes are heated through and lightly browned and peppers are crisp-tender, turning once.

4 On cutting board, place an ear of corn pointed end down. While holding corn firmly at stem end to keep it in place, use a sharp knife to cut corn from cob; rotate cob as needed to cut corn from all sides. Repeat with the remaining ear of corn. Place 1 slice of the tofu on each of four dinner plates. Top tofu with half of the corn and half of the pepper-tomato mixture. Repeat layers. Serve with lime wedges and, if desired, fresh cilantro.

NUTRITION FACTS PER SERVING:
306 cal., 16 g total fat (2 g sat. fat), 0 mg chol., 382 mg sodium, 28 g carb., 4 g dietary fiber, 15 g protein.

203

Meatless

Kale–Goat Cheese Frittata ⏱ 🥕

START TO FINISH **30 minutes**   MAKES **6 servings**

2   **teaspoons olive oil**

2   **cups coarsely chopped fresh kale or spinach (about 4 ounces)**

1   **medium onion, halved and thinly sliced**

6   **eggs**

4   **egg whites**

¼   **teaspoon salt**

⅛   **teaspoon ground black pepper**

¼   **cup oil-pack dried tomatoes, drained and thinly sliced**

1   **ounce soft goat cheese (chèvre), crumbled (¼ cup)**

1 Preheat broiler. In a large ovenproof nonstick skillet heat oil over medium heat. Add kale and onion. Cook and stir about 10 minutes or until onion is tender.

2 Meanwhile, in a medium bowl whisk together eggs, egg whites, salt, and pepper. Pour egg mixture over kale mixture in skillet. Cook over medium-low heat. As egg mixture sets, run a spatula around the edge of the skillet, lifting egg mixture so the uncooked portion flows underneath. Continue cooking and lifting edge until egg mixture is almost set but still glossy and moist.

3 Sprinkle egg mixture with dried tomatoes and goat cheese. Place skillet under the broiler, 4 to 5 inches from the heat. Broil for 1 to 2 minutes or until eggs are set. Cut into wedges to serve.

NUTRITION FACTS PER SERVING:
145 cal., 9 g total fat (3 g sat. fat), 216 mg chol., 242 mg sodium, 6 g carb., 1 g dietary fiber, 11 g protein.

tip

Kale is a super green packed with whopping amounts of health-boosting antioxidants and vitamins. Its leaves can be curly or flat, but whichever variety you choose, pick small leaves for the mildest flavor. Larger leaves provide a stronger, slightly bitter taste—which many people love. Store it in the refrigerator for no more than three days, otherwise the leaves will be unpleasantly strong. Use kale in egg dishes, soups, and stir-fries.

Two-Potato Frittata

START TO FINISH **30 minutes** OVEN **450°F/400°F** MAKES **4 servings**

2 small sweet potatoes, scrubbed and thinly sliced or chopped

1 medium Yukon gold potato, chopped

1 small red onion, cut into thin wedges or chopped

2 tablespoons olive oil

Salt

8 eggs

½ of a 5.2-ounce package semisoft cheese with garlic and roasted pepper

Fresh oregano (optional)

1 Preheat oven to 450°F. In a 13×9×2-inch rectangular baking pan combine potatoes and red onion. Toss with oil and sprinkle with salt. Roast, uncovered, for 15 minutes.

2 Meanwhile, in a medium bowl whisk together eggs, cheese, and a pinch salt until combined. Reduce oven temperature to 400°F. Pour egg mixture over vegetables; return to oven. Bake for 7 to 9 minutes more or until eggs are set.

3 Invert frittata onto a large cutting board; cut into wedges. Flip wedges topsides up and place on serving plates. Top with oregano, if desired.

NUTRITION FACTS PER SERVING: *344 cal., 25 g total fat (10 g sat. fat), 424 mg chol., 566 mg sodium, 17 g carb., 2 g dietary fiber, 15 g protein.*

205

tip

Another time, use leftover cooked vegetables instead of potatoes and onion. Arrange vegetables on the pan and place in the oven to reheat for 5 minutes. Top with the egg mixture and bake as directed.

Meatless

Veggie Frittata

START TO FINISH **30 minutes** MAKES **4 servings**

⅓ cup dried orzo pasta (rosamarina)

2 tablespoons olive oil

2 medium red, yellow, and/or orange sweet peppers, seeded and chopped

8 eggs

¼ cup milk

½ cup chopped pitted ripe olives

¼ cup snipped fresh basil

¼ teaspoon salt

¼ teaspoon ground black pepper

2 tablespoons shredded Parmesan cheese

1 Preheat broiler. In a large saucepan cook pasta according to package directions; drain. Meanwhile, in a large ovenproof skillet heat oil over medium-high heat. Add sweet peppers; cook until tender. Stir in cooked pasta.

2 In a large bowl beat together eggs and milk. Stir in olives, basil, salt, and black pepper. Pour over vegetable mixture in skillet; cook over medium heat. As mixture sets, run a spatula around the skillet edge, lifting egg mixture so uncooked portion flows underneath. Continue cooking and lifting edges until egg mixture is almost set. Reduce heat as necessary to prevent overcooking.

3 Place skillet under the broiler, 4 to 5 inches from heat. Broil about 3 minutes or until top is set. Sprinkle with cheese. Cover and let stand for 5 minutes. Cut into wedges to serve.

NUTRITION FACTS PER SERVING: *319 cal., 20 g total fat (5 g sat. fat), 426 mg chol., 525 mg sodium, 17 g carb., 3 g dietary fiber, 17 g protein.*

206

Pasta

A simple ingredient deliciously transforms into something extraordinary in these pasta dishes ranging from simply tossed to super-sauced.

6

Stack-and-Steam Halibut with Angel Hair Pasta

START TO FINISH 30 minutes MAKES 4 servings

- 4   **4- to 5-ounce fresh or frozen halibut fillets**
- 4   **coiled nests dried angel hair pasta (about 4 ounces)**
- 5   **cloves garlic**
- 1   **medium lemon**
- 2   **medium tomatoes, sliced**
- 2   **tablespoons snipped fresh Italian (flat-leaf) parsley (optional)**
     Salt
     Ground black pepper
- 1   **5- to 6-ounce package fresh baby spinach**
- ¼   **cup olive oil**
- 2   **tablespoons balsamic vinegar**

208

1 Thaw fish, if frozen. Fill a 12-inch skillet or a Dutch oven with a steamer basket insert half full with lightly salted water (steamer basket insert should not touch the water).* Bring water to boiling. Add pasta to boiling water. Cook, covered, for 4 minutes. Using a slotted spoon, transfer pasta to a large bowl; cover and keep warm.

2 Meanwhile, slice 4 cloves of the garlic; mince the remaining one clove of garlic. Set aside. Cut lemon in half; squeeze juice from one lemon half. Slice the remaining lemon half; set aside.

3 Rinse fish; pat dry with paper towels. In the steamer basket arrange fish, lemon slices, and tomatoes in single layers. Top with garlic slices; sprinkle with parsley (if using), salt, and pepper. Steam, covered, for 3 to 5 minutes or until fish flakes easily when tested with a fork. Top with spinach. Cook, covered, about 30 seconds more or just until spinach is wilted.

4 Divide pasta, fish, and spinach among dinner plates. Top fish with lemon and tomato slices.

5 For vinaigrette, in a screw-top jar combine minced garlic, lemon juice, oil, and vinegar. Cover and shake well. Drizzle each serving with vinaigrette.

NUTRITION FACTS PER SERVING: *388 cal., 17 g total fat (2 g sat. fat), 36 mg chol., 243 mg sodium, 31 g carb., 4 g dietary fiber, 29 g protein.*

*tip
If you do not have a pan with a steamer insert that will leave room to cook the pasta, cook the pasta in a separate pot.

Coconut-Chicken Pasta

START TO FINISH **25 minutes**   MAKES **4 servings**

6   ounces dried angel hair pasta

3   cups cooked chicken cut
    into strips

1   14-ounce can unsweetened
    coconut milk

⅓   cup thinly sliced green onions

⅓   cup shredded carrot (1 small)

2   teaspoons Thai seasoning

½   cup chopped dry-roasted
    peanuts

    Snipped fresh Italian
    (flat-leaf) parsley (optional)

1 In a Dutch oven cook pasta according to package directions; drain. Return pasta to hot Dutch oven.

2 Meanwhile, in a large skillet combine chicken, coconut milk, green onions, carrot, and Thai seasoning. Cook and stir over medium heat until heated through.

3 Pour hot chicken mixture over cooked pasta; toss gently to coat. Sprinkle each serving with peanuts and, if desired, parsley.

NUTRITION FACTS PER SERVING:
653 cal., 36 g total fat (20 g sat. fat), 93 mg chol., 287 mg sodium, 41 g carb., 3 g dietary fiber, 42 g protein.

Lime-Dressed Chicken and Pasta

START TO FINISH **25 minutes**   MAKES **4 servings**

6   **ounces dried angel hair pasta**

3   **ears of corn, husks and silks removed**

4   **skinless, boneless chicken breast halves (about 1 pound total)**

$1\frac{1}{2}$ **teaspoons chili powder**

$\frac{1}{4}$ **teaspoon salt**

$\frac{1}{4}$ **teaspoon freshly ground black pepper**

$\frac{1}{4}$ **cup olive oil or vegetable oil**

3   **tablespoons lime juice or lemon juice**

2   **medium tomatoes, sliced**

Salt

Freshly ground black pepper

Snipped fresh parsley (optional)

Lime halves (optional)

1 Cook pasta according to package directions, adding corn to the water with pasta; drain in a colander. Rinse pasta and corn under cold running water until cool; drain well. On cutting board, place an ear of corn pointed end down. While holding corn firmly at stem end to keep it in place, use a sharp knife to cut corn from cobs; rotate cob as needed to cut corn from all sides. Repeat with the remaining ears of corn.

2 Meanwhile, sprinkle chicken with 1 teaspoon of the chili powder, the $\frac{1}{4}$ teaspoon salt, and $\frac{1}{4}$ teaspoon pepper. In a large skillet heat 1 tablespoon of the oil over medium heat. Add chicken; cook for 8 to 10 minutes or until chicken is no longer pink (170°F), turning once.

3 For dressing, in a screw-top jar combine the remaining $\frac{1}{2}$ teaspoon chili powder, the remaining 3 tablespoons oil, and lime juice. Cover and shake well.

4 Divide cooked pasta, corn, and tomatoes among dinner plates. Arrange chicken on top; drizzle with dressing. Lightly sprinkle with additional salt and pepper. If desired, garnish with parsley and serve with lime halves.

NUTRITION FACTS PER SERVING:
515 cal., 17 g total fat (3 g sat. fat), 66 mg chol., 226 mg sodium, 58 g carb., 5 g dietary fiber, 36 g protein.

⏱ Sautéed Chicken with Pasta

START TO FINISH **30 minutes**   MAKES **4 servings**

8   ounces dried angel hair pasta

½   teaspoon salt

½   teaspoon dried thyme, crushed

¼   teaspoon ground black pepper

2   skinless, boneless chicken breast halves (about 12 ounces total), halved horizontally

2   tablespoons olive oil

3   cups sliced fresh mushrooms (8 ounces)

1   small red onion, halved and sliced

3   cloves garlic, minced

1½   cups reduced-sodium chicken broth

1   tablespoon all-purpose flour

1   teaspoon Dijon-style mustard

4   roma tomatoes, cut into thin wedges

¼   cup snipped fresh Italian (flat-leaf) parsley

1 Cook pasta according to package directions; drain. Return pasta to hot pan; cover and keep warm.

2 Meanwhile, in a small bowl combine ¼ teaspoon of the salt, the thyme, and pepper. Sprinkle thyme mixture on both sides of chicken. In a 12-inch skillet heat 1 tablespoon of the oil over medium-high heat. Add chicken; reduce heat to medium. Cook about 6 minutes or until chicken is no longer pink, turning once. Remove from skillet; cover and keep warm.

3 Add the remaining 1 tablespoon oil to skillet. Add mushrooms, red onion, and garlic. Cook about 5 minutes or until onion is tender, stirring occasionally. In a medium bowl whisk together broth, flour, mustard, and the remaining ¼ teaspoon salt. Add to mushroom mixture in skillet, Cook and stir until slightly thickened and bubbly. Stir in tomatoes and parsley; heat through.

4 Divide cooked pasta among dinner plates. Top with chicken and mushroom mixture.

211

NUTRITION FACTS PER SERVING:
426 cal., 9 g total fat (2 g sat. fat), 49 mg chol., 604 mg sodium, 53 g carb., 4 g dietary fiber, 31 g protein.

Shrimp and Mushroom Pasta ⏱ 🥕

START TO FINISH **30 minutes**   MAKES **4 servings**

9   **ounces fresh or frozen peeled and deveined medium shrimp***

8   **ounces dried whole grain angel hair pasta or spaghetti**

1   **tablespoon olive oil**

3   **cups chopped fresh stemmed shiitake mushrooms (8 ounces)**

3   **cups sliced fresh cremini or button mushrooms (8 ounces)**

2   **cloves garlic, minced**

1   **14.5-ounce can no-salt-added diced tomatoes, undrained**

2   **teaspoons snipped fresh oregano**

¼   **teaspoon salt**

¼   **teaspoon freshly ground black pepper**

   Fresh oregano sprigs or snipped fresh parsley

1 Thaw shrimp, if frozen. Cook pasta according to package directions; drain. Return pasta to hot pan; cover and keep warm.

2 Meanwhile, rinse shrimp; pat dry with paper towels. Set aside. In a 12-inch nonstick skillet heat oil over medium-high heat. Add mushrooms and garlic; cook for 4 minutes.

3 Stir in tomatoes, snipped oregano, salt, and pepper. Bring to boiling; reduce heat. Simmer, uncovered, for 5 to 10 minutes or until mixture is thickened. Stir in shrimp. Simmer, covered, for 2 to 3 minutes more or until shrimp are opaque.

4 Serve shrimp mixture over cooked pasta. Garnish with oregano sprigs.

NUTRITION FACTS PER SERVING:
371 cal., 6 g total fat (1 g sat. fat), 129 mg chol., 343 mg sodium, 49 g carb., 7 g dietary fiber, 31 g protein.

212

*tip

For a more dramatic presentation, use shrimp with the tails left on. Start with 12 ounces shrimp; peel and devein shrimp, leaving tails intact.

Vermicelli with Sausage and Spinach

START TO FINISH **25 minutes** MAKES **4 to 6 servings**

2 teaspoons olive oil

1 pound cooked smoked sausage links, halved lengthwise and cut into $\frac{1}{2}$-inch pieces

$\frac{3}{4}$ cup chopped onion

2 large cloves garlic, minced

2 14-ounce cans reduced-sodium chicken broth

$\frac{1}{4}$ cup water

8 ounces dried vermicelli or angel hair pasta, broken in half

1 9-ounce package fresh baby spinach

$\frac{1}{4}$ teaspoon ground black pepper

$\frac{1}{3}$ cup whipping cream

1 In a Dutch oven heat oil over medium heat. Add sausage, onion, and garlic. Cook until sausage is light brown and onion is tender, stirring occasionally.

2 Add broth and the water; bring to boiling. Stir in pasta; cook for 3 minutes, stirring frequently. Stir in spinach and pepper; cook about 1 minute more or just until spinach is wilted. Stir in cream.

NUTRITION FACTS PER SERVING:
782 cal., 47 g total fat (18 g sat. fat), 104 mg chol., 2,556 mg sodium, 52 g carb., 4 g dietary fiber, 38 g protein.

213

Summer Pasta Your Way ⏱ 🥕

START TO FINISH 25 minutes MAKES 4 servings

- **10** ounces dried spinach or whole grain spaghetti
- **1** tablespoon olive oil
- **2** tablespoons sliced green onion (1)
- **1½** cups assorted summer vegetables, such as halved sugar snap peas, chopped eggplant, quartered and sliced zucchini or yellow summer squash, sliced mushrooms, chopped sweet pepper, cooked lima beans, sliced asparagus, and/or sliced carrot
- **¼** cup snipped oil-pack dried tomato
- **2** cups assorted cherry tomatoes, halved, or seeded and chopped tomatoes
- **½** cup dry white wine, chicken broth, or vegetable broth
- **¼** cup pitted kalamata olives, sliced (optional)
- Salt
- Ground black pepper
- **½** cup crumbled garlic-and-herb or plain feta cheese, crumbled goat cheese (chèvre), or chopped smoked Gouda cheese (2 ounces) or **¼** cup shredded Parmigiano-Reggiano cheese (1 ounce)
- **2** tablespoons snipped fresh basil

1 In a Dutch oven cook spaghetti according to package directions; drain. Return spaghetti to hot Dutch oven; cover and keep warm.

2 Meanwhile, in a large skillet heat oil over medium heat. Add green onion. Cook about 30 seconds. Stir in assorted vegetables and dried tomato. Cook, covered, for 5 minutes, stirring once. Stir in fresh tomatoes, wine, and, if desired, olives; cook for 30 seconds more.

3 Add vegetable mixture to cooked spaghetti; toss gently to combine. Season to taste with salt and pepper. Sprinkle each serving with cheese and basil.

NUTRITION FACTS PER SERVING:
399 cal., 9 g total fat (3 g sat. fat), 13 mg chol., 356 mg sodium, 62 g carb., 10 g dietary fiber, 14 g protein.

Take advantage of the flexibility of this summer-fresh pasta to create several dishes. Use the pasta of your choice, vary the vegetables depending on what's in season, and use your favorite cheese. You can vary the seasoning as well (add 1 tablespoon thyme, sage, or rosemary and a clove or two of garlic along with the onion instead of basil or replace the basil at the end with Italian parsley or cilantro).

214

Pasta Puttanesca

START TO FINISH **30 minutes** MAKES **4 servings**

- 6 **ounces dried thin spaghetti**
- 2 **tablespoons olive oil**
- 1 **clove garlic, thinly sliced**
- 2 **cups peeled and chopped roma tomatoes (6 medium)**
- ½ **cup coarsely chopped, pitted kalamata or ripe olives**
- 4 **to 5 anchovy fillets, chopped**
- 1 **teaspoon drained capers, chopped**
- ½ **teaspoon ground black pepper**
- ¼ **to ½ teaspoon crushed red pepper**
- ¼ **cup snipped fresh Italian (flat-leaf) parsley**

1 Cook spaghetti according to package directions; drain. Return spaghetti to hot pan; cover and keep warm.

2 Meanwhile, for sauce, in a large skillet heat oil over medium heat. Add garlic. Cook and stir for 30 seconds. Stir in tomatoes, olives, anchovies, capers, black pepper, and crushed red pepper.

3 Bring just to boiling; reduce heat. Simmer, uncovered, for 5 to 7 minutes or until slightly thickened, stirring occasionally.

4 Serve sauce over cooked spaghetti. Sprinkle with parsley.

NUTRITION FACTS PER SERVING:
265 cal., 10 g total fat (1 g sat. fat), 3 mg chol., 323 mg sodium, 37 g carb., 3 g dietary fiber, 8 g protein.

Winter Garden Pasta

START TO FINISH **30 minutes** MAKES **6 servings**

8 ounces dried whole grain spaghetti

3 cups broccoli florets

1 15-ounce can cannellini beans (white kidney beans), rinsed and drained

1 14.5-ounce can no-salt-added diced tomatoes, drained

2 tablespoons no-salt-added tomato paste

2 cloves garlic, minced

¼ teaspoon salt

¼ teaspoon ground black pepper

2 tablespoons snipped fresh Italian (flat-leaf) parsley

¼ cup grated Parmesan cheese

1 In a Dutch oven cook spaghetti according to package directions, adding broccoli for the last 3 minutes of cooking; drain. Return spaghetti mixture to hot Dutch oven.

2 Stir beans, tomatoes, tomato paste, garlic, salt, and pepper into spaghetti mixture; heat through. Stir in parsley. Sprinkle each serving with cheese.

NUTRITION FACTS PER SERVING: *221 cal., 2 g total fat (1 g sat. fat), 2 mg chol., 313 mg sodium, 46 g carb., 9 g dietary fiber, 13 g protein.*

Four-Cheese Linguine with Prosciutto

START TO FINISH 30 minutes MAKES 8 servings

1¼   **pounds dried linguine**

1   **cup shredded Emmentaler or Swiss cheese (4 ounces)**

1   **cup shredded fontina cheese (4 ounces)**

1   **cup crumbled Gorgonzola or other blue cheese (4 ounces)**

¾   **cup finely shredded Parmesan cheese (3 ounces)**

2   **tablespoons all-purpose flour**

2   **cups whipping cream**

8   **ounces thinly sliced prosciutto, coarsely chopped**

Milk (optional)

Freshly ground black pepper

1 In a Dutch oven cook linguine according to package directions; drain. Return linguine to hot Dutch oven.

2 Meanwhile, for sauce, in a large saucepan combine Emmentaler cheese, fontina cheese, Gorgonzola cheese, and Parmesan cheese. Sprinkle with flour; toss gently to coat. Stir in cream and prosciutto. Cook and stir over medium heat just until mixture comes to boiling.

3 Pour sauce over cooked linguine; stir gently to coat. If desired, thin with a little milk. Sprinkle each serving with pepper.

NUTRITION FACTS PER SERVING: *768 cal., 46 g total fat (24 g sat. fat), 133 mg chol., 1,023 mg sodium, 58 g carb., 2 g dietary fiber, 32 g protein.*

217

Chicken and Sweet Pepper Linguine Alfredo

START TO FINISH 25 minutes   MAKES 4 servings

1   9-ounce package refrigerated whole wheat linguine
    Nonstick cooking spray
1   cup red sweet pepper strips (1 medium)
2   medium zucchini and/or yellow summer squash, halved lengthwise and sliced (about 2$\frac{1}{2}$ cups)
8   ounces packaged chicken stir-fry strips*
1   10-ounce container refrigerated light Alfredo pasta sauce
$\frac{1}{3}$ cup finely shredded Parmesan, Romano, or Asiago cheese (optional)
2   teaspoons snipped fresh thyme
$\frac{1}{8}$ teaspoon freshly ground black pepper

1 Using kitchen scissors, cut linguine in half. In a Dutch oven cook linguine according to package directions; drain. Return linguine to hot Dutch oven; cover and keep warm.

2 Meanwhile, coat a large skillet with cooking spray; heat skillet over medium-high heat. Add sweet pepper; cook and stir for 2 minutes. Add squash; cook and stir for 2 to 3 minutes more or until vegetables are crisp-tender. Remove from skillet.

3 Add chicken to skillet. Cook and stir for 3 to 4 minutes or until chicken is no longer pink. Return vegetables to skillet. Stir in pasta sauce; heat through.

4 Add chicken mixture, cheese, if desired, and thyme to cooked linguine; toss gently to combine. Sprinkle each serving with black pepper.

NUTRITION FACTS PER SERVING:
371 cal., 11 g total fat (5 g sat. fat), 66 mg chol., 461 mg sodium, 43 g carb., 7 g dietary fiber, 26 g protein.

*tip
If you prefer, cut skinless, boneless chicken breast halves into bite-size strips.

Shrimp and Pasta Diavolo

START TO FINISH **25 minutes**   MAKES **4 servings**

9   ounces fresh or frozen peeled and deveined medium shrimp*

1   9-ounce package refrigerated linguine

2   tablespoons olive oil

1   medium onion, cut into thin wedges

3   cloves garlic, minced

¼   teaspoon crushed red pepper

1   14.5-ounce can diced tomatoes, undrained

2   cups fresh baby spinach

½   cup torn fresh basil

½   cup finely shredded Parmesan cheese (2 ounces)

     Fresh basil leaves

1 Thaw shrimp, if frozen. In a Dutch oven cook linguine according to package directions; drain. Return linguine to hot Dutch oven; cover and keep warm.

2 Meanwhile, rinse shrimp; pat dry with paper towels. Set aside. In a large skillet heat oil over medium heat. Add onion, garlic, and crushed red pepper. Cook until onion is tender, stirring occasionally.

3 Stir in tomatoes. Bring to boiling; reduce heat. Simmer, uncovered, for 3 minutes. Stir in shrimp. Simmer, covered, for 2 to 3 minutes or until shrimp are opaque.

4 Add shrimp mixture, spinach, and torn basil to cooked pasta; toss gently to combine. Sprinkle each serving with cheese and garnish with basil leaves.

NUTRITION FACTS PER SERVING:
412 cal., 13 g total fat (4 g sat. fat), 204 mg chol., 528 mg sodium, 44 g carb., 4 g dietary fiber, 30 g protein.

219

*tip

For a more dramatic presentation, use shrimp with the tails left on. Start with 12 ounces shrimp; peel and devein shrimp, leaving tails intact.

Linguine with Shrimp and Pine Nuts ⏱

START TO FINISH **30 minutes** MAKES **4 servings**

9	ounces fresh or frozen peeled and deveined medium shrimp*
8	ounces dried linguine
¾	cup chicken broth
⅓	cup dry sherry or chicken broth
2	tablespoons lemon juice
¼	teaspoon salt
¼	teaspoon crushed red pepper
1	tablespoon olive oil
¼	cup pine nuts
2	cloves garlic, minced
1½	cups sliced assorted fresh mushrooms, such as button, cremini, and/or stemmed shiitake (4 ounces)
1	tablespoon butter
4	cups fresh baby spinach
¼	cup freshly grated Asiago cheese (1 ounce)
	Pine nuts, toasted (optional)

1 Thaw shrimp, if frozen. Cook linguine according to package directions; drain. Return linguine to hot pan; cover and keep warm.

2 Meanwhile, in a small bowl combine broth, sherry, lemon juice, salt, and crushed red pepper; set aside.

3 Rinse shrimp; pat dry with paper towels. In a large skillet heat oil over medium heat. Add shrimp, ¼ cup pine nuts, and garlic. Cook for 2 to 3 minutes or until shrimp are opaque, stirring frequently. Remove shrimp mixture from skillet.

4 Add mushrooms and butter to skillet. Cook about 3 minutes or until mushrooms are nearly tender, stirring occasionally. Carefully add broth mixture. Bring to boiling; reduce heat. Boil gently, uncovered, for 5 minutes. Return shrimp mixture to skillet; heat through.

5 Divide cooked linguine among shallow bowls. Top with shrimp mixture, spinach, cheese, and, if desired, additional pine nuts.

NUTRITION FACTS PER SERVING: *492 cal., 17 g total fat (5 g sat. fat), 145 mg chol., 577 mg sodium, 50 g carb., 2 g dietary fiber, 31 g protein.*

220

*tip
For a more dramatic presentation, use shrimp with the tails left on. Start with 12 ounces shrimp; peel and devein shrimp, leaving tails intact.

⏱ Salmon and Mozzarella Fettuccine

START TO FINISH **30 minutes** MAKES **6 to 8 servings**

1¼ **pounds fresh or frozen skinless salmon fillets**

12 **to 16 ounces dried fettuccine**
   Salt

3 **tablespoons olive oil**

4 **cloves garlic, minced**

3 **cups chopped roma tomatoes (6 medium)**

1 **cup sliced green onions (8)**

⅔ **cup sliced pitted ripe olives or kalamata olives**

⅓ **cup snipped fresh basil**

¼ **cup dry white wine**

½ **teaspoon coarse ground black pepper**

8 **ounces fresh mozzarella cheese, coarsely chopped**
   Snipped fresh basil (optional)

1 Thaw fish, if frozen. In a Dutch oven cook fettuccine according to package directions; drain. Return fettuccine to hot Dutch oven; cover and keep warm.

2 Meanwhile, rinse fish; pat dry with paper towels. Cut fish into 1-inch pieces. Lightly sprinkle fish with salt.

3 In a skillet heat 1 tablespoon of the oil over medium-high heat. Add garlic; cook and stir for 15 seconds. Add fish. Cook for 4 to 6 minutes or until fish flakes easily when tested with a fork, turning pieces occasionally. Stir in tomatoes, green onions, olives, ⅓ cup basil, wine, and pepper; heat through.

4 Add fish mixture, the remaining 2 tablespoons oil, and cheese to cooked pasta; toss gently to combine. If desired, sprinkle each serving with additional basil.

NUTRITION FACTS PER SERVING:
624 cal., 30 g total fat (10 g sat. fat), 79 mg chol., 408 mg sodium, 49 g carb., 4 g dietary fiber, 35 g protein.

221

Chicken and Fettuccine with Artichokes

START TO FINISH **30 minutes** MAKES **4 servings**

8 ounces dried fettuccine or linguine

2 tablespoons olive oil

12 ounces skinless, boneless chicken breast halves

$\frac{1}{4}$ cup butter

3 cloves garlic, minced

1 9-ounce package frozen artichoke hearts, thawed and halved lengthwise

$\frac{3}{4}$ cup dry white wine

$\frac{1}{4}$ cup coarsely chopped pistachio nuts

$\frac{1}{4}$ teaspoon salt

2 tablespoons snipped fresh Italian (flat-leaf) parsley

Chopped pistachio nuts (optional)

Cracked black pepper

1 Cook fettuccine according to package directions; drain. Return fettuccine to hot pan; cover and keep warm.

2 Meanwhile, in a 12-inch skillet heat oil over medium heat. Add chicken. Cook for 8 to 12 minutes or until chicken is no longer pink (170°F), turning once. Remove chicken from skillet; discard pan drippings.

3 In the same skillet heat butter over medium heat. Add garlic; cook and stir for 15 seconds. Stir in artichokes, wine, $\frac{1}{4}$ cup pistachio nuts, and salt. Bring to boiling; reduce heat. Simmer, uncovered, for 5 minutes. Return chicken to skillet; cook for 1 to 2 minutes or until heated through. Transfer chicken to a cutting board; cut diagonally into 1-inch slices.

4 Arrange cooked fettuccine on a large serving platter or dinner plates. Arrange chicken on top of fettuccine. Spoon artichoke mixture over chicken and fettuccine. Sprinkle with parsley, and if desired, additional pistachio nuts. Sprinkle with pepper.

NUTRITION FACTS PER SERVING: *583 cal., 25 g total fat (8 g sat. fat), 82 mg chol., 325 mg sodium, 51 g carb., 6 g dietary fiber, 31 g protein.*

222

Fettuccine with Chicken and Cherry Tomatoes

START TO FINISH **20 minutes**   MAKES **4 servings**

1   6- to 9-ounce package refrigerated or frozen cooked Italian or grilled chicken breast strips
1   9-ounce package refrigerated fettuccine
½   cup shredded Parmesan cheese (2 ounces)
2   tablespoons olive oil
2   cups cherry tomatoes, halved
½   cup pitted ripe olives, halved
    Salt
    Freshly ground black pepper

1 Thaw chicken, if frozen. Using kitchen scissors, cut fettuccine into thirds. In a Dutch oven cook fettuccine according to package directions; drain. Return fettuccine to hot Dutch oven.

2 Add chicken, cheese, and oil to cooked fettuccine; toss gently to combine. Cook over low heat until heated through. Remove from heat. Add tomatoes and olives; toss gently to combine. Season to taste with salt and pepper.

NUTRITION FACTS PER SERVING:
371 cal., 15 g total fat (4 g sat. fat), 76 mg chol., 866 mg sodium, 39 g carb., 3 g dietary fiber, 22 g protein.

223

Bacon and Tomato Fettuccine ⏱ ★

START TO FINISH **30 minutes** MAKES **6 servings**

¾ cup butter, cut up and softened

1 pound dried fettuccine

1½ cups finely shredded Parmigiano-Reggiano cheese (6 ounces)

⅓ cup seeded and chopped roma tomato (1 medium; optional)

¼ cup small fresh basil leaves (optional)

2 slices bacon, crisp-cooked, drained, and crumbled (optional)

Finely shredded Parmigiano-Reggiano cheese (optional)

Freshly ground black pepper

1 Place half of the butter in a large bowl; set aside.

2 Cook fettuccine according to package directions. Remove ½ cup of the cooking water; set aside. Drain pasta lightly, leaving some cooking water with the pasta.

3 Add cooked pasta to butter in bowl; toss vigorously to coat. Add the remaining butter and 1½ cups cheese; toss to combine, adding enough of the reserved ½ cup cooking water to reach a creamy consistency. If desired, top with tomato, basil, and bacon.

4 If desired, sprinkle each serving with additional cheese. Sprinkle with pepper.

NUTRITION FACTS PER SERVING: *613 cal., 33 g total fat (20 g sat. fat), 83 mg chol., 685 mg sodium, 58 g carb., 3 g dietary fiber, 21 g protein.*

224

Chicken and Pasta Primavera

START TO FINISH **30 minutes**   MAKES **6 servings**

1   9-ounce package refrigerated plain or spinach fettuccine

1   medium zucchini, halved lengthwise and thinly sliced (1¼ cups)

1   cup thinly sliced carrots (2 medium)

¾   cup frozen whole kernel corn

3   cups shredded cooked chicken

1   10-ounce carton original cream cheese for cooking*

½   cup sour cream

2   tablespoons Dijon-style mustard

2   teaspoons finely shredded lemon peel

1   teaspoon dried basil, crushed

Cracked black pepper (optional)

¼   cup finely shredded Parmesan cheese (1 ounce)

1 In a Dutch oven cook fettuccine according to package directions, adding zucchini, carrots, and corn to the water with pasta; drain. Return fettuccine mixture to hot Dutch oven; add chicken.

2 Meanwhile, in a medium saucepan combine cream cheese for cooking, sour cream, mustard, lemon peel, and basil; cook and stir until heated through.

3 Add cream cheese mixture to hot fettuccine mixture; toss gently to coat. If desired, sprinkle each serving with pepper. Serve with cheese.

NUTRITION FACTS PER SERVING:
421 cal., 18 g total fat (8 g sat. fat), 129 mg chol., 562 mg sodium, 32 g carb., 2 g dietary fiber, 32 g protein.

*tip

If you can't find cream cheese for cooking, in a medium saucepan combine 1½ cups chicken broth, 4 teaspoons cornstarch, the lemon peel, and basil. Cook and stir over medium heat until thickened and bubbly. Cook and stir for 2 minutes more. Remove from heat. Stir in sour cream and mustard. Add to hot fettuccine mixture and continue as directed.

Pasta

Chicken and Olives Fettuccine ⏱

START TO FINISH 30 minutes MAKES 6 to 8 servings

12 to 16 ounces dried fettuccine

2 tablespoons olive oil

1 pound skinless, boneless chicken breast halves, cut into 1-inch pieces

1 large onion, cut into thin wedges

2 cloves garlic, minced

1 28-ounce can Italian-style whole peeled tomatoes in puree

1/2 teaspoon coarse ground black pepper

1/4 teaspoon salt

1/2 cup whipping cream

1 1/2 cups large pimento-stuffed green olives and/or pitted kalamata or other Italian olives, sliced

1/2 cup finely shredded fresh basil

1/4 cup grated Parmesan cheese

1 In a Dutch oven cook fettuccine according to package directions; drain. Return fettuccine to hot Dutch oven; cover and keep warm.

2 Meanwhile, in a large skillet heat oil over medium-high heat. Add chicken, onion, and garlic. Cook about 5 minutes or until chicken is no longer pink, stirring occasionally. Place half of the tomatoes in a blender or food processor. Cover and blend or process until smooth. Snip the remaining tomatoes into bite-size pieces.

3 Stir pureed tomatoes, tomato pieces in puree, pepper, and salt into chicken mixture. Bring to boiling; reduce heat. Boil gently, uncovered, for 2 minutes. Stir in cream. Boil gently, uncovered, for 3 minutes more, stirring occasionally. Stir in olives; heat through.

4 Add chicken mixture, basil, and cheese to cooked fettuccine; toss gently to combine.

NUTRITION FACTS PER SERVING:
499 cal., 20 g total fat (7 g sat. fat), 74 mg chol., 891 mg sodium, 53 g carb., 5 g dietary fiber, 28 g protein.

Easy Sausage Lasagna

START TO FINISH **25 minutes**   MAKES **4 to 6 servings**

8   ounces dried campanelle or mafalda pasta

1   pound hot or sweet bulk Italian sausage

3   cups sliced fresh mushrooms (8 ounces)

¾   cup chopped green sweet pepper (1 medium)

½   cup chopped onion (1 medium)

1   26-ounce jar mushroom pasta sauce

1   cup shredded Italian cheese blend (4 ounces)

     Snipped fresh parsley (optional)

1 Cook pasta according to package directions; drain.

2 Meanwhile, in a 12-inch skillet cook sausage, mushrooms, sweet pepper, and onion over medium-high heat until meat is brown and vegetables are tender, using a wooden spoon to break up meat as it cooks. Drain off fat.

3 Add cooked pasta and pasta sauce to meat mixture; stir to combine. Return to simmering. Sprinkle with cheese. Cook, covered, over low heat until cheese is melted. If desired, sprinkle with parsley.

NUTRITION FACTS PER SERVING:
892 cal., 49 g total fat (19 g sat. fat), 106 mg chol., 1,881 mg sodium, 78 g carb., 8 g dietary fiber, 36 g protein.

227

Quick Skillet Lasagna ★ 🥕

START TO FINISH **30 minutes** MAKES **6 servings**

8 ounces uncooked lean ground chicken or turkey

$\frac{1}{2}$ cup chopped onion (1 medium)

2 cups pasta sauce

1 cup water

2 cups dried extra-wide noodles

$1\frac{1}{2}$ cups coarsely chopped zucchini

$\frac{1}{2}$ cup fat-free ricotta cheese

2 tablespoons grated Parmesan or Romano cheese

1 tablespoon snipped fresh parsley

$\frac{1}{2}$ cup shredded mozzarella cheese (2 ounces)

Snipped fresh parsley (optional)

1 In a large skillet cook ground chicken and onion over medium heat until meat is brown, using a wooden spoon to break up meat as it cooks. Drain off any fat.

2 Stir in pasta sauce and the water. Bring to boiling. Stir in noodles and zucchini. Return to boiling; reduce heat. Simmer, covered, about 10 minutes or until noodles are tender, stirring occasionally.

3 Meanwhile, in a small bowl combine ricotta cheese, Parmesan cheese, and 1 tablespoon parsley. Drop cheese mixture by spoonfuls on top of pasta mixture. Sprinkle with mozzarella cheese.

4 Cook, covered, over low heat for 4 to 5 minutes or until cheese mixture is heated through and mozzarella cheese is melted. If desired, sprinkle with additional parsley.

NUTRITION FACTS PER SERVING:
186 cal., 3 g total fat (2 g sat. fat), 45 mg chol., 519 mg sodium, 21 g carb., 2 g dietary fiber, 17 g protein

Parmesan Chicken and Noodles

START TO FINISH **30 minutes** OVEN **450°F** MAKES **4 servings**

6 **ounces dried extra-wide egg noodles**

1 **2- to 2¼-pound purchased roasted chicken**

1 **cup frozen peas**

4 **cloves garlic, minced**

1¾ **cups whole milk, half-and-half, or light cream**

½ **of a slice white or whole wheat bread**

¾ **cup shredded Parmesan cheese (3 ounces)**

2 **tablespoons butter, melted**

Snipped fresh thyme (optional)

1 Preheat oven to 450°F. Cook noodles according to package directions; drain.

2 Meanwhile, remove chicken from bones; discard skin and bones. Using two forks, pull chicken apart into shreds. In a large saucepan combine shredded chicken, peas, and garlic. Stir in milk; heat through. Cover and keep warm.

3 Place bread in a blender or food processor. Cover and blend or process until coarse crumbs form. Transfer to a small bowl; stir in ¼ cup of the cheese and the melted butter.

4 Stir cooked noodles and the remaining ½ cup cheese into chicken mixture. Cook and stir until bubbly. Divide chicken mixture among four 16-ounce individual casseroles. Top with bread crumb mixture. Bake about 5 minutes or until tops begin to brown. If desired, garnish with fresh thyme.

NUTRITION FACTS PER SERVING:
701 cal., 37 g total fat (16 g sat. fat), 222 mg chol., 1,388 mg sodium, 45 g carb., 3 g dietary fiber, 50 g protein.

229

Lemon-Caper Tuna and Noodles

START TO FINISH 20 minutes MAKES 4 servings

12 ounces dried extra-wide
     egg noodles

1   lemon

1   15-ounce jar light garlic
     Alfredo pasta sauce or
     one 10-ounce container
     refrigerated light Alfredo
     pasta sauce

1   tablespoon drained capers

1   12-ounce can solid white tuna
     (water-pack), drained and
     broken into chunks

     Cracked black pepper
     (optional)

     Snipped fresh chives
     (optional)

1 Cook noodles according to package directions; drain.

2 Meanwhile, finely shred peel from lemon. Cut lemon in half; squeeze juice from lemon. In a medium saucepan combine lemon juice, pasta sauce, and capers. Cook and stir until heated through.

3 Gently stir in cooked noodles and tuna. Cook just until heated through. Sprinkle with lemon peel and, if desired, pepper and chives.

NUTRITION FACTS PER SERVING:
655 cal., 19 g total fat (11 g sat. fat), 154 mg chol., 1,384 mg sodium, 78 g carb., 4 g dietary fiber, 41 g protein.

Chicken Lo Mein

START TO FINISH **25 minutes** MAKES **4 servings**

8   ounces dried Chinese egg
    noodles, rice noodles, or udon
    (broad, white noodles)

2   tablespoons peanut oil or
    canola oil

1   16-ounce package frozen stir-
    fry vegetables

1   tablespoon finely chopped
    fresh ginger

1   pound skinless, boneless
    chicken breast halves, cut
    into 1/2-inch pieces

1/3 cup stir-fry sauce

    Sliced green onions or
    snipped fresh cilantro
    (optional)

1 Cook noodles according to package directions; drain. Return noodles to hot pan.

2 Meanwhile, in a large skillet heat 1 tablespoon of the oil over medium-high heat. Add frozen vegetables and ginger; cook and stir for 4 to 6 minutes or until vegetables are crisp-tender. Remove from skillet. Add the remaining 1 tablespoon oil to skillet; add chicken. Cook and stir for 3 to 4 minutes or until chicken is no longer pink.

3 Return vegetable mixture to skillet. Add cooked noodles and stir-fry sauce; cook and stir until heated through. If desired, garnish each serving with green onions.

NUTRITION FACTS PER SERVING:
455 cal., 8 g total fat (2 g sat. fat), 66 mg chol., 907 mg sodium, 60 g carb., 2 g dietary fiber, 30 g protein.

Penne Chicken in Red Sauce

START TO FINISH 25 minutes   MAKES 4 servings

- 6 ounces dried penne pasta
- 1 9-ounce package fresh spinach
- 2 tablespoons olive oil
- 1½ pounds skinless, boneless chicken breast halves, cut into thin bite-size strips
- ¼ teaspoon salt
- ⅛ teaspoon ground black pepper
- 1 14-ounce jar desired-flavor red pasta sauce
- 1 cup shredded mozzarella cheese (4 ounces)

1 Cook pasta according to package directions. Place spinach in a large colander set in the sink. When pasta is done, pour pasta and cooking water over spinach in colander. Set aside.

2 Meanwhile, in a 12-inch skillet heat oil over medium-high heat. Add half the chicken. Cook for 2 to 3 minutes or until no longer pink. Add remaining chicken; cook for 2 to 3 minutes or until no longer pink. Drain off fat. Return all of the chicken to skillet. Sprinkle with salt and pepper.

3 Add pasta sauce to skillet. Bring to boiling. Stir in cooked pasta mixture; heat through. Remove from heat. Sprinkle with cheese. Let stand for 3 to 5 minutes or until cheese is melted.

NUTRITION FACTS PER SERVING:
538 cal., 16 g total fat (5 g sat. fat), 114 mg chol., 789 mg sodium, 42 g carb., 4 g dietary fiber, 55 g protein.

Chicken-Veggie Pasta Toss

START TO FINISH **30 minutes** MAKES **4 servings**

6 ounces dried multigrain penne pasta

1 tablespoon olive oil or canola oil

4 cloves garlic, minced

¼ teaspoon crushed red pepper

1 16-ounce package frozen broccoli stir-fry vegetables

12 ounces skinless, boneless chicken breast halves, cut into bite-size strips

1 15-ounce can no-salt-added cannellini beans (white kidney beans), rinsed and drained

½ to ¾ cup reduced-sodium chicken broth

1 tablespoon snipped fresh oregano

1 Cook penne according to package directions; drain.

2 Meanwhile, in a 12-inch nonstick skillet heat oil over medium-high heat. (Add more oil as necessary during cooking.) Add garlic and crushed red pepper; cook and stir for 30 seconds. Add frozen vegetables; cook and stir for 5 minutes. Remove vegetables from skillet.

3 Add chicken to skillet; cook and stir for 3 to 4 minutes or until chicken is no longer pink. Return vegetables to skillet. Add penne, beans, and enough of the broth to moisten. Cook until heated through, stirring occasionally. Sprinkle each serving with oregano.

NUTRITION FACTS PER SERVING:
399 cal., 6 g total fat (1 g sat. fat), 49 mg chol., 214 mg sodium, 50 g carb., 10 g dietary fiber, 35 g protein.

233

tip

Today pasta comes in many shapes and sizes. Many new pastas—including gluten-free and multigrain—can be substituted for most pastas in recipes. Make your pasta dishes more healthful by using whole grain pasta. Consider gradually introducing whole grain pasta by starting with equal parts whole grain and refined (regular) pasta. Cook according to package directions.

Salmon and Asparagus–Sauced Pasta

START TO FINISH **25 minutes** MAKES **4 servings**

- 1 **pound fresh asparagus spears**
- 8 **ounces dried cavatappi or penne pasta**
- 1 **tablespoon butter**
- ¾ **cup red or yellow sweet pepper strips (1 small)**
- ½ **cup chopped onion (1 medium)**
- 1 **10-ounce container refrigerated Alfredo pasta sauce**
- ¼ **cup milk**
- ⅛ **teaspoon ground black pepper**
- 1 **3-ounce package thinly sliced, smoked salmon (lox-style), coarsely chopped**
- 2 **teaspoons snipped fresh tarragon or ½ teaspoon dried tarragon, crushed**

1 Snap off and discard woody bases from asparagus. Cut asparagus diagonally into 2-inch pieces.

2 In a Dutch oven cook cavatappi according to package directions, adding asparagus for the last 3 minutes of cooking; drain. Return pasta mixture to hot Dutch oven; cover and keep warm.

3 Meanwhile, in a medium saucepan heat butter over medium heat until melted. Add sweet pepper and onion. Cook until vegetables are tender, stirring occasionally. Stir in pasta sauce, milk, and black pepper; heat through. Stir in smoked salmon and tarragon; heat through.

4 Pour salmon mixture over pasta mixture; stir gently to combine.

NUTRITION FACTS PER SERVING:
446 cal., 18 g total fat (11 g sat. fat), 54 mg chol., 910 mg sodium, 53 g carb., 4 g dietary fiber, 18 g protein.

234

Antipasti Bow Ties

START TO FINISH 25 minutes MAKES 4 servings

4   ounces dried farfalle pasta
    (bow ties)

1   12-ounce jar marinated
    artichoke salad (artichokes,
    sweet pepper, and olives)
    or 1½ cups deli marinated
    artichoke salad, undrained

1   tablespoon olive oil

1   teaspoon dried Italian
    seasoning, crushed

½   of a medium cantaloupe

6   ounces salami, chopped

4   ounces bocconcini (small
    fresh mozzarella balls),
    halved

    Salt

    Ground black pepper

1 Cook pasta according to package directions; drain. Rinse with cold water; drain again.

2 Meanwhile, drain artichoke salad, reserving ¼ cup liquid. In a small bowl combine the reserved artichoke liquid, oil, and Italian seasoning; set aside. Peel cantaloupe. Cut cantaloupe into wedges; halve wedges.

3 In a large bowl combine cooked pasta, artichoke salad, cantaloupe, salami, and bocconcini. Pour oil mixture over pasta mixture; toss gently to coat. Season to taste with salt and pepper.

NUTRITION FACTS PER SERVING:
448 cal., 24 g total fat (9 g sat. fat), 58 mg chol., 1,057 mg sodium, 34 g carb., 3 g dietary fiber, 22 g protein.

235

Bow Ties with Sausage and Sweet Peppers

START TO FINISH 25 minutes MAKES 4 to 6 servings

- 8 ounces dried farfalle pasta (bow ties)
- 12 ounces sweet Italian or apple-flavor cooked chicken sausage links, cut into 1-inch pieces
- 2 medium red and/or yellow sweet peppers, seeded and cut into ¾-inch pieces
- ½ cup beef broth or chicken broth
- ¼ cup snipped fresh basil or Italian (flat-leaf) parsley
- ¼ cup finely shredded Parmigiano-Reggiano cheese or Parmesan cheese (1 ounce)

1 In a Dutch oven cook pasta according to package directions; drain. Return pasta to hot Dutch oven; cover and keep warm.

2 Meanwhile, in a large skillet cook sausage and sweet peppers over medium heat about 8 minutes or until sausage is brown, stirring occasionally.

3 Stir broth into sausage mixture. Bring to boiling; reduce heat. Simmer, uncovered, for 5 minutes. Add sausage mixture and basil to cooked pasta; toss gently to coat. Sprinkle each serving with cheese.

NUTRITION FACTS PER SERVING:
379 cal., 10 g total fat (4 g sat. fat), 29 mg chol., 687 mg sodium, 48 g carb., 3 g dietary fiber, 24 g protein.

★ Garden-Fresh Wagon Wheel Pasta

START TO FINISH **25 minutes**   MAKES **4 servings**

1   **12-ounce package frozen, cooked breaded chicken nuggets**

8   **ounces dried wagon wheel pasta**

4   **cups chopped or sliced assorted vegetables, such as broccoli, carrots, summer squash, cauliflower, and/or sweet peppers**

½   **of an 8-ounce tub-style cream cheese spread with chive and onion**

¼   **to ½ cup milk**

   Salt

   Ground black pepper

   Shredded Parmesan cheese

1 Heat chicken nuggets according to package directions.

2 Meanwhile, in a Dutch oven cook pasta in a large amount of boiling, lightly salted water for 4 minutes. Add vegetables. Cook about 5 minutes more or until pasta is tender; drain. Return pasta mixture to hot Dutch oven.

3 Add cream cheese spread to pasta mixture; heat through. Thin with enough of the milk to reach desired consistency. Season to taste with salt and pepper.

4 Serve chicken nuggets with pasta mixture. Sprinkle each serving with cheese.

NUTRITION FACTS PER SERVING: *643 cal., 27 g total fat (12 g sat. fat), 81 mg chol., 811 mg sodium, 72 g carb., 4 g dietary fiber, 25 g protein.*

237

Speedy and Spicy Tuna Noodle Casserole

START TO FINISH 25 minutes MAKES 4 servings

8 ounces dried wagon wheel and/or elbow macaroni

1 10.75-ounce can condensed nacho cheese soup

½ cup milk

1 12-ounce can solid white tuna (water-pack), drained and broken into chunks

1 4-ounce can diced green chile peppers, drained

Rich round crackers, tortilla chips, or corn chips (optional)

1 In a Dutch oven cook macaroni according to package directions; drain. Return macaroni to hot Dutch oven.

2 Add soup and milk to cooked macaroni, stirring until macaroni is coated and creamy. Gently fold in tuna and chile peppers; heat through. If desired, serve with crackers.

NUTRITION FACTS PER SERVING:
414 cal., 9 g total fat (4 g sat. fat), 44 mg chol., 905 mg sodium, 51 g carb., 2 g dietary fiber, 31 g protein.

⭐ Bucatini and Bacon

START TO FINISH **25 minutes**   MAKES **4 servings**

8   **ounces dried bucatini or fusilli pasta**

3   **cups fresh baby spinach**

1   **28-ounce can whole peeled tomatoes with basil, undrained**

6   **slices bacon, crisp-cooked, drained, and crumbled**

3   **cloves garlic, minced**

½   **cup freshly grated Pecorino Romano cheese**

   Salt

   Ground black pepper

   Freshly grated Pecorino Romano cheese (optional)

1 In a Dutch oven cook pasta according to package directions; drain. Return pasta to hot Dutch oven. Stir in spinach; cover and keep warm.

2 Meanwhile, drain tomatoes, reserving liquid. Snip tomatoes into bite-size pieces. In a medium saucepan combine tomatoes, bacon, and garlic. Bring to boiling; reduce heat. Simmer, uncovered, for 10 minutes, stirring occasionally.

3 Add tomato mixture to pasta mixture; heat through, tossing gently to coat and adding some of the reserved tomato liquid if mixture is dry. Stir in ½ cup cheese. Season to taste with salt and pepper. If desired, sprinkle each serving with additional cheese.

NUTRITION FACTS PER SERVING: *355 cal., 9 g total fat (4 g sat. fat), 24 mg chol., 845 mg sodium, 51 g carb., 4 g dietary fiber, 17 g protein.*

239

Fusilli with Greens and Pecorino Romano Cheese

START TO FINISH **30 minutes** MAKES **6 servings**

- 1 **pound dried fusilli pasta**
- 2 **tablespoons olive oil**
- 4 **cups chopped onions (4 large)**
- 1 **large bunch escarole (about 14 ounces), coarsely chopped**
- 1 **10-ounce package fresh spinach, coarsely chopped**
- ½ **teaspoon freshly ground black pepper**
- ¼ **teaspoon salt**
- 2 **cups shredded Pecorino Romano cheese (8 ounces)**

1 Cook pasta according to package directions; drain, reserving ⅓ cup of the cooking water. Return pasta and the reserved water to hot pan; cover and keep warm.

2 Meanwhile, in a Dutch oven heat oil over medium-high heat. Add onions; cook about 10 minutes or until golden brown, stirring occasionally. Stir in escarole, spinach, pepper, and salt. Reduce heat to medium-low. Cook, covered, about 5 minutes or until greens are wilted and tender.

3 Stir cheese into cooked pasta. Add pasta mixture to greens mixture; stir to combine.

NUTRITION FACTS PER SERVING:
489 cal., 13 g total fat (5 g sat. fat), 28 mg chol., 473 mg sodium, 72 g carb., 6 g dietary fiber, 21 g protein.

240

Vegetable Pasta with Provolone

START TO FINISH **30 minutes** MAKES **4 servings**

- 1 **cup dried small alphabet-shape pasta, acini de pepe, or large couscous**
- 1½ **cups assorted vegetables, such as finely chopped carrots, red sweet pepper, broccoli and/or frozen baby peas, edamame, and whole kernel corn**
- 1 **tablespoon olive oil**
- ⅛ **teaspoon ground black pepper**
- ⅓ **cup finely chopped provolone or cheddar cheese**

1 In a large saucepan cook pasta according to package directions, adding vegetables for the last 5 minutes of cooking; drain. Return pasta mixture to hot saucepan.

2 Add oil and pepper to pasta mixture; toss gently to coat. Cool slightly. Add cheese; toss gently to combine.

NUTRITION FACTS PER SERVING:
314 cal., 8 g total fat (3 g sat. fat), 11 mg chol., 159 mg sodium, 47 g carb., 3 g dietary fiber, 12 g protein.

Chicken and Sausage with Acini di Pepe

START TO FINISH **30 minutes** MAKES **6 servings**

1 tablespoon butter

1 pound skinless, boneless chicken breast halves, cut into 1-inch pieces

1 pound cooked smoked sausage links, cut into ½-inch slices

1 cup chopped sweet onion (1 large)

½ cup chopped red sweet pepper (1 small)

3 cloves garlic, minced

1 14-ounce can reduced-sodium chicken broth

¾ cup water

1 tablespoon balsamic vinegar

⅛ teaspoon cayenne pepper

1½ cups dried acini di pepe

½ cup sliced green onions (4)

1 In a 4-quart Dutch oven heat butter over medium heat until melted. Add chicken, sausage, onion, sweet pepper, and garlic. Cook for 5 minutes, stirring occasionally. Add broth, the water, vinegar, and cayenne pepper.

2 Bring just to boiling. Stir in acini de pepe; reduce heat. Simmer, covered, about 10 minutes or until chicken is no longer pink and pasta is tender, stirring occasionally. Remove from heat. Stir in green onions.

NUTRITION FACTS PER SERVING:
583 cal., 27 g total fat (9 g sat. fat), 97 mg chol., 898 mg sodium, 49 g carb., 3 g dietary fiber, 36 g protein.

Acini di pepe, which means "peppercorns" in Italian, is a teeny round pasta, often used in soups. Any small pasta makes a good substitute for acini di pepe. Try orzo. Or substitute small alphabet-shape pasta for a child-friendly dish.

Chicken with Greek Orzo Risotto

START TO FINISH **30 minutes**   MAKES **4 servings**

4   **skinless, boneless chicken breast halves (about 1¼ pounds total)**
    Salt
    Freshly ground black pepper
2   **tablespoons olive oil**
3   **cups reduced-sodium chicken broth**
2   **cloves garlic, minced**
1   **cup dried orzo pasta (rosamarina)**
¾   **cup quartered cherry tomatoes**
½   **cup crumbled feta cheese (2 ounces)**
¼   **cup sliced pitted ripe olives**
1   **tablespoon snipped fresh oregano**

242

1 Lightly sprinkle chicken with salt and pepper. In a 12-inch skillet heat 1 tablespoon of the oil over medium heat. Add chicken; cook for 8 to 12 minutes or until chicken is no longer pink (170°F), turning once.

2 Meanwhile, for risotto, in a medium saucepan bring broth and garlic to boiling; reduce heat and simmer. In a large saucepan heat the remaining 1 tablespoon oil over medium heat. Add orzo; cook and stir for 1 minute. Slowly add ½ cup of the hot broth to orzo, stirring constantly. Continue to cook and stir over medium heat until broth is absorbed. Continue adding broth, ½ cup at a time, stirring constantly until broth is absorbed and mixture is creamy. (This should take about 15 minutes.) Remove from heat.

3 Stir tomatoes, cheese, olives, and oregano into risotto. Serve chicken with risotto.

NUTRITION FACTS PER SERVING:
451 cal., 14 g total fat (4 g sat. fat), 99 mg chol., 952 mg sodium, 35 g carb., 2 g dietary fiber, 44 g protein.

Greek Skillet Supper

START TO FINISH **30 minutes** MAKES **4 servings**

8 ounces lean ground lamb or ground beef

¾ cup chopped onion

2 cloves garlic, minced

1 14-ounce can beef broth

1½ cups dried medium shell macaroni

2 cups frozen mixed vegetables

1 14.5-ounce can whole tomatoes, undrained and cut up

2 tablespoons tomato paste

2 teaspoons snipped fresh marjoram or 1 teaspoon dried marjoram, crushed

⅛ teaspoon ground cinnamon

⅛ teaspoon ground nutmeg

½ cup crumbled feta cheese (2 ounces)

1 teaspoon snipped fresh marjoram

1 In a large skillet cook meat, onion, and garlic over medium-high heat until meat is brown, using a wooden spoon to break up meat as it cooks. Drain off fat. Stir in broth and macaroni. Bring to boiling; reduce heat. Simmer, covered, for 10 minutes.

2 Stir in frozen vegetables, tomatoes, tomato paste, dried marjoram (if using), cinnamon, and nutmeg. Return to boiling; reduce heat. Simmer, uncovered, for 5 to 10 minutes more or until vegetables are tender. Stir in 2 teaspoons fresh marjoram (if using). Sprinkle each serving with cheese and 1 teaspoon fresh marjoram.

NUTRITION FACTS PER SERVING:
400 cal., 12 g total fat (6 g sat. fat), 50 mg chol., 783 mg sodium, 51 g carb., 3 g dietary fiber, 22 g protein.

243

Salmon and Ravioli

START TO FINISH **25 minutes**   MAKES **4 servings**

- 2   **6-ounce fresh or frozen skinless salmon fillets**
- 1   **9-ounce package refrigerated 4-cheese ravioli**
- 1   **lemon**
      Salt
      Ground back pepper
- 2   **tablespoons olive oil**
- 1   **5- to 6-ounce package fresh baby spinach**
- 2   **tablespoons butter**
- 3   **cloves garlic, thinly sliced**
      Shredded Parmesan cheese

1 Thaw salmon, if frozen. Cook ravioli according to package directions; drain. Return ravioli to hot pan; cover and keep warm.

2 Meanwhile, cut lemon in half; squeeze juice from one lemon half. Cut the remaining lemon half into small wedges. Set lemon juice and lemon wedges aside. Rinse fish; pat dry with paper towels. Sprinkle fish with salt and pepper.

3 In a large skillet heat oil over medium heat. Add fish. Cook for 6 to 8 minutes or until fish flakes easily when tested with a fork, turning once. Remove fish. Add spinach to skillet. Cook and stir about 1 minute or just until spinach begins to wilt. Remove spinach. Add lemon juice, butter, and garlic to skillet. Cook and stir over medium heat until butter is melted. Cook and stir for 1 minute more.

4 Slice fish; arrange on dinner plates. Add cooked ravioli and spinach; drizzle with butter mixture. Sprinkle each serving with cheese and serve with lemon wedges.

NUTRITION FACTS PER SERVING:
525 cal., 31 g total fat (12 g sat. fat), 102 mg chol., 689 mg sodium, 31 g carb., 3 g dietary fiber, 29 g protein.

Apple-Sausage Rigatoni

START TO FINISH 25 minutes   MAKES 4 servings

6   ounces dried rigatoni pasta

8   ounces cooked smoked
    sausage links, halved
    lengthwise and cut into
    1-inch pieces

$1\frac{1}{2}$ pounds McIntosh or Braeburn
    apples, cored and cut into
    $\frac{1}{2}$-inch slices

$\frac{1}{2}$ cup whipping cream

$\frac{1}{2}$ cup crumbled Gorgonzola or
    other blue cheese (2 ounces)

    Fresh herbs (optional)

1 In a Dutch oven cook pasta according to package directions; drain.

2 In the same Dutch oven cook sausage over medium heat until light brown. Add apples; cook about 5 minutes or until apples are light golden brown, stirring occasionally. Stir in cooked pasta, cream, and cheese; heat through. If desired, garnish with fresh herbs.

NUTRITION FACTS PER SERVING:
613 cal., 34 g total fat (16 g sat. fat),
92 mg chol., 1,056 mg sodium, 56 g carb.,
5 g dietary fiber, 26 g protein.

245

Rotini with Shrimp and Spinach

START TO FINISH **20 minutes** MAKES **4 servings**

12 ounces fresh or frozen peeled and deveined medium shrimp

6 ounces dried rotini or other pasta

1 tablespoon olive oil

3 cloves garlic, minced

1 cup chicken broth

1 tablespoon cornstarch

1 teaspoon dried basil, crushed

1 teaspoon dried oregano, crushed

4 cups fresh baby spinach or torn spinach

Finely shredded Parmesan cheese

1 Thaw shrimp, if frozen. In a Dutch oven cook pasta according to package directions; drain. Return pasta to hot Dutch oven; cover and keep warm.

2 Meanwhile, rinse shrimp; pat dry with paper towels. In a skillet heat oil over medium-high heat. Add garlic; cook and stir for 15 seconds. Add shrimp; cook and stir for 2 to 3 minutes or until shrimp are opaque. Remove from skillet.

3 In a small bowl combine broth, cornstarch, basil, and oregano. Add to skillet; cook and stir until thickened and bubbly. Add spinach. Cook and stir for 1 to 2 minutes or just until spinach starts to wilt. Return shrimp; heat through.

4 Add shrimp mixture to cooked pasta; toss gently to combine. Sprinkle each serving with cheese.

NUTRITION FACTS PER SERVING:
333 cal., 7 g total fat (1 g sat. fat), 136 mg chol., 422 mg sodium, 39 g carb., 3 g dietary fiber, 25 g protein.

246

⏱ Chicken and Gorgonzola Cheese Pasta

START TO FINISH **30 minutes**   MAKES **6 to 8 servings**

12   to 16 ounces dried pasta

1½   pounds skinless, boneless chicken breast halves, cut crosswise into ½-inch slices

½   teaspoon salt

½   teaspoon freshly ground black pepper

3   tablespoons olive oil

3   cups sliced fresh cremini, stemmed shiitake, and/or button mushrooms (8 ounces)

2   cups whipping cream

1   cup crumbled Gorgonzola or other blue cheese (4 ounces)

⅔   cup grated Parmesan cheese

¼   cup snipped fresh Italian (flat-leaf) parsley

1 In a Dutch oven cook pasta according to package directions; drain. Return pasta to hot Dutch oven; cover and keep warm. Meanwhile, sprinkle chicken with ¼ teaspoon of the salt and ¼ teaspoon of the pepper.

2 In a large nonstick skillet heat 1 tablespoon of the oil over medium-high heat. Add half of the chicken; cook and stir until brown. Remove from skillet. Repeat with another 1 tablespoon oil and the remaining chicken. Remove from skillet. Add the remaining 1 tablespoon oil to skillet. Add mushrooms. Cook for 5 to 8 minutes or until mushrooms are softened and liquid is evaporated, stirring occasionally.

3 Return chicken to skillet; stir in cream. Bring to boiling; reduce heat. Boil gently, uncovered, for 3 minutes. Stir in ½ cup of the Gorgonzola cheese, the Parmesan cheese, the remaining ¼ teaspoon salt, and the remaining ¼ teaspoon pepper. Cook and stir about 1 minute or until cheeses are melted.

4 Add chicken mixture, the remaining ½ cup Gorgonzola cheese, and parsley to cooked pasta; toss gently to combine.

NUTRITION FACTS PER SERVING:
800 cal., 48 g total fat (26 g sat. fat), 200 mg chol., 753 mg sodium, 47 g carb., 2 g dietary fiber, 45 g protein.

247

Pasta with Broccoli Raab and Clams

START TO FINISH 25 minutes   MAKES 6 to 8 servings

12   to 16 ounces dried pasta
2   tablespoons olive oil
1   pound broccoli raab, trimmed
     and cut into 2-inch pieces, or
     3 cups broccoli florets
3   cloves garlic, sliced
2   6.5-ounce cans chopped
     clams, undrained
¼   cup butter
½   cup dry white wine
½   teaspoon crushed red pepper
¼   teaspoon ground black pepper
¼   cup grated Parmesan cheese

1 Cook pasta according to package directions; drain. Return pasta to hot pan; cover and keep warm.

2 Meanwhile, in a 12-inch skillet heat oil over medium-high heat. Add broccoli and garlic. Cook for 5 minutes, stirring occasionally. Stir in clams and butter. Cook over medium heat until butter is melted.

3 Stir in wine, crushed red pepper, and black pepper. Bring just to boiling; reduce heat. Simmer, uncovered, about 2 minutes or until mixture is slightly reduced.

4 Serve broccoli mixture over cooked pasta. Sprinkle each serving with cheese.

NUTRITION FACTS PER SERVING:
469 cal., 15 g total fat (6 g sat. fat), 64 mg chol., 219 mg sodium, 49 g carb., 4 g dietary fiber, 27 g protein.

Beef, Pork, and Lamb

Variety is the spice of quick-cooking cuts of beef, pork, and lamb. Meat takes on a new dimension when accented with enticing ingredients.

7

Caprese Pasta and Steak ⏱

START TO FINISH **30 minutes**   MAKES **4 servings**

8 **ounces dried large
   rigatoni pasta**

½ **cup purchased basil pesto**

1 **pound boneless beef shoulder
   top blade (flat-iron) or tri-tip
   steak, cut into 4 portions**

4 **ounces fresh mozzarella
   cheese, sliced**

4 **roma tomatoes, sliced**

   Fresh basil leaves (optional)

1 Cook pasta according to package directions; drain. Return to hot pan.

2 Meanwhile, remove 2 tablespoons of the pesto and brush it on the steaks. Heat a large heavy skillet over medium heat; add steaks. Cook about 10 minutes or to desired doneness, turning once.

3 Add the remaining 6 tablespoons pesto to pasta; toss to coat. Divide pasta among four dinner plates. Top with steaks, cheese, and tomato slices. If desired, top with fresh basil.

NUTRITION FACTS PER SERVING:
*695 cal., 35 g total fat (6 g sat. fat),
94 mg chol., 486 mg sodium, 53 g carb.,
3 g dietary fiber, 40 g protein.*

Beef Stroganoff

START TO FINISH **30 minutes** MAKES **4 servings**

- 12 ounces boneless beef sirloin steak
- 1 8-ounce carton sour cream
- 2 tablespoons all-purpose flour
- ½ cup water
- 2 teaspoons instant beef bouillon granules
- ¼ teaspoon ground black pepper
- 2 tablespoons butter or margarine
- 2 cups sliced mixed fresh mushrooms, such as button, cremini, and/or stemmed shiitake
- ½ cup chopped onion (1 medium)
- 1 clove garlic, minced
- 2 cups hot cooked noodles

1 If desired, partially freeze meat for easier slicing. Trim fat from steak. Thinly slice steak across the grain into bite-size strips. In a small bowl stir together sour cream and flour. Stir in the water, bouillon granules, and pepper; set aside.

2 In a large skillet heat butter over medium-high heat until melted. Add meat, mushrooms, onion, and garlic; cook and stir about 5 minutes or until meat is desired doneness. Drain off fat.

3 Stir sour cream mixture into meat mixture. Cook and stir until thickened and bubbly. Cook and stir for 1 minute more. Serve over hot cooked noodles.

NUTRITION FACTS PER SERVING:
486 cal., 30 g total fat (15 g sat. fat), 108 mg chol., 573 mg sodium, 30 g carb., 2 g dietary fiber, 24 g protein.

251

Beef, Mango, and Spiced Bulgur Bowls

START TO FINISH **30 minutes** MAKES **4 servings**

1 cup reduced-sodium
   chicken broth

²⁄₃ cup bulgur

1 clove garlic, minced

½ teaspoon ground cumin

¼ teaspoon ground coriander

⅛ teaspoon ground cinnamon

⅛ teaspoon cayenne pepper

6 ounces lower-sodium
   deli roast beef, cut into
   thin strips*

½ of a medium mango, peeled
   and cut up*

½ cup fresh snow pea pods,
   halved crosswise*

2 green onions, sliced*

¼ cup snipped fresh cilantro *

¼ cup unsalted peanuts,
   chopped (optional)

1 In a 1½-quart microwave-safe casserole combine broth, bulgur, garlic, cumin, coriander, cinnamon, and cayenne pepper. Microwave, covered, on 100 percent power (high) about 4 minutes or until boiling. Remove from microwave. Let stand about 20 minutes or until bulgur is tender. Drain, if necessary.

2 Divide bulgur mixture among four serving bowls. Top with beef, mango, pea pods, green onions, cilantro, and, if desired, peanuts.

NUTRITION FACTS PER SERVING:
164 cal., 2 g total fat (1 g sat. fat), 26 mg chol., 421 mg sodium, 25 g carb., 5 g dietary fiber, 13 g protein.

*tip
Maximize your time by cutting up the beef, mango, vegetables, and cilantro during the bulgur's standing time.

✪ Beef Stew and Garlic Mash

START TO FINISH **30 minutes** MAKES **4 servings**

1   16-ounce package frozen
    assorted vegetable blend
    (carrots, peas, and onions)

½   cup water

1   17-ounce package refrigerated
    cooked beef tips with gravy

2   teaspoons Worcestershire
    sauce

6   cloves garlic

2   tablespoons water

1   pound Yukon gold or red
    potatoes, halved

2   tablespoons olive oil

¼   teaspoon salt

¼   teaspoon freshly ground
    black pepper

2   tablespoons fresh
    oregano leaves

1 In a 4-quart Dutch oven combine vegetables and the ½ cup water. Bring to boiling over medium heat. Meanwhile, microwave beef tips according to package directions. Add beef tips and Worcestershire to vegetables. Reduce heat to low. Cook, covered, about 5 minutes or until vegetables are tender.

2 In a small microwave-safe bowl combine garlic and the 2 tablespoons water; cover with vented plastic wrap. Microwave on 100 percent power (high) for 1 minute; set aside. In a large microwave-safe bowl microwave potatoes on 100 percent power (high) for 8 to 10 minutes or just until tender, stirring once halfway through cooking.

3 Peel and mash garlic. Add garlic, oil, salt, and pepper to potatoes; mash with a potato masher. Divide potato mixture among four serving dishes; top with beef mixture. Sprinkle with oregano.

NUTRITION FACTS PER SERVING:
368 cal., 14 g total fat (3 g sat. fat), 47 mg chol., 888 mg sodium, 42 g carb., 8 g dietary fiber, 24 g protein.

Barbecue Beef Cups ☆

START TO FINISH **30 minutes** OVEN **400°F** MAKES **5 servings (2 cups each)**

1   **pound ground beef**
¼   **cup chopped onion**
⅔   **cup barbecue sauce**
2   **tablespoons packed brown sugar**
1   **10- to 12-ounce package refrigerated biscuits (10 biscuits)**
½   **cup shredded cheddar cheese (2 ounces)**

1 Preheat oven to 400°F. In a large skillet cook ground beef and onion until meat is brown, using a wooden spoon to break up meat as it cooks. Drain off fat. Stir barbecue sauce and brown sugar into meat mixture.

2 Press a biscuit into the bottom and up the side of a 2½-inch muffin cup; repeat with the remaining biscuits to make 10 biscuit-lined muffin cups. Spoon ground beef mixture into biscuit-lined cups. Sprinkle with cheese.

3 Bake about 12 minutes or until biscuit edges are golden. Loosen and carefully remove from muffin cups. Serve warm.

NUTRITION FACTS PER SERVING:
483 cal., 24 g total fat (10 g sat. fat), 76 mg chol., 1,011 mg sodium, 44 g carb., 1 g dietary fiber, 22 g protein.

Beef and Bean Stir-Fry

START TO FINISH 25 minutes MAKES 4 servings

2   tablespoons vegetable oil
1   pound boneless beef top loin
    steak, trimmed and cut into
    thin strips
2   cloves garlic, minced
1   teaspoon grated fresh ginger
3½ cups broccoli florets
2   carrots, thinly
    diagonally sliced
6   green onions, cut into long
    thin strips
¼   cup orange juice concentrate,
    thawed, or orange juice
2   tablespoons reduced-sodium
    soy sauce
¼   teaspoon crushed red pepper
1   15-ounce can cannellini beans
    (white kidney beans) rinsed
    and drained

1 In a 12-inch skillet with flared sides or a large wok heat 1 tablespoon of the oil over medium-high heat. Add beef, garlic, and ginger; cook and stir for 2 to 3 minutes or until beef is brown. Remove from skillet. In the same skillet heat the remaining 1 tablespoon oil. Add broccoli and carrots; cook and stir for 3 minutes. Add green onions; cook for 1 minute more.

2 Add orange juice concentrate, soy sauce, and crushed red pepper; toss to coat. Add cooked beef and beans; cook until heated through.

NUTRITION FACTS PER SERVING:
470 cal., 28 g total fat (9 g sat. fat), 76 mg chol., 557 mg sodium, 30 g carb., 8 g dietary fiber, 31 g protein.

255

Sweet-and-Spicy Edamame-Beef Stir-Fry

START TO FINISH **30 minutes** MAKES **4 servings**

8   ounces beef sirloin steak

4   teaspoons canola oil

2   teaspoons grated fresh ginger

2   cups broccoli florets

1   cup red and/or yellow sweet pepper strips

1   cup frozen shelled sweet soybeans (edamame)

3   tablespoons hoisin sauce

2   tablespoons rice vinegar

1   teaspoon red chili paste

2   cups hot cooked brown or white rice

1 If desired, partially freeze meat for easier slicing. Trim fat from steak. Thinly slice steak across the grain into bite-size strips; set aside.

2 In a nonstick wok or large skillet heat 2 teaspoons of the oil over medium-high heat. Add ginger; cook and stir for 15 seconds. Add broccoli and sweet pepper. Cook and stir about 4 minutes or until crisp-tender. Remove vegetables from wok.

3 Add the remaining 2 teaspoons oil to wok. Add meat and edamame; cook and stir about 2 minutes or until meat is desired doneness. Return vegetables to wok.

4 In a small bowl combine hoisin, vinegar, and chili paste. Add to meat mixture; toss to coat. Heat through. Serve over hot cooked rice.

NUTRITION FACTS PER SERVING: *340 cal., 11 g total fat (2 g sat. fat), 24 mg chol., 262 mg sodium, 38 g carb., 6 g dietary fiber, 22 g protein.*

Skillet Pot Roast with Mushrooms and Cherries

START TO FINISH **30 minutes** MAKES **4 to 6 servings**

1 **12-ounce package frozen unsweetened pitted dark sweet cherries**

1 **tablespoon olive oil or vegetable oil**

1 **8-ounce package fresh mushrooms, halved**

1 **medium red sweet pepper, seeded and cut into bite-size strips**

1 **cup chopped onion (1 large)**

2 **teaspoons dried sage or thyme, crushed**

2 **16- or 17-ounce packages refrigerated cooked beef pot roast with juices**

2 **tablespoons balsamic vinegar**

1 Place frozen cherries in a colander in sink. Run cold water over cherries to partially thaw. Drain well; set aside.

2 In a 12-inch skillet heat oil over medium heat. Add mushrooms, sweet pepper, onion, and 1 teaspoon of the sage; cook about 7 minutes or until tender. Add roast and juices, cherries, and balsamic vinegar to skillet. Bring to boiling; reduce heat. Simmer, uncovered, about 10 minutes or until heated through and juices thicken slightly, stirring occasionally. Stir in the remaining 1 teaspoon sage.

NUTRITION FACTS PER SERVING: *451 cal., 18 g total fat (7 g sat. fat), 120 mg chol., 727 mg sodium, 27 g carb., 4 g dietary fiber, 49 g protein.*

Mexican Beef and Veggies

START TO FINISH 30 minutes   MAKES 4 to 6 servings

1   medium butternut squash
    (1¼ pounds), peeled, seeded,
    and cubed (about 3 cups)

12 ounces lean ground beef

2   cloves garlic, minced

1   teaspoon ground cumin

½   teaspoon salt

⅛   teaspoon ground cinnamon

1   14.5-ounce can diced
    tomatoes, undrained

1   medium zucchini, halved
    lengthwise and cut into
    ¼-inch slices

¼   cup water

¼   cup snipped fresh cilantro

2   to 3 cups hot cooked white
    rice or brown rice

    Bottled hot pepper
    sauce (optional)

1 In a large skillet cook butternut squash, meat, garlic, cumin, salt, and cinnamon over medium heat until meat is brown, using a wooden spoon to break up meat as it cooks. Drain off fat.

2 Stir tomatoes into meat mixture. Bring to boiling; reduce heat. Simmer, covered, about 8 minutes or just until butternut squash is tender. Stir in zucchini and the water. Simmer, covered, about 4 minutes more or until zucchini is tender. Stir in cilantro. Serve over hot cooked rice. If desired, season to taste with bottled hot pepper sauce.

NUTRITION FACTS PER SERVING:
*313 cal., 9 g total fat (3 g sat. fat),
54 mg chol., 504 mg sodium, 39 g carb.,
3 g dietary fiber, 20 g protein.*

Herbed Steaks with Horseradish

START TO FINISH **20 minutes** MAKES **4 servings**

2 **12- to 14-ounce beef top loin steaks, cut 1 inch thick**
   Salt
   Ground black pepper
2 **tablespoons prepared horseradish**
1 **tablespoon Dijon-style mustard**
2 **teaspoons snipped fresh Italian (flat-leaf) parsley**
1 **teaspoon snipped fresh thyme**
   Broiled cherry tomatoes (optional)
   Broiled sweet pepper strips (optional)

1 Preheat broiler. Season steaks with salt and black pepper. Place steaks on the unheated rack of a broiler pan. Broil 4 inches from heat for 7 minutes. Meanwhile, in a small bowl combine horseradish, mustard, parsley, and thyme.

2 Turn steaks. Broil for 8 to 9 minutes more or to medium doneness (160°F). For the last 1 minute of broiling, spread horseradish mixture over steaks. If desired, serve with tomatoes and sweet peppers.

NUTRITION FACTS PER SERVING: *284 cal., 15 g total fat (6 g sat. fat), 84 mg chol., 351 mg sodium, 1 g carb., 0 g dietary fiber, 33 g protein.*

Espresso-Rubbed Steak with Green Chile Pesto ⏱ 🥕

START TO FINISH **30 minutes**   MAKES **8 servings**

- 1   **1½-pound beef flank steak**
- 2   **teaspoons chili powder**
- 1   **teaspoon kosher salt or regular salt**
- 1   **teaspoon instant espresso coffee powder**
- ½   **teaspoon garlic powder**
- ½   **teaspoon dried oregano, crushed**
- ½   **teaspoon ground black pepper**
     Nonstick cooking spray
- 1   **recipe Green Chile Pesto**

1 Trim fat from steak. Score both sides of steak in a diamond pattern by making shallow diagonal cuts at 1-inch intervals. In a small bowl stir together chili powder, salt, espresso powder, garlic powder, oregano, and pepper. Sprinkle chili powder mixture evenly over steak; rub in with your fingers.

2 Coat a large nonstick skillet with cooking spray; heat over medium-high heat until very hot. Add steak; reduce heat to medium. Cook to desired doneness, turning once halfway through cooking. Allow 12 to 14 minutes for medium-rare (145°F) or 14 to 16 minutes for medium (160°F). Transfer to a cutting board. Cover with foil; let stand for 10 minutes before slicing.

3 Meanwhile, prepare Green Chile Pesto. To serve, thinly slice steak against grain. Pass Green Chile Pesto.

NUTRITION FACTS PER SERVING: *244 cal., 17 g total fat (3 g sat. fat), 31 mg chol., 335 mg sodium, 4 g carb., 1 g dietary fiber, 20 g protein.*

Green Chile Pesto

Halve 2 medium fresh Anaheim or poblano chile peppers lengthwise; remove stems, seeds, and veins.* Coarsely chop peppers. In a food processor combine peppers, ½ cup fresh cilantro leaves, ¼ cup crumbled Cotija cheese, 2 tablespoons pine nuts, 2 cloves garlic, ¼ teaspoon crushed red pepper, dash salt, and dash ground black pepper. Cover and process to finely chop mixture. With the processor running, add ⅓ cup olive oil in a steady stream through feed tube; process until mixture is a coarse paste. Makes about 1⅓ cups pesto.

*tip

Because chile peppers contain volatile oils that can burn your skin and eyes, avoid direct contact with them as much as possible. When working with chile peppers, wear plastic or rubber gloves. If your bare hands do not touch the peppers, wash your hands and nails well with soap and warm water.

Pan-Fried Garlic Steak with White Beans

START TO FINISH **20 minutes** MAKES **4 servings**

4 **4- to 5-ounce beef rib-eye steaks, cut $\frac{1}{2}$ inch thick**

Olive oil

Salt

Ground black pepper

6 **cloves garlic, peeled and thinly sliced**

2 **tablespoons butter**

1 **15- to 19-ounce can cannellini beans (white kidney beans) rinsed and drained**

$\frac{1}{4}$ **cup snipped fresh Italian (flat-leaf) parsley**

1 Drizzle steaks lightly with olive oil; sprinkle with salt and pepper.

2 Heat a 12-inch heavy skillet over medium-high heat. Add steaks; reduce heat to medium. Cook steaks to desired doneness, turning once halfway through cooking. Allow 6 to 8 minutes for medium-rare (145°F). Remove steaks from skillet; cover and keep warm. Add garlic to skillet; cook and stir about 1 minute or until softened; remove from skillet.

3 Add butter to skillet; stir in beans. Heat through. Add parsley; cook for 1 minute more. Top steaks with garlic. Serve with bean mixture.

NUTRITION FACTS PER SERVING:
326 cal., 18 g total fat (7 g sat. fat), 81 mg chol., 415 mg sodium, 16 g carb., 5 g dietary fiber, 29 g protein.

261

Steak and Mushrooms ⏱🥕

START TO FINISH **30 minutes**   MAKES **4 servings**

4   beef tenderloin steaks, cut 1 inch thick (about 1 pound total)

Salt

Ground black pepper

1   tablespoon olive oil

1   8-ounce package sliced fresh mushrooms

1   medium green sweet pepper, seeded and cut into thin strips

½   cup chopped red onion (1 medium)

1   tablespoon bottled minced garlic

¼   cup beef broth

¼   cup whipping cream

1 Season meat lightly with salt and pepper. In a large skillet heat oil over medium-high heat until very hot. Add steaks; reduce heat to medium. Cook for 10 to 13 minutes or to desired doneness, turning once. Transfer steaks to a serving platter; cover and keep warm.

2 In the same skillet cook and stir mushrooms, sweet pepper, red onion, and garlic over medium-high heat about 6 minutes or until tender and most of the liquid has evaporated. Stir in broth and cream. Bring to boiling; reduce heat to medium. Boil gently, uncovered, about 4 minutes or until slightly thickened, stirring occasionally. Spoon mushroom mixture over steaks.

NUTRITION FACTS PER SERVING:
298 cal., 18 g total fat (7 g sat. fat), 90 mg chol., 191 mg sodium, 7 g carb., 1 g dietary fiber, 26 g protein.

Hanger Steak with Asian Noodles

START TO FINISH **25 minutes** MAKES **4 servings**

- ½ **cup beef broth**
- ¼ **cup water**
- ¼ **cup reduced-sodium soy sauce**
- 1 **tablespoon oyster sauce***
- 1 **tablespoon rice vinegar**
- 2 **teaspoons cornstarch**
- 1 **teaspoon sugar**
- 1 **1½-pound beef hanger steak****
- ¼ **teaspoon salt**
- 2 **tablespoons cream sherry**
- ⅓ **cup chopped green onions**
- 1 **tablespoon grated fresh ginger**
- 2 **cloves garlic, minced**
- 3 **cups hot cooked ramen noodles or rice**
- **Radish strips (optional)**
- **Sliced green onions (optional)**

1 In a small bowl combine broth, the water, soy sauce, oyster sauce, vinegar, cornstarch, and sugar; set aside. Trim fat from steak. Sprinkle steak with salt.

2 For a charcoal grill, grill steak on the rack of an uncovered grill directly over medium-hot coals about 10 minutes or until medium (160°F), turning once halfway through grilling. (For a gas grill, preheat grill. Reduce heat to medium-high. Place steak on grill rack over heat. Cover and grill as above.)

3 Meanwhile, for sauce, in a saucepan bring sherry to simmering over medium heat; simmer for 1 minute. Stir in the ⅓ cup green onions, the ginger, and garlic; simmer for 1 minute. Add broth mixture; simmer about 2 minutes more or until slightly thickened. Cool slightly.

4 Thinly slice steak diagonally across the grain. Serve sliced meat with sauce and hot cooked noodles. If desired, garnish with radish strips and additional green onions.

NUTRITION FACTS PER SERVING: *438 cal., 10 g total fat (4 g sat. fat), 56 mg chol., 1,442 mg sodium, 40 g carb., 1 g dietary fiber, 42 g protein.*

263

*tip
Oyster sauce—a thick, dark concoction made from a concentrated mixture of oysters, brine, and soy sauce—brings richness and a sweet-smoky flavor to recipes. It can also be used as a condiment.

**tip
Hanger steak, part of the diaphragm that hangs between the last rib and the loin, is sometimes known as butcher's steak because butchers tended to set aside the intensely flavored but not well-known cut for themselves. Hanger steak is better known in France (as onglet) than in the United States, so you might have to ask your butcher to cut it for you. You can substitute flank steak or skirt steak.

Flat-Iron Steak with BBQ Beans ☆

START TO FINISH **20 minutes** MAKES **4 servings**

2 **boneless beef shoulder top blade (flat-iron) steaks, halved (1 to 1¼ pounds total)**

2 **teaspoons fajita seasoning**

1 **15-ounce can black beans, rinsed and drained**

⅓ **cup barbecue sauce**

2 **to 3 medium tomatoes, sliced**

Pickled jalapeño chile pepper slices (optional)

1 Lightly grease a grill pan; heat the pan over medium-high heat. Trim fat from steaks. Sprinkle steaks with fajita seasoning. Place steaks on hot grill pan; grill until desired doneness, turning once. Allow 8 to 12 minutes for medium-rare (145°F) or 12 to 15 minutes for medium (160°F). Remove steaks from pan. Cover with foil; let stand for 5 minutes.

2 Meanwhile, in a medium microwave-safe bowl stir together beans and barbecue sauce. Cover loosely with plastic wrap. Microwave on 100 percent power (high) about 3 minutes or until heated through, stirring once.

3 Serve steaks with beans and sliced tomatoes. If desired, garnish with pickled jalapeño chile pepper slices.

NUTRITION FACTS PER SERVING:
305 cal., 11 g total fat (4 g sat. fat), 74 mg chol., 678 mg sodium, 25 g carb., 6 g dietary fiber, 29 g protein.

Flat-Iron Steak with Avocado Butter

START TO FINISH **30 minutes**   MAKES **6 servings**

6   boneless beef shoulder top
     blade (flat-iron) steaks or
     boneless rib-eye steaks, cut
     ³/₄ inch thick
1   tablespoon olive oil
1   tablespoon herbes de
     Provence, crushed
¹/₂ teaspoon salt
¹/₂ teaspoon freshly ground
     black pepper
1   recipe Avocado Butter

1 Trim fat from steaks. Brush steaks with the olive oil. For rub, in a small bowl combine herbes de Provence, salt, and pepper. Sprinkle evenly over both sides of each steak; rub in with your fingers.

2 For a charcoal grill, grill steaks on the rack of an uncovered grill directly over medium coals for 7 to 9 minutes for medium-rare (145°F) or 10 to 12 minutes for medium (160°F), turning once halfway through grilling. (For a gas grill, preheat grill. Reduce heat to medium. Place steaks on the grill rack over heat. Cover and grill as above.) Serve steaks with Avocado Butter.

Avocado Butter

Halve, seed, peel, and chop 1 ripe avocado. In a medium bowl combine the chopped avocado, ¹/₄ cup softened butter, 3 tablespoons lime juice, 2 tablespoons snipped fresh chervil or parsley, 1 tablespoon snipped fresh tarragon, ¹/₄ teaspoon salt, and, if desired, ¹/₈ teaspoon cayenne pepper. Using a fork, gently mash the ingredients together until thoroughly combined (if desired, leave mixture somewhat chunky). Spoon mixture into a small bowl; chill until almost firm.

NUTRITION FACTS PER SERVING:
369 cal., 25 g total fat (10 g sat. fat), 109 mg chol., 463 mg sodium, 3 g carb., 2 g dietary fiber, 33 g protein.

265

Wine-Balsamic Glazed Steak ⏱

START TO FINISH **30 minutes** MAKES **4 servings**

- 2 teaspoons vegetable oil
- 4 boneless beef top loin or top sirloin steaks, cut $\frac{1}{2}$ to $\frac{3}{4}$ inch thick ($1\frac{1}{2}$ to 2 pounds total)
- 3 cloves garlic, minced
- $\frac{1}{8}$ teaspoon crushed red pepper
- $\frac{3}{4}$ cup dry red wine
- 2 cups sliced fresh mushrooms
- 3 tablespoons balsamic vinegar
- 2 tablespoons soy sauce
- 4 teaspoons honey
- 2 tablespoons butter

1 In a large skillet heat oil over medium-high heat. Add steaks; reduce heat to medium. Cook for 10 to 13 minutes or to desired doneness, turning occasionally. If meat browns too quickly, reduce heat to medium low. Transfer meat to serving platter; cover and keep warm.

2 Add garlic and crushed red pepper to skillet; cook for 10 seconds. Remove skillet from heat. Carefully add wine; return to heat. Boil gently, uncovered, about 5 minutes or until most of the liquid is evaporated. Add mushrooms, vinegar, soy sauce, and honey; return to simmering. Cook and stir about 4 minutes or until mushrooms are tender. Add butter, stirring until melted. Spoon over steaks.

NUTRITION FACTS PER SERVING:
535 cal., 33 g total fat (14 g sat. fat), 110 mg chol., 633 mg sodium, 13 g carb., 1 g dietary fiber, 37 g protein.

Beef, Mushroom, and Onion Tart

START TO FINISH **30 minutes**   OVEN **425°F**   MAKES **4 servings**

12   ounces lean ground beef

1   8-ounce package sliced fresh mushrooms

½   of a medium red onion, cut into thin wedges

¼   teaspoon salt

¼   teaspoon ground black pepper

1   13.8-ounce package refrigerated pizza dough

3   ounces blue cheese, crumbled

   Fresh oregano and/or pizza seasoning (optional)

1 Preheat oven to 425°F. In a 12-inch skillet cook meat, mushrooms, and red onion over medium heat about 8 minutes or until meat is brown and onion is tender, using a wooden spoon to break up meat as it cooks. Drain off fat. Stir in salt and pepper.

2 Meanwhile, grease a large baking sheet or line with parchment. Unroll pizza dough on baking sheet. Roll or pat dough to a 15×12-inch rectangle. Top dough with beef mixture, keeping filling within 1½ inches of all edges. Fold edges over the filling, pleating as needed.

3 Bake about 15 minutes or until crust is golden. Top with blue cheese. If desired, sprinkle with oregano and/or pizza seasoning.

NUTRITION FACTS PER SERVING:
525 cal., 23 g total fat (10 g sat. fat), 74 mg chol., 1,041 mg sodium, 49 g carb., 2 g dietary fiber, 31 g protein.

267

Veal Scaloppine with Marsala ⏱ 🥕

START TO FINISH 25 minutes MAKES 4 servings

- 4 tablespoons butter
- 3 cups fresh mushrooms, quartered, halved, or sliced
- ½ cup sliced green onions (4)
- ¼ teaspoon salt
- ¼ teaspoon ground black pepper
- 1 pound veal scaloppine*
- ¾ cup dry Marsala or dry sherry
- ⅓ cup chicken broth
- 2 tablespoons snipped fresh Italian (flat-leaf) parsley

  Hot cooked pasta and/or Italian bread (optional)

1 In an extra-large skillet heat 2 tablespoons of the butter over medium heat until melted. Add mushrooms and green onions. Cook for 4 to 5 minutes or until tender. Remove from skillet; set aside.

2 Sprinkle salt and pepper over veal. In the same skillet heat remaining 2 tablespoons butter over medium-high heat until melted. Cook veal, half at time if necessary about 2 minutes or until light brown, turning once. Transfer veal to four warm dinner plates; cover and keep warm.

3 Add Marsala and broth to drippings in skillet. Bring to boiling; reduce heat. Simmer, uncovered, for 2 to 3 minutes, stirring to scrape up any browned bits. Return mushroom mixture to skillet. Stir in parsley; heat through.

4 To serve, spoon mushroom mixture over veal. If desired, serve with hot cooked pasta and/or Italian bread.

NUTRITION FACTS PER SERVING:
311 cal., 15 g total fat (8 g sat. fat), 119 mg chol., 373 mg sodium, 7 g carb., 1 g dietary fiber, 27 g protein.

*tip

Veal scaloppine is very thinly sliced veal. If you like, you can substitute chicken. Horizontally halve 4 skinless, boneless chicken breast halves. Place each chicken breast half between two pieces of plastic wrap. Using the flat side of a meat mallet, pound chicken lightly, working from the center to the edges, until about ⅛ inch thick and the breast half is rectangular. Remove plastic wrap.

★ Crispy Baked Pork Chops and Potatoes

START TO FINISH **30 minutes** OVEN **425°F** MAKES **4 servings**

1   egg
2   tablespoons fat-free milk
1   cup packaged corn bread
    stuffing mix, crushed
4   bone-in pork loin chops,
    cut $\frac{1}{2}$ inch thick (1 to
    $1\frac{1}{2}$ pounds total)
    Salt
    Ground black pepper
1   20-ounce package frozen
    roasted potato pieces

1 Preheat oven to 425°F. In a shallow dish beat egg with a fork; stir in milk. Place crushed stuffing mix in another shallow dish. Trim fat from chops. Sprinkle chops with salt and pepper. Dip chops into egg mixture. Coat both sides with stuffing mix.

2 Arrange chops in a single layer in one side of a 15×10×1-inch baking pan. Add potato pieces to the other side of the same pan, mounding potatoes as needed to fit.

3 Bake for 20 to 25 minutes or until chops are slightly pink in centers and juices run clear (160°F) and potatoes are lightly browned and crisp, turning pork and stirring potatoes once.

NUTRITION FACTS PER SERVING: *442 cal., 18 g total fat (4 g sat. fat), 92 mg chol., 1,407 mg sodium, 51 g carb., 2 g dietary fiber, 18 g protein.*

Apple-Pecan Pork Chops

START TO FINISH **20 minutes** MAKES **4 servings**

- **4** **boneless pork loin chops, cut ¾ to 1 inch thick**
- **Salt**
- **Ground black pepper**
- **2** **tablespoons butter**
- **1** **medium red apple, cored and thinly sliced**
- **¼** **cup pecan halves**
- **2** **tablespoons packed brown sugar**

1 Trim fat from chops. Sprinkle chops with salt and pepper; set aside.

2 In a large skillet melt butter over medium heat until it sizzles. Add apples; cook and stir for 2 minutes. Push apples to side of skillet. Add chops; cook for 4 minutes. Turn chops, moving apples aside as needed. Spoon apples over chops. Sprinkle with pecans and brown sugar.

3 Cook, covered, for 4 to 8 minutes more or until chops are slightly pink in centers and juices run clear (160°F). Serve apples and cooking juices over chops.

NUTRITION FACTS PER SERVING: *250 cal., 13 g total fat (5 g sat. fat), 66 mg chol., 360 mg sodium, 12 g carb., 1 g dietary fiber, 22 g protein.*

Pork Chops and Squash

4   **bone-in pork loin chops, cut
    ³⁄₄ inch thick**

4   **small zucchini and/or yellow
    summer squash, halved
    lengthwise**

1   **tablespoon olive oil**

    Salt

    Ground black pepper

1   **orange, peeled and chopped**

½   **cup chipotle salsa**

1 Brush chops and squash lightly with olive oil; sprinkle with salt and pepper. For a charcoal grill, grill chops and squash, cut sides down, directly over medium coals until chops are slightly pink in centers and juices run clear (160°F) and squash are tender, turning once halfway through grilling. Allow 11 to 13 minutes for chops and 6 to 8 minutes for squash. (For gas grill, preheat grill. Reduce heat to medium. Place chops and squash, cut sides down, on grill rack over heat. Cover and grill as above.)

2 Meanwhile, stir together chopped orange and salsa. Cut grilled squash into bite-size pieces; serve with chops. Spoon orange mixture over chops.

NUTRITION FACTS PER SERVING:
*268 cal., 14 g total fat (4 g sat. fat),
78 mg chol., 340 mg sodium, 10 g carb.,
3 g dietary fiber, 26 g protein.*

Beef, Pork, and Lamb

Smoked Pork Chops with Mustard-Dill Sauce

START TO FINISH 25 minutes   MAKES 6 servings

6   smoked pork loin chops, cut
     1 inch thick
3   tablespoons packed brown
     sugar
3   tablespoons cider vinegar or
     white wine vinegar
1/2 cup Dijon-style mustard
3   tablespoons olive oil
1/2 teaspoon dried dill
     Dash ground black pepper

1 Preheat broiler. Place chops on the unheated rack of a broiler pan. Broil 3 to 4 inches from the heat for 9 to 12 minutes or until heated through, turning once halfway through broiling.

2 Meanwhile, for sauce, in a small bowl combine brown sugar and vinegar, stirring until sugar dissolves. Whisk in mustard, oil, dill, and pepper until well mixed. Transfer warm chops to a serving platter. Drizzle chops with some of the sauce. Pass the remaining sauce.

NUTRITION FACTS PER SERVING:
208 cal., 11 g total fat (2 g sat. fat),
45 mg chol., 1,453 mg sodium, 7 g carb.,
0 g dietary fiber, 15 g protein.

Quick Skillet Lasagna page 228

273

Shrimp Pasta Diavolo page 219

Coconut Chicken Pasta page 209

274

Caprese Pasta and Steak
page 250

275

Mediterranean Lamb Skillet **page 310**

Chicken and Pasta Primavera **page 225**

276

Hanger Steaks with Asian Noodles **page 263**

Jerk Chicken and Pineapple Slaw **page 319**

Bacon and Blue Cheese
Dinner Pies

page 307

Wine-Balsamic Glazed Steak
page 266

278

Quick Chicken Pot Pie
page 331

279

280

Lemony Cod with Asparagus page 341

Mexican Shrimp Tostadas page 367

Simple Salmon, Greens, and Couscous page 349

Curried Sea Scallops
page 372

Cowboy Steak and Whiskey Butter
page 384

283

Crab-Fennel Salad
page 374

Apricot-Glazed Pork Chop Skillet

START TO FINISH **25 minutes**   MAKES **4 servings**

1   to 1½ pounds boneless pork sirloin chops, cut ½ inch thick

⅛   teaspoon salt

⅛   teaspoon ground black pepper

1   tablespoon olive oil

2   medium apricots, cut into thin wedges

1   teaspoon snipped fresh rosemary

¼   cup reduced-sodium chicken broth

2   tablespoons orange juice

1   tablespoon apricot spreadable fruit

1   tablespoon reduced-sodium teriyaki sauce

1 Trim fat from chops, if necessary. Sprinkle chops with salt and pepper. In a 12-inch skillet heat oil over medium-high heat. Add chops to skillet. Reduce heat to medium; cook for 8 to 10 minutes or until slightly pink in centers and juices run clear (160°F), turning once halfway through cooking and adding apricots and rosemary to the skillet for the last 3 minutes of cooking. Turn apricots occasionally during cooking. Transfer chops and apricots to a serving platter; cover and keep warm.

2 In a small bowl combine broth, orange juice, spreadable fruit, and teriyaki sauce. Add to hot skillet, stirring to scrape up any browned bits. Bring to boiling; reduce heat. Simmer, uncovered, about 1 minute or until slightly thickened. Serve over chops and apricots.

NUTRITION FACTS PER SERVING:
201 cal., 8 g total fat (2 g sat. fat), 71 mg chol., 230 mg sodium, 6 g carb., 0 g dietary fiber, 25 g protein.

Glazed Teriyaki Pork Chops with Potatoes ⏱

START TO FINISH **30 minutes** MAKES **4 servings**

4   **boneless pork loin chops, cut**
     ³⁄₄ inch thick

¹⁄₄ **cup teriyaki glaze**

12   **ounces tiny new potatoes,**
     quartered

1   **tablespoon olive oil**

1   **tablespoon toasted sesame oil**

¹⁄₄ **teaspoon salt**

¹⁄₈ **teaspoon ground black pepper**

1   **cup fresh snow pea pods,**
     halved lengthwise

     Teriyaki glaze

1 Preheat broiler. Brush all sides of chops with ¹⁄₄ cup teriyaki glaze. Arrange chops on half of the unheated rack of a broiler pan; set aside.

2 In a large bowl add potatoes, olive oil, sesame oil, salt, and pepper; toss to coat. Arrange potatoes in a single layer on rack next to chops.

3 Broil 4 inches from heat for 9 to 11 minutes or until chops are slightly pink in centers and juices run clear (160°F) and potatoes are tender, turning chops and potatoes once.

4 Place pea pods in a large bowl. Add potatoes and toss to combine. Serve chops with potatoes and pea pods. Pass additional teriyaki glaze.

NUTRITION FACTS PER SERVING: *394 cal., 15 g total fat (4 g sat. fat), 86 mg chol., 626 mg sodium, 23 g carb., 2 g dietary fiber, 38 g protein.*

Skillet Pork Chops with Apples

START TO FINISH 25 minutes   MAKES 4 servings

4 **boneless pork loin chops, cut ³⁄₄ inch thick (about 1¹⁄₄ pounds total)**

Salt

Ground black pepper

2 **tablespoons canola oil**

2 **medium onions, sliced and separated into rings (about 1 cup)**

1 **teaspoon dried marjoram, crushed**

2 **to 4 teaspoons coarse-grain brown mustard or Dijon-style mustard**

2 **red and/or green cooking apples, cored and cut into thin wedges**

1 Season pork chops with salt and pepper. In a large skillet heat oil over medium-high heat. Add chops; cook for 4 minutes, turning once. Remove chops from skillet, reserving drippings in skillet.

2 Cook onion rings in reserved drippings over medium heat for 4 to 5 minutes or until crisp-tender, stirring occasionally. Reduce heat to medium low. Sprinkle onions with about half of the marjoram. Place chops on onions in skillet. Spread mustard over chops. Arrange apple wedges around and on top of chops; sprinkle chops and apples with the remaining marjoram.

3 Cook, covered, for 5 to 8 minutes or until chops are slightly pink in centers and juices run clear (160°F). Serve apples, onions, and cooking juices with chops.

NUTRITION FACTS PER SERVING:
313 cal., 12 g total fat (2 g sat. fat), 94 mg chol., 278 mg sodium, 18 g carb., 3 g dietary fiber, 33 g protein.

291

tip

Certain kinds of apples are better for cooking than others because they keep their shape and don't turn mushy when exposed to heat. Good apple options for this skillet dish include Golden Delicious, Granny Smith, Jonathan, or Rome Beauty.

Beef, Pork, and Lamb

Southwest Pork Chops

START TO FINISH **30 minutes** MAKES **6 servings**

6 **bone-in pork rib chops, cut
   3/4 inch thick (about
   2 1/2 pounds total)**

   Nonstick cooking spray

1 **15-ounce can Mexican-style or
   Tex-Mex-style chili beans**

1 **cup salsa**

1 **cup frozen whole kernel corn**

3 **cups hot cooked rice**

   **Snipped fresh cilantro
   (optional)**

1 Trim fat from chops. Coat an unheated 12-inch nonstick skillet with cooking spray. Heat skillet over medium-high heat. Add chops, three at a time if necessary; cook about 4 minutes or until brown, turning once. Remove chops from skillet.

2 Add chili beans, salsa, and corn to skillet; stir to combine. Place chops on top of bean mixture. Bring to boiling; reduce heat. Simmer, covered, for 15 to 20 minutes or until chops are slightly pink in centers and juices run clear (160°F). Serve over hot cooked rice. If desired, sprinkle with cilantro.

NUTRITION FACTS PER SERVING: *379 cal., 10 g total fat (3 g sat. fat), 71 mg chol., 490 mg sodium, 38 g carb., 5 g dietary fiber, 33 g protein.*

Pork Chops with Black Bean Salsa

START TO FINISH **30 minutes** MAKES **4 servings**

4   **bone-in pork loin chops, cut 1$\frac{1}{4}$ inches thick (about 3 pounds total)**

1   **teaspoon Jamaican jerk seasoning or Cajun seasoning**

$\frac{1}{8}$ **teaspoon ground black pepper**

$\frac{3}{4}$ **cup canned black beans, rinsed and drained ($\frac{1}{2}$ of a 15-ounce can)**

$\frac{2}{3}$ **cup corn relish**

1$\frac{1}{2}$ **teaspoons lime juice**

$\frac{1}{4}$ **teaspoon ground cumin**

    Sour cream (optional)

1 Preheat broiler. Trim fat from chops. Sprinkle Jamaican jerk seasoning and pepper evenly over all sides of chops; rub in with your fingers. Place chops on the unheated rack of a broiler pan. Broil 3 to 4 inches from the heat for 16 to 20 minutes or until slightly pink in centers and juices run clear (160°F), turning once halfway through broiling.

2 Meanwhile, for salsa, in a small bowl combine black beans, corn relish, lime juice, and cumin. Serve chops with salsa and, if desired, sour cream.

NUTRITION FACTS PER SERVING:
442 cal., 9 g total fat (3 g sat. fat), 185 mg chol., 457 mg sodium, 20 g carb., 2 g dietary fiber, 66 g protein.

293

Grilled Pork Chops with Chile Rub and Chutney ⏱ 🥕

START TO FINISH **30 minutes** MAKES **4 servings**

1 tablespoon olive oil

1 medium sweet onion, such as Vidalia or Maui, thinly sliced

½ teaspoon cumin seeds

¼ teaspoon sea salt

4 bone-in pork loin chops,* cut ¾ inch thick (about 2 pounds total)

1 large canned chipotle chile pepper in adobo sauce, finely chopped**

2 oranges, peeled, seeded, and sectioned

¼ cup orange juice

1 In a large skillet heat olive oil over medium heat. Add onion, cumin seeds, and sea salt. Cook for 12 to 15 minutes or until onion is tender and golden, stirring occasionally.

2 Meanwhile, trim fat from chops. Rub chile pepper onto chops.** For a charcoal grill, grill chops on the rack of an uncovered grill directly over medium coals for 11 to 13 minutes or until chops are slightly pink in centers and juices run clear (160°F), turning once halfway through grilling. (For a gas grill, preheat grill; reduce heat to medium. Place chops on grill rack over heat. Cover and grill as above.)

3 Stir orange sections and orange juice into onion mixture. Heat to boiling; reduce heat. Simmer, uncovered, for 5 minutes, stirring occasionally. Serve over grilled chops.

NUTRITION FACTS PER SERVING: *289 cal., 14 g total fat (4 g sat. fat), 78 mg chol., 207 mg sodium, 16 g carb., 3 g dietary fiber, 25 g protein.*

294

*tip

If using pork chops that have not been injected with a sodium solution, sprinkle chops with ¼ teaspoon salt before grilling.

**tip

Because chile peppers contain volatile oils that can burn your skin and eyes, avoid direct contact with them as much as possible. When working with chile peppers, wear plastic or rubber gloves. If your bare hands do touch the peppers, wash your hands and nails well with soap and warm water.

Grilled Pork Tenderloin with Pineapple-Bean Salsa

START TO FINISH 30 minutes   MAKES 4 servings

1	1¼-pound pork tenderloin
¾	cup light lime vinaigrette dressing
½	teaspoon ground cumin
1	10-ounce can pineapple tidbits (juice-pack), drained
1	cup canned black beans, rinsed and drained
½	of a red sweet pepper, finely chopped
⅛	teaspoon salt
⅛	teaspoon ground black pepper

1 Place tenderloin in a large resealable plastic bag. In a glass measuring cup whisk together vinaigrette and cumin. Pour ½ cup of the vinaigrette mixture into bag with pork; reserve the remaining vinaigrette mixture to use in salsa. Let pork stand at room temperature while heating grill.

2 Drain pork, discarding marinade. For a charcoal grill, grill pork over medium-hot coals about 18 minutes or until slightly pink in center and juices run clear (160°F), turning frequently. (For a gas grill, preheat grill. Reduce heat to medium-high. Place pork on grill rack over heat. Cover and grill as above.)

3 Meanwhile, for salsa, in a small bowl stir together pineapple, black beans, sweet pepper, salt, and black pepper. Stir in the reserved vinaigrette mixture. Serve salsa with pork.

NUTRITION FACTS PER SERVING:
290 cal., 10 g total fat (3 g sat. fat), 94 mg chol., 763 mg sodium, 25 g carb., 4 g dietary fiber, 32 g protein.

Ginger Pork Stir-Fry

START TO FINISH **30 minutes** MAKES **4 servings**

1 tablespoon vegetable oil

1 small onion, cut into thin wedges

2 cloves garlic, minced

8 ounces boneless pork loin, cut into bite-size strips, or cubed firm tofu (fresh bean curd)

2 medium carrots, thinly bias-sliced

1½ cups fresh snow pea pods

1 tablespoon sesame seeds

2 tablespoons reduced-sodium soy sauce

1 tablespoon grated fresh ginger

1 teaspoon toasted sesame oil

¼ to ½ teaspoon crushed red pepper

¼ cup plum sauce

¼ cup water

2 to 3 cups hot cooked cellophane noodles, rice vermicelli noodles, or rice

Snipped fresh cilantro and/or chopped roasted cashews (optional)

1 In a wok or large skillet heat vegetable oil over medium-high heat. Add onion and garlic. Cook for 2 minutes. Add pork and carrots; cook for 2 minutes more. Add pea pods and sesame seeds; cook and stir for 3 minutes. Add soy sauce, ginger, sesame oil, and crushed red pepper. Cook and stir for 1 minute. Stir in plum sauce and the water; heat through.

2 Serve over hot cooked noodles. If desired, top with cilantro and/or cashews.

NUTRITION FACTS PER SERVING:
326 cal., 13 g total fat (3 g sat. fat), 34 mg chol., 418 mg sodium, 37 g carb., 3 g dietary fiber, 14 g protein.

Pork and Hash Brown Skillet

START TO FINISH **30 minutes** MAKES **4 servings**

4 **4-ounce boneless pork loin chops, cut $\frac{3}{4}$ inch thick**

$\frac{3}{4}$ **teaspoon seasoned salt**

2 **tablespoons vegetable oil**

$\frac{1}{3}$ **cup chopped onion (1 small)**

1 **medium red sweet pepper, cut into $\frac{3}{4}$-inch pieces**

3 **cups frozen diced hash brown potatoes**

2 **cups frozen peas and carrots**

1 **teaspoon dried thyme, crushed**

1 Sprinkle all sides of chops evenly with $\frac{1}{2}$ teaspoon of the seasoned salt. In a very large skillet heat 1 tablespoon of the oil over medium-high heat. Add chops; cook about 6 minutes or until brown, turning once halfway through cooking. Remove chops from skillet.

2 Carefully add the remaining 1 tablespoon oil to skillet. Add onion and sweet pepper; cook and stir for 1 minute. Stir in potatoes, peas and carrots, thyme, and the remaining $\frac{1}{4}$ teaspoon seasoned salt. Cook for 6 minutes, stirring frequently.

3 Place chops on top of potato mixture in skillet. Reduce heat to medium. Cook, covered, for 6 to 9 minutes or until chops are slightly pink in centers and juices run clear and potatoes are brown.

NUTRITION FACTS PER SERVING:
406 cal., 15 g total fat (3 g sat. fat), 72 mg chol., 422 mg sodium, 39 g carb., 5 g dietary fiber, 29 g protein.

Thai Pork and Vegetable Curry

START TO FINISH 30 minutes MAKES 4 servings

1⅓	cups jasmine rice
12	ounces pork tenderloin or lean boneless pork
	Salt
	Ground black pepper
2	tablespoons vegetable oil
8	ounces green beans, bias-sliced into 1½-inch pieces (2 cups)*
1	red sweet pepper, cut into thin bite-size strips
2	green onions, bias-sliced into ¼-inch pieces
1	14-ounce can unsweetened coconut milk
4	teaspoons curry paste
1	teaspoon sugar
⅛	teaspoon crushed red pepper
1	lime, cut into wedges

1 Cook rice according to package directions; drain. Cover and keep warm.

2 Meanwhile, thinly slice pork into bite-size pieces. Sprinkle with salt and black pepper. In a large nonstick skillet heat 1 tablespoon of the oil over medium-high heat. Add pork; cook and stir about 4 minutes or until no pink remains. Remove from skillet.

3 Add the remaining 1 tablespoon oil to the skillet. Add green beans; cook and stir for 3 minutes. Add sweet pepper and green onions; cook and stir about 2 minutes more or until vegetables are crisp-tender. Remove from skillet. Add coconut milk, curry paste, sugar, and crushed red pepper to skillet. Bring mixture to boiling; reduce heat. Simmer, uncovered, about 2 minutes or until mixture is slightly thickened. Stir in pork and vegetables; heat through. Serve over hot cooked rice. Serve with lime wedges.

NUTRITION FACTS PER SERVING:
490 cal., 16 g total fat (5 g sat. fat), 47 mg chol., 593 mg sodium, 63 g carb., 3 g dietary fiber, 23 g protein.

298

*tip

A 9-ounce package of frozen cut green beans, thawed, can be substituted for the fresh beans. Add them to the skillet along with the sweet pepper and green onions; cook as directed.

Zucchini-Wrapped Pork

START TO FINISH **30 minutes** OVEN **450°F** MAKES **4 servings**

1   **small zucchini**

12   **ounces pork tenderloin**

     Olive oil

     Salt

     Ground black pepper

⅓   **cup basil pesto**

     Small fresh basil leaves (optional)

     Watercress or arugula (optional)

1 Preheat oven to 450°F. Line a 15×10×1-inch baking pan with foil; set aside. With a vegetable peeler* or sharp knife, cut zucchini lengthwise into thin slices (you'll need eight slices). Cut pork tenderloin crosswise into four equal portions. Using the palm of your hand, press each pork portion down to flatten slightly.

2 Wrap each pork portion with two zucchini slices (reserve remaining zucchini for another use). Place in prepared pan. Lightly brush with oil; sprinkle with salt and pepper.

3 Roast for 18 to 20 minutes or until slightly pink in centers and juices run clear. To serve, spoon some of the pesto over each pork portion. If desired, sprinkle with basil leaves. Serve with the remaining pesto and, if desired, watercress.

NUTRITION FACTS PER SERVING: *203 cal., 11 g total fat (2 g sat. fat), 62 mg chol., 382 mg sodium, 4 g carb., 1 g dietary fiber, 21 g protein.*

299

*tip

A vegetable peeler works great for making the zucchini slices. If using a knife, first cut a thin lengthwise piece off so the zucchini lies flat and doesn't roll on the cutting board, then slice thinly.

Jamaican Pork Kabobs

START TO FINISH **30 minutes**   MAKES **4 servings**

2 ears of corn, husked and cleaned, or 2 medium red and/or yellow sweet peppers, seeded and cut into 1-inch pieces

1 12- to 14-ounce pork tenderloin

¼ cup mango chutney, finely chopped

3 tablespoons Pickapeppa sauce*

1 tablespoon vegetable oil

1 tablespoon water

16 baby pattypan squash (each about 1 inch in diameter) or 2 small zucchini or yellow summer squash, halved lengthwise and cut into 1-inch slices

1 small red onion, cut into ½-inch wedges

1 Preheat broiler. Cut ears of corn (if using) crosswise into 1-inch pieces. In a medium saucepan cook corn pieces in a small amount of boiling water for 3 minutes; drain and rinse with cold water.

2 Meanwhile, cut tenderloin into 1-inch slices. In a small bowl combine chutney, Pickapeppa sauce, oil, and the water; set aside.

3 For kabobs, on eight long metal skewers, alternately thread corn or sweet pepper pieces, pork slices, squash, and red onion wedges, leaving a ¼-inch space between pieces.

4 Place kabobs on the unheated rack of a broiler pan. Broil 3 to 4 inches from the heat for 12 to 14 minutes or until no pink remains and the vegetables are tender, turning once halfway through broiling and brushing with the chutney mixture for the last 2 minutes of broiling.

NUTRITION FACTS PER SERVING:
254 cal., 6 g total fat (1 g sat. fat), 50 mg chol., 264 mg sodium, 26 g carb., 3 g dietary fiber, 23 g protein.

300

*tip

If you can't find Pickapeppa sauce, substitute 3 tablespoons Worcestershire sauce mixed with a dash of bottled hot pepper sauce.

Pork Medallions with Broccoli Raab

START TO FINISH **25 minutes**   MAKES **4 servings**

- 2 **tablespoons butter**
- 2 **cups sliced fresh mushrooms**
- 2 **cups chopped broccoli raab, small broccoli florets, or chopped broccolini**
- 12 **ounces pork tenderloin**
  Salt
  Ground black pepper
- 2 **ounces prosciutto or thinly sliced ham, cut into bite-size strips**
- ¼ **cup balsamic vinegar**
- 1 **tablespoon packed brown sugar**

1 In a large skillet heat 1 tablespoon of the butter over medium-high heat until melted. Add mushrooms and broccoli. Cook about 3 minutes or until crisp-tender, stirring occasionally. Remove vegetables from skillet; set aside.

2 Meanwhile, trim fat from pork; cut pork into ½-inch slices. Sprinkle pork slices with salt and pepper. Add the remaining 1 tablespoon butter to skillet. Add pork slices. Cook for 4 to 6 minutes or until juices run clear, turning once.

3 Add prosciutto, vinegar, brown sugar, and vegetables to skillet; heat through.

NUTRITION FACTS PER SERVING:
238 cal., 10 g total fat (5 g sat. fat), 80 mg chol., 559 mg sodium, 10 g carb., 0 g dietary fiber, 25 g protein.

301

Gorgonzola-Sauced Tortellini with Sausage

START TO FINISH 30 minutes   MAKES 4 servings

1   9-ounce package refrigerated spinach-cheese tortellini or three-cheese tortellini

8   ounces bulk sweet or hot Italian sausage

1½ cups cremini, stemmed shiitake, or button mushrooms, sliced (6 ounces)

1   small onion, cut into thin wedges

2   ounces Gorgonzola cheese, crumbled (½ cup)

1   14.5-ounce can diced tomatoes with basil, garlic, and oregano, drained

1   6-ounce jar marinated artichoke hearts, drained and quartered

1   tablespoon finely shredded Parmesan cheese

2   tablespoons thinly sliced fresh basil

1 In a large saucepan cook pasta according to package directions; drain.

2 Meanwhile, in a 3-quart saucepan cook sausage, mushrooms, and onion until sausage is brown and onion is tender, using a wooden spoon to break up meat as it cooks. Drain off fat.

3 Add Gorgonzola cheese; cook and stir over low heat until melted. Gently stir in pasta, tomatoes, and artichokes; heat through. Sprinkle with Parmesan cheese and basil.

NUTRITION FACTS PER SERVING:
464 cal., 24 g total fat (11 g sat. fat), 71 mg chol., 1,384 mg sodium, 37 g carb., 3 g dietary fiber, 23 g protein.

Kielbasa and Sauerkraut Skillet

START TO FINISH **20 minutes** MAKES **4 servings**

1 pound cooked kielbasa, bias-sliced into 2-inch pieces

1 small red onion, thinly sliced

1 15-ounce can sauerkraut, undrained

1 tablespoon coarse-grain brown mustard

¼ to ½ teaspoon caraway seeds

¼ teaspoon salt

¼ teaspoon ground black pepper

1 In a large skillet cook kielbasa pieces and red onion over medium heat just until onion is tender. Stir in sauerkraut, mustard, caraway seeds, salt, and pepper. Cook, covered, about 10 minutes or until heated through.

NUTRITION FACTS PER SERVING:
392 cal., 34 g total fat (16 g sat. fat), 50 mg chol., 1,755 mg sodium, 6 g carb., 2 g dietary fiber, 14 g protein.

303

Beef, Pork, and Lamb

Sausage and Polenta with Balsamic Vinaigrette ⏱

START TO FINISH 30 minutes Oven: 400°F MAKES 4 servings

½ of a 16-ounce tube refrigerated cooked polenta (plain or flavored)

1 tablespoon olive oil

4 uncooked sweet Italian sausage links (about 1 pound total), each cut into 4 pieces

½ cup apple juice or apple cider

¼ cup balsamic vinegar

2 tablespoons snipped dried tomatoes (not oil-pack)

1 8-ounce package mixed salad greens

¼ cup pine nuts or slivered almonds, toasted (optional)

1 Preheat oven to 400°F. Cut polenta crosswise into ¼-inch slices; cut each slice in half. Brush polenta with oil. Arrange in a single layer in a shallow baking pan. Bake about 15 minutes or until light brown, turning once halfway through baking.

2 Meanwhile, in a large skillet cook sausage pieces over medium heat for 5 minutes, turning to brown evenly. Remove sausage from skillet. Drain off fat; wipe skillet with paper towels.

3 Return sausage to skillet; add apple juice, vinegar, and dried tomatoes. Bring to boiling; reduce heat. Simmer, covered, for 8 to 10 minutes or until sausage is cooked through (160°F).

4 To serve, divide greens among four serving plates. Arrange polenta slices and sausage next to greens. Spoon tomato mixture over greens, polenta, and sausage. If desired, sprinkle with nuts.

NUTRITION FACTS PER SERVING: *380 cal., 22 g total fat (8 g sat. fat), 57 mg chol., 741 mg sodium, 23 g carb., 4 g dietary fiber, 15 g protein.*

Polenta, a dish made from cooked cornmeal, is a staple in Italy. To drastically cut preparation time, look for tubes of cooked polenta, available in the refrigerated section of the market. Find it plain or in flavors such as Italian herb or sun-dried tomato.

Pork Loin with Parsnips and Pears

START TO FINISH **30 minutes** MAKES **4 servings**

1½ pounds boneless pork loin

Salt

Ground black pepper

3 tablespoons Pickapeppa sauce or Worcestershire sauce

1 tablespoon olive oil

3 or 4 small parsnips, peeled and sliced

2 pears, cored and sliced and/or chopped

½ cup pear nectar or apple juice

Fresh Italian (flat-leaf) parsley (optional)

1 Cut pork into ½-inch slices; sprinkle lightly with salt and pepper. Brush with some of the Pickapeppa sauce.

2 In a 12-inch skillet heat oil over medium heat. Add pork slices; cook until brown, turning to brown evenly. Transfer to a plate; cover and keep warm.

3 In the same skillet cook parsnips and pears about 5 minutes or until parsnips are crisp-tender, stirring occasionally. Stir the remaining Pickapeppa sauce and the pear nectar into the skillet. Return pork to skillet; cook about 5 minutes more or until juices run clear. Remove pork and pear mixture to a serving platter. Continue to boil sauce, uncovered, until slightly thickened.

4 Pour sauce over pork and pear mixture. If desired, sprinkle with parsley.

NUTRITION FACTS PER SERVING:
399 cal., 15 g total fat (4 g sat. fat), 94 mg chol., 318 mg sodium, 28 g carb., 4 g dietary fiber, 38 g protein.

305

Glazed Ham with Vegetables

START TO FINISH 20 minutes MAKES 4 servings

2 medium sweet potatoes, peeled and cut into 1-inch cubes

12 ounces Brussels sprouts, trimmed and halved

2 tablespoons butter or margarine

1 to 1¼ pounds sliced cooked ham, about ¼ inch thick

½ cup apple butter

2 tablespoons cider vinegar

Baguette slices (optional)

Salt

Ground black pepper

1 In a covered large saucepan cook sweet potatoes and Brussels sprouts in lightly salted boiling water for 8 to 10 minutes or just until tender. Drain.

2 Meanwhile, in a 12-inch skillet heat butter over medium-high heat until melted. Add ham; cook for 4 to 5 minutes or until brown, turning occasionally. Remove ham from skillet. Place ham and vegetables on serving plates; cover to keep warm.

3 In the same skillet stir together apple butter and vinegar; heat through. Serve apple butter mixture with ham, vegetables, and, if desired, baguette slices. Season to taste with salt and pepper.

NUTRITION FACTS PER SERVING: *513 cal., 16 g total fat (7 g sat. fat), 80 mg chol., 1,664 mg sodium, 70 g carb., 8 g dietary fiber, 23 g protein.*

Bacon and Blue Cheese Dinner Pies

START TO FINISH **30 minutes**   OVEN **400°F**   MAKES **4 servings**

6   slices bacon

1   8.5-ounce package corn muffin mix

⅔   cup all-purpose flour

1   teaspoon chili powder

1   egg, lightly beaten

¼   cup milk

2   Granny Smith apples, cored and thinly sliced

⅓   cup crumbled blue cheese

Fresh thyme (optional)

1 Preheat oven to 400°F. Grease two baking sheets; set aside. In a skillet cook bacon until crisp. Using a slotted spoon, remove bacon and drain on paper towels; reserve 1 tablespoon drippings. Chop bacon.

2 Meanwhile, in a medium bowl combine corn muffin mix, flour, and chili powder. Add egg and milk; stir until well mixed. Divide dough into four portions. Place two portions on each prepared baking sheet. Press each dough portion into a 6- to 7-inch circle.

3 Top each circle with a layer of apple slices, leaving a 1-inch border. Fold edges around apple slices. Brush apples and crusts with the reserved bacon drippings.

4 Bake for 10 minutes. Top with blue cheese and the bacon; bake for 5 to 7 minutes more or until edges are golden and centers of crusts are set. If desired, sprinkle with thyme.

NUTRITION FACTS PER SERVING: *524 cal., 19 g total fat (6 g sat. fat), 79 mg chol., 890 mg sodium, 72 g carb., 3 g dietary fiber, 15 g protein.*

307

Spicy Apricot Lamb Chops

START TO FINISH 25 minutes MAKES 4 servings

8 lamb rib chops, cut
   1 inch thick

1 tablespoon packed
   brown sugar

1 teaspoon garlic salt

1 teaspoon chili powder

1 teaspoon paprika

½ teaspoon dried oregano,
   crushed

¼ teaspoon ground cinnamon

¼ teaspoon ground allspice

¼ teaspoon ground black pepper

¼ cup apricot preserves

1 Preheat broiler. Trim fat from chops. In a small bowl combine brown sugar, garlic salt, chili powder, paprika, oregano, cinnamon, allspice, and pepper. Sprinkle spice mixture on all sides of the chops; rub in with your fingers.

2 Place chops on the unheated rack of a broiler pan. Broil 4 to 5 inches from the heat for 10 to 15 minutes or until medium (160°F), turning chops and spooning preserves over chops once halfway through broiling.

NUTRITION FACTS PER SERVING:
311 cal., 8 g total fat (3 g sat. fat), 119 mg chol., 345 mg sodium, 18 g carb., 1 g dietary fiber, 39 g protein.

308

Lamb with Two-Pepper Bulgur

START TO FINISH **30 minutes** MAKES **6 servings**

2 cups water

1 cup bulgur

½ cup chopped onion
(1 medium)

1 cup small fresh spinach leaves
or shredded fresh spinach

¾ cup chopped red sweet
pepper (1 medium)

2 teaspoons lemon-pepper
seasoning

½ teaspoon salt

6 lamb loin chops, cut 1 inch
thick (about 1¾ pounds total)
or 6 boneless pork loin chops,
cut 1 inch thick (about
2 pounds total)

1 Preheat broiler. In a medium saucepan combine the water, bulgur, and onion. Bring to boiling; reduce heat. Simmer, covered, for 12 to 15 minutes or until bulgur is tender and most of the liquid is absorbed. Drain, if necessary. Stir in spinach, sweet pepper, 1 teaspoon of the lemon-pepper seasoning, and the salt. Cover and keep warm.

2 Meanwhile, trim fat from chops. Sprinkle chops with the remaining 1 teaspoon lemon-pepper seasoning. Place chops on the unheated rack of a broiler pan. Broil 4 to 5 inches from the heat until done, turning once halfway through broiling. For the lamb, allow 10 to 15 minutes for medium (160°F). For the pork, allow 9 to 11 minutes (160°F).

3 To serve, divide bulgur mixture among six dinner plates. Top with lamb or pork.

NUTRITION FACTS PER SERVING:
191 cal., 4 g total fat (1 g sat. fat), 49 mg chol., 602 mg sodium, 21 g carb., 5 g dietary fiber, 19 g protein.

309

Mediterranean Lamb Skillet ⏱

START TO FINISH 25 minutes MAKES 4 servings

½ cup dried orzo pasta
(rosamarina)

8 lamb rib chops, cut
1 inch thick

Salt

Ground black pepper

2 teaspoons olive oil

3 cloves garlic, minced

1 14.5-ounce can diced tomatoes
with basil, garlic, and
oregano, undrained

1 tablespoon balsamic vinegar

2 teaspoons snipped
fresh rosemary

⅓ cup halved, pitted
kalamata olives

2 tablespoons pine nuts, toasted

Fresh rosemary sprigs
(optional)

1 Cook pasta according to package directions; drain and cover and keep warm. Meanwhile, trim fat from chops. Sprinkle chops with salt and pepper. In a large skillet heat oil over medium heat. Add chops; cook for 9 to 11 minutes or until medium (160°F), turning once halfway through cooking. Remove chops from skillet, reserving drippings in skillet. Keep chops warm.

2 Add garlic to the reserved drippings; cook and stir for 1 minute. Stir in tomatoes, vinegar, and the snipped rosemary. Bring to boiling; reduce heat. Simmer, uncovered, for 5 minutes. Stir in cooked pasta and olives.

3 Spoon pasta mixture into four shallow bowls; arrange two chops in each bowl. Sprinkle with pine nuts and, if desired, garnish with rosemary sprigs.

NUTRITION FACTS PER SERVING:
678 cal., 51 g total fat (20 g sat. fat),
105 mg chol., 886 mg sodium, 28 g carb.,
2 g dietary fiber, 27 g protein.

Chicken and Turkey

Its versatility makes poultry ideal for flaunting many creative flourishes. These chicken and turkey dishes are easy to make and hard to resist.

8

Farfalle with Chicken and Tomato Pesto

START TO FINISH **30 minutes** MAKES **6 servings**

8   ounces dried farfalle pasta
    (bow ties)
2   cups frozen peas, chopped
    roasted red sweet peppers,
    and/or chopped marinated
    artichoke hearts
½   cup oil-pack dried tomatoes,
    drained
⅓   cup olive oil
½   cup slivered almonds, toasted
    if desired
2   cloves garlic
¼   teaspoon salt
¼   teaspoon ground black pepper
¼   cup freshly grated Parmesan
    cheese (1 ounce)
2   cups chopped or shredded
    purchased roasted chicken or
    cooked chicken
¼   cup snipped fresh basil
    Freshly grated Parmesan
    cheese (optional)

1 Cook pasta according to package directions, adding peas (if using) for the last 2 minutes of cooking. Drain, reserving ½ cup of the cooking water. Return pasta and peas to hot pan.

2 Meanwhile, for dried tomato pesto, in a food processor or blender combine dried tomatoes, oil, almonds, garlic, salt, and black pepper. Cover and process or blend until almost smooth. Add the ¼ cup Parmesan cheese. Cover and process or blend just until combined.

3 Add the ½ cup reserved cooking water, dried tomato pesto, and roasted red peppers and/or artichoke hearts (if using) to pasta in pan. Add chicken and basil. Toss gently to mix well. If desired, serve with additional Parmesan cheese.

NUTRITION FACTS PER SERVING:
484 cal., 27 g total fat (6 g sat. fat), 56 mg chol., 605 mg sodium, 40 g carb., 5 g dietary fiber, 23 g protein.

Rosemary-Maple Chicken Fettuccine

START TO FINISH **30 minutes**   MAKES **5 servings**

10   ounces dried fettuccine

5   skinless, boneless chicken breast halves (about 1$\frac{1}{2}$ pounds total)

$\frac{1}{4}$ teaspoon salt

$\frac{1}{4}$ teaspoon ground black pepper

1   tablespoon olive oil

2   medium red, green, and/or yellow sweet peppers, seeded and cut into bite-size strips

1   medium onion, sliced

$\frac{3}{4}$ cup reduced-sodium chicken broth

1   tablespoon cornstarch

1   teaspoon snipped fresh rosemary

$\frac{1}{8}$ teaspoon ground black pepper

$\frac{1}{4}$ cup pure maple syrup or maple-flavor syrup

1 Cook pasta according to package directions; drain. Set aside, cover and keep warm.

2 Meanwhile, sprinkle chicken with salt and the $\frac{1}{4}$ teaspoon black pepper. In a very large skillet heat oil over medium heat. Add chicken; cook for 10 to 12 minutes or until tender and no longer pink (170°F), turning once halfway through cooking. Remove chicken from skillet; cover and keep warm.

3 Increase heat to medium-high. Add sweet peppers and onion to skillet; cook and stir for 4 to 6 minutes or until vegetables are crisp-tender.

4 In a small bowl stir together broth, cornstarch, rosemary, and the $\frac{1}{8}$ teaspoon black pepper. Add to skillet. Cook and stir until thickened and bubbly. Cook and stir for 1 minute more; stir in maple syrup.

5 To serve, divide hot pasta among five serving plates or shallow bowls. Top with chicken. Spoon sweet peppers and sauce over chicken.

NUTRITION FACTS PER SERVING:
466 cal., 6 g total fat (1 g sat. fat), 79 mg chol., 285 mg sodium, 60 g carb., 2 g dietary fiber, 40 g protein.

313

Pasta Stackups with Chicken Sausage

START TO FINISH 30 minutes MAKES 4 servings

6   dried lasagna noodles
1   cup coarsely chopped dried
     tomatoes (not oil-pack)
6   cloves garlic, minced
2   tablespoons olive oil
1   pound cooked chicken
     sausage links, halved
     lengthwise and cut into large
     pieces
1   5-ounce package baby spinach
½   teaspoon salt
½   teaspoon ground black pepper
     Shaved Parmesan cheese
     (optional)

1 Cook lasagna noodles according to package directions; drain, reserving 1 cup of the cooking water. In a medium bowl combine dried tomatoes and garlic; pour the 1 cup reserved cooking water over. Set aside.

2 Meanwhile, in a 12-inch skillet heat the oil over medium-high heat. Add sausage. Cook until lightly browned and heated through, turning occasionally. Add tomato mixture. Cook, uncovered, for 2 minutes. Stir in spinach, salt, and pepper; cover and remove from heat.

3 Cut each cooked lasagna noodle in half. To serve, layer noodles and sausage mixture onto serving plates. If desired, pass Parmesan cheese.

NUTRITION FACTS PER SERVING:
430 cal., 19 g total fat (4 g sat. fat), 97 mg chol., 1,074 mg sodium, 36 g carb., 4 g dietary fiber, 30 g protein.

Fast Chicken and Rice

START TO FINISH **15 minutes**   MAKES **4 servings**

½ cup frozen peas

1 **8.8-ounce pouch cooked brown rice or white rice**

1 **tablespoon vegetable oil**

1 **pound chicken breast tenderloins, halved crosswise**

¼ **cup stir-fry sauce**

1 **2-ounce package oven-roasted sliced almonds**

1 Stir peas into rice in pouch. Heat in microwave according to rice package directions.

2 Meanwhile, in a large skillet heat oil over medium-high heat. Add chicken; cook and stir for 2 to 3 minutes or until tender and no longer pink. Stir rice mixture into chicken mixture. Stir in stir-fry sauce; heat through. Sprinkle with almonds.

NUTRITION FACTS PER SERVING:
311 cal., 9 g total fat (1 g sat. fat), 66 mg chol., 453 mg sodium, 25 g carb., 2 g dietary fiber, 31 g protein.

When handling raw chicken or turkey, practice safe handling techniques to avoid health risks.

- Set aside a cutting board exclusively for raw poultry and meat that will be cooked. Have another cutting board for breads and foods that don't need to be cooked.
- Wash work surfaces and utensils in hot, soapy water before and after handling poultry and meat to prevent the spread of bacteria. And wash hands immediately after handling raw meat or poultry.
- Serve cooked poultry and meat immediately; refrigerate leftovers within 2 hours.

Rice-Stuffed Peppers

START TO FINISH **30 minutes** MAKES **4 servings**

4   **small (about 5 ounces each) or 2 large (about 8 ounces each) red and/or yellow sweet peppers**

    Salt

    Ground black pepper

1   **cup 1-inch pieces asparagus or broccoli florets**

1   **8.8-ounce pouch cooked long grain rice**

1   **cup cubed cooked chicken**

½   **cup finely shredded Parmesan or Romano cheese (2 ounces)**

¼   **cup milk**

½   **to 1 teaspoon dried oregano, crushed**

¼   **teaspoon salt**

⅛   **teaspoon ground black pepper**

¼   **cup broken walnuts, toasted if desired**

    Shaved or shredded Parmesan or Romano cheese (optional)

1 Cut sweet peppers in half lengthwise. Remove seeds and membranes. If necessary, cut a thin slice from the bottom of each sweet pepper half so it stays upright. In a Dutch oven cook sweet peppers in enough boiling water to cover for 3 minutes; drain well. Place on a serving platter, cut sides up. Sprinkle lightly with salt and black pepper; set aside.

2 Meanwhile, for filling, in a covered medium saucepan cook asparagus in a small amount of boiling water for 1 to 2 minutes or just until tender. Drain; return to hot pan. Stir in rice, chicken, the ½ cup Parmesan cheese, the milk, oregano, the ¼ teaspoon salt, and the ⅛ teaspoon black pepper. Cook and stir over medium heat until heated through. Stir in walnuts.

3 Divide filling among sweet peppers. If desired, top with additional Parmesan cheese.

NUTRITION FACTS PER SERVING:
321 cal., 13 g total fat (4 g sat. fat), 43 mg chol., 581 mg sodium, 32 g carb., 5 g dietary fiber, 21 g protein.

Cinnamon Roasted Chicken with Pumpkin-Sage Grits

START TO FINISH 30 minute   OVEN 400°F   MAKES 4 servings

4   4- to 6-ounce skinless,
    boneless chicken breast
    halves
1   tablespoon vegetable oil
1½ teaspoons salt
1   teaspoon ground cinnamon
½   teaspoon ground black pepper
1½ cups water
⅔   cup instant grits (two 1-ounce
    packages)
½   cup canned pumpkin
1   tablespoon snipped fresh sage
⅓   cup shredded cheddar cheese
    Fresh sage leaves

1 Preheat oven to 400°F. Arrange chicken breast halves in 13×9×2-inch baking pan. Drizzle all sides of chicken with oil. Sprinkle chicken with 1 teaspoon of the salt, the cinnamon, and pepper; rub in with your fingers. Roast for 18 to 20 minutes or until tender and no longer pink (170°F).

2 Meanwhile, in a medium saucepan bring the water to boiling. Add grits, stirring until combined. Stir in pumpkin, snipped sage, and the remaining ½ teaspoon salt. Return to boiling; reduce heat. Cook, uncovered, for 5 to 7 minutes or until thickened, stirring frequently. Remove from heat; stir in cheese.

3 To serve, spoon grits onto four serving plates; top with chicken breast halves. Top with sage leaves.

NUTRITION FACTS PER SERVING:
253 cal., 8 g total fat (3 g sat. fat), 76 mg chol., 1,162 mg sodium, 14 g carb., 2 g dietary fiber, 30 g protein.

Indian-Spiced Chicken Pitas

START TO FINISH **30 minutes** MAKES **4 pita halves**

1 **cup plain fat-free yogurt**

1 **teaspoon garam masala**

½ **teaspoon bottled hot pepper sauce**

¼ **teaspoon salt**

12 **ounces skinless, boneless chicken breast halves, cut into bite-size strips**

Nonstick cooking spray

2 **whole wheat pita bread rounds, halved crosswise**

1 **cup refrigerated mango and papaya slices, drained and coarsely chopped***

1 **tablespoon tiny fresh mint leaves**

1 In a small bowl combine yogurt, garam masala, hot pepper sauce, and salt, reserving one-fourth of mixture in the refrigerator for serving. Pour the remaining yogurt mixture into a resealable plastic bag; add chicken. Seal bag; turn to coat chicken. Marinate in the refrigerator for 15 minutes. Drain chicken; discard marinade.

2 Coat an unheated large nonstick skillet with cooking spray. Heat skillet over medium heat. Add chicken to hot skillet; cook about 5 minutes or until tender and no longer pink, turning once.

3 To serve, divide chicken evenly among pita bread halves. Drizzle with the reserved yogurt mixture. Top with chopped fruit; sprinkle with fresh mint.

NUTRITION FACTS PER PITA HALF:
249 cal., 2 g total fat (0 g sat. fat), 51 mg chol., 430 mg sodium, 32 g carb., 3 g dietary fiber, 26 g protein.

*tip
Substitute peaches for mango, if desired.

Jerk Chicken and Pineapple Slaw

START TO FINISH **30 minutes** MAKES **4 servings**

3 **heads baby bok choy, trimmed and thinly sliced**

2 **cups shredded red cabbage**

½ **of a peeled, cored fresh pineapple, coarsely chopped**

2 **tablespoons cider vinegar**

4 **teaspoons packed brown sugar**

2 **teaspoons all-purpose flour**

2 **teaspoons Jamaican jerk seasoning**

4 **small skinless, boneless chicken breast halves**

1 For pineapple slaw, in a very large bowl combine bok choy, cabbage, and pineapple. In a small bowl stir together vinegar and 2 teaspoons of the brown sugar. Drizzle over bok choy mixture; toss to coat. Set aside.

2 In a large resealable plastic bag combine the remaining 2 teaspoons brown sugar, the flour, and jerk seasoning. Add chicken; shake well to coat.

3 On a lightly greased grill pan or 12-inch heavy skillet cook chicken over medium heat for 6 to 8 minutes or until tender and no longer pink (170°F), turning once. Remove chicken to cutting board.

4 Slice chicken; serve with pineapple slaw.

NUTRITION FACTS PER SERVING:
205 cal., 2 g total fat (0 g sat. fat), 66 mg chol., 318 mg sodium, 19 g carb., 3 g dietary fiber, 29 g protein.

Blackened Chicken with Avocado Salsa

START TO FINISH 25 minutes   OVEN 375°F   MAKES 4 servings

- 4   skinless, boneless chicken breast halves (about 1 pound total)
- 2   teaspoons blackened steak seasoning
- 1   tablespoon olive oil
- 2   tablespoons rice vinegar
- 2   tablespoons olive oil
- ¼   teaspoon ground cumin
- ⅛   teaspoon salt
-      Dash ground black pepper
- 1   avocado, halved, seeded, peeled, and chopped
- ⅔   cup chopped fresh or refrigerated papaya
- ⅓   cup finely chopped red sweet pepper
- ¼   cup snipped fresh cilantro

1 Preheat oven to 375°F. Lightly sprinkle both sides of each chicken breast half with blackened steak seasoning.

2 In a large ovenproof skillet heat the 1 tablespoon oil over medium heat. Add chicken; cook until brown, turning to brown evenly. Bake about 15 minutes or until the chicken is tender and no longer pink (170°F). Do not turn.

3 Meanwhile, for salsa, in a large bowl whisk together rice vinegar, the 2 tablespoons oil, the cumin, salt, and black pepper. Add avocado, papaya, sweet pepper, and cilantro; toss together.

4 To serve, spoon some of the salsa over the chicken. Pass the remaining salsa.

NUTRITION FACTS PER SERVING:
323 cal., 17 g total fat (3 g sat. fat), 82 mg chol., 513 mg sodium, 7 g carb., 3 g dietary fiber, 34 g protein.

Chipotle Chile Chicken with Blueberry-Pepper Salsa

START TO FINISH **25 minutes** OVEN **400°F** MAKES **4 servings**

Nonstick cooking spray

2 **tablespoons honey**

1 **tablespoon butter or margarine, melted**

2 **teaspoons finely chopped canned chipotle chile pepper in adobo sauce***

1 **teaspoon dried oregano, crushed**

$\frac{1}{2}$ **teaspoon salt**

4 **skinless, boneless chicken breast halves (about 1$\frac{1}{4}$ pounds total)**

1$\frac{1}{2}$ **cups frozen blueberries, thawed and drained**

1 **11-ounce can mandarin oranges, drained**

3 **tablespoons finely chopped red onion**

1 **teaspoon finely shredded lime peel**

2 **teaspoons lime juice**

1 Preheat oven to 400°F. Coat a 13×9×2-inch baking pan with cooking spray; set aside. In a small bowl stir together 1 tablespoon of the honey, the melted butter, 1 teaspoon of the chile pepper, the oregano, and salt. Brush both sides of each chicken breast half with the chile pepper mixture. Arrange chicken in prepared pan. Bake for 15 to 20 minutes or until tender and no longer pink (170°F).

2 Meanwhile, for salsa, in a medium bowl combine blueberries, oranges, red onion, lime peel, lime juice, the remaining 1 tablespoon honey, and the remaining 1 teaspoon chile pepper. Serve salsa with chicken.

NUTRITION FACTS PER SERVING:
279 cal., 5 g total fat (2 g sat. fat), 90 mg chol., 420 mg sodium, 25 g carb., 2 g dietary fiber, 34 g protein.

*tip
Because chile peppers contain volatile oils that can burn your skin and eyes, avoid direct contact with them as much as possible. When working with chile peppers, wear plastic or rubber gloves. If your bare hands do touch the peppers, wash your hands and nails well with soap and warm water.

Chicken and Turkey

Spicy Chicken with Fruit

START TO FINISH **30 minutes**   MAKES **4 servings**

- 2 teaspoons Jamaican jerk seasoning
- 2 fresh serrano chile peppers, seeded and finely chopped*
- 4 skinless, boneless chicken breast halves (about 1¼ pounds total)
- Nonstick cooking spray
- ½ cup peach nectar
- 3 green onions, cut into 1-inch pieces
- 2 cups sliced peeled peaches
- 1 cup sliced plums
- 1 tablespoon packed brown sugar
- ⅛ teaspoon salt
- ½ cup pitted dark sweet cherries
- 2 cups hot cooked brown rice

1 In a small bowl combine jerk seasoning and half of the chopped chile peppers. Sprinkle seasoning mixture over all sides of chicken breast halves; rub in with your fingers.*

2 Lightly coat an unheated large nonstick skillet with cooking spray; heat skillet over medium heat. Add chicken. Cook for 8 to 10 minutes or until tender and no longer pink (170°F), turning once halfway through cooking. Transfer to a serving platter; cover and keep warm.

3 Add 2 tablespoons of the peach nectar and the green onions to skillet. Cook and stir for 2 minutes.

4 In a small bowl combine the remaining 6 tablespoons peach nectar, half of the peaches, half of the plums, the remaining chile peppers, the brown sugar, and salt. Add to skillet. Cook and stir over medium-high heat for 3 to 4 minutes or until slightly thickened and bubbly. Remove from heat. Stir in cherries and the remaining peaches and plums. Spoon over chicken. Serve with hot cooked rice.

NUTRITION FACTS PER SERVING:
372 cal., 3 g total fat (1 g sat. fat), 82 mg chol., 330 mg sodium, 48 g carb., 5 g dietary fiber, 37 g protein.

*tip

Because chile peppers contain volatile oils that can burn your skin and eyes, avoid direct contact with them as much as possible. When working with chile peppers, wear plastic or rubber gloves. If your bare hands do touch the peppers, wash your hands and nails well with soap and warm water.

Smoky Lime-Chicken-Succotash Skillet

START TO FINISH **25 minutes** MAKES **4 to 6 servings.**

1   **lime**

1   **16-ounce package frozen corn**

1   **12-ounce package frozen shelled sweet soybeans (edamame) or one 16-ounce package frozen baby lima beans**

1¾   **cups water**

1   **2- to 2½-pound purchased roasted chicken, cut into serving-size pieces**

1   **16-ounce jar chipotle salsa**

1 Finely shred peel from lime; juice lime. Set aside. In a very large skillet combine corn and edamame; add the water. Bring to boiling; reduce heat. Simmer, uncovered, for 5 to 6 minutes or just until edamame is tender. Stir in lime peel and lime juice.

2 Place chicken pieces on top of corn mixture. Pour salsa over all. Cook, covered, over medium heat about 10 minutes or until heated through.

NUTRITION FACTS PER SERVING:
621 cal., 28 g total fat (7 g sat. fat), 134 mg chol., 823 mg sodium, 41 g carb., 8 g dietary fiber, 58 g protein.

Time-saving packages of frozen vegetables such as corn, peas, and sweet soybeans (edamame) are as nutritious as fresh vegetables. They typically are frozen shortly after picking, locking in the flavor and nutrients.

323

Saucy BBQ Chicken

START TO FINISH 30 minutes   MAKES 4 servings

8   small chicken drumsticks
    Vegetable oil
1   large onion, cut into 6 slices
1   cup ketchup
¼   cup molasses
3   to 4 tablespoons cider vinegar
2   tablespoons packed brown sugar
1   teaspoon smoked paprika
    Several dashes bottled hot pepper sauce
    Fresh Italian (flat-leaf) parsley (optional)

1 Preheat broiler. Arrange chicken on the unheated rack of a broiler pan. Broil 4 to 5 inches from the heat for 10 minutes.

2 Brush onion with oil. Remove pan from oven; turn chicken and move chicken to one side of the broiler pan. Arrange onion slices in a single layer on the other side of the pan. Broil about 15 minutes or until chicken is tender and no longer pink (180°F).

3 Meanwhile, for sauce, in a small saucepan combine ketchup, molasses, vinegar, brown sugar, smoked paprika, and hot pepper sauce. Bring to boiling over medium heat; cover and keep warm. Remove onions from pan. Broil chicken for 1 to 2 minutes more, brushing with some of the sauce during the last minute of broiling.

4 Chop two of the onion slices; stir chopped onion into sauce.

5 Serve chicken with the remaining four onion slices and sauce. If desired, garnish with parsley.

NUTRITION FACTS PER SERVING:
426 cal., 16 g total fat (4 g sat. fat), 118 mg chol., 802 mg sodium, 41 g carb., 1 g dietary fiber, 30 g protein.

tip
Cover and chill any remaining sauce; use within 3 days.

Extra Saucy Chicken Sandwiches

START TO FINISH **30 minutes** MAKES **6 servings**

- 2 tablespoons vegetable oil
- 1 large onion, halved crosswise and thinly sliced
- 2 pounds skinless, boneless chicken breast halves, cut into bite-size strips
- 1 14- to 16-ounce jar cheddar cheese pasta sauce
- 2 tablespoons Worcestershire sauce
- 12 slices marble rye bread, toasted
- 1 tomato, sliced
- 12 slices bacon, crisp-cooked and drained (optional)

1 In a very large skillet heat 1 tablespoon of the oil over medium-high heat. Add onion and half of the chicken; cook for 4 to 5 minutes or until chicken is no longer pink. Remove from skillet to a medium bowl. Add the remaining 1 tablespoon oil and the remaining chicken to skillet. Cook for 4 to 5 minutes more or until chicken is tender and no longer pink. Return chicken-onion mixture to skillet. Stir in pasta sauce and Worcestershire sauce; heat through.

2 To serve, spoon chicken and sauce mixture over half of the bread slices. Top with tomato slices and, if desired, bacon. Top with the remaining bread slices.

NUTRITION FACTS PER SERVING:
491 cal., 18 g total fat (5 g sat. fat), 114 mg chol., 1,084 mg sodium, 38 g carb., 4 g dietary fiber, 43 g protein.

325

Lemon-Ginger Chicken Thighs

START TO FINISH **30 minutes** MAKES **4 servings**

1 **lemon**

1 **tablespoon grated fresh ginger**

½ **teaspoon salt**

2 **tablespoons honey**

2 **tablespoons water**

1 **tablespoon reduced-sodium soy sauce**

8 **bone-in chicken thighs**

2 **teaspoons vegetable oil**

Sliced green onions and/or lemon wedges (optional)

1 Finely shred peel from lemon; juice lemon. In a small bowl combine the lemon peel, ginger, and salt. In another small bowl combine lemon juice, honey, the water, and soy sauce.

2 Rub lemon peel mixture under the skin of the chicken thighs. In a 12-inch skillet heat oil over medium-high heat. Add chicken, skin sides down. Cook about 7 minutes or until well-browned. Turn chicken; add lemon juice mixture. Reduce heat; cover and cook for 14 to 18 minutes more or until chicken is tender and no longer pink (180°F).

3 Transfer chicken to plates. If desired, skim fat from pan juices. Drizzle chicken with pan juices. Top with green onions and/or serve with lemon wedges.

NUTRITION FACTS PER SERVING: *459 cal., 31 g total fat (8 g sat. fat), 158 mg chol., 567 mg sodium, 12 g carb., 1 g dietary fiber, 33 g protein.*

Lickety-Split Lemon Chicken

START TO FINISH **30 minutes** MAKES **4 servings**

2 tablespoons butter or margarine

12 ounces chicken breast tenderloins

1 8-ounce package sliced mushrooms

1 medium red sweet pepper, seeded and cut into strips

2 tablespoons all-purpose flour

1 14-ounce can chicken broth

1 teaspoon finely shredded lemon peel

2 tablespoons lemon juice

1 teaspoon dried thyme, crushed

Salt

Ground black pepper

1 14.8-ounce pouch cooked long grain rice

Lemon wedges (optional)

1 In a very large skillet heat butter over medium heat until melted. Add chicken; cook for 6 to 8 minutes or until tender and no longer pink, adding mushrooms and sweet pepper for the last 5 minutes of cooking. Stir in flour. Cook and stir for 1 minute more. Add broth, lemon peel, lemon juice, and thyme. Cook and stir until thickened and bubbly. Cook and stir for 2 minutes more. Season to taste with salt and black pepper.

2 Meanwhile, prepare rice according to package directions. Serve chicken mixture over rice. If desired, serve with lemon wedges.

NUTRITION FACTS PER SERVING:
361 cal., 10 g total fat (4 g sat. fat), 66 mg chol., 643 mg sodium, 41 g carb., 2 g dietary fiber, 25 g protein.

327

Rosemary Chicken with Vegetables

START TO FINISH **30 minutes** MAKES **4 servings**

- 4 **skinless, boneless chicken breast halves (1$\frac{1}{4}$ to 1$\frac{1}{2}$ pounds total)**
- $\frac{1}{2}$ **teaspoon lemon-pepper seasoning**
- 2 **tablespoons olive oil**
- 1 **teaspoon bottled minced garlic**
- 2 **medium zucchini and/or yellow summer squash, cut into $\frac{1}{4}$-inch slices (2$\frac{1}{2}$ cups)**
- $\frac{1}{2}$ **cup apple juice or apple cider**
- 2 **teaspoons snipped fresh rosemary or $\frac{1}{2}$ teaspoon dried rosemary, crushed**
- 4 **ounces refrigerated linguine**
- 2 **tablespoons dry white wine**
- 2 **teaspoons cornstarch**
- 12 **cherry tomatoes, halved**

  Fresh rosemary sprigs (optional)

1 Sprinkle chicken with lemon-pepper seasoning. In a large skillet heat oil over medium heat. Add chicken; cook for 8 to 10 minutes or until chicken is tender and no longer pink (170°F), turning once halfway through cooking. Transfer chicken to a serving platter; cover and keep warm.

2 Add garlic to hot skillet; cook for 15 seconds. Add zucchini and/or summer squash, apple juice, and snipped rosemary. Bring to boiling; reduce heat. Simmer, covered, for 2 minutes.

3 Meanwhile, cook pasta according to package directions; drain. In a small bowl combine wine and cornstarch. Add to zucchini mixture in skillet; cook and stir until thickened and bubbly. Cook and stir for 2 minutes more. Stir in tomato halves. Serve vegetables and pasta with chicken. If desired, garnish with rosemary sprigs.

NUTRITION FACTS PER SERVING:
356 cal., 10 g total fat (2 g sat. fat), 103 mg chol., 235 mg sodium, 27 g carb., 2 g dietary fiber, 38 g protein.

Nutty Chicken Stir-Fry

START TO FINISH **30 minutes**   MAKES **6 servings**

$2\frac{1}{2}$ **cups shredded cabbage**

$1\frac{1}{4}$ **cups sliced zucchini (1 medium)**

$\frac{3}{4}$ **cup red sweet pepper strips**

$\frac{1}{2}$ **cup sliced carrot (1 medium)**

$\frac{1}{2}$ **cup sliced onion (1 medium)**

1 **tablespoon vegetable oil**

12 **ounces skinless, boneless chicken breast halves, cut into 1-inch pieces**

$\frac{1}{2}$ **cup stir-fry sauce**

$\frac{1}{2}$ **teaspoon ground ginger**

3 **to 4 cups hot cooked white rice or brown rice**

$\frac{3}{4}$ **cup chopped peanuts or cashews**

1 In a large bowl combine cabbage, zucchini, sweet pepper, carrot, and onion. In a large skillet or wok heat oil over medium-high heat. Add half of the vegetable mixture; cook and stir about 2 minutes or until crisp-tender. Remove cooked vegetables from skillet or wok. Repeat with the remaining vegetable mixture, adding more oil, if necessary.

2 If necessary, add more oil to skillet. Add chicken; cook and stir for 3 to 5 minutes or until tender and no longer pink. Push chicken to side of skillet. Add stir-fry sauce and ginger to center of skillet; cook and stir until bubbly. Return vegetables to skillet; stir in chicken from sides of skillet. Cook and stir about 1 minute or until heated through. Serve over rice. Sprinkle with nuts.

NUTRITION FACTS PER SERVING: *355 cal., 14 g total fat (2 g sat. fat), 33 mg chol., 816 mg sodium, 37 g carb., 5 g dietary fiber, 22 g protein.*

329

Crunchy Chicken Strips ✮

START TO FINISH **30 minutes** OVEN **425°F** MAKES **8 servings**

Nonstick cooking spray

7 **cups bite-size cheddar fish-shape crackers or 14 cups pretzels (14 ounces pretzels)**

1½ **cups bottled buttermilk ranch salad dressing**

2 **pounds chicken breast tenderloins**

Bottled buttermilk ranch salad dressing (optional)

1 Preheat oven to 425°F. Line two 15×10×1-inch baking pans with foil; lightly coat foil with cooking spray. Set aside.

2 Crush crackers or pretzels (you should have 5 cups crushed mixture); transfer to a shallow dish. Pour the 1½ cups ranch dressing into another shallow dish. Dip chicken tenderloins into the dressing, allowing excess to drip off; dip into cracker crumbs, turning to coat. Arrange chicken in a single layer on prepared pans. Lightly coat chicken with cooking spray.

3 Bake, uncovered, for 10 to 15 minutes or until tender and no longer pink (170°F), rotating pans halfway through baking. If desired, serve with additional ranch dressing.

NUTRITION FACTS PER SERVING:
582 cal., 35 g total fat (7 g sat. fat), 90 mg chol., 765 mg sodium, 34 g carb., 1 g dietary fiber, 33 g protein.

Chicken and Biscuit Pockets ✮

START TO FINISH **30 minutes** OVEN **400°F** MAKES **5 servings**

2 **10.2-ounce packages (10 biscuits total) refrigerated large flaky biscuits**

1 **cup finely chopped cooked chicken or turkey (about 5 ounces)**

⅔ **cup coarsely shredded yellow summer squash**

½ **cup shredded Monterey Jack or cheddar cheese (2 ounces)**

½ **cup mayonnaise or salad dressing**

1 **tablespoon honey mustard**

1 Preheat oven to 400°F. Separate biscuits; use the palm of your hand to flatten each to a 4-inch circle. Divide chicken, squash, and cheese among dough circles, placing fillings on one side of each dough circle. Fold the other sides of dough circles over fillings; pinch edges well to seal.* Arrange filled biscuits about 2 inches apart on an ungreased baking sheet. Bake about 12 minutes or until golden on top and edges are set.

2 Meanwhile, in a small bowl stir together mayonnaise and mustard. Serve as dipping sauce for warm biscuits.

NUTRITION FACTS PER SERVING:
626 cal., 39 g total fat (10 g sat. fat), 43 mg chol., 1,359 mg sodium, 48 g carb., 0 g dietary fiber, 19 g protein.

330

＊tip

For a tighter seal, press edges with the tines of a fork.

★ Chicken Pot Pie

START TO FINISH **30 minutes**   OVEN **450°F**   MAKES **6 servings**

½ of a 15-ounce package
    (1 crust) rolled refrigerated
    unbaked piecrust
1   10.75-ounce can condensed
    cream of onion soup
2   cups low-fat milk
1   8-ounce package reduced-fat
    cream cheese (Neufchâtel)
⅓ cup water
1   teaspoon dried sage, crushed
¼ teaspoon ground black pepper
3   cups chopped cooked chicken
1   16-ounce package frozen
    mixed vegetables
1   cup instant white rice

1 Preheat oven to 450°F. Let piecrust stand at room temperature for 15 minutes as directed on package. Unroll piecrust onto a large baking sheet. Using a pizza cutter or sharp knife, cut piecrust into strips ½- to 1-inch wide. Separate strips slightly. Bake for 8 to 10 minutes or until golden.

2 Meanwhile, for filling, in a 4-quart Dutch oven combine soup, milk, cream cheese, the water, sage, and pepper. Cook and stir over medium-high heat until cream cheese melts. Stir in chicken, vegetables, and rice. Bring to boiling, stirring frequently; reduce heat. Simmer, covered, about 10 minutes or until vegetables and rice are tender, stirring occasionally.

3 Transfer filling to a serving dish. Top with pastry strips.

NUTRITION FACTS PER SERVING:
574 cal., 26 g total fat (11 g sat. fat), 104 mg chol., 728 mg sodium, 51 g carb., 4 g dietary fiber, 32 g protein.

331

Chicken and Turkey

Turkey and Bean Burritos ★

START TO FINISH 30 minutes OVEN 350°F MAKES 8 burritos

- 8   8-inch flour tortillas
- 12 ounces uncooked ground turkey
- 1   cup chopped onion (1 large)
- 2   cloves garlic, minced
- 1   15-ounce can black beans or pinto beans, rinsed and drained
- 1/2 cup salsa
- 2   teaspoons chili powder
- 1/2 cup shredded cheddar cheese (2 ounces)
- 1/2 cup shredded lettuce
  Salsa (optional)
  Sour cream mixed with snipped fresh cilantro (optional)

1 Preheat oven to 350°F. Stack tortillas; wrap in foil. Heat in the oven for 10 minutes to soften.

2 Meanwhile, for filling, in a large skillet cook turkey, onion, and garlic over medium heat until meat is brown and onion is tender, using a wooden spoon to break up meat as it cooks. Drain off fat. Stir beans, the 1/2 cup salsa, and the chili powder into turkey mixture in skillet; heat through.

3 Spoon about 1/3 cup of the filling onto each tortilla; top each with 1 tablespoon of the cheese and 1 tablespoon of the lettuce. Fold bottom edge up and over filling, just until covered. Fold in opposite sides. Roll up, tucking in sides.

4 If desired, serve burritos with additional salsa and/or sour cream mixed with snipped cilantro.

NUTRITION FACTS PER BURRITO:
231 cal., 8 g total fat (3 g sat. fat), 41 mg chol., 439 mg sodium, 25 g carb., 4 g dietary fiber, 15 g protein.

Layered Turkey Enchiladas

START TO FINISH **25 minutes**   OVEN **450°F**   MAKES **4 servings**

- 1 **tablespoon vegetable oil**
- 1 **pound turkey breast tenderloin, cut into bite-size strips**
- 1 **16-ounce package frozen (yellow, green, and red) sweet peppers and onion stir-fry vegetables**
- 1 **10-ounce can enchilada sauce**
- ½ **cup canned whole berry cranberry sauce**
- **Salt**
- **Ground black pepper**
- 9 **6-inch corn tortillas, halved**
- 1 **8-ounce package shredded Mexican blend cheese (2 cups)**
- **Lime wedges (optional)**
- **Fresh cilantro sprigs (optional)**

1 Position oven rack in the top third of the oven. Preheat oven to 450°F. In an extra-large skillet heat oil over medium heat. Add turkey; cook about 4 minutes or until no longer pink. Add frozen vegetables, enchilada sauce, and cranberry sauce. Bring to boiling; remove from heat. Sprinkle to taste with salt and pepper.

2 In a 2-quart baking dish layer one-third of the tortillas and one-third of the cheese. Using a slotted spoon, top with half of the turkey-vegetable mixture. Layer one-third of the tortillas, one-third of the cheese, and the remaining turkey-vegetable mixture. Top with the remaining tortillas. Spoon sauce remaining in the skillet over layers in baking dish; sprinkle with the remaining cheese.

3 Bake about 5 minutes or until cheese is melted. Cut into squares. If desired, serve with lime and cilantro.

NUTRITION FACTS PER SERVING: *615 cal., 25 g total fat (11 g sat. fat), 120 mg chol., 1,171 mg sodium, 52 g carb., 6 g dietary fiber, 45 g protein.*

Turkey Alfredo with Green Beans

START TO FINISH 20 minutes   MAKES 4 servings

2   cups frozen whole green beans

12 ounces turkey breast tenderloin or skinless, boneless chicken breast halves

1   tablespoon canola oil

1   10-ounce container refrigerated Alfredo pasta sauce

4   English muffins or bagels, split and toasted

1 Cook the green beans according to package directions; drain. Cover and keep warm. Meanwhile, cut turkey into bite-size strips. In a large skillet heat oil over medium-high heat. Add turkey; cook for 3 to 4 minutes or until tender and no longer pink.

2 Stir Alfredo sauce into turkey; heat through. Place toasted English muffin or bagel halves on serving plates. Arrange green beans on top of English muffins or bagels. Spoon turkey and sauce over all.

NUTRITION FACTS PER SERVING: 441 cal., 19 g total fat (9 g sat. fat), 94 mg chol., 817 mg sodium, 36 g carb., 3 g dietary fiber, 30 g protein.

Turkey Salisbury Steaks

START TO FINISH **30 minutes** MAKES **4 servings**

1 pound uncooked ground turkey

1 envelope (half of a 2.2-ounce package) beefy onion soup mix

2 tablespoons Worcestershire sauce

2 teaspoons olive oil

1 tablespoon butter or margarine

1 clove garlic, minced

2 cups sliced fresh mushrooms

½ cup reduced-sodium chicken broth

¼ cup dry red wine or reduced-sodium chicken broth

¼ cup tomato paste

Fresh thyme leaves (optional)

1 In a large bowl stir together turkey, 2 tablespoons of the dry soup mix, and 1 tablespoon of the Worcestershire sauce. Shape turkey mixture into four ½-inch thick oval patties.

2 In a large skillet heat oil over medium-high heat. Add patties; cook about 3 minutes or until browned, turning once halfway through cooking. Remove from skillet; set aside.

3 In same skillet heat butter over medium-high heat until melted. Add garlic. Cook for 30 seconds. Add mushrooms. Cook and stir about 5 minutes or until tender. Add broth, wine, tomato paste, the remaining dry soup mix, and the remaining 1 tablespoon Worcestershire sauce, stirring to scrape up any browned bits.

4 Return patties to skillet; spoon sauce over patties. Cover and cook on medium-low heat about 8 minutes or until done (165°F),* spooning sauce over patties halfway through cooking. If desired, sprinkle with thyme.

NUTRITION FACTS PER SERVING:
285 cal., 15 g total fat (5 g sat. fat), 97 mg chol., 1,008 mg sodium, 12 g carb., 1 g dietary fiber, 23 g protein.

*tip
The internal color of a burger is not a reliable doneness indicator. A turkey patty cooked to 165°F is safe, regardless of color. To measure the doneness of a patty, insert an instant-read thermometer through the side of the patty to a depth of 2 to 3 inches.

Turkey Steaks with Pear and Blue Cheese

START TO FINISH **30 minutes** MAKES **4 servings**

2   **turkey breast tenderloins (1 to 1¼ pounds total)**

1   **teaspoon dried sage, crushed**

¼   **teaspoon salt**

¼   **teaspoon ground black pepper**

1   **tablespoon butter or margarine**

1   **tablespoon olive oil**

1   **large ripe pear, cored and thinly sliced**

2   **cups fresh baby spinach**

¼   **cup crumbled blue cheese (1 ounce)**

1 Horizontally split tenderloins to make four ½-inch steaks. Rub one side of each turkey steak with sage; sprinkle with salt and pepper. In an extra-large skillet heat butter and oil over medium-high heat. Add turkey steaks; cook for 14 to 16 minutes or until tender and no longer pink (170°F), turning once halfway through cooking. (If turkey browns too quickly, reduce heat to medium.) Remove from skillet, reserving the butter and oil in the skillet. Cover turkey and keep warm.

2 Add pear slices to hot skillet. Cook over medium heat about 2 minutes or until tender and lightly browned, stirring occasionally.

3 Serve turkey and pears over spinach; sprinkle with blue cheese.

NUTRITION FACTS PER SERVING:
247 cal., 10 g total fat (4 g sat. fat), 84 mg chol., 352 mg sodium, 9 g carb., 2 g dietary fiber, 30 g protein.

Turkey Saltimbocca

START TO FINISH **30 minutes** MAKES **4 servings**

¼ **cup all-purpose flour**

½ **teaspoon salt**

½ **teaspoon dried sage, crushed**

¼ **teaspoon ground black pepper**

4 **turkey cutlets or slices (about 12 ounces total)**

2 **tablespoons vegetable oil**

4 **slices cooked ham (about 3 ounces)**

4 **slices fontina or Swiss cheese (about 2 ounces)**

¼ **cup dry white wine**

¼ **cup reduced-sodium chicken broth**

2 **tablespoons snipped fresh Italian (flat-leaf) parsley (optional)**

1 In a shallow dish combine flour, salt, sage, and pepper; set aside.

2 Place each turkey cutlet between two pieces of plastic wrap. Using the flat side of a meat mallet, pound turkey lightly, working from the center to the edges, until about ¼ inch thick. Remove plastic wrap. Dip cutlets into flour mixture, turning to coat both sides; shake off excess.

3 In an extra-large nonstick skillet heat oil over medium-high heat. Add cutlets; cook about 2 minutes or until brown. Turn cutlets over; top with ham and cheese. Add wine and broth; cook about 2 minutes more or until cheese melts and sauce thickens.

4 Transfer cutlets to a serving platter. Spoon pan drippings over cutlets. If desired, garnish with parsley.

NUTRITION FACTS PER SERVING:
282 cal., 14 g total fat (4 g sat. fat), 66 mg chol., 774 mg sodium, 7 g carb., 1 g dietary fiber, 28 g protein.

337

Turkey Reuben Loaf

START TO FINISH **30 minutes** OVEN **400°F** MAKES **4 servings**

½ cup mayonnaise or salad dressing

¼ cup sweet pickle relish

1 tablespoon ketchup

2 cups shredded cabbage

2 teaspoons vinegar

1 teaspoon caraway seeds

½ of an unsliced oblong loaf of bread

6 ounces Havarti cheese, sliced

8 ounces cooked turkey, sliced or chopped

1 Preheat oven to 400°F. For sauce, in a small bowl combine mayonnaise, pickle relish, and ketchup. In a medium bowl combine cabbage, vinegar, and caraway seeds.

2 Slice bread lengthwise. Remove some of the soft bread, reserving it for another use. Spread some of the sauce on cut sides of bread; reserve the remaining sauce for serving. Arrange half of the cheese slices on the bottom half of the bread. Top with cabbage mixture, turkey, and the remaining cheese. Top with the top half of the bread.

3 Wrap filled bread loaf tightly in foil; place on baking sheet. Bake for 10 minutes. Remove from oven; carefully unwrap. Bake for 2 to 3 minutes more or until bread is crisp and cheese is melted.

4 To serve, use a sharp serrated knife to cut loaf into slices. Pass the remaining sauce.

NUTRITION FACTS PER SERVING:
640 cal., 40 g total fat (13 g sat. fat), 85 mg chol., 931 mg sodium, 37 g carb., 5 g dietary fiber, 31 g protein.

338

Seafood

Bask in the bounty of the sea and watch
weekday dinner demands float away with
the help of fast-to-fix fish and seafood.

9

Broiled Salmon Orzo

START TO FINISH **30 minutes**   MAKES **4 servings**

- 4 **4- to 5-ounce fresh or frozen skinless salmon fillets**
- ¼ **teaspoon salt**
- ⅛ **teaspoon ground black pepper**
- ⅓ **cup dried orzo pasta (rosamarina)**
- 1 **tablespoon chopped pitted ripe olives**
- 1 **tablespoon snipped fresh parsley**
- 1 **teaspoon olive oil**
- ½ **teaspoon finely shredded lemon peel**
  Lemon wedges

1 Preheat broiler. Thaw fish, if frozen. Rinse fish; pat dry with paper towels. Place fish on the greased unheated rack of a broiler pan, tucking under any thin edges. Sprinkle with ⅛ teaspoon of the salt and half of the pepper. Set aside.

2 Cook pasta according to package directions; drain. Return to hot pan. Stir in olives, parsley, oil, lemon peel, the remaining ⅛ teaspoon salt, and the remaining pepper.

3 Meanwhile, broil fish about 4 inches from the heat for 4 to 6 minutes per ½-inch thickness or just until fish flakes easily when tested with a fork. (If fillets are 1 inch or more thick, carefully turn once halfway through broiling.)

4 Serve fish with pasta mixture and lemon wedges.

NUTRITION FACTS PER SERVING:
304 cal., 17 g total fat (4 g sat. fat), 62 mg chol., 220 mg sodium, 12 g carb., 1 g dietary fiber, 25 g protein.

> To test fish for doneness, gently place the tines of a fork into the fish and twist the fork slightly. If ready, the fish should flake and easily pull apart.

Baked Mediterranean Cod and Asparagus

START TO FINISH **30 minutes** OVEN **475°F** MAKES **4 servings**

1½ **pounds fresh or frozen skinless cod fillets, ½- to ¾-inch thick**

2 **tablespoons olive oil**

Salt

Ground black pepper

1 **pound asparagus spears, trimmed**

1 **recipe Olive Relish**

1 Preheat oven to 475°F. Thaw fish, if frozen. Rinse fish; pat dry with paper towels. Cut fish into four serving-size pieces, if necessary. Lightly coat a 15×10×1-inch baking pan with some of the olive oil. In one side of the pan arrange fish fillets, turning under any thin portions. Brush fish with 1 teaspoon of the remaining olive oil. Sprinkle fish with salt and pepper.

2 Bake for 5 minutes. Place asparagus in opposite side of pan; brush with the remaining olive oil and sprinkle with salt and pepper. Bake for 7 to 10 minutes more or until fish flakes easily when tested with a fork. Serve fish with Olive Relish and the asparagus.

NUTRITION FACTS PER SERVING:
257 cal., 12 g total fat (2 g sat. fat), 73 mg chol., 738 mg sodium, 5 g carb., 3 g dietary fiber, 32 g protein.

Olive Relish

In a small bowl combine ¾ cup whole pimiento-stuffed olives, coarsely chopped; ⅓ cup chopped onion (1 small); ¼ cup snipped fresh Italian (flat-leaf) parsley; 2 tablespoons capers, drained; 1 small fresh jalapeño chile pepper, seeded and chopped;* and 1 tablespoon white wine vinegar. Season to taste with ground black pepper. Makes 1⅓ cups.

*tip

Because chile peppers contain volatile oils that can burn your skin and eyes, avoid direct contact with them as much as possible. When working with chile peppers, wear plastic or rubber gloves. If your bare hands do touch the peppers, wash your hands and nails well with soap and warm water.

Lemony Cod with Asparagus

START TO FINISH 25 minutes   MAKES 4 servings

1 pound fresh or frozen skinless cod or flounder fillets, about $\frac{1}{2}$ inch thick

4 soft breadsticks

2 tablespoons butter or margarine, melted

$\frac{1}{4}$ teaspoon garlic salt

12 ounces asparagus spears, trimmed

1 tablespoon lemon juice

$\frac{1}{2}$ teaspoon dried thyme, crushed

$\frac{1}{8}$ teaspoon ground black pepper

Lemon wedges, halved crosswise (optional)

1 Thaw fish, if frozen. Preheat broiler. Place breadsticks on the unheated rack of a broiler pan. Brush with 1 tablespoon of the melted butter and sprinkle with the garlic salt. Broil 4 inches from heat for 1 to 2 minutes or until golden brown, turning breadsticks once. Remove from pan cover and keep warm.

2 Meanwhile, rinse fish; pat dry with paper towels. Arrange fish and asparagus in a single layer on the same broiler pan rack.

3 In a small bowl stir together the remaining 1 tablespoon butter and the lemon juice. Drizzle some of the butter mixture over fish; brush remaining butter mixture over asparagus. Sprinkle fish and asparagus with thyme and pepper.

4 Broil 4 inches from heat for 4 to 6 minutes or until fish flakes easily when tested with a fork and asparagus is crisp-tender, turning asparagus once. Serve fish and asparagus with breadsticks and, if desired, lemon wedges.

NUTRITION FACTS PER SERVING: *293 cal., 8 g total fat (4 g sat. fat), 64 mg chol., 454 mg sodium, 29 g carb., 3 g dietary fiber, 27 g protein.*

⏱ Prosciutto-Wrapped Fish

START TO FINISH 30 minutes MAKES 4 servings

2   fresh or frozen skinless cod
     fillets, about $\frac{1}{2}$ inch thick,
     or 4 skinless flounder,
     catfish, or trout fillets,
     about $\frac{1}{4}$ inch thick

4   2-inch sprigs fresh rosemary
     or 2 teaspoons dried
     rosemary, crushed

4   thin slices prosciutto or
     cooked ham

3   tablespoons lemon juice
     Freshly ground black pepper

2   medium roma tomatoes,
     halved lengthwise
     Olive oil

1   19-ounce can cannellini beans
     (white kidney beans), rinsed
     and drained

1   tablespoon olive oil

1   clove garlic, minced

2   teaspoons snipped fresh
     rosemary or $\frac{1}{2}$ teaspoon
     dried rosemary, crushed

$\frac{1}{4}$ teaspoon smoked sea salt,
     crushed, or $\frac{1}{8}$ teaspoon
     regular salt

1 Thaw fish, if frozen. Rinse fish; pat dry with paper towels. Cut each fillet in half crosswise. If using cod, place a rosemary sprig on top of each fillet half or sprinkle with the 2 teaspoons dried rosemary. If using thinner fish fillets, place rosemary sprigs or sprinkle dried rosemary on half of the pieces and top with the remaining fish pieces to make 4 stacks. Wrap 1 slice of the prosciutto around cod fillet or fish stack. Sprinkle fish with 1 tablespoon of the lemon juice and the pepper. Set aside.

2 Heat a nonstick or well-seasoned grill pan over medium heat. Brush tomatoes lightly with oil. Add tomato halves to grill pan, cut sides down. Cook for 6 to 8 minutes or until tomatoes are very tender, turning once. Remove tomatoes from grill pan; set aside to cool slightly.

3 Place fish fillets on grill pan,* rosemary sprig sides up if fillets are not stacked. Cook for 4 to 6 minutes or until fish flakes easily when tested with a fork, turning once halfway through cooking.

4 Meanwhile, in a medium serving bowl gently toss together the remaining 2 tablespoons lemon juice, the beans, 1 tablespoon oil, garlic, 2 teaspoons snipped rosemary, and salt. Serve fish and grilled tomatoes with bean mixture.

NUTRITION FACTS PER SERVING:
*276 cal., 7 g total fat (1 g sat. fat),
49 mg chol., 989 mg sodium, 21 g carb.,
7 g dietary fiber, 39 g protein.*

*tip
If the grill pan is large enough, tomatoes and fish may be grilled
at the same time.

Cioppino with Basil Gremolata

START TO FINISH **25 minutes** MAKES **4 servings**

6 ounces fresh or frozen cod fillets

6 ounces fresh or frozen peeled and deveined shrimp*

1 tablespoon olive oil or vegetable oil

1 cup green sweet pepper strips (1 medium)

1 cup chopped onion (1 large)

2 cloves garlic, minced

2 14.5-ounce cans Italian-style stewed tomatoes, undrained and cut up

½ cup water

¼ teaspoon salt

¼ teaspoon ground black pepper

3 tablespoons snipped fresh basil

1 tablespoon finely shredded lemon peel

2 cloves garlic, minced

1 Thaw cod and shrimp, if frozen. Rinse cod and shrimp; pat dry with paper towels. Cut cod into 1-inch pieces; set aside. In a large pot heat oil over medium heat. Add sweet pepper, onion, and 2 cloves minced garlic. Cook and stir until tender. Stir in tomatoes, the water, salt, and black pepper. Bring to boiling. Stir in cod and shrimp. Return to boiling; reduce heat. Simmer, covered, for 2 to 3 minutes or just until cod flakes easily when tested with a fork and shrimp are opaque.

2 In a small bowl combine basil, lemon peel, and 2 cloves minced garlic. Sprinkle each serving with basil mixture.

NUTRITION FACTS PER SERVING: *188 cal., 5 g total fat (1 g sat. fat), 83 mg chol., 921 mg sodium, 20 g carb., 5 g dietary fiber, 19 g protein.*

*tip

For a more dramatic presentation, use shrimp with the tails left on. Start with 8 ounces shrimp; peel and devein shrimp, leaving tails intact.

Maple-Bourbon Glazed Salmon

4   4- to 5-ounce fresh or frozen skinless, salmon fillets

⅓   cup pure maple syrup or maple-flavor syrup

⅓   cup orange juice

3   tablespoons bourbon or orange juice

    Salt

    Ground black pepper

¼   cup coarsely chopped pecans or walnuts

1 Thaw fish, if frozen. Preheat broiler. For glaze, in a small saucepan combine maple syrup, orange juice, and bourbon. Cook, uncovered, over medium heat for 5 minutes.

2 Meanwhile, rinse fish; pat dry with paper towels. Lightly sprinkle salmon with salt and pepper. Place on a lightly greased broiler pan. Broil 3 to 4 inches from heat for 5 minutes. Remove 2 tablespoons of the glaze and brush salmon on all sides. Turn salmon; broil about 5 minutes more or until salmon flakes easily when tested with a fork. Discard remainder of the glaze used to brush fish.

3 Stir pecans into the remaining glaze; cook over high heat about 5 minutes or until glaze reaches the consistency of syrup. Serve salmon topped with pecan mixture.

NUTRITION FACTS PER SERVING: *386 cal., 20 g total fat (4 g sat. fat), 62 mg chol., 215 mg sodium, 21 g carb., 1 g dietary fiber, 24 g protein.*

Salmon with Roasted Vegetables

START TO FINISH 30 minutes OVEN 450°F MAKES 4 servings

4   4- to 5-ounce fresh or frozen skinless salmon fillets, about 1 inch thick
    Nonstick cooking spray
1   tablespoon snipped fresh dill or 1 teaspoon dried dill
½   teaspoon salt
¼   teaspoon ground black pepper
2   medium zucchini and/or yellow summer squash, cut crosswise into ¼-inch slices (about 2½ cups)
1   cup grape tomatoes or cherry tomatoes, halved
4   green onions, cut into 1-inch pieces
1   tablespoon Dijon-style mustard

1 Preheat oven to 450°F. Thaw fish, if frozen. Rinse fish; pat dry with paper towels. Set aside. Line a 15×10×1-inch baking pan with foil; lightly coat foil with cooking spray. Set aside.

2 In a small bowl combine dill, salt, and pepper; set aside. In a large bowl combine zucchini, tomatoes, and green onions. Generously coat vegetables with cooking spray, tossing to coat evenly. Sprinkle with half of the dill mixture, tossing to coat evenly.

3 In one side of the foil-lined pan spoon vegetable mixture. Arrange fish in other side of pan. Stir mustard into the remaining dill mixture. Spread mustard-dill mixture evenly over fish.

4 Bake, uncovered, for 4 to 6 minutes per ½-inch thickness of fish or until fish flakes easily when tested with a fork and zucchini is crisp-tender.

NUTRITION FACTS PER SERVING: *239 cal., 12 g total fat (3 g sat. fat), 66 mg chol., 463 mg sodium, 6 g carb., 2 g dietary fiber, 24 g protein.*

346

Salmon with Tropical Rice

START TO FINISH **30 minutes**   MAKES **4 servings**

1   1½-pound fresh or frozen skinless salmon fillet, about 1 inch thick

2   teaspoons olive oil

1   teaspoon lemon-pepper seasoning

1   8.8-ounce pouch cooked brown or white rice

1   medium mango,* peeled, seeded, and chopped

1   tablespoon snipped fresh cilantro

1   teaspoon finely shredded lemon peel

Lemon wedges (optional)

Fresh cilantro sprigs (optional)

1 Thaw salmon, if frozen. Rinse fish; pat dry with paper towels. Preheat oven to 450°F. Grease a 3-quart rectangular baking dish; place fish in prepared dish. Drizzle oil over fish. Sprinkle with lemon-pepper seasoning.

2 In a medium bowl stir together cooked rice, mango, snipped cilantro, and lemon peel, breaking up rice with a spoon. Spoon rice mixture around fish. Bake, uncovered, about 15 minutes or until fish flakes easily when tested with a fork.

3 To serve, cut fish into four serving-size pieces. Serve fish on top of rice mixture. If desired, garnish with lemon wedges and cilantro sprigs.

NUTRITION FACTS PER SERVING: *462 cal., 22 g total fat (4 g sat. fat), 99 mg chol., 104 mg sodium, 27 g carb., 2 g dietary fiber, 36 g protein.*

*tip

Because the meat from the mango holds tightly to the seed, this fruit require a little effort before yielding its fragrant meat. An easy way to remove the meat is to make a cut through the mango, sliding a sharp knife next to the seed along one side. Repeat on the other side of the seed, resulting in two large pieces. Then cut away all of the meat that remains around the seed. Remove peel on all pieces and cut up the meat.

Seafood

Salmon and Couscous Casserole

START TO FINISH **25 minutes** MAKES **4 servings**

1 cup water

2 cloves garlic, minced

2/3 cup whole wheat couscous

1 14.75-ounce can salmon, drained, flaked, and skin and bones removed

2 cups fresh baby spinach leaves

1/2 cup bottled roasted red sweet peppers, drained and chopped

1/3 cup bottled tomato bruschetta topper

2 tablespoons purchased toasted almonds*

1 In a 2-quart microwave-safe casserole combine the water and garlic. Microwave, uncovered, on 100 percent power (high) for 2½ to 3 minutes or until mixture is boiling. Remove from microwave; stir in couscous. Spoon salmon on top of couscous mixture. Cover and let stand for 5 minutes.

2 Add spinach, roasted peppers, and bruschetta topper to couscous mixture. Toss to combine. Divide mixture among four serving plates. Top with almonds.

NUTRITION FACTS PER SERVING: *335 cal., 9 g total fat (2 g sat. fat), 41 mg chol., 616 mg sodium, 34 g carb., 6 g dietary fiber, 30 g protein.*

348

*tip
If you cannot find toasted almonds at the supermarket, you can toast your own. Preheat oven to 350°F. Spread whole almonds in a single layer in a pie pan. Bake for 8 to 10 minutes or until lightly browned, stirring occasionally. Cool completely before using.

Simple Salmon, Greens, and Couscous

START TO FINISH **30 minutes** MAKES **4 servings**

Nonstick cooking spray

4 **skinless salmon fillets, about 1 inch thick (about 1 pound total)**

¼ **teaspoon salt**

¼ **teaspoon ground black pepper**

2 **teaspoons reduced-sodium soy sauce**

1 **tablespoon olive oil**

3 **cups trimmed and coarsely chopped mustard greens or collard greens**

1 **14-ounce can chicken broth**

1 **cup couscous**

Lemon wedges (optional)

1 Preheat oven to 450°F. Line a shallow baking pan with foil and lightly coat with cooking spray; set aside.

2 Sprinkle fish fillets with salt and pepper. Arrange fillets in prepared pan. Drizzle with soy sauce. Bake, uncovered, for 15 to 18 minutes or just until fish flakes easily when tested with a fork.

3 Meanwhile, heat oil in a 2-quart saucepan over medium heat. Stir in greens; cover and cook for 5 minutes or until greens are nearly tender, stirring once or twice. Add broth; bring to boiling.

4 Stir in couscous; remove from heat and let stand for 5 minutes.

5 Divide couscous mixture among four serving plates. Top with fish fillets. If desired, serve with lemon wedges.

NUTRITION FACTS PER SERVING:
603 cal., 16 g total fat (3 g sat. fat), 67 mg chol., 562 mg sodium, 74 g carb., 6 g dietary fiber, 37 g protein.

349

Salmon, Rice, and Pesto Salad

START TO FINISH **25 minutes** MAKES **4 servings**

1½	**cups fresh sugar snap peas or 1-inch pieces fresh asparagus**
1	**8.8-ounce pouch cooked long grain and wild rice**
¼	**cup basil or dried tomato pesto**
¼	**cup light mayonnaise or salad dressing**
1	**8-ounce piece smoked salmon, flaked and skin and bones removed**
1	**cup cherry tomatoes, halved**
⅓	**cup thinly sliced radishes**
	Lettuce leaves

1 In a medium saucepan cook sugar snap peas in a small amount of boiling lightly salted water for 2 minutes; drain. Place in a bowl of ice water to chill; drain.

2 In a large bowl combine cooked rice, pesto, and mayonnaise. Gently stir in sugar snap peas, smoked salmon, tomatoes, and radishes. Arrange lettuce among dinner plates. Spoon salad on top of lettuce.

NUTRITION FACTS PER SERVING:
312 cal., 14 g total fat (3 g sat. fat), 23 mg chol., 892 mg sodium, 28 g carb., 3 g dietary fiber, 16 g protein.

Poached Salmon on Ciabatta

START TO FINISH **30 minutes**   MAKES **4 sandwiches**

½   cup dry white wine or water

½   cup water

12   ounces fresh or frozen skinless salmon fillet, about 1 inch thick

¼   cup tub-style whipped cream cheese with garlic and herbs

2   tablespoons fat-free milk

1   tablespoon snipped fresh dill

1   teaspoon finely shredded lemon peel

⅛   teaspoon cracked black pepper

4   2-ounce ciabatta rolls, split and toasted, if desired

1   cup fresh baby spinach

1 In a large nonstick skillet combine wine and the water. Bring to boiling; add fish. Reduce heat. Cover and simmer for 8 to 12 minutes or just until fish flakes easily when tested with a fork. Remove fish from cooking liquid; discard liquid. Let fish cool to room temperature; break into large chunks.

2 Meanwhile, in a small bowl combine cream cheese, milk, dill, lemon peel, and cracked pepper. Spread cream cheese mixture on cut sides of the ciabatta rolls. Arrange spinach and fish chunks on bottoms of rolls. Add tops of rolls, spread sides down.

NUTRITION FACTS PER SANDWICH:
395 cal., 16 g total fat (5 g sat. fat), 57 mg chol., 458 mg sodium, 30 g carb., 2 g dietary fiber, 23 g protein.

351

Sesame-Teriyaki Sea Bass

START TO FINISH 25 minutes   MAKES 4 servings

- 4   4-ounce fresh or frozen sea bass, rockfish, or other fish fillets, $\frac{1}{2}$ to $\frac{3}{4}$ inch thick
- $\frac{1}{4}$ teaspoon ground black pepper
- $\frac{1}{4}$ cup sweet rice wine (mirin)
- 3   tablespoons soy sauce
- 2   teaspoons honey
- 2   teaspoons vegetable oil
- 2   teaspoons sesame seeds and/or black sesame seeds, toasted*

1 Thaw fish, if frozen. Rinse fish; pat dry with paper towels. Sprinkle fish with pepper; set aside.

2 For glaze, in a small saucepan combine rice wine, soy sauce, and honey. Bring to boiling; reduce heat. Simmer, uncovered, about 10 minutes or until glaze is slightly thickened and reduced to $\frac{1}{3}$ cup; set aside.

3 Meanwhile, in a large nonstick skillet heat oil over medium heat. Add fish; cook 4 to 6 minutes per $\frac{1}{2}$-inch thickness of fish or until fish is golden and flakes easily when tested with a fork, turning once. Drain fish on paper towels.

4 Transfer fish to a serving platter; drizzle glaze over fish. Sprinkle with sesame seeds.

NUTRITION FACTS PER SERVING:
181 cal., 5 g total fat (1 g sat. fat), 46 mg chol., 968 mg sodium, 11 g carb., 0 g dietary fiber, 22 g protein.

352

*tip
To toast sesame seeds, spread seeds in a dry skillet; cook over medium heat for 3 to 5 minutes or until toasted, stirring often and watching closely so seeds don't burn. Remove immediately from skillet.

Crispy Fish and Peppers

START TO FINISH **20 minutes** MAKES **4 servings**

1 **pound fresh or frozen small fish fillets, such as grouper, catfish, or tilapia**

¾ **cup buttermilk**

1 **egg**

1 **teaspoon Cajun seasoning**

1 **cup all-purpose flour**

3 **to 4 tablespoons vegetable oil**

1 **cup sliced and/or chopped miniature sweet peppers**

1 **lemon, cut into wedges**

1 Thaw fish, if frozen. Rinse fish; pat dry with paper towels.

2 In a shallow dish whisk together buttermilk, egg, and Cajun seasoning. Place flour into another shallow dish. Dip fish in buttermilk mixture, then into flour, turning to coat. Repeat twice to coat fish well.

3 In a large heavy skillet heat 3 tablespoons of the oil over medium-high heat. Carefully add fish to hot oil (working in batches, if necessary). Cook for 6 to 10 minutes or until golden, turning once halfway through cooking. Add more oil, if necessary. Drain fish on paper towels.

4 Drain oil from skillet; wipe skillet clean with paper towels. Add sweet peppers to skillet; cook about 2 minutes or until crisp-tender.

5 Serve fish with peppers and lemon.

NUTRITION FACTS PER SERVING: *251 cal., 13 g total fat (2 g sat. fat), 97 mg chol., 188 mg sodium, 8 g carb., 2 g dietary fiber, 26 g protein.*

353

tip

When cooking fish in a skillet, it's important to dry the fish thoroughly after rinsing. The drier the fish, the easier it is for any buttermilk or egg wash mixture and flour coating to cling to the fish.

Pan-Fried Fish with Peppers and Pecans

START TO FINISH **25 minutes** MAKES **4 servings**

- 1 **pound fresh or frozen thin white fish fillets, such as trout, tilapia, or catfish (skinned, if desired)**
- $\frac{1}{3}$ **cup all-purpose flour**
- $\frac{1}{4}$ **teaspoon salt**
- 6 **tablespoons butter or margarine**
- 1 **tablespoon packed brown sugar**
- $\frac{1}{2}$ **cup chopped pecans**
- $\frac{1}{2}$ **of a red sweet pepper, seeded and cut into strips**
- $\frac{1}{8}$ **teaspoon cayenne pepper**
  Juice from 1 small lime
  Green onions, sliced

1 Thaw fish, if frozen. Rinse fish; pat dry with paper towels. If necessary, cut fish into serving-size pieces. In a shallow dish combine flour and salt. Dip fish into flour mixture to coat.

2 In a large skillet heat 3 tablespoons of the butter over medium-high heat until melted. Add fish in a single layer. Reduce heat to medium. Cook for 6 to 8 minutes or until golden and fish flakes easily when tested with a fork, turning once. Remove fish from skillet; cover and keep warm.

3 Wipe out skillet. Add the remaining 3 tablespoons butter to skillet; heat over medium heat until melted. Add brown sugar, stirring until dissolved. Stir in pecans, sweet pepper, and cayenne. Cook and stir for 3 to 4 minutes or until pecans are lightly toasted and pepper strips are just tender. Remove from heat. Stir in lime juice. Spoon pecan mixture over fish. Top with green onions.

NUTRITION FACTS PER SERVING:
364 cal., 24 g total fat (10 g sat. fat), 97 mg chol., 268 mg sodium, 11 g carb., 1 g dietary fiber, 26 g protein.

Thai-Style Tilapia and Vegetables

4 4- to 6-ounce fresh or frozen skinless tilapia, cod, or other fish fillets, about $\frac{1}{2}$ inch thick

1 red sweet pepper, seeded and cut into thin, bite-size strips

1 cup thin asparagus spears or green beans trimmed and cut into 2-inch pieces

1 medium carrot, cut into thin, bite-size strips

$\frac{1}{4}$ teaspoon salt

$\frac{1}{8}$ teaspoon ground black pepper

$\frac{3}{4}$ cup canned unsweetened light coconut milk

2 teaspoons lime juice

2 teaspoons fish sauce or soy sauce

1 teaspoon grated fresh ginger or $\frac{1}{2}$ teaspoon ground ginger

$\frac{1}{8}$ to $\frac{1}{4}$ teaspoon crushed red pepper

2 tablespoons chopped peanuts

1 tablespoon snipped fresh cilantro

1 Thaw fish, if frozen. Rinse fish; pat dry with paper towels.

2 Fill a 12-inch skillet with water to a depth of 1 inch. Bring water to boiling; reduce heat. Arrange sweet pepper, asparagus, and carrot in a steamer basket. Place fish on top of vegetables. Sprinkle fish and vegetables with salt and black pepper. Place steamer basket over the simmering water; cover and simmer gently for 6 to 8 minutes or until fish flakes easily when tested with a fork.

3 Meanwhile, for sauce, in a small saucepan combine coconut milk, lime juice, fish sauce, ginger, and crushed red pepper. Bring to boiling; reduce heat. Boil gently, uncovered, for 2 to 3 minutes or until slightly thickened.

4 Arrange fish and vegetables among dinner plates; drizzle with sauce and sprinkle with peanuts and cilantro.

NUTRITION FACTS PER SERVING:
173 cal., 5 g total fat (2 g sat. fat), 48 mg chol., 557 mg sodium, 8 g carb., 2 g dietary fiber, 23 g protein.

355

Tilapia Puttanesca

START TO FINISH **30 minutes** MAKES **4 servings**

1	**pound fresh or frozen skinless tilapia fillets**
⅛	**teaspoon salt**
1	**tablespoon olive oil**
½	**of a medium red onion, cut into wedges**
1	**14.5-ounce can diced tomatoes, undrained**
2	**cloves garlic, minced**
2	**teaspoons dried oregano, crushed**
¼	**teaspoon crushed red pepper**
¼	**cup pitted ripe olives**
1	**tablespoon capers, drained (optional)**
2	**tablespoons coarsely snipped fresh Italian (flat-leaf) parsley**

1 Thaw fish, if frozen. Rinse fish; pat dry with paper towels. Sprinkle with salt; set aside.

2 For sauce, in a large skillet heat oil over medium heat. Add red onion; cook about 8 minutes or until tender, stirring occasionally. Stir in tomatoes, garlic, oregano, and crushed red pepper. Bring to boiling; reduce heat. Simmer, uncovered, for 5 minutes.

3 Add olives and, if desired, capers to sauce. Top with fish fillets. Return to boiling; reduce heat. Cook, covered, for 6 to 10 minutes or until fish flakes easily when tested with fork. Remove fish. Simmer sauce, uncovered, for 1 to 2 minutes more or until thickened. To serve, spoon sauce over fish. Sprinkle with parsley.

NUTRITION FACTS PER SERVING:
182 cal., 6 g total fat (1 g sat. fat), 56 mg chol., 431 mg sodium, 8 g carb., 2 g dietary fiber, 24 g protein.

Cumin-Spiced Fish Tacos

START TO FINISH **25 minutes**   OVEN **450°F**   MAKES **4 servings**

12	ounces fresh or frozen skinless fish fillets
1	tablespoon olive oil
¼	teaspoon salt
¼	teaspoon ground cumin
⅛	teaspoon garlic powder
1½	cups shredded lettuce
1	medium tomato, seeded and chopped
8	corn taco shells, warmed according to package directions
½	cup salsa

1 Thaw fish, if frozen. Preheat oven to 450°F. Grease a shallow baking pan; set aside. Rinse fish; pat dry with paper towels. Cut fish crosswise into ¾-inch slices. Place fish in a single layer in prepared baking pan. In a small bowl combine oil, salt, cumin, and garlic powder; brush over fish. Bake, uncovered, for 4 to 6 minutes or just until fish flakes easily when tested with a fork.

2 To serve, divide lettuce and tomato among taco shells; add fish slices and top with salsa.

NUTRITION FACTS PER SERVING:
322 cal., 19 g total fat (3 g sat. fat), 44 mg chol., 353 mg sodium, 21 g carb., 3 g dietary fiber, 17 g protein.

Add more flavor-packed interest to any tacos by offering a variety of topping options.
- Fresh fruit salsa made with kiwifruit, red onion, strawberries, mango, and green onion.
- Black bean salsa (black beans, tomato, corn, chopped jalapeño chile pepper, and cilantro) or other bean salsa.
- Coleslaw mix combined with a little mayonnaise and lime juice.
- Chopped fresh tomato and basil, cubed mozzarella cheese, and a drizzle of balsamic vinaigrette.
- Sweet pepper strips and mayonnaise mixed with a chopped chipotle chile pepper.
- Crumbled crisp-cooked bacon and a spoonful of mayonnaise.

Catfish and Slaw Tacos

START TO FINISH **30 minutes** MAKES **8 tacos**

1 pound fresh or frozen catfish fillets
1 lime
¼ cup mayonnaise or salad dressing
½ teaspoon bottled hot pepper sauce
½ of a small head cabbage, shredded (about 2½ cups)
1 tablespoon Cajun seasoning
¼ cup cornmeal
¼ cup all-purpose flour
¼ cup vegetable oil
16 4-inch corn tortillas or eight 8-inch flour tortillas
   Lime wedges
   Bottled hot pepper sauce (optional)

1 Thaw fish, if frozen. Rinse fish; pat dry with paper towels. Cut fish into 1-inch strips; set aside.

2 Meanwhile, for slaw, cut whole lime in half; squeeze about 3 tablespoons juice. In a medium bowl combine lime juice, mayonnaise, and the ½ teaspoon hot pepper sauce. Add cabbage; toss to coat. Set aside.

3 Toss fish strips with Cajun seasoning. In a large bowl combine cornmeal and flour. Add fish strips; toss to coat.

4 In a large skillet heat oil over medium heat. Cook fish strips, half at a time, in hot oil for 4 to 6 minutes or until golden and fish flakes easily when tested with a fork, turning to brown evenly. Remove from skillet.

5 Wrap tortillas in paper towels. Microwave on 100 percent power (high) for 1 minute (or toast in a dry skillet). If using corn tortillas, stack 2 for each taco, or use 1 flour tortilla for each taco. Divide fish and slaw among tortillas. Reserve any dressing left in bowl to serve with tacos. Serve tacos immediately with reserved dressing, lime wedges, and additional hot pepper sauce.

NUTRITION FACTS PER SERVING:
620 cal., 36 g total fat (5 g sat. fat), 59 mg chol., 300 mg sodium, 53 g carb., 3 g dietary fiber, 24 g protein.

Grilled Tuna Steaks and Vegetables

4 **5-ounce fresh or frozen tuna steaks, cut 1 inch thick**

2 **tablespoons canola oil**

2 **tablespoons lime juice**

$\frac{1}{2}$ **teaspoon ground ancho chile pepper or chili powder**

$\frac{1}{4}$ **teaspoon ground cumin**

1 **clove garlic, minced**

$\frac{1}{4}$ **teaspoon salt**

1 **large zucchini, trimmed and halved lengthwise**

1 **large red sweet pepper, seeded and quartered**

2 **$\frac{1}{4}$-inch slices red onion**

2 **tablespoons coarsely chopped walnuts, toasted**

Fresh cilantro

Lime wedges

1 Thaw fish, if frozen. Rinse fish; pat dry with paper towels. In a small bowl whisk together oil, lime juice, ground chile pepper, cumin, garlic, and salt. Brush about half of the oil mixture onto both sides of each zucchini half, pepper quarter, and onion slice. Brush the remaining oil mixture on the tuna.

2 For a charcoal grill, grill fish and vegetables on the greased rack of an uncovered grill directly over medium coals for 8 to 12 minutes or just until fish flakes easily when tested with a fork and vegetables are crisp-tender, gently turning fish and vegetables once halfway through grilling. (For a gas grill, preheat grill. Reduce heat to medium. Place fish and vegetables on greased grill rack over heat. Cover and grill as above.)

3 Cut zucchini pieces crosswise in half and then cut lengthwise into thick slices. Cut pepper quarters lengthwise into thick slices. Using tongs, separate onion slices into rings.

4 To serve, place vegetables on dinner plates. Arrange tuna on top of vegetables; sprinkle with nuts. Garnish with cilantro. Pass lime wedges.

NUTRITION FACTS PER SERVING:
265 cal., 11 g total fat (1 g sat. fat), 63 mg chol., 209 mg sodium, 7 g carb., 2 g dietary fiber, 35 g protein.

359

Tuna Caponata

START TO FINISH **30 minutes** MAKES **4 servings**

12   ounces fresh or frozen tuna
     steaks, cut 1 inch thick

5   tablespoons olive oil

1   medium eggplant, peeled and
     cut into 1-inch pieces

1   medium onion, cut into thin
     wedges

3   cloves garlic, minced

1   19-ounce can cannellini beans
     (white kidney beans), rinsed
     and drained

1   8- or 9-ounce package frozen
     artichoke hearts, thawed and
     coarsely chopped

1   cup chopped tomatoes (2)

2   tablespoons red wine vinegar

1   tablespoon capers, drained

2   teaspoons snipped fresh
     rosemary

1   teaspoon sugar

$\frac{1}{2}$ teaspoon salt

$\frac{1}{4}$ teaspoon crushed red pepper

$\frac{1}{4}$ cup pine nuts, toasted
     Salt
     Ground black pepper
     Fresh rosemary sprigs
     and/or snipped fresh Italian
     (flat-leaf) parsley

1 Thaw fish, if frozen. In a 12-inch skillet heat 4 tablespoons of the oil over medium-high heat. Add eggplant; cook about 5 minutes or until golden, stirring occasionally. Using a slotted spoon, remove eggplant from skillet; set aside.

2 Add the remaining 1 tablespoon oil to skillet. Add onion and garlic; cook over medium heat about 4 minutes or until onion is tender, stirring occasionally.

3 Stir in beans, artichokes, tomatoes, vinegar, capers, the snipped rosemary, the sugar, the $\frac{1}{2}$ teaspoon salt, and crushed red pepper. Bring to boiling; reduce heat. Simmer, uncovered, for 5 minutes, stirring occasionally. Remove from heat; stir in eggplant and pine nuts. Cool to room temperature.

4 Meanwhile, rinse fish; pat dry with paper towels. Sprinkle tuna lightly with salt and black pepper. Preheat a greased grill pan over medium-high heat. Place tuna in grill pan. Cook for 8 to 12 minutes or just until tuna flakes easily when tested with a fork but is still slightly pink in center, turning once.

5 Arrange eggplant mixture on a serving platter. Arrange tuna on top of eggplant mixture. Garnish with rosemary sprigs and/or parsley. To serve, cut tuna into four serving-size pieces.

NUTRITION FACTS PER SERVING:
496 cal., 28 g total fat (4 g sat. fat), 32 mg chol., 784 mg sodium, 38 g carb., 16 g dietary fiber, 32 g protein.

★ Tuna and Biscuits

START TO FINISH **30 minutes**   OVEN **400°F**   MAKES **4 servings**

1   10-ounce container reduced-fat Alfredo pasta sauce

1   10-ounce package frozen peas and carrots

1   4-ounce can (drained weight) sliced mushrooms, drained

1   teaspoon lemon juice

¼   teaspoon dried dill

1   12-ounce can tuna, drained and flaked

1   cup packaged biscuit mix

⅓   cup fat-free milk

¼   cup shredded cheddar cheese (1 ounce)

1 Preheat oven to 400°F. In a large ovenproof skillet combine pasta sauce, peas and carrots, mushrooms, lemon juice, and dill. Cook and stir over medium heat until bubbly and heated through. Stir in tuna; cover and keep warm.

2 In a medium bowl stir together biscuit mix, milk, and half of the cheese. Drop mixture into four mounds on top of tuna mixture. Sprinkle with the remaining cheese.

3 Bake for 12 to 15 minutes or until biscuits are golden.

NUTRITION FACTS PER SERVING:
487 cal., 20 g total fat (9 g sat. fat), 74 mg chol., 1,540 mg sodium, 46 g carb., 3 g dietary fiber, 33 g protein.

Greek Leeks and Shrimp Stir-Fry

START TO FINISH 30 minutes   MAKES 4 servings

1¼	pounds fresh or frozen peeled and deveined medium shrimp
⅔	cup water
⅓	cup lemon juice
1	tablespoon cornstarch
¾	teaspoon bouquet garni seasoning or dried oregano, crushed
1	cup quick-cooking couscous
½	teaspoon dried oregano, crushed
¼	teaspoon salt
1½	cups boiling water
1	tablespoon olive oil
1⅓	cups thinly sliced leeks
½	cup crumbled feta cheese (2 ounces)

1 Thaw shrimp, if frozen. Rinse shrimp; pat dry with paper towels. Set aside.

2 In a small bowl combine the ⅔ cup water, the lemon juice, cornstarch, and ¼ teaspoon of the bouquet garni seasoning; set aside.

3 In another small bowl combine couscous, oregano, salt, and the remaining ½ teaspoon bouquet garni seasoning. Pour the 1½ cups boiling water over couscous mixture. Cover and let stand for 5 minutes.

4 Meanwhile, in a wok or 12-inch skillet heat oil over medium-high heat. Add leeks; cook and stir for 2 to 3 minutes or until tender. Remove leeks from wok; set aside. Stir lemon juice mixture; add to wok. Bring to boiling. Add shrimp; cook for 2 to 3 minutes or until shrimp are opaque. Stir in cooked leeks and ¼ cup of the feta cheese.

5 To serve, fluff couscous mixture with a fork. Transfer couscous mixture to a serving platter. Spoon shrimp mixture over couscous; sprinkle with the remaining ¼ cup feta cheese.

NUTRITION FACTS PER SERVING: *433 cal., 10 g total fat (4 g sat. fat), 232 mg chol., 548 mg sodium, 45 g carb., 3 g dietary fiber, 38 g protein.*

Shrimp and Couscous Jambalaya

START TO FINISH **30 minutes** MAKES **4 servings**

12 ounces fresh or frozen
   medium shrimp in shells
2 tablespoons vegetable oil
1 cup sliced celery (2 stalks)
¾ cup chopped green sweet
   pepper (1 medium)
½ cup chopped onion
   (1 medium)
½ teaspoon Cajun seasoning
¼ teaspoon dried oregano,
   crushed
1 14.5-ounce can reduced-
   sodium chicken broth
1 cup couscous
½ cup chopped tomato
   (1 medium)
   Bottled hot pepper sauce
   (optional)
   Lemon wedges (optional)

1 Thaw shrimp, if frozen. Peel and devein shrimp.* Rinse shrimp; pat dry with paper towels. Set aside.

2 In a large skillet heat oil over medium heat. Add celery, sweet pepper, onion, Cajun seasoning, and oregano. Cook and stir until vegetables are tender. Carefully add broth. Bring to boiling.

3 Stir in shrimp; remove from heat. Stir in couscous and tomato. Cover and let stand for 5 minutes. To serve, fluff mixture with a fork. Transfer mixture to a shallow serving bowl. If desired, serve with hot pepper sauce and lemon wedges.

NUTRITION FACTS PER SERVING:
317 cal., 8 g total fat (1 g sat. fat), 98 mg chol., 462 mg sodium, 42 g carb., 9 g dietary fiber, 18 g protein.

*tip

To peel shrimp, use your fingers to open the shell lengthwise down the body's underside. Starting at the head end, peel the shell back from the body. Then gently pull on the tail portion of the shell and remove it. To devein shrimp, use a sharp knife to make a shallow slit along the shrimp's back from the head end to the tail. Rinse under cold running water to remove the vein, using the tip of knife, if necessary.

Seafood

Shrimp and Tomato Piccata ⏱ 🥕

START TO FINISH **20 minutes**   MAKES **4 servings**

1   **pound fresh or frozen peeled and deveined medium shrimp**

3   **tablespoons olive oil**

8   **ounces small, thin green beans, trimmed (2 cups)**

3   **small tomatoes, cut into wedges**

1   **teaspoon finely shredded lemon peel**

3   **tablespoons lemon juice**

1   **tablespoon capers, drained**
    Hot cooked pasta (optional)

1 Thaw shrimp, if frozen. Rinse shrimp; pat dry with paper towels. Set aside.

2 In a very large skillet heat 1 tablespoon of the oil over medium-high heat. Add green beans; cook for 3 minutes. Add shrimp; cook and stir about 3 minutes or until shrimp are opaque. Add tomato wedges; cook for 1 minute more. Divide shrimp mixture among four dinner plates.

3 For sauce, in a small bowl whisk together the remaining 2 tablespoons oil, the lemon peel, lemon juice, and capers. Drizzle sauce over shrimp mixture. If desired, serve with hot cooked pasta.

NUTRITION FACTS PER SERVING:
244 cal., 12 g total fat (2 g sat. fat), 172 mg chol., 239 mg sodium, 10 g carb., 4 g dietary fiber, 25 g protein.

Spicy Shrimp Pasta

1 **pound fresh or frozen peeled and deveined shrimp with tails**

8 **ounces dried angel hair pasta**

3 **cups broccoli florets**

1 **6.5-ounce jar oil-pack dried tomato strips with Italian herbs**

   Olive oil

2 **shallots, finely chopped**

¼ **to ½ teaspoon crushed red pepper**

   Salt

   Ground black pepper

¼ **cup snipped fresh basil**

1 Thaw shrimp, if frozen. Rinse shrimp; pat dry with paper towels. In a 4-quart Dutch oven cook pasta according to pasta package directions, adding broccoli to the water with pasta; drain. Return to Dutch oven; cover to keep warm.

2 Meanwhile, drain dried tomatoes, reserving oil. If necessary, add enough olive oil to equal ¼ cup total. In an extra-large skillet heat reserved oil over medium-high heat. Add shallots; cook and stir for 1 to 2 minutes or until tender. Add shrimp and crushed red pepper; cook and stir for 2 minutes. Add dried tomatoes; cook and stir about 1 minute more or until shrimp are opaque.

3 Toss shrimp mixture with cooked pasta. Season to taste with salt and black pepper. Drizzle with additional olive oil. Transfer to a serving bowl. Sprinkle with fresh basil.

NUTRITION FACTS PER SERVING:
526 cal., 19 g total fat (3 g sat. fat), 172 mg chol., 394 mg sodium, 55 g carb., 5 g dietary fiber, 34 g protein.

Shrimp Po' Boy

START TO FINISH 30 minutes MAKES 4 servings

1   12-ounce package frozen medium shrimp
2   teaspoons Old Bay seasoning
¼   teaspoon ground black pepper
1   tablespoon vegetable oil
1   cup deli coleslaw
2   teaspoons prepared horseradish
½   teaspoon bottled hot pepper sauce
4   individual French or hoagie rolls, split and toasted
    Potato chips or corn chips (optional)

1 Place shrimp in a medium bowl half-filled with cool water. Let stand for 5 minutes; drain. Remove tails from shrimp, if present. In the same bowl toss shrimp with Old Bay seasoning and black pepper.

2 In a large skillet heat oil over medium-high heat. Add shrimp; cook about 3 minutes or until opaque.

3 In a small bowl combine coleslaw, horseradish, and hot pepper sauce. To serve, divide shrimp among bottoms of rolls. Top with coleslaw mixture. Add tops of rolls. If desired, serve with chips.

NUTRITION FACTS PER SERVING:
545 cal., 14 g total fat (3 g sat. fat), 132 mg chol., 1,158 mg sodium, 77 g carb., 4 g dietary fiber, 29 g protein.

Mexican Shrimp Tostadas

START TO FINISH **20 minutes**   MAKES **4 servings**

1   **pound fresh or frozen cooked shrimp**

8   **tostada shells**

1   **8-ounce can no-salt-added tomato sauce**

1   **1.25-ounce envelope reduced-sodium taco seasoning mix**

Canned refried beans or black beans, warmed (optional)

Shredded lettuce

Sliced green onions

½   **cup shredded Monterey Jack cheese (2 ounces)**

¼   **cup sour cream**

Salsa

Green onions, sliced

1 Thaw shrimp, if frozen; remove tails, if present. Heat tostada shells according to package directions.

2 In a large nonstick skillet combine shrimp, tomato sauce, and taco seasoning. Bring to boiling; reduce heat. Simmer, uncovered, for 2 to 3 minutes or until shrimp are heated through, stirring occasionally.

3 To serve, spread warmed tostada shells with refried beans, if desired. Arrange lettuce, black beans, if desired, and green onions on tostada shells; top with shrimp mixture. Serve with cheese, sour cream, salsa, and additional sliced green onions.

NUTRITION FACTS PER SERVING:
362 cal., 16 g total fat (6 g sat. fat), 190 mg chol., 920 mg sodium, 27 g carb., 3 g dietary fiber, 30 g protein.

Easy Shrimp and Saffron Rice

START TO FINISH 30 minutes MAKES 4 servings

2 tablespoons vegetable oil

2 cloves garlic, minced

2 teaspoons mustard seeds

1 8- to 10-ounce package yellow rice mix

1/4 teaspoon saffron threads, crushed, or 1/8 teaspoon ground saffron (optional)

2 2/3 cups water

1 16-ounce jar mild or medium thick-and-chunky salsa

12 ounces frozen peeled and deveined shrimp, thawed and tails removed, if present

1 8- to 9-ounce package frozen sugar snap peas

1 In a 12-inch skillet heat oil over medium heat. Add garlic and mustard seeds. Cook and stir for 2 minutes. Stir in rice mix and, if desired, saffron. Stir in the water and salsa. Bring to boiling; reduce heat. Simmer, covered, for 20 minutes, stirring once halfway through cooking.

2 Add shrimp and pea pods. Cook, covered, about 5 minutes or until shrimp are opaque. Remove from heat. Let stand for 5 minutes before serving.

NUTRITION FACTS PER SERVING:
430 cal., 9 g total fat (1 g sat. fat), 129 mg chol., 1,900 mg sodium, 63 g carb., 2 g dietary fiber, 23 g protein.

Scallops with Watercress and Fennel

START TO FINISH **30 minutes** MAKES **4 servings**

12 fresh or frozen sea scallops
    (1 to 1½ pounds total)
 1 medium fennel bulb
⅛ teaspoon salt
⅛ teaspoon ground black pepper
⅓ cup plain low-fat yogurt
 1 to 1½ teaspoons grated fresh
    ginger or ⅛ to ¼ teaspoon
    ground ginger
½ teaspoon finely shredded
    orange peel
 1 teaspoon orange juice
 1 teaspoon honey
 2 medium oranges, peeled and
    thinly sliced crosswise
 4 cups watercress, tough stems
    removed

1 Preheat broiler. Thaw scallops, if frozen. Cut off and discard upper stalks from fennel bulb. Remove any wilted outer layers and cut off and discard a thin slice from fennel base. Cut fennel bulb into very thin slices.* Set aside.

2 Meanwhile, rinse scallops; pat dry with paper towels. Sprinkle scallops with salt and pepper. Place scallops on the unheated rack of a broiler pan. Broil 4 inches from heat about 8 minutes or until scallops are opaque, turning once halfway through broiling.

3 Meanwhile, for dressing, in a small bowl whisk together yogurt, ginger, orange peel, orange juice, and honey. Set aside.

4 Cut orange slices in half. Divide sliced fennel and watercress among four dinner plates. Arrange scallops and orange slices on top of vegetables; drizzle with dressing.

NUTRITION FACTS PER SERVING:
*172 cal., 1 g total fat (0 g sat. fat),
39 mg chol., 314 mg sodium, 18 g carb.,
4 g dietary fiber, 22 g protein.*

369

*tip
Use a mandolin to slice fennel very thinly.

Mediterranean Scallops and Pasta

START TO FINISH 30 minutes   MAKES 4 servings

1   pound fresh or frozen sea
    scallops
2   tablespoons olive oil
2   tablespoons lemon juice
2   teaspoons dried
    Mediterranean seasoning,
    crushed
8   ounces dried fettuccine
1   6-ounce jar quartered
    marinated artichoke hearts,
    drained
¼   cup oil-pack dried tomatoes,
    well drained and sliced
¼   cup purchased basil pesto

1 Thaw scallops, if frozen. Rinse scallops; pat dry with paper towels. Halve any large scallops. In a medium bowl combine oil, lemon juice, and Mediterranean seasoning. Add scallops; toss to coat. Cover and chill for 15 minutes.

2 Meanwhile, in a 4-quart Dutch oven or saucepan cook pasta according to package directions; drain. Return to hot Dutch oven. Add artichokes, tomatoes, and pesto to cooked pasta. Toss to coat; cover and keep warm.

3 In a large skillet bring scallop mixture to boiling over medium-high heat. Boil gently, uncovered, for 3 to 4 minutes or until scallops are opaque, turning scallops occasionally. Add scallop mixture to pasta mixture; toss to coat. Heat through. Serve immediately.

NUTRITION FACTS PER SERVING:
537 cal., 22 g total fat (1 g sat. fat), 40 mg chol., 592 mg sodium, 54 g carb., 2 g dietary fiber, 29 g protein.

Pan-Seared Scallops with Spinach

START TO FINISH **20 minutes** MAKES **4 servings**

1 **pound fresh or frozen sea scallops**

2 **tablespoons all-purpose flour**

1 **to 2 teaspoons blackened steak seasoning or Cajun seasoning**

1 **tablespoon vegetable oil**

1 **10-ounce package fresh spinach**

1 **tablespoon water**

2 **tablespoons balsamic vinegar**

¼ **cup cooked bacon pieces**

1 Thaw scallops, if frozen. Rinse scallops; pat dry with paper towels. In a plastic bag combine flour and seasoning. Add scallops; toss to coat. In a large skillet heat oil over medium heat. Add scallops; cook about 6 minutes or until browned and opaque, turning once. Remove scallops from skillet; set aside.

2 Add spinach to the same skillet; sprinkle with the water. Cook, covered, over medium-high heat about 2 minutes or until spinach is wilted. Add vinegar; toss to coat evenly. Return scallops to skillet; heat through. Sprinkle with bacon.

NUTRITION FACTS PER SERVING:
195 cal., 7 g total fat (0 g sat. fat), 43 mg chol., 538 mg sodium, 10 g carb., 2 g dietary fiber, 23 g protein.

As suggested by their name, sea scallops are the larger of the two most widely available varieties of this kind of shellfish. Bay scallops, the smaller variety, have a sweet flavor similar to sea scallops. Scallops should be firm, sweet smelling, and free of excess cloudy liquid. Chill scallops covered with their own liquid in a closed container for up to 2 days.

Curried Sea Scallops

START TO FINISH **25 minutes** MAKES **4 servings**

1 **pound fresh or frozen sea scallops**
1 **teaspoon curry powder**
¼ **teaspoon ground ginger**
⅛ **teaspoon cracked black pepper**
⅛ **teaspoon chili powder**
2 **cups cherry tomatoes or grape tomatoes, halved**
1 **tablespoon olive oil**
2 **tablespoons snipped fresh cilantro**
 Lemon wedges (optional)

1 Thaw scallops, if frozen. Rinse scallops; pat dry with paper towels. Sprinkle scallops with curry powder, ginger, pepper, and chili powder; set aside. Tear off four 24×18-inch pieces of heavy-duty foil. Fold each piece in half to make an 18×12-inch rectangle.

2 Divide seasoned scallops and tomatoes among foil rectangles. Drizzle with oil. For each packet, bring up two opposite edges of foil; seal with a double fold. Fold the remaining ends to completely enclose the food, leaving space for steam to build.

3 For a charcoal grill, grill foil packets on the rack of an uncovered grill directly over medium coals for 8 to 10 minutes or until scallops are opaque, carefully opening packets to check doneness. (For a gas grill, preheat grill. Reduce heat to medium. Place foil packets on grill rack over heat. Cover and grill as above.)

4 Sprinkle with cilantro. If desired, serve with lemon wedges.

NUTRITION FACTS PER SERVING:
149 cal., 5 g total fat (1 g sat. fat), 37 mg chol., 189 mg sodium, 7 g carb., 1 g dietary fiber, 20 g protein.

Oven Method: Preheat oven to 450°F. Prepare as directed through Step 2. Bake packets directly on the oven rack for 10 to 12 minutes or until scallops are opaque, carefully opening packets to check doneness. Serve as directed in Step 4.

tip
Serve over brown rice with a splash of low-sodium soy sauce.

Crab and Corn Chowder

START TO FINISH **20 minutes**   MAKES **4 servings**

1   14.75-ounce can cream-style corn
1   4- to 6-ounce container semisoft cheese with garlic and herbs, cut up
1½   cups milk
1   8-ounce package flake-style imitation crabmeat
1   cup grape tomatoes, halved
2   tablespoons snipped fresh Italian (flat-leaf) parsley

1 In a large saucepan combine corn and cheese; heat and stir until cheese melts. Gradually stir in milk; cook and stir until heated through.

2 Stir in crabmeat and tomatoes. Sprinkle with parsley.

NUTRITION FACTS PER SERVING:
289 cal., 12 g total fat (8 g sat. fat), 45 mg chol., 816 mg sodium, 35 g carb., 2 g dietary fiber, 12 g protein.

Veggie Fish Chowder

START TO FINISH **25 minutes**   MAKES **4 servings**

1   pound fresh or frozen firm-texture white fish, such as cod or haddock
    Ground black pepper
1   tablespoon olive oil
1   cup thinly sliced carrots (2 medium)
1   cup fresh sugar snap pea pods, halved diagonally
2¼   cups water
1   14-ounce can vegetable broth
1   4-ounce package or half of a 7.2-ounce package butter-and-herb-flavor instant mashed potatoes
    Salt
    Shaved Parmesan cheese

1 Thaw fish, if frozen. Cut fish into four portions. Rinse fish; pat dry with paper towels. Lightly sprinkle fish with pepper. In a 4-quart Dutch oven heat oil over medium-high heat. Add fish, carrots, and sugar snap peas; cook for 3 minutes.

2 Add the water and broth. Bring to boiling; reduce heat. Simmer, covered, about 3 minutes or until fish flakes easily when tested with a fork. Remove from heat.

3 Place instant mashed potatoes in a small bowl. Carefully remove 1¼ cups of the hot broth mixture and stir into potatoes (mashed potatoes will be thick).

4 Divide mashed potatoes among soup bowls. Break fish into bite-size pieces. Ladle chowder over mashed potatoes. Season to taste with salt and additional pepper. Top each serving with cheese.

NUTRITION FACTS PER SERVING:
264 cal., 7 g total fat (2 g sat. fat), 49 mg chol., 1,001 mg sodium, 27 g carb., 3 g dietary fiber, 23 g protein.

Crab-Fennel Salad

START TO FINISH **20 minutes** MAKES **3 servings**

- 1/3 cup plain low-fat yogurt
- 2 tablespoons mayonnaise or salad dressing
- 2 tablespoons milk
- 1/2 teaspoon curry powder
- 2 cups coarsely chopped fresh fruit, such as cantaloupe, strawberries, honeydew melon, and/or pineapple
- 1 6- to 8-ounce package chunk-style imitation crabmeat or lobster
- 3/4 cup sliced fennel
- 4 cups torn mixed salad greens or three 1-inch slices romaine lettuce

1 For dressing, in a small bowl stir together yogurt, mayonnaise, milk, and curry powder. If desired, thin dressing with additional milk.*

2 In a large bowl combine fresh fruit, crabmeat, and fennel; set aside. Divide salad greens among salad plates. Top with crabmeat mixture; drizzle with dressing.

NUTRITION FACTS PER SERVING: *176 cal., 5 g total fat (1 g sat. fat), 16 mg chol., 601 mg sodium, 24 g carb., 3 g dietary fiber, 10 g protein.*

*Make-Ahead Directions: Dressing can be made up to 24 hours in advance and stored, covered, in the refrigerator to enhance the curry flavor.

Pasta with White Clam Sauce

START TO FINISH **30 minutes**   MAKES **4 servings**

- 10 ounces dried linguine or fettuccine
- 2 6.5-ounce cans chopped or minced clams, undrained
- Half-and-half, light cream, or whole milk (about 2 cups)
- 2 tablespoons butter
- 1/2 cup chopped onion (1 medium)
- 2 cloves garlic, minced
- 1/4 cup all-purpose flour
- 2 teaspoons snipped fresh oregano or 1/2 teaspoon dried oregano, crushed
- 1/4 teaspoon salt
- 1/8 teaspoon ground black pepper
- 1/4 cup snipped fresh parsley
- 1/4 cup dry white wine, nonalcoholic dry white wine, or chicken broth
- 1/4 cup finely shredded or grated Parmesan cheese
- Fresh oregano (optional)

1 Cook linguine according to package directions; drain. Return linguine to hot pan; cover and keep warm.

2 Meanwhile, drain clams, reserving juices from 1 of the cans (you should have about 1/2 cup juices). Add enough half-and-half to the reserved juice to measure 2 1/2 cups total liquid. Set clams and liquid aside.

3 In a medium saucepan heat butter over medium heat until melted. Add onion and garlic; cook until onion is tender. Stir in flour, dried oregano (if using), salt, and pepper. Gradually stir in clam juices mixture. Cook and stir until thickened and bubbly. Cook and stir for 1 minute more.

4 Stir in drained clams, 2 teaspoons snipped oregano (if using), parsley, and wine; heat through. Serve clam mixture over warm linguine. Sprinkle with cheese and, if desired, garnish with additional fresh oregano.

NUTRITION FACTS PER SERVING: *595 cal., 23 g total fat (13 g sat. fat), 88 mg chol., 369 mg sodium, 69 g carb., 2 g dietary fiber, 25 g protein.*

Classic Oyster Stew

START TO FINISH **30 minutes**   MAKES **10 servings**

3 **dozen shucked oysters, undrained (about 1 pound total)**

4 **cups whole milk**

2 **cups whipping cream**

7 **tablespoons unsalted butter**

1 **cup finely chopped yellow onion (1 large)**

½ **cup finely chopped celery (1 stalk)**

¾ **teaspoon kosher salt**

3 **tablespoons all-purpose flour**

Freshly ground black pepper

Dash cayenne pepper

Snipped fresh Italian (flat-leaf) parsley

1 Drain oysters, reserving liquid. Inspect oysters and remove any bits of shell. Set aside oysters and liquid.

2 In a medium saucepan heat milk and cream just until simmering; cover and keep warm.

3 In a Dutch oven heat 4 tablespoons of the butter over medium heat until melted and bubbling. Add onion, celery, and ½ teaspoon of the salt, stirring well to coat with butter. Cook slowly about 10 minutes or until onion is tender and translucent, stirring frequently. Sprinkle flour over vegetable mixture; cook for 2 minutes more, stirring well to blend in the flour. Slowly whisk in the hot milk mixture; bring mixture back to a low simmer, stirring occasionally.

4 Meanwhile, in a 12-inch nonstick skillet heat the remaining 3 tablespoons butter over medium heat until melted and bubbly. Add drained oysters in a single layer. Sprinkle with the remaining ¼ teaspoon salt and a few grinds of black pepper. Cook just until oysters begin to curl around the edges and gills are slightly exposed. Transfer oysters to the milk mixture in Dutch oven. Turn off heat.

5 Add oyster liquid to hot skillet. Cook for 2 to 3 minutes or until liquid comes to boiling. Immediately transfer to stew in Dutch oven; stir. Stir in cayenne pepper. If desired, cover and let stand for 10 minutes before serving. Sprinkle with parsley.

NUTRITION FACTS PER SERVING:
342 cal., 30 g total fat (18 g sat. fat), 121 mg chol., 303 mg sodium, 11 g carb., 0 g dietary fiber, 8 g protein.

Grilling

Just about everything tastes better after it has sizzled on the grill. These main-dish delights easily entice appetites and appease hunger.

10

Chimichurri Burgers

START TO FINISH **30 minutes**   MAKES **6 servings**

1   recipe Chimichurri Topping

1   pound 95% or higher lean ground beef

8   ounces lean ground pork

1   tablespoon chili powder

½   teaspoon onion powder

¼   teaspoon ground cumin

⅛   teaspoon salt

3   whole wheat pita bread rounds, quartered and toasted

¾   cup roasted red sweet pepper strips

1 Prepare Chimichurri Topping; set aside. In a large bowl combine ground beef, ground pork, chili powder, onion powder, cumin, and salt; mix well. Shape meat mixture into six ½-inch-thick patties.

2 For a charcoal grill, grill patties on the rack of an uncovered grill directly over medium coals for 10 to 13 minutes or until done (160°F), turning once halfway through grilling. (For a gas grill, preheat grill. Reduce heat to medium. Place patties on grill rack over heat. Cover and grill as above.)

3 Arrange each grilled burger on two of the toasted pita quarters. Top with roasted pepper strips and Chimichurri Topping.

NUTRITION FACTS PER SERVING: *325 cal., 15 g total fat (5 g sat. fat), 74 mg chol., 407 mg sodium, 21 g carb., 4 g dietary fiber, 26 g protein.*

Chimichurri Topping

In a small bowl combine ½ cup finely snipped fresh Italian (flat-leaf) parsley; ½ cup finely snipped fresh cilantro; 2 tablespoons red wine vinegar; 1 tablespoon olive oil; 2 cloves garlic, minced; ¼ teaspoon salt; ¼ teaspoon ground black pepper; and ⅛ teaspoon cayenne pepper.

Chimichurri is a condiment that's used in Argentina in much the same way as ketchup is used in the United States. The Chimichurri Topping used here includes fresh cilantro instead of the more traditional oregano.

Garden Beef Burgers

START TO FINISH **30 minutes**   MAKES **4 servings**

1 egg white, lightly beaten

½ cup shredded carrot
   (1 medium)

¼ cup thinly sliced green
   onions (2)

¼ cup shredded zucchini

2 cloves garlic, minced

⅛ teaspoon ground black pepper

12 ounces 90% or higher lean
   ground beef

8 ½-inch slices whole wheat
   baguette-style French bread,
   toasted

¾ cup fresh spinach

1 small tomato, thinly sliced

½ cup thinly shaved zucchini*

1 In a large bowl combine egg white, carrot, green onions, shredded zucchini, garlic, and pepper. Add ground beef; mix well. Shape meat mixture into four ¾-inch-thick patties.

2 For a charcoal grill, grill patties on the rack of an uncovered grill directly over medium coals for 14 to 18 minutes or until patties are done (160°F), turning once halfway through grilling. (For a gas grill, preheat grill. Reduce heat to medium. Place patties on grill rack over heat. Cover and grill as above.)

3 Serve each burger between two toasted bread slices with spinach, tomato, and shaved zucchini.

NUTRITION FACTS PER SERVING:
258 cal., 10 g total fat (3 g sat. fat), 55 mg chol., 229 mg sodium, 19 g carb., 3 g dietary fiber, 21 g protein.

*tip
Use a vegetable peeler to thinly shave the zucchini.

Fennel and Pork Burgers with Grape Relish

START TO FINISH 30 minutes   MAKES 4 servings

1 egg, lightly beaten
1 tablespoon bourbon (optional)
1/2 cup quick-cooking rolled oats
1 tablespoon fennel seeds, crushed
1 teaspoon paprika
1 teaspoon finely shredded lemon peel
1 clove garlic, minced
1/2 teaspoon salt
1/2 teaspoon ground black pepper
1 pound lean ground pork
1 1/2 cups seedless red grapes, halved
1 cup chopped fennel (1 medium)
2 tablespoons balsamic vinegar
1 tablespoon butter
Salt
Ground black pepper
4 slices bread, toasted (optional)
1/4 cup snipped fresh parsley

1. In a large bowl combine egg and, if desired, bourbon. Stir in oats, fennel seeds, paprika, lemon peel, garlic, 1/2 teaspoon salt, and 1/2 teaspoon pepper. Add ground pork; mix well. Shape meat mixture into four 3/4-inch-thick patties; set aside.

2. Fold a 36×18-inch piece of heavy foil in half to make an 18-inch square. For relish, place grapes, fennel, vinegar, and butter in the center of foil. Sprinkle with additional salt and pepper. Bring up two opposite edges of foil; seal with a double fold. Fold the remaining ends to completely enclose grape mixture, leaving space for steam to build.

3. For a charcoal grill, grill patties and relish packet on the rack of an uncovered grill directly over medium coals for 14 to 18 minutes or until patties are done (160°F),* turning once halfway through grilling. (For a gas grill, preheat grill. Reduce heat to medium. Place patties and relish packet on grill rack over heat. Cover and grill as above.)

4. If desired, serve burgers on toasted bread slices. Spoon relish over burgers. Sprinkle with parsley.

NUTRITION FACTS PER SERVING:
284 cal., 14 g total fat (6 g sat. fat), 114 mg chol., 409 mg sodium, 23 g carb., 7 g dietary fiber, 18 g protein.

Fennel's slightly sweet licorice flavor adds impact to this chunky relish cooked on the grill in a foil packet. Buy fennel with a firm white bulb and green celerylike stalks. The feathery fronds on the stalks will remind you of fresh dill. Snip a few fennel fronds and sprinkle them over burgers, salads, or other dishes to add a pop of flavor.

*tip

The internal color of a burger is not a reliable doneness indicator. A pork patty cooked to 160°F is safe, regardless of color. To measure the doneness of a patty, insert an instant-read thermometer through the side of the patty to a depth of 2 to 3 inches.

Tex-Mex Turkey Patties

START TO FINISH **30 minutes** MAKES **2 servings**

8 ounces uncooked ground turkey breast or 90% or higher lean ground beef

¼ cup salsa

¼ teaspoon ground cumin

⅛ teaspoon ground black pepper

Dash salt

½ cup thinly sliced sweet onion (such as Vidalia or Walla Walla)

½ cup red sweet pepper strips

1 teaspoon canola oil

2 tostada shells

¼ of a medium avocado, seeded, peeled, and sliced or chopped

1 In a medium bowl combine ground turkey, salsa, cumin, black pepper, and salt; mix well. Shape turkey mixture into two ½-inch-thick patties.

2 Fold a 24×12-inch piece of heavy foil in half to make a 12-inch square. Place onion and sweet pepper in the center of foil; drizzle with oil. Bring up two opposite edges of foil; seal with a double fold. Fold the remaining ends to completely enclose vegetables, leaving space for steam to build.*

3 For a charcoal grill, grill patties and vegetable packet on the rack of an uncovered grill directly over medium coals for 10 to 13 minutes or until patties are done (165°F for turkey, 160°F for beef) and vegetables are tender, turning once halfway through grilling. (For a gas grill, preheat grill. Reduce heat to medium. Place patties and vegetable packet on grill rack over heat. Cover and grill as above.)

4 Serve burgers on tostada shells. Top with vegetables and avocado.

NUTRITION FACTS PER SERVING: *285 cal., 10 g total fat (1 g sat. fat), 55 mg chol., 430 mg sodium, 20 g carb., 5 g dietary fiber, 29 g protein.*

*tip

Instead of encasing the vegetables in foil, the onion and sweet pepper may be cooked in a skillet on the side burner of the grill or on the rangetop. In a covered medium skillet cook onion and sweet pepper in hot oil over medium heat for 10 minutes, stirring occasionally. Cook, uncovered, about 3 minutes more or until pepper is very tender and onion is golden brown, stirring occasionally.

Greek-Style Turkey Burgers

START TO FINISH **30 minutes**   MAKES **4 servings**

- 1 **egg white, lightly beaten**
- 1/3 **cup fine dry whole wheat bread crumbs***
- 1 **tablespoon crumbled feta cheese**
- 1 **tablespoon plain low-fat yogurt**
- 1 **teaspoon snipped fresh rosemary or 1/2 teaspoon dried rosemary, crushed**
- 1 **teaspoon snipped fresh oregano or 1/2 teaspoon dried oregano, crushed**
- 1/8 **teaspoon ground black pepper**
- 1 **pound uncooked ground turkey breast or chicken breast**
  Torn mixed salad greens (optional)
- 1 **recipe Olive-Tomato Salsa**
- 1/4 **cup crumbled feta cheese (1 ounce)**
  Plain low-fat yogurt (optional)
- 2 **whole wheat pita bread rounds, quartered and lightly toasted**

1 In a medium bowl combine egg white, bread crumbs, 1 tablespoon feta cheese, 1 tablespoon yogurt, rosemary, oregano, and pepper. Add ground turkey; mix well. Shape turkey mixture into four 3/4-inch-thick patties.

2 For a charcoal grill, grill patties on the rack of an uncovered grill directly over medium coals for 14 to 18 minutes or until patties are no longer pink (165°F), turning once halfway through grilling. (For a gas grill, preheat grill. Reduce heat to medium. Place patties on grill rack over heat. Cover and grill as above.)

3 If desired, divide salad greens among dinner plates. Place burgers on plates. Top with Olive-Tomato Salsa, 1/4 cup feta cheese, and, if desired, additional yogurt. Serve burgers with toasted pita bread.

NUTRITION FACTS PER SERVING:
275 cal., 6 g total fat (2 g sat. fat), 53 mg chol., 507 mg sodium, 23 g carb., 4 g dietary fiber, 35 g protein.

Olive-Tomato Salsa

In a small bowl combine 1 cup seeded and chopped tomatoes (2 medium); 1/4 cup seeded and chopped cucumber; 1/4 cup chopped pitted kalamata or other ripe olives; 1/2 teaspoon snipped fresh rosemary or 1/4 teaspoon dried rosemary, crushed; and 1/2 teaspoon snipped fresh oregano or 1/4 teaspoon dried oregano, crushed. Makes about 1 1/2 cups.

*tip

For 1/3 cup fine dry whole wheat bread crumbs, place 1 slice whole wheat bread, toasted, in a food processor. Cover and process until fine crumbs form.

Cheesy Eggplant Burgers

START TO FINISH 25 minutes   MAKES 6 servings

1 teaspoon garlic powder

½ teaspoon ground black pepper

⅛ teaspoon salt

½ cup seeded and chopped tomato (1 medium)

2 tablespoons olive oil

1 tablespoon snipped fresh oregano

2 teaspoons snipped fresh thyme

2 teaspoons cider vinegar

6 ½-inch slices eggplant

6 ¾-ounce slices smoked Gouda cheese

6 ½-inch slices whole grain baguette-style French bread, toasted

1 In a small bowl combine garlic powder, pepper, and salt. In another small bowl combine half of the garlic powder mixture, the tomato, 1 tablespoon of the oil, the oregano, thyme, and vinegar; set aside.

2 Brush eggplant slices with the remaining 1 tablespoon oil and sprinkle with the remaining garlic powder mixture.

3 For a charcoal grill, grill eggplant on the rack of an uncovered grill directly over medium coals for 6 to 8 minutes or just until tender and golden brown, turning once halfway through grilling and topping with cheese for the last 2 minutes of grilling. (For a gas grill, preheat grill. Reduce heat to medium. Place eggplant on grill rack over heat. Cover and grill as above.)

4 Divide grilled eggplant slices among toasted bread slices. Top with tomato mixture.

NUTRITION FACTS PER SERVING:
201 cal., 11 g total fat (4 g sat. fat), 17 mg chol., 506 mg sodium, 19 g carb., 4 g dietary fiber, 7 g protein.

Cowboy Steak and Whiskey Butter ⏱

START TO FINISH **30 minutes** MAKES **4 servings**

- 2 tablespoons **Whiskey Butter**
- 1 tablespoon **turbinado sugar or packed brown sugar**
- 1 tablespoon **ground New Mexican chile pepper or chili powder**
- 1 tablespoon **ground chipotle chile pepper**
- 1½ teaspoons **smoked paprika**
- 1½ teaspoons **ground white pepper**
- 1 teaspoon **freshly ground black pepper**
- 2 **1-pound bone-in beef rib-eye steaks, cut 1 inch thick**
- 2 teaspoons **olive oil**
  Snipped fresh parsley (optional)

1 Prepare Whiskey Butter. Cover and chill until ready to serve. For rub, in a small bowl combine sugar, New Mexican chile pepper, chipotle chile pepper, paprika, white pepper, and black pepper.

2 Trim fat from steaks. Brush both sides of steaks with oil. Sprinkle about 1 tablespoon of the rub evenly over both sides of steaks; rub in with your fingers.

3 For a charcoal grill, grill steaks on the rack of an uncovered grill directly over medium coals for 10 to 13 minutes for medium-rare (145°F) or 12 to 15 minutes for medium (160°F), turning once halfway through grilling. (For a gas grill, preheat grill. Reduce heat to medium. Place steaks on grill rack over heat. Cover and grill as above.)

4 Spoon Whiskey Butter onto steaks. If desired, sprinkle with parsley. Before serving, cut each steak in half.

NUTRITION FACTS PER SERVING:
423 cal., 28 g total fat (13 g sat. fat), 130 mg chol., 189 mg sodium, 7 g carb., 2 g dietary fiber, 35 g protein.

Whiskey Butter

In a medium bowl combine 1 cup softened unsalted butter, ¼ cup finely chopped shallots, 1 tablespoon snipped fresh parsley, 1 tablespoon whiskey, ½ teaspoon sea salt or salt, ½ teaspoon Dijon-style mustard, ½ teaspoon Worcestershire sauce, and dash ground white pepper. Makes about 1 cup.

*tip

Store the remaining Whiskey Butter in the refrigerator for up to 1 week or freeze for up to 3 months. Store the remaining rub in a covered container at room temperature for up to 3 months.

Peach and Horseradish–Sauced Rib-Eyes

START TO FINISH **25 minutes** MAKES **4 servings**

2 **boneless beef rib-eye steaks, cut 1 inch thick (about 1½ pounds total)**

1 **tablespoon olive oil**

1 **tablespoon steak seasoning**

2 **peaches, halved**

⅓ **cup peach preserves**

2 **tablespoons prepared horseradish**

2 **tablespoons plum sauce**

1 Trim fat from steaks. Brush both sides of steaks with oil; sprinkle steak seasoning evenly over both sides of steaks.

2 For a charcoal grill, grill steaks on the rack of an uncovered grill directly over medium coals for 10 to 12 minutes for medium-rare (145°F) or 12 to 15 minutes for medium (160°F), turning once halfway through grilling. (For a gas grill, preheat grill. Reduce heat to medium. Place steaks on grill rack over heat. Cover and grill as above.)

3 While steaks are grilling, add peach halves to grill. Grill for 8 to 10 minutes or until tender and lightly browned, turning once halfway through grilling.

4 For sauce, in a small bowl stir together preserves, horseradish, and plum sauce. Slice steaks. Serve steak slices with grilled peaches and sauce.

NUTRITION FACTS PER SERVING:
399 cal., 18 g total fat (6 g sat. fat), 100 mg chol., 700 mg sodium, 23 g carb., 1 g dietary fiber, 35 g protein.

Pepper-Punched T-Bones

START TO FINISH **25 minutes** MAKES **4 servings**

- ½ cup steak sauce
- 2 tablespoons snipped fresh thyme
- 2 tablespoons whole green peppercorns in brine, drained and chopped
- 2 teaspoons cracked black pepper
- ½ teaspoon cayenne pepper
- 4 beef T-bone steaks, cut ¾ inch thick

1 In a small bowl combine steak sauce, thyme, green peppercorns, black pepper, and cayenne pepper. Trim fat from steaks. Spread half of the pepper mixture on one side of steaks.

2 For a charcoal grill, place steaks, pepper sides down, on the rack of an uncovered grill directly over medium coals. Carefully spread the remaining pepper mixture on tops of steaks. Grill for 7 to 10 minutes for medium-rare (145°F) or 10 to 13 minutes for medium (160°F), turning once halfway through grilling. (For a gas grill, preheat grill. Reduce heat to medium. Place steaks, pepper sides down, on grill rack over heat. Cover and grill as above.)

NUTRITION FACTS PER SERVING: 583 cal., 38 g total fat (15 g sat. fat), 146 mg chol., 567 mg sodium, 5 g carb., 1 g dietary fiber, 52 g protein.

Strip Steaks with Lime and Sweet Onion Salsa

START TO FINISH **30 minutes** MAKES **4 servings**

1 **recipe Lime and Sweet Onion Salsa**

4 **boneless beef top loin (strip) steaks, cut 1 inch thick**

2 **tablespoons snipped fresh sage**

1 **fresh habañero chile pepper, seeded and finely chopped***

½ **teaspoon salt**

1 Prepare Lime and Sweet Onion Salsa. Cover and chill until ready to serve.

2 Trim fat from steaks. In a small bowl combine sage, chile pepper, and salt. Wearing plastic or rubber gloves, sprinkle mixture evenly over both sides of steaks; rub in with your fingers.**

3 For a charcoal grill, grill steaks on the rack of an uncovered grill directly over medium coals for 10 to 12 minutes for medium-rare (145°F) or 12 to 15 minutes for medium (160°F), turning once halfway through grilling. (For a gas grill, preheat grill. Reduce heat to medium. Place steaks on grill rack over heat. Cover and grill as above.) Serve steaks with salsa.

NUTRITION FACTS PER SERVING:
431 cal., 17 g total fat (6 g sat. fat), 166 mg chol., 581 mg sodium, 4 g carb., 1 g dietary fiber, 62 g protein.

Lime and Sweet Onion Salsa

Peel and section 2 large limes; chop lime segments. In a medium bowl stir together chopped lime, ½ cup finely chopped sweet onion (1 medium), 3 tablespoons snipped fresh cilantro, ½ teaspoon sugar, and ¼ teaspoon salt.

*tip

Because chile peppers contain volatile oils that can burn your skin and eyes, avoid direct contact with them as much as possible. When working with chile peppers, wear plastic or rubber gloves. If your bare hands do touch the peppers, wash your hands and nails well with soap and warm water.

**tip

If time permits, rub the steaks with the habañero mixture, then cover and marinate in the refrigerator for up to 24 hours before grilling.

387

Ham Steaks with Fresh Peach Chutney

START TO FINISH **30 minutes**   MAKES **6 servings**

1   **pound ripe peaches, peeled and chopped, or nectarines, chopped**

½   **cup finely chopped, peeled and seeded cucumber**

½   **cup orange juice**

¼   **cup finely chopped red onion**

1   **tablespoon finely snipped fresh mint**

1   **tablespoon tequila**

¼   **teaspoon salt**

⅛   **teaspoon ground black pepper**

½   **cup orange juice**

2   **tablespoons tequila**

2   **1- to 1¼-pound cooked ham steaks, cut ½ inch thick**

1 For chutney, in a medium bowl combine peaches, cucumber, ½ cup orange juice, red onion, mint, 1 tablespoon tequila, salt, and pepper. Set aside.

2 For marinade, in a shallow glass dish combine ½ cup orange juice and 2 tablespoons tequila. Remove ¼ cup of the marinade to serve with the grilled ham.

3 Add ham steaks to the remaining marinade in dish. Marinate at room temperature for 5 to 10 minutes, turning once. Remove ham from marinade, reserving marinade.

4 For a charcoal grill, grill ham on the rack of an uncovered grill directly over medium-hot coals about 8 minutes or until heated through (140°F), turning and brushing once with the reserved marinade halfway through grilling. (For a gas grill, preheat grill. Reduce heat to medium-high. Place ham on grill rack over heat. Cover and grill as above.) Discard any remaining marinade.

5 Cut ham into serving-size pieces. Transfer to a serving platter. Pour the reserved ¼ cup marinade over ham. Serve with chutney.

NUTRITION FACTS PER SERVING:
251 cal., 7 g total fat (2 g sat. fat), 68 mg chol., 2,017 mg sodium, 12 g carb., 1 g dietary fiber, 31 g protein.

Tomato-Topped Lamb Chops and Rice

START TO FINISH **20 minutes**   MAKES **4 servings**

8   **lamb loin chops, cut 1 inch thick**

Salt

Ground black pepper

1   **8.8-ounce pouch cooked long grain rice**

4   **medium roma tomatoes, cut up**

4   **green onions, cut into 1-inch pieces**

1   **tablespoon snipped fresh oregano**

1   **tablespoon balsamic vinegar**

1 Trim fat from chops. Sprinkle chops with salt and pepper. For a charcoal grill, grill chops on the rack of an uncovered grill directly over medium coals for 12 to 14 minutes for medium-rare (145°F) or 15 to 17 minutes for medium (160°F), turning once halfway through grilling. (For a gas grill, preheat grill. Reduce heat to medium. Place chops on grill rack over heat. Cover and grill as above.)

2 Meanwhile, heat rice in the microwave oven according to package directions. In a food processor combine tomatoes, green onions, and oregano. Cover and process with on/off pulses until coarsely chopped. Transfer to a small bowl; stir in vinegar. Season to taste with additional salt and pepper.

3 Divide rice among dinner plates; top with chops. Serve with tomato mixture.

NUTRITION FACTS PER SERVING:
273 cal., 7 g total fat (2 g sat. fat), 70 mg chol., 153 mg sodium, 26 g carb., 3 g dietary fiber, 25 g protein.

Sesame-Ginger Barbecued Chicken ⏱

START TO FINISH **30 minutes** MAKES **6 servings**

⅓ cup plum sauce or sweet-and-sour sauce

¼ cup water

3 tablespoons hoisin sauce

1½ teaspoons sesame seeds, toasted if desired

1 teaspoon grated fresh ginger or ¼ teaspoon ground ginger

1 clove garlic, minced

¼ to ½ teaspoon Asian chili sauce or several dashes bottled hot pepper sauce

6 skinless, boneless chicken breast halves or 12 skinless, boneless chicken thighs

Hot cooked noodles or rice (optional)*

Sesame seeds, toasted if desired (optional)

Green onion curls (optional)

1 For sauce, in a small saucepan combine plum sauce, the water, hoisin sauce, 1½ teaspoons sesame seeds, ginger, garlic, and chili sauce. Bring to boiling over medium heat, stirring frequently. Reduce heat. Simmer, covered, for 3 minutes.

2 For a charcoal grill, grill chicken on the rack of an uncovered grill directly over medium coals for 12 to 15 minutes or until chicken is no longer pink (170°F for breasts, 180°F for thighs), turning once halfway through grilling and brushing with some of the sauce during the last 5 minutes of grilling. (For a gas grill, preheat grill. Reduce heat to medium. Place chicken on grill rack over heat. Cover and grill as above.)

3 Reheat the remaining sauce. Slice chicken. If desired, serve chicken on top of hot cooked noodles. Spoon the remaining sauce over chicken. if desired, sprinkle with additional sesame seeds and garnish with green onion curls.

NUTRITION FACTS PER SERVING:
190 cal., 2 g total fat (0 g sat. fat), 77 mg chol., 278 mg sodium, 9 g carb., 0 g dietary fiber, 31 g protein.

*tip

For a touch of color, add some halved fresh snow pea pods or sugar snap pea pods to the noodles or rice for the last few minutes of cooking.

Grilled Chicken and Creamy Corn

START TO FINISH **20 minutes**   MAKES **4 servings**

2   **tablespoons olive oil**

1   **teaspoon smoked paprika**

3   **ears sweet corn, husks and silks removed**

4   **skinless, boneless chicken breast halves (1$\frac{1}{4}$ to 1$\frac{1}{2}$ pounds total)**

   Salt

   Ground black pepper

$\frac{1}{3}$ **cup sour cream**

   Milk

$\frac{1}{4}$ **cup shredded fresh basil**

1 In a small bowl combine olive oil and paprika. Brush corn and chicken with oil mixture. Lightly sprinkle with salt and pepper.

2 For a charcoal grill, grill chicken on the rack of an uncovered grill directly over medium coals for 12 to 15 minutes or until chicken is no longer pink (170°F), turning once halfway through grilling. (For a gas grill, preheat grill. Reduce heat to medium. Place chicken on grill rack over heat. Cover and grill as above.)

3 On cutting board place an ear of corn pointed end down. While holding corn firmly at stem end to keep it in place, use a sharp knife to cut corn from cobs; rotate cob as needed to cut corn from all sides. Repeat with the remaining ears of corn. Transfer kernels to a medium bowl; stir in sour cream. Season with additional salt and pepper. Stir in enough milk to make mixture of desired creaminess. Slice chicken breasts. Serve with corn and sprinkle with shredded basil.

NUTRITION FACTS PER SERVING:
309 cal., 13 g total fat (4 g sat. fat), 89 mg chol., 238 mg sodium, 14 g carb., 2 g dietary fiber, 2 g sugar, 36 g protein.

391

Mahi Mahi with Black Bean and Avocado Relish ⏱ 🥕

START TO FINISH 30 minutes   MAKES 4 servings

1   pound fresh or frozen skinless mahi mahi fillets

2   tablespoons snipped fresh cilantro

2   tablespoons snipped fresh oregano

½   teaspoon finely shredded lime peel

2   tablespoons lime juice

1   tablespoon olive oil

1   to 2 cloves garlic, minced

¼   to ½ teaspoon bottled hot pepper sauce

1   15-ounce can black beans, rinsed and drained

1   medium avocado, seeded, peeled, and chopped

Salt

Ground black pepper

1 Thaw fish, if frozen. In a small bowl combine cilantro, oregano, lime peel, lime juice, oil, garlic, and hot pepper sauce. For relish, in a medium bowl combine beans and avocado; stir in half of the cilantro mixture. Cover and chill relish until ready to serve.

2 Rinse fish; pat dry with paper towels. Lightly sprinkle fish with salt and pepper. Brush the remaining cilantro mixture over both sides of fish.

3 For a charcoal grill, grill fish on the greased rack of an uncovered grill directly over medium coals for 4 to 6 minutes per ½-inch thickness or until fish flakes easily when tested with a fork, carefully turning once halfway through grilling. (For a gas grill, preheat grill. Reduce heat to medium. Place fish on greased grill rack over heat. Cover and grill as above.)

4 Cut fish into serving-size portions. Divide three-fourths of the relish among dinner plates. Arrange fish on top of relish; spoon the remaining relish over fish.

NUTRITION FACTS PER SERVING:
255 cal., 10 g total fat (1 g sat. fat), 83 mg chol., 369 mg sodium, 18 g carb., 6 g dietary fiber, 29 g protein.

Mahi mahi is a mild-flavored, almost sweet fish. If it's not available at your grocery store, substitute: mackerel, tuna, or catfish. Catfish will be a little fattier than mahi mahi, but is readily available in most markets.

⏱ Salmon and Asparagus with Herb Mayonnaise

START TO FINISH **25 minutes**   MAKES **4 servings**

4 6- to 8-ounce fresh or frozen skinless salmon fillets, about 1 inch thick
½ cup finely chopped celery (1 stalk)
⅓ cup mayonnaise
¼ cup thinly sliced green onions (2)
1 tablespoon lemon juice
2 teaspoons snipped fresh tarragon or ½ teaspoon dried tarragon, crushed
1 pound fresh asparagus spears
1 tablespoon olive oil
   Sea salt or salt
   Freshly ground black pepper
   Lemon wedges (optional)

1 Thaw fish, if frozen. For herb mayonnaise, in a small bowl stir together celery, mayonnaise, green onions, lemon juice, and tarragon. Cover and chill until ready to serve.

2 Rinse fish; pat dry with paper towels. Snap off and discard woody bases from asparagus. Lightly brush asparagus and fish with oil. Sprinkle with salt and pepper.

3 For a charcoal grill, grill fish and asparagus on the greased rack of an uncovered grill directly over medium coals for 8 to 12 minutes or until fish flakes easily when tested with a fork and asparagus is tender, carefully turning fish once halfway through grilling and turning asparagus occasionally. (For a gas grill, preheat grill. Reduce heat to medium. Place fish and asparagus on greased grill rack over heat. Cover and grill as above.)

4 To serve, arrange fish and asparagus on dinner plates. Top fish with herb mayonnaise. If desired, serve with lemon wedges.

NUTRITION FACTS PER SERVING:
545 cal., 41 g total fat (8 g sat. fat), 100 mg chol., 314 mg sodium, 6 g carb., 3 g dietary fiber, 37 g protein.

Broiler Method: Prepare as directed, except preheat broiler. Place fish and asparagus on the greased unheated rack of a broiler pan. Broil about 4 inches from the heat for 8 to 12 minutes or until fish flakes easily when tested with a fork and asparagus is tender, carefully turning fish once halfway through broiling and turning asparagus occasionally.

Salmon with Cilantro-Pineapple Salsa ⏱ 🥕

START TO FINISH **30 minutes** MAKES **4 servings**

- 1 **1-pound fresh or frozen skinless salmon fillet, about 1 inch thick**
- 2 **cups coarsely chopped fresh pineapple**
- ½ **cup chopped red or green sweet pepper (1 small)**
- ¼ **cup finely chopped red onion**
- 3 **tablespoons lime juice**
- 2 **tablespoons snipped fresh cilantro or parsley**
- ½ **teaspoon finely shredded lime peel (set aside)**
- 1 **small fresh jalapeño chile pepper, seeded and finely chopped***
- ½ **teaspoon chili powder**
- ¼ **teaspoon salt**
  Dash cayenne pepper
  Lime wedges (optional)

1 Thaw fish, if frozen. For salsa, in a medium bowl combine pineapple, sweet pepper, red onion, 2 tablespoons of the lime juice, 1 tablespoon of the cilantro, and the jalapeño pepper. Set aside.

2 Rinse fish; pat dry with paper towels. In a small bowl combine the remaining 1 tablespoon lime juice, the remaining 1 tablespoon cilantro, lime peel, chili powder, salt, and cayenne pepper. Brush lime mixture on both sides of fish. Place fish in a well-greased wire grill basket, tucking under any thin edges to make fish of uniform thickness.

3 For a charcoal grill, grill fish in basket on the rack of an uncovered grill directly over medium coals for 8 to 12 minutes or until fish flakes easily when tested with a fork, turning basket once halfway through grilling. (For a gas grill, preheat grill. Reduce heat to medium. Place fish in basket on grill rack over heat. Cover and grill as above.)

4 Cut fish into four serving-size portions. Top with salsa and, if desired, serve with lime wedges.

NUTRITION FACTS PER SERVING:
257 cal., 12 g total fat (2 g sat. fat), 66 mg chol., 219 mg sodium, 13 g carb., 2 g dietary fiber, 23 g protein.

*tip
Because chile peppers contain volatile oils that can burn your skin and eyes, avoid direct contact with them as much as possible. When working with chile peppers, wear plastic or rubber gloves. If your bare hands do touch the peppers, wash your hands and nails well with soap and warm water.

Grilled Fish Tacos

START TO FINISH **30 minutes**   MAKES **6 servings**

1   **pound fresh or frozen skinless cod, sole, or flounder fillets, about $\frac{1}{2}$ inch thick**

1   **tablespoon lemon juice**

1   **tablespoon olive oil**

1   **teaspoon chili powder**

$\frac{1}{2}$ **teaspoon ground cumin**

$\frac{1}{4}$ **teaspoon salt**

$\frac{1}{4}$ **teaspoon ground black pepper**

12   **7- to 8-inch fat-free flour tortillas**

1   **recipe Pineapple Salsa**

1 Thaw fish, if frozen. Rinse fish; pat dry with paper towels. Arrange fish in a 2-quart square baking dish; set aside. For marinade, in a small bowl whisk together lemon juice, oil, chili powder, cumin, salt, and pepper. Pour marinade over fish; turn fish to coat with marinade. Cover and marinate in the refrigerator for 15 minutes. Drain fish, discarding any marinade. Meanwhile, stack tortillas and wrap in foil; set aside.

2 For a charcoal grill, grill fish and tortilla packet on the greased rack of an uncovered grill directly over medium coals for 4 to 6 minutes or until fish flakes easily when tested with a fork and tortillas are warmed, turning tortilla packet once halfway through grilling. (For a gas grill, preheat grill. Reduce heat to medium. Place fish and tortilla packet on greased grill rack over heat. Cover and grill as above.)

3 Transfer fish to a cutting board. Cut or flake fish into 1-inch pieces. Serve in warmed tortillas topped with Pineapple Salsa.

NUTRITION FACTS PER SERVING: *305 cal., 3 g total fat (0 g sat. fat), 33 mg chol., 823 mg sodium, 49 g carb., 0 g dietary fiber, 18 g protein.*

Pineapple Salsa

In a medium bowl stir together 1 cup chopped fresh pineapple; $\frac{1}{4}$ cup chopped red sweet pepper; $\frac{1}{4}$ cup chopped red onion; 2 tablespoons snipped fresh cilantro; 1 fresh serrano or jalapeño chile pepper, seeded and finely chopped*; 1 teaspoon finely shredded lime peel; and $\frac{1}{2}$ teaspoon salt.

*tip

Because chile peppers contain volatile oils that can burn your skin and eyes, avoid direct contact with them as much as possible. When working with chile peppers, wear plastic or rubber gloves. If your bare hands do touch the peppers, wash your hands and nails well with soap and warm water.

395

Lemon and Herb–Grilled Trout Sandwiches

START TO FINISH 25 minutes MAKES 4 sandwiches

1 **pound fresh or frozen ruby or rainbow trout fillets**

1 **large lemon**

¹⁄₂ **cup mayonnaise**

¹⁄₄ **cup snipped fresh basil or 2 tablespoons snipped fresh dill**

¹⁄₄ **teaspoon salt**

¹⁄₄ **teaspoon ground black pepper**

4 **ciabatta buns, split**

Fresh basil leaves (optional)

1 Thaw fish, if frozen. Rinse fish; pat dry with paper towels. Cut lemon in half. Finely shred peel and squeeze juice from one lemon half; thinly slice the remaining lemon half and set aside.

2 In a small bowl combine lemon peel, lemon juice, mayonnaise, ¹⁄₄ cup basil, salt, and pepper. Remove 2 tablespoons of the mayonnaise mixture and brush over fish.

3 For a charcoal grill, grill fish, skin sides up, on the rack of an uncovered grill directly over medium-hot coals for 1 minute. Carefully turn fish; grill for 5 to 7 minutes more or until fish flakes easily when tested with a fork. (For a gas grill, preheat grill. Reduce heat to medium-high. Place fish, skin sides up, on grill rack over heat. Cover and grill as above.)

4 While fish is grilling, add lemon slices and buns, cut sides down, to grill. Grill until grill marks appear on lemon slices and buns are toasted, turning lemon slices once halfway through grilling. Remove fish, lemon slices, and buns from grill.

5 If desired, remove skin from fish. Cut fish into bun-size pieces. Spread some of the mayonnaise mixture on buns. Top with fish, lemon slices, and, if desired, basil leaves. Add tops of buns. Serve with the remaining mayonnaise mixture.

NUTRITION FACTS PER SANDWICH:
518 cal., 30 g total fat (6 g sat. fat), 77 mg chol., 667 mg sodium, 32 g carb., 3 g dietary fiber, 29 g protein.

Cajun Shrimp Stir-Fry in a Grill Wok

START TO FINISH **30 minutes**   MAKES **4 servings**

12   **ounces fresh or frozen peeled and deveined medium shrimp**

2   **tablespoons vegetable oil**

2   **cups red and/or yellow sweet pepper strips (2 medium)**

1   **cup thin onion wedges**

1   **cup broccoli florets or zucchini chunks**

1   **teaspoon Cajun seasoning**

    Nonstick cooking spray

¼   **cup chopped pecans, toasted**

1   **tablespoon snipped fresh parsley**

    Lime wedges

1 Thaw shrimp, if frozen. Rinse shrimp; pat dry with paper towels. In a small bowl combine shrimp and 1 tablespoon of the oil; toss gently to coat. Set aside.

2 In a large bowl combine sweet pepper strips, onion wedges, broccoli, and Cajun seasoning. Drizzle with the remaining 1 tablespoon oil; toss gently to coat.

3 Lightly coat a grill wok with cooking spray. For a charcoal grill, place grill wok on the rack of an uncovered grill directly over medium-hot coals. Heat wok for 5 minutes. Carefully add shrimp; grill for 2 to 3 minutes or until shrimp begin to brown, stirring occasionally. Add vegetable mixture; grill and stir for 4 to 6 minutes or until shrimp are opaque and vegetables are tender. (For a gas grill, preheat grill. Reduce heat to medium-high. Place grill wok on grill rack directly over heat. Cover and heat wok, then grill as above.)

4 Sprinkle shrimp mixture with pecans and parsley. Serve with lime wedges.

NUTRITION FACTS PER SERVING:
249 cal., 14 g total fat (1 g sat. fat), 129 mg chol., 185 mg sodium, 13 g carb., 4 g dietary fiber, 20 g protein.

Grilled Shrimp and Pineapple Skewers

START TO FINISH **30 minutes**   MAKES **4 servings**

12 ounces fresh or frozen peeled and deveined jumbo shrimp

$\frac{1}{2}$ of a fresh pineapple

$\frac{1}{2}$ cup water

6 tablespoons orange marmalade

1 tablespoon soy sauce

1 8.8-ounce pouch cooked long grain rice

$\frac{1}{4}$ cup snipped fresh cilantro

1 Thaw shrimp, if frozen. Rinse shrimp; pat dry with paper towels. Thread shrimp onto four metal skewers. Cut pineapple into 4 slices; core, if desired, and cut each slice into fourths to make 16 small wedges. Thread pineapple wedges onto four metal skewers.

2 In a small saucepan combine the water, 4 tablespoons of the marmalade, and the soy sauce. Brush shrimp and pineapple with some of the soy mixture.

3 For a charcoal grill, grill shrimp and pineapple skewers on the rack of an uncovered grill directly over medium coals for 7 to 9 minutes or until shrimp are opaque and pineapple is heated through, turning once halfway through grilling. (For a gas grill, preheat grill. Reduce heat to medium. Place shrimp and pineapple skewers on grill rack over heat. Cover and grill as above.) Remove from grill; cover and keep warm.

4 In a small saucepan bring the remaining soy mixture to a full boil. Heat rice in the microwave oven according to package directions. Transfer rice to a serving bowl; stir in the remaining 2 tablespoons marmalade and cilantro. Serve shrimp and pineapple skewers with rice and the remaining soy mixture.

NUTRITION FACTS PER SERVING:
322 cal., 3 g total fat (0 g sat. fat), 172 mg chol., 451 mg sodium, 49 g carb., 2 g dietary fiber, 25 g protein.

tip

If time permits, you may use wooden skewers. But you'll need to soak them in water for at least 30 minutes. Drain before using.

Shrimp and Fruit Kabobs

START TO FINISH **30 minutes**   MAKES **4 servings**

1   pound fresh or frozen peeled and deveined large shrimp*

$\frac{1}{2}$ teaspoon finely shredded lemon peel

2   tablespoons lemon juice

1   tablespoon canola oil

2   cloves garlic, minced

1   teaspoon snipped fresh dill or tarragon or $\frac{1}{2}$ teaspoon dried dill or tarragon

$\frac{1}{4}$ teaspoon ground black pepper

$1\frac{1}{2}$ cups peeled papaya cut into $1\frac{1}{2}$-inch pieces

$\frac{1}{4}$ of a fresh pineapple, cut into 1- to $1\frac{1}{2}$-inch pieces

3   red plums, pitted and quartered lengthwise

1 Thaw shrimp, if frozen. Rinse shrimp; pat dry with paper towels. In a small bowl stir together lemon peel, lemon juice, oil, garlic, dill, and pepper.

2 On eight 12-inch metal skewers** thread shrimp, papaya, pineapple, and plums, leaving $\frac{1}{4}$ inch between pieces. Brush with some of the lemon juice mixture.

3 For a charcoal grill, grill skewers on the rack of an uncovered grill directly over medium-hot coals for 5 to 8 minutes or until shrimp are opaque and fruit is heated through, turning occasionally during grilling and brushing once with the remaining lemon juice mixture halfway through grilling. (For a gas grill, preheat grill. Reduce heat to medium. Place skewers on grill rack over heat. Cover and grill as above.)

NUTRITION FACTS PER SERVING:
213 cal., 6 g total fat (1 g sat. fat), 172 mg chol., 170 mg sodium, 17 g carb., 2 g dietary fiber, 24 g protein.

*tip

For a more dramatic presentation, use shrimp with the tails left on. Start with $1\frac{1}{2}$ pounds shrimp; peel and devein shrimp, leaving tails intact.

**tip

If time permits, you may use wooden skewers. But you'll need to soak them in water for at least 30 minutes. Drain before using.

Grilled Shrimp and Romaine ⏱

START TO FINISH **25 minutes**   MAKES **4 servings**

- 12 ounces fresh or frozen peeled and deveined large shrimp
- ¼ cup olive oil
- ½ teaspoon kosher salt or ¼ teaspoon salt
- 2 hearts of romaine lettuce, halved lengthwise
- ¼ cup finely shredded Parmesan cheese (1 ounce)
- 2 lemons
  Olive oil
  Kosher salt or salt
  Freshly ground black pepper

1 Thaw shrimp, if frozen. Rinse shrimp; pat dry with paper towels. Thread shrimp onto four 10-inch metal skewers. In a small bowl whisk together ¼ cup oil and ½ teaspoon kosher salt. Brush shrimp and cut sides of lettuce with oil mixture.

2 For a charcoal grill, grill shrimp skewers on the rack of an uncovered grill directly over medium coals for 5 to 8 minutes or until shrimp are opaque, turning once halfway through grilling. (For a gas grill, preheat grill. Reduce heat to medium. Place shrimp skewers on grill rack over heat. Cover and grill as above.)

3 While shrimp are grilling, add lettuce, cut sides down, to grill. Grill for 2 to 4 minutes or until grill marks appear on lettuce and lettuce is slightly wilted.

4 Remove shrimp from skewers and place in a serving bowl; add lettuce to bowl. Sprinkle with cheese. Cut 1 of the lemons in half; squeeze juice over shrimp and lettuce. Drizzle with additional oil and sprinkle with additional kosher salt and pepper. Cut the remaining lemon into wedges; serve with shrimp and lettuce.

NUTRITION FACTS PER SERVING:
267 cal., 20 g total fat (3 g sat. fat), 133 mg chol., 514 mg sodium, 2 g carb., 0 g dietary fiber, 19 g protein.

*tip
If you own a grill wok, preheat it on the grill and toss in the shrimp instead of threading them onto skewers. Grill for 5 to 8 minutes or until shrimp are opaque, stirring frequently.

Tomato and Grilled Veggie Stacks

START TO FINISH **30 minutes**   MAKES **6 servings**

1   **medium eggplant,* cut crosswise into 6 slices**

2   **medium yellow sweet peppers, seeded and each cut lengthwise into thirds**

3   **tablespoons olive oil**

   Salt

   Ground black pepper

2   **large tomatoes, each cut into 6 slices**

1   **pound fresh mozzarella cheese, cut into 12 slices**

6   **thin slices prosciutto**

   Small fresh basil leaves

1   **tablespoon balsamic vinegar**

1 Brush eggplant slices and sweet pepper pieces with 2 tablespoons of the oil. Sprinkle with salt and pepper.

2 For a charcoal grill, grill eggplant and sweet peppers on the rack of an uncovered grill directly over medium coals about 8 minutes or until tender, turning once halfway through grilling. (For a gas grill, preheat grill. Reduce heat to medium. Place eggplant and sweet peppers on grill rack over heat. Cover and grill as above.) Remove from grill. Cool to room temperature. If desired, cut each sweet pepper piece in half.

3 On dinner plates layer tomatoes, eggplant, cheese, sweet peppers, and prosciutto. Top with several basil leaves. Drizzle with the remaining 1 tablespoon oil and vinegar.

NUTRITION FACTS PER SERVING:
396 cal., 29 g total fat (11 g sat. fat), 60 mg chol., 911 mg sodium, 13 g carb., 4 g dietary fiber, 23 g protein.

*tip

For best results, select an eggplant that has a diameter similar in size to the diameter of the tomatoes.

401

Index

Note: Page references in *italics* indicate photographs.

403

411

Metric Information

The charts on this page provide a guide for converting measurements from the U.S. customary system, which is used throughout this book, to the metric system.

PRODUCT DIFFERENCES

Most of the ingredients called for in the recipes in this book are available in most countries. However, some are known by different names. Here are some common American ingredients and their possible counterparts:

• All-purpose flour is enriched, bleached, or unbleached white household flour. When self-rising flour is used in place of all-purpose flour in a recipe that calls for leavening, omit the leavening agent (baking soda or baking powder) and salt.
• Baking soda is bicarbonate of soda.
• Cornstarch is cornflour.
• Golden raisins are sultanas.
• Light-colored corn syrup is golden syrup.
• Powdered sugar is icing sugar.
• Sugar (white) is granulated, fine granulated, or castor sugar.
• Vanilla or vanilla extract is vanilla essence.

VOLUME AND WEIGHT

The United States traditionally uses cup measures for liquid and solid ingredients. The chart below shows the approximate imperial and metric equivalents. If you are accustomed to weighing solid ingredients, the following approximate equivalents will be helpful.

• 1 cup butter, castor sugar, or rice = 8 ounces = $1/2$ pound = 250 grams
• 1 cup flour = 4 ounces = $1/4$ pound = 125 grams
• 1 cup icing sugar = 5 ounces = 150 grams

Canadian and U.S. volume for a cup measure is 8 fluid ounces (237 ml), but the standard metric equivalent is 250 ml.

1 British imperial cup is 10 fluid ounces.

In Australia, 1 tablespoon equals 20 ml, and there are 4 teaspoons in the Australian tablespoon.

Spoon measures are used for smaller amounts of ingredients. Although the size of the tablespoon varies slightly in different countries, for practical purposes and for recipes in this book, a straight substitution is all that's necessary. Measurements made using cups or spoons always should be level unless stated otherwise.

COMMON WEIGHT RANGE REPLACEMENTS

Imperial / U.S.	Metric
$1/2$ ounce	15 g
1 ounce	25 g or 30 g
4 ounces ($1/4$ pound)	11 5 g or 125 g
8 ounces ($1/2$ pound)	225 g or 250 g
16 ounces (1 pound)	450 g or 500 g
$11/4$ pounds	625 g
$11/2$ pounds	750 g
2 pounds or $21/4$ pounds	1,000 g or 1 Kg

OVEN TEMPERATURE EQUIVALENTS

Fahrenheit Setting	Celsius Setting*	Gas Setting
300°F	150°C	Gas Mark 2 (very low)
325°F	160°C	Gas Mark 3 (low)
350°F	180°C	Gas Mark 4 (moderate)
375°F	190°C	Gas Mark 5 (moderate)
400°F	200°C	Gas Mark 6 (hot)
425°F	220°C	Gas Mark 7 (hot)
450°F	230°C	Gas Mark 8 (very hot)
475°F	240°C	Gas Mark 9 (very hot)
500°F	260°C	Gas Mark 10 (extremely hot)
Broil	Broil	Grill

Electric and gas ovens may be calibrated using celsius. However, for an electric oven, increase celsius setting 10 to 20 degrees when cooking above 160°C. For convection or forced air ovens (gas or electric), lower the temperature setting 25°F/10°C when cooking at all heat levels.

BAKING PAN SIZES

Imperial / U.S.	Metric
9x1½-inch round cake pan	22- or 23x4-cm (1.5 L)
9x1½-inch pie plate	22- or 23x4-cm (1 L)
8x8x2-inch square cake pan	20x5-cm (2 L)
9x9x2-inch square cake pan	22- or 23x4.5-cm (2.5 L)
11x7x1½-inch baking pan	28x17x4-cm (2 L)
2-quart rectangular baking pan	30x19x4.5-cm (3 L)
13x9x2-inch baking pan	34x22x4.5-cm (3.5 L)
15x10x1-inch jelly roll pan	40x25x2-cm
9x5x3-inch loaf pan	23x13x8-cm (2 L)
2-quart casserole	2 L

U.S. / STANDARD METRIC EQUIVALENTS

$1/8$ teaspoon = 0.5 ml	
$1/4$ teaspoon = 1 ml	
$1/2$ teaspoon = 2 ml	
1 teaspoon = 5 ml	
1 tablespoon = 15 ml	
2 tablespoons = 25 ml	
$1/4$ cup = 2 fluid ounces = 50 ml	
$1/3$ cup = 3 fluid ounces = 75 ml	
$1/2$ cup = 4 fluid ounces = 125 ml	
$2/3$ cup = 5 fluid ounces = 150 ml	
$3/4$ cup = 6 fluid ounces = 175 ml	
1 cup = 8 fluid ounces = 250 ml	
2 cups = 1 pint = 500 ml	
1 quart = 1 litre	

288

287

Shrimp and Fruit Kabobs
page 399

Tomato and Grilled Veggie Stack

page 401

286

Greek-Style Turkey Burgers page 382

Sesame-Ginger Barbecued Chicken page 390

285

Salmon and Asparagus with Herbed Mayonnaise page 393